"*Invitation to Biblical Hebrew Syntax: An Intermediate Grammar* is a needed resource that is long overdue for all who desire to better understand the syntax of biblical Hebrew. One of the greatest strengths of this approach is it teaches Hebrew syntax actively. Not only does it explain the syntax and provide examples of the syntax, it also includes drills with answer keys so students can put the concepts into practice and measure their progress. The following compositions give students a guided approach to applying the concepts of Hebrew syntax to Hebrew text. The addition of new concepts in each following composition, along with the repetition of already introduced concepts, helps students solidify their understanding. Finally, the section on accents provides a way of clearly understanding an aspect of the Hebrew Bible that has been difficult for many Hebrew students. Fuller and Choi lift the veil of mystery many students experience and shine light on the beauty of biblical Hebrew."

—T. J. Betts,
Associate Professor of Old Testament Interpretation,
The Southern Baptist Theological Seminary

"For several years now I have used the early stages of Fuller and Choi's *Invitation to Biblical Hebrew Syntax: An Intermediate Grammar*. The presentation of the verbal system is clear and concise, following the classical models of Arabic and Jewish grammarians. The grammar presents the material in the traditional categories of noun, verb, and particle. It is descriptive and helpful for students—offering many Hebrew verse examples, with the Hebrew issue at hand underlined and at times with graphics. The examples include an English translation with the key phrasing highlighted in bold. The chapters present syntactical questions and many practice drills to give students an opportunity to analyze Hebrew syntax (an answer key is offered in an appendix). One fifth of the grammar's content focuses on a discussion of clausal syntax with many helpful examples and drills. At the end, there is an excellent and comprehensive treatment of the Hebrew accent system and its usefulness in Hebrew syntax and exegesis. The composition section is one of the most helpful features of this book. Students learn syntax by putting simple English paragraphs into biblical Hebrew. These assignments offer detailed syntactical notes on how the student should compose the Hebrew syntax. Then the student works with their composition to the point where they can recite their Hebrew composition when looking at the English text. While this is an 'old school' method, students learn to think in biblical Hebrew! I have seen students come away with an excellent grasp of Hebrew syntax and superb biblical Hebrew reading speed. As an early student of Fuller, I was taught in this method and it greatly improved all aspects of my understanding, translation, and reading speed."

—Eric Alan Mitchell,
Associate Professor of Old Testament & Archaeology,
Southwestern Baptist Theological Seminary

"Russell Fuller and Kyoungwon Choi possess an encyclopedic knowledge of biblical Hebrew and the Masoretic text. Their latest work, *Invitation to Biblical Hebrew Syntax: An Intermediate Grammar*, distills a lifetime of study and presents it in a single volume. The discussions demonstrate a mastery of the technical details of Hebrew linguistics but are free of the jargon that renders many studies of biblical Hebrew inaccessible to most students. The principles taught are grounded in centuries of scholarly analysis and not based in ephemeral theory. This volume will serve two purposes: as a textbook for an advanced course in Hebrew syntax and as a *vade mecum* for reference. It is a most welcome contribution."

—Duane Garrett,
John R. Sampey Professor of Old Testament Interpretation,
The Southern Baptist Theological Seminary

INVITATION TO THEOLOGICAL STUDIES SERIES

INVITATION TO BIBLICAL HEBREW SYNTAX

An Intermediate Grammar

RUSSELL T. FULLER
KYOUNGWON CHOI

Invitation to Biblical Hebrew Syntax: An Intermediate Grammar

Published by Kregel Publications, a division of Kregel, Inc., 2450 Oak Industrial Dr. NE, Grand Rapids, MI 49505-6020.

The translation of the Hebrew Bible portions used throughout is the authors' own English rendering of the Hebrew.

The Hebrew font NewJerusalemU is available from www.linguistsoftware.com/lgku.htm, +1-425-775-1130.

ISBN 978-0-8254-4257-5

Printed in the United States of America

17 18 19 20 21/ 6 5 4 3 2

CONTENTS

SYNTAX

COMPOSITION

HEBREW ACCENTS

APPENDIXES

PREFACE

We wish to thank those who helped us and encouraged us along the way. In particular, we thank the many students who gave many suggestions and corrections to improve the work, most notably: Andrew Ellis, Anthony Ferguson, Ryan Cheung, and Adam Howell. Special recognition goes to Michael Jones, Stephen DeKuyper, Michael Lyons, and Robert Brunansky for their careful reading of the work and their many hours of help. We thank Chip Hardy, John Beckman, and Bill Arnold for their suggestions and criticisms (their help does not imply endorsement). Also, we appreciate the support and encouragement of Eric Mitchell of Southwestern Theological Seminary and his students who worked through the materials.

Two deserve special mention. Richard MacDonald prepared the Scripture and subject indexes. Moreover, he furnished many corrections and suggestions. His many hours of reading and re-reading the work were invaluable. We also thank Ihab Griess for his advice and encouragement. His insights into Semitic languages greatly influenced our thinking on many aspects of Semitic syntax.

We also acknowledge two of our teachers at Hebrew Union College-Jewish Institute of Religion, in Cincinnati, Ohio: Isaac Jerusalmi and Samuel Greengus, who first encouraged us in the study of a traditional Semitic approach to Hebrew and other Semitic languages. Their influence, instruction, and friendship will always be cherished.

This project took many years to complete. Family support is vital for such tasks. We thank our wives Donna and Jiyoun; and our children David, Christine, Katherine and Hayyiym, Aayin. We again thank our parents Thomas and Melba Fuller and Youngsam and Jung-Eun Choi, whose help and support are beyond words.

Finally, we thank Kregel Publications for all of their support and patience. In particular, we appreciate Dennis and Paul Hillman, Jim Weaver, Fred Mabie, and especially Shawn Vander Lugt, for their help and support.

We hope this book will assist the learning of Biblical Hebrew syntax to glorify God and His Son, Jesus Christ.

Russell T. Fuller
Kyoungwon Choi

INTRODUCTION

This book is divided into three parts: the syntax, the compositions, and the accents. The syntax is explained with numerous examples. These examples are given with a larger font to identify the proper word. For the chapters on the clauses, only the chapter on the substantival clause will be given larger font, since the other chapters are straightforward for identifying the proper words. The translation for these examples will often be woodenly literal to aid the understanding. Exercises for the syntax, including questions and drills, furnish more practice to comprehend and to identify the syntactical constructions. Keys to the drills are supplied to further aid the student, especially the self-taught student. Technical terms given in small caps (ACCUSATIVE) are defined in the glossary in the appendix. Since these technical terms include common terms (for example, perfect and imperfect), they will be given in small caps only occasionally. The compositions are comprehensive exercises designed to ingrain the principles of the syntax by writing and reciting Biblical Hebrew idiom. Finally, the accents are presented for their syntactical and exegetical value. The accents reinforce and complement the syntax, furnishing a solid foundation for understanding Biblical Hebrew and the Masoretic text.

THE SYNTAX

The syntax imitates traditional Semitic models, as expressed by medieval and modern Arabic grammarians and by medieval Jewish grammarians. In grammar, and particularly in syntax, Biblical Hebrew closely resembles Arabic. Since Arabic is the dominate living Semitic language and since modern Arabic preserves much of classical Arabic, it furnishes the best model for Biblical Hebrew grammar and syntax (and for Biblical Aramaic as well, therefore, many categories that apply to Biblical Aramaic are also included). This does not suggest, of course, that classical Arabic resembles Biblical Hebrew in every respect. Most differences are easily discernable, especially for native Arabic speakers. The syntactical categories for this syntax, therefore, follow the categories of native Arabic grammarians as appropriate, rather than arbitrary or novel linguistic categories. This methodology emulates the study of classical languages for centuries.

Traditional Semitic grammar recognizes three parts of speech: noun, verb, and particle. The noun is a word with inherent meaning. Participles, infinitives, adjectives, and some adverbs are subcategories of nouns. A verb is a word with inherent meaning and time/aspect. A particle is a word without inherent meaning and without time/aspect, its meaning determined by context. Those adverbs that are not regarded as nouns are particles.

The verb will follow native Semitic categories with some exceptions. First, because the terms "perfect" and "imperfect" are so embedded in Hebrew studies for hundreds of years, they will be retained instead of the native Arabic terms, past and present. Second, English tenses will be used as subcategories to aid students in understanding the translational and semantic equivalents between Biblical Hebrew and English. Semitic subcategories for the verb will be mentioned where appropriate.

The Semitic noun possessed a case system—nominative, genitive, and accusative – still found in Arabic. Although Biblical Hebrew dropped most case endings, the meaning and function of the case system still prevailed in Biblical Hebrew (and Biblical Aramaic). As the case system faded, prepositions took over most case functions, so that, for instance, a prepositional phrase sometimes replaced or substituted for an accusative construction. An understanding of the Semitic cases, therefore, is essential to comprehend the noun in Biblical Hebrew.

Particles, in contrast to nouns and verbs, do not have subcategories. Particles that affect verbs will be discussed with the verb. Particles with case functions will be discussed with nouns. Finally, particles will be discussed with their governing of clauses.

THE COMPOSITIONS

The compositions imitate the idioms of Hebrew to ingrain the principles of syntax. The drills furnished in the syntax require the student to identify the syntactical construction; the compositions require the student to compose the constructions. The drills are usually partial, involving a single word, phrase, or clause in a verse; the compositions are comprehensive, encompassing every word in the verse. The drills passively teach the syntax; the compositions actively inculcate the syntax. Though each has benefits, composition is more thorough and useful.

Composition is the traditional method for learning syntax for classical languages. Modern languages are learned by speaking them. Biblical Hebrew and other dead languages are learned by composing and by reciting them. Composition with recitation engages more senses than the eyes, virtually reviving the dormant language and energizing the eyes, mouth, and ears for the mind to grasp the syntax. Composition with recitation, used for centuries in classical Greek and Latin, most effectively and efficiently instills the syntax and idiom of Biblical Hebrew.

THE HEBREW ACCENTS

Although often neglected and dismissed, the Masoretic accents represent the traditional chanting of the text, which reflects the traditional understanding of the syntax and meaning of the text. The accents divide a verse into halves and then subdivide the halves continually until the verse is grouped into syntactical units of one, two, or three words (usually). This dividing of verses and grouping of words essentially diagrams the syntax by indicating which words go together and which words are separated.

In addition to grouping words and diagramming the syntax, the accents divulge many subtleties of syntax. The accents show distinctive patterns for verbal and nominal clauses, often highlighting emphatic word order. Similarly, they often mark the words most important for the meaning of a verse or a clause. For a verse with multiple clauses, the accents group related clauses. This is especially important in poetry, as the accents variously combine parallel clauses/words and non-parallel clauses/words in a verse. In both poetry and prose, the first half of the verse as marked by the accents often represents the general ideal of the whole verse, with the second half of the verse explaining, complementing, or specifying the first half of the verse. "The latter part of the verse as indicated by the accents," says Ihab Griess, a native Arabic speaker, "is often the tail on the dog."

HOW TO USE THIS BOOK

Follow these three steps to get the full benefit of this textbook: First, carefully read the syntax, mastering the examples, then work the exercises by answering the questions without looking back at the syntax and by identifying correctly the syntactical constructions in the drills. Second, compose and recite the compositions according to the instructions given in the introduction to the compositions. Look up the references in the footnotes and review the syntax. Third, study the accents, memorizing the accents and learning their value for the syntax and meaning of the text.

SELECTED BIBLIOGRAPHY

Addeweesh, Rashid Abdulrahman. *A Syntactic and Semantic Study of Hal "Circumstantial" Structures in Modern Literary Arabic Prose Literature.* Ph.D. Dissertation. University of Michigan, Ann Arbor, 1985.

Allen and Greenough. *New Latin Grammar*. Edited by Greenough, Howard, Kittredge, and D'ooge. Boston: Ginn & Co., 1903.

Ben-Asher, Aaron b. Moses. *Dikduke ha-Teamim*. Edited by H. L. Strack, and S. Baer. Leipzig: L. Fernau, 1879.

Blau, Joshua. *Topics in Hebrew and Semitic Linguistics*. Jerusalem: Magnes, 1998.

Brown, Francis, S. R. Driver, A. Briggs. *A Hebrew and English Lexicon of the Old Testament*. Oxford: Clarendon, 1907.

Delitzsch, Franz, *Commentary on the Old Testament: Proverbs, Ecclesiastes, Song of Solomon*. Vol. VI. Grand Rapids: Eerdmans, reprint 1984.

Driver, S. R. *A Treatise on the Use of the Tenses in Hebrew*. 3rd ed. Oxford: Clarendon, 1892.

Ewald, Heinrich. *Syntax of the Hebrew Language of the Old Testament*. Edinburgh: T&T Clark, 1978.

Fuller, Russell T. and Kyoungwon Choi. *Invitation to Biblical Hebrew: A Beginning Grammar*. Grand Rapids: Kregel, 2006.

Griess, Ihab Joseph. *Syntactical Comparisons between Classical Hebrew and Classical Arabic: A Study Based on the Translation of Mohammad ʿId's Arabic Grammar*. Lewiston, NY: E. Mellen, 2008.

Hodge, A. A. *Outlines of Theology*. Edinburgh: The Banner of Truth, 1879.

Howell, Mortimer S. *A Grammar of the Classical Arabic Language: Translated and Compiled from the Works of the Most Approved Native or Naturalized Authorities*. 4 vols in 7. New Delhi: Gian Publishing House, 1880-1911; reprinted 1990.

Joüon, P. *Grammaire de l'hebreu biblique*. Rome: Institut Biblique Pontifical, 1923; reprinted with corrections, 1965.

Joüon, P. *A Grammar of Biblical Hebrew*. 2 vols. Translated and revised by T. Muraoka. Rome: Editrice Pontificio Istituto Biblico, 1991.

Kautzsch, E., ed. *Gesenius' Hebrew Grammar*. 2nd ed. Translated by A. E. Cowley. Oxford: Clarendon, 1910.

Koehler, Ludwig and Walter Baumgartner. *The Hebrew and Aramaic Lexicon of the Old Testament.* Translated by M. E. J. Richardson. Lieden: E. J. Brill, 1994-2000.

Moscati, S. et al. *An Introduction to the Comparative Grammar of the Semitic Languages: Phonology and Morphology*. Wiesbaden: Harrassowitz, 1964.

Price, James D. *The Syntax of Masoretic Accents in the Hebrew Bible: Studies in the Bible and Early Christianity*. New York: Mellen, 1990.

________. *Concordance of the Hebrew Accents in the Hebrew Bible*. 5 vols. New York: Mellen, 1996.

Revell, E. J. *The Oldest Evidence for the Hebrew Accent System*. Bulletin of John Rylands Library, LIV, 1971.

Roberts, C. H. *Two Biblical Papyri in the John Rylands Library*. Manchester: Manchester University Press, 1936.

Schürer, Emil. *The History of the Jewish People in the Age of Jesus Christ, A New English Edition*. Revised and edited by G. Vermes and F. Millar. Edinburgh: T & T Clark, 1973.

Smyth, Herbert. *Greek Grammar*. Cambridge: Havard University Press, 1984.

Thackston, W. M. *An Introduction to Koranic and Classical Arabic*. Bethesda, MD: Ibex, 1994.

Wechter, Pinchas. *Ibn Barūn's Arabic Works on Hebrew Grammar and Lexicography*. Philadelphia: The Dropsie College for Hebrew and Cognate Learning, 1964.

Wickes, W. *Two Treatises on the Accentuation of the Old Testament: Ta'ame emet on Pslams, Proverbs and Job; Ta'ame kaf-alef Sefarim on the Twenty-One Prose Books*. New York: Ktav Publishing House, 1970.

Wright, W. *A Grammar of the Arabic Language*. 2 vols. Cambridge: Cambridge University Press, 1971.

Yamauchi, Edwin. *Ezra and Nehemiah*. EBC 4. Grand Rapids: Zondervan, 1988.

Ziadeh, F. J. and R. Bayly Winder. *An Introduction to Modern Arabic*. Princeton, NJ: Princeton University Press, 1957.

ABBREVIATIONS

Allen and Greenough	Allen and Greenough. *New Latin Grammar*. Edited by Greenough, Howard, Kittredge, and D'ooge. Boston: Ginn & Co., 1903.
BA	Biblical Aramaic
BDB	Brown, Francis, S. R. Driver, A. Briggs. *A Hebrew and English Lexicon of the Old Testament*. Oxford: Clarendon, 1907.
BHS	Elliger, K and W. Rudolph. *Biblica Hebraica Stuttgartensia*. Stuttgart: Deutsche Bibelgesellschaft, 1983.
Ewald	Ewald, Heinrich. *Syntax of the Hebrew Language of the Old Testament*. Edinburgh: T&T Clark, 1978.
GKC	Kautzsch, E., ed. *Gesenius' Hebrew Grammar*. 2nd ed. Translated by A. E. Cowley. Oxford: Clarendon, 1910.
Griess	Griess, Ihab Joseph. Syntactical Comparisons between Classical Hebrew and Classical Arabic: A Study Based on the Translation of Mohammad ᶜId's Arabic Grammar. Lewiston, NY: E. Mellen, 2008.
Howell	Howell, Mortimer S. *A Grammar of the Classical Arabic Language: Translated and Compiled from the Works of the Most Approved Native or Naturalized Authorities*. 4 vols in 7. New Delhi: Gian Publishing House, 1880-1911; reprinted 1990.
IBH	Fuller, Russell T. and Kyoungwon Choi. *Invitation to Biblical Hebrew: A Beginning Grammar*. Grand Rapids: Kregel, 2006.
JM	Joüon, P. *A Grammar of Biblical Hebrew*. 2 vols. Translated and revised by T. Muraoka. Rome: Editrice Pontificio Istituto Biblico, 1991.
Joüon	Joüon, P. *Grammaire de l'hebreu biblique*. Rome: Institut Biblique Pontifical, 1923; reprinted with corrections, 1965.
KBL	Koehler, L and Walter Baumgartner. *The Hebrew and Aramaic Lexicon of the Old Testament*. Translated by M. E. J. Richardson. Lieden: E. J. Brill, 1994-2000.
Moscati	Moscati, S., et al. *An Introduction to the Comparative Grammar of the Semitic Languages: Phonology and Morphology*. Wiesbaden: Harrassowitz, 1964.

Smyth	Smyth, Herbert. *Greek Grammar*. Cambridge: Harvard University Press, 1984.
Thackston	Thackston, W. M. *An Introduction to Koranic and Classical Arabic*. Bethesda, MD: Ibex, 1994.
Wechter	Wechter, Pinchas. *Ibn Barūn's Arabic Works on Hebrew Grammar and Lexicography*. Philadelphia: The Dropsie College for Hebrew and Cognate Learning, 1964.
Wright	Wright, W. *A Grammar of the Arabic Language*. 2 vols. Cambridge: Cambridge University Press, 1971.
WW	Wickes, W. *Two Treatises on the Accentuation of the Old Testament: Ta'ame emet on Pslams, Proverbs and Job; Ta'ame kaf-alef Sefarim on the Twenty-One Prose Books*. New York: Ktav Publishing House, 1970
ZW	Ziadeh, F. J. and R. Bayly Winder. *An Introduction to Modern Arabic*. Princeton, NJ: Princeton University Press, 1957.

Chapter 1
THE HEBREW VERBAL SYSTEM

§1. Introduction

Verbs have inherent meaning, along with aspect, tense, and mood.[1] Nouns have inherent meaning, but are without aspect, tense, and mood. Particles, by contrast, do not have inherent meaning, aspect, tense, or mood.[2]

The verbal system of Hebrew has two primary finite forms: the PERFECT and the IMPERFECT.[3] What Indo-European languages express by several finite verbal forms, the Hebrew verbal system expresses by two forms. For Hebrew to express the various shades of meaning of other verbal systems, the perfect and imperfect must be flexible. To understand and translate Hebrew verbs properly, consider the context, especially nearby adverbs and particles.[4]

§2. Aspect, Tense, and Mood *a*

ASPECT is the manner of the verbal action, as conceived or portrayed by the author. For Hebrew, the perfect represents the manner of action as completed, finished, or done;[5] the imperfect represents the manner of action as incomplete: in progress, about to begin, or just begun. The verbal root of the perfect with the suffixed pronouns indicates the aspect as completed. Thus, with the verbal root קטל "killing," the suffix is attached: קָטַלְתִּי = killing I, = killing (completed by) me, = I killed, to indicate the action as completed, finished. In the imperfect, the preformative letters (איתן) indicate the aspect as incomplete, so אֶקְטֹל, I killing = I (am in the process, or am about to begin, or have just begun) killing.[6] The perfect is static or motionless, like a snapshot; the imperfect is dynamic or moving, like a motion picture.[7]

The perfect and the imperfect also express TENSE; hence, Arab grammarians refer to the perfect as the "past tense" and the imperfect as the "present tense." Tense is simply time: past, present, and future. Because it represents completed action, the perfect *b*

1. Verbs are also distinguished from nouns and particles by expressing actions and states of being (stative verbs) and by having AGENT (subject) suffixes.
2. Griess, 21–23; Howell §1, 402, 497; ZW, 20–23.
3. These two forms may be expanded by particles, such as the Vav. Of course, Hebrew also has an imperative as a finite form, limited mostly to commands.
4. ZW, 21.
5. Sometimes, the Hebrew perfect can be like a GREEK PERFECT—a completed action with continuing results, as Ps 1:1, "Blessed is the man who has walked (completed in the past and does so still in the present)."
6. Wright I, §94. Primarily, the preformative letters of the imperfect (איתן) are aspect indicators of the imperfect. Secondarily, they substitute for pronouns, but they are not regarded as pronouns. The suffixes of the perfect are pronouns. The pronouns of the imperfect are the suffixed forms of the second and third feminine (תקטלי, תקטלנה). The initial ת indicates the imperfect aspect; the suffixed י and נה express the pronouns of the feminine singular and plural.
7. The meaning of some words imply "motion"; the meaning of other words are static or motionless. For example, מצא (to find) is motionless; בקש (to seek) implies motion.

is naturally past tense. The imperfect, representing an action in progress, is naturally present/future tense. Although those are the "natural" tenses, the Hebrew verbal forms do not express time in themselves. Indeed, while the forms have aspect indicators, they do not have tense indicators.[8] If an action is present or future but viewed as completed or done, the perfect is used; if an action is past but viewed as about to begin, in progress, or ongoing, the imperfect is used. Context, including adverbs and particles, must determine the proper tense for a given perfect or imperfect.[9]

c The MOOD of a verb refers to an author's attitude toward a statement. The Hebrew perfect expresses the INDICATIVE mood, a statement of fact (or what the author considers fact), indicating reality in the past, present, or future. "He walked," "he walks," or "he will walk" are indicative statements representing fact or reality. Most statements in Hebrew are indicative statements. The Hebrew imperfect may express the INDICATIVE, SUBJUNCTIVE, or JUSSIVE/PRETERIT. The subjunctive mood represents a contingent, desirable, or hypothetical statement. "He should (would, could, may, ought to) walk" is a subjunctive statement of what should (could, might, ought to, etc.), but not necessarily will, happen. For Hebrew, the subjunctive mood is restricted to purpose/result clauses in the imperfect.[10] The jussive/preterit[11] expresses a wish, desire, or command in the jussive—Let him walk—or a past completed action in the preterit—he walked. Finally, the imperative mood expresses the will of the speaker to a second person (you), often conveying a command—walk (you).

How does an author or speaker choose which verbal form he wants to use? Considering tense, an author uses the perfect when the verbal action occurred before the time of its enunciation or narration (and sometimes at the time of enunciation, see §3g–k and especially §3j, and sometimes after the time of enunciation, especially in prophetic and emphatic statements, §3l–m). An author uses the imperfect when the verbal action occurs during or after the time of its enunciation or narration (and occasionally before the time of enunciation when describing past actions vividly, §4d). Considering aspect, an author uses the perfect for completed action and for declarative statements. An author uses an imperfect for actions in progress, about to be in progress, and for statements of description or volition.[12]

How does an author or speaker choose between tense and aspect? Tense usually surpasses aspect in narrative contexts (Gen 1); aspect usually surpasses tense in direct speech (Gen 37:7) and poetry (Ps 23). Of course, if the direct speech or poetry narrates an account, then tense becomes stronger. In Psalm 18, for instance, David praises God and describes his distresses with strong verbal aspect (Ps 18:2–7). Then David narrates God's deliverance with strong verbal

8. Arabic adds a particle (سوف or in shortened form سـ) to the imperfect to indicate explicitly a future.
9. Griess, 248–255; Wright I, §77.
10. The infinitive construct, V^{ə}yiqtol, or V^{ə}qatal may substitute for the imperfect subjunctive.
11. The jussive/preterit is a mood form of the imperfect. The jussive resembles the imperative in mood. The term "preterit," a tense designation instead of a mood, is indicative in mood. See §4a and footnote 20.
12. Griess, 248–255; Howell §403–404.

tense (Ps 18:8–20). Although the tense or aspect may surpass the other in a given context, every verb in every context has both tense and aspect. The one never completely eclipses the other.[13]

§3. The Perfect (Qatal) *a*

A. Form

To indicate completed action, the perfect receives or implies a suffixed pronoun. The third masculine singular and the third common plural imply a pronoun. The Vav of the third common plural is a "Vav of plurality."

	Perfect Forms	Pronominal Suffixes: Explicit and Implicit Vav of Plurality	
1cs	קָטַלְתִּי	explicit pronoun	(cf. אָנֹכִי/אֲנִי)
2ms	קָטַלְתָּ	explicit pronoun	(cf. אַתָּה)
2fs	קָטַלְתְּ[9]	explicit pronoun	(cf. אַתְּ)
3ms	קָטַל	implicit pronoun	
3fs	קָטְלָה	explicit pronoun	ה ָ » ה ַ » ת (cf. קְטָלַתְנִי)
1cp	קָטַלְנוּ	explicit pronoun	(cf. אֲנַחְנוּ)
2mp	קְטַלְתֶּם	explicit pronoun	(cf. אַתֶּם)
2fp	קְטַלְתֶּן	explicit pronoun	(cf. אַתֶּן)
3mp/ 3fp	קָטְלוּ	implicit pronoun (Vav of plurality)	

B. Aspect, Tense, and Mood *b*

The perfect represents completed action in aspect; past, present, or future in tense; and indicative in mood.[15]

1. Aspect: The aspect of the perfect is action completed, finished, done. Gen 1:1, 5; 4:1; 13:12
2. Tense: The perfect may be used for past, present, or future actions. *c*
    a) Past time: Usually, the perfect is past tense, the completed verbal action occurring before the time of enunciation or narration. The following English tenses are given for translation purposes. They do not represent Hebrew or Semitic categories.

---

13. Griess, 248–255.
14. The second person feminine singular independent pronoun was originally אַנְתִּי as in Aramaic (אַנְתִּי), Syriac (ܐܢܬܝ), and Arabic (أَنْتِ). This form with Yod occurs seven times as *Kᵉthīb* (Judg 17:2; 1 Kgs 14:2; 2 Kgs 4:16; 4:23; 8:1; Jer 4:30; Ezek 36:13) and appears before pronominal suffixes to the finite verbal forms, as the perfect קְטַלְתִּינִי. See Moscati §13.8 and GKC §32h.
15. Griess, 248–251; Howell §403.

d i. PAST: An English past tense often renders an Hebrew perfect, especially as a tense of narration.

בְּרֵאשִׁית בָּרָא אֱלֹהִים אֵת הַשָּׁמַיִם וְאֵת הָאָרֶץ׃ Gen 1:1

In the beginning God **created** the heavens and the earth.

Gen 1:5; 4:1; Exod 5:1; BA Ezra 5:3

e ii. PERFECT: An English perfect (he has forsaken; they have forsaken) may render a Hebrew perfect. Context determines whether a verb should be translated as an English past or perfect. English perfects are common in direct speech and poetry.

וַיֹּאמֶר יְהוָה אֶל־קָיִן לָמָּה חָרָה לָךְ וְלָמָּה נָפְלוּ פָנֶיךָ׃ Gen 4:6

And the Lord said to Cain, Why **has it become hot** to you, and why **has** your face **fallen**?

Gen 6:13(בָּא); 24:27(עָזַב, נָחַנִי) Isa 1:4(עָזְבוּ, נִאֲצוּ, נָזֹרוּ) 66:8 (שָׁמַע, רָאָה); BA Dan 2:9(הִזְדְּמִנְתּוּן), 10(שְׁאֵל)

f iii. PAST PERFECT (Pluperfect): The English past perfect can also render a Hebrew perfect. The English past perfect conveys a past action that precedes another action in the past, or an action completed in the past with continuing results in the past, for example, he *had walked* down the street. The past perfect translation, more common in narrative than in direct speech or in poetry, is sometimes appropriate in NOMINAL CLAUSES or in various subordinate clauses, such as relative clauses or כִּי clauses.

וַאֲבִימֶלֶךְ לֹא קָרַב אֵלֶיהָ Gen 20:4[a]

And Abimelek **had** not **come** near to her.

In Gen 20:4, the perfect in a nominal clause conveys a past perfect notion.

וַיַּרְא אֱלֹהִים אֶת־כָּל־אֲשֶׁר עָשָׂה וְהִנֵּה־טוֹב מְאֹד Gen 1:31[a]

And God saw all that he **had made** and behold (it was) very good.

In Gen 1:31, the perfect in a relative clause conveys a past perfect notion.

עִם אֲשֶׁר תִּמְצָא אֶת־אֱלֹהֶיךָ לֹא יִחְיֶה נֶגֶד אַחֵינוּ הַכֶּר־לְךָ מָה עִמָּדִי וְקַח־לָךְ וְלֹא־יָדַע יַעֲקֹב כִּי רָחֵל גְּנָבָתַם׃ Gen 31:32

With whom(ever) you find your gods, he will not live. Before our brothers recognize for yourself what(ever is) with me and take for yourself. But Jacob did not know that Rachel **had stolen them**.

In Gen 31:32, the perfect in a כִּי clause conveys a past perfect notion.

Gen 2:3, 5, 8, 22; 4:5; 6:12; 8:6; 34:7; Exod 1:5; 1 Sam 1:5; 23:13

g b) Present time: The following categories express completed action occurring up to or during the time of enunciation or narration.

i. Stative verbs: In addition to expressing action, Hebrew verbs may express states of being – to be big, small, great, etc. These verbs are called stative verbs. Originally, stative verbs were adjectives converted into verbs.[16] When adjectives are predicates (The man is *great*) in nominal clauses, the sentence is naturally in the present: הָאִישׁ זָקֵן, The man is old. When these adjectives are converted into a stative verb in the perfect, they are often translated as an English present tense. Stative verbs, however, may also be translated as an English past or perfect tense according to the context.

וַיֹּאמֶר יְהוָה אֶל־אַבְרָהָם לָמָּה זֶּה צָחֲקָה שָׂרָה לֵאמֹר הַאַף אֻמְנָם אֵלֵד וַאֲנִי זָקַנְתִּי׃ Gen 18:13

And the Lord said to Abraham, Why did Sarah laugh saying, Will, in fact, I give birth? And I, **I am old**.

Gen 6:13; 29:21; 32:11; 44:20; Exod 10:7; Num 14:8; 21:30; Deut 32:22; 1 Sam 10:2; 12:2; 25:17; Ps 104:1

ii. Greek perfect: The Hebrew perfect may resemble the aspect of the Greek perfect, completed action with present condition or results. This is more common in poetry and direct speech than in narrative. *h*

הוֹי גּוֹי חֹטֵא עַם כֶּבֶד עָוֺן זֶרַע מְרֵעִים בָּנִים מַשְׁחִיתִים עָזְבוּ אֶת־יְהוָה נִאֲצוּ אֶת־קְדוֹשׁ יִשְׂרָאֵל נָזֹרוּ אָחוֹר׃ Isa 1:4

Woe sinning nation, a people heavy of iniquity, seed of wicked ones, corrupt sons. They **have abandoned** the Lord (and they abandon Him still). They **have spurned** the Holy One of Israel (and they spurn Him still). They **have turned** backwards (and they turn backwards still).

Gen 4:6; 32:27; 33:17; Exod 16:28; Lev 5:3; 14:35; 20:19; Num 19:13; 21:5; 31:49; Isa 66:8; Ps 34:18; 37:13; 38:11

iii. Perfect of certitude: When the perfect occurs in present time, it may express certainty or strong confidence. The action, though in progress in the present, is represented as done, hence, the certainty of the action. Verbs relating mental actions (know, hope, wait, trust, despise, choose, remember, love, hate, etc.), usually occurring in the first person and in direct speech and poetry, may express a statement with strong certainty and confidence. *i*

יְהוָה אֱלֹהַי בְּךָ חָסִיתִי Ps 7:2[a]

O Lord my God, in you **I take refuge**.

Gen 27:46; 1 Sam 2:16; Ps 11:5 (שָׂנְאָה נַפְשׁוֹ, a rare example of a third person perfect of certitude); 40:2; Ezra 9:6

16. Apparently, some non-stative verbs evolved into stative verbs, at least in form. Also, some stative verbs may have become non-stative in meaning: עָמֵל, עָמַל; שָׁכֵן, שָׁכַן; שָׁמֵעַ, שָׁמַע.

j iv. Verbs of speaking: Verbs of speaking in the first person and in direct speech, such as שָׁבַע, נָגַד, אָמַר, are completed in the present.

וַיֹּאמֶר בִּי נִשְׁבַּעְתִּי נְאֻם־יְהוָה Gen 22:16[a]

And he said, By myself **I swear**, declares the Lord.

1 Sam 17:10; 2 Sam 17:11; 19:30

k v. General truths or maxims: These perfects are commonly found in direct speech and poetry.

Jer 8:7[a] גַּם־חֲסִידָה בַשָּׁמַיִם יָֽדְעָה מוֹעֲדֶיהָ וְתֹר וְסִיס וְעָגוּר שָׁמְרוּ
אֶת־עֵת בֹּאָנָה

Even a stork in the heavens **knows** her appointed seasons.
And a turtledove and a swallow and a crane **keep** the time of their coming.

Ps 84:4; Job 7:9

l c) Future time: The following categories have the completed action occurring after the time of enunciation or narration.

i. Perfect of certitude: This is the same perfect of certainty with the present, except the verbal action occurs in the future. Often occurring in the first person and in direct speech and poetry, these perfects express strong certainty and confidence. Context determines whether a perfect of certitude occurs in the present or future.

בַּיּוֹם הַהוּא כָּרַת יְהוָה אֶת־אַבְרָם בְּרִית לֵאמֹר לְזַרְעֲךָ Gen 15:18
נָתַתִּי אֶת־הָאָרֶץ הַזֹּאת

On that day, the Lord cut with Abraham a covenant saying,
To your seed **I will give** this land.

Gen 17:16; 23:11; Exod 9:15; Judg 1:2; 1 Sam 2:16; Isa 54:8; 65:6; Job 40:4

m ii. Prophetic perfect: The prophets frequently describe future actions with the perfect as already completed, furnishing certainty to a future event, similar to the perfect of certitude.

Isa 9:1 הָעָם הַהֹלְכִים בַּחֹשֶׁךְ רָאוּ אוֹר גָּדוֹל יֹשְׁבֵי בְּאֶרֶץ צַלְמָוֶת
אוֹר נָגַהּ עֲלֵיהֶם׃

The people, who walk in the darkness, **saw (will see)** a great light; the dwellers in the land of the deep darkness, a light **shined (will shine)** upon them.

Jer 31:33; Isa 9:2(3x)-3, 5; 24:14; 25:8; 26:9; 30:19; 51:3

n iii. Future perfect: A future perfect is an action in the future that precedes another future action. For instance, in the statement—I will forgive them when they *will have repented* of their sins—the action of repenting occurs in the future before the action of forgiving. The verb, *will have repented*, is a future perfect. Of course, the future perfect is not a Hebrew or Semitic category.

Deut 8:10 וְאָכַלְתָּ וְשָׂבָעְתָּ וּבֵרַכְתָּ אֶת־יְהוָה אֱלֹהֶיךָ עַל־הָאָרֶץ הַטֹּבָה אֲשֶׁר נָתַן־לָךְ׃

And you will eat and be satisfied. And you will bless the Lord, your God, upon the good land which **he will have given** to you.

Exod 20:25(2x); 1 Sam 1:28; Isa 4:4; Jer 8:3

3. Mood: The perfect is indicative in prose. In poetry or direct speech the perfect may rarely express a wish or desire of the speaker. Usually, the particle לוּ will precede the perfect when expressing a wish or desire. *o*

Num 14:2[b] וַיֹּאמְרוּ אֲלֵהֶם כָּל־הָעֵדָה לוּ־מַתְנוּ בְּאֶרֶץ מִצְרַיִם אוֹ בַּמִּדְבָּר הַזֶּה לוּ־מָתְנוּ׃

And the whole congregation said to them, **Would that we had died** in the land of Egypt, or in this wilderness **would that we had died**!

C. Usages in the Old Testament *p*

1. Narrative: When an author wishes to interrupt the succession of Vav-consecutives but still wishes to describe a completed action, he uses a perfect. The perfect will then usually be preceded by words and/or particles to express a variety of clauses (but not succession) including:[17] nominal, causal, temporal, relative, interrogative, or negative clauses. The perfect with preceding words or particles may begin a book (Genesis) or a narrative (Gen 3:1), though the Vav-consecutive more frequently begins books (Judg 1:1) and narratives (Gen 14:1).

   The first chapter of Genesis furnishes a typical example of the usage of the perfect in narrative. Because Moses chose to begin Genesis with a prepositional phrase, and not a Vav-consecutive, and because he wanted completed/past action for the verb, he used a perfect. The perfect of verse one is followed by three nominal clauses (a clause with the subject before the verb or a clause without a finite verb) in verse two. The first nominal clause of verse two has a verb, and because Moses desired to express a completed action, a perfect verb after the subject (initiator) was required. Then verses three through five furnish a series of Vav-consecutive constructions with the successive notion (and then . . . and then . . . and then, etc.), characteristic of Hebrew narrative. After the first verb in verse five, Moses departs from the successive Vav-consecutive to contrast the darkness with the light by placing the contrasted word first (darkness), followed by a perfect to express a completed action.[18] Finally, after a long chain of Vav-consecutives in the second half of verse twenty-seven, Moses again avoids the successive Vav-consecutive construction by placing the nouns before the perfect, with its completed aspect. Now the statement without succession describes how God made man—male and female.

17. Exod 14:3 has a perfect without a preceding particle.
18. Gen 1:10 supplies another example of interrupting the Vav-consecutive for contrast.

The perfect in narrative, therefore, is the default when an author desires to express a completed action without the notion of succession. Various words or particles usually precede the perfect. In narrative, tense trumps aspect.

q 2. Direct speech and poetry: As is natural and expected, the perfect in direct speech and poetry is more flexible than in narrative. First, whereas in narrative the perfect is often preceded by words and particles; in direct speech and poetry, the perfect often occurs without preceding words and particles. Second, the perfect in direct speech and poetry often occurs in present and future contexts with usages such as prophetic perfect, perfect of certitude, perfects with verbs of speaking, general truths and maxims, and many of the same uses as in narrative.[19] In direct speech and poetry, aspect trumps tense.

r **D. Emphasizing the Perfect**

Usually, the infinitive absolute (the absolute object, §13b–j; 17d–j) and various particles, such as רַק, אַף, and גַּם emphasize the perfect. Exod 3:9; 6:4

s **E. Negation of the Perfect (§41a)**

The negative לֹא negates the perfect.

§4. Imperfect (Yiqtol)

a The Hebrew imperfect represents three MOODS/forms: INDICATIVE, SUBJUNCTIVE, JUSSIVE/PRETERIT. Moreover, the imperfect may add an energic particle to emphasize the form. While classical Arabic uses final short vowels to distinguish all these moods into three imperfect forms, Biblical Hebrew has lost these final short vowels and has, therefore, collapsed most of these into one imperfect form.[20] Traces of the various moods and forms, however, may be still found in Biblical Hebrew.[21]

The prefixed letters (איתן) indicate the imperfect aspect and substitute for pronouns. The pronouns for the imperfect are the suffixes found in the second feminine singular and the second/third feminine plural forms. The second and third masculine plural forms imply a pronoun with the "Vav of plurality." All other forms (1cs, 2ms, 3ms, 3fs, 1cp)[22] imply the pronoun.[23]

19. English translations of the perfect as past perfect and future perfect are rare in direct speech and poetry.
20. Short vowels with the final root letter indicated the indicative and subjunctive. The lack of short vowels indicated the jussive/preterit. When Hebrew dropped all final short vowels, almost all imperfects resembled jussives/preterits in form.
21. Griess, 251–255; Howell §408–427.
22. The imperative forms demonstrate that the pronouns are the suffixes for the imperfect and the imperative. The Yod of the imperfect (3ms, 3mp) preformatives is not a pronoun, but a pronominal substitute. In Biblical Aramaic the ל is the preformative for the third person verbs (Dan 2:20, 28–29; 5:17). Moreover, in Syriac, the third person verbal forms have Nun instead of Yod as the aspect indicator.
23. Griess, 58–60; Howell §404; Wright I, §89.

	Imperfect Forms	Suffixed Element: Explicit Pronouns and Vav of Plurality		Prefixed Element: Imperfect Indicators/Pronoun Substitutes
1cs	אֶקְטֹל			א
2ms	תִּקְטֹל			תִּ
2fs	תִּקְטְלִי	ִ י		תִּ
3ms	יִקְטֹל			י
3fs	תִּקְטֹל			תִּ
1cp	נִקְטֹל			נ
2mp	תִּקְטְלוּ	וּ	(Vav of plurality)	תִּ
2fp	תִּקְטֹלְנָה	נָה		תִּ
3mp	יִקְטְלוּ	וּ	(Vav of plurality)	י
3fp	תִּקְטֹלְנָה	נָה		תִּ

The imperfect, like the imperative, is a volitional form expressing the will or volition of the writer/speaker.[24] Hence, the common translation of the imperfect, I *will* come, often indicates volition instead of (or as much as) tense. Independent pronouns and energic forms may emphasize the volition of the imperfect.

A. Indicative Mood *b*

The indicative expresses an event, situation, or state as actual or real. As the name suggests, the indicative *indicates* an actual occurrence or situation.[25]

1. Form: Final Nuns occasionally found on imperfect forms with vocalic endings (2mp, 3mp) are remnants of the old indicative form. Context must now determine whether a word is in the indicative.

2. Aspect: The imperfect indicative, the most common type of imperfect, is used for any action that is (or is considered by the author as) incomplete. Ihab Griess states, "(The aspect of the imperfect indicative) is simply an action in the process of realization with no notion of completion."[26] The author, therefore, perceives the action as in process, about to start, or ongoing in some manner. This includes repeated or constant (durative) action. As such, the imperfect is more descriptive than the perfect. *c*

3. Tense: The imperfect indicative may be used for past, present, or future incomplete actions, though the action of the imperfect indicative usually occurs in present/future time. Context determines whether the unfinished action occurs in the past, present, or future. *d*

24. This is particularly true of the jussive and first person indicatives.
25. Howell §408–409; Wright II, §8–14.
26. Griess, 251.

a) Past time: The imperfect indicative expresses action in progress, including repeated or durative action. This action is also called FREQUENTATIVE since the action occurs frequently. The imperfect vividly describes a past action in process.

Job 1:5[b] כָּכָה יַעֲשֶׂה אִיּוֹב כָּל־הַיָּמִים׃

According to this, Job **would do** all the days.

Gen 2:6; 29:2; 37:7; Exod 13:22; 17:11; 40:36; Deut 2:11, 20; Judg 11:40; 1 Sam 9:9; 23:13; BA Dan 4:9(3x), 16; 5:6; 7:10, 14–15

e b) Present time: The event is in process at the time of enunciation. The imperfect indicative used in present time often implies a future orientation as well. This imperfect indicates what is going on now and what is expected to continue in the future. Moreover, the imperfect indicative may indicate an action that has just begun or an action that one customarily does, like a habit, occupation, or general pattern in life. In present time, the imperfect indicative is often found in direct speech and poetry, especially with expressions of general truths, maxims, and questions. In addition to context, adverbial particles of the present time, negations (excluding prohibitions), and interrogative sentences often indicate a present tense for the imperfect indicative. Furthermore, after verbs of thinking, knowing, supposing, doubting, etc., the imperfect indicative is often a present tense (1 Sam 1:10), with the action viewed as just about to begin (1 Sam 14:43) or in progress, including repeated or durative action.

Gen 32:33[a] עַל־כֵּן לֹא־יֹאכְלוּ בְנֵי־יִשְׂרָאֵל אֶת־גִּיד הַנָּשֶׁה אֲשֶׁר עַל־כַּף הַיָּרֵךְ עַד הַיּוֹם הַזֶּה

Therefore, the sons of Israel do not **eat** the sinew of the hip which is on the socket of the thigh unto this day.

Gen 24:31 וַיֹּאמֶר בּוֹא בְּרוּךְ יְהוָה לָמָּה תַעֲמֹד בַּחוּץ

And he said, Come, blessed of the Lord! Why do you **stand** outside?

Exod 23:8 וְשֹׁחַד לֹא תִקָּח כִּי הַשֹּׁחַד יְעַוֵּר פִּקְחִים וִיסַלֵּף דִּבְרֵי צַדִּיקִים׃

And a bribe you shall not take, because a bribe **blinds** the seeing ones and **subverts** the words of the just.

Repeated action, Gen 32:33; Deut 1:44; 1 Sam 18:5; durative action (questions), Gen 32:30; Exod 2:7, 13; 17:2(2x); (In an indirect question, Exod 3:3); Deut 2:20; 1 Sam 1:8; 9:9; 16:23; 24:10; general truths, Exod 23:8; Prov 15:20; present time in general, Exod 11:7; 14:14; 1 Sam 23:23; 24:11, 13–14; BA Dan 4:14(3x)

f c) Future time: The event occurs after the time of enunciation or narration. In future time, the imperfect indicative usually represents a future action without process or progress. It may also represent something that is about to begin or imminent, and therefore, incomplete, but not necessarily in progress or started yet (Ps 1:6, action just about to begin). In addition to context, adverbial particles of the future, an expected event, formal requests (including commands and prohibitions), prayers (including wishes, hopes, and fears), promises, oaths, conditions, and negatives often indicate a future tense for the imperfect indicative. In future time, the imperfect may represent a command, similar to an imperative.

Gen 42:37[a] וַיֹּאמֶר רְאוּבֵן אֶל־אָבִיו לֵאמֹר אֶת־שְׁנֵי בָנַי תָּמִית אִם־לֹא אֲבִיאֶנּוּ אֵלֶיךָ

And Reuben spoke to his father, saying, My two sons you **may put to death** if I do not **cause him to come back** to you.

Exod 5:8; 19:11; 1 Sam 24:21; Jer 1:7(2x); questions 1 Sam 23:11–12; BA Dan 2:7; volitions and commands Exod 12:46–47; 22:28–29; 23:14–15, 17, 19; Jer 1:17

4. Usage in the Old Testament *g*
   a) Narrative: In narrative, the imperfect indicative is often the tense of description, especially in past and present contexts. For example, a series of frequentative imperfects in 1 Samuel chapter one describe the actions as occurring every year: Elkanah would go up to Shiloh; Peninnah would provoke Hannah; and Hannah would not eat. These Hebrew imperfects are similar to the descriptive nature of Greek and Latin imperfect and present tenses. Likewise in Exod 17:11, when Moses would raise his hands (from time to time), Israel would prevail. When Moses would drop his hands (from time to time), Amelek would prevail. These ongoing actions are vivid and descriptive, like a motion picture. The perfect, by contrast, represents finished, motionless action, like a snapshot.
   b) Direct speech and poetry: In direct speech and poetry, the imperfect indicative may be past, present, or future in time. The action is usually descriptive, viewed as in progress. If the action has not begun, the action can be near future (imminent) or remote future (non-imminent), usually without progress. Often in the Psalms, the author views a past, completed action as ongoing to make the account more vivid. In Ps 18:5, David describes the cords of death as having surrounded (perfect) him. Then he describes the cords of destruction as terrorizing (imperfect) him, as if the terrorizing were still ongoing. *h*

5. Negations and prohibitions with indicatives and jussives (§42): The imperfect indicative is negated with לֹא (see §41b). In prohibitions, the imperfect indicative with לֹא expresses a stronger, more emphatic negative than אַל with the jussive—you *must* not, you *will* not. לֹא with the indicative is the emphatic prohibition; אַל with the jussive is the simple prohibition. A preceding infinitive absolute may strengthen a prohibition. *i*

B. Subjunctive Mood (§52) *j*

The SUBJUNCTIVE is more hypothetical or contingent than the indicative.

What the indicative declares as actual, the subjunctive declares as possible. For Hebrew, the subjunctive is restricted to purpose/result statements.[27]

1. Form: Particles such as פֶּן, לְמַעַן, בַּעֲבוּר, אֲשֶׁר (BA דִּי) may indicate that the imperfect verb is subjunctive.

k 2. Aspect: The aspect of the subjunctive is usually without progress.[28]

Gen 21:30 וַיֹּאמֶר כִּי אֶת־שֶׁבַע כְּבָשֹׂת תִּקַּח מִיָּדִי בַּעֲבוּר תִּהְיֶה־לִּי לְעֵדָה כִּי חָפַרְתִּי אֶת־הַבְּאֵר הַזֹּאת׃

And he said, Indeed, these seven ewe lambs you will take from my hand, in order that (for the intent that, for the reason that) **it may exist** for me as a witness that I dug this well.

Gen 3:22; 11:4; 19:15; 27:25; Exod 4:5; BA Ezra 5:10

l 3. Tense: The subjunctive is future.

m 4. Usage in the Old Testament: The subjunctive occurs in direct speech (most commonly), poetry, and narrative.

C. Jussive/Preterit Mood

n The JUSSIVE/PRETERIT form represents two verbal moods/forms. The jussive expresses a command, wish, or advice (common in prayers and prohibitions with אַל); the preterit, an indicative in mood, expresses a past tense, essentially equivalent to a perfect. The jussive is usually action without progress; the preterit is always action without progress. The form and context may imply a jussive or preterit. The particles אָז or (בְּ)טֶרֶם often indicate a preterit.[29] The jussive may be strengthened with the energic particle נָא.[30]

1. Form: Originally, short vowels at the end of the imperfect indicated the indicative and the subjunctive. The absence of a short vowel (implying a silent shewa) indicated the jussive/preterit. When Hebrew dropped final short vowels from the indicative and subjunctive, all imperfects looked like jussive/preterits.

   The jussive/preterit form, however, may occasionally be distinguished in certain verbal stems. In the strong verb, for example, the thematic vowel (יַקְטִיל versus יַקְטֵל) of the Hiphil imperfect distinguishes the indicative and subjunctive from the jussive/preterit. Similarly, in some weak verbs, the thematic vowels (יָקוּם versus יָקֹם and וַיָּקָם) distinguish the indicative and subjunctive from the jussive/preterit. Preterits are often preceded by the particles אָז or (בְּ)טֶרֶם in prose, but they may be without the particle, as indicated by context.

27. Howell §410–418; Wright II, §15–16. For the negative with the subjunctive, see §41c.
28. Other words or particles may indicate if the action is in progress.
29. Most preterits are connected to the Vav-consecutive, for example, וַיַּקְטֵל.
30. Jussive: Howell §419-427; Wright II, §17; Preterit: Howell §419, 548; Wright II, §18. For the negative with the jussive/preterit, see §41d.

1 Kgs 3:16 אָ֣ז תָּבֹ֗אנָה שְׁתַּ֛יִם נָשִׁ֥ים זֹנ֖וֹת אֶל־הַמֶּ֑לֶךְ וַֽתַּעֲמֹ֖דְנָה לְפָנָֽיו׃
Then two women, harlots, **came** to the king and stood before him.

1 Kgs 8:1[a] אָ֣ז יַקְהֵ֣ל שְׁלֹמֹ֣ה אֶת־זִקְנֵ֣י יִשְׂרָאֵ֡ל אֶת־כָּל־רָאשֵׁ֣י הַמַּטּוֹת֩ נְשִׂיאֵ֨י הָאָב֜וֹת לִבְנֵ֧י יִשְׂרָאֵ֛ל אֶל־הַמֶּ֥לֶךְ שְׁלֹמֹ֖ה יְרוּשָׁלָ֑͏ִם
Then Solomon **assembled** the elders of Israel and all the heads of the tribes, the leaders of the fathers belonging to the sons of Israel, to King Solomon in Jerusalem.

Preterits with particles: Exod 12:34; 15:1, 15; Jer 1:5(2x); BA Ezra 5:5

Ps 8:6 וַתְּחַסְּרֵ֣הוּ מְּ֭עַט מֵאֱלֹהִ֑ים וְכָב֖וֹד וְהָדָ֣ר תְּעַטְּרֵֽהוּ׃
And you made him a little lower than the angels; and with honor and glory **you crowned him**.

Preterits without particles: Exod 15:14; Deut 32:10; Isa 42:6; Job 3:3; BA Dan 6:20
Jussive in meaning: Exod 5:21; 7:9; 10:10; 1 Sam 24:13; BA Dan 5:10(2x); Ezra 4:15; 5:17

2. Aspect: The jussive is incomplete in aspect, but usually not in process. The preterit is always completed action. The jussive expresses the wish or desire of the speaker, sometimes with a modal nuance—*may, should, would, want, ought*, etc.; the preterit indicates a statement of fact. *o*

3. Tense: The jussive is a future tense; the preterit a past tense. *p*

4. Usage in the Old Testament: *q*
   a) Narrative: In narrative, the jussive is rare; the preterit occurs occasionally (though common in Vayyiqtol forms).
   b) Direct speech and poetry: The jussive is common; the preterit occurs occasionally.

D. Energic Particles with the Moods *r*

1. Form: There are three ENERGIC forms:[31]
   a) The particle נָא with an imperfect (usually an indicative or jussive) or imperative. נָא רְפָא נָא (Num 12:13 has a נָא before and after the verb); Exod 3:3, 18; 4:18; 5:3
   b) Imperfects (cohortatives) and imperatives (emphatic) ending in ָה.[32] הָבָה

31. Wright (I, §78) regards the energic forms as a mood; Howell (§610) regards the energic forms as particles attached to mood forms. For the negative with the energic particles, see §41e. For a comparison of energic forms of Arabic and Hebrew, see Griess, 276–279.

32. These forms ending in ָה are connected to the -an syllable of Arabic energic forms, that are pronounced long "a" in pause, similar to the pronunciation of the Hebrew cohortative and emphatic imperative (Wright I, §97c). These forms may also take the particle נָא, similar to the -ann syllable of the energic Arabic forms. Compare these energic Arabic forms to the cohortative with נָא in Hebrew (Gen 18:21). Most authorities see these constructions (-an, -ann) as equal in emphasis; some view -ann as more emphatic than -an. The cohortative

Exod 1:10; 4:18; 5:8; 9:28; 14:4, 25; 15:1; 1 Sam 14:1, 6; 17:44; Jer 7:3

c) Suffixed forms with energic Nun (usually with an indicative, rarely with a jussive, Num 6:25). Exod 5:18 (תִּתֵּנוּ); 7:2; 15:2; 16:4; 19:19; 20:19; 21:14, 26–27; 22:15, 20; 23:4; Deut 1:36, 38–39; 1 Sam 6:2; 17:25, 27, 44; 18:5, 21

s 2. Aspect: The energic element adds energy, emphasis, or emotion to the verb. It usually stresses the will, desire, request, command, exhortation, or interrogation of the speaker or author, with the notion of fixed determination or the self interest of the speaker, or both. The energic nuance may be rendered by an exclamation mark or by a variety of emphatic English words: please, now, I pray, indeed, in fact, really, etc. Although Arabic restricts energic particles to the indicative and the future, Hebrew allows the energic particles with an indicative (Num 23:25), jussive (נָא), subjunctive (Gen 27:19), or a Vav-perfect (Vᵊqatal, Gen 40:14; Deut 24:13). The indicative, subjunctive, or jussive maintain their aspect with the energic nuance.

t 3. Tense: The energic forms occur in present and future tenses but not in past tense.

u 4. Usage in the Old Testament: The energic forms are rare in narrative, but common in direct speech and poetry. The imperfect indicative (1 Kgs 1:5) and subjunctive may have a volitional nuance; the jussive always has a volitional nuance. The energic forms emphasize this volitional nuance.

v **E. Emphasizing the Imperfect**

In addition to the energic particles, the infinitive absolute (the absolute object) and particles, such as רַק, אַף, and גַּם, etc., may emphasize the imperfect.

§5. Imperative (Qᵊtol)

The Imperative mood expresses a command or desire of the speaker.[33]

a **A. Form**

The imperative form resembles the imperfect form except the imperatives are without the aspect indicators (preformatives) of the imperfect. The masculine forms imply the pronouns, with the plural form taking the "Vav of plurality." Suffixed pronouns indicate the feminine.

b **B. Aspect**

The aspect of the imperative is usually action without progress, but context may suggest action in process.

---

ending ָה may be "hidden" by the addition of pronominal suffixes. Context then determines if a first person imperfect verb with a pronominal suffix is a cohortative.

33. Howell §428–431.

C. Tense *c*

The imperative is a future tense.

D. Usage in the Old Testament *d*

The imperative expresses only positive commands. Negative commands require אַל and the jussive or לֹא and the indicative or subjunctive. The imperative expresses commands (Gen 12:1), requests (2 Kgs 5:22), permission (2 Sam 18:23), or assured promises (Isa 37:30).

2 Kgs 5:22[b] תְּנָה־נָּא לָהֶם כִּכַּר־כֶּסֶף וּשְׁתֵּי חֲלִפוֹת בְּגָדִים׃

Give to them please a talent of silver and two changes of clothes.

In 2 Kgs 5:22, the imperative expresses a request.

E. Emphasizing the Imperative *e*

The imperative may be emphasized variously. An energic particle emphasizes the imperative: an energic suffix (1 Sam 21:10), energic ה ָ (1 Sam 16:11; 20:21), or particle נָא (Exod 4:6; 10:11, 17) following the imperative (1 Sam 14:29; 15:25; 17:17; 23:11). The infinitive absolute after the imperative emphasizes the imperative (Num 11:15). The infinitive absolute, by itself, often implies and emphasizes an imperative (§17f). Particles, such as רַק and גַּם, etc., also emphasize the imperative.

§6. Verbal Forms with Vav *a*

Like all particles, the Vav derives its meaning from context. The Vav adds two nuances to the verb. First, it may be a connecting "and" linking two forms. Second, the Vav may add greater energy (meaning) than a connecting "and," hence the term "energic Vav."[34] The energic Vav communicates: temporal succession (and then), logical succession (and therefore, and so), and purpose/result. Moreover, the energic Vav and its verbal form may be dependent on the preceding verbal form, or it may be independent of (or loosely dependent on) the preceding verbal form. This dependency does not always imply that the verbal form with Vav is equivalent with the preceding form in meaning, especially if the preceding form is a participle or an infinitive construct. When the verbal form with Vav follows a participle or infinitive construct, it does not become a participle or an infinitive construct (§16a). Commonly, the Vav-perfect introduces an apodosis for various clauses.

A. Vav-perfect (V^{ə}qatal) *b*

Context determines whether a Vav connected to a perfect is a connecting Vav or energic Vav.

1. Connecting Vav: A Vav joins a perfect to another form, usually a perfect. Translate this Vav as a connecting "and" or as an adversative "but."
   a) And: The Vav joins two or more perfects.

34. In Arabic, *Waw* is a connector, usually translated "and." The Arabic particle *Fa* is energic, "and so," "and then." Hebrew Vav represents both Arabic *Waw* and *Fa*. Wright I, §366.

וּֽלְיִשְׁמָעֵאל שְׁמַעְתִּיךָ הִנֵּה ׀ בֵּרַכְתִּי אֹתוֹ וְהִפְרֵיתִי אֹתוֹ
וְהִרְבֵּיתִי אֹתוֹ בִּמְאֹד מְאֹד Gen 17:20[a]

And with respect to Ishmael, I have heard you, behold I will bless him **and will make** him **fruitful and will multiply** him very greatly.

In Gen 17:20, the perfect (bless) is a perfect of certitude continued by the connecting Vavs and perfects.

Deut 33:2; 1 Sam 17:38; 24:11; 2 Sam 23:20; 1 Kgs 8:47; 20:27; 2 Kgs 19:22; Isa 1:2; Jer 7:31

c b) But: The Vav may express the adversative notion of "but." The adversative notion often occurs after a negative.

וַיֹּאמֶר אֱלֹהִים אֵלָיו יַעַן אֲשֶׁר שָׁאַלְתָּ אֶת־הַדָּבָר הַזֶּה וְלֹא־
שָׁאַלְתָּ לְּךָ יָמִים רַבִּים וְלֹא־שָׁאַלְתָּ לְּךָ עֹשֶׁר וְלֹא שָׁאַלְתָּ
נֶפֶשׁ אֹיְבֶיךָ וְשָׁאַלְתָּ לְּךָ הָבִין לִשְׁמֹעַ מִשְׁפָּט׃ 1 Kgs 3:11

And God said to him, Because you asked this matter, and you did not ask for yourself many days, and you did not ask for yourself wealth, and you did not ask for the life of your enemies, **but you asked** for yourself to understand to hear justice.

Gen 17:5; 47:30; 48:21; Exod 3:22; 21:18

d 2. Energic Vav: The energic Vav also "converts" the perfect into an imperfect in aspect and tense. Like the imperfect, the Vav-perfect often overlaps present and future time, expressing what is going on now and what you expect will go on in the future. In other contexts, the present and the future are clearly distinguished. Vav-perfects are often joined consecutively to other Vav-perfects or other verbal forms. This consecutive use, called Vav-consecutive, usually expresses succession, either temporal ("and then") or logical ("and so" Deut 2:6).

e a) Past time: The Vav-perfect expresses action in progress, including repeated (FREQUENTATIVE) or durative action in past time. This Vav "converts" the perfect into an imperfect in aspect.

וְאֵד יַעֲלֶה מִן־הָאָרֶץ וְהִשְׁקָה אֶת־כָּל־פְּנֵי־הָאֲדָמָה׃ Gen 2:6

And a mist used to go up from the ground **and it would water** all the face of the ground.

In Gen 2:6, a Vav-perfect is dependent on a preceding imperfect frequentative.

וְעָלָה הָאִישׁ הַהוּא מֵעִירוֹ מִיָּמִים ׀ יָמִימָה לְהִשְׁתַּחֲוֹת
וְלִזְבֹּחַ לַיהוָה צְבָאוֹת בְּשִׁלֹה 1 Sam 1:3[a]

And that man **would go up** from his city from the days to the days to bow down and to sacrifice to the Lord of hosts in Shiloh.

In 1 Sam 1:3, the Vav-perfect (frequentative) is not dependent on a preceding verbal form.

Exod 33:11; 1 Sam 7:16; 16:23; 17:34–35; 2 Sam 15:2; 2 Kgs 3:4; Job 1:4

b) Present time: The Vav-perfect continues a preceding present tense imperfect. *f*

וְאַתָּה יְהוָה יְדַעְתָּנִי תִּרְאֵנִי וּבָחַנְתָּ לִבִּי אִתָּךְ Jer 12:3[a]

And you, O Lord, you know me, you see me **and you test** my heart with yourself.

Isa 28:18, 25; 44:15; Ps 46:10; 49:10; 90:6

c) Future time: The Vav-perfect may be dependent (more or less) on a preceding finite verbal form in the future or on a participle with an imperfect tense/aspect. These Vav-perfects often express temporal succession or sometimes logical succession. *g*

i. A preceding imperfect (jussive, cohortative): This is the narrative tense for future actions.

הֵן גֵּרַשְׁתָּ אֹתִי הַיּוֹם מֵעַל פְּנֵי הָאֲדָמָה וּמִפָּנֶיךָ אֶסָּתֵר וְהָיִיתִי נָע וָנָד Gen 4:14

Behold, you have driven me away this day from upon the face of the ground, and from your face I will hide myself. **And I will exist** as a wanderer and a nomad.

Gen 6:21; 24:4; 27:40; 32:12; Exod 1:10; 2:7; 5:7; 15:26; 1 Sam 24:13 (Jussive)

ii. A preceding imperative (very common): Here the Vav-perfect functions as an imperative. *h*

וּקְחוּ אִישׁ מַחְתָּתוֹ וּנְתַתֶּם עֲלֵיהֶם קְטֹרֶת Num 61:17[a]

And take each his fire holder, **and place** upon them incense.

Gen 44:4; 45:9; Exod 6:6–8; 7:26; 9:8; 1 Sam 23:2

iii. A preceding participle: The Vav-perfect continues the tense and aspect of the preceding participle. *i*

כִּי לְיָמִים עוֹד שִׁבְעָה אָנֹכִי מַמְטִיר עַל־הָאָרֶץ אַרְבָּעִים יוֹם וְאַרְבָּעִים לָיְלָה וּמָחִיתִי אֶת־כָּל־הַיְקוּם אֲשֶׁר עָשִׂיתִי מֵעַל פְּנֵי הָאֲדָמָה׃ Gen 7:4

For with respect to days, yet seven, I am causing rain upon the earth for forty days and forty nights **and I will blot out** every established which I made from upon the face of the ground.

Gen 17:19; 48:4; Exod 3:13; 8:25; 10:5; 16:4; 21:16(2x); Deut 4:22; 1 Sam 24:5

d) The following Vav-perfects relate actions in process in the past, present, or future, and they may be used independently of preceding finite verbal forms (imperfects or imperatives) or preceding verbal nouns (participles and infinitive constructs). *j*

i. After perfects:

אֶת־קַשְׁתִּי נָתַתִּי בֶּעָנָן וְהָיְתָה לְאוֹת בְּרִית בֵּינִי וּבֵין הָאָרֶץ׃ Gen 9:13

And my bow I placed in the clouds, **and it will exist** for a sign of the covenant between me and the earth.

Gen 27:45; Exod 3:13

k ii. After nominal clauses:

Gen 17:4 אֲנִי הִנֵּה בְרִיתִי אִתָּךְ וְהָיִיתָ לְאַב הֲמוֹן גּוֹיִם׃

My – behold, my covenant is with you. **And you will exist** as a father of a multitude of nations.

Gen 28:15; 47:23; Exod 8:17; 12:44; 16:7; 1 Sam 24:16 (2x as jussives)

l iii. After an infinitive construct with preposition:

Exod 1:16[a] וַיֹּאמֶר בְּיַלֶּדְכֶן אֶת־הָעִבְרִיּוֹת וּרְאִיתֶן עַל־הָאָבְנָיִם

And he said, When you assist Hebrew women in child birth, **and you look** upon the birthstool.

Lev 26:26; 1 Sam 1:12; 2 Sam 7:14; 15:10; 1 Kgs 13:31; Jer 51:61

m iv. Beginning a narrative or section, usually with וְהָיָה:

Deut 7:12[a] וְהָיָה ׀ עֵקֶב תִּשְׁמְעוּן אֵת הַמִּשְׁפָּטִים הָאֵלֶּה וּשְׁמַרְתֶּם וַעֲשִׂיתֶם אֹתָם

And it will happen because you listen to these judgments **and you carefully keep** them.

Deut 6:10; 8:18; 11:13

Observation: These forms often express a command, wish, question, or function frequentatively.

Deut 10:19 וַאֲהַבְתֶּם אֶת־הַגֵּר כִּי־גֵרִים הֱיִיתֶם בְּאֶרֶץ מִצְרָיִם׃

And love the alien, for as aliens you existed in the land of Egypt.

Gen 18:26 וַיֹּאמֶר יְהוָה אִם־אֶמְצָא בִסְדֹם חֲמִשִּׁים צַדִּיקִם בְּתוֹךְ הָעִיר וְנָשָׂאתִי לְכָל־הַמָּקוֹם בַּעֲבוּרָם׃

And the Lord said, if I find in Sodom fifty righteous in the midst of the city, **then I will forgive** all the place on account of them.

In Gen 18:26, a Vav-perfect introduces the apodosis with a perfect of certitude.

n **B. Vav-imperfect (Vayyiqtol and Vᵊyiqtol)**

The Vav-imperfects come in two forms: Vayyiqtol and Vᵊyiqtol

1. Vayyiqtol:[35] The energic Vav (pointed like the article) connects to a PRETERIT (or a jussive form). The aspect is completed, similar to a perfect, with the added nuance of the energic Vav. Sometimes in poetry and direct speech, the Vayyiqtol continues the tense and aspect of the preceding finite verbal form (perfect) or a preceding verbal noun (participle or infinitive construct).

   The common uses of the Vayyiqtol form include:[36]

---

35. This form in the first person may have the energic ending of the cohortative, ָה, וָאֶקְטְלָה. This ending adds emotion and/or energy to the verbal form. In later biblical books (Chronicles, Ezra/Nehemiah, for example), the "energy" of this ending is debatable. Context must decide whether the ending conveys energy or not.

36. The Vayyiqtol is the narrative tense for past tense actions. The reader must always notice

a) Temporal succession: An action succeeds another action in time. This is usually translated "and then" or simply "and" or "then." (Gen 1:3–2:3) *o*

וַיִּיצֶר֩ יְהוָ֨ה אֱלֹהִ֜ים אֶת־הָֽאָדָ֗ם עָפָר֙ מִן־הָ֣אֲדָמָ֔ה Gen 2:7[a]

Then the Lord God **formed** man from the soil of the ground.

וַיֹּ֨אמֶר אַבְרָ֜ם אֶל־שָׂרַ֗י הִנֵּ֤ה שִׁפְחָתֵךְ֙ בְּיָדֵ֔ךְ עֲשִׂי־לָ֖הּ הַטּ֣וֹב בְּעֵינָ֑יִךְ וַתְּעַנֶּ֣הָ שָׂרַ֔י Gen 16:6

And Abram said to Sarai, Behold your handmaid is in your hand, do to her the good in your eyes. **Then** Sarai **humiliated her**.

b) Logical succession: An action succeeds another action logically. Translate "and so," "and therefore," or "and consequently." *p*

וַיְהִ֤י יְהוָה֙ אֶת־יוֹסֵ֔ף וַיְהִ֖י אִ֣ישׁ מַצְלִ֑יחַ וַיְהִ֕י בְּבֵ֖ית אֲדֹנָ֥יו הַמִּצְרִֽי׃ Gen 39:2

And the Lord was with Joseph, and he existed as a successful man. **And so he existed** in the house of his master, the Egyptian.

Gen 37:7; Num 31:16; Josh 5:9; 2 Sam 6:13; 2 Kgs 7:20; Job 2:3; 2 Chr 14:12

c) Adversative: This is usually preceded by a negative. *q*

וַתַּ֨עַן חַנָּ֤ה וַתֹּ֙אמֶר֙ לֹ֣א אֲדֹנִ֔י אִשָּׁ֤ה קְשַׁת־ר֙וּחַ֙ אָנֹ֔כִי וְיַ֥יִן וְשֵׁכָ֖ר לֹ֣א שָׁתִ֑יתִי וָאֶשְׁפֹּ֥ךְ אֶת־נַפְשִׁ֖י לִפְנֵ֥י יְהוָֽה׃ 1 Sam 1:15

But Hannah answered and said, No, my lord, a woman harsh of spirit I am. And wine and strong drink I have not drunk, **but I have poured out** my soul before the Lord.

Gen 16:6; 19:10, 14; 20:3; 24:33; 37:35; 39:8, 21; Exod 1:17

d) Explanatory: The Vayyiqtol explains a preceding verb. *r*

וַיִּקְרָ֤א מֶֽלֶךְ־מִצְרַ֙יִם֙ לַֽמְיַלְּדֹ֔ת וַיֹּ֣אמֶר לָהֶ֔ן מַדּ֥וּעַ עֲשִׂיתֶ֖ן הַדָּבָ֣ר הַזֶּ֑ה וַתְּחַיֶּ֖יןָ אֶת־הַיְלָדִֽים׃ Exod 1:18

And the king of Egypt called for the midwives, and said to them, Why have you done this thing, **(namely that) you preserved** the boys **alive**?

1 Sam 8:8; cf. Exod 14:5 (second כִּי)

e) Continuing a preceding finite verbal form or a preceding verbal noun: The Vayyiqtol may continue the tense and aspect of the preceding form, as it may also express succession. This is more common in poetry and direct speech than in narrative. *s*

i. Participle: The Vayyiqtol form may continue the aspect and tense of the participle, but the Vayyiqtol is a verb, not a participle. The following examples could also be interpreted as past tense, completed actions.

---

when this form is avoided. Sometimes it is avoided for routine matters, such as negating the verb; at other times, it is avoided for important syntactical and exegetical reasons, such as introducing a nominal clause.

Ps 34:8 חֹנֶה מַלְאַךְ־יְהוָה סָבִיב לִירֵאָיו וַיְחַלְּצֵם׃

The angel of the Lord is encamping around (to) his fearers **and he rescues them.**

2 Sam 19:2; Ps 2 9:5; 104:32; 107:40

ii. Infinitive:

Ps 92:8 בִּפְרֹחַ רְשָׁעִים כְּמוֹ עֵשֶׂב וַיָּצִיצוּ כָּל־פֹּעֲלֵי אָוֶן לְהִשָּׁמְדָם עֲדֵי־עַד׃

When the wicked sprout as grass, **and** all the doers of iniquity **bloom**, in order for their being destroyed forever.

Ps 34:1; 59:1

iii. Imperfect (present):

Job 14:10 וְגֶבֶר יָמוּת וַיֶּחֱלָשׁ וַיִּגְוַע אָדָם וְאַיּוֹ׃

And man dies and **is prostrate**. **And** man **expires**, and where is he?

Isa 59:16; Hab 1:10; Job 11:3

iv. Perfect (This is common for past tense perfects, but it also occurs for present and future perfects in poetry):

Isa 9:5 כִּי־יֶלֶד יֻלַּד־לָנוּ בֵּן נִתַּן־לָנוּ וַתְּהִי הַמִּשְׂרָה עַל־שִׁכְמוֹ
וַיִּקְרָא שְׁמוֹ פֶּלֶא יוֹעֵץ אֵל גִּבּוֹר אֲבִיעַד שַׂר־שָׁלוֹם׃

For a child is born for us. A son is given to us, and the government will exist upon his shoulders. And his name **shall be called** Wonderful Counselor.

Isa 9:12–13, 18–19; 51:3, 53:1–2, 8–9 Most of these examples are prophetic perfects, but they can be used in other contexts as well.

t 2. Vəyiqtol: The Vav may be connecting or energic. The imperfects may be indicative or jussive/preterit, and they may take energic forms. Most Vəyiqtols with connecting Vavs are indicative, jussive/preterit, or energic; most Vəyiqtols with energic Vavs are jussive in form, but subjunctive (purpose) in meaning.[37]

a) Connecting Vav: This is more common in poetry and direct speech than in narrative. Vəyiqtol often connects with an imperfect (or sometimes with another verbal form or grammatical construction) with the meaning "and."

Exod 23:8[b] כִּי הַשֹּׁחַד יְעַוֵּר פִּקְחִים וִיסַלֵּף דִּבְרֵי צַדִּיקִים׃

For a bribe blinds the seeing **and distorts** the words of the righteous.

Exod 5:21; 19:3; 24:12; Deut 2:4; 1 Sam 10:5; 24:16 (3x as jussives); Ps 2:12; 5:12; 6:11; 9:4

u b) Energic (§53b): In direct speech, Vəyiqtol frequently has an energic meaning expressing purpose, similar to a Greek ἵνα clause. These

37. The Vəyiqtol form often stands in the place of a subjunctive (Lev 9:6).

Vᵊyiqtols are subjunctive ("in order that," "so that"), and often follow a cohortative, jussive, or imperative.

כֹּה־אָמַר יְהוָה אֱלֹהֵי יִשְׂרָאֵל שַׁלַּח אֶת־עַמִּי וְיָחֹגּוּ לִי בַּמִּדְבָּר׃ Exod 5:1[b]

Thus said the Lord, the God of Israel, Send away my people **that they might keep the feast** to me in the wilderness.

In Exod 5:1, the Vᵊyiqtol (subjunctive) follows an imperative.

Gen 19:34; 23:9; Exod 5:5; 8:4 (jussive), 10:17, 21(2x); 11:2; 12:3; 14:4, 12; 1 Sam 11:12; 12:10 (with energic ending); BA Dan 5:2

C. Vav-imperative (Uqᵊtol) *v*

Similar to Vav-imperfects, the Vav of the Vav-imperative may be connecting or energic. Vav-Imperatives usually occur in poetry and direct speech.

1. Connecting Vav: Uqᵊtol often connects to a preceding imperative with the meaning "and."

פְּרוּ וּרְבוּ וּמִלְאוּ אֶת־הַמַּיִם בַּיַּמִּים Gen 1:22[b]

Be fruitful **and multiply and fill** the waters in the seas.

Gen 12:19; 18:6; 34:10; Exod 7:9; 8:12; 14:16

2. Energic (§53c): In direct speech, Uqᵊtol occasionally has an energic meaning expressing purpose. The energic Uqᵊtol normally occurs after a cohortative, imperative, jussive, or rarely an indicative. *w*

וַיֹּאמֶר אֲלֵהֶם יוֹסֵף בַּיּוֹם הַשְּׁלִישִׁי זֹאת עֲשׂוּ וִחְיוּ אֶת־הָאֱלֹהִים אֲנִי יָרֵא׃ Gen 42:18

And Joseph said to them on the third day, this do that **you might live**. God I fear.

Gen 42:18; 45:18; 47:19; Exod 3:10; Judg 19:24; 1 Sam 12:17; 28:22; 2 Kgs 5:10; Amos 5:4, 6

§7. The Qal and the Derived Conjugations of the Verb *a*

In addition to the Qal, Hebrew possesses other conjugations or stems said to be derived from the primary Qal conjugation. Usually, these derived conjugations add nuances to the basic meaning of the Qal. Some Hebrew verbs do not occur in the Qal, but only in a derived stem (Niphal, Piel, Pual, Hithpael, Hiphil, or Hophal). Including the Qal stem, most Hebrew verbs occur in a few (one to three) stems. Few verbs occur in all stems.

In addition to aspect, tense, and mood, the Qal and its derived conjugations have voice: active (Qal, Piel, Hiphil), passive (Pual, Hophal), and REFLEXIVE (Niphal, Hithpael). In the active voice, the agent does the action of the verb. For stative verbs, the agent becomes a state or exists in a state. Verbs in the active voice may take an object (transitive) or may not take an object (intransitive). Transitive verbs take their objects directly or indirectly through a preposition.

In the passive voice, the subject receives the verbal action. The object of the active verb becomes the subject of the passive verb. In Hebrew and other Semitic languages, the agent or doer of the verbal action of the passive cannot be expressed as the English passive, "John was hit *by Paul*." Instead, Hebrew must use the active construction, "Paul hit John." Although Hebrew and other Semitic languages "hide" the agent of passive verbs, the agent is implied or assumed in the mind of the speaker—"John was hit (by someone or something)." The passive of the imperfect and participle may have the nuance of "worthy of," "ought to be," or "liable to be."[38]

The Hebrew and Semitic reflexive, by contrast, is "agentless," that is, the agent of the verbal action is irrelevant, being neither implied nor assumed in the mind of the speaker. The context may make the agent known, but the reflexive form neither assumes or implies the agent. Moreover, reflexive action often expresses the result, state, or effect for the object of an active verb—יִסַּרְתַּנִי וָאִוָּסֵר, You disciplined me, and so (as a result) I got myself disciplined (Jer 17:14[2x]; 20:17; 31:4; 31:18; 51:9), or נִחֲמוֹ וַיִּתְנַחֵם, He comforted him, and so (as a result) he got himself comforted (compare Gen 37:35). The action of the active verb (he comforted) affected the object (him). The reflexive expresses the result, state, or effect of the active verbal action on the object (he got himself comforted), with agency irrelevant for the reflexive verb. Reflexive verbs properly occur with physical actions (break, cut, hit, mourn), though non-physical actions of the senses (know, understand) or states may also take reflexives occasionally. The Semitic grammarians say these verbs express actions that are "preceptable by the senses." As the reflexive Hithpael takes direct objects or objects through a preposition, the reflexive nuance is weaken, but not completely lost. As the name "reflexive" implies, the verbal action in some manner comes back to the subject.[39]

Summary of Voice in Hebrew for Translation into English:

Active:	"He broke it."
Passive:	"It was broken (by someone or something)." Agency is implied, though the agency may be unknown.
Reflexive:	"It got itself broken," "it broke," or "it broke by itself." Agency is irrelevant.

A. Qal

The Qal is the "light" or simple form of the verb without the "heavy" prefixes (Niphal, Hithpael, Hiphil, or Hophal) or internal modifications of the verbal root (Piel, Pual, or Hithpael). The Qal preserved a passive in the participle and rare forms resembling the Pual or Hophal. If a verbal form resembles the Pual perfect (Gen 4:26) or Hophal imperfect (Gen 18:4), but does not occur in the Piel perfect or Hiphil imperfect, the form is probably Qal passive.[40]

Qal verbs express actions and states. The verbs conveying actions usually have Patach for their thematic vowel in the perfect. The verbs conveying a state

38. Thackston §58.

39. Thackston §58; Wright I, §47, 50, 52.

40. GKC §52e; 53u. GKC §52e correctly states, "In these cases there is no need to assume any error on the part of the punctuators; the sharpening of the second radical may have taken place in order to retain the characteristic 'u' of the first syllable, and the 'a' of the second syllable is in accordance with the vocalization of all the other passives." Indeed, the Masoretes were fluent in Arabic and Aramaic, languages with Qal passive forms. These masters of Hebrew, Arabic, and Aramaic undoubtedly grasped the difference between a Qal passive and a Pual or Hophal. Also see GKC §52e fn 5 for the opinion of Ibn Janach, who also regarded these forms as Qal passives.

(to be heavy, great, small) usually have Sere or Holem for thematic vowels in the perfect. Originally, the Sere thematic vowel of stative verbs indicated temporary or acquired states (old, guilty, fat); the Holem thematic vowel of stative verbs indicated permanent or innate states (be powerful, be light). The Sere vowels still may indicate temporary ailments and griefs (hungry, faint, unclean) and their opposites (full, clean, rejoice, glad). Over time, this distinction began to fade between the Sere and Holem vowels, producing exceptions.[41]

B. Piel, Pual, and Hithpael *b*

The Piel, Pual, and Hithpael are INTENSIVE/EXTENSIVE verbal forms. The doubling of the second radical strengthens the form, often exaggerating the meaning of the Qal by adding force to the verbal action and/or extending the verbal action to many subjects or objects. Of course, these forms are not always intensive/extensive, as the Hiphil is not always causative. The Pual is the passive of the Piel; the Hithpael is the REFLEXIVE of the Piel (and sometimes to the Qal), the ת adding a reflexive nuance and often a personal interest/privilege nuance to the intensives (Exod 8:5; 19:22; 1 Sam 23:19; BA Dan 5:23). A few verbs occur in the Piel, Pual, or Hithpael without "fitting" any of the following categories.[42]

1. Intensive/extensive: Intensive action communicates action with great force or energy. Extensive action extends or repeats the action to many subjects (frequentatively extensive, the subject does the action many times) or to many objects (numerically extensive, the action is extended to many objects). Extensive action can also extend the time of the action (temporally extensive, that is, the time is extended, as for example, to weep for a long time or much).[43] Extensive action often occurs without intensive action, but intensive action usually occurs with the extension of the action. Intensive/extensive action, therefore, conveys a "busying oneself eagerly in an action"[44] or a "constant, firm action."[45] Intensive/extensive formations of nouns are naturally used for professions (Gen 39:1, הַטַּבָּחִים) or any adjective that signifies intensive/extensive action (Exod 21:29, נַגָּח). *c*
   Examples:
   a) שׁבר: The Qal signifies "break"; the Piel intensifies the "breaking" with force—"smash to pieces"—and extends the smashing to all objects one after another until all are smashed to pieces.

      קוֹל יְהוָה שֹׁבֵר אֲרָזִים וַיְשַׁבֵּר יְהוָה אֶת־אַרְזֵי הַלְּבָנוֹן׃ Ps 29:5

      The voice of the Lord (is) a breaker (of) the cedars; **and** the Lord **smashes to pieces** the cedars of Lebanon.
   b) קבר: The Qal denotes burying; the Piel extends the burying to all corpses one after another until none are left (numerically extensive). This verb

41. Howell §484; Wright I, §38.
42. Howell §489; Wright I, §39–41; ZW, 61.
43. Wright I, §40
44. GKC §52f
45. Franz Delitzsch, *Commentary on the Old Testament: Proverbs, Ecclesiastes, Song of Solomon*, Vol VI (Grand Rapids: Eerdmans, reprint 1984), 182.

is extensive, but not intensive since the force of burying cannot be intensified.

1 Kgs 11:15 וַיְהִי בִּהְיוֹת דָּוִד אֶת־אֱדוֹם בַּעֲלוֹת יוֹאָב שַׂר הַצָּבָא לְקַבֵּר אֶת־הַחֲלָלִים וַיַּךְ כָּל־זָכָר בֶּאֱדוֹם׃

And it happened when David was in Edom when Joab, the commander of the army, went up **to bury** the slain **one after the other** that he smote every male in Edom.

c) הלך: The Qal conveys "to walk"; the Piel intensifies the walking (trampling, marching) and extends the walking—all about, all around—"to trample all around or to march about." The Hithpael adds the notion of personal interest/privilege, "to march all around at one's own discretion, privilege, or leisure."

Prov 6:28 אִם־יְהַלֵּךְ אִישׁ עַל־הַגֶּחָלִים וְרַגְלָיו לֹא תִכָּוֶינָה׃

Or **can** a man **walk about** on hot coals, and his feet not be scorched?

Gen 13:17 קוּם הִתְהַלֵּךְ בָּאָרֶץ לְאָרְכָּהּ וּלְרָחְבָּהּ כִּי לְךָ אֶתְּנֶנָּה׃

Arise, **walk about at your leisure** through the land with respect to its length and breadth; for to you I will give it.

Exod 14:27; 1 Sam 23:23; 24:8, 19; BA Dan 2:14, 44; 4:11

d) **אזר**: The Qal conveys a simple girding. The Piel intensifies the force of the girding and extends the girding to many items. The Hithpael furnishes the reflexive meaning.

Isa 8:9 רֹעוּ עַמִּים וָחֹתּוּ וְהַאֲזִינוּ כֹּל מֶרְחַקֵּי־אָרֶץ הִתְאַזְּרוּ וָחֹתּוּ הִתְאַזְּרוּ וָחֹתּוּ׃

Be broken, O peoples, and be shattered; And give ear, all remote places of the earth. **Get yourselves securely girded** and be dismayed. **Get yourselves securely girded** and be dismayed.

With these imperatives, the Hithpael expresses the result of doing the action of the Piel to yourself.

d 2. Factitive: The word factitive comes from a Latin word (*facere*) meaning "to make." The Piel factitive often makes Qal intransitive verbs transitive and Qal transitive verbs doubly transitive (taking two objects, Job 38:12). Factitives occur with non-physical Qal intransitive verbs that cannot be intensified or extended. They make Qal stative verbs transitive and denote the placing of someone or something (the direct object) into the state of the Qal.

a) למד: The intransitive non-stative Qal becomes transitive in the Piel. (Qal) to learn; (Piel) to make learn, to teach.

Deut 4:5 רְאֵה׀ לִמַּדְתִּי אֶתְכֶם חֻקִּים וּמִשְׁפָּטִים כַּאֲשֶׁר צִוַּנִי יְהוָה אֱלֹהָי לַעֲשׂוֹת כֵּן בְּקֶרֶב הָאָרֶץ אֲשֶׁר אַתֶּם בָּאִים שָׁמָּה לְרִשְׁתָּהּ׃

See, **I have taught you** statutes and judgments just as the Lord my God commanded me, that you should do thus in the land where you are entering to possess it.

b) חיה: Qal, be alive; Piel, to make or preserve alive

Gen 12:12 וְהָיָה כִּי־יִרְאוּ אֹתָךְ הַמִּצְרִים וְאָמְרוּ אִשְׁתּוֹ זֹאת וְהָרְגוּ אֹתִי
וְאֹתָךְ יְחַיּוּ׃

And it will come about when the Egyptians see you, that they will say, "This is his wife"; and they will kill me, **and you they will preserve alive**.

c) כבד: The intransitive Qal stative means to be heavy; the transitive Piel puts the subject of the Qal into a state—make heavy (honor) your parents, or put your parents in a heavy state.

Exod 20:12 כַּבֵּד אֶת־אָבִיךָ וְאֶת־אִמֶּךָ לְמַעַן יַאֲרִכוּן יָמֶיךָ עַל הָאֲדָמָה
אֲשֶׁר־יְהוָה אֱלֹהֶיךָ נֹתֵן לָךְ׃

Make heavy your father and your mother so that your days may be prolonged upon the land which the Lord your God is giving to you.

d) קדשׁ: In Exod 19:23, God commanded the Israelites to put Sinai in a holy state, that is, to make holy or sanctify Sinai.

Exod 19:23 וַיֹּאמֶר מֹשֶׁה אֶל־יְהוָה לֹא־יוּכַל הָעָם לַעֲלֹת אֶל־הַר סִינָי
כִּי־אַתָּה הַעֵדֹתָה בָּנוּ לֵאמֹר הַגְבֵּל אֶת־הָהָר וְקִדַּשְׁתּוֹ׃

And Moses said to the Lord, The people are not able to go up to Mount Sinai, for you have testified against them saying, Mark off the mountain **and put it in a holy condition**.

Num 11:18[a] וְאֶל־הָעָם תֹּאמַר הִתְקַדְּשׁוּ לְמָחָר וַאֲכַלְתֶּם בָּשָׂר

And to the people say, **Get yourselves in a holy condition** for tomorrow, and you shall eat flesh.

The reflexive Hithpael in Num 11:18 means to get oneself into a holy condition.

e) Num 12:6

Num 12:6 וַיֹּאמֶר שִׁמְעוּ־נָא דְבָרָי אִם־יִהְיֶה נְבִיאֲכֶם יְהוָה בַּמַּרְאָה
אֵלָיו אֶתְוַדָּע בַּחֲלוֹם אֲדַבֶּר־בּוֹ׃

He said, Hear now my words: If a prophet with respect to you exists, the Lord—in a vision **I make myself known** to him. I shall speak with him in a dream.

This Hithpael may be the reflexive to the Piel doubly transitive verb (Job 28:12), with a retained object through the preposition (to him).

f) Gen 37:18

Gen 37:18 וַיִּרְאוּ אֹתוֹ מֵרָחֹק וּבְטֶרֶם יִקְרַב אֲלֵיהֶם וַיִּתְנַכְּלוּ אֹתוֹ לַהֲמִיתוֹ׃

When they saw him from a distance; And when he came near to him, **they put him in a naïve state** for themselves.

When the Hithpael takes a direct object, it may weaken its reflexive nuance, as in Gen 37:18 and Num 12:6 above. In these cases, the Hithpael may be similar in meaning to the Piel, but with the reflexive nuance of "for himself/themselves" or "for his/their benefit."

1 Sam 21:14 (Hithpoel); 23:16; Jer 7:30; BA Dan 6:8; Ezra 4:21, 23; 6:12, 20, 22

3. Declarative/Estimative: The declarative Piels, often associated with verbs of speech or with verbs having an adjectival meaning in the Qal, declare, estimate, or consider someone or something to be the meaning of the verb. *e*

a) ברך: To declare or estimate someone or something as blessed.
b) צדק: To declare or estimate someone as righteous.

וַיִּחַר אַף׀ אֱלִיהוּא בֶן־בַּרַכְאֵל הַבּוּזִי מִמִּשְׁפַּחַת רָם בְּאִיּוֹב חָרָה אַפּוֹ עַל־צַדְּקוֹ נַפְשׁוֹ מֵאֱלֹהִים׃ Job 32:2

And the anger of Elihu, the son of Barachel the Buzite, from the family of Ram was hot. Against Job his anger burned, because **he declared** his soul **righteous** more than God.

וַיֹּאמֶר יְהוּדָה מַה־נֹּאמַר לַאדֹנִי מַה־נְּדַבֵּר וּמַה־נִּצְטַדָּק Gen 44:16[a]

So Judah said, What shall we say to our lord? What shall we speak? And how shall **we get ourselves declared as righteous**?

The Hithpael adds the reflexive notion in Gen 44:16, "Someone declared us righteous, and so (the result is) we got ourselves declared righteous." The agent who did the declaring is irrelevant to the reflexive verb, though the context may indicate the agent.

Gen 24:1; Exod 20:11; Deut 33:1; 2 Sam 6:12; BA Dan 2:19; 4:19

f 4. DENOMINATIVE: The word denominative means "(derived) from the noun." English has denominative verbs such as "to phone" or "to email." Denominatives derive their meaning from a noun and usually do not occur in the Qal unless the meaning of the Qal differs from the denominative Piel. The other Piels (intensive/extensive, factitive, and declarative/estimative), by contrast, are associated with a Qal verb of similar meaning. The Hiphil also expresses denominatives.

a) כהן: to priest, that is, to act or function as a priest, to do all the priestly functions.

וְכִפֶּר הַכֹּהֵן אֲשֶׁר־יִמְשַׁח אֹתוֹ וַאֲשֶׁר יְמַלֵּא אֶת־יָדוֹ לְכַהֵן תַּחַת אָבִיו Lev 16:32[a]

The priest who anoints him and who fills his hand **to function as a priest** in place of his father will make atonement.

b) שרש: to root, that is, to deprive of roots, uproot. This denominative has a depriving sense.

גַּם־אֵל יִתָּצְךָ לָנֶצַח יַחְתְּךָ וְיִסָּחֲךָ מֵאֹהֶל וְשֵׁרֶשְׁךָ מֵאֶרֶץ חַיִּים סֶלָה׃ Ps 52:7

Even God will tear you down forever. He will snatch you away and rip you away from your tent; **he will uproot you** from the land of the living.

1 Sam 23:7

The Hithpael has other rare usages, including reciprocal (Gen 42:1) and possibly passive (Prov 31:30), though these may also be reflexives with a slight variation of nuance. Moreover, the Hithpael may occasionally be reflexive to the Qal (Ps 18:26).

g Determining whether a Piel is intensive, extensive, or both may be difficult. Usually, intensive/extensive Piels occur in the Qal with a similar meaning, but without the intensive/extensive nuance. Intensive/extensive Piels are usually physical actions, done with the hands or feet, not with the senses; their objects are usually concrete and plural, not abstract or singular. Sometimes their action happens with such force and/or occurrences (extensions) that the object is no more. In 1 Kgs 18:38, for example, the fire from heaven licks the water repeatedly and intensively until all was gone—not a drop left. In Ps 106:38, an extensive Piel relates Israel's sacrificing of their children (note the concrete plural object) one after another, until none were left to sacrifice. The action of sacrificing in 1 Kgs 8:5 and the action of burying in 1 Kgs 11:15 (again both with concrete plural objects) illustrate the extension of the action to many (numeric) objects—"to bury one body after another." Such actions cannot be done with more bodily force or intensity. Naturally, many Piel participles have the extensity (and sometimes the intensity) of occurrences, since they depict the repetitive actions inherent in occupations and professions (§23h).

Three considerations usually disqualify a Piel, Pual, or Hithpael from being intensive/extensive. First, a stative verb in the Qal is factitive, not intensive. Second, a verb that does not occur in a finite Qal form (perfect, imperfect, or imperative), but only in the Piel, Pual, or Hithpael, is usually factitive, denominative, or declarative (exceptions כבשׁ, נתח). Third, Piel, Pual, or Hithpael do not intensify or extend classes of verbs expressing speech or exercises of the mind, emotions, and senses, such as hoping, trusting, remembering, loving, hating, seeing, speaking, or hearing.

For determining whether rare roots are intensive, consider the meaning of the root and check the root in Mishnaic Hebrew, cognate Semitic languages, and the ancient versions (Septuagint and Vulgate), for any hint of intensification.

C. Hiphil and Hophal *h*

These conjugations are CAUSATIVE verbal forms. Of course, these forms have a variety of uses, like the Piel. The Hophal is the passive of the Hiphil (Exod 10:8). The Niphal may express the reflexive to the Hiphil, especially with verbs that occur only in the Niphal and Hiphil. A few verbs occur in the Hiphil or Hophal without "fitting" any of the following categories.[46]

1. Causative/Factitive: The causative makes an intransitive Qal transitive and a transitive Qal doubly transitive. The subject of the intransitive Qal becomes the object of the causative element (הִ, הַ). The subject of the transitive Qal becomes the object of the causative element, and the object of the transitive Qal become the object of the verbal root of the Hiphil.[47]

2 Kgs 3:19 וְהִכִּיתֶם כָּל־עִיר מִבְצָר וְכָל־עִיר מִבְחוֹר וְכָל־עֵץ טוֹב
תַּפִּילוּ וְכָל־מַעַיְנֵי־מַיִם תִּסְתֹּמוּ וְכֹל הַחֶלְקָה
הַטּוֹבָה תַּכְאִבוּ בָּאֲבָנִים׃

And you will strike every fortified city and every choice city, and every good tree **you will cause to fall** and all springs of water you will stop up, and every good plot of land **you will cause pain (mar)** with stones.

46. Howell §488; Wright I, §44–45; ZW, 61.
47. §13k–u and footnote 39.

The intransitive Qal would be, "every good tree fell." The Hiphil makes the subject of the intransitive Qal the object of the causative element in the Hiphil, "you will cause every good tree (to fall)."

Gen 48:11 וַיֹּ֤אמֶר יִשְׂרָאֵל֙ אֶל־יוֹסֵ֔ף רְאֹ֥ה פָנֶ֖יךָ לֹ֣א פִלָּ֑לְתִּי וְהִנֵּ֨ה הֶרְאָ֥ה אֹתִ֛י אֱלֹהִ֖ים גַּ֥ם אֶת־זַרְעֶֽךָ׃

And Israel said to Joseph, I never expected to see your face, and behold, **God caused me to see** even your seed.

The transitive Qal would be, "I saw your seed." The Hiphil makes the subject of the transitive Qal the object of the causative element in the Hiphil, "God cause me (to see)." And the Hiphil make the object of the transitive Qal the object of the verbal root of the Hiphil, "(God caused me) to see even your seed."

Exod 5:4; 15:22; BA Dan 2:25; Ezra 4:10

a) Allowance: For English purposes, some causatives may be translated: "to allow" or "to let."

Ps 119:10 בְּכָל־לִבִּ֥י דְרַשְׁתִּ֑יךָ אַל־תַּ֝שְׁגֵּ֗נִי מִמִּצְוֺתֶֽיךָ׃

With all my heart I have sought you; **let me** not **wander** from your commandments.

Exod 12:36

b) Inner causative: The subject is also the object, so the object is *within* the verb. These verbs are usually stative in the Qal, with a reflexive translation for the inner causative for English.

Neh 9:25[b] וַיֹּאכְל֤וּ וַֽיִּשְׂבְּעוּ֙ וַיַּשְׁמִ֔ינוּ

And they ate and became satisfied **and they made themselves fat**.

Exod 10:21

i 2. Declarative/Estimative: Like the Piel, the Hiphil may declare, estimate, or consider someone to be the meaning of the verb. These declarative verbs are usually associated with verbs of speech or with verbs having an adjectival nuance in the Qal.

Prov 17:15 מַצְדִּ֣יק רָ֭שָׁע וּמַרְשִׁ֣יעַ צַדִּ֑יק תּוֹעֲבַ֥ת יְ֝הוָ֗ה גַּם־שְׁנֵיהֶֽם׃

He who justifies the wicked, **and he who condemns** the righteous, both of them alike are an abomination to the Lord.

A more interpretive translation of the declarative is, "The man who *declares* the righteous to be the wicked (the justifier of the wicked); and the man who *declares* the wicked to be righteous (the condemner of the righteous), both of them alike are an abomination to the Lord."

Exod 23:7

j 3. Denominative: Like the Piel, the Hiphil may express a denominative. The meaning between the Piel and Hiphil denominative is similar. The denominative Hiphil has various nuances:

Gen 2:5[b] כִּי֩ לֹ֨א הִמְטִ֜יר יְהוָ֤ה אֱלֹהִים֙ עַל־הָאָ֔רֶץ

For the Lord God had not yet caused rain upon the earth.

Gen 1:12; Jer 14:22, 50:9

פִּנִּיתָ לְפָנֶיהָ וַתַּשְׁרֵשׁ שָׁרָשֶׁיהָ וַתְּמַלֵּא־אָרֶץ׃ Ps 80:10

You cleared before her **and you uprooted** her roots and you filled earth.

This denominative has a depriving sense.

אִם־הַשְּׂמֹאל וְאֵימִנָה וְאִם־הַיָּמִין וְאַשְׂמְאִילָה׃ Gen 13:9[b]

If to the left, then I will go to the right. If to the right, then I will go to the left.

וַיַּשְׁכֵּם אַבְרָהָם בַּבֹּקֶר Gen 19:27[a]

And Abraham got up in the morning

Denominatives may communicate time and place. Gen 13:9 expresses movement towards a place; Gen 19:27 expresses the occurrence of a period of time.

As the intensives are not always intensive, the Hiphil is not always causative. As the Piel, Pual, and Hithpael are usually non-intensive if the verbal root is without a Qal finite verbal form, so the Hiphil is often non-causative if the verbal root is without a Qal finite verbal form, for example, הִשְׁלִיךְ. As Qal stative verbs become factitives in the Piel, so Qal stative verbs become inner causatives in the Hiphil.

D. Niphal *k*

The Niphal is the reflexive of the Qal and frequently of the Hiphil. Properly, for the reflexive Niphal, the Qal or Hiphil should be transitive, expressing a physical or visible action. The reflexive Niphal describes the result or effect of the Qal action on its object. גְּאָלוֹ וַיִּגָּאֵל—He redeemed him, and so he (the object of the Qal verb) got himself redeemed. The agent of the reflexive verb is irrelevant. Personal interest may occasionally be implied in the Niphal. Personal interest is more clearly indicated by the ת of the Hithpael. Later, in Hebrew (and in Arabic) the Niphal reflexive was used for non-physical actions or actions "not perceptable to the senses." These later Niphals that are "not perceptable to the senses" may also be interpreted as passives. The other uses of the Niphal are secondary and less common. Moreover, they may be variations of the reflexive. A few verbs occur in the Niphal without "fitting" any of the following categories.[48]

1. Reflexive:

   וַתִּבָּקַע הָאֲדָמָה אֲשֶׁר תַּחְתֵּיהֶם׃ Num 16:31[b]

   The ground which was under them got (itself) split.

   Gen 1:9; 2:4, 10; 3:5; 19:17; Exod 7:15; 10:3; 1 Sam 21:5

2. Personal interest: This occasional usage expresses the personal interest of the speaker. This may be a nuance of the reflexive since the reflexive also frequently implies personal interest as well. *l*

48. Howell §491; Wright I, §52–53; ZW, 62.

1 Sam 20:6 אִם־פָּקֹד יִפְקְדֵנִי אָבִיךָ וְאָמַרְתָּ נִשְׁאֹל נִשְׁאַל מִמֶּנִּי דָוִד
לָרוּץ בֵּית־לֶחֶם עִירוֹ כִּי זֶבַח הַיָּמִים שָׁם לְכָל־הַמִּשְׁפָּחָה׃

If your father misses me in any way, then say, David **earnestly asked (for himself or for his own personal interest)** of me to run to Bethlehem his city, because the yearly sacrifice (was) there for the whole family.

m 3. Tolerative: The subject allows (tolerates) the verbal action to happen to himself. The Israelites allowed themselves to be defeated, or they feigned defeat against Ai. This is probably a reflexive with an added nuance.

Josh 8:15 וַיִּנָּגְעוּ יְהוֹשֻׁעַ וְכָל־יִשְׂרָאֵל לִפְנֵיהֶם וַיָּנֻסוּ דֶּרֶךְ הַמִּדְבָּר׃

And Joshua and all Israel **allowed themselves** to be smitten before them, and fled to the way of the wilderness.

Isa 65:1; Jer 6:8, 31:18

n 4. Reciprocal: The action is reciprocated by two or more individuals or groups.

1 Kgs 12:6[a] וַיִּוָּעַץ הַמֶּלֶךְ רְחַבְעָם אֶת־הַזְּקֵנִים אֲשֶׁר־הָיוּ עֹמְדִים
אֶת־פְּנֵי שְׁלֹמֹה אָבִיו

And King Rehoboam **counseled together** with the elders who existed as those who stand before Solomon, his father.

Again, this is probably a variation of the reflexive: He got himself counsel with the elders.

Exod 21:22

Exercises

I. Questions and Discussions

1. In view of Hebrew having only two main tenses (perfect and imperfect), discuss the issues that must be considered in understanding and translating verbs.
2. Define aspect. Discuss how aspect is expressed in the perfect and imperfect.
3. Define tense. How do the Arab grammarians refer to the perfect and imperfect?
4. How are the tenses related to the perfect and imperfect?
5. Define mood. List and discuss the moods of Hebrew.
6. How is mood related to the perfect and imperfect?
7. From the perspective of tense, what is the general principle that decides whether a Hebrew author uses the perfect or imperfect?
8. From the perspective of aspect, what is the general principle that decides whether a Hebrew author uses the perfect or imperfect?
9. When is tense stronger than aspect? When is aspect stronger than tense?
10. Can a verb ever have tense without aspect or aspect without tense?
11. How does the form of the perfect indicate completed action?
12. List and discuss the uses of the perfect for past, present, and future actions.
13. Discuss the mood of the perfect.
14. Generally, how is the perfect used in Old Testament narrative, direct speech, and poetry?
15. How is the perfect emphasized?
16. List the moods/forms represented in the imperfect.
17. How should the prefixed letters of the imperfect be understood?
18. What are the pronouns of the imperfect?
19. Define volitional forms. What are the volitional forms and how are they emphasized?
20. Define indicative mood. What forms shows remnants of the indicative form?
21. Discuss the aspect of the indicative mood.
22. Discuss the usage of the indicative in the past, present, and future tense.
23. Generally, how is the imperfect used in Old Testament narrative, direct speech, and poetry?
24. Discuss prohibitions with indicatives and jussives.
25. Define subjunctive mood. Compare and contrast it with the indicative.
26. How is the subjunctive indicated?
27. What is the aspect and tense of the subjunctive?
28. Define jussive and preterit.
29. How is the jussive and preterit indicated?
30. Discuss the form of the jussive and preterit.
31. What is the aspect and tense of the jussive and preterit? Discuss their usage in the Old Testament.
32. List the three energic particles.
33. Discuss the usage of the energic particles with the imperfect and imperative.

34. How is the imperfect emphasized?
35. Contrast the form of the imperative and the imperfect.
36. Discuss the aspect, tense, and usage of the imperative.
37. How is the imperative emphasized?
38. Define connecting and energic Vav.
39. Discuss the two nuances (translations) of the connecting Vav with the perfect.
40. Discuss the usages of the energic Vav with the imperfect in the past, present, and future. Also discuss the independent use of the energic Vav with the imperfect.
41. Discuss the Vayyiqtol form in narrative, poetry, and direct speech.
42. List and discuss the common uses of the Vayyitqtol form.
43. When is the connecting Vav more common than energic Vav for Vᵊyiqtol forms?
44. What nuance does the Vᵊyiqtol with energic Vav usually express?
45. What nuance does energic Vav express with Vav imperative forms?
46. Define "derived conjugations."
47. Define and contrast the three voices of Hebrew: active, passive, and reflexive. Summarize how to translate them into English.
48. Define the Qal. Discuss the Qal passive. How is the Qal passive indicated? Did the Masoretes misunderstand these forms?
49. Define Piel, Pual, and Hithpael. Define intensive and extensive verbal action. List and discuss the various types of extensive verbal actions.
50. Define and discuss the terms: factitive, declarative/estimative, and denominative.
51. How can it be determined whether the Piel, Pual, or Hithpael is intensive/extensive?
52. Define Hiphil and Hophal.
53. Discuss the usages of the Hiphil and Hophal. Define "inner causative." How do the Piel and Hiphil denominatives differ?
54. Define Niphal.
55. Discuss the usages of the Niphal.

II. Drills

1. **Analyze the tense and usage (e.g. present, certitude) of the following perfects. The verses follow the numbering of the Masoretic Text.**

Gen 42:38 (1)
וַיֹּ֕אמֶר לֹֽא־יֵרֵ֥ד בְּנִ֖י עִמָּכֶ֑ם כִּֽי־אָחִ֨יו מֵ֜ת וְה֧וּא לְבַדּ֣וֹ נִשְׁאָ֗ר וּקְרָאָ֤הוּ אָסוֹן֙ בַּדֶּ֙רֶךְ֙ אֲשֶׁ֣ר תֵּֽלְכוּ־בָ֔הּ וְהוֹרַדְתֶּ֧ם אֶת־שֵׂיבָתִ֛י בְּיָג֖וֹן שְׁאֽוֹלָה׃

Isa 10:28 (2)
בָּ֥א עַל־עַיַּ֖ת עָבַ֣ר בְּמִגְר֑וֹן לְמִכְמָ֖שׂ יַפְקִ֥יד כֵּלָֽיו׃

Exod 7:26 (3)
וַיֹּ֤אמֶר יְהוָה֙ אֶל־מֹשֶׁ֔ה בֹּ֖א אֶל־פַּרְעֹ֑ה וְאָמַרְתָּ֣ אֵלָ֗יו כֹּ֚ה אָמַ֣ר יְהוָ֔ה שַׁלַּ֥ח אֶת־עַמִּ֖י וְיַֽעַבְדֻֽנִי׃

Gen 13:12 (4)
אַבְרָ֖ם יָשַׁ֣ב בְּאֶֽרֶץ־כְּנָ֑עַן וְל֗וֹט יָשַׁב֙ בְּעָרֵ֣י הַכִּכָּ֔ר וַיֶּאֱהַ֖ל עַד־סְדֹֽם׃

Gen 6:6 (5)
וַיִּנָּ֣חֶם יְהוָ֔ה כִּֽי־עָשָׂ֥ה אֶת־הָֽאָדָ֖ם בָּאָ֑רֶץ וַיִּתְעַצֵּ֖ב אֶל־לִבּֽוֹ׃

Deut 26:3 (6)
וּבָאתָ֙ אֶל־הַכֹּהֵ֔ן אֲשֶׁ֥ר יִהְיֶ֖ה בַּיָּמִ֣ים הָהֵ֑ם וְאָמַרְתָּ֣ אֵלָ֗יו הִגַּ֤דְתִּי הַיּוֹם֙ לַיהוָ֣ה אֱלֹהֶ֔יךָ כִּי־בָ֙אתִי֙ אֶל־הָאָ֔רֶץ אֲשֶׁ֨ר נִשְׁבַּ֧ע יְהוָ֛ה לַאֲבֹתֵ֖ינוּ לָ֥תֶת לָֽנוּ׃

Exod 7:1 (7)
וַיֹּ֤אמֶר יְהוָה֙ אֶל־מֹשֶׁ֔ה רְאֵ֛ה נְתַתִּ֥יךָ אֱלֹהִ֖ים לְפַרְעֹ֑ה וְאַהֲרֹ֥ן אָחִ֖יךָ יִהְיֶ֥ה נְבִיאֶֽךָ׃

Gen 43:14 (8)
וְאֵ֣ל שַׁדַּ֗י יִתֵּ֨ן לָכֶ֤ם רַחֲמִים֙ לִפְנֵ֣י הָאִ֔ישׁ וְשִׁלַּ֥ח לָכֶ֛ם אֶת־אֲחִיכֶ֥ם אַחֵ֖ר וְאֶת־בִּנְיָמִ֑ין וַאֲנִ֕י כַּאֲשֶׁ֥ר שָׁכֹ֖לְתִּי שָׁכָֽלְתִּי׃

Gen 19:19 (9)
הִנֵּה־נָ֠א מָצָ֨א עַבְדְּךָ֥ חֵן֮ בְּעֵינֶ֒יךָ֒ וַתַּגְדֵּ֣ל חַסְדְּךָ֗ אֲשֶׁ֤ר עָשִׂ֙יתָ֙ עִמָּדִ֔י לְהַחֲי֖וֹת אֶת־נַפְשִׁ֑י וְאָנֹכִ֗י לֹ֤א אוּכַל֙ לְהִמָּלֵ֣ט הָהָ֔רָה פֶּן־תִּדְבָּקַ֥נִי הָרָעָ֖ה וָמַֽתִּי׃

1 Sam 2:1 (10)
וַתִּתְפַּלֵּ֤ל חַנָּה֙ וַתֹּאמַ֔ר עָלַ֤ץ לִבִּי֙ בַּֽיהוָ֔ה רָ֥מָה קַרְנִ֖י בַּֽיהוָ֑ה רָ֤חַב פִּי֙ עַל־א֣וֹיְבַ֔י כִּ֥י שָׂמַ֖חְתִּי בִּישׁוּעָתֶֽךָ׃

Gen 31:34 (11)
וְרָחֵ֞ל לָקְחָ֣ה אֶת־הַתְּרָפִ֗ים וַתְּשִׂמֵ֛ם בְּכַ֥ר הַגָּמָ֖ל וַתֵּ֣שֶׁב עֲלֵיהֶ֑ם וַיְמַשֵּׁ֥שׁ לָבָ֛ן אֶת־כָּל־הָאֹ֖הֶל וְלֹ֥א מָצָֽא׃

Gen 6:7 (12)
וַיֹּ֣אמֶר יְהוָ֗ה אֶמְחֶ֨ה אֶת־הָאָדָ֤ם אֲשֶׁר־בָּרָ֙אתִי֙ מֵעַל֙ פְּנֵ֣י הָֽאֲדָמָ֔ה מֵֽאָדָם֙ עַד־בְּהֵמָ֔ה עַד־רֶ֖מֶשׂ וְעַד־ע֣וֹף הַשָּׁמָ֑יִם כִּ֥י נִחַ֖מְתִּי כִּ֥י עֲשִׂיתִֽם׃

Ps 33:20 (13)
נַפְשֵׁ֗נוּ חִכְּתָ֥ה לַיהוָ֑ה עֶזְרֵ֖נוּ וּמָגִנֵּ֣נוּ הֽוּא׃

(14) Gen 21:17 וַיִּשְׁמַע אֱלֹהִים אֶת־קוֹל הַנַּעַר וַיִּקְרָא מַלְאַךְ אֱלֹהִים׀ אֶל־הָגָר מִן־
הַשָּׁמַיִם וַיֹּאמֶר לָהּ מַה־לָּךְ הָגָר אַל־תִּירְאִי כִּי־שָׁמַע אֱלֹהִים אֶל־קוֹל
הַנַּעַר בַּאֲשֶׁר הוּא־שָׁם׃

(15) Deut 8:10 וְאָכַלְתָּ וְשָׂבָעְתָּ וּבֵרַכְתָּ אֶת־יְהוָה אֱלֹהֶיךָ עַל־הָאָרֶץ הַטֹּבָה אֲשֶׁר נָתַן־
לָךְ׃

2. **Analyze the mood, tense, and usage of the following imperfects.**

(1) Gen 12:13 אִמְרִי־נָא אֲחֹתִי אָתְּ לְמַעַן יִיטַב־לִי בַעֲבוּרֵךְ וְחָיְתָה נַפְשִׁי בִּגְלָלֵךְ׃

(2) Exod 9:5 וַיָּשֶׂם יְהוָה מוֹעֵד לֵאמֹר מָחָר יַעֲשֶׂה יְהוָה הַדָּבָר הַזֶּה בָּאָרֶץ׃

(3) Exod 5:9 תִּכְבַּד הָעֲבֹדָה עַל־הָאֲנָשִׁים וְיַעֲשׂוּ־בָהּ וְאַל־יִשְׁעוּ בְּדִבְרֵי־שָׁקֶר׃

(4) 1 Sam 2:8 מֵקִים מֵעָפָר דָּל מֵאַשְׁפֹּת יָרִים אֶבְיוֹן לְהוֹשִׁיב עִם־נְדִיבִים וְכִסֵּא
כָבוֹד יַנְחִלֵם כִּי לַיהוָה מְצֻקֵי אֶרֶץ וַיָּשֶׁת עֲלֵיהֶם תֵּבֵל׃

(5) 1 Sam 18:5 וַיֵּצֵא דָוִד בְּכֹל אֲשֶׁר יִשְׁלָחֶנּוּ שָׁאוּל יַשְׂכִּיל וַיְשִׂמֵהוּ שָׁאוּל עַל אַנְשֵׁי
הַמִּלְחָמָה וַיִּיטַב בְּעֵינֵי כָל־הָעָם וְגַם בְּעֵינֵי עַבְדֵי שָׁאוּל׃

(6) 1 Sam 24:14 כַּאֲשֶׁר יֹאמַר מְשַׁל הַקַּדְמֹנִי מֵרְשָׁעִים יֵצֵא רֶשַׁע וְיָדִי לֹא תִהְיֶה־בָּךְ׃

(7) Deut 2:11 רְפָאִים יֵחָשְׁבוּ אַף־הֵם כָּעֲנָקִים וְהַמֹּאָבִים יִקְרְאוּ לָהֶם אֵמִים׃

(8) Deut 2:12 וּבְשֵׂעִיר יָשְׁבוּ הַחֹרִים לְפָנִים וּבְנֵי עֵשָׂו יִירָשׁוּם וַיַּשְׁמִידוּם מִפְּנֵיהֶם
וַיֵּשְׁבוּ תַּחְתָּם כַּאֲשֶׁר עָשָׂה יִשְׂרָאֵל לְאֶרֶץ יְרֻשָּׁתוֹ אֲשֶׁר־נָתַן יְהוָה לָהֶם׃

(9) Exod 3:19 וַאֲנִי יָדַעְתִּי כִּי לֹא־יִתֵּן אֶתְכֶם מֶלֶךְ מִצְרַיִם לַהֲלֹךְ וְלֹא בְּיָד חֲזָקָה׃

(10) Exod 5:8 וְאֶת־מַתְכֹּנֶת הַלְּבֵנִים אֲשֶׁר הֵם עֹשִׂים תְּמוֹל שִׁלְשֹׁם תָּשִׂימוּ עֲלֵיהֶם לֹא
תִגְרְעוּ מִמֶּנּוּ כִּי־נִרְפִּים הֵם עַל־כֵּן הֵם צֹעֲקִים לֵאמֹר נֵלְכָה נִזְבְּחָה
לֵאלֹהֵינוּ׃

(11) Exod 19:19 וַיְהִי קוֹל הַשֹּׁפָר הוֹלֵךְ וְחָזֵק מְאֹד מֹשֶׁה יְדַבֵּר וְהָאֱלֹהִים יַעֲנֶנּוּ בְקוֹל׃

(12) Exod 23:7 מִדְּבַר־שֶׁקֶר תִּרְחָק וְנָקִי וְצַדִּיק אַל־תַּהֲרֹג כִּי לֹא־אַצְדִּיק רָשָׁע׃

(13) Gen 37:15 וַיִּמְצָאֵהוּ אִישׁ וְהִנֵּה תֹעֶה בַּשָּׂדֶה וַיִּשְׁאָלֵהוּ הָאִישׁ לֵאמֹר מַה־תְּבַקֵּשׁ׃

Josh 3:1 (14) וַיַּשְׁכֵּם יְהוֹשֻׁעַ בַּבֹּקֶר וַיִּסְעוּ מֵהַשִּׁטִּים וַיָּבֹאוּ עַד־הַיַּרְדֵּן הוּא וְכָל־בְּנֵי יִשְׂרָאֵל וַיָּלִנוּ שָׁם טֶרֶם יַעֲבֹרוּ׃

Exod 33:7 (15) וּמֹשֶׁה יִקַּח אֶת־הָאֹהֶל וְנָטָה־לוֹ מִחוּץ לַמַּחֲנֶה הַרְחֵק מִן־הַמַּחֲנֶה וְקָרָא לוֹ אֹהֶל מוֹעֵד וְהָיָה כָּל־מְבַקֵּשׁ יְהוָה יֵצֵא אֶל־אֹהֶל מוֹעֵד אֲשֶׁר מִחוּץ לַמַּחֲנֶה׃

Gen 3:3 (16) וּמִפְּרִי הָעֵץ אֲשֶׁר בְּתוֹךְ־הַגָּן אָמַר אֱלֹהִים לֹא תֹאכְלוּ מִמֶּנּוּ וְלֹא תִגְּעוּ בּוֹ פֶּן־תְּמֻתוּן׃

3. **Analyze the following Vav-perfect forms: connecting or energic Vav, then usage.**

Exod 16:21 (1) וַיִּלְקְטוּ אֹתוֹ בַּבֹּקֶר בַּבֹּקֶר אִישׁ כְּפִי אָכְלוֹ וְחַם הַשֶּׁמֶשׁ וְנָמָס׃

Ps 10:10 (2) יִדְכֶּה יָשֹׁחַ וְנָפַל בַּעֲצוּמָיו חֵיל כָּאִים׃

Exod 7:9 (3) כִּי יְדַבֵּר אֲלֵכֶם פַּרְעֹה לֵאמֹר תְּנוּ לָכֶם מוֹפֵת וְאָמַרְתָּ אֶל־אַהֲרֹן קַח אֶת־מַטְּךָ וְהַשְׁלֵךְ לִפְנֵי־פַרְעֹה יְהִי לְתַנִּין׃

1 Sam 12:2 (4) וְעַתָּה הִנֵּה הַמֶּלֶךְ מִתְהַלֵּךְ לִפְנֵיכֶם וַאֲנִי זָקַנְתִּי וָשַׂבְתִּי וּבָנַי הִנָּם אִתְּכֶם וַאֲנִי הִתְהַלַּכְתִּי לִפְנֵיכֶם מִנְּעֻרַי עַד־הַיּוֹם הַזֶּה׃

Exod 3:16 (5) לֵךְ וְאָסַפְתָּ אֶת־זִקְנֵי יִשְׂרָאֵל וְאָמַרְתָּ אֲלֵהֶם יְהוָה אֱלֹהֵי אֲבֹתֵיכֶם נִרְאָה אֵלַי אֱלֹהֵי אַבְרָהָם יִצְחָק וְיַעֲקֹב לֵאמֹר פָּקֹד פָּקַדְתִּי אֶתְכֶם וְאֶת־הֶעָשׂוּי לָכֶם בְּמִצְרָיִם׃

Gen 47:23 (6) וַיֹּאמֶר יוֹסֵף אֶל־הָעָם הֵן קָנִיתִי אֶתְכֶם הַיּוֹם וְאֶת־אַדְמַתְכֶם לְפַרְעֹה הֵא־לָכֶם זֶרַע וּזְרַעְתֶּם אֶת־הָאֲדָמָה׃

Gen 26:22 (7) וַיַּעְתֵּק מִשָּׁם וַיַּחְפֹּר בְּאֵר אַחֶרֶת וְלֹא רָבוּ עָלֶיהָ וַיִּקְרָא שְׁמָהּ רְחֹבוֹת וַיֹּאמֶר כִּי־עַתָּה הִרְחִיב יְהוָה לָנוּ וּפָרִינוּ בָאָרֶץ׃

Gen 6:18 (8) וַהֲקִמֹתִי אֶת־בְּרִיתִי אִתָּךְ וּבָאתָ אֶל־הַתֵּבָה אַתָּה וּבָנֶיךָ וְאִשְׁתְּךָ וּנְשֵׁי־בָנֶיךָ אִתָּךְ׃

Gen 4:14 (9) הֵן גֵּרַשְׁתָּ אֹתִי הַיּוֹם מֵעַל פְּנֵי הָאֲדָמָה וּמִפָּנֶיךָ אֶסָּתֵר וְהָיִיתִי נָע וָנָד בָּאָרֶץ וְהָיָה כָל־מֹצְאִי יַהַרְגֵנִי׃

Josh 6:8 (10)
וַיְהִי כֶּאֱמֹר יְהוֹשֻׁעַ אֶל־הָעָם וְשִׁבְעָה הַכֹּהֲנִים נֹשְׂאִים שִׁבְעָה שׁוֹפְרוֹת
הַיּוֹבְלִים לִפְנֵי יְהוָה עָבְרוּ וְתָקְעוּ בַּשּׁוֹפָרוֹת וַאֲרוֹן בְּרִית יְהוָה הֹלֵךְ
אַחֲרֵיהֶם׃

4. Analyze the following Vav-imperfect and Vav-imperative forms.

Exod 18:19 (1)
עַתָּה שְׁמַע בְּקֹלִי אִיעָצְךָ וִיהִי אֱלֹהִים עִמָּךְ הֱיֵה אַתָּה לָעָם מוּל
הָאֱלֹהִים וְהֵבֵאתָ אַתָּה אֶת־הַדְּבָרִים אֶל־הָאֱלֹהִים׃

Exod 5:1 (2)
וְאַחַר בָּאוּ מֹשֶׁה וְאַהֲרֹן וַיֹּאמְרוּ אֶל־פַּרְעֹה כֹּה־אָמַר יְהוָה אֱלֹהֵי
יִשְׂרָאֵל שַׁלַּח אֶת־עַמִּי וְיָחֹגּוּ לִי בַּמִּדְבָּר׃

Exod 3:8 (3)
וָאֵרֵד לְהַצִּילוֹ מִיַּד מִצְרַיִם וּלְהַעֲלֹתוֹ מִן־הָאָרֶץ הַהִוא אֶל־אֶרֶץ טוֹבָה
וּרְחָבָה אֶל־אֶרֶץ זָבַת חָלָב וּדְבָשׁ אֶל־מְקוֹם הַכְּנַעֲנִי וְהַחִתִּי וְהָאֱמֹרִי
וְהַפְּרִזִּי וְהַחִוִּי וְהַיְבוּסִי׃

Ps 18:48 (4)
הָאֵל הַנּוֹתֵן נְקָמוֹת לִי וַיַּדְבֵּר עַמִּים תַּחְתָּי׃

Gen 18:5 (5)
וְאֶקְחָה פַת־לֶחֶם וְסַעֲדוּ לִבְּכֶם אַחַר תַּעֲבֹרוּ כִּי־עַל־כֵּן עֲבַרְתֶּם עַל־
עַבְדְּכֶם וַיֹּאמְרוּ כֵּן תַּעֲשֶׂה כַּאֲשֶׁר דִּבַּרְתָּ׃

Isa 31:1 (6)
הוֹי הַיֹּרְדִים מִצְרַיִם לְעֶזְרָה עַל־סוּסִים יִשָּׁעֵנוּ וַיִּבְטְחוּ עַל־רֶכֶב כִּי
רָב וְעַל פָּרָשִׁים כִּי־עָצְמוּ מְאֹד וְלֹא שָׁעוּ עַל־קְדוֹשׁ יִשְׂרָאֵל וְאֶת־יְהוָה
לֹא דָרָשׁוּ׃

Gen 6:1 (7)
וַיְהִי כִּי־הֵחֵל הָאָדָם לָרֹב עַל־פְּנֵי הָאֲדָמָה וּבָנוֹת יֻלְּדוּ לָהֶם׃

Gen 20:7 (8)
וְעַתָּה הָשֵׁב אֵשֶׁת־הָאִישׁ כִּי־נָבִיא הוּא וְיִתְפַּלֵּל בַּעַדְךָ וֶחְיֵה וְאִם־אֵינְךָ
מֵשִׁיב דַּע כִּי־מוֹת תָּמוּת אַתָּה וְכָל־אֲשֶׁר־לָךְ׃

Isa 9:13 (9)
וַיַּכְרֵת יְהוָה מִיִּשְׂרָאֵל רֹאשׁ וְזָנָב כִּפָּה וְאַגְמוֹן יוֹם אֶחָד׃

Gen 4:1 (10)
וְהָאָדָם יָדַע אֶת־חַוָּה אִשְׁתּוֹ וַתַּהַר וַתֵּלֶד אֶת־קַיִן וַתֹּאמֶר קָנִיתִי אִישׁ
אֶת־יְהוָה׃

Gen 19:26 (11)
וַתַּבֵּט אִשְׁתּוֹ מֵאַחֲרָיו וַתְּהִי נְצִיב מֶלַח׃

Gen 23:9 (12)
וְיִתֶּן־לִי אֶת־מְעָרַת הַמַּכְפֵּלָה אֲשֶׁר־לוֹ אֲשֶׁר בִּקְצֵה שָׂדֵהוּ בְּכֶסֶף מָלֵא
יִתְּנֶנָּה לִּי בְּתוֹכְכֶם לַאֲחֻזַּת־קָבֶר׃

5. Analyze the usages of the intensive/extensive conjugation.

Exod 23:26 (1) לֹא תִהְיֶה מְשַׁכֵּלָה וַעֲקָרָה בְּאַרְצֶךָ אֶת־מִסְפַּר יָמֶיךָ אֲמַלֵּא׃

Exod 3:20 (2) וְשָׁלַחְתִּי אֶת־יָדִי וְהִכֵּיתִי אֶת־מִצְרַיִם בְּכֹל נִפְלְאֹתַי אֲשֶׁר אֶעֱשֶׂה
בְּקִרְבּוֹ וְאַחֲרֵי־כֵן יְשַׁלַּח אֶתְכֶם׃

Exod 10:27 (3) וַיְחַזֵּק יְהוָה אֶת־לֵב פַּרְעֹה וְלֹא אָבָה לְשַׁלְּחָם׃

Exod 2:17 (4) וַיָּבֹאוּ הָרֹעִים וַיְגָרְשׁוּם וַיָּקָם מֹשֶׁה וַיּוֹשִׁעָן וַיַּשְׁקְ אֶת־צֹאנָם׃

Job 33:32 (5) אִם־יֵשׁ־מִלִּין הֲשִׁיבֵנִי דַּבֵּר כִּי־חָפַצְתִּי צַדְּקֶךָּ׃

Exod 9:25 (6) וַיַּךְ הַבָּרָד בְּכָל־אֶרֶץ מִצְרַיִם אֵת כָּל־אֲשֶׁר בַּשָּׂדֶה מֵאָדָם וְעַד־בְּהֵמָה
וְאֵת כָּל־עֵשֶׂב הַשָּׂדֶה הִכָּה הַבָּרָד וְאֶת־כָּל־עֵץ הַשָּׂדֶה שִׁבֵּר׃

Exod 28:41 (7) וְהִלְבַּשְׁתָּ אֹתָם אֶת־אַהֲרֹן אָחִיךָ וְאֶת־בָּנָיו אִתּוֹ וּמָשַׁחְתָּ אֹתָם וּמִלֵּאתָ
אֶת־יָדָם וְקִדַּשְׁתָּ אֹתָם וְכִהֲנוּ לִי׃

6. Analyze the usages of the causative conjugation.

Gen 1:15 (1) וְהָיוּ לִמְאוֹרֹת בִּרְקִיעַ הַשָּׁמַיִם לְהָאִיר עַל־הָאָרֶץ וַיְהִי־כֵן׃

Isa 1:18 (2) לְכוּ־נָא וְנִוָּכְחָה יֹאמַר יְהוָה אִם־יִהְיוּ חֲטָאֵיכֶם כַּשָּׁנִים כַּשֶּׁלֶג יַלְבִּינוּ
אִם־יַאְדִּימוּ כַתּוֹלָע כַּצֶּמֶר יִהְיוּ׃

Gen 1:12 (3) וַתּוֹצֵא הָאָרֶץ דֶּשֶׁא עֵשֶׂב מַזְרִיעַ זֶרַע לְמִינֵהוּ וְעֵץ עֹשֶׂה־פְּרִי אֲשֶׁר
זַרְעוֹ־בוֹ לְמִינֵהוּ וַיַּרְא אֱלֹהִים כִּי־טוֹב׃

Exod 21:8 (4) אִם־רָעָה בְּעֵינֵי אֲדֹנֶיהָ אֲשֶׁר־לוֹ יְעָדָהּ וְהֶפְדָּהּ לְעַם נָכְרִי לֹא־יִמְשֹׁל
לְמָכְרָהּ בְּבִגְדוֹ־בָהּ׃

Exod 23:7 (5) מִדְּבַר־שֶׁקֶר תִּרְחָק וְנָקִי וְצַדִּיק אַל־תַּהֲרֹג כִּי לֹא־אַצְדִּיק רָשָׁע׃

Gen 19:2 (6) וַיֹּאמֶר הִנֶּה נָּא־אֲדֹנַי סוּרוּ נָא אֶל־בֵּית עַבְדְּכֶם וְלִינוּ וְרַחֲצוּ רַגְלֵיכֶם
וְהִשְׁכַּמְתֶּם וַהֲלַכְתֶּם לְדַרְכְּכֶם וַיֹּאמְרוּ לֹּא כִּי בָרְחוֹב נָלִין׃

7. **Analyze the usages of the Niphal conjugation.**

Exod 22:1 (1) אִם־בַּמַּחְתֶּ֛רֶת יִמָּצֵ֥א הַגַּנָּ֖ב וְהֻכָּ֣ה וָמֵ֑ת אֵ֥ין ל֖וֹ דָּמִֽים׃

Exod 10:3 (2) וַיָּבֹ֨א מֹשֶׁ֣ה וְאַהֲרֹן֮ אֶל־פַּרְעֹה֒ וַיֹּאמְר֣וּ אֵלָ֗יו כֹּֽה־אָמַ֤ר יְהוָה֙ אֱלֹהֵ֣י
הָֽעִבְרִ֔ים עַד־מָתַ֣י מֵאַ֔נְתָּ לֵעָנֹ֖ת מִפָּנָ֑י שַׁלַּ֥ח עַמִּ֖י וְיַֽעַבְדֻֽנִי׃

1 Kgs 12:8 (3) וַיַּעֲזֹ֛ב אֶת־עֲצַ֥ת הַזְּקֵנִ֖ים אֲשֶׁ֣ר יְעָצֻ֑הוּ וַיִּוָּעַ֗ץ אֶת־הַיְלָדִים֙ אֲשֶׁ֣ר גָּדְל֣וּ
אִתּ֔וֹ אֲשֶׁ֥ר הָעֹמְדִ֖ים לְפָנָֽיו׃

Exod 23:13 (4) וּבְכֹ֛ל אֲשֶׁר־אָמַ֥רְתִּי אֲלֵיכֶ֖ם תִּשָּׁמֵ֑רוּ וְשֵׁ֨ם אֱלֹהִ֤ים אֲחֵרִים֙ לֹ֣א תַזְכִּ֔ירוּ
לֹ֥א יִשָּׁמַ֖ע עַל־פִּֽיךָ׃

Exod 14:4 (5) וְחִזַּקְתִּ֣י אֶת־לֵב־פַּרְעֹה֮ וְרָדַ֣ף אַחֲרֵיהֶם֒ וְאִכָּבְדָ֤ה בְּפַרְעֹה֙ וּבְכָל־חֵיל֔וֹ
וְיָדְע֥וּ מִצְרַ֖יִם כִּֽי־אֲנִ֣י יְהוָ֑ה וַיַּעֲשׂוּ־כֵֽן׃

Exod 9:15 (6) כִּ֤י עַתָּה֙ שָׁלַ֣חְתִּי אֶת־יָדִ֔י וָאַ֥ךְ אוֹתְךָ֛ וְאֶֽת־עַמְּךָ֖ בַּדָּ֑בֶר וַתִּכָּחֵ֖ד מִן־הָאָֽרֶץ׃

Chapter 2
THE NOUN

§8. Introduction

Nouns have inherent meaning, but lack aspect, tense, or mood. They have at least one of the following characteristics: functioning as a vocative, predicate, subject, the first word in a construct package; or having the ability to take an article. Nouns are usually divided into two classes: primary and descriptive. A DESCRIPTIVE NOUN is an adjective or participle;[1] PRIMARY NOUNS are all other nouns that are not adjectives or participles.[2]

Moreover, there are verbal nouns, that is, nouns related to verbs: infinitive absolute, infinitive construct, and participle (§15–18). Numerals in Hebrew are usually viewed as nouns (§28–32). Of course, pronouns may substitute for nouns (§19–21). Apposition is used to modify one noun by another noun (§22–27). Every Hebrew noun has four grammatical categories: gender (§9), number (§9), case (§10–14), and definiteness/indefiniteness (§33–36).

§9. Gender and Number *a*

A. Gender

Hebrew has feminine and masculine gender, but not neuter. With animate objects, gender may indicate sex; with inanimate objects, gender is grammatical. An accented ָ֫ה usually indicates a feminine noun and always indicates a feminine adjective or participle. Many animate objects are feminine without the accented ָ֫ה: אֵם mother, רָחֵל ewe, עֵז female goat, אָתוֹן female donkey. Some animate objects, especially collectives, may be masculine or feminine (context determining): בָּקָר cattle. Strong or fierce animals are frequently masculine, זְאֵב wolf; weak or timid animals are often feminine, יוֹנָה dove.

The following categories are feminine with or without the ending ָ֫ה.[3]

1. Names of countries and towns: These feminine nouns are regarded as the mother of the inhabitants (motherland): אַשּׁוּר Asshur, אֱדוֹם Edom. Some place names, that were originally not proper nouns, retain their masculine gender: בֵּית־אֵל Bethel.

2. Common nouns of a circumscribed space: אֶ֫רֶץ land, תֵּבֵל world, כִּכָּר plain.

3. Parts of the body, tools, and instruments: רֶ֫גֶל feet, חֶ֫רֶב sword.

4. Some natural objects or forces: אֵשׁ fire, אֶ֫בֶן stone, רוּחַ wind.

---

1. Native Semitic grammarians regard the adjective and participle as subsets of nouns, §22.
2. Griess, 74; Wechter, 26; Wright I, §191.
3. The following categories may also have some nouns that are both feminine and masculine or that are only masculine.

5. Classes
   a) Abstracts: צְדָקָה righteousness, גְּבוּרָה strength
   b) Titles and offices: קֹהֶלֶת preacher
   c) Collectives: גּוֹלָה exiles, חַיָּה living animals

6. Used for a single example of a class (the masculine furnishes the class, usually a collective): שֵׂעָר (masc. hair, a collective), שַׂעֲרָה (fem. a single hair); אֳנִי (masc. fleet of ships, collective), אֳנִיָּה (fem. a single ship)

7. Feminine used with the masculine of the same stem to express totality of the class. For example, "sons and daughters" (all the young) in Isa 60:4, בָּנַיִךְ מֵרָחוֹק יָבֹאוּ וּבְנֹתַיִךְ עַל־צַד תֵּאָמַנָה׃, "Your sons come from afar; your daughters will be carried on the side."

b **B. Number**

Hebrew nouns may be singular, dual, or plural.

1. Singular: In addition to its normal meaning of a single thing or category, the singular may express a collective or, by repetition of a singular noun, a distributive notion.
   a) Collective: Some nouns may be singular or collective, context determining—אָדָם man/mankind, נֶפֶשׁ soul(s), אִישׁ man, men.
   b) Distributive (§24f, 31): שָׁנָה שָׁנָה every year *or* year by year, יוֹם יוֹם every day *or* day by day.
      Exod 3:15; 16:5, 21; Jer 7:25 (without repeating the noun); BA Dan 3:33

2. Dual: The dual, a plural of two, is often limited to body parts occurring in pairs and to certain common nouns such as יוֹם day, שָׁנָה year, שָׁמַיִם heaven and מַיִם water.

3. Plural: The plural expresses more than one or two things. Other notable uses of the plural include:
   a) Extensive plural (including some duals):
      i. Place: The plurality extends over an area or surface—מַיִם (surfaces of) water, פָּנִים (areas of the) face, מַרְגְּלוֹת (places) at the feet, צַוָּארִים (areas of the) neck. BA Dan 5:9

      ii. Time: The plurality extends over time—עוֹלָמִים ages. BA Dan 2:44
   b) Intensive plural: Intensive plurals, often abstract nouns or natural objects, intensify the noun. Intensive plurals are often found in poetry and direct speech: אוֹנִים might(s), אֱמוּנוֹת faithfulness(es), אַשְׁרֵי blessedness(es); יַמִּים seas, הָרִים mountains.

      כִּי־אֱלֹהִים קְדֹשִׁים הוּא Josh 24:19
      For He is a holy God.

The plural adjective for "holy" is an intensive plural. For abstract nouns this often means, "He is holy *with all kinds and with every kind* (the notion of the plural) of holiness—He is the perfection of holiness." He, therefore, possesses holiness in an infinite degree, and there is nothing in him contrary to holiness.
Exod 12:12; 15:5(2x), 11; Jer 7:24; BA Dan 2:18

c) Plural of quality/condition: These plurals describe a quality/condition of the noun:
   i. זְקֻנִים "the conditions, circumstances, or times of old age;" מְגוּרִים "the conditions, circumstances, or times of sojourning."

   ii. נְעוּרִים "the conditions or qualities that constitute youth;" בְּתוּלִים "the conditions, qualities, or times that constitute virginity."
   Deut 22:14

Exercises

Questions and Discussions

1. Define a noun. What are the distinguishing characteristics of a noun?
2. What are primary and descriptive nouns?
3. What are the four grammatical categories that every noun has?
4. What are the gender categories of Hebrew? Which English gender category does Hebrew lack?
5. List the noun types that are often feminine.
6. What are the three numbers of a Semitic noun?
7. What are the usages of the singular other than expressing a single item or category?
8. When is the dual used?
9. Discuss the usages of the plural other than expressing more than one or two items or categories.

Chapter 3
THE CASES

§10. Introduction

Hebrew originally possessed case endings for nouns, as formal Arabic still does. Although most case endings have fallen off Hebrew nouns, the case functions still operated in Biblical Hebrew. Hebrew has three cases: NOMINATIVE, for almost all subjects and for the predicate in clauses without a finite verb; GENITIVE, for the packaging of nouns to modify or limit one noun by another noun; and the ACCUSATIVE, for objects of verbs and for adverbial expressions.

§11. Nominative *a*

The nominative functions according to the type of clause: NOMINAL or VERBAL.[1] In a nominal clause, the subject precedes the verb, or the clause is verbless. In a verbal clause, the verb precedes the subject. Semitic grammarians employed separate terms for the subjects and predicates of these clauses to stress the difference between these clauses. For nominal clauses, the subject is the INITIATOR, and its predicate (a verb, noun, participle, or adjective, etc.) is the ANNOUNCEMENT. For verbal clauses, the subject is the AGENT, and its predicate is the VERB. When a noun is an initiator, an announcement, or an agent, it is in the nominative case.[2]

A. Nominative in Nominal Clauses (§38) *b*

The subject of a nominal clause, the initiator or "that which begins," starts a new beginning by placing the noun (initiator) before its verb, rendering the initiator the focal point of the clause. As the focal point, Hebrew separates[3] or disconnects the initiator from its announcement (its verb).[4] The nominal clause, as its label suggests, focuses on the noun (the initiator), especially its identity, character, and description.

---

1. The adverbial clause (Howell, Introduction iv), a third category of clauses often found in relative clauses, usually expresses time or place when an adverbial word or phrase (usually a prepositional phrase) functions as the announcement (predicate). These clauses usually have definite initiators (subjects).The word order may vary: "David (is) in the temple" or "In the temple (is) David." According to Wright's grammar (II, §115), "the logical emphasis always falls on that part of the sentence that is put in the second place." The meaning expressed, therefore, is: "David (is) in the temple (and not elsewhere)" or "In the temple (is) David (and no one else)." Some authorities consider the adverbial clause as a variant of the nominal clause.
2. Griess, 74–84, 129–136; Howell, Introduction iv, §20–34; Wright II, §113; ZW, 23–24.
3. The Hebrew accents indicate this separation. Disjunctive accents separate an initiator from its announcement (verb). Conjunctive accents connect the agent to its verb. Similarly, Arabic often separates the initiator from its announcement (verb) by pausing in speech and often connects the agent to its verb without pausing in speech.
4. This assumes that the initiator has a finite verb as its announcement. If a nominal clause is verbless, the word order of initiator and announcement may vary (§11dd–ii).

c The predicate of a nominal clause is called the announcement or the enunciation because it furnishes an announcement or an enunciation concerning its initiator. If the announcement is a finite verb, the initiator precedes its announcement. If the announcement is a noun, adjective, participle, etc., then the announcement usually follows its initiator, but the announcement may precede the initiator for emphasis.[5]

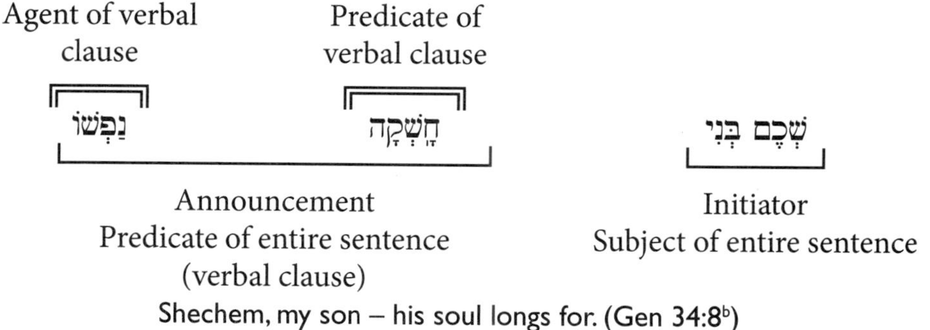

Shechem, my son – his soul longs for. (Gen 34:8[b])

Exod 12:15 (כִּי כָּל־אֹכֵל חָמֵץ וְנִכְרְתָה הַנֶּפֶשׁ הַהִוא); 1 Sam 2:10 (יְהוָה יֵחַתּוּ מְרִיבָיו); BA Dan 5:6 (מַלְכָּא זִיוֺהִי שְׁנוֹהִי וְרַעְיֹנֹהִי יְבַהֲלוּנֵּהּ)
In Genesis 34:8, the initiator is the subject of the entire nominal clause (sentence), not the subject of the verb.[6] The agent (subject) of the verb is "his soul." The announcement of the nominal clause (sentence) is a verbal clause since its agent (subject) follows its verb. In the English translation, the hyphen separates the initiator from its announcement.

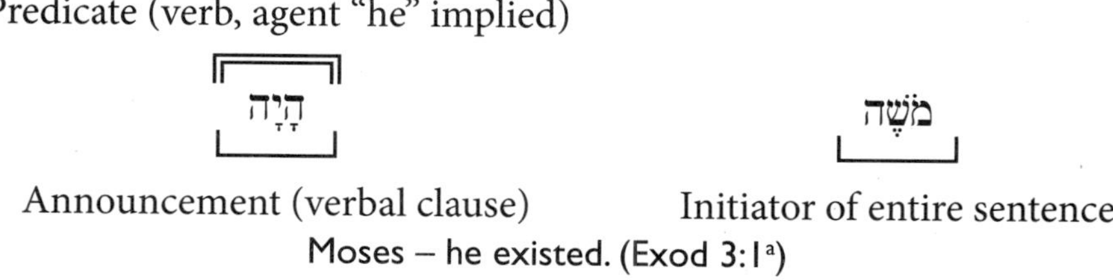

Moses – he existed. (Exod 3:1[a])

The initiator is the subject of the announcement, a verbal clause, not just a verb. The subject (agent) of the verb is the implied pronoun of the verb—"he." Again, the hyphen in the English translation separates the initiator from its announcement.

רָעִים — וְאַנְשֵׁי סְדֹם

Announcement (adjective) — Initiator

The men of Sodom were wicked. (Gen 13:13[a])

The initiator is subject of the nominal clause; the adjective is the announcement. This verbless clause is purely descriptive, without verbal action or

5. ZW, 24.
6. Such initiators are also considered to be in "preoccupation" or in Casus Pendens. See §14a-b.

movement. The initiator is similar or equivalent to its announcement in some manner.

1. Nominative as initiator of nominal clauses (in verbless clauses) *d*
   a) The initiator may be a word(s) or clause.
      i. Word or words

וְעֵלִ֖י שֹׁמֵ֥ר אֶת־פִּֽיהָ׃ 1 Sam 1:12[b]

And Eli was a watcher of her mouth.

מְק֣וֹר חַ֭יִּים פִּ֣י צַדִּ֑יק Prov 10:11[a]

A well of life is the mouth of the righteous.

      ii. Clause

וַיֹּ֣אמֶר לָבָ֗ן ט֚וֹב תִּתִּ֣י אֹתָ֣הּ לָ֔ךְ מִתִּתִּ֥י אֹתָ֖הּ לְאִ֣ישׁ אַחֵ֑ר Gen 29:19[a]

And Laban said, **My giving her to you** is better than my giving her to another man.

   b) The initiator may be definite or indefinite. *e*
      i. Definite

The initiator is usually definite.[7]

וְעֵינֵ֥י לֵאָ֖ה רַכּ֑וֹת Gen 29:17[a]

And the eyes of Leah were weak.

BA Dan 2:11 (וּמִלְּתָ֨א . . . יַקִּירָ֗ה "The word . . . is rare")

      ii. Indefinite *f*

Exceptionally, the initiator is indefinite for a variety of reasons, including:

① A prepositional or adverbial phrase precedes the initiator. The preposition ל with a definite object followed by an indefinite initiator asserts possession.

וּלְלָבָ֖ן שְׁתֵּ֣י בָנ֑וֹת Gen 29:16[a]

And to Laban were **a couple of daughters**.

Assertion of possession: Gen 18:14 (וּלְשָׂרָ֥ה בֵֽן׃); Exod 2:16 (וּלְכֹהֵ֥ן מִדְיָ֖ן שֶׁ֣בַע בָּנ֑וֹת); 1 Sam 1:2 (וְלוֹ֙ שְׁתֵּ֣י נָשִׁ֔ים); 17:12 (וְל֛וֹ שְׁמֹנָ֥ה בָנִ֖ים). Rarely, the inverse word order occurs, probably due to emphasis (Exod 22:2, the previous verse has normal word order).

The preposition ב and adverbs (שָׁם) followed by an indefinite initiator asserts existence. (See §42g for the negative of existence.)

7. According to Arab grammarians, the subject of a nominal clause must be definite (Wright II, §127). Some exceptions to this rule are given in the following section (§11f–j). Sometimes numbers as initiators, though indefinite in form, may become definite by a definite modifier (Gen 9:19). This may also happen when the number is not functioning as an initiator (Gen 22:23). Moreover, not limited to numbers, indefinite nouns may also become definite by a definite modifier (1 Sam 16:23).

Gen 40:10[a] וּבַגֶּפֶן שְׁלֹשָׁה שָׂרִיגִם

And in the vine, there were three branches

Assertion of existence: Exod 25:34 (וּבַמְּנֹרָה אַרְבָּעָה גְבִעִים); 1 Sam 20:18 (מָחָר חֹדֶשׁ); 1 Sam 21:8–9 (וְשָׁם אִישׁ מֵעַבְדֵי שָׁאוּל); 1 Sam 24:4 (וְשָׁם מְעָרָה). Occasionally, an indefinite initiator may precede the prepositional phrase to assert existence (1 Sam 25:2; Neh 6:7; 1 Chr 12:41).

g ② An interrogative, exclamation, or negation precedes the initiator (or a negative clause follows the initiator).

Gen 37:26 וַיֹּאמֶר יְהוּדָה אֶל־אֶחָיו מַה־בֶּצַע כִּי נַהֲרֹג אֶת־אָחִינוּ

And Judah said to his brothers, **What profit (is it)** that we kill our brother?

Num 23:23[a] כִּי לֹא־נַחַשׁ בְּיַעֲקֹב וְלֹא־קֶסֶם בְּיִשְׂרָאֵל

For **no omen is** against Jacob, and **no divination** is against Israel.

Exod 12:19 (שְׂאֹר לֹא יִמָּצֵא), 13:7 (וְלֹא־יֵרָאֶה לְךָ חָמֵץ וְלֹא־יֵרָאֶה לְךָ שְׂאֹר); Deut 32:47 (לֹא־דָבָר רֵק הוּא); 1 Sam 20:21 (וְאֵין דָּבָר); 2 Sam 20:1 (אֵין־לָנוּ חֵלֶק בְּדָוִד וְלֹא נַחֲלָה־לָנוּ בְּבֶן־יִשַׁי); 2 Kgs 20:8 (מָה אוֹת); Jer 7:32 (הִנֵּה־יָמִים בָּאִים); Ezek 24:6 (אוֹי עִיר); Mal 3:14 (וּמַה־בֶּצַע); Ps 8:5 (מָה־אֱנוֹשׁ); BA Dan 3:25 (וַחֲבָל לָא־אִיתַי); Ezra 6:9 (וּמָה חַשְׁחָן)

h ③ An adjective, clause, or a genitive qualifies[8] the initiator. In the following example (Josh 10:11), the relative clause SPECIALIZES an adjective.

Josh 10:11 רַבִּים אֲשֶׁר־מֵתוּ בְּאַבְנֵי הַבָּרָד מֵאֲשֶׁר הָרְגוּ בְּנֵי יִשְׂרָאֵל בֶּחָרֶב׃

Many who died by the stones of hail were more than those whom the Israelites killed by the sword.

Exod 2:19 (אִישׁ מִצְרִי); 11:6 (צְעָקָה גְדֹלָה); 12:16 " (מִקְרָא־קֹדֶשׁ); 1 Sam 1:1 (אִישׁ אֶחָד); 9:6 (אִישׁ־אֱלֹהִים); 20:29 (זֶבַח מִשְׁפָּחָה); Jer 26:11 (מִשְׁפַּט־מָוֶת); Prov 10:11 (מְקוֹר חַיִּים); BA Ezra 4:20 (וּמַלְכִין תַּקִּיפִין); 5:11 (וּמֶלֶךְ לְיִשְׂרָאֵל רַב); Dan 2:34 (אֶבֶן דִּי־לָא בִידַיִן)

i ④ The initiator is a supplication or desire.

Gen 43:23[a] וַיֹּאמֶר שָׁלוֹם לָכֶם

And he said, **Peace be to you**.

Gen 1:3 (יְהִי אוֹר), 14 (יְהִי מְאֹרֹת בִּרְקִיעַ הַשָּׁמַיִם); 29:6 (הֲשָׁלוֹם לוֹ); 43:28 (שָׁלוֹם לְעַבְדְּךָ לְאָבִינוּ); 1 Sam 21:3 (אִישׁ אַל־יֵדַע מְאוּמָה)

8. When an indefinite noun is qualified in some way, such as by an adjective or by an indefinite word in the genitive, the indefinite noun is SPECIALIZED. Though indefinite, specialized nouns are not completely indefinite since an adjective or a genitive limits them (§12b).

⑤ For emphasis, especially in poetry and direct speech nominal clauses may have indefinite initiators. *j*

וְנִכְשָׁלִ֔ים אָ֥זְרוּ חָֽיִל׃ 1 Sam 2:4[b]

שְׂבֵעִ֤ים בַּלֶּ֙חֶם֙ נִשְׂכָּ֔רוּ וּרְעֵבִ֖ים חָדֵ֑לּוּ 1 Sam 2:5[a]

And (the ones) stumbling – they girded up with strength.
(The ones) filled with bread – they got themselves hired out **and (the) hungry** – they ceased (to hunger).

2. Nominative as announcement (predicate) of nominal clauses *k*
   a) The announcement may be a word(s), phrase, or clause.
      i. Word or words

וְעֵלִ֖י שֹׁמֵ֥ר אֶת־פִּֽיהָ׃ 1 Sam 1:12[b]

And Eli was **a watcher** of her mouth.

Prov 10:11 (פִּ֣י צַדִּ֑יק)

      ii. Phrase *l*
Functioning as a nominative, a prepositional or adverbial phrase may be an announcement.[9]

יְהוָ֤ה ׀ בְּהֵ֘יכַ֤ל קָדְשׁ֗וֹ Ps 11:4[a]

The Lord is **in his holy temple.**

Exod 9:29 (לַיהוָ֖ה הָאָֽרֶץ׃); 25:34 (וּבַמְּנֹרָ֖ה אַרְבָּעָ֣ה גְבִעִ֑ים); 1 Sam 19:16 (הַתְּרָפִ֖ים אֶל־הַמִּטָּ֑ה), 19 (דָוִ֖ד בְּנָי֥וֹת בָּרָמָֽה׃); BA Dan 4:7 (וְחֶזְוֵ֥י רֵאשִׁ֖י עַל־מִשְׁכְּבִ֑י)

      iii. Clause *m*
A nominal clause (sentence) may have a nominal[10] or verbal clause as an announcement in the place of a nominative.

① Nominal clause

יְהוָה֮ בַּשָּׁמַ֪יִם כִּ֫סְא֥וֹ Ps 11:4[a]

The Lord – **in the heavens is his throne.**

The initiator of the entire sentence (a nominal clause) is "The Lord." The announcement, "in the heavens is his throne," is also a nominal clause. (or an adverbial clause. See §11a, footnote 1) "His throne" functions as a nominative to the preposition phrase, "in the heavens."

---

9. This construction expresses various nuances: Ps 11:4, an adverbial clause (See §11a, footnote 1); Exod 9:29, an assertion of possession (§11f); Exod 25:34, an assertion of existence (§11f). Similarly, distinguish the following constructions: אָחִי (my brother), a definite construct package (§12a); אָח לִי, an indefinite construction, implying more brothers (§12r); לִי אָח, an assertion of possession—"I have a brother."

10. Consider a nominal clause functioning as an announcement as definite. Also, some of these examples may be considered adverbial clauses, which are perhaps variations or subsets of the nominal clause. See §11a, footnote 1.

בַּשָּׁמַיִם כִּסְאוֹ	יְהוָה
Announcement (nominal clause)	Initiator of entire sentence

The Lord – in the heavens is his throne.

BA Dan 2:32 (הוּא צַלְמָא רֵאשֵׁהּ דִּי־דְהַב טָב);
5:6 (אֱדַיִן מַלְכָּא זִיוֺהִי שְׁנוֺהִי)

n ② Verbal clause

אַבְרָם יָשַׁב בְּאֶרֶץ־כְּנָעַן Gen 13:12[a]

Abram – **he dwelt in the land of Canaan.**

The initiator of the sentence is "Abram." The announcement, "he dwelt in the land of Canaan," is a verbal clause.

יָשַׁב בְּאֶרֶץ־כְּנָעַן	אַבְרָם
Announcement (verbal clause)	Initiator of entire sentence

Abram – he dwelt in the land of Canaan.

In sentences with verbal clauses as an announcement, the announcement usually has a connecting link (often a pronoun, explicit or implicit) referring back to the initiator. In Gen 13:12 above, the pronoun (he) is implicit in the verb (dwelt). Moreover, the initiator is often emphatic, especially in direct speech and poetry.
Jer 23:3 (וַאֲנִי אֲקַבֵּץ)

o b) The announcement may be definite or indefinite.

i. Definite

① A proper name (usually with a pronoun as the initiator)

אֲנִי יְהוָה הוּא שְׁמִי Isa 42:8[a]

I am **the Lord**, it is my name.

Gen 27:19 (אָנֹכִי עֵשָׂו); Exod 6:2 (אֲנִי יְהוָה׃)

p ② A pronoun (usually with a pronoun as the initiator)

לְמַעַן תֵּדְעוּ וְתַאֲמִינוּ לִי וְתָבִינוּ כִּי־אֲנִי הוּא Isa 43:10[b]

So that you may know and believe me and understand that I am **he.**

אֲנִי אֲנִי הוּא Deut 32:39[a]

I, I – am **He.**

Exod 3:11 (מִי אָנֹכִי); 16:8 (וְנַחְנוּ מָה); Isa 41:4 (אֲנִי־הוּא׃);
Ps 102:28 (וְאַתָּה־הוּא)

q ③ A noun annexed to a separate word(s) that is definite or a noun annexed to a pronominal suffix

וַיֹּאמֶר אִישׁ הָאֱלֹהִים הוּא 1 Kgs 13:26[a]

And he said, He is **the man of God.**

In 1 Kgs 13:26, the initiator (הוּא) is a pronoun (§11dd–ii).
Lev 6:2 (זֹאת תּוֹרַת הָעֹלָה); 13:23 (צָרֶבֶת הַשְּׁחִין הִוא)

יְהוָ֗ה סַֽלְעִ֣י וּמְצוּדָתִ֣י וּמְפַלְטִ֑י Ps 18:3[a]

The Lord (is) **my rock and my fortress and my deliverer**.

The nouns in Ps 18:3 are annexed to a pronominal suffixes. Exod 15:3 (יְהוָ֖ה אִ֣ישׁ מִלְחָמָ֑ה יְהוָ֖ה שְׁמֽוֹ׃); 1 Sam 24:7 (כִּֽי־מְשִׁ֥יחַ יְהוָ֖ה הֽוּא׃)

④ A noun with the article (usually with a pronoun as the initiator) *r*

וַיֹּ֧אמֶר נָתָ֛ן אֶל־דָּוִ֖ד אַתָּ֣ה הָאִ֑ישׁ 2 Sam 12:7[a]

And Nathan said to David, You are **the man**.

Exod 16:15-16 (ה֣וּא הַלֶּ֔חֶם...זֶ֤ה הַדָּבָר֙); Jer 7:28 (זֶ֣ה הַגּ֗וֹי)

⑤ An adjective or participle with the article *s*

These emphatic constructions absolutely and exclusively identify the definite initiator with its definite announcement. They probably assume or imply a SEPARATING PRONOUN between the initiator and the announcement.

וַיִּשְׁלַ֣ח פַּרְעֹ֗ה וַיִּקְרָא֙ לְמֹשֶׁ֣ה וּֽלְאַהֲרֹ֔ן וַיֹּ֥אמֶר אֲלֵהֶ֖ם חָטָ֣אתִי הַפָּ֑עַם יְהוָה֙ הַצַּדִּ֔יק וַאֲנִ֥י וְעַמִּ֖י הָרְשָׁעִֽים׃ Exod 9:27

And Pharaoh sent and summoned Moses and Aaron, and said to them, I have sinned this time; the Lord is **the righteous one**, and I and my people are **the wicked ones**.

עֵינֵיכֶם֙ הָֽרֹא֔וֹת אֵ֛ת אֲשֶׁר־עָשָׂ֥ה יְהוָ֖ה בְּבַ֣עַל פְּע֑וֹר Deut 4:3[a]

Your eyes are **the ones seeing** what the Lord has done in Baal-peor.

Adjectives—1 Kgs 3:22–23 (בְּנִ֥י הַחַ֖י וּבְנֵ֣ךְ הַמֵּ֑ת); Participles—Deut 3:21 (עֵינֶ֣יךָ הָרֹאֹ֗ת); 8:18 (ה֗וּא הַנֹּתֵ֥ן לְךָ֛); 11:7 (כִּ֤י עֵֽינֵיכֶם֙ הָֽרֹאֹ֔ת); 1 Sam 4:16 (אָנֹכִ֙י הַבָּ֣א); 9:19 (אָנֹכִ֣י הָרֹאֶ֔ה); Isa 14:27 (וְיָד֥וֹ הַנְּטוּיָ֖ה)

⑥ A clause *t*

יְהוָ֗ה בְּסוּפָ֤ה וּבִשְׂעָרָה֙ דַּרְכּ֔וֹ Nah 1:3[b]

The Lord – **in the storm and whirlwind is his way**.

When clauses function as announcements, consider them definite.

ii. Indefinite *u*

The announcement of a nominal clause is usually indefinite.[11]

אַ֤ךְ ט֖וֹב לְיִשְׂרָאֵ֥ל אֱלֹהִ֗ים Ps 73:1

Indeed, God is **good** to Israel.

Ps 145:17 (צַדִּ֣יק יְ֭הוָה); BA Dan 4:31 (דִּ֤י שָׁלְטָנֵהּ֙ שָׁלְטָ֣ן עָלַ֔ם); Ezra 4:15 (דִּ֣י קִרְיְתָ֣א דָ֡ךְ קִרְיָ֣א מָֽרָדָ֡א), 19 (מִתְנַשְּׂאָ֑ה ... דִּ֚י קִרְיְתָ֣א)

3. Nominatives and nominal clauses with SEPARATING PRONOUN *v*

Nominal clauses may sometimes insert a third person pronoun *between* the initiator and the announcement. Arab grammarians calls this construction a separating pronoun.[12] By contrast, the Arab grammarians do

11. This excludes announcements that are clauses. See §11t.
12. Howell §166; Wright II, §124.

not regard the third person pronoun that *follows* the announcement as a separating pronoun. Though both constructions are similar in "separating" the initiator from its announcement as a Casus Pendens, their differences distinguish the constructions.

a) The separating pronoun between the initiator and its announcement: The separating pronoun emphasizes the initiator by repeating or corroborating it. Moreover, the separating pronoun itself is also emphatic in this construction. The definite initiator and the (almost always) definite announcement are absolutely and exclusively identified with each other (ABSOLUTE INDENTIFICATION, §16h; 27a fn 6, 9).[13] This separating pronoun prevents the reading of two nouns (initiator and announcement) as an apposition instead of as a statement. Finally, this highly emphatic construction is a Casus Pendens (§14c). These constructions should be analyzed as follows.

יְהוָ֖ה ה֥וּא הָאֱלֹהִֽים׃ 1 Kgs 18:39[b]

The Lord – **He** is the God.

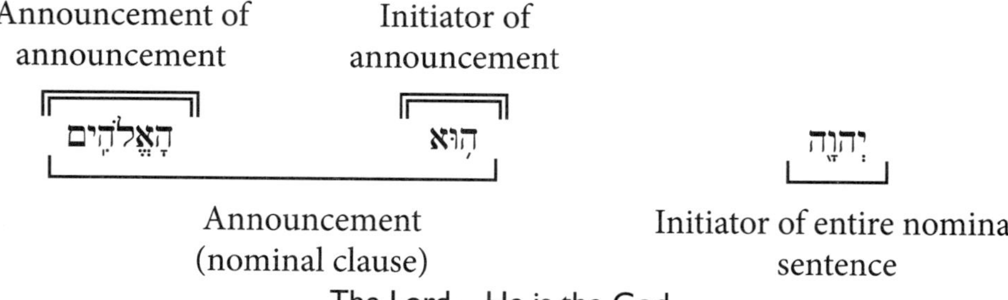

The Lord – He is the God.

The Lord is absolutely and exclusively identified as the God.
Deut 4:39 (כִּ֤י יְהוָה֙ ה֣וּא הָֽאֱלֹהִ֔ים); 10:9 (יְהוָ֖ה ה֣וּא נַחֲלָת֑וֹ), 17
(כִּ֚י יְהוָ֣ה אֱלֹהֵיכֶ֔ם ה֚וּא אֱלֹהֵ֣י הָֽאֱלֹהִ֔ים); 12:23 (כִּ֥י הַדָּ֖ם ה֣וּא הַנָּ֑פֶשׁ);
Josh 13:14 (אִשֵּׁ֨י יְהוָ֜ה אֱלֹהֵ֤י יִשְׂרָאֵל֙ ה֣וּא נַחֲלָת֔וֹ); 1 Sam 4:8
(אֵ֤לֶּה הֵם֙ הָֽאֱלֹהִ֔ים); 1 Kgs 18:39
(יְהוָה֙ ה֣וּא הָֽאֱלֹהִ֔ים יְהוָ֖ה ה֥וּא הָאֱלֹהִֽים׃); Isa 33:6 (יִרְאַ֥ת יְהוָ֖ה הִ֥יא אוֹצָרֽוֹ׃);
Hos 11:5 (וְאַשּׁ֖וּר ה֣וּא מַלְכּ֑וֹ); Neh 8:10 (כִּֽי־חֶדְוַ֥ת יְהוָ֖ה הִ֥יא מָֽעֻזְּכֶֽם׃);
Num 16:7 (אֲשֶׁר־יִבְחַ֥ר יְהוָ֖ה ה֣וּא הַקָּד֑וֹשׁ)

w b) The pronoun after the initiator and announcement: This pronoun also "separates" the initiator (now a Casus Pendens) from its announcement. This construction's usage and emphasis vary by context. Generally, the initiator is definite; the announcement, indefinte. The emphasis ranges from strong emphasis almost like the highly emphatic separating pronoun above to virtually

13. Participles as announcements furnish an exception to the rule of a definite announcement with this construction. They may be definite (Deut 3:22; 9:3; 31:8; Josh 24:17) or indefinite (Deut 31:3; Josh 22:22; 23:3). Arabic also has exceptions to the rule that the predicate is definite in these constructions, but the predicates in those cases are generally SPECIALIZED, and so they are practically definite.

no emphasis or to a stylistic emphasis. Also the announcement may receive emphasis since it precedes the pronoun, though its emphasis is less than the initiator. The pronoun, in contrast to the preceding separating pronoun, is without emphasis.

Subject of predicate — Predicate of predicate

הָ֑וא — אֵ֥שׁ אֹכְלָ֖ה — כִּ֚י יְהוָ֣ה אֱלֹהֶ֔יךָ

Predicate of entire sentence (nominal clause) — Subject of entire nominal sentence

For the Lord, your God – a consuming fire he (is). (Deut 4:24[a])

Subject of predicate — Predicate of predicate

הָ֑וא — 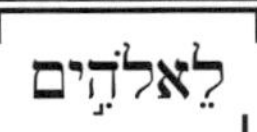 לֵאלֹהִ֣ים — כִּ֥י הַמִּשְׁפָּ֖ט

Predicate of entire sentence (nominal clause) — Subject of entire nominal sentence

For justice – (belonging) to the God, it (is) (Deut 1:17[a])

As the last example illustrates, a prepositional phrase may occur as the announcement. Notice the ל with a definite noun furnishes exclusiveness for this construction: Judgment belongs to God (and God alone). This construction, similar to the separating pronoun, may distinguish between an apposition and a statement.

חֲל֥וֹם אֶחָ֖ד הֽוּא׃ Gen 41:26[b]

(The) dream, one it (is) = The dream is one

Without the pronoun, the words could be understood appositionally (adjective): "one dream." This example, though without emphasis, has the Semitic style of the Casus Pendens. (Jer 10:3)

שֶׁ֣בַע פָּרֹ֣ת הַטֹּבֹ֗ת שֶׁ֤בַע שָׁנִים֙ הֵ֔נָּה Gen 41:26[a]

The seven good cows, seven years they (are) = The seven good cows are seven years

In this example, the pronoun is not necessary, but it furnishes the Semitic style of the Casus Pendens. This example is without emphasis.

כִּ֣י הַמָּק֗וֹם אֲשֶׁ֤ר אַתָּה֙ עוֹמֵ֣ד עָלָ֔יו אַדְמַת־קֹ֖דֶשׁ הֽוּא׃ Exod 3:5[b]

For the place, upon which you are standing, holy ground it (is)

Because the construction is expanded with a relative clause, the Casus Pendens (the place) is both emphatic and stylistic.

Exod 16:36 (וְהָעֹ֕מֶר עֲשִׂרִ֥ית הָאֵיפָ֖ה הֽוּא׃); Josh 5:15 (כִּ֣י הַמָּק֗וֹם אֲשֶׁ֛ר אַתָּ֛ה עֹמֵ֥ד עָלָ֖יו קֹ֣דֶשׁ ה֑וּא); 2 Kgs 4:9 (כִּ֛י אִ֥ישׁ אֱלֹהִ֖ים קָד֥וֹשׁ ה֑וּא); BA Dan 2:28 (וְחֶזְוֵ֥י רֵאשָׁ֛ךְ עַֽל־מִשְׁכְּבָ֖ךְ דְּנָ֥ה הֽוּא׃)

x 4. The word order of nominal clauses

Because the announcement qualifies the initiator, the initiator usually precedes the announcement.

a) Nominal clause with a verb as announcement
The initiator *must* precede the verb.[14] Gen 13:12[a] אַבְרָ֖ם יָשַׁ֣ב "Abram—he dwelt."

y b) Nominal clause with a nominal clause (or adverbial clause) as announcement
The initiator *must* precede a nominal (or adverbial) clause that functions as an announcement. Nah 1:3[b] יְהוָ֗ה בְּסוּפָ֤ה וּבִשְׂעָרָה֙ דַּרְכּ֔וֹ "the Lord – in the storm and the whirlwind is his way"

z c) Nominal clause with a word or phrase, but not a clause, as announcement
The word order varies.

i. The initiator *must* precede the announcement:

① When both the initiator and the announcement are definite:

Exod 9:27[b] יְהוָה֙ הַצַּדִּ֔יק וַאֲנִ֥י וְעַמִּ֖י הָרְשָׁעִֽים׃

The Lord is the righteous one, **and I and my people** are the wicked ones.

aa ② When both the initiator and the announcement are indefinite, so that either could be the initiator (§11h):

Prov 10:11[a] מְק֣וֹר חַ֭יִּים פִּ֣י צַדִּ֑יק

A well of life is the mouth of the righteous.

Prov 14:30 (חַיֵּ֣י בְ֭שָׂרִים לֵ֣ב מַרְפֵּ֑א); 15:4 (מַרְפֵּ֣א לָ֭שׁוֹן עֵ֣ץ חַיִּ֑ים)

bb ③ When following certain particles, the initiator must precede the announcement: הִנֵּה, אֵין/אַיִן, etc.:

1 Sam 19:11[b] אִם־אֵ֨ינְךָ֜ מְמַלֵּ֤ט אֶת־נַפְשְׁךָ֙ הַלַּ֔יְלָה

If **you are not** fleeing for your life tonight . . .

Gen 20:3 (הִנְּךָ֥ מֵת֙), 7 (וְאִם־אֵֽינְךָ֣ מֵשִׁ֗יב); Exod 4:18 (הַעוֹדָ֣ם חַיִּ֑ים); 5:10 (אֵינֶ֛נִּי נֹתֵ֥ן לָכֶ֖ם); 1 Sam 20:5 (הִנֵּה־חֹ֙דֶשׁ֙ מָחָ֔ר)

cc ④ When the initiator is emphatic:

Exod 3:15[a] יְהוָ֞ה אֱלֹהֵ֣י אֲבֹתֵיכֶ֗ם אֱלֹהֵ֨י אַבְרָהָ֜ם אֱלֹהֵ֥י יִצְחָ֛ק וֵאלֹהֵ֥י יַעֲקֹ֖ב שְׁלָחַ֣נִי אֲלֵיכֶ֑ם

The Lord, God of your fathers, the God of Abraham, the God of Isaac, and the God of Jacob – He has sent me to you.

Exod 12:29 (וַֽיהוָה֙ הִכָּ֣ה); 1 Sam 24:20 (וַֽיהוָה֙ יְשַׁלֶּמְךָ֣)

dd ii. The announcement *must* precede the initiator:

① When an indefinite initiator follows a definite prepositional phrase with ל and the construction asserts possession (§11f):

1 Sam 1:2[a] וְלוֹ֙ שְׁתֵּ֣י נָשִׁ֔ים

And to him **were a couple of wives.**

Gen 16:1 (וְלָ֛הּ שִׁפְחָ֥ה מִצְרִ֖ית); 1 Sam 2:8 (כִּ֤י לַֽיהוָה֙ מְצֻ֣קֵי אֶ֔רֶץ); 2 Sam 17:18 (וְל֥וֹ בְאֵ֛ר בַּחֲצֵר֖וֹ)

14. Although the initiator must precede the verb, other words or phrases may precede the initiator, such as an adverbial word or phrase (כִּי, Gen 43:5).

② When the announcement is an interrogative pronoun: *ee*

מָֽה־אֱנ֥וֹשׁ כִּֽי־תִזְכְּרֶ֑נּוּ Ps 8:5[a]

What is man that you should in fact remember him?

1 Sam 11:12 (מִ֣י הָאֹמֵ֔ר); Mic 6:8 (מַה־טּ֑וֹב); Job 7:17 (מָֽה־אֱנוֹשׁ)

③ When the announcement is emphatic: *ff*

כִּֽי־קָ֝ד֗וֹשׁ יְהוָ֥ה אֱלֹהֵֽינוּ׃ Ps 99:9[b]

For **holy** is the Lord, our God.

Isa 6:3 (קָד֧וֹשׁ ׀ קָד֛וֹשׁ קָד֖וֹשׁ יְהוָ֣ה); Ps 48:2 (גָּ֘ד֤וֹל יְהוָ֣ה); 103:8 (רַח֣וּם וְחַנּ֣וּן יְהוָ֑ה); 135:5 (גָד֣וֹל יְהוָ֑ה)

iii. The announcement *may* precede the initiator: *gg*

① When the announcement is a prepositional phrase or adverbial, indicating place or time (This word order may be reversed if the initiator is SPECIALIZED.):

וְאֵלֶ֙יךָ֙ תְּשׁ֣וּקָת֔וֹ Gen 4:7[b]

And to you is its desire.

Exod 16:26 (וּבַיּ֥וֹם הַשְּׁבִיעִ֛י שַׁבָּ֖ת); 1 Sam 1:3 (וְשָׁ֞ם שְׁנֵ֣י בְנֵי־עֵלִ֗י); 6:14 (וְשָׁ֖ם אֶ֣בֶן גְּדוֹלָ֑ה); 21:8 (וְשָׁ֡ם אִישׁ֩ מֵעַבְדֵ֨י שָׁא֜וּל); 24:4 (וְשָׁ֣ם מְעָרָ֔ה); Hab 3:4 (וְשָׁ֖ם חֶבְי֥וֹן עֻזֹּֽה׃); Neh 10:40 (וְשָׁם֙ כְּלֵ֣י הַמִּקְדָּ֔שׁ). This construction with the preposition ב or the adverbial particle שָׁם and an indefinite initiator often asserts existence (Exod 16:26; 1 Sam 6:14; §11f). These constructions that do not assert existence, like Gen 4:7, are adverbial clauses (§11a, footnote 1).

② When the initiator and announcement cannot be confused, as for example, when the initiator is definite and the announcement is indefinite: *hh*

כִּֽי־נַ֖עַר אָנֹֽכִי׃ Jer 1:6[b]

Because a lad I am.

Exod 4:25 (חֲתַן־דָּמִ֥ים אַתָּ֖ה לִֽי׃); Prov 20:1 (לֵ֣ץ הַ֭יַּיִן); 31:30 (שֶׁ֣קֶר הַ֭חֵן וְהֶ֣בֶל הַיֹּ֑פִי)

5. Agreement of initiator and announcement *ii*

The initiator agrees with its verb in gender and number, but there are exceptions. A plural initiator may have a singular announcement (Gen 27:29[b] וּמְבָרֲכֶ֖יךָ בָּרֽוּךְ׃; Ps 119:137[b] וְ֝יָשָׁ֗ר מִשְׁפָּטֶֽיךָ׃)

B. Nominative in Verbal Clauses (§38c) *jj*

In the verbal clause, the verb precedes the subject (agent). The subject of the verbal clause is called the "agent" or "the doer" because the verbal action exists in (for example, Moses knew) or proceeds from (for example, Moses struck) the agent.[15] Indeed, the agent may be viewed as connected to the verb, as the suffixed pronouns are connected to the perfect, imperfect, and

15. Howell, Vol 1, 46-47. This definition, of course, excludes passive verbs. The subject of passive verbs is said "to stand in the place of the agent," because the action happens to the subject.

imperative. In nominal clauses, by contrast, the initiator is separated from its verb (announcement).[16]

מֹשֶׁה — Subject (agent) | דִּבֶּר — Predicate (verb)

Moses spoke.

דִּבֶּר

Verb with agent implied ("he")

He spoke.

kk 1. Nominative as agent of verbal clauses

a) The agent may be a word or words.

וַיְהִי דְבַר־יְהוָה אֵלָיו 1 Kgs 17:8

And **the word of the Lord** came to him.

ll b) The agent may be definite or indefinite.

i. Definite

The agent of verbal clauses is usually definite. Exod 17:3 (וַיִּצְמָא שָׁם הָעָם); BA Ezra 4:17 (פִּתְגָמָא שְׁלַח מַלְכָּא)

mm ii. Indefinite

כַּאֲשֶׁר יֹאמַר מְשַׁל הַקַּדְמֹנִי מֵרְשָׁעִים יֵצֵא רֶשַׁע וְיָדִי לֹא תִהְיֶה־בָּךְ׃ 1 Sam 24:14

As the proverb of the ancients says, Out of the wicked comes forth **wickedness**; but my hand shall not be against you.

An indefinite agent is more common in poetry and direct speech than in prose, as 1 Sam 24:14 illustrates. In prose, the agent may be indefinite for a variety of reasons, including:

① An adjective, clause, or annexation to another noun (construct package) specializes an indefinite agent.[17]

וַיֹּאמֶר דָּוִד אֶל־שָׁאוּל אַל־יִפֹּל לֵב־אָדָם עָלָיו 1 Sam 17:32[a]

And David said to Saul, Let not **the heart of man** fall upon him.

Exod 1:8 (וַיָּקָם מֶלֶךְ־חָדָשׁ); 12:30 (וַתְּהִי צְעָקָה גְדֹלָה); 20:3 (לֹא יִהְיֶה־לְךָ אֱלֹהִים אֲחֵרִים); Jer 26:17 (וַיָּקֻמוּ אֲנָשִׁים מִזִּקְנֵי הָאָרֶץ); BA Dan 3:8 (קְרִבוּ גֻּבְרִין כַּשְׂדָּאִין)

nn ② The verb הָיָה sometimes takes an indefinite agent.

וַיְהִי רָעָב בָּאָרֶץ Gen 12:10[a]

Then **a famine** existed in the land.

---

16. ZW, 24. The conjunctive accents usually join verb and agent, and the disjunctive accents usually separate initiator and announcement (§11b fn 3). If a compound apposition modifies the agent, the verb may take a disjunctive accent (Gen 20:2b).

17. The agent is not completely indefinite, but specialized, §12b.

Exod 7:19 (וְהָיָה דָם); 19:16 (וַיְהִי קֹלֹת וּבְרָקִים);
1 Sam 1:2 (וַיְהִי לִפְנִנָּה יְלָדִים); 2:32 (וְלֹא־יִהְיֶה זָקֵן);
Isa 39:8 (יִהְיֶה שָׁלוֹם וֶאֱמֶת)

③ Negative clauses often take an indefinite agent. *oo*

Exod 11:7[a] וּלְכֹל בְּנֵי יִשְׂרָאֵל לֹא יֶחֱרַץ־כֶּלֶב לְשֹׁנוֹ לְמֵאִישׁ וְעַד־בְּהֵמָה

But against any of the sons of Israel **a dog shall not bark**, whether from man even unto beast.

Exod 12:13[b] וְלֹא־יִהְיֶה בָכֶם נֶגֶף לְמַשְׁחִית בְּהַכֹּתִי בְּאֶרֶץ מִצְרָיִם׃

And no plague will befall you to destroy youwhen I strike the land of Egypt.

Exod 13:3 (וְלֹא יֵאָכֵל חָמֵץ׃); 19:13 (לֹא־תִגַּע בּוֹ יָד);
Isa 39:6 (לֹא־יִוָּתֵר דָּבָר)

④ Conditional clauses (especially in laws) often take an indefinite agent. *pp*

Exod 21:14 וְכִי־יָזִד אִישׁ עַל־רֵעֵהוּ לְהָרְגוֹ בְעָרְמָה מֵעִם מִזְבְּחִי תִּקָּחֶנּוּ לָמוּת׃

And if a man acts presumptuously against his neighbor to kill him deceitfully, from my altar you will indeed take him to put (him) to death.

Gen 42:4 (פֶּן־יִקְרָאֶנּוּ אָסוֹן׃); Exod 21:18
(וְכִי־יְרִיבֻן אֲנָשִׁים), 20 (וְכִי־יַכֶּה אִישׁ)

⑤ Abstract agents are often indefinite. *qq*

Jer 8:3[a] וְנִבְחַר מָוֶת מֵחַיִּים

And **death** will be chosen rather than life.

1 Sam 24:14 (מֵרְשָׁעִים יֵצֵא רֶשַׁע)

2. The agreement of subject (agent or initiator) and verb *rr*

a) Gender and number

The agent agrees with its verb in gender and number, but there are exceptions. A masculine pronoun may reflect a feminine agent (Ruth 1:8[b] עֲשִׂיתֶם). A singular verb may have a plural agent (Joel 1:20[b] גַּם־בַּהֲמוֹת שָׂדֶה תַּעֲרוֹג). Collective nouns may occur with a singular verb or with a plural verb (Exod 1:20[b] וַיִּרֶב הָעָם). When the subject is a thing or animal, the gender/number of the agent often differs with the verb.

Exod 1:10 (וְהָיָה כִּי־תִקְרֶאנָה מִלְחָמָה), 16 (וְאִם־בַּת הִיא וָחָיָה׃);
10:23 (וְלֹא־קָמוּ אִישׁ... לֹא־רָאוּ אִישׁ); 13:7 (מַצּוֹת יֵאָכֵל); 16:1
(וַיִּסְעוּ מֵאֵילִם וַיָּבֹאוּ כָּל־עֲדַת בְּנֵי־יִשְׂרָאֵל)
Exod 19:16; 20:3; 1 Sam 20:33; 1 Kgs 22:36

b) Multiple agents to a singular verb *ss*

Often multiple agents connect to a singular verb. Like Arabic, the first agent often determines the number and gender of the verb.

Num 12:1[a] וַתְּדַבֵּר מִרְיָם וְאַהֲרֹן בְּמֹשֶׁה

And **Miriam and Aaron** spoke against Moses

Gen 13:1 וַיַּעַל אַבְרָם מִמִּצְרַיִם הוּא וְאִשְׁתּוֹ וְכָל־אֲשֶׁר־לוֹ וְלוֹט עִמּוֹ הַנֶּגְבָּה׃

And Abram went up from Egypt – he, **his wife, and all that belonged to him** and Lot with him to the Negev.

Exod 1:6 (וַיָּמָת יוֹסֵף וְכָל־אֶחָיו); 4:29 (וַיֵּלֶךְ מֹשֶׁה וְאַהֲרֹן); 7:6 (וַיַּעַשׂ מֹשֶׁה וְאַהֲרֹן); Num 12:1 (וַתְּדַבֵּר מִרְיָם וְאַהֲרֹן בְּמֹשֶׁה); Exod 9:34; 12:30; 14:20; 15:1, 16; 18:5; 21:4; 23:12(2x); 1 Sam 12:14; 23:5; Jer 26:21; BA Dan 5:11 (נַהִירוּ וְשָׂכְלְתָנוּ וְחָכְמָה כְּחָכְמַת־אֱלָהִין הִשְׁתְּכַחַת בֵּהּ); Dan 4:10; 5:16; Ezra 5:3

tt c) אֱלֹהִים

אֱלֹהִים, when used for the true God, is a plural of intensity (§9b), taking a singular verb and singular modifiers. When אֱלֹהִים means "judges," "gods," "angels," etc., it usually takes a plural verb and modifiers (Exod 22:8).

uu 3. The word order of verbal clauses

The word order of a verbal clause must be the verb before the agent. Although word order may vary within the verbal clause—an object, adverb, or prepositional phrase may occur before a verb and its agent, and usually with emphasis—the principle of verb before agent is inviolate.

vv 4. Omission of the agent by the passive verb

When an author uses an active verb, the agent of the action is usually revealed. When the author wishes to conceal the agent of the action, he transforms an active verb into a passive verb or uses a third person active verb impersonally.[18] Reasons for transforming an active verb to a passive verb or for using third person active verbs impersonally include:

a) When the agent of the action is unknown or hidden for security purposes:

1 Kgs 1:51[a] וַיֻּגַּד לִשְׁלֹמֹה לֵאמֹר הִנֵּה אֲדֹנִיָּהוּ יָרֵא אֶת־הַמֶּלֶךְ שְׁלֹמֹה

And it was reported to Solomon saying, Behold, Adonijah (is) a fearer of the king, Solomon.

1 Sam 19:19 (וַיֻּגַּד לְשָׁאוּל), 22 (וַיֹּאמֶר); 23:7 (וַיֻּגַּד לְשָׁאוּל), 22 (כִּי אָמַר אֵלַי); 24:11 (וְאָמַר)

ww b) When the agent of the action is well-known, therefore, without need of mention:[19]

Isa 1:20 וְאִם־תְּמָאֲנוּ וּמְרִיתֶם חֶרֶב תְּאֻכְּלוּ כִּי פִּי יְהוָה דִּבֵּר׃

But if you refuse and rebel, **you will be devoured by the sword**. Truly, the mouth of the Lord has spoken.

18. Of course, the active verb may also subtly hide the actual agents by using vague agents (Ruth 4:1, "sit here so and so"). For the contrast between passive and reflexive, see §7a.

19. The active construction would be, "I (God) will cause the sword to consume you."

1 Kgs 3:24 (וַיָּבִאוּ הַחֶרֶב); BA Dan 3:4 (וְכָרוֹזָא קָרֵא); 4:23 (אֲמַרִין); 7:5 (וְכֵן אָמְרִין)

c) When the agent is unimportant, without need of mention: *xx*

וַתָּמָת רָחֵל וַתִּקָּבֵר בְּדֶרֶךְ אֶפְרָתָה Gen 35:19

So Rachel died **and was buried** on the way to Ephrath.

Gen 22:20 (וַיֻּגַּד לְאַבְרָהָם); 31:22 (וַיֻּגַּד לְלָבָן); BA Dan 5:3 (הַיְתִיו מָאנֵי דַהֲבָא)

§12. Genitive *a*

A noun is in the genitive case when it is a non-initial noun of a construct package; the first word of the package, called the governing noun, may be in any case (NOMINATIVE, GENITIVE, or ACCUSATIVE) according to its function in the clause.[20] Native Semitic grammarians call the construct package ANNEXATION because the governing noun is annexed or attached to the last noun (the genitive). Annexation occurs when a noun is attached to another noun, when a noun is attached to a pronominal suffix, or when a preposition is attached to a noun.[21] Annexation may be proper and improper. Furthermore, variations of annexation include: nouns of relation, clause in the place of the genitive, and ל with a noun substituting for a genitive.[22]

A. Proper Annexation *b*

PROPER ANNEXATION occurs when the second word (the genitive) limits and identifies the first word (the governing noun) in some manner, forming one unit of meaning or one conceptual unit.[23] Hence, proper annexation is also called "meaning annexation" or "sense annexation." For example, the words סֵפֶר and הָאִישׁ are two unattached words having two units of meaning. When they are annexed—סֵפֶר הָאִישׁ—the two attached words now form one meaning or concept, the genitive now identifying and making definite the first noun[24] – the-book-of-the-man.[25] The genitive with its article—הָאִישׁ—defines, limits, and describes the governing noun (סֵפֶר). Words in proper annexation cannot be separated without changing the meaning of the annexation. Of course, the genitive may limit its noun without making it definite. In the annexation, כַּף אִישׁ, the annexation is proper because the genitive (אִישׁ) limits and identifies the governing noun (כַּף).

20. The governing noun of a construct package may be in any case (nominative, genitive, or accusative) according to its syntactic role in the sentence. In longer construct packages, such as בֵּית אִישׁ אֱלֹהִים, the first word (בֵּית) is the governing noun to אִישׁ אֱלֹהִים, its genitive; אִישׁ governs אֱלֹהִים and is genitive to בֵּית, and אֱלֹהִים is genitive to אִישׁ and בֵּית.
21. All prepositions are in the place of accusatives (unless it is the predicate in a verbless clause, then it is in the place of a nominative), usually adverbial accusatives; their objects are in the genitive.
22. Griess, 180–188; Howell §110–117; Wright II, §75, 77.
23. Proper annexation may also express the superlative, §23d.
24. The concept of proper annexation as having one meaning or concept is seen by the definite genitive making the indefinite governing noun definite. Normally, a word is definite if: it has the article, it has a pronominal suffix, or it is a proper name.
25. English compound adjectives connected by dashes, such as, "a run-of-the-mill house," resemble annexation by expressing one unit of meaning. The words cannot be separated without changing the meaning of the adjective, similar to Hebrew annexation.

Although the genitive does not make its governing noun definite, the genitive SPECIALIZES[26] its governing noun. Specializing annexation, being proper, forms one conceptual unit, which cannot be separated without changing the meaning (Exod 4:25b חֲתַן־דָּמִים "bridegroom of blood"; 1 Sam 11:2[a] עֵין יָמִין "eye of the right"; 21:5[a] לֶחֶם חֹל "bread of common," לֶחֶם קֹדֶשׁ "bread of holiness"; Jer 7:34[a] קוֹל שָׂשׂוֹן וְקוֹל שִׂמְחָה קוֹל חָתָן וְקוֹל כַּלָּה "voice of mirth, voice of gladness, voice of the bridegroom, voice of the bride"; BA Dan 7:4[b] וּלְבַב אֱנָשׁ "heart of a man").

Proper annexation communicates various meanings. The meaning or relationship between the genitive and its governing noun may be understood by inserting one of three prepositions between them: ב, מִן, or ל.

c 1. The ב preposition—in, at, by

The genitive is a noun of place or time to the governing noun. In 2 Sam 1:21[a], the ב appears between the annexation: "O Mountains in Gilboa" (הָרֵי בַגִּלְבֹּעַ).[27] The following examples assume the meaning of the ב preposition between the annexed members.

לֹא־תִירָא מִפַּחַד לָיְלָה Ps 91:5[a]

You must not be afraid of terror **in night**.

The genitive (לָיְלָה) is a noun of time specializing its governing noun (מִפַּחַד)—terror *in* night.

1 Sam 13:23 (אֶל־מַעֲבַר מִכְמָשׂ)

לְזַרְעֲךָ נָתַתִּי אֶת־הָאָרֶץ הַזֹּאת מִנְּהַר מִצְרַיִם עַד־הַנָּהָר הַגָּדֹל נְהַר־פְּרָת׃ Gen 15:18[b]

To your seed I gave this land, from the river **at Egypt** unto the great river, Euphrates.

The genitive (מִצְרַיִם) is an adverb of place for its governing noun (מִנְּהַר) – river *at* Egypt.

Gen 2:13 (אֶרֶץ כּוּשׁ); 18:1 (בְּאֵלֹנֵי מַמְרֵא), 20 (זַעֲקַת סְדֹם וַעֲמֹרָה); Exod 7:11 (חַרְטֻמֵּי מִצְרָיִם); 1 Sam 20:25 (מוֹשַׁב הַקִּיר); 24:2 (בְּמִדְבַּר עֵין גֶּדִי); Jer 1:1 (בְּאֶרֶץ בִּנְיָמִן); 26:2 (בַּחֲצַר בֵּית־יְהוָה ... עַל־כָּל־עָרֵי יְהוּדָה); BA Dan 2:12 (חַכִּימֵי בָבֶל)

d 2. The מִן preposition—from, out of

This annexation usually occurs for a part/whole (partitive genitive) relationship, often expressing a superlative or the material out of which the governing noun is made. In 2 Sam 1:15, the מִן appears between the annexation: "And David called to one of the young men" (לְאַחַד מֵהַנְּעָרִים). The following examples assume the meaning of the מִן preposition between the annexed members.

חַכְמוֹת שָׂרוֹתֶיהָ תַּעֲנֶינָּה Judg 5:29[a]

The wise (women) of her princesses would answer.

---

26. SPECIALIZATION limits a noun without making it definite (§11h; Wright II, §75; ZW, 33, footnote 1).

27. The insertion of a ב between a construct and its governing noun of place or time occurs several times. Judg 8:11; 2 Sam 10:9; Isa 5:11; 9:1; 19:8; 22:16; Hos 14:8; Obad 3; Ps 84:7; 136:8-9.

The governing noun (חֲכְמוֹת), an adjective used substantivally, is the part; the genitive (שָׂרוֹתֶיהָ) is the whole—the wise (women) *out of* her princesses = the wisest women of her princesses (a superlative).[28]

Ps 2:9 תְּרֹעֵם בְּשֵׁבֶט בַּרְזֶל כִּכְלִי יוֹצֵר תְּנַפְּצֵם׃

You will break them **with a rod out of iron,** as a vessel of a potter you will shatter them.

The genitive (בַּרְזֶל) is the material out of which the governing noun (בְּשֵׁבֶט) is made—the rod (made) out of iron.

Exod 2:3 (תֵּבַת גֹּמֶא); 20:23–25 (אֱלֹהֵי כֶסֶף וֵאלֹהֵי זָהָב; מִזְבַּח אֲדָמָה; אֲבָנִים מִזְבַּח); 1 Sam 17:5–6 (וְכוֹבַע נְחֹשֶׁת; וְשִׁרְיוֹן קַשְׂקַשִּׂים; וּמִצְחַת נְחֹשֶׁת; וְכִידוֹן נְחֹשֶׁת); Jer 1:18 (וּלְעַמּוּד בַּרְזֶל וּלְחֹמוֹת נְחֹשֶׁת); BA Dan 3:5 (לְצֶלֶם דַּהֲבָא); 4:14 (וּשְׁפַל אֲנָשִׁים); Ezra 7:12 (מֶלֶךְ מַלְכַיָּא)

3. The ל preposition—(with reference) to[29] *e*

This is the most common category, which includes the possessive. This is a flexible category with many nuances. In Prov 24:9, the ל appears between the annexation: "The scoffer (is) an abomination with reference to man" (וְתוֹעֲבַת לְאָדָם לֵץ׃). The following examples assume the meaning of the ל preposition between the annexed members.

Exod 40:6 וְנָתַתָּה אֵת מִזְבַּח הָעֹלָה לִפְנֵי פֶּתַח מִשְׁכַּן אֹהֶל־מוֹעֵד׃

And you will set **the altar of burnt offering** before the door of the dwelling place of the tabernacle.

The governing noun (מִזְבַּח) has reference to (and is identified by) the genitive (הָעֹלָה) – "the altar with respect to burnt offering." Compare this construction with the following example:

1 Chr 22:1 וַיֹּאמֶר דָּוִיד זֶה הוּא בֵּית יְהוָה הָאֱלֹהִים וְזֶה־מִּזְבֵּחַ לְעֹלָה לְיִשְׂרָאֵל׃

And David said, This is the house of the Lord God, and this is **(the) altar with reference to burnt offering** for Israel.

Notice the same meaning of the two preceding examples, Exod 40:6 and 1 Chr 22:1. In 1 Chr 22:1, the ל "breaks" the annexation of Exod 40:6.

Lev 17:6[a] וְזָרַק הַכֹּהֵן אֶת־הַדָּם עַל־מִזְבַּח יְהוָה פֶּתַח אֹהֶל מוֹעֵד

And the priest will sprinkle the blood upon **the altar of the Lord** at the door of the tabernacle.

The governing noun (מִזְבַּח) has reference to, belongs to, and is identified by the genitive (יְהוָה). Compare the same words with the ל preposition in Gen 8:20 (מִזְבֵּחַ לַיהוָה "an altar to the Lord").

Gen 2:7 (נִשְׁמַת חַיִּים); 3:19 (בְּזֵעַת אַפֶּיךָ); 4:11 (דְּמֵי אָחִיךָ), 26 (בְּשֵׁם יְהוָה׃); 7:7 (מֵי הַמַּבּוּל׃, וּנְשֵׁי־בָנָיו); 1 Sam 20:29 (שֻׁלְחַן הַמֶּלֶךְ׃); BA Dan 2:23 (מִלַּת מַלְכָּא, אֱלָהּ אֲבָהָתִי)

B. Improper Annexation *f*

Improper annexation, as the name implies, is a pseudo-annexation. In

28. §23e
29. Related to this annexation with the meaning of the ל preposition is the construction of §12r.

improper annexation, the genitive does not limit or identify the first word, a definite genitive will not make its first noun definite,[30] and an indefinite genitive will not SPECIALIZE its first noun. Improper annexation, therefore, does not form one unit of meaning. It merely attaches words using the annexation construction, a grammatical expediency for ease of expression. Hence, improper or pseudo-annexation is also called "verbal annexation" since it merely annexes words without forming one unit of meaning. The attached words can be separated by changing the genitive into an accusative without changing the meaning. In improper annexation, the first word must be a participle (active or passive) or an adjective.[31] The genitive functions as an accusative of the direct object with transitive active participles and as an ACCUSATIVE OF SPECIFICATION (§13jj) with intransitive participles, and adjectives.

g 1. Adjectives

The governing noun is an adjective with the genitive functioning as a GENITIVE OF SPECIFICATION, specifying the area of application for the governing noun.

Gen 39:6[b] וַיְהִ֣י יוֹסֵ֔ף יְפֵה־תֹ֖אַר וִיפֵ֥ה מַרְאֶֽה׃

And Joseph became **beautiful (in the area) of form and beautiful (in the area) of appearance**.

The genitive (תֹּאַר) specifies the area of application for the governing noun (יְפֵה)—"beautiful specifically in the area of form."

1 Sam 1:15[a] וַתַּ֨עַן חַנָּ֤ה וַתֹּ֙אמֶר֙ לֹ֣א אֲדֹנִ֔י אִשָּׁ֤ה קְשַׁת־ר֙וּחַ֙ אָנֹ֔כִי וְיַ֥יִן
וְשֵׁכָ֖ר לֹ֣א שָׁתִ֑יתִי

And Hannah answered and said, No, my lord, a woman **harsh (in the area) of spirit** I am, and wine and strong drink I have not drunken.

Gen 18:4 (מְעַט־מַ֔יִם); 34:21 (רַֽחֲבַת־יָדַ֖יִם); 35:29 (וּשְׂבַ֣ע יָמִ֑ים); Exod 4:10 (כְבַד־פֶּ֛ה וּכְבַ֥ד לָשׁ֖וֹן); 16:14 (דַּ֥ק מְחֻסְפָּ֖ס דַּ֥ק כַּכְּפֹ֖ר), 36 (עֲשִׂרִ֥ית הָאֵיפָ֖ה); 1 Sam 1:10 (מָ֣רַת נָ֑פֶשׁ); 16:12 (יְפֵ֥ה עֵינַ֖יִם וְט֣וֹב רֹ֑אִי); 20:20 (שְׁלֹ֥שֶׁת הַחִצִּ֖ים); 21:16 (חֲסַ֤ר מְשֻׁגָּעִים֙); 25:3 (טֽוֹבַת־שֶׂ֙כֶל֙ וִ֣יפַת תֹּ֔אַר); BA Dan 4:14 (וּשְׁפַ֥ל אֲנָשִׁ֖ים)

h 2. Participles

The governing noun is a transitive participle with the genitive functioning as an accusative of direct object.

Ps 106:3 אַ֭שְׁרֵי שֹׁמְרֵ֣י מִשְׁפָּ֑ט עֹשֵׂ֖ה צְדָקָ֣ה בְכָל־עֵֽת׃

Blessed **(are they who are) keeping** justice and (blessed is he who is) **doing** righteousness all the time.

Gen 3:5 (יֹדְעֵ֖י ט֥וֹב וָרָֽע׃); 4:2 (רֹ֣עֵה צֹ֔אן); 14:19 (קֹנֵ֖ה שָׁמַ֥יִם וָאָֽרֶץ׃); 18:25 (הֲשֹׁפֵט֙ כָּל־הָאָ֔רֶץ)

Exod 3:8; 15:11; 20:6; 21:12; BA Dan 2:29; Ezra 4:15; 7:11

If the governing noun is an intransitive participle, the genitive functions

30. 1 Sam 15:32[b] (מַר־הַמָּֽוֶת׃ "bitterness with respect to death"). The article is probably generic of an abstract noun, not a particularizing article, §35c.

31. This definition excludes participles that have become pure nouns like כֹּהֵן and adjectives that are use substantivally, חָכָם = wise *man*.

as an accusative of specification, similar to the adjective, as the following example illustrates.

2 Sam 13:31 וַיָּקָם הַמֶּלֶךְ וַיִּקְרַע אֶת־בְּגָדָיו וַיִּשְׁכַּב אָרְצָה וְכָל־עֲבָדָיו נִצָּבִים קְרֻעֵי בְגָדִים׃

And the king rose up and tore his clothes and lay down on the ground and (as) all his servants were standing, **torn (in the area of)** garments.

Gen 4:20 (יֹשֵׁב אֹהֶל); Isa 14:19 (מְטֹעֲנֵי חָרֶב); Jer 41:5 (מְגֻלְּחֵי זָקָן וּקְרֻעֵי בְגָדִים); Cant 3:6 (מְקֻטֶּרֶת מוֹר וּלְבוֹנָה)

C. Nouns of Relation *i*

Nouns of relation are annexations with the governing nouns אִישׁ, בַּ֫עַל, or בֵּן (or their plurals or their feminine forms) with the genitive being a quality, characteristic, or class. The governing noun is, metaphorically speaking, related to the quality, characteristic, class, or group. These annexations are quasi-adjectives, which may be used substantivally, like any other adjective.

1. אִישׁ

Exod 4:10[a] וַיֹּאמֶר מֹשֶׁה אֶל־יְהוָה בִּי אֲדֹנָי לֹא אִישׁ דְּבָרִים אָנֹכִי

And Moses said to the Lord, Please, my Lord, I am not **a man of words**.

Moses claims not to be a part of the class of eloquent men.

Prov 15:18 אִישׁ חֵמָה יְגָרֶה מָדוֹן וְאֶרֶךְ אַפַּיִם יַשְׁקִיט רִיב׃

A man of heat stirs up strife, but the long of anger pacifies contention.

A man of heat belongs to the class of the hot-tempered.

Gen 9:20 (אִישׁ הָאֲדָמָה); Num 31:28 (אַנְשֵׁי הַמִּלְחָמָה)
Judg 3:29; 1 Kgs 2:26; Ps 5:7; Job 34:8, 36; Prov 10:23; 16:28

2. בַּ֫עַל *j*

Gen 14:13[b] וְהֵם בַּעֲלֵי בְרִית־אַבְרָם׃

And they were **the owners of the covenant of Abram**.

They belong to the class of those who covenant with Abram.

Gen 37:19 וַיֹּאמְרוּ אִישׁ אֶל־אָחִיו הִנֵּה בַּעַל הַחֲלֹמוֹת הַלָּזֶה בָּא׃

And they said to one another, Behold, **this owner of dreams** (is) coming.

Joseph belongs to the class of dreamers.

Gen 49:23 (בַּעֲלֵי חִצִּים׃); Prov 1:17 (בַּעַל כָּנָף׃); 29:22 (וּבַעַל חֵמָה); BA Ezra 4:8 (בְּעֵל־טְעֵם)

3. בֵּן *k*

Gen 6:2[a] וַיִּרְאוּ בְנֵי־הָאֱלֹהִים אֶת־בְּנוֹת הָאָדָם

And **the sons of God** saw the daughters of man.

Ezek 2:1 וַיֹּאמֶר אֵלָי בֶּן־אָדָם עֲמֹד עַל־רַגְלֶיךָ וַאֲדַבֵּר אֹתָךְ׃

And he said to me, **Son of man**, stand upon your feet, and I will speak with you.

The annexation expresses a man who belongs to the class of Adam.

Gen 5:32 (בֶּן־חֲמֵשׁ מֵאוֹת שָׁנָה); Ps 89:23 (וּבֶן־עַוְלָה); 102:21 (בְּנֵי תְמוּתָה׃);

Job 5:7 (וּבְנֵי־רֶשֶׁף)
Job 41:26; Prov 15:11; BA Dan 2:25; 3:25; 6:1; 7:13

l **D. Clauses (phrases) in the Place of the Genitive (§39b–c)**

As a clause may stand in the place of the nominative or accusative, so a clause may stand in the place of a genitive.

1. The clause is in the place of the genitive after:
   a) A preposition

אַחֲרֵי נִמְכַּר גְּאֻלָּה תִּהְיֶה־לּוֹ Lev 25:48[a]

After he is sold, (the right of) redemption exists to him.

The verbal clause, נִמְכַּר, is in the position of the genitive after the preposition אַחֲרֵי.

הַכֹּהֲנִים לֹא אָמְרוּ אַיֵּה יְהוָה וְתֹפְשֵׂי הַתּוֹרָה לֹא יְדָעוּנִי וְהָרֹעִים פָּשְׁעוּ בִי וְהַנְּבִיאִים נִבְּאוּ בַבַּעַל וְאַחֲרֵי לֹא־יוֹעִלוּ הָלָכוּ׃ Jer 2:8

The priests did not say, Where is the Lord? and the handlers of the law did not know me. And the shepherds transgressed against me, and the prophets prophesied by Baal. **And after they (who) do not profit,** they walked.

Deut 33:11 (מִן־יְקוּמוּן׃); 2 Sam 21:10 (עַד נִתַּךְ־מַיִם); Isa 14:9 (מִתַּחַת רָגְזָה); 59:18 (כְּעַל גְּמֻלוֹת); Jer 41:16 (אַחַר הִכָּה)

m b) A noun

כִּי יֹדֵעַ אֱלֹהִים כִּי בְּיוֹם אֲכָלְכֶם מִמֶּנּוּ וְנִפְקְחוּ עֵינֵיכֶם וִהְיִיתֶם כֵּאלֹהִים יֹדְעֵי טוֹב וָרָע׃ Gen 3:5

For God (is) knowing that **on the day of** your eating from it, that your eyes will be opened and you will exist as gods knowing good and evil.

תְּחִלַּת דִּבֶּר־יְהוָה בְּהוֹשֵׁעַ Hos 1:2a

The beginning of (the time when) the Lord spoke to Hosea.

The verbal clause, דִּבֶּר, is in the position of the genitive after the construct noun תְּחִלַּת.

Exod 10:28 (בְּיוֹם רְאֹתְךָ פָנַי); Lev 7:9 (וְכָל־נַעֲשָׂה); 1 Sam 25:15 (כָּל־יְמֵי הִתְהַלַּכְנוּ אִתָּם); Isa 15:1 (בְּלֵיל שֻׁדַּד עָר); 29:1 (קִרְיַת חָנָה דָוִד); 40:4 (כָּל־גֶּיא יִנָּשֵׂא); Hos 14:3 (כָּל־תִּשָּׂא עָוֹן); Ps 104:9 (גְּבוּל־שַׂמְתָּ)

n 2. The clause or phrase in the place of the genitive may be:
   a) A verbal clause

וַיֹּאמֶר בִּי אֲדֹנָי שְׁלַח־נָא בְּיַד־תִּשְׁלָח׃ Exod 4:13

And he said, Please my Lord, send please **by the hand of (whom) you send**.

The verbal clause, תִּשְׁלָח, is in the place of the genitive to the governing noun בְּיַד.

וַיְהִי בְּיוֹם דִּבֶּר יְהוָה אֶל־מֹשֶׁה בְּאֶרֶץ מִצְרָיִם׃ Exod 6:28

And it happened **on the day of (which) God spoke to Moses in the land of Egypt**.

The verbal clause, דִּבֶּר יְהוָה אֶל־מֹשֶׁה בְּאֶרֶץ מִצְרָיִם, is in the place of the genitive to the governing noun בְּיוֹם.

Ps 71:18 (עַד־אַגִּיד ... לְכָל־יָבוֹא); 90:15 (כִּימוֹת עִנִּיתָנוּ שְׁנוֹת רָאִינוּ); 148:6 (חָק־נָתַן); Job 21:30 (אֵיד יֵחָשֶׂךְ רָע)

b) A relative clause *o*

i. Nominal clause

Gen 39:3 וַיַּרְא אֲדֹנָיו כִּי יְהוָה אִתּוֹ וְכֹל אֲשֶׁר־הוּא עֹשֶׂה יְהוָה מַצְלִיחַ בְּיָדוֹ׃

And his master saw that the Lord (was) with him, **and all of which he (was) doing**, the Lord (was) prospering in his hand.

The nominal relative clause, אֲשֶׁר־הוּא עֹשֶׂה, is in the place of the genitive after the governing noun וְכֹל.

Gen 40:3 וַיִּתֵּן אֹתָם בְּמִשְׁמַר בֵּית שַׂר הַטַּבָּחִים אֶל־בֵּית הַסֹּהַר מְקוֹם אֲשֶׁר יוֹסֵף אָסוּר שָׁם׃

And he put them in the place of keeping of the house of the chief of the bodyguards, to the house of roundness, **the place of which Joseph was bound there (the place where Joseph was bound)**.

The relative clause is in the place of the genitive after the governing noun מְקוֹם.

Lev 14:32 (תּוֹרַת אֲשֶׁר־בּוֹ נֶגַע צָרָעַת); Jer 22:25 (וּבְיַד אֲשֶׁר־אַתָּה יָגוֹר)

ii. Verbal clause *p*

Josh 7:8 בִּי אֲדֹנָי מָה אֹמַר אַחֲרֵי אֲשֶׁר הָפַךְ יִשְׂרָאֵל עֹרֶף לִפְנֵי אֹיְבָיו׃

Please my Lord, what can I say **after that Israel has turned a back of the neck before his enemies?**

The verbal relative clause, אֲשֶׁר הָפַךְ יִשְׂרָאֵל עֹרֶף לִפְנֵי אֹיְבָיו, is in the place of the genitive after the governing preposition אַחֲרֵי.

Lev 4:24 (בִּמְקוֹם אֲשֶׁר־יִשְׁחַט אֶת־הָעֹלָה); 7:2 (בִּמְקוֹם אֲשֶׁר יִשְׁחֲטוּ אֶת־הָעֹלָה); 27:8 (עַל־פִּי אֲשֶׁר תַּשִּׂיג יַד); Deut 22:24 (עַל־דְּבַר אֲשֶׁר לֹא־צָעֲקָה); 1 Sam 3:13 (בַּעֲוֹן אֲשֶׁר־יָדַע)

c) A prepositional phrase *q*

Isa 9:1 הָעָם הַהֹלְכִים בַּחֹשֶׁךְ רָאוּ אוֹר גָּדוֹל יֹשְׁבֵי בְּאֶרֶץ צַלְמָוֶת אוֹר נָגַהּ עֲלֵיהֶם׃

The people, the ones walking in darkness, they saw a great light; **the dwellers of (those who were) in the land of deep darkness**, a light has shone upon them.

The prepositional phrase, בְּאֶרֶץ צַלְמָוֶת, is in the place of the genitive after the governing noun יֹשְׁבֵי. Notice the ב preposition between the governing noun and its genitive (§12c).

Isa 9:2 הִרְבִּיתָ הַגּוֹי לוֹ הִגְדַּלְתָּ הַשִּׂמְחָה שָׂמְחוּ לְפָנֶיךָ כְּשִׂמְחַת בַּקָּצִיר כַּאֲשֶׁר יָגִילוּ בְּחַלְּקָם שָׁלָל׃

You will multiply the nation; to him you will make great joy. They will be glad before you **as the gladness (which is) in the harvest** as they rejoice in their dividing of spoil.

The prepositional phrase (בַּקָּצִיר) is in the place of the genitive after the governing noun (כְּשִׂמְחַת).

Num 28:10 (עֹלַת שַׁבַּת בְּשַׁבַּתּוֹ); Josh 15:6 (מִצְּפוֹן לְבֵית הָעֲרָבָה); Judg 5:10 (יֹשְׁבֵי עַל־מִדִּין וְהֹלְכֵי עַל־דֶּרֶךְ); 1 Kgs 7:8 (מִבֵּית לָאוּלָם); Isa 14:19 (יוֹרְדֵי אֶל־אַבְנֵי־בוֹר); Ezek 13:2 (לִנְבִיאֵי מִלִּבָּם); Hos 7:5 (חֲמַת מִיָּיִן)

r **E. The ל with a Noun Substituting for a Genitive**

As the ל preposition often communicates the nuance of annexation (§12e), so the ל preposition with its noun may substitute for a genitive for a preceding noun. This allows the first word to be indefinite, and the second word with the ל to be indefinite (See §11l, the latter part of footnote 9). Furthermore, it relieves a long chain of annexations.

וַיַּעַן אֶחָד מֵהַנְּעָרִים וַיֹּאמֶר הִנֵּה רָאִיתִי בֵּן לְיִשַׁי בֵּית הַלַּחְמִי 1 Sam 16:18[a]

And one of the young men answered and said, Behold I saw a son **of Jesse**, the Bethlehemite.

וַיֹּאמֶר אֵלִיָּהוּ אֶל־הָעָם אֲנִי נוֹתַרְתִּי נָבִיא לַיהוָה לְבַדִּי 1 Kgs 18:22[a]

And Elijah said to the people, I – I am left as a prophet **of the Lord**, I alone.

מִזְמוֹר לְדָוִד Ps 3:1[a]

A psalm (with respect) **to David**

Gen 8:20 (מִזְבֵּחַ לַיהוָה); 32:14 (מִנְחָה לְעֵשָׂו); Exod 12:14 (חַג לַיהוָה), 48 (פֶּסַח לַיהוָה); 16:23 (שַׁבָּתוֹן שַׁבַּת־קֹדֶשׁ לַיהוָה)

בִּשְׁנַת שָׁלֹשׁ לְאָסָא מֶלֶךְ יְהוּדָה 1 Kgs 15:28[a]

In the year of third **to Asa**, king of Judah

The ל with אָסָא allows the numeral "three" to be close to the word "year." Otherwise the word "three" would have to be placed at the end of the phrase, as reconstructed below:

בִּשְׁנַת אָסָא מֶלֶךְ יְהוּדָה שָׁלֹשׁ

In the year of Asa, king of Judah, three

Exod 13:12 (כָּל־פֶּטֶר־רֶחֶם לַיהוָה); Lev 1:9 (אִשֵּׁה רֵיחַ־נִיחוֹחַ לַיהוָה׃); Num 3:35 (וּנְשִׂיא בֵית־אָב לְמִשְׁפְּחֹת מְרָרִי); 18:4 (אֶת־מִשְׁמֶרֶת אֹהֶל מוֹעֵד לְכֹל עֲבֹדַת הָאֹהֶל);
Jer 1:3 (עַד־תֹּם עַשְׁתֵּי עֶשְׂרֵה שָׁנָה לְצִדְקִיָּהוּ);
2 Chr 35:5 (לִפְלֻגּוֹת בֵּית הָאָבוֹת לַאֲחֵיכֶם ... וַחֲלֻקַּת בֵּית־אָב לַלְוִיִּם׃);
BA Ezra 6:15 (עַד יוֹם תְּלָתָה לִירַח אֲדָר ... שְׁנַת־שֵׁת לְמַלְכוּת דָּרְיָוֶשׁ מַלְכָּא׃)

§13. Accusative

a As the genitive limits nouns and is governed by another noun, so the accusative usually limits verbs[32] (or participles and infinitives). Accusatives limit the verb as to its object, or as to its place, time, manner, situation, specification, or rarely as to its purpose/intent. Because the accusative endings have almost completely disappeared in Hebrew, determining whether a word is in the accusative is sometimes difficult, except when the accusative marker אֵת is employed. As a general rule, if a word is not a subject, a predicate in a verbless clause, a verb, a genitive, a vocative, or a word in apposition to these, the word is in the accusative. There are three types of accusatives: the ABSOLUTE OBJECT, the DIRECT OBJECT, and the ADVERBIAL OBJECT.[33]

32. Adverbial accusatives may also limit the subject or objects of verbs.
33. Griess, 137–147, 260–275; Howell §39–44, 64–85; Wechter, 51–52; Wright II, §22–26, 43–44.

A. Absolute Object *b*

Absolute objects are infinitive absolutes or abstract nouns expressing verbal actions or states, usually having the same root letters as their governing verb (שָׂמַח שִׂמְחָה גְּדוֹלָה "he rejoiced a great rejoicing," שִׂמְחָה שָׂמֵחַ "rejoicing he rejoiced"). This object is called absolute because the verb is not restricted by the person or thing (accusative of direct object) and because the verb is not restricted by the time, place, manner, or specification (adverbial accusatives), but *the object is the verbal action itself.* Being absolute or unrestricted,[34] the absolute object must be indefinite. The absolute object is, therefore, the purest object, being intimately connected to its governing verb and expressing, in the purest manner, the fundamental essence of the verbal action in the abstract. Hence, the absolute object must be an abstract, not a concrete, noun. The subject of the verb, according to Ibn Barun, must "execute, occasion and bring into existence" the absolute object—he rejoiced a rejoicing.[35] The absolute object may occur before (slightly more emphatic) or after its verb. Absolute objects either emphasize or explain their verbs.

1. Emphasizing the verb (§17e–i) *c*

This absolute object is usually an infinitive absolute unrestricted by adjectives, adverbs, articles, etc. Moreover, it cannot be pluralized. The unrestricted or absolute nature of the infinitive absolute furnishes strong emphasis.

Exod 22:5 כִּי־תֵצֵא אֵשׁ וּמָצְאָה קֹצִים וְנֶאֱכַל גָּדִישׁ אוֹ הַקָּמָה אוֹ הַשָּׂדֶה שַׁלֵּם יְשַׁלֵּם הַמַּבְעִר אֶת־הַבְּעֵרָה׃

When fire goes out and finds thorn bushes and consumes the stacked or standing grain or the field, the one who started the conflagration **paying he will pay** (he will most certainly pay).

Exod 2:19 (וְגַם־דָּלֹה דָלָה); 3:16 (פָּקֹד פָּקַדְתִּי אֶתְכֶם); 5:23 (וְהַצֵּל לֹא־הִצַּלְתָּ); 8:24 (הַרְחֵק לֹא־תַרְחִיקוּ); 11:1 (גָּרֵשׁ יְגָרֵשׁ אֶתְכֶם)

Exod 13:19(2x); 15:1; 17:14; 18:18; 19:5, 13(2x); 21:12, 20; 22:2–3, 22(3x); 1 Sam 6:3; 12:25; 14:28, 30, 39; 20:5–7; 23:22; 24:21; 2 Sam 12:14; Jer 7:5(2x); 26:15

Omitting the absolute object: The absolute object emphasizing the verb may be omitted, though assumed, when מְאֹד is present,[36] especially when מְאֹד is repeated. This is common with stative verbs and with Vav-consecutive constructions, because stative verbs rarely use infinitive absolutes and because the Vav-consecutive is rarely preceded by an infinitive absolute.[37] *d*

34. Some absolute objects may be restricted or limited by adjectives or adverbs, Gen 12:17.
35. Wechter, 52. Of course, not every object related to its verb is an absolute object. For example, the idiomatic expressions, "to dream a dream" and "to sacrifice a sacrifice," are not absolute objects. All absolute objects must be either an infinitive absolute or an abstract noun. Exod 5:7; 1 Sam 24:16; BA Ezra 5:7
36. Griess, 142–143.
37. The infinitive absolute also may occasionally emphasize a Vayyitqol form by following it, Gen 19:9; 31:15; Num 11:32; Josh 24:10; Ezek 25:12.

וַיִּרְאוּ מְאֹד מְאֹד וַיֹּאמְרוּ הִנֵּה שְׁנֵי הַמְּלָכִים לֹא עָמְדוּ לְפָנָיו 2 Kgs 10:4[a]

And they feared **exceedingly, exceedingly**, and they said, Behold both kings – they have not stood before him.

The repetition of מְאֹד implies an omitted absolute object.

כָּבְדָה מְאֹד יַד הָאֱלֹהִים שָׁם׃ 1 Sam 5:11[b]

And the hand of God was **very** heavy there.

וַיִּשְׂמַח שָׁם שָׁאוּל וְכָל־אַנְשֵׁי יִשְׂרָאֵל עַד־מְאֹד׃ 1 Sam 11:15[b]

And Saul and the men of Israel rejoiced there **very greatly**.

Gen 7:19 (גָּבְרוּ מְאֹד מְאֹד); 17:2 (וְאַרְבֶּה אוֹתְךָ בִּמְאֹד מְאֹד׃), 20 (וְהִרְבֵּיתִי אֹתוֹ בִּמְאֹד מְאֹד); 30:43 (וַיִּפְרֹץ הָאִישׁ מְאֹד מְאֹד) Exod 1:7, 20; 14:10; 1 Sam 12:18; 14:31; 18:30; Ezek 16:13

e 2. Explaining the verb (§17j)

This absolute object explains the verb by expressing the quality or manner of the verbal action, functioning adverbially to their governing verbs. These absolute objects still emphasize the verb, though to a lesser degree than the preceding category.

a) An abstract noun limited by adjectives or adverbs (but not the article) This absolute object may be pluralized.

וַיְנַגַּע יְהוָה אֶת־פַּרְעֹה נְגָעִים גְּדֹלִים וְאֶת־בֵּיתוֹ עַל־דְּבַר שָׂרַי אֵשֶׁת אַבְרָם׃ Gen 12:17

And the Lord struck Pharaoh **with great strokes** and his house because of Sarai, the wife of Abram.

This pluralized absolute object and its modifier (נְגָעִים גְּדֹלִים) explains the manner and quality of how the Lord struck Pharaoh and his house.

Gen 27:33–34 (וַיֶּחֱרַד יִצְחָק חֲרָדָה גְּדֹלָה עַד־מְאֹד ... וַיִּצְעַק צְעָקָה גְּדֹלָה וּמָרָה עַד־מְאֹד); 30:20 (זְבָדַנִי אֱלֹהִים אֹתִי זֵבֶד טוֹב); 50:10 (וַיִּסְפְּדוּ־שָׁם מִסְפֵּד גָּדוֹל וְכָבֵד מְאֹד); Exod 32:30 (אַתֶּם חֲטָאתֶם חֲטָאָה גְדֹלָה); Deut 7:23 (וְהָמָם מְהוּמָה גְדֹלָה); Judg 21:2 (וַיִּבְכּוּ בְּכִי גָדוֹל׃); 1 Sam 4:5 (כָל־יִשְׂרָאֵל תְּרוּעָה גְדוֹלָה) 1 Sam 6:19; 17:25; 19:8; 2 Sam 13:15; 23:5; Isa 38:3; Jonah 1:16

f b) Two infinitive absolutes

The infinitive absolutes may not be pluralized.

קְבוּרַת חֲמוֹר יִקָּבֵר סָחוֹב וְהַשְׁלֵךְ מֵהָלְאָה לְשַׁעֲרֵי יְרוּשָׁלִָם׃ Jer 22:19

With the burial of a donkey he will be buried, **a dragging and throwing down** from the outside (with respect) to the gates of Jerusalem.

The infinitive absolutes explain the manner of the burial—with a dragging and a throwing down.

וְנָגַף יְהוָה אֶת־מִצְרַיִם נָגֹף וְרָפוֹא Isa 19:22[a]

And the Lord will smite Egypt **a smiting and a healing**.

The infinitive absolutes explain the quality or manner that the Lord will smite—with a smiting that heals.

1 Sam 6:12 (הָלְכוּ הָלֹךְ וְגָעוֹ); 1 Kgs 20:37 (וַיַּכֵּהוּ הָאִישׁ הַכֵּה וּפָצֹעַ׃);

Jer 7:13 (וָאֲדַבֵּר אֲלֵיכֶם הַשְׁכֵּם וְדַבֵּר); 12:17
(וְנָתַשְׁתִּי אֶת־הַגּוֹי הַהוּא נָתוֹשׁ וְאַבֵּד); 25:3 (וָאֲדַבֵּר אֲלֵיכֶם אַשְׁכֵּים וְדַבֵּר);
50:4 (הָלוֹךְ וּבָכוֹ יֵלֵכוּ); Joel 2:26 (וַאֲכַלְתֶּם אָכוֹל וְשָׂבוֹעַ)

c) An infinitive absolute and a Vav-perfect or Vav-imperfect *g*

The verb may be pluralized.

Josh 6:13[a] וְשִׁבְעָה הַכֹּהֲנִים נֹשְׂאִים שִׁבְעָה שׁוֹפְרוֹת הַיֹּבְלִים לִפְנֵי אֲרוֹן יְהוָה הֹלְכִים הָלוֹךְ וְתָקְעוּ בַּשּׁוֹפָרוֹת

And seven priests (were) lifting seven horn, ram's horns, before the ark of the Lord as walkers **walking, and they would blow** on the horns.

A smoother translation reads, "They would blow on their horns as they walked."

2 Sam 13:19[b] וַתָּשֶׂם יָדָהּ עַל־רֹאשָׁהּ וַתֵּלֶךְ הָלוֹךְ וְזָעָקָה׃

And she placed her hand upon her head, and she went, **going and she would cry out**.

A smoother translation reads, "She would cry as she walked."

The infinitive absolutes and the Vav-perfects explain the manner of her going—with a going in which she would cry out.

1 Sam 19:23[b] וַתְּהִי עָלָיו גַּם־הוּא רוּחַ אֱלֹהִים וַיֵּלֶךְ הָלוֹךְ וַיִּתְנַבֵּא

And the Spirit of God was upon him – even him, and he went, **going and he prophesied (prophesying as he went)**.

Dan 11:10 (וּבָא בוֹא וְשָׁטַף וְעָבָר)

d) An infinitive absolute and a participle or adjective *h*

The participle or adjective is not pluralized. The participle or adjective may be an ACCUSATIVE OF SITUATION (§13z) substituting for absolute objects.

Gen 26:13 וַיִּגְדַּל הָאִישׁ וַיֵּלֶךְ הָלוֹךְ וְגָדֵל עַד כִּי־גָדַל מְאֹד׃

And the man became great, and he went, **a going and a becoming great (becoming great as he went)** until he became very great.

1 Sam 14:19[a] וַיֵּלֶךְ הָלוֹךְ וָרָב

And it proceeded, **proceeding and great (becoming great as it proceeded)**.

Judg 4:24 (וַתֵּלֶךְ יַד בְּנֵי־יִשְׂרָאֵל הָלוֹךְ וְקָשָׁה);
2 Sam 18:25 (וַיֵּלֶךְ הָלוֹךְ וְקָרֵב׃)

e) Two participles *i*

The participles are not pluralized. The participles are probably accusatives of situation (§13z) substituting for absolute objects.

1 Sam 17:41[a] וַיֵּלֶךְ הַפְּלִשְׁתִּי הֹלֵךְ וְקָרֵב אֶל־דָּוִד

And the Philistine went **(in the status of) one who goes and draws near** to David.

Exod 19:19 וַיְהִי קוֹל הַשּׁוֹפָר הוֹלֵךְ וְחָזֵק מְאֹד מֹשֶׁה יְדַבֵּר וְהָאֱלֹהִים יַעֲנֶנּוּ בְקוֹל׃

When the sound of the trumpet **grew louder and louder**, Moses spoke and God answered him with thunder. (lit. And the sound of the trumpet happened, proceeding and becoming strong greatly.)

2 Sam 15:30 (וְדָוִד עֹלֶה בְמַעֲלֵה הַזֵּיתִים עֹלֶה וּבוֹכֶה); Ezra 10:1
(וּכְהִתְפַּלֵּל עֶזְרָא וּכְהִתְוַדֹּתוֹ בֹּכֶה וּמִתְנַפֵּל)

j **Final observations on the absolute object**:

a) Participles and (theoretically) infinitives (2 Sam 6:20 כְּהִגָּלוֹת נִגְלוֹת) may also have absolute objects.
Josh 6:13 (הֹלְכִים הָלוֹךְ וְתָקְעוּ); 2 Sam 16:5 (יֹצֵא יָצוֹא וּמְקַלֵּל׃); Isa 22:17 (וְעֹטְךָ עָטֹה׃); Jer 23:17 (אֹמְרִים אָמוֹר); 41:6 (הֹלֵךְ הָלֹךְ וּבֹכֶה)

b) Infinitive absolutes and abstract nouns of a different root but similar meaning may sometimes substitute for an absolute object.
Jer 22:19 (יִקָּבֵר סָחוֹב וְהַשְׁלֵךְ)

c) Verbs may take an absolute object along with a direct object and/or an adverbial accusative.

1 Kgs 3:27 וַיַּעַן הַמֶּלֶךְ וַיֹּאמֶר תְּנוּ־לָהּ אֶת־הַיָּלוּד הַחַי וְהָמֵת לֹא תְמִיתֻהוּ הִיא אִמּוֹ׃

And the king answered and said, Give to her the living child, **and killing you must not kill him** (you must certainly not kill him). She is his mother.

The verb has a direct object connected to it and is preceded by an absolute object.
Gen 22:17 (כִּי־בָרֵךְ אֲבָרֶכְךָ); 28:22 (עַשֵּׂר אֲעַשְּׂרֶנּוּ); Exod 3:7 (רָאֹה רָאִיתִי אֶת־עֳנִי עַמִּי), 16 (פָּקֹד פָּקַדְתִּי אֶתְכֶם)
Exod 22:15; 23:4, 24; Lev 7:24

k **B. Direct Object**

The object is direct because the verbal action of the agent goes directly to the object. This constrasts with the absolute object which is *itself* the verbal action and with the adverbial object which is related to the verb indirectly or *adverbially*. Moreover, the absolute object and the adverbial object are usually indefinite; the direct object is usually definite with the אֵת particle.[38] Verbs may take one or two direct objects.

l 1. One object[39]

a) The אֵת particle

i. The אֵת particle may occur with an indefinite object, but usually a genitive or adjective limits or SPECIALIZES the indefinite object.

Exod 40:2[b] תָּקִים אֶת־מִשְׁכַּן אֹהֶל מוֹעֵד׃

You will set up **the dwelling place** of the tent of meeting.

In Exod 40:2, the אֵת particle occurs with an indefinite noun, specialized by the last two words.
Gen 1:29 (אֶת־כָּל־עֵשֶׂב); Exod 29:44 (אֶת־אֹהֶל מוֹעֵד); 38:30 (אֶת־אַדְנֵי פֶּתַח אֹהֶל מוֹעֵד); Lev 7:8 (אֶת־עֹלַת אִישׁ); 1 Sam 24:10 (אֶת־דִּבְרֵי אָדָם); 2 Sam 5:24 (אֶת־קוֹל צְעָדָה)
Num 21:9; 1 Kgs 12:31; 2 Kgs 18:17; 23:20

38. The אֵת particle may precede a direct object or adverbial object, but not an absolute object.
39. Intransitive verbs, of course, do not take direct objects. Qal intransitive verbs may become transitive by the causative element of the Hiphil (הִ, הַ), by the doubled second letter of the factitive Piel, and sometimes by the presence of prepositions on the object (IMPROPER OBJECT). A Qal transitive verb may take two objects in the Hiphil, Piel, and sometimes with the presence of prepositions on the object (§7h).

ii. Indefinite words may use the אֵת to clarify the accusative from the nominative. *m*

וְהִשִּׂיג לָכֶם דַּיִשׁ אֶת־בָּצִיר וּבָצִיר יַשִּׂיג אֶת־זָרַע Lev 26:5[a]

Threshing will overtake for you **(the harvest of) vintage** and the vintage will overtake seedtime.

In Lev 26:5, the indefinite accusatives (אֶת־בָּצִיר and אֶת־זָרַע) take the אֶת־ particle to distinguish them from the indefinite nominatives (דַּיִשׁ and וּבָצִיר). Isa 34:14 (וּפָגְשׁוּ צִיִּים אֶת־אִיִּים)

iii. The definite direct object occurring before its verb usually requires the אֵת particle. The אֵת particle is also required if it occurs on a second direct object after a pronominal suffix connected to a verb (Gen 32:24 וַיַּעֲבִרֵם אֶת־הַנָּחַל). *n*

וְאֵת כְּבִיר הָעִזִּים שָׂמָה מְרַאֲשֹׁתָיו 1 Sam 19:13[a]

And a quilt of goatskin she placed at its head.

Gen 15:10 (וְאֶת־הַצִּפֹּר לֹא בָתָר׃); 19:10 (וְאֶת־הַדֶּלֶת סָגָרוּ׃); 42:34 (וְאֶת־הָאָרֶץ תִּסְחָרוּ׃); 47:21 (וְאֶת־הָעָם הֶעֱבִיר אֹתוֹ לֶעָרִים); Exod 3:7 (וְאֶת־צַעֲקָתָם שָׁמַעְתִּי); 4:17 (וְאֶת־הַמַּטֶּה הַזֶּה תִּקַּח); 23:27 (אֶת־אֵימָתִי אֲשַׁלַּח); Deut 2:36 (אֶת־הַכֹּל נָתַן יְהוָה)

iv. Poetry and direct speech tend to attach their direct objects to the verb; prose uses the אֵת particle more commonly than poetry and direct speech. In direct speech, the object before its verb often requires the particle אֵת. *o*

b) The direct object before its verb is emphatic and usually requires the אֵת particle. Exod 26:29 (וְאֶת־הַקְּרָשִׁים תְּצַפֶּה זָהָב וְאֶת־טַבְּעֹתֵיהֶם תַּעֲשֶׂה זָהָב); Deut 3:12 (וְאֶת־הָאָרֶץ הַזֹּאת יָרַשְׁנוּ); 22:7 (וְאֶת־הַבָּנִים תִּקַּח־לָךְ), 14 (אֶת־הָאִשָּׁה הַזֹּאת לָקַחְתִּי); 1 Kgs 17:4 (וְאֶת־הָעֹרְבִים צִוִּיתִי) Exod 4:17; 1 Sam 31:10; Ezek 34:3(2x) *p*

c) A clause[40] may function as the direct object, especially after verbs of the senses. *q*

וַיַּרְא יְהוָה כִּי רַבָּה רָעַת הָאָדָם בָּאָרֶץ Gen 6:5[a]

And the Lord saw **that great was the wickedness of man on the earth**.

Gen 3:6–7 (וְכִי תַאֲוָה־הוּא לָעֵינַיִם ... וַיֵּדְעוּ כִּי עֵירֻמִּם הֵם) (וַתֵּרֶא הָאִשָּׁה כִּי טוֹב הָעֵץ לְמַאֲכָל); 8:11 (וַיֵּדַע נֹחַ כִּי־קַלּוּ הַמַּיִם); 15:13 (יָדֹעַ תֵּדַע כִּי־גֵר יִהְיֶה זַרְעֲךָ); 21:30 (וַיֹּאמֶר כִּי אֶת־שֶׁבַע כְּבָשֹׂת תִּקַּח מִיָּדִי); BA Dan 2:23 (הוֹדַעְתַּנִי דִּי־בְעֵינָא מִנָּךְ)

d) Pronominal objects may be omitted, but implied, if obvious from the context. *r*

וַיְשַׁלְּחוּ אֶת־כְּתֹנֶת הַפַּסִּים וַיָּבִיאוּ אֶל־אֲבִיהֶם Gen 37:32[a]

And they sent away the tunic of many colors and brought **(it)** to their father.

40. These clauses are called substantival since the clause functions as a noun or substantive, §39d.

Gen 12:19 (קַח אִתָּהּ); 48:14 (וַיָּשֶׁת אִתָּהּ); Exod 2:6 (וַתִּפְתַּח אִתָּהּ); 4:9 (וְשָׁפַכְתָּ אֹתָם הַיַּבָּשָׁה); 15:25 (וַיַּשְׁלֵךְ אֹתוֹ אֶל־הַמַּיִם); 1 Sam 6:13 (וַיִּשְׂמְחוּ אֹתוֹ לִרְאוֹת׃); 20:40 (לֵךְ הָבֵיא אֹתָם הָעִיר׃); Jer 7:29 (וְהַשְׁלִיכִי אִתָּהּ); BA Dan 6:17 (וּרְמוֹ יָתֵהּ לְגֻבָּא)

s e) A preposition with its genitive may sometimes substitute for the accusative receiving the action of the verb directly. This is considered an IMPROPER OBJECT, to be contrasted with the accusative, the "proper" object.[41]

Ps 115:9 יִשְׂרָאֵל בְּטַח בַּיהוָה עֶזְרָם וּמָגִנָּם הוּא׃

Israel, trust **in the Lord**; their help and their shield He (is).

Exod 4:1 (לֹא־יַאֲמִינוּ לִי), 4 (וַיַּחֲזֶק בּוֹ); 7:20 (וַיָּרֶם בַּמַּטֶּה); 1 Sam 21:12 (הִכָּה שָׁאוּל בַּאֲלָפָיו וְדָוִד בְּרִבְבֹתָיו׃); 23:5 (וַיַּךְ בָּהֶם); Num 14:31 (מְאַסְתֶּם בָּהּ׃)

t 2. Two objects

Some verbs take two direct objects.[42] The two objects may be unrelated, unable to form an initiator and announcement in a nominal clause; or the two objects may be related, able to form an initiator and announcement in a nominal clause.

a) Unrelated objects

Most of these verbs, especially verbs of filling, satisfying, depriving, forbidding, and asking, take a single object in the Qal and a double object in the Piel and the Hiphil. Commonly, one of the double objects is a person; the other object is usually a thing.

Gen 12:12[a] וְהָיָה כִּי־יִרְאוּ אֹתָךְ הַמִּצְרִים

And it will happen when the Egyptians see **you**

In Gen 12:12, the Qal has a single object. The next example, Deut 3:24, is the same verb in the Hiphil having a double object, an object of the person (your servant) and the object of the thing (your greatness and your strong hand).

Deut 3:24[a] אֲדֹנָי יְהוִה אַתָּה הַחִלּוֹתָ לְהַרְאוֹת אֶת־עַבְדְּךָ אֶת־גָּדְלְךָ וְאֶת־יָדְךָ הַחֲזָקָה

Lord God, You have begun to show **your servant your greatness and your strong hand**.

In Deut 3:24 the same verb (ראה in the infinitive form), in the Hiphil, takes two objects (אֶת־עַבְדְּךָ and אֶת־גָּדְלְךָ וְאֶת־יָדְךָ הַחֲזָקָה). Gen 37:23 (וַיַּפְשִׁיטוּ אֶת־יוֹסֵף אֶת־כֻּתָּנְתּוֹ); Exod 33:13 (הוֹדִעֵנִי נָא אֶת־דְּרָכֶךָ), 18 (הַרְאֵנִי נָא אֶת־כְּבֹדֶךָ׃); Num 20:26 (וְהַפְשֵׁט אֶת־אַהֲרֹן אֶת־בְּגָדָיו וְהִלְבַּשְׁתָּם אֶת־אֶלְעָזָר); Deut 4:10 (וְאַשְׁמִעֵם אֶת־דְּבָרָי); BA Dan 2:23 (דִּי־מִלַּת מַלְכָּא הוֹדַעְתֶּנָא׃); 5:17 (וּפִשְׁרָא אֲהוֹדְעִנֵּהּ׃)

41. Compare the terms "proper" and "improper" annexation, §12b, f.

42. A verb that takes two objects will often retain one object when it becomes passive. Contrast the use of רָאָה in Num 13:26 in the Hiphil with two objects and in Exod 26:30 in the Hophal with one object.

b) Related objects *u*

The two objects could form a nominal clause as initiator and announcement.[43] Two classes of verbs are involved: verbs of making, appointing, calling, naming, and verbs that express actions of the mind (heart), such as thinking, doubting, believing, knowing, and reckoning, etc.

וַיִּיצֶר יְהוָה אֱלֹהִים אֶת־הָאָדָם עָפָר מִן־הָאֲדָמָה Gen 2:7[a]

And the Lord God formed **the man (out of) dirt** from the ground.

The two objects could form a nominal clause, הָאָדָם עָפָר "the man is dirt."

וַיִּקְרָא הָאָדָם שֵׁם אִשְׁתּוֹ חַוָּה Gen 3:20[a]

And the man called **the name of his wife Eve**.

In Gen 3:20, the two objects could form a nominal clause—"Eve is the name of his wife."

וַיָּשֶׂם שָׁאוּל אֶת־הָעָם שְׁלֹשָׁה רָאשִׁים 1 Sam 11:11[a]

And Saul placed **the people into three heads (companies)**.

The nominal clause would be, "The people (were) three companies." Here, as commonly, the first object is a direct object, and the second object is an ACCUSATIVE OF SITUATION (§13z).

Exod 8:10 (וַיִּצְבְּרוּ אֹתָם חֳמָרִם חֳמָרִם); 20:25 (לֹא־תִבְנֶה אֶתְהֶן גָּזִית); 22:12 (יְבִאֵהוּ עֵד); Deut 2:5 (כִּי־יְרֻשָּׁה לְעֵשָׂו נָתַתִּי אֶת־הַר שֵׂעִיר׃); 1 Sam 19:20 (וַיַּרְא אֶת־לַהֲקַת הַנְּבִיאִים נִבְּאִים); 1 Kgs 18:32 (וַיִּבְנֶה אֶת־הָאֲבָנִים מִזְבֵּחַ); Jer 1:5 (נָבִיא לַגּוֹיִם נְתַתִּיךָ׃)

Observation: When translating the two direct objects, you may render one object as the direct object and the other as an English indirect object. Commonly, the ל preposition expresses the English indirect object.

וַתֹּאמֶר תְּנָה־לִּי בְרָכָה כִּי אֶרֶץ הַנֶּגֶב נְתַתָּנִי Josh 15:19[a]

And she said, Give to me a blessing because **the land of the Negev** you have given **to me**.

In Josh 15:19, the verb takes two objects: the first object (אֶרֶץ הַנֶּגֶב) is a direct object, and the second object is the pronominal suffix on the verb, which English would render as an indirect object. Also note the ל preposition indicating the English indirect object in תְּנָה־לִּי.

C. Adverbial Object *v*

The ADVERBIAL OBJECT (accusative) limits the verb, or its subject or object, adverbially. Since it receives the action of the verb indirectly, the adverbial accusative is also called the indirect accusative. Almost always indefinite,[44] the adverbial accusative answers the questions: where, when, how, in what situation, in terms of what, or for what purpose—relative to the verb, subject, or object.

43. In English grammar, the second object is a predicate accusative.
44. Some adverbial accusatives have the particle ה, such as הַיּוֹם, הַלַּיְלָה. Often these particles (ה) are not definite articles, "the day," but they have become part of the meaning of the noun, "today." The non-definite particle (ה) is also found with certain place names, הַגִּלְגָּל and pronouns, הַזֶּה, §36a.

1. Place
Adverbial accusatives of place answer the question of "where," "how far," "how high." Adverbial accusatives of place have two categories.[45]
   a) Unspecified place
   The unspecified place indicates general directions or locations, such as the particles שָׁם (Ps 133:3), אֲשֶׁר (where), זֶה (here, at this place), הֵנָּה, etc.; prepositions לִפְנֵי, אַחַר, and all other directional prepositions; and unspecified nouns such as מָקוֹם.

   וְלֹא־סָרוּ יָמִין וּשְׂמֹאול 1 Sam 6:12[a]

   And they did not turn **to the right or to the left**.

   Gen 13:9 (הַשְּׂמֹאל. . . הַיָּמִין); Exod 2:4 (מֵרָחֹק – מִן substitutes for accusative of place), 12 (כֹּה וָכֹה); 12:46 (חוּצָה); 19:12 (סָבִיב); Jer 1:15 (צָפוֹנָה); BA Ezra 6:3 (אֲתַר דִּי־דָבְחִין)

w b) Specified place
   This may be a common noun (house, city, country) or a proper noun (Jerusalem, Judea). Both the common and proper nouns often occur after verbs of motion, resting, and dwelling.

   מִן־הָאָרֶץ הַהִוא יָצָא אַשּׁוּר וַיִּבֶן אֶת־נִינְוֵה וְאֶת־רְחֹבֹת עִיר וְאֶת־כָּלַח׃ Gen 10:11

   From that land he went forth into **Assyria**, and built Nineveh and Rehoboth-Ir and Calah.

   Gen 38:11 (בֵּית־אָבִיךְ); Exod 4:9 (הַיַּבָּשָׁה, בַּיַּבָּשֶׁת׃); 13:17–18 (דֶּרֶךְ אֶרֶץ פְּלִשְׁתִּים ... דֶּרֶךְ הַמִּדְבָּר), 21 (הַדֶּרֶךְ); 18:5 (הַר הָאֱלֹהִים׃); Deut 1:19 (אֵת כָּל־הַמִּדְבָּר הַגָּדוֹל וְהַנּוֹרָא הַהוּא); 1 Sam 2:29 (מָעוֹן); 11:15 (הַגִּלְגָּל); 13:11 (מִכְמָשׂ׃); 19:13 (מְרַאֲשֹׁתָיו); 20:35 (הַשָּׂדֶה); 21:1-2 (הָעִיר׃ ... נֹבֶה); Jer 1:15 (יְרוּשָׁלַ͏ִם); 26:10 (בֵּית יְהוָה), 21 (מִצְרָיִם׃); Num 16:18 (פֶּתַח אֹהֶל מוֹעֵד)

   Observation: Clauses, especially relative clauses, may function as an accusative of place.

x 2. Time
Adverbial accusatives of time answer the questions of "when" and "how long."
   a) Unspecified time
   This includes particles כִּי, אֲשֶׁר (Job 1:5), אָז, בְּטֶרֶם, עַתָּה (Gen 12:19, note the accusative ending on עַתָּה) etc.; prepositions (sometimes used with אֲשֶׁר) לִפְנֵי, אַחַר, עַד (Prov 8:26); and unspecified nouns, עֵת (Hos 10:12).

   וְעַתָּה הִנֵּה אִשְׁתְּךָ קַח וָלֵךְ׃ Gen 12:19[b]

   And now, behold your wife, take (her) and go.

y b) Specified time
   This includes words like יוֹם, הַיּוֹם, יוֹמָם, לַיְלָה, הַלַּיְלָה (Note the accusative endings on the last three words.), בֹּקֶר, עֶרֶב. (Ps 1:2) The accusative may convey the nuance of "throughout" as in Ps 1:2.

45. Hebrew also uses the accusative ending Qames-He (ה ָ) to represent direction towards a place: to the Negeb (הַנֶּגְבָּה, Gen 12:9), to the land of Canaan (אַרְצָה כְּנַעַן, Gen 11:31; IBH 10.11).

Ps 1:2 כִּ֤י אִ֥ם בְּתוֹרַ֥ת יְהוָ֗ה חֶ֫פְצ֥וֹ וּֽבְתוֹרָת֥וֹ יֶהְגֶּ֗ה יוֹמָ֥ם וָלָֽיְלָה׃

But his delight (is) in the law of the Lord, and in His law he meditates **(throughout the) day and night**.

Observation: Temporal clauses may function in the place of an accusative of time.
Exod 4:10 (מִן – גַּ֤ם מִתְּמוֹל֙ גַּ֣ם מִשִּׁלְשֹׁ֔ם with its genitive substitutes for accusative of time); 12:30–31 (לַ֫יְלָה); 13:4 (הַיּ֖וֹם), 7 (אֵ֖ת שִׁבְעַ֣ת הַיָּמִ֑ים —Note the accusative marker אֵת), 14 (מָחָ֖ר), 21–22 (יוֹמָ֥ם וָלָֽיְלָה׃ . . . יוֹמָ֔ם ...לָ֑יְלָה); 15:22 (שְׁלֹֽשֶׁת־יָמִ֛ים); 16:6–7 (עֶ֕רֶב ... וּבֹ֗קֶר), 25 (הַיּ֔וֹם); 21:2 (שֵׁ֣שׁ שָׁנִ֣ים); 24:18 (אַרְבָּעִ֣ים י֔וֹם וְאַרְבָּעִ֖ים לָֽיְלָה׃); 1 Sam 20:27 (גַּם־תְּמ֖וֹל גַּם־הַיּ֑וֹם); 23:14 (כָּל־הַיָּמִ֔ים); Jer 7:25 (י֖וֹם – This word is also distributive, §9b)

3. Situation (Hal[46], §15e, l; 48-50): *z*
The ACCUSATIVE OF SITUATION describes the situation, condition, or status for a noun; or the manner of the action for a verb.[47] It is frequently an indefinite, DESCRIPTIVE NOUN, that is, a participle (Num 16:27 יָצְא֣וּ נִצָּבִ֗ים) or adjective (Lev 20:20 עֲרִירִ֥ים). It can also be an indefinite (usually) primary noun[48] if it has the sense of the כ preposition (as) implied before it (Gen 38:11 אַלְמָנָ֤ה; 1 Sam 2:33 אֲנָשִֽׁים׃). The accusative of situation furnishes explanatory details for a verb or noun. The accusative of situation does this for a verb by answering the questions "how" or "in what manner" in relation to the verbal action (Gen 34:25 בֶּ֑טַח; 1 Sam 20:10 קָשָֽׁה׃). It furnishes explanatory details for a noun by answering the questions "in what situation, condition or status" in relation to the (usually) definite subject or definite direct object. The accusative of situation may occur before (with emphasis, 1 Sam 17:34 רֹעֶ֨ה; 1 Kgs 5:15 אֹהֵ֛ב) or after its verb. The accusative of situation may occur in a nominal clause, including verbless sentences. Finally, a clause or phrase frequently functions as an accusative of situation (§48–50).

Accusatives of situation are divided into illustrating or strengthening and permanent or temporary.

a) Illustrating or Strengthening *aa*

i. Illustrating

This accusative of situation illustrates its subject by providing new information or an attribute to its noun. In 1 Kgs 5:15, the verb הָיָה takes an illustrating accusative of situation.[49]

1 Kgs 5:15[b] כִּ֣י אֹהֵ֛ב הָיָ֥ה חִירָ֛ם לְדָוִ֖ד כָּל־הַיָּמִֽים׃

For **(in the status of) friend** Hiram existed to David always.

---

46. The Arabic word, Hal, means, "situation, condition."
47. The accusative of situation may also limit another noun.
48. PRIMARY NOUNS, by contrast, are not participles or adjectives, but are common nouns such as king, son, tree, etc.
49. The verb הָיָה often takes an illustrating accusative of situation, but never a nominative, to complete its meaning. אֵין (construct form of אַ֫יִן) and יֵשׁ, the "sisters" of הָיָה, may also take an illustrating accusative of situation (§41x).

The accusative of situation illustrates the subject (Hiram) by furnishing information (he existed as a friend to David).
Exod 2:11 (מַכֶּה); 5:20 (נִצָּבִים); 6:8 (מוֹרָשָׁה); 7:1
(אֱלֹהִים ... נְבִיאֶךָ:), 19 (דָם); 9:3 (דֶּבֶר כָּבֵד מְאֹד:), 10
(שְׁחִין אֲבַעְבֻּעֹת); 11:1 (כָּלָה); 12:9
(וּבָשֵׁל מְבֻשָּׁל בַּמָּיִם כִּי אִם־צְלִי־אֵשׁ), 14 (חַג לַיהוָה ... חֻקַּת עוֹלָם);
13:18 (וַחֲמֻשִׁים); 14:9 (חֹנִים עַל־הַיָּם), 30 (מֵת); 17:12 (אֱמוּנָה),
14 (זִכָּרוֹן), 18:3 (גֵּר), 25 (רָאשִׁים ... שָׂרֵי); 19:5–6
(סְגֻלָּה ... מַמְלֶכֶת כֹּהֲנִים וְגוֹי קָדוֹשׁ), 11 (נְכֹנִים), 19
(הוֹלֵךְ וְחָזֵק מְאֹד); 20:16 (עֵד שָׁקֶר:); 21:5 (חָפְשִׁי:); 22:12 (עֵד),
20 (גֵרִים), 23 (אַלְמָנוֹת ... יְתֹמִים:), 30 (טְרֵפָה); 23:1 (עֵד חָמָס:), 4–5
(תֹּעֶה ... רֹבֵץ), 15 (רֵיקָם:); 1 Sam 11:2 (חֶרְפָּה), 11 (שְׁנַיִם יָחַד:);
12:11 (בֶּטַח:); 15:8 (חָי), 32 (מַעֲדַנֹּת); 18:14 (מַשְׂכִּיל), 29 (אֹיֵב);
21:6 (קֹדֶשׁ), 9 (נָחוּץ:); 23:26 (נֶחְפָּז); Jer 7:11 (הַמְעָרַת פָּרִצִים);
26:18 (נִבָּא ... שָׂדֶה ... עִיִּים); BA Dan 2:5 (הַדָּמִין ... נְוָלִי), 31
(חֶזֵה); 3:23 (אַתּוּן־נוּרָא); 5:11 (רַב חַרְטֻמִּין), 19
(זָיְעִין וְדָחֲלִין ... צָבֵא ... קָטֵל ... מַחֵא ... מָרִים ... מַשְׁפִּיל:),
27 (חַסִּיר:); 6:3 (נָזִק:), 12 (בָּעֵא וּמִתְחַנַּן); Ezra 4:12 (יְדִיעַ), 24
(בָּטְלָא); 5:11 (בְּנֵה); 6:6 (רַחִיקִין); Num 14:37; 16:27, 30; 22:23

bb ii. Strengthening

This accusative of situation strengthens or confirms its verb, noun, or a (verbless) nominal clause.

① Verb

This accusative of situation emphasizes the verb by restating the verb or by virtually restating the verb.

cc ❶ Restating the verb with the same verbal root:

וַיֵּלֶךְ הַפְּלִשְׁתִּי הֹלֵךְ וְקָרֵב אֶל־דָּוִד 1 Sam 17:41[a]

And the Philistine went **(in the status of) one who goes** and draws near to David.

These participles probably also function as substitutes for absolute objects, §13f, §16m.

Num 8:19 (נְתֻנִים); Isa 22:16 (חֹצְבִי מָרוֹם)

dd ❷ Virtually restating the verb with a different verbal root:

וַיֵּצֵא יִשְׁמָעֵאל בֶּן־נְתַנְיָה לִקְרָאתָם מִן־הַמִּצְפָּה הֹלֵךְ הָלֹךְ וּבֹכֶה Jer 41:6[a]

Ishmael, son of Nathaniah, went out to meet them from Mizpah, **(in the status of) one who goes, going** and weeping.

The participle and infinitive absolute restate the verb, since their meanings are similar to the verb.

Isa 22:16 (קֶבֶר)

ee ② Noun

Particles, such as רַק ,גַּם ,אַךְ, which are in the place of the accusative of situation, strengthen (emphasize) their nouns.

Gen 41:40 אַתָּה תִּהְיֶה עַל־בֵּיתִי וְעַל־פִּיךָ יִשַּׁק כָּל־עַמִּי רַק הַכִּסֵּא אֶגְדַּל מִמֶּךָּ׃

You shall be over my house, and upon your mouth all my people will kiss. **Only** in terms of the throne I will be greater than you.

Gen 9:4[b] אַךְ־בָּשָׂר בְּנַפְשׁוֹ דָמוֹ לֹא תֹאכֵלוּ׃

Only flesh, in its life, that is, its blood, you must not eat.

1 Sam 12:52[b] גַּם־אַתֶּם גַּם־מַלְכְּכֶם תִּסָּפוּ׃

Even you, even your king will be swept away.

Exod 8:24 (רַק), 28 (גַּם); 10:17 (רַק), 26 (וְגַם); 11:3 (גַּם); 12:15 (אַךְ), 31-32 (גַּם: 5x)

Exod 12:32; 18:18; 19:22; 21:19, 21, 35; 1 Sam 20:39; Jer 26:15

③ Verbless nominal clause *ff*

The accusative of situation describes the entire clause. In these verbless nominal clauses, the subject (initiator) and the predicate (announcement) must both be definite.

Ps 104:25[a] זֶה הַיָּם גָּדוֹל וּרְחַב יָדַיִם

This is the sea **(in the status of) great and broad of hands (on both sides, everywhere)**.

b) Permanent or temporary *gg*

i. Permanent

The status or condition of the accusative of situation is permanent.

Gen 37:53[a] כִּי־אֵרֵד אֶל־בְּנִי אָבֵל שְׁאֹלָה

Surely I am going down to my son **(in the permanent status of) a mourner** to Sheol.

Deut 2:9 (יְרֻשָּׁה, יְרֻשָּׁה:); 1 Sam 2:33 (וְאִישׁ); 11:2 (חֶרְפָּה); Jer 26:18 (עִיִּים); BA Ezra 5:14 (פֶּחָה); 6:11 (נְוָלוּ)

ii. Temporary *hh*

The status or condition of the accusative of situation is temporary.

Deut 3:18 וָאֲצַו אֶתְכֶם בָּעֵת הַהִוא לֵאמֹר יְהוָה אֱלֹהֵיכֶם נָתַן לָכֶם אֶת־הָאָרֶץ הַזֹּאת לְרִשְׁתָּהּ חֲלוּצִים תַּעַבְרוּ לִפְנֵי אֲחֵיכֶם בְּנֵי־יִשְׂרָאֵל כָּל־בְּנֵי־חָיִל׃

And I commanded you at that time, saying, The Lord your God has given to you this land to possess it. **(In the temporary status of) girded** all the warriors shall cross over before your brothers, the sons of Israel.

1 Sam 6:14 (עֹלָה); 14:52 (חֲזָקָה); 15:8 (חָי); 19:9 (רָעָה); 23:26 (נֶחְפָּז); Jer 26:7 (מְדַבֵּר)

Observation: Frequently, nouns with the prepositions ל and sometimes כ substitute for an accusative of situation, especially after היה. *ii*

1 Sam 10:12[b] עַל־כֵּן הָיְתָה לְמָשָׁל

Therefore, it existed **as a proverb**.

הֲלוֹא כִּי־מְשָׁחֲךָ יְהוָה עַל־נַחֲלָתוֹ לְנָגִיד׃ 1 Sam 10:1[b]

Is (it) not that the Lord has anointed you over his inheritance **as a leader**?

וַיְהִי כְּמַחֲרִישׁ׃ 1 Sam 10:27[b]

And he existed **as a silent one**.

Exod 2:14 (לְאִישׁ); 4:3-4 (לְנָחָשׁ ... לְמַטֶּה), 9 (לְדָם), 18 (לְשָׁלוֹם׃); 6:7 (לְעָם ... לֵאלֹהִים); 7:9 (לְתַנִּין׃), 17 (לְדָם׃); 8:12 (לְכִנִּם); 9:9 (לְאָבָק ... לִשְׁחִין), 24 (לְגוֹי׃); 10:7 (לְמוֹקֵשׁ); 12:6 (לְמִשְׁמֶרֶת), 13 (לְאֹת ... לְמַשְׁחִית), 24 (לְחָק); 13:9 (לְאוֹת ... וּלְזִכָּרוֹן); 15:2 (לִישׁוּעָה); 16:3 (לָשֹׂבַע); 21:2 (לַחָפְשִׁי), 7 (לְאָמָה); 22:24 (כְּנֹשֶׁה); 23:33 (לְמוֹקֵשׁ׃); 1 Sam 11:7 (כְּאִישׁ אֶחָד׃); 12:22 (לְעָם׃); 17:9 (לַעֲבָדִים); 18:17 (לְאִשָּׁה), 21 (לְמוֹקֵשׁ); 20:42 (לְשָׁלוֹם); 23:17 (לְמִשְׁנֶה); 24:16 (לְדַיָּן); Jer 1:18 (לְעִיר מִבְצָר וּלְעַמּוּד בַּרְזֶל וּלְחֹמוֹת נְחֹשֶׁת); 7:24 (לְאָחוֹר), 33-34 (לְמַאֲכָל ... לְחָרְבָּה); 8:2 (לְדֹמֶן); 26:6 (לִקְלָלָה), 18 (לְבָמוֹת יָעַר׃—Notice the preceding accusative of situations without preposition in parallel constructions, "as a field . . . as ruins"); Num 22:22 (לְשָׂטָן); Ezra 6:17 (לְחַטָּאָה); BA Dan 2:35 (לְטוּר רַב)

jj 4. Specification (Tamyiz[50]):

The ACCUSATIVE OF SPECIFICATION specifies the area of application for another noun, for a subject and its verb, a verb and its object, or for impersonal passive verbs. The accusative of specification resembles the accusative of situation: they are both indefinite (usually) and clarifying, occurring in both verbal or nominal clauses, including verbless clauses. They are, however, dissimilar in many important aspects. The accusative of specification is usually a PRIMARY NOUN, rarely an adjective, and never a participle. It can never imply the meaning "as" of a כ preposition. The sentence would be ambiguous without the accusative of specification, so it clarifies a statement by answering the questions, "in what terms of," "by what specifically," or "with respect to what."

Accusatives of specification are categorized as specification of nature or of attribution.

kk a) Specification of nature

This specification clarifies the *entire* nature or essence of something;[51] therefore, the specification and its noun could form a nominal clause.

This is common with:

i. Numbers (§29a–b, e)

---

50. The Arabic word Tamyiz means specification.

51. These resemble apposition (all-for-all substitution), clarifying the entire nature of something. They differ from substitution, however, in that they are not corroborative or emphatic, §27a.

Gen 37:9 וַיַּחֲלֹם עוֹד֙ חֲלוֹם אַחֵר וַיְסַפֵּר אֹתוֹ לְאֶחָיו וַיֹּאמֶר הִנֵּה
חָלַמְתִּי חֲלוֹם֙ עוֹד וְהִנֵּה הַשֶּׁמֶשׁ וְהַיָּרֵחַ וְאַחַד עָשָׂר֙ כּוֹכָבִים
מִשְׁתַּחֲוִים לִי׃

And he dreamed yet another dream, and he related it to his brothers, and said, Behold, I have dreamed another dream. And behold, the sun and the moon **and eleven (specifically as to) stars** were bowing down to me.

The specification is the NUMERABLE "stars." The nominal clause would be, "The stars are eleven."

Gen 2:10 (לְאַרְבָּעָה רָאשִׁים׃); 5:5-23 (שָׁנָה); Lev 27:4 (שְׁלֹשִׁים שָׁקֶל׃);
1 Sam 21:4 (חֲמִשָּׁה־לֶחֶם)

ii. Nouns of measure *ll*

2 Kgs 5:23[b] וַיִּפְרָץ־בּוֹ וַיָּצַר כִּכְּרַיִם כֶּסֶף

And he urged him, and bound **two talents (specifically as to) silver.**

The nominal clause would be, "Two talents are silver."

Exod 25:39 (כִּכָּר זָהָב); 1 Sam 25:18 (סְאִים קָלִי); 1 Kgs 16:24 (בְּכִכְּרַיִם כָּסֶף)

iii. Nouns of quality *mm*

1 Chr 28:18[a] וּלְמִזְבַּח הַקְּטֹרֶת זָהָב מְזֻקָּק בַּמִּשְׁקָל

And for the altar of incense **(specifically as to) gold** refined by weight.

The nominal clause would be, "The altar of incense is gold."

Exod 24:10 (לִבְנַת הַסַּפִּיר); 26:29 (זָהָב); 30:3 (זָהָב); 37:17 (זָהָב); 1 Kgs 6:28 (זָהָב׃); 7:27 (נְחֹשֶׁת)

b) Specification of attribute *nn*

This specification clarifies an *attribute*, but not the entire nature or essence of something; therefore, the specification and its noun cannot form a nominal clause.

i. Clarifying subject and verb (or predicate):

In 1 Kgs 15:23, the specification clarifies in what terms "he was sick"—specifically as to his feet. Moreover, the noun (subject) and its specification cannot make a nominal clause —"he was feet." "He" is clarified only in the attribute of "his feet," not in his entire nature. Notice that 2 Chr 16:12 (בְּרַגְלָיו "in his feet"), the parallel passage of 1 Kgs 15:23, substitutes a prepositional phrase with ב for the accusative of specification. Notice אֵת marks the accusative (of specification), not the direct object, in some of the following examples.

1 Kgs 15:23[b] רַק לְעֵת זִקְנָתוֹ חָלָה אֶת־רַגְלָיו׃

Only in the time of his old age he was diseased **(specifically as to) his feet.**

2 Chr 16:12[a] וַיֶּחֱלֶא אָסָא בִּשְׁנַת שְׁלוֹשִׁים וָתֵשַׁע לְמַלְכוּתוֹ בְּרַגְלָיו

And Asa became sick in the thirty-ninth year of his reign in his feet.

In 2 Chr 16:12, the prepositional phrase (בְּרַגְלָיו) substitutes for the accusative of specification of 1 Kgs 15:23.

Gen 17:11 וּנְמַלְתֶּם אֵת בְּשַׂר עָרְלַתְכֶם וְהָיָה לְאוֹת בְּרִית בֵּינִי וּבֵינֵיכֶם׃

And you shall be circumcised **(specifically as to) the flesh of your foreskin**; and it shall exist in terms of a sign of covenant between me and you.

In Gen 17:11, the specification clarifies in what terms you shall be circumcised—in terms of the flesh of the foreskin.

Gen 41:40[b] רַק הַכִּסֵּא אֶגְדַּל מִמֶּךָּ׃

Only **(specifically as to) the throne** I will be greater than you.

Deut 2:9 (מִלְחָמָה); BA Ezra 4:14 (דִּי־מְלַח הֵיכְלָא)

oo ii. Clarifying the verb and object:

In these examples, the specification clarifies the verb and its object, usually specifying something about the object.

Ps 3:8[a] כִּי־הִכִּיתָ אֶת־כָּל־אֹיְבַי לֶחִי

For you have smitten all my enemies **(specifically as to) the cheek**.

Gen 37:21[b] לֹא נַכֶּנּוּ נָפֶשׁ׃

Let us not smite him **(specifically as to) the soul**.

Gen 37:23 (אֶת־כֻּתָּנְתּוֹ); Exod 23:27 (עֹרֶף׃)

pp c) Accusatives of specification also occur after impersonal passive verbs. In these cases, the accusative marker אֵת marks the accusative of specification, not the direct object or the subject.

1 Kgs 2:21 וַתֹּאמֶר יֻתַּן אֶת־אֲבִישַׁג הַשֻּׁנַמִּית לַאֲדֹנִיָּהוּ אָחִיךָ לְאִשָּׁה׃

So she said, Let **Abishag** the Shunammite be given to Adonijah your brother as a wife.

This may be rendered more literally, “May it be given—specifically as to Abishag.

Gen 27:42[a] וַיֻּגַּד לְרִבְקָה אֶת־דִּבְרֵי עֵשָׂו בְּנָהּ הַגָּדֹל

Now when the words of her elder son **Esau were reported** to Rebekah,

Exod 21:28 (אֶת־בְּשָׂרוֹ); 27:7 (אֶת־בַּדָּיו); Lev 10:18 (אֶת־דָּמָהּ); 13:49 (אֶת־הַכֹּהֵן׃); Num 32:5 (אֶת־הָאָרֶץ הַזֹּאת); Josh 9:24 (אֵת אֲשֶׁר צִוָּה יְהוָה אֱלֹהֶיךָ); 2 Sam 21:11 (אֵת אֲשֶׁר־עָשְׂתָה רִצְפָּה); Jer 35:14 (אֶת־דִּבְרֵי יְהוֹנָדָב); 50:20 (אֶת־עֲוֹן יִשְׂרָאֵל)

qq 5. Purpose (cause, reason, motive):

The accusative of purpose, a rare construction, is usually found with verbs of motion.[52]

Num 10:9[a] וְכִי־תָבֹאוּ מִלְחָמָה בְּאַרְצְכֶם

And when you come **for the purpose of war** in your land.

Isa 7:25[a] לֹא־תָבוֹא שָׁמָּה יִרְאַת שָׁמִיר וָשָׁיִת

You will not come there **because of the fear of briers and thorns**.

52. This construction resembles the supine construction of Latin.

§14. Casus Pendens (Preoccupation) *a*

The Casus Pendens construction refers to a noun with indirect case function. Such a noun is said to be "hanging" (Pendens) in the sentence; hence, the term Casus Pendens, "the hanging case." The "hanging" noun is later referred to in the sentence by another noun or pronoun. For example, in the sentence, "That girl, I like her," the noun "girl" hangs in the sentence since it functions indirectly as an accusative. Later in the sentence, the pronoun, "her," which functions directly as an accusative (object), refers back to "girl."

This construction, though rare in English, commonly occurs in Semitic. Native Semitic grammarians label this construction "preoccupation" because a noun or verb is said to be preoccupied with the pronoun or noun referring back[53] to the suspended (hanging) noun, the Casus Pendens.[54] In Gen 34:8[b], שְׁכֶם בְּנִי חָשְׁקָה נַפְשׁוֹ, the verb (longs for) is preoccupied with the noun and its pronoun (the subject), "his soul," which refers to its suspended noun, "Shechem, my son." This construction always places the suspended noun first in the sentence or clause and almost always emphasizes the suspended noun, with a style pleasing to the Semitic ear. Then a pronoun or noun in the nominative, genitive, or accusative resumes the suspended noun. The suspended or hanging noun (the Casus Pendens) may be resumed by a noun or pronoun in the nominative, genitive, or accusative.

I. Suspended Noun (Casus Pendens) Resumed by a Nominative *b*

A noun or pronoun as a nominative (subject) resumes the suspended noun (the Casus Pendens).

A. The Subject in a Nominal Clause with a Verb

Lev 18:29 כִּי כָּל־אֲשֶׁר יַעֲשֶׂה מִכֹּל הַתּוֹעֵבוֹת הָאֵלֶּה וְנִכְרְתוּ הַנְּפָשׁוֹת
הָעֹשֹׂת מִקֶּרֶב עַמָּם׃

For everyone who does from any of these abominations – even the souls doing (them) will be cut off from the midst of their people.

The first half of the verse is the suspended noun—more precisely, "everyone who does." The noun, "souls," resumes the suspended noun in the second half of the verse. Gen 15:4; 17:14; Josh 15:16

Lev 7:25 כִּי כָּל־אֹכֵל חֵלֶב מִן־הַבְּהֵמָה אֲשֶׁר יַקְרִיב מִמֶּנָּה אִשֶּׁה
לַיהוָה וְנִכְרְתָה הַנֶּפֶשׁ הָאֹכֶלֶת מֵעַמֶּיהָ׃

For any man who eats fat from the animal from which is offered as a fire-offering of the Lord – even the soul eating (of it) will be cut off from his people.

This example is virtually identical to the preceding example except for a participle as the suspended noun. The participle, of course, is equivalent to

53. The Casus Pendens construction with its "retrospective pronoun" can be confused with retrospective pronouns within relatives clauses. The retrospective pronoun in relative clauses simply clarifies the role of the antecedent within the relative clause. They are not suspended or emphatic.
54. Griess, 232–235. The accents normally confirm its emphatic character by giving the Casus Pendens the most important disjunctive accent in the clause.

אֲשֶׁר with a perfect or imperfect (here with an imperfect as the preceding example indicates). Participles are frequently employed as suspended nouns. Gen 9:6; Exod 12:15, 19; 21:12

וַיהוָה פָּקַד אֶת־שָׂרָה Gen 21:1[a]

And **the Lord** – he visited Sarah.

Native Semitic grammarians also consider these nominal clauses as preoccupation. The suspended noun in nominal clauses (especially in narrative, but not direct speech) are usually not as emphatic as other constructions of preoccupation. The implied pronoun of the verb, "he," resumes the suspended noun, "the Lord." Gen 3:1; 4:1; 37:3

הוּא יְשׁוּפְךָ רֹאשׁ וְאַתָּה תְּשׁוּפֶנּוּ עָקֵב׃ Gen 3:15[b]

He – he will bruise your head, and **you** – you will indeed bruise (his) heel.

This example is similar to the preceding example except for the suspended pronouns. The implied third person singular pronouns of the imperfect verbs resume the suspended noun. Gen 3:16; 4:7

וַיֹּאמֶר הָאָדָם הָאִשָּׁה אֲשֶׁר נָתַתָּה עִמָּדִי הִוא נָתְנָה־לִּי מִן־הָעֵץ וָאֹכֵל׃ Gen 3:12

And the man said, **The woman that you gave to me – she** – she gave to me from the tree, and I ate.

The pronominal suffix of the verb resumes the suspended noun and the suspended pronoun. The double suspension (Casus Pendens) of noun and pronoun is very emphatic. Gen 4:22 (וְצִלָּה גַם־הִוא יָלְדָה); Num 35:19 (גֹּאֵל הַדָּם הוּא יָמִית), 33 (כִּי הַדָּם הוּא יַחֲנִיף אֶת־הָאָרֶץ); Deut 1:36 (זוּלָתִי כָּלֵב בֶּן־יְפֻנֶּה הוּא יִרְאֶנָּה), 38-39 (יְהוֹשֻׁעַ בִּן־נוּן הָעֹמֵד לְפָנֶיךָ הוּא יָבֹא שָׁמָּה...וְטַפְּכֶם...וּבְנֵיכֶם...הֵמָּה יָבֹאוּ שָׁמָּה); 31:8 (וַיהוָה הוּא הַהֹלֵךְ לְפָנֶיךָ הוּא יִהְיֶה); Josh 22:23 (יְהוָה הוּא יְבַקֵּשׁ׃); 23:5 (וַיהוָה אֱלֹהֵיכֶם הוּא יֶהְדֳּפֵם); 1 Sam 17:37 (יְהוָה אֲשֶׁר הִצִּלַנִי מִיַּד הָאֲרִי וּמִיַּד הַדֹּב הוּא יַצִּילֵנִי); 21:10 (חֶרֶב גָּלְיָת הַפְּלִשְׁתִּי אֲשֶׁר־הִכִּיתָ בְּעֵמֶק הָאֵלָה הִנֵּה־הִיא לוּטָה); Gen 24:7; 2 Sam 14:19; Isa 13:22; 7:8; Prov 10:22; 19:21; BA Dan 2:38, 47.

c **B. Subject in a Nominal Clause without a Verb**

A SEPARATING PRONOUN resumes the suspended noun.[55]

כִּי יהוה הוּא הָאֱלֹהִים Deut 4:39[a]

For **the Lord** – he is God

The separating pronoun, occurring after the suspended noun, resumes the suspended noun, "the Lord." Deut 4:39; 10:9, 17; 12:23

כִּי הַמָּקוֹם אֲשֶׁר אַתָּה עוֹמֵד עָלָיו אַדְמַת־קֹדֶשׁ הוּא׃ Exod 3:5[b]

For **the place upon which you are standing** – it is holy ground.

The separating pronoun, occurring after the suspended noun, resumes the suspended noun, "the place." These constructions are always emphatic. Deut 4:39; 10:9, 17; 12:23

55. For SEPARATING PRONOUN, see §11v–w.

וְהַלֻּחֹת מַעֲשֵׂה אֱלֹהִים הֵמָּה וְהַמִּכְתָּב מִכְתַּב אֱלֹהִים הוּא חָרוּת עַל־הַלֻּחֹת׃ Exod 32:16

The tablets, (the) work of God they (are); the writing, (the) writing of God it (is), engraved on the tablets

The pronouns, occurring after the announcements, resume the suspended nouns. The pronoun after the announcement has varied emphasis. In Exod 32:16, the construction has style with some emphasis. In certain contexts, they stylistically connect initiator and announcement without emphasis (§11w). Gen 41:25–26

II. Suspended Noun (Casus Pendens) Resumed by a Genitive *d*

A pronominal suffix on a noun resumes the suspended noun. Pronominal suffixes are always in the genitive to their nouns. Pronominal suffixes on participles may be genitive or accusative, depending on the context.

A pronominal suffix resumes the suspended noun.

יהוה בְּסוּפָה וּבִשְׂעָרָה דַּרְכּוֹ Nah 1:3[b]

The Lord – in the storm and whirlwind is his way.

The suspended noun, "the Lord," is resumed by the pronominal suffix. Ps 11:4

כִּי־זֶה מֹשֶׁה הָאִישׁ אֲשֶׁר הֶעֱלָנוּ מֵאֶרֶץ מִצְרַיִם לֹא יָדַעְנוּ מֶה־הָיָה לוֹ׃ Exod 32:1[b]

For **this man Moses, who brought us up from the land of Egypt** – we do not know what happened to him.

The pronominal suffix on the preposition, "to him," resumes the suspended noun, "this man Moses." Gen 34:8; Isa 34:3; Ps 10:5; 46:5; 89:3; 90:10; Neh 9:36

אֲנִי הִנֵּה בְרִיתִי אִתָּךְ Gen 17:4[a]

As for **me** – behold my covenant is with you.

The pronominal suffix on בְּרִית resumes the suspended pronoun, "me." Gen 40:16; Jos 23:9

III. Suspended Noun (Casus Pendens) Resumed by an Accusative *e*

The accusative is the object of a verb.

כִּי אֶת־כָּל־הָאָרֶץ אֲשֶׁר־אַתָּה רֹאֶה לְךָ אֶתְּנֶנָּה Gen 13:15[a]

For **all the land which you are seeing** – to you I will give it.

The object pronoun, "it," resumes the suspended noun and its modifiers. The verb is "preoccupied" with the pronoun, thereby suspending or hanging the noun, "the land." Gen 24:27; 28:13; 35:12

וְהָיָה הַנַּעֲרָ אֲשֶׁר אֹמַר אֵלֶיהָ הַטִּי־נָא כַדֵּךְ וְאֶשְׁתֶּה וְאָמְרָה שְׁתֵה וְגַם־גְּמַלֶּיךָ אַשְׁקֶה אֹתָהּ הֹכַחְתָּ לְעַבְדְּךָ לְיִצְחָק Gen 24:14

And it happened, **the maiden to whom I say, Extend please your jar that I may drink, and should she say, Drink, and even your camels I will cause to drink** – her you have chosen for your servant, for Isaac.

The object pronoun, "her," resumes the suspended noun, "the maiden." Gen 21:13; 47:21; Exod 12:44

Exercises

I. Questions and Discussions

1. List the original cases of Hebrew and discuss their usages. Discuss the two types of clauses in Hebrew. Discuss the nomenclature for subjects and predicates in the two types of clauses.
2. Discuss the subject of the entire sentence and the subject of a verb in nominal clauses.
3. When is the nominative as the initiator indefinite? Discuss the assertion of possession and existence.
4. When is the nominative as the announcement definite?
5. Define separating pronoun. Define the construction similar to the separating pronoun.
6. Discuss the use of and the word order of the separating pronoun and the similar construction in nominal clauses.
7. When must the initiator precede its announcement?
8. When must the announcement precede its initiator?
9. When may the announcement precede its initiator?
10. When is the nominative as the agent indefinite?
11. How does Hebrew often handle multiple agents with a verb?
12. When is the agent omitted by a passive verb?
13. When is a word in the genitive?
14. What case is the first word in a construct package (annexation)?
15. What are the two types of annexation? Define them.
16. When does the genitive specialize its governing noun?
17. Which prepositions may be understood between annexed words in proper annexation? What determines which preposition is appropriate?
18. What parts of speech must be the governing noun in improper annexation?
19. How does the genitive function in improper annexation?
20. Define nouns of relation.
21. Discuss clauses and phrases in the place of the genitive.
22. Discuss when the לְ preposition substitutes for a genitive.
23. How does the accusative limit its verb?
24. How can it be determined that a word is in the accusative?
25. List the three types of accusatives.
26. Define the absolute object.
27. List and discuss the two uses of the absolute object.
28. When may the absolute object be omitted?
29. List and discuss the five ways that the absolute object explains the verb.
30. Define direct object.
31. List and discuss the four usages of the אֵת particle.
32. How is the direct object emphasized?
33. When may pronominal objects be omitted?
34. Define improper object.
35. List and define the two categories of verbs with two objects. Contrast and compare these categories.
36. Define adverbial object.
37. List and define the five categories of adverbial accusatives.

38. Define accusative of situation. List and define the categories of accusative of situations.
39. What prepositions with nouns may substitute for an accusative of situation?
40. What case is the predicate of the verb הָיָה?
41. Define the accusative of specification. Discuss the three usages of the accusative of specification.
42. Define and discuss the accusative of purpose. What kind of verb is usually found with the accusative of purpose?
43. Describe the Casus Pendens construction. What does the term Casus Pendens mean?
44. How do native Semitic grammarians describe the Casus Pendens construction?
45. Explain the terms "suspended noun" and "preoccupation."
46. What is the word order of Casus Pendens constructions?
47. What cases may resume the Casus Pendens?

II. Drills: Analyze the usage of case for the following nouns. (The verses follow the numbering of the Masoretic Text.)

1. **Analyze why the initiator or agent is indefinite.**

Exod 12:38 (1) וְגַם־עֵרֶב רַב עָלָה אִתָּם וְצֹאן וּבָקָר מִקְנֶה כָּבֵד מְאֹד׃

Exod 9:24 (2) וַיְהִי בָרָד וְאֵשׁ מִתְלַקַּחַת בְּתוֹךְ הַבָּרָד כָּבֵד מְאֹד אֲשֶׁר לֹא־הָיָה כָמֹהוּ
בְּכָל־אֶרֶץ מִצְרַיִם מֵאָז הָיְתָה לְגוֹי׃

Exod 16:24 (3) וַיַּנִּיחוּ אֹתוֹ עַד־הַבֹּקֶר כַּאֲשֶׁר צִוָּה מֹשֶׁה וְלֹא הִבְאִישׁ וְרִמָּה
לֹא־הָיְתָה בּוֹ׃

1 Sam 25:2 (4) וְאִישׁ בְּמָעוֹן וּמַעֲשֵׂהוּ בַכַּרְמֶל וְהָאִישׁ גָּדוֹל מְאֹד וְלוֹ צֹאן שְׁלֹשֶׁת־
אֲלָפִים וְאֶלֶף עִזִּים וַיְהִי בִּגְזֹז אֶת־צֹאנוֹ בַּכַּרְמֶל׃

1 Sam 8:19[b] (5) וַיֹּאמְרוּ לֹּא כִּי אִם־מֶלֶךְ יִהְיֶה עָלֵינוּ׃

Exod 12:16 (6) וּבַיּוֹם הָרִאשׁוֹן מִקְרָא־קֹדֶשׁ וּבַיּוֹם הַשְּׁבִיעִי מִקְרָא־קֹדֶשׁ יִהְיֶה לָכֶם
כָּל־מְלָאכָה לֹא־יֵעָשֶׂה בָהֶם אַךְ אֲשֶׁר יֵאָכֵל לְכָל־נֶפֶשׁ הוּא לְבַדּוֹ
יֵעָשֶׂה לָכֶם׃

Exod 2:1 (7) וַיֵּלֶךְ אִישׁ מִבֵּית לֵוִי וַיִּקַּח אֶת־בַּת־לֵוִי׃

Gen 13:8 (8) וַיֹּאמֶר אַבְרָם אֶל־לוֹט אַל־נָא תְהִי מְרִיבָה בֵּינִי וּבֵינֶיךָ וּבֵין רֹעַי וּבֵין
רֹעֶיךָ כִּי־אֲנָשִׁים אַחִים אֲנָחְנוּ׃

2. Analyze why the announcement is definite.

Exod 8:15 (1) וַיֹּאמְר֤וּ הַֽחַרְטֻמִּים֙ אֶל־פַּרְעֹ֔ה אֶצְבַּ֥ע אֱלֹהִ֖ים הִ֑וא וַיֶּחֱזַ֤ק לֵב־פַּרְעֹה֙
וְלֹֽא־שָׁמַ֣ע אֲלֵהֶ֔ם כַּאֲשֶׁ֖ר דִּבֶּ֥ר יְהוָֽה׃

Exod 21:1 (2) וְאֵ֙לֶּה֙ הַמִּשְׁפָּטִ֔ים אֲשֶׁ֥ר תָּשִׂ֖ים לִפְנֵיהֶֽם׃

Deut 4:35 (3) אַתָּה֙ הָרְאֵ֣תָ לָדַ֔עַת כִּ֥י יְהוָ֖ה ה֣וּא הָֽאֱלֹהִ֑ים אֵ֥ין ע֖וֹד מִלְבַדּֽוֹ׃

Gen 41:44 (4) וַיֹּ֧אמֶר פַּרְעֹ֛ה אֶל־יוֹסֵ֖ף אֲנִ֣י פַרְעֹ֑ה וּבִלְעָדֶ֗יךָ לֹֽא־יָרִ֨ים אִ֜ישׁ אֶת־יָד֛וֹ
וְאֶת־רַגְל֖וֹ בְּכָל־אֶ֥רֶץ מִצְרָֽיִם׃

Exod 3:15 (5) וַיֹּאמֶר֩ ע֨וֹד אֱלֹהִ֜ים אֶל־מֹשֶׁ֗ה כֹּֽה־תֹאמַר֮ אֶל־בְּנֵ֣י יִשְׂרָאֵל֒ יְהוָ֞ה אֱלֹהֵ֣י
אֲבֹתֵיכֶ֗ם אֱלֹהֵ֨י אַבְרָהָ֜ם אֱלֹהֵ֥י יִצְחָ֛ק וֵאלֹהֵ֥י יַעֲקֹ֖ב שְׁלָחַ֣נִי אֲלֵיכֶ֑ם זֶה־
שְּׁמִ֣י לְעֹלָ֔ם וְזֶ֥ה זִכְרִ֖י לְדֹ֥ר דֹּֽר׃

Deut 4:3 (6) עֵֽינֵיכֶם֙ הָֽרֹאֹ֔ת אֵ֛ת אֲשֶׁר־עָשָׂ֥ה יְהוָ֖ה בְּבַ֣עַל פְּע֑וֹר כִּ֣י כָל־הָאִ֗ישׁ אֲשֶׁ֤ר
הָלַךְ֙ אַחֲרֵ֣י בַֽעַל־פְּע֔וֹר הִשְׁמִיד֛וֹ יְהוָ֥ה אֱלֹהֶ֖יךָ מִקִּרְבֶּֽךָ׃

3. Analyze the word order of the initiator and announcement.

1 Sam 24:17 (1) וַיְהִ֣י׀ כְּכַלּ֣וֹת דָּוִ֗ד לְדַבֵּ֞ר אֶת־הַדְּבָרִ֤ים הָאֵ֙לֶּה֙ אֶל־שָׁא֔וּל וַיֹּ֣אמֶר שָׁא֔וּל
הֲקֹלְךָ֥ זֶ֖ה בְּנִ֣י דָוִ֑ד וַיִּשָּׂ֥א שָׁא֛וּל קֹל֖וֹ וַיֵּֽבְךְּ׃

Exod 7:16 (2) וְאָמַרְתָּ֣ אֵלָ֗יו יְהוָ֞ה אֱלֹהֵ֤י הָֽעִבְרִים֙ שְׁלָחַ֣נִי אֵלֶ֔יךָ לֵאמֹ֔ר שַׁלַּח֙ אֶת־עַמִּ֔י
וְיַֽעַבְדֻ֖נִי בַּמִּדְבָּ֑ר וְהִנֵּ֥ה לֹא־שָׁמַ֖עְתָּ עַד־כֹּֽה׃

Exod 8:17[a] (3) כִּ֣י אִם־אֵינְךָ֮ מְשַׁלֵּ֣חַ אֶת־עַמִּי֒ הִנְנִ֨י מַשְׁלִ֜יחַ בְּךָ֗ וּבַעֲבָדֶ֧יךָ וּבְעַמְּךָ֛
וּבְבָתֶּ֖יךָ אֶת־הֶעָרֹ֑ב

Exod 19:5 (4) וְעַתָּ֗ה אִם־שָׁמ֤וֹעַ תִּשְׁמְעוּ֙ בְּקֹלִ֔י וּשְׁמַרְתֶּ֖ם אֶת־בְּרִיתִ֑י וִהְיִ֨יתֶם לִ֤י סְגֻלָּה֙
מִכָּל־הָ֣עַמִּ֔ים כִּי־לִ֖י כָּל־הָאָֽרֶץ׃

1 Sam 1:1 (5) וַיְהִי֩ אִ֨ישׁ אֶחָ֜ד מִן־הָרָמָתַ֛יִם צוֹפִ֖ים מֵהַ֣ר אֶפְרָ֑יִם וּשְׁמ֡וֹ אֶ֠לְקָנָה
בֶּן־יְרֹחָ֧ם בֶּן־אֱלִיה֛וּא בֶּן־תֹּ֥חוּ בֶן־צ֖וּף אֶפְרָתִֽי׃

Judg 20:27 (6) וַיִּשְׁאֲל֥וּ בְנֵֽי־יִשְׂרָאֵ֖ל בַּֽיהוָ֑ה וְשָׁ֗ם אֲרוֹן֙ בְּרִ֣ית הָאֱלֹהִ֔ים בַּיָּמִ֖ים הָהֵֽם׃

Prov 16:14[a] (7) חֲמַת־מֶ֥לֶךְ מַלְאֲכֵי־מָ֑וֶת

4. **Analyze the following genitives as proper or improper. If proper, which preposition should be understood between the annexation? If improper, analyze its function.**

Exod 6:12 (1) וַיְדַבֵּר מֹשֶׁה לִפְנֵי יְהוָה לֵאמֹר הֵן בְּנֵי־יִשְׂרָאֵל לֹא־שָׁמְעוּ אֵלַי וְאֵיךְ
יִשְׁמָעֵנִי פַרְעֹה וַאֲנִי עֲרַל שְׂפָתָיִם׃

1 Sam 6:4 (2) וַיֹּאמְרוּ מָה הָאָשָׁם אֲשֶׁר נָשִׁיב לוֹ וַיֹּאמְרוּ מִסְפַּר סַרְנֵי פְלִשְׁתִּים חֲמִשָּׁה
טְחֹרֵי זָהָב וַחֲמִשָּׁה עַכְבְּרֵי זָהָב כִּי־מַגֵּפָה אַחַת לְכֻלָּם וּלְסַרְנֵיכֶם׃

Gen 3:23 (3) וַיְשַׁלְּחֵהוּ יְהוָה אֱלֹהִים מִגַּן־עֵדֶן לַעֲבֹד אֶת־הָאֲדָמָה אֲשֶׁר לֻקַּח מִשָּׁם׃

Gen 9:6 (4) שֹׁפֵךְ דַּם הָאָדָם בָּאָדָם דָּמוֹ יִשָּׁפֵךְ כִּי בְּצֶלֶם אֱלֹהִים עָשָׂה אֶת־הָאָדָם׃

Gen 1:2 (5) וְהָאָרֶץ הָיְתָה תֹהוּ וָבֹהוּ וְחֹשֶׁךְ עַל־פְּנֵי תְהוֹם וְרוּחַ אֱלֹהִים מְרַחֶפֶת
עַל־פְּנֵי הַמָּיִם׃

Exod 11:5 (6) וּמֵת כָּל־בְּכוֹר בְּאֶרֶץ מִצְרַיִם מִבְּכוֹר פַּרְעֹה הַיֹּשֵׁב עַל־כִּסְאוֹ עַד
בְּכוֹר הַשִּׁפְחָה אֲשֶׁר אַחַר הָרֵחָיִם וְכֹל בְּכוֹר בְּהֵמָה׃

Exod 15:11 (7) מִי־כָמֹכָה בָּאֵלִם יְהוָה מִי כָּמֹכָה נֶאְדָּר בַּקֹּדֶשׁ נוֹרָא תְהִלֹּת עֹשֵׂה פֶלֶא׃

Gen 1:27 (8) וַיִּבְרָא אֱלֹהִים ׀ אֶת־הָאָדָם בְּצַלְמוֹ בְּצֶלֶם אֱלֹהִים בָּרָא אֹתוֹ זָכָר
וּנְקֵבָה בָּרָא אֹתָם׃

Gen 4:15 (9) וַיֹּאמֶר לוֹ יְהוָה לָכֵן כָּל־הֹרֵג קַיִן שִׁבְעָתַיִם יֻקָּם וַיָּשֶׂם יְהוָה לְקַיִן אוֹת
לְבִלְתִּי הַכּוֹת־אֹתוֹ כָּל־מֹצְאוֹ׃

Gen 3:8 (10) וַיִּשְׁמְעוּ אֶת־קוֹל יְהוָה אֱלֹהִים מִתְהַלֵּךְ בַּגָּן לְרוּחַ הַיּוֹם וַיִּתְחַבֵּא
הָאָדָם וְאִשְׁתּוֹ מִפְּנֵי יְהוָה אֱלֹהִים בְּתוֹךְ עֵץ הַגָּן׃

Exod 8:18 (11) וְהִפְלֵיתִי בַיּוֹם הַהוּא אֶת־אֶרֶץ גֹּשֶׁן אֲשֶׁר עַמִּי עֹמֵד עָלֶיהָ לְבִלְתִּי
הֱיוֹת־שָׁם עָרֹב לְמַעַן תֵּדַע כִּי אֲנִי יְהוָה בְּקֶרֶב הָאָרֶץ׃

Gen 24:2 (12) וַיֹּאמֶר אַבְרָהָם אֶל־עַבְדּוֹ זְקַן בֵּיתוֹ הַמֹּשֵׁל בְּכָל־אֲשֶׁר־לוֹ שִׂים־נָא יָדְךָ
תַּחַת יְרֵכִי׃

Exod 11:2 (13) דַּבֶּר־נָא בְּאָזְנֵי הָעָם וְיִשְׁאֲלוּ אִישׁ ׀ מֵאֵת רֵעֵהוּ וְאִשָּׁה מֵאֵת רְעוּתָהּ
כְּלֵי־כֶסֶף וּכְלֵי זָהָב׃

5. Analyze the following annexations.

Exod 24:14 (1) וְאֶל־הַזְּקֵנִ֤ים אָמַר֙ שְׁבוּ־לָ֣נוּ בָזֶ֔ה עַ֥ד אֲשֶׁר־נָשׁ֖וּב אֲלֵיכֶ֑ם וְהִנֵּ֨ה אַהֲרֹ֤ן
וְחוּר֙ עִמָּכֶ֔ם מִי־בַ֥עַל דְּבָרִ֖ים יִגַּ֥שׁ אֲלֵהֶֽם׃

Gen 18:10 (2) וַיֹּ֗אמֶר שׁ֣וֹב אָשׁ֤וּב אֵלֶ֙יךָ֙ כָּעֵ֣ת חַיָּ֔ה וְהִנֵּה־בֵ֖ן לְשָׂרָ֣ה אִשְׁתֶּ֑ךָ וְשָׂרָ֥ה
שֹׁמַ֛עַת פֶּ֥תַח הָאֹ֖הֶל וְה֥וּא אַחֲרָֽיו׃

Lev 14:46 (3) וְהַבָּא֙ אֶל־הַבַּ֔יִת כָּל־יְמֵ֖י הִסְגִּ֣יר אֹת֑וֹ יִטְמָ֖א עַד־הָעָֽרֶב׃

Josh 2:22 (4) וַיֵּלְכוּ֙ וַיָּבֹ֣אוּ הָהָ֔רָה וַיֵּ֤שְׁבוּ שָׁם֙ שְׁלֹ֣שֶׁת יָמִ֔ים עַד־שָׁ֖בוּ הָרֹדְפִ֑ים וַיְבַקְשׁ֧וּ
הָרֹדְפִ֛ים בְּכָל־הַדֶּ֖רֶךְ וְלֹ֥א מָצָֽאוּ׃

Exod 9:4 (5) וְהִפְלָ֣ה יְהוָ֔ה בֵּ֚ין מִקְנֵ֣ה יִשְׂרָאֵ֔ל וּבֵ֖ין מִקְנֵ֣ה מִצְרָ֑יִם וְלֹ֥א יָמ֛וּת
מִכָּל־לִבְנֵ֥י יִשְׂרָאֵ֖ל דָּבָֽר׃

Exod 6:28 (6) וַיְהִ֗י בְּי֨וֹם דִּבֶּ֧ר יְהוָ֛ה אֶל־מֹשֶׁ֖ה בְּאֶ֥רֶץ מִצְרָֽיִם׃

Gen 25:27 (7) וַֽיִּגְדְּלוּ֙ הַנְּעָרִ֔ים וַיְהִ֣י עֵשָׂ֗ו אִ֛ישׁ יֹדֵ֥עַ צַ֖יִד אִ֣ישׁ שָׂדֶ֑ה וְיַעֲקֹב֙ אִ֣ישׁ תָּ֔ם
יֹשֵׁ֖ב אֹהָלִֽים׃

6. Find the accusatives in the following verses. Analyze the absolute objects, double direct objects, and adverbial accusatives (and their substitutes).

Exod 2:22[b] (1) כִּ֣י אָמַ֔ר גֵּ֣ר הָיִ֔יתִי בְּאֶ֖רֶץ נָכְרִיָּֽה׃

1 Sam 9:6 (2) וַיֹּ֣אמֶר ל֗וֹ הִנֵּה־נָ֨א אִישׁ־אֱלֹהִים֙ בָּעִ֣יר הַזֹּ֔את וְהָאִ֣ישׁ נִכְבָּ֔ד כֹּ֛ל
אֲשֶׁר־יְדַבֵּ֖ר בּ֣וֹא יָב֑וֹא עַתָּה֙ נֵ֣לְכָה שָּׁ֔ם אוּלַ֛י יַגִּ֥יד לָ֖נוּ אֶת־דַּרְכֵּ֥נוּ
אֲשֶׁר־הָלַ֥כְנוּ עָלֶֽיהָ׃

Exod 8:5[b] (3) רַ֥ק בַּיְאֹ֖ר תִּשָּׁאַֽרְנָה׃

Num 11:33 (4) הַבָּשָׂ֗ר עוֹדֶ֙נּוּ֙ בֵּ֣ין שִׁנֵּיהֶ֔ם טֶ֖רֶם יִכָּרֵ֑ת וְאַ֤ף יְהוָה֙ חָרָ֣ה בָעָ֔ם וַיַּ֤ךְ
יְהוָה֙ בָּעָ֔ם מַכָּ֖ה רַבָּ֥ה מְאֹֽד׃

Exod 15:23 (5) וַיָּבֹ֣אוּ מָרָ֔תָה וְלֹ֣א יָֽכְל֗וּ לִשְׁתֹּ֥ת מַ֙יִם֙ מִמָּרָ֔ה כִּ֥י מָרִ֖ים הֵ֑ם עַל־כֵּ֥ן
קָרָֽא־שְׁמָ֖הּ מָרָֽה׃

1 Sam 8:1 (6) וַיְהִ֕י כַּאֲשֶׁ֖ר זָקֵ֣ן שְׁמוּאֵ֑ל וַיָּ֧שֶׂם אֶת־בָּנָ֛יו שֹׁפְטִ֖ים לְיִשְׂרָאֵֽל׃

Jer 1:5 (7) בְּטֶ֨רֶם אֶצָּרְךָ֤ בַבֶּ֙טֶן֙ יְדַעְתִּ֔יךָ וּבְטֶ֛רֶם תֵּצֵ֥א מֵרֶ֖חֶם הִקְדַּשְׁתִּ֑יךָ נָבִ֥יא
לַגּוֹיִ֖ם נְתַתִּֽיךָ׃

Gen 7:4 (8) כִּי֩ לְיָמִ֨ים ע֜וֹד שִׁבְעָ֗ה אָנֹכִי֙ מַמְטִ֣יר עַל־הָאָ֔רֶץ אַרְבָּעִ֣ים י֔וֹם וְאַרְבָּעִ֖ים
לָ֑יְלָה וּמָחִ֗יתִי אֶֽת־כָּל־הַיְקוּם֙ אֲשֶׁ֣ר עָשִׂ֔יתִי מֵעַ֖ל פְּנֵ֥י הָאֲדָמָֽה׃

Jer 7:25 (9) לְמִן־הַיּ֗וֹם אֲשֶׁ֨ר יָצְא֤וּ אֲבֽוֹתֵיכֶם֙ מֵאֶ֣רֶץ מִצְרַ֔יִם עַ֖ד הַיּ֣וֹם הַזֶּ֑ה וָאֶשְׁלַ֤ח
אֲלֵיכֶם֙ אֶת־כָּל־עֲבָדַ֣י הַנְּבִיאִ֔ים י֖וֹם הַשְׁכֵּ֥ם וְשָׁלֹֽחַ׃

Exod 25:28 (10) וְעָשִׂ֤יתָ אֶת־הַבַּדִּים֙ עֲצֵ֣י שִׁטִּ֔ים וְצִפִּיתָ֥ אֹתָ֖ם זָהָ֑ב וְנִשָּׂא־בָ֖ם אֶת־הַשֻּׁלְחָֽן׃

Exod 4:19 (11) וַיֹּ֨אמֶר יְהוָ֤ה אֶל־מֹשֶׁה֙ בְּמִדְיָ֔ן לֵ֖ךְ שֻׁ֣ב מִצְרָ֑יִם כִּי־מֵ֙תוּ֙ כָּל־הָ֣אֲנָשִׁ֔ים
הַֽמְבַקְשִׁ֖ים אֶת־נַפְשֶֽׁךָ׃

Exod 10:8 (12) וַיּוּשַׁ֞ב אֶת־מֹשֶׁ֤ה וְאֶֽת־אַהֲרֹן֙ אֶל־פַּרְעֹ֔ה וַיֹּ֣אמֶר אֲלֵהֶ֔ם לְכ֖וּ עִבְד֣וּ
אֶת־יְהוָ֣ה אֱלֹהֵיכֶ֑ם מִ֥י וָמִ֖י הַהֹלְכִֽים׃

Exod 2:10[a] (13) וַֽיְהִי־לָ֖הּ לְבֵ֑ן

Exod 8:25 (14) וַיֹּ֣אמֶר מֹשֶׁ֗ה הִנֵּ֨ה אָנֹכִ֜י יוֹצֵ֣א מֵעִמָּ֗ךְ וְהַעְתַּרְתִּ֤י אֶל־יְהוָה֙ וְסָ֣ר הֶעָרֹ֗ב
מִפַּרְעֹ֛ה מֵעֲבָדָ֥יו וּמֵעַמּ֖וֹ מָחָ֑ר רַ֗ק אַל־יֹסֵ֤ף פַּרְעֹה֙ הָתֵ֔ל לְבִלְתִּי֙ שַׁלַּ֣ח
אֶת־הָעָ֔ם לִזְבֹּ֖חַ לַיהוָֽה׃

Exod 3:7 (15) וַיֹּ֣אמֶר יְהוָ֔ה רָאֹ֥ה רָאִ֛יתִי אֶת־עֳנִ֥י עַמִּ֖י אֲשֶׁ֣ר בְּמִצְרָ֑יִם וְאֶת־צַעֲקָתָ֤ם
שָׁמַ֙עְתִּי֙ מִפְּנֵ֣י נֹגְשָׂ֔יו כִּ֥י יָדַ֖עְתִּי אֶת־מַכְאֹבָֽיו׃

Exod 15:25 (16) וַיִּצְעַ֣ק אֶל־יְהוָ֗ה וַיּוֹרֵ֤הוּ יְהוָה֙ עֵ֔ץ וַיַּשְׁלֵךְ֙ אֶל־הַמַּ֔יִם וַיִּמְתְּק֖וּ הַמָּ֑יִם שָׁ֣ם
שָׂ֥ם ל֛וֹ חֹ֥ק וּמִשְׁפָּ֖ט וְשָׁ֥ם נִסָּֽהוּ׃

Exod 7:24 (17) וַיַּחְפְּר֧וּ כָל־מִצְרַ֛יִם סְבִיבֹ֥ת הַיְאֹ֖ר מַ֣יִם לִשְׁתּ֑וֹת כִּ֣י לֹ֤א יָֽכְלוּ֙ לִשְׁתֹּ֔ת
מִמֵּימֵ֖י הַיְאֹֽר׃

Exod 4:14 (18) וַיִּֽחַר־אַ֨ף יְהוָ֜ה בְּמֹשֶׁ֗ה וַיֹּ֙אמֶר֙ הֲלֹ֨א אַהֲרֹ֤ן אָחִ֙יךָ֙ הַלֵּוִ֔י יָדַ֕עְתִּי כִּֽי־דַבֵּ֥ר
יְדַבֵּ֖ר ה֑וּא וְגַ֤ם הִנֵּה־הוּא֙ יֹצֵ֣א לִקְרָאתֶ֔ךָ וְרָאֲךָ֖ וְשָׂמַ֥ח בְּלִבּֽוֹ׃

Exod 3:21 (19) וְנָתַתִּ֛י אֶת־חֵ֥ן הָֽעָם־הַזֶּ֖ה בְּעֵינֵ֣י מִצְרָ֑יִם וְהָיָה֙ כִּ֣י תֵֽלֵכ֔וּן לֹ֥א תֵלְכ֖וּ
רֵיקָֽם׃

Josh 6:5 (20) וְהָיָה בִּמְשֹׁךְ בְּקֶרֶן הַיּוֹבֵל כְּשָׁמְעֲכֶם אֶת־קוֹל הַשּׁוֹפָר יָרִיעוּ כָל־הָעָם
תְּרוּעָה גְדוֹלָה וְנָפְלָה חוֹמַת הָעִיר תַּחְתֶּיהָ וְעָלוּ הָעָם אִישׁ נֶגְדּוֹ׃

Num 8:19 (21) וָאֶתְּנָה אֶת־הַלְוִיִּם נְתֻנִים לְאַהֲרֹן וּלְבָנָיו מִתּוֹךְ בְּנֵי יִשְׂרָאֵל לַעֲבֹד
אֶת־עֲבֹדַת בְּנֵי־יִשְׂרָאֵל בְּאֹהֶל מוֹעֵד וּלְכַפֵּר עַל־בְּנֵי יִשְׂרָאֵל וְלֹא יִהְיֶה
בִּבְנֵי יִשְׂרָאֵל נֶגֶף בְּגֶשֶׁת בְּנֵי־יִשְׂרָאֵל אֶל־הַקֹּדֶשׁ׃

Ps 3:8 (22) קוּמָה יְהוָה הוֹשִׁיעֵנִי אֱלֹהַי כִּי־הִכִּיתָ אֶת־כָּל־אֹיְבַי לֶחִי שִׁנֵּי רְשָׁעִים
שִׁבַּרְתָּ׃

Exod 12:15 (23) שִׁבְעַת יָמִים מַצּוֹת תֹּאכֵלוּ אַךְ בַּיּוֹם הָרִאשׁוֹן תַּשְׁבִּיתוּ שְּׂאֹר מִבָּתֵּיכֶם
כִּי כָּל־אֹכֵל חָמֵץ וְנִכְרְתָה הַנֶּפֶשׁ הַהִוא מִיִּשְׂרָאֵל מִיּוֹם הָרִאשֹׁן
עַד־יוֹם הַשְּׁבִעִי׃

Exod 2:11 (24) וַיְהִי בַּיָּמִים הָהֵם וַיִּגְדַּל מֹשֶׁה וַיֵּצֵא אֶל־אֶחָיו וַיַּרְא בְּסִבְלֹתָם וַיַּרְא
אִישׁ מִצְרִי מַכֶּה אִישׁ־עִבְרִי מֵאֶחָיו׃

Exod 14:21 (25) וַיֵּט מֹשֶׁה אֶת־יָדוֹ עַל־הַיָּם וַיּוֹלֶךְ יְהוָה אֶת־הַיָּם בְּרוּחַ קָדִים עַזָּה
כָּל־הַלַּיְלָה וַיָּשֶׂם אֶת־הַיָּם לֶחָרָבָה וַיִּבָּקְעוּ הַמָּיִם׃

2 Sam 15:30 (26) וְדָוִד עֹלֶה בְמַעֲלֵה הַזֵּיתִים עֹלֶה וּבוֹכֶה וְרֹאשׁ לוֹ חָפוּי וְהוּא הֹלֵךְ
יָחֵף וְכָל־הָעָם אֲשֶׁר־אִתּוֹ חָפוּ אִישׁ רֹאשׁוֹ וְעָלוּ עָלֹה וּבָכֹה׃

Exod 21:32 (27) אִם־עֶבֶד יִגַּח הַשּׁוֹר אוֹ אָמָה כֶּסֶף שְׁלֹשִׁים שְׁקָלִים יִתֵּן לַאדֹנָיו
וְהַשּׁוֹר יִסָּקֵל׃

Exod 25:18 (28) וְעָשִׂיתָ שְׁנַיִם כְּרֻבִים זָהָב מִקְשָׁה תַּעֲשֶׂה אֹתָם מִשְּׁנֵי קְצוֹת הַכַּפֹּרֶת׃

7. Find the words in Casus Pendens. Then identify the case that resumes the Casus Pendens.

Num 14:38 (1) וִיהוֹשֻׁעַ בִּן־נוּן וְכָלֵב בֶּן־יְפֻנֶּה חָיוּ מִן־הָאֲנָשִׁים הָהֵם הַהֹלְכִים לָתוּר
אֶת־הָאָרֶץ׃

Isa 15:7 (2) עַל־כֵּן יִתְרָה עָשָׂה וּפְקֻדָּתָם עַל נַחַל הָעֲרָבִים יִשָּׂאוּם׃

Num 22:38 (3) וַיֹּאמֶר בִּלְעָם אֶל־בָּלָק הִנֵּה־בָאתִי אֵלֶיךָ עַתָּה הֲיָכֹל אוּכַל דַּבֵּר
מְאוּמָה הַדָּבָר אֲשֶׁר יָשִׂים אֱלֹהִים בְּפִי אֹתוֹ אֲדַבֵּר׃

Gen 22:24 (4) וּפִֽילַגְשׁ֖וֹ וּשְׁמָ֣הּ רְאוּמָ֑ה וַתֵּ֤לֶד גַּם־הִוא֙ אֶת־טֶ֣בַח וְאֶת־גַּ֔חַם וְאֶת־תַּ֖חַשׁ
וְאֶת־מַעֲכָֽה׃

Num 14:36 (5) וְהָ֣אֲנָשִׁ֔ים אֲשֶׁר־שָׁלַ֥ח מֹשֶׁ֖ה לָת֣וּר אֶת־הָאָ֑רֶץ וַיָּשֻׁ֗בוּ וַיַּלִּ֤ינוּ עָלָיו֙
אֶת־כָּל־הָ֣עֵדָ֔ה לְהוֹצִ֥יא דִבָּ֖ה עַל־הָאָֽרֶץ׃

Exod 38:24 (6) כָּל־הַזָּהָ֗ב הֶֽעָשׂוּי֙ לַמְּלָאכָ֔ה בְּכֹ֖ל מְלֶ֣אכֶת הַקֹּ֑דֶשׁ וַיְהִ֣י ׀ זְהַ֣ב הַתְּנוּפָ֗ה
תֵּ֤שַׁע וְעֶשְׂרִים֙ כִּכָּ֔ר וּשְׁבַ֨ע מֵא֤וֹת וּשְׁלֹשִׁים֙ שֶׁ֔קֶל בְּשֶׁ֖קֶל הַקֹּֽדֶשׁ׃

Exod 32:16 (7) וְהַ֨לֻּחֹ֔ת מַעֲשֵׂ֥ה אֱלֹהִ֖ים הֵ֑מָּה וְהַמִּכְתָּ֗ב מִכְתַּ֤ב אֱלֹהִים֙ ה֔וּא חָר֖וּת עַל־
הַלֻּחֹֽת׃

Gen 24:43 (8) הִנֵּ֛ה אָנֹכִ֥י נִצָּ֖ב עַל־עֵ֣ין הַמָּ֑יִם וְהָיָ֤ה הָֽעַלְמָה֙ הַיֹּצֵ֣את לִשְׁאֹ֔ב וְאָמַרְתִּ֣י
אֵלֶ֔יהָ הַשְׁקִֽינִי־נָ֥א מְעַט־מַ֖יִם מִכַּדֵּֽךְ׃

Num 24:13 (9) אִם־יִתֶּן־לִ֨י בָלָ֜ק מְלֹ֣א בֵיתוֹ֮ כֶּ֣סֶף וְזָהָב֒ לֹ֣א אוּכַ֗ל לַעֲבֹר֙ אֶת־פִּ֣י יְהוָ֔ה
לַעֲשׂ֥וֹת טוֹבָ֛ה א֥וֹ רָעָ֖ה מִלִּבִּ֑י אֲשֶׁר־יְדַבֵּ֥ר יְהוָ֖ה אֹת֥וֹ אֲדַבֵּֽר׃

Gen 17:15 (10) וַיֹּ֤אמֶר אֱלֹהִים֙ אֶל־אַבְרָהָ֔ם שָׂרַ֣י אִשְׁתְּךָ֔ לֹא־תִקְרָ֥א אֶת־שְׁמָ֖הּ שָׂרָ֑י כִּ֥י
שָׂרָ֖ה שְׁמָֽהּ׃

Gen 26:15 (11) וְכָל־הַבְּאֵרֹ֗ת אֲשֶׁ֤ר חָֽפְרוּ֙ עַבְדֵ֣י אָבִ֔יו בִּימֵ֖י אַבְרָהָ֣ם אָבִ֑יו סִתְּמ֣וּם
פְּלִשְׁתִּ֔ים וַיְמַלְא֖וּם עָפָֽר׃

1 Sam 2:10 (12) יְהוָ֞ה יֵחַ֣תּוּ מְרִיבָ֗יו עָלָיו֙ בַּשָּׁמַ֣יִם יַרְעֵ֔ם יְהוָ֖ה יָדִ֣ין אַפְסֵי־אָ֑רֶץ וְיִתֶּן־עֹ֣ז
לְמַלְכּ֔וֹ וְיָרֵ֖ם קֶ֥רֶן מְשִׁיחֽוֹ׃

Isa 9:1 (13) הָעָם֙ הַהֹלְכִ֣ים בַּחֹ֔שֶׁךְ רָא֖וּ א֣וֹר גָּד֑וֹל יֹשְׁבֵי֙ בְּאֶ֣רֶץ צַלְמָ֔וֶת א֖וֹר נָגַ֥הּ
עֲלֵיהֶֽם׃

Exod 4:21 (14) וַיֹּ֣אמֶר יְהוָה֮ אֶל־מֹשֶׁה֒ בְּלֶכְתְּךָ֙ לָשׁ֣וּב מִצְרַ֔יְמָה רְאֵ֗ה כָּל־הַמֹּֽפְתִים֙
אֲשֶׁר־שַׂ֣מְתִּי בְיָדֶ֔ךָ וַעֲשִׂיתָ֖ם לִפְנֵ֣י פַרְעֹ֑ה וַאֲנִי֙ אֲחַזֵּ֣ק אֶת־לִבּ֔וֹ וְלֹ֥א
יְשַׁלַּ֖ח אֶת־הָעָֽם׃

Exod 3:1 (15) וּמֹשֶׁ֗ה הָיָ֥ה רֹעֶ֛ה אֶת־צֹ֛אן יִתְר֥וֹ חֹתְנ֖וֹ כֹּהֵ֣ן מִדְיָ֑ן וַיִּנְהַ֤ג אֶת־הַצֹּאן֙ אַחַ֣ר
הַמִּדְבָּ֔ר וַיָּבֹ֛א אֶל־הַ֥ר הָאֱלֹהִ֖ים חֹרֵֽבָה׃

2 Kgs 10:29 (16) רַ֣ק חֲטָאֵ֞י יָרָבְעָ֤ם בֶּן־נְבָט֙ אֲשֶׁ֣ר הֶחֱטִ֣יא אֶת־יִשְׂרָאֵ֔ל לֹא־סָ֥ר יֵה֖וּא
מֵאַחֲרֵיהֶ֑ם עֶגְלֵי֙ הַזָּהָ֔ב אֲשֶׁ֥ר בֵּֽית־אֵ֖ל וַאֲשֶׁ֥ר בְּדָֽן׃

(17) 1 Kgs 15:13 וְגַ֣ם ׀ אֶת־מַעֲכָ֣ה אִמּ֗וֹ וַיְסִרֶ֙הָ֙ מִגְּבִירָ֔ה אֲשֶׁר־עָשְׂתָ֥ה מִפְלֶ֖צֶת לָאֲשֵׁרָ֑ה
וַיִּכְרֹ֤ת אָסָא֙ אֶת־מִפְלַצְתָּ֔הּ וַיִּשְׂרֹ֖ף בְּנַ֥חַל קִדְרֽוֹן׃

(18) 1 Sam 25:27 וְעַתָּה֙ הַבְּרָכָ֣ה הַזֹּ֔את אֲשֶׁר־הֵבִ֥יא שִׁפְחָתְךָ֖ לַֽאדֹנִ֑י וְנִתְּנָה֙ לַנְּעָרִ֔ים
הַמִּֽתְהַלְּכִ֖ים בְּרַגְלֵ֥י אֲדֹנִֽי׃

(19) 2 Sam 14:10 וַיֹּ֖אמֶר הַמֶּ֑לֶךְ הַֽמְדַבֵּ֤ר אֵלַ֙יִךְ֙ וַהֲבֵאת֣וֹ אֵלַ֔י וְלֹֽא־יֹסִ֥יף ע֖וֹד לָגַ֥עַת בָּֽךְ׃

(20) Exod 16:36 וְהָעֹ֕מֶר עֲשִׂרִ֥ית הָאֵיפָ֖ה הֽוּא׃

(21) Gen 37:3 וְיִשְׂרָאֵ֗ל אָהַ֤ב אֶת־יוֹסֵף֙ מִכָּל־בָּנָ֔יו כִּֽי־בֶן־זְקֻנִ֥ים ה֖וּא ל֑וֹ וְעָ֥שָׂה ל֖וֹ
כְּתֹ֥נֶת פַּסִּֽים׃

(22) Ps 46:5 נָהָ֗ר פְּלָגָ֗יו יְשַׂמְּח֥וּ עִיר־אֱלֹהִ֑ים קְ֝דֹ֗שׁ מִשְׁכְּנֵ֥י עֶלְיֽוֹן׃

(23) Ps 65:4 דִּבְרֵ֣י עֲ֭וֺנֹת גָּ֣בְרוּ מֶ֑נִּי פְּ֝שָׁעֵ֗ינוּ אַתָּ֥ה תְכַפְּרֵֽם׃

(24) 1 Sam 3:11 וַיֹּ֣אמֶר יְהוָה֮ אֶל־שְׁמוּאֵל֒ הִנֵּ֨ה אָנֹכִ֜י עֹשֶׂ֥ה דָבָ֖ר בְּיִשְׂרָאֵ֑ל אֲשֶׁר֙ כָּל־
שֹׁ֣מְע֔וֹ תְּצִלֶּ֖ינָה שְׁתֵּ֥י אָזְנָֽיו׃

(25) Ps 74:17 אַתָּ֣ה הִ֭צַּבְתָּ כָּל־גְּבוּל֣וֹת אָ֑רֶץ קַ֥יִץ וָ֝חֹ֗רֶף אַתָּ֥ה יְצַרְתָּֽם׃

CHAPTER 4
VERBAL NOUNS

§15. Introduction

The infinitive absolute, infinitive construct, and participle are VERBAL NOUNS, that is, nouns related to verbs. The term INFINITIVE means without limits or bounds, that is, without the limits of person, number, and gender of "finite" verbs. Infinitives are *abstract* verbal nouns, communicating abstract verbal notions such as sacrificing (abstract), but not a sacrifice (concrete), or dreaming (abstract), but not a dream (concrete). As nouns, they communicate "the act of sacrificing" or "the event of dreaming." By contrast, PARTICIPLES, so called because they participate in or partake of the verb and the adjective, are *concrete* verbal nouns (more precisely, verbal adjectives), indicating the person or thing doing the verbal idea inherent in the participle. As such, they do not relate "the event or act of sacrificing" as the infinitive, but "the person who sacrifices/dreams" or "the thing which shines." They are, therefore, referred to as "nouns of the agent" or "nouns of the one who does the action." The participle, קֹטֵל, therefore, strictly means, "The man (or thing) by whom the coming into existence and occurrence of the verbal event of killing can be asserted." Like infinitives, participles may be used similar to, but not identical to, verbs.[1]

§16. Participles *a*

Participles are similar to verbs. In form, the participle and the imperfect share the same thematic vowel in the derived stems, with the initial Mem of the participle replacing the aspect indicators of the imperfect (excluding the Niphal). Participles also possess tense, aspect, and voice (active and passive). In syntax, the participle may govern an accusative like a verb.[2] Indeed, the participle often translates so smoothly as an English verb that it appears, at least in some contexts, to be a verb.

This, of course, is illusionary—the participle is a noun, not a verb. As a noun, the participle has gender, number, case, definiteness/indefiniteness, and sometimes the suffixes of the genitive. Moreover, the participle may function as a vocative, predicate, subject, or the first word of an annexation. Finally, the article may define a participle.

Although a noun, the participle is more precisely a *verbal* noun. The participle, therefore, differs from a noun in some particulars. The noun is merely subsistence without verbal aspect; the participle has verbal aspect, expressing a *habitual* or *abiding* state or activity, ideal for occupations or professions. When conveying a habitual or abiding *activity*, the participle resembles the imperfect in aspect; therefore, the participle שֹׁמֵר would equal אֲשֶׁר יִשְׁמֹר. When conveying a habitual or abiding *state*, the participle resembles the perfect in aspect; therefore, the participle צֹדֶה would equal אֲשֶׁר צָדָה (Exod 21:13). Like the verb, the participle can be active, when the person or thing is viewed as doing the continual activity, or passive, when the continual activity is being done to the person or thing.

1. Griess, 221–228; Howell §331, 343–347; Wright I, §195, 229–230; ZW, 27, 70.
2. The participle occasionally takes the pronominal suffixes of the accusative, like a verb, Ps 18:33.

As the participle differs from a noun in particulars, so it differs from verbs as well. The perfect and imperfect denote origination and occurrence of an action or state, that is, the action *coming into existence and happening*. This is natural for the imperfect whose meaning implies origination with *constant renewal* or *repetition*. Similarly, the perfect also expresses origination, particularly with stative verbs. For example, in 1 Kgs 1:50, the word יָרֵא is a perfect, "Adonijah *became* afraid." In 1 Kgs 1:51, the same word and form occurs as a participle, "Adonijah was afraid."[3] In the first example, the perfect indicates that an event occurred, happened, and came into existence—this is verbal *movement* or *action* with point of origin; in the second example, the participle does not convey the movement or action of an event coming into existence and occurring, but the *fixedness* of a habitual or abiding state (or activity). This "fixedness" reveals the nominal (noun) nature of the participle.

In many contexts, a participle or an imperfect could be appropriate. But they are not interchangeable. The imperfect conveys action; the participle, description. The participle, however, is often more efficient than the imperfect since the participle combines implied *verbal* actions of the subject—if Jacob is a man who seeks (a seeker), this assumes verbal (usually imperfect) acts or events of seeking—with maximum *adjectival* description of the subject. The Semitic author or speaker, therefore, relishes the compact, yet vibrant, participle in direct speech and poetical statements. In Genesis 37:7, for example, Joseph begins with a participle, achieving maximum description with its implied imperfect actions in the past (we were binders of bindings). Then he relates a verbal event with two perfect verbs, expressing completed, past actions (my binding stood up and stood itself upright). Then he reports another verbal event in process with the imperfect: Your bindings were going around and around, then (suddenly) their bindings bowed down to Joseph's bindings (completed, past action of the Vav-consecutive). Joseph could have used an imperfect for the participle if he wanted repeated verbal occurrences, but he would have lost the vivid description with the implied imperfect verbal actions of the participle. Later in the verse, he could have used a participle for the imperfect, but he would have then lost the bold contrast of verbal actions and aspects of the perfects, the imperfect, and the Vav-consecutive. In many contexts, either a participle or verb could be used, but the skillful Semitic author or speaker chooses deliberately and revealingly, knowing the power and nuance of the participle and of the verb.

This usage of the participle is characteristically Semitic, as Arabic and Aramaic attest. Western languages, such as Greek and Latin, do not use participles in the same manner. Western languages would normally use a verb to render this Semitic participial construction.

This usage of the participle is characteristically Semitic, as Arabic and Aramaic attest. Western languages, such as Greek and Latin, do not use participles in the same manner. Western languages would normally use a verb to render this Semitic participial construction.

The participle, then, is a verbal noun (or adjective), not a nominal verb, an adjectival noun with verbal characteristics. It may function as a SUBSTANTIVE, adjective, or predicate. Yet, whatever its function, the participle is always descriptive,

3. Literally, "Adonijah (was) a fearer."

either in itself (substantive) or to another word as an attribute (adjective) or as a predicate (ANNOUNCEMENT).

A. Nominative *b*

1. Subject: The participle as a subject usually has the article, with the verbal aspect of a perfect (past) or imperfect (present or future), context determining.
   a) Agent: The participle as AGENT always follows its verb. Gen 38:28; 50:2; Exod 21:19; 22:5; Lev 15:8; 20:10; Num 15:4
   b) Initiator: The participle as INITIATOR always precedes its verb (announcement). Gen 21:6; Exod 21:34; Lev 27:15; Num 11:32; Deut 19:20; 1 Sam 20:36; 21:3; BA Dan 2:5

2. Predicate (Announcement): Usually the participle as an announcement is without the article (like the adjective), with the aspect of an imperfect (past frequentative, present, or future) or of a perfect (in Biblical Aramaic). Like the adjective, the participle as an announcement is always descriptive. When the participle functions as an announcement, the participle has or implies an agent. This predicate use of the participle is characteristically Semitic. This predicate use of the participle is characteristically Semitic. *c*

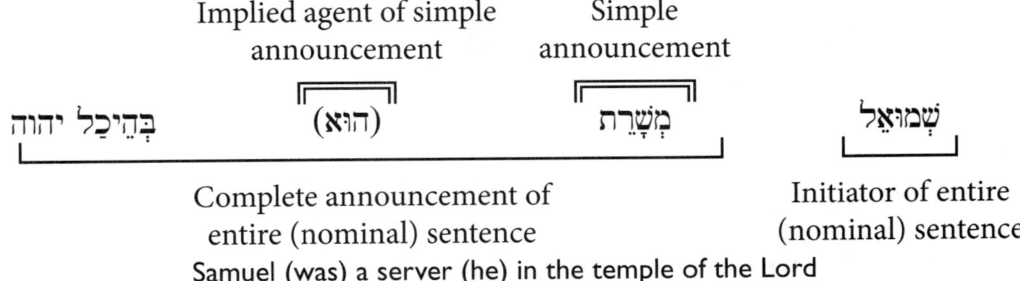

The participle as an announcement may be used in a variety of clauses.

a) In independent nominal clauses: *d*

וַאֲדֹנִיָּה בֶן־חַגִּית מִתְנַשֵּׂא לֵאמֹר אֲנִי אֶמְלֹךְ 1 Kgs 1:5a

And Adonijah, the son of Haggith, **was exalting himself**, saying, I rule.

Gen 2:10; Exod 25:32; Lev 7:10; Num 36:8; Jos 6:13; Judg 16:9; 1 Sam 2:26; 3:1; 29:2; 2 Sam 15:18; 1 Kgs 2:45; 8:7

As a concrete verbal noun, a more precise translation would be, "Adonijah was an exalter of himself," as if he had made it his profession. The participle has the aspect of an imperfect; therefore, the verbal equivalent would be אֲשֶׁר יִתְנַשֵּׂא.

Perfect: The participle with a perfect meaning may occur in Biblical Aramaic when the participle occurs before its agent. BA Dan 2:5; 3:9, 26; Ezra 5:3, 6:14

Imperfect: Gen 41:1–2; Exod 3:9, 13; 5:13; 7:17; 1 Sam 1:13 (with separating pronoun); 2:6–8; 5:3–4; 6:13; 19:11, 14; 24:5, 15; Jer 7:17(2x), 18(3x), 19; BA Dan 2:21–22; 3:14; Ezra 4:19

e b) In SITUATION CLAUSES (§13z; 48–49a-b): These dependent clauses are adverbial to another clause, furnishing the condition, status, or situation for its independent clause. These clauses function as accusatives of situation to their independent clause. For situation clauses, the tense is determined by the main verb in the independent clause. The word order for this construction is frequently Vav+(pro) noun+participle.

Gen 18:1 וַיֵּרָא אֵלָיו יְהוָה בְּאֵלֹנֵי מַמְרֵא וְהוּא יֹשֵׁב פֶּתַח־הָאֹהֶל כְּחֹם הַיּוֹם׃

And the Lord appeared to him in the oaks of Mamre, **and (while, as) he was sitting** in the tent door in the heat of the day.

As a concrete verbal noun, a precise translation would be, "He was a sitter."

1 Sam 4:12; 5:4 (וְרֹאשׁ); 6:12; 10:5; 17:41; 19:9(2x), 20; 2 Kgs 22:14; Jer 14:15; 26:19; 27:15; 33:1; 36:18; BA Ezra 5:8(4x)

f c) In הִנֵּה clauses: Participles often occur in הִנֵּה clauses. הִנֵּה clauses may be independent or situation clauses.

In independent clauses: Gen 41:29; 45:12; Exod 8:17, Num 27:7; Judg 19:16; 1 Sam 2:31; 5:3–4; 23:1; 1 Kgs 13:25; Isa 13:9; 30:27; Jer 1:15; Zech 5:7. In situation clauses: Gen 15:3; 28:12

g d) In a variety of dependent clauses (§43–46; 77–79): This includes, for example, כִּי, relative, and temporal clauses. Consecutive clauses with participles as announcements often introduce a temporal clause (§79d).

1 Sam 9:14 וַיַּעֲלוּ הָעִיר הֵמָּה בָּאִים בְּתוֹךְ הָעִיר וְהִנֵּה שְׁמוּאֵל יֹצֵא לִקְרָאתָם לַעֲלוֹת הַבָּמָה׃

And they went up to the city, (just as) they were entering into the midst of the city, **then behold Samuel was going out** to meet them to go up to the high place.

temporal clause—1 Sam 17:23; relative clause—Gen 39:6, 22–23; 40:3; 1 Sam 10:19; כִּי clause—Gen 3:5; 19:13–14; 29:9; 31:20

h e) In ABSOLUTE IDENTIFICATION (§11v; 27a fn 6, 9): Rarely, the participle as an announcement with the article expresses absolute identification with its subject. This construction resembles the definite adjective as a predicate (Exod 9:27). These constructions, all highly emphatic, imply a "separating pronoun." First Kings 18:39 demonstrates a separating pronoun between two nouns, showing absolute identification.

1 Kgs 18:39 וַיַּרְא כָּל־הָעָם וַיִּפְּלוּ עַל־פְּנֵיהֶם וַיֹּאמְרוּ יְהוָה הוּא הָאֱלֹהִים יְהוָה הוּא הָאֱלֹהִים׃

And when all the people saw it, they fell on their faces; and they said, The Lord – **He** is God; the Lord – **He** is God.

Yet, the initiator and participle may be brought together without the mortar of the separating pronoun, the language of direct, impassioned speech, as the following example illustrates.

Deut 3:21 וְאֶת־יְהוֹשׁוּעַ צִוֵּיתִי בָּעֵת הַהִוא לֵאמֹר עֵינֶיךָ הָרֹאֹת אֵת כָּל־אֲשֶׁר עָשָׂה יְהוָה אֱלֹהֵיכֶם לִשְׁנֵי הַמְּלָכִים הָאֵלֶּה

And Joshua I commanded at that time saying, **Your eyes are the ones seeing** all which the Lord, your God, did to both of these kings.

The construction, "Your eyes are the ones seeing," expresses absolute identification, "Your eyes *exclusively* are the ones seeing."
Deut 4:3; 8:18; 11:7; Isa 14:27

3. Special considerations: *i*
   a) Like other nominal clauses, the participle as an announcement may omit the subject, especially a pronoun, if the context implies it (Ps 16:8). This is common for participles as announcements in הִנֵּה clauses.

      Gen 37:15 וַיִּמְצָאֵהוּ אִישׁ וְהִנֵּה תֹעֶה בַּשָּׂדֶה וַיִּשְׁאָלֵהוּ הָאִישׁ לֵאמֹר מַה־תְּבַקֵּשׁ׃

      And a man found him, **and behold, (he was) a wanderer** in the field, and the man asked him saying, What are you seeking?

      The subject הוּא is implied between הִנֵּה and the participle תֹעֶה.
      Gen 24:30; 41:1; Exod 7:15; 8:16; Num 12:10; 23:6; 1 Sam 20:1; BA Ezra 4:12; 6:3
   b) The participle as an announcement is negated by אֵין (§41z). Gen 41:8, 24, 39; Exod 5:11; 8:17; 1 Sam 19:11; BA Dan 3:14
   c) The participle as an announcement is emphasized by placing the participle before its subject or rarely by a following infinitive absolute. Participle before subject: Gen 3:14; 15:14; 19:13; 29:9, 33; 30:1. Participle followed by infinitive absolute: Josh 6:13; 2 Sam 16:5; 2 Kgs 2:11; Isa 22:17; Jer 23:17; 41:6

B. Genitive (12b, f) *j*

Participles as substantives may be used in the genitive as part of a PROPER or IMPROPER ANNEXATION (§12b, f). In proper annexation, the participle (genitive) and its governing word may be understood by a ל preposition between them or very rarely by a מִן preposition between them, but never by a ב preposition between them.

1. Proper Annexation:

   Lev 21:11[a] וְעַל כָּל־נַפְשֹׁת מֵת לֹא יָבֹא

   And upon all persons **of the dead**, he will not come.

   Deut 33:21; Josh 16:10; Judg 2:14, 1 Sam 17:7

2. Improper Annexation:

   1 Sam 21:16[a] חֲסַר מְשֻׁגָּעִים אָנִי

   Am I lacking **of madmen**

   1 Sam 21:16; Jer 6:28; Ps 72:18; 86:10

k **C. Accusative**

Participles as substantives are used in the accusative as a direct object, as an accusative of situation, or rarely as a substitute for an absolute object. The participle never functions as an accusative of time, place, or specification.

1. Direct object (§13k–u): The participle as the direct object is usually definite. Gen 50:2; Exod 3:16; 12:23; 21:35; 29:34

l 2. ACCUSATIVE OF SITUATION (§13z): As a DESCRIPTIVE NOUN conveying a "*habitual* or *abiding* state or activity," the participle ideally functions as an accusative of situation. Always without the article, the participle as an accusative of situation often resembles the aspect of the imperfect and rarely the aspect of the perfect.

Ps 18:4 מְהֻלָּל אֶקְרָא יְהוָה וּמִן־אֹיְבַי אִוָּשֵׁעַ׃

I call to the Lord, in the status of **one who is to be praised**, and from my enemies I am being saved.

Gen 3:8; 27:6; Exod 2:11; 12:11; 14:9; 33:10; Num 5:21; 8:19; Deut 21:1; Ps 19:11; 76:8

When a participle is a predicate to הָיָה, the participle is an accusative of situation, not a periphrastic verbal construction, as in English (is doing, are making) or in Greek. הָיָה is not equivalent to the English verb "to be."

Exod 3:1[a] וּמֹשֶׁה הָיָה רֹעֶה אֶת־צֹאן

Moses **existed** in the status of **(one who) shepherds** the sheep.

Gen 1:6; 4:2, 17; 21:20; 39:22; 42:31; Exod 19:11; BA Dan 3:25(2x); 4:1

m 3. Substitute for absolute objects (§13h): Consecutive participles, singular and indefinite, rarely substitute for absolute objects.

1 Sam 17:41 וַיֵּלֶךְ הַפְּלִשְׁתִּי הֹלֵךְ וְקָרֵב אֶל־דָּוִד וְהָאִישׁ נֹשֵׂא הַצִּנָּה לְפָנָיו׃

The Philistine went, **drawing ever closer** to David, with the man bearing his shield before him.

Exod 19:19 וַיְהִי קוֹל הַשֹּׁפָר הוֹלֵךְ וְחָזֵק מְאֹד מֹשֶׁה יְדַבֵּר וְהָאֱלֹהִים יַעֲנֶנּוּ בְקוֹל׃

When the sound of the trumpet **grew louder and louder**, Moses spoke and God answered him with thunder.

Gen 26:13[b] וַיֵּלֶךְ הָלוֹךְ וְגָדֵל

And he went, **going and becoming great**.

Notice in Gen 26:13 that the participle substitutes for one of the infinitive absolutes. In the preceding examples, 1 Sam 17:41 and Exod 19:19, the participles (probably accusative of situations) substitute for both infinitive absolutes.

n **D. Participle as an Adjective (Descriptive Noun) in the Nominative, Genitive, and Accusative (§23f–g)**

The participle, when used as an adjective (attributive use of the participle), agrees with its governing noun in number, gender, and case. The attributive participle is often definite.

Adjectival (attributive): This is very common.

וְנָקוּמָה וְנַעֲלֶה בֵּית־אֵל וְאֶעֱשֶׂה־שָּׁם מִזְבֵּחַ לָאֵל הָעֹנֶה אֹתִי
בְּיוֹם צָרָתִי וַיְהִי עִמָּדִי בַּדֶּרֶךְ אֲשֶׁר הָלָכְתִּי׃ Gen 35:3

And let us rise and go up to Bethel that I might make there an altar, to the God **who answered** me in the day of my distress, and He was with me in the path that I have gone.

אֲנִי הָאִשָּׁה הַנִּצֶּבֶת עִמְּכָה בָּזֶה 1 Sam 1:26[b]

I am the woman **who stood** with you here.

In Gen 35:3 and 1 Sam 1:26, the participle has the aspect of the perfect. Gen 1:26, 29 (These two examples have the aspect of the imperfect); 2:9; 3:24; 7:21; 14:19; 15:9(3x); 31:12; Exod 1:1; 11:5; 1 Sam 24:15; BA Dan 3:6; Ezra 4:8

§17. Infinitive Absolute *a*

The infinitive absolute emphasizes the meaning of the verb abstractly. As such, the infinitive absolute is almost always emphatic. Being an abstract verbal noun, the infinitive absolute has nominal (substantive) usages.

A. Nominative

This rare usage, without emphasis and usually confined to poetry and direct speech, functions similar to an English gerund.

אָכֹל דְּבַשׁ הַרְבּוֹת לֹא־טוֹב וְחֵקֶר כְּבֹדָם כָּבוֹד׃ Prov 25:27

Eating much honey is not good. And the search of their own glory is (not) glory.

Job 25:2; Prov 15:22; 28:21

B. Genitive *b*

Like the nominative, this usage is rare, without emphasis, and usually confined to poetry and direct speech.

וְטֵאטֵאתִיהָ בְּמַטְאֲטֵא הַשְׁמֵד נְאֻם יְהוָה צְבָאוֹת׃ Isa 14:23[b]

And I will sweep her with the broom **of destroying**, declares the Lord of hosts.

Ezek 16:49; Prov 1:3; 21:16

C. Accusative *c*

As an accusative, the infinitive absolute expresses the essence of the verbal action purely as an ABSOLUTE OBJECT, either strengthening the verb or expressing the manner of the action adverbially. Rarely and without emphasis, the infinitive absolute may also function as a direct object.

1. Absolute object (§13b–j). The infinitive absolute will usually be the same root as the verb, like a cognate accusative. Occasionally, absolute object constructions are abbreviated with the verb omitted but implied. The infinitive absolute as the absolute object, whether fully expressed or abbreviated, is always emphatic, especially before the perfect or imperfect and after the participle or imperative. They strengthen the verbal idea by intensifying a statement or by intensifying the verbal action. Moreover, they may express the manner of the action, like an adverb. *d*

e a) Strengthening (Emphasizing) the verb[4] (§13c–d)

i. Intensifying a statement (a strong assertion): This infinitive absolute, occurring before the perfect and imperfect but after the imperative and participle, intensifies a statement into a strong assertion (Jer 7:5[2x]; 26:15). This applies to a variety of statements including conditional (Exod 15:26), interrogative (Gen 37:8), causal (Ps 118:13), and adversative statements (2 Sam 24:24). These constructions may be abbreviated by omitting but implying the verb.

Gen 2:17 וּמֵעֵ֗ץ הַדַּ֙עַת֙ ט֣וֹב וָרָ֔ע לֹ֥א תֹאכַ֖ל מִמֶּ֑נּוּ כִּ֗י בְּי֛וֹם אֲכָלְךָ֥ מִמֶּ֖נּוּ מ֥וֹת תָּמֽוּת׃

And from the tree of the knowledge of good and evil you shall not eat, because in the day of your eating from it you shall **surely** die.

In Gen 2:17, the infinitive absolute strengthens the verbal assertion.

f ① Imperative: The imperative is usually omitted but implied.

Isa 6:9 וַיֹּ֕אמֶר לֵ֖ךְ וְאָמַרְתָּ֣ לָעָ֣ם הַזֶּ֑ה שִׁמְע֤וּ שָׁמ֙וֹעַ֙ וְאַל־תָּבִ֔ינוּ וּרְא֥וּ רָא֖וֹ וְאַל־תֵּדָֽעוּ׃

And he said, Go and say to this people, hear **a hearing (hear intently or indeed)**, but do not understand, see **a seeing (see intently or indeed)**, but do not understand.

Deut 1:16 וָאֲצַוֶּה֙ אֶת־שֹׁ֣פְטֵיכֶ֔ם בָּעֵ֥ת הַהִ֖וא לֵאמֹ֑ר שָׁמֹ֤עַ בֵּין־אֲחֵיכֶם֙ וּשְׁפַטְתֶּ֣ם צֶ֔דֶק בֵּין־אִ֥ישׁ וּבֵין־אָחִ֖יו וּבֵ֥ין גֵּרֽוֹ׃

And I commanded your judges at that time saying, **Hear** between your brothers and judge in terms of righteousness between a man and his brother and his sojourner.

In Isa 6:9, the imperative verb is explicit; in Deut 1:16, the imperative is implied before the infinitive absolute (שִׁמְעוּ). Both verses are equally emphatic.

With explicit imperative: Num 11:15; Judg 5:23; Jer 22:10; Job 13:17; 21:2; 37:2; with implied imperative: Exod 13:3; 20:8; Lev 2:6; Num 4:2

g ② Perfect:

1 Sam 2:27 וַיָּבֹ֥א אִישׁ־אֱלֹהִ֖ים אֶל־עֵלִ֑י וַיֹּ֣אמֶר אֵלָ֗יו כֹּ֚ה אָמַ֣ר יְהוָ֔ה הֲנִגְלֹ֤ה נִגְלֵ֙יתִי֙ אֶל־בֵּ֣ית אָבִ֔יךָ בִּֽהְיוֹתָ֥ם בְּמִצְרַ֖יִם לְבֵ֥ית פַּרְעֹֽה׃

4. The categories of "intensifying a statement" and "intensifying the action of the verb" may overlap, with the result that both the statement and the verbal action are intensified. Context determines the suitable interpretation.

1 Sam 2:28a וּבָחֹר אֹתוֹ מִכָּל־שִׁבְטֵי יִשְׂרָאֵל לִי לְכֹהֵן לַעֲלוֹת עַל־מִזְבְּחִי

And the man of God came to Eli and said to him, Thus says the Lord, **Revealing myself** I revealed myself (I indeed revealed myself) to the house of your father while they were in Egypt to the house of Pharaoh. **And choosing** I chose (I indeed chose) him from all the tribes of Israel for myself for a priest to cause to go up upon my altar.

1 Sam 2:27 gives the full absolute object construction; 1 Sam 2:28 abbreviates the construction, both being equally emphatic.

Gen 26:28; 27:30; 30:16; 31:30; 40:15; 43:3, 7, 20; Exod 3:7; 8:11; Lev 5:19; 1 Sam 2:27–28; 20:3, 6, 28; 23:10; Hos 4:2; 10:4

③ Imperfect: *h*

Exod 15:26 וַיֹּאמֶר אִם־שָׁמוֹעַ תִּשְׁמַע לְקוֹל׀ יְהוָה אֱלֹהֶיךָ

And he said, If you will **indeed** hear the voice of the Lord, your God.

2 Kgs 4:43 וַיֹּאמֶר מְשָׁרְתוֹ מָה אֶתֵּן זֶה לִפְנֵי מֵאָה אִישׁ וַיֹּאמֶר תֵּן לָעָם
וְיֹאכֵלוּ כִּי כֹה אָמַר יְהוָה אָכֹל וְהוֹתֵר׃

And his attendant said, How can I give this before a hundred men? And he said, Give to the people that they may eat, for thus says the Lord, **eating they will eat (they will certainly eat) and a leaving over they will have left over (they will certainly have left over)**.

The first verse (Exod 15:26) has the full construction with the imperfect; the second verse (2 Kgs 4:43) abbreviates the construction by implying the imperfect.

Full constructions: Exod 22:16; 23:4; 1 Sam 20:5, 6, 7, 9; 23:22; 2 Kgs 19:29;

Abbreviated constructions: Exod 18:22 (implied indicative); Ezek 21:31 (implied cohortative); Lev 6:7 (implied jussive); Jer 7:9 (6x implied indicatives)

Gen 2:16–17; 15:13; 17:13; 18:10, 18; 28:22; 32:13; 37:8(2x)

ii. Intensifying the action of the verb: This infinitive absolute, usually occurring before the verb, intensifies the force of the verbal action. *i*

Gen 20:18 כִּי־עָצֹר עָצַר יְהוָה בְּעַד כָּל־רֶחֶם לְבֵית אֲבִימֶלֶךְ עַל־
דְּבַר שָׂרָה אֵשֶׁת אַבְרָהָם׃

Because the Lord **closing** (he) closed (the Lord closed firmly and completely) every womb belonging to the house of Abimelech because of Sarah, Abraham's wife.

Judg 15:13[a] וַיֹּאמְרוּ לוֹ לֵאמֹר לֹא כִּי־אָסֹר נֶאֱסָרְךָ וּנְתַנּוּךָ בְיָדָם

And they said to him, No, but **binding** we will bind (we will securely bind) you, and we will give you into their hand. . . .

Gen 37:33; Exod 11:1; 15:26; 17:14; 21:19; 22:16; 23:24(2x); Lev

10:16; Judg 11:35; 15:2; 1 Kgs 19:10

j iii. Explaining the manner or quality of the verb (adverbial, §13e–i): These are often consecutive infinitive absolutes, occurring after the verb.

Jer 22:19 קְבוּרַת חֲמוֹר יִקָּבֵר סָחוֹב וְהַשְׁלֵךְ מֵהָלְאָה לְשַׁעֲרֵי יְרוּשָׁלִָם׃

With the burial of a donkey he will be buried, **a dragging and throwing down** from the outside (with respect) to the gates of Jerusalem.

Gen 8:3[a] וַיָּשֻׁבוּ הַמַּיִם מֵעַל הָאָרֶץ הָלוֹךְ וָשׁוֹב

And the waters returned from upon the earth **a going and a returning**.

A smoother translation renders, "And the waters were continually returning from upon the earth."

Gen 8:5, 7; Josh 6:9; Judg 14:9; 1 Sam 3:12; 17:16; 19:23 (note the Vav-Consecutive substituting for an absolute object); 2 Sam 3:16; 1 Kgs 20:37; Isa 3:16; Jer 12:17

Deut 13:15[a] וְדָרַשְׁתָּ וְחָקַרְתָּ וְשָׁאַלְתָּ הֵיטֵב

And you will **thoroughly** seek, search, and ask.

Rarely, a single infinitive absolute expresses manner or quality of the verbal action.

Deut 17:4; 2 Kgs 11:18

k 2. Direct object

Like the nominative and the genitive, the direct object usage is rare, without emphasis, and usually confined to poetry and direct speech.

Isa 1:17 לִמְדוּ הֵיטֵב דִּרְשׁוּ מִשְׁפָּט אַשְּׁרוּ חָמוֹץ שִׁפְטוּ יָתוֹם רִיבוּ אַלְמָנָה׃

Learn **(the act of) doing good**, seek justice; set straight the ruthless; judge (properly) the orphan; plead for the widow.

§18. Infinitive Construct

a The infinitive construct is not an emphatic form like the infinitive absolute, but its usage is more varied than the infinitive absolute. The infinitive construct functions similarly, but not identically, to the English infinitive. Being an abstract verbal noun, the infinitive construct has nominal (substantive) usages. Commonly, the infinitive construct is used as an accusative of cause/reason or of specification/explanation. Moreover, the infinitive construct, in the position of the genitive annexed to a preposition, expresses cause/reason or specification/explanation. Finally, it may substitute for an accusative of time.

A. Nominative (subject) *b*

Gen 2:18 וַיֹּאמֶר יְהוָה אֱלֹהִים לֹא־טוֹב הֱיוֹת הָאָדָם לְבַדּוֹ אֶעֱשֶׂה־לּוֹ עֵזֶר כְּנֶגְדּוֹ׃

And the Lord God said, **(the) existing** of man alone is not good; I will make him a helper corresponding to him.

Gen 29:7; 30:15; Exod 14:12; 1 Sam 15:22 (שׁמע)

B. Genitive *c*

1. Without a preposition (§79b):

These constructions are often equivalent to temporal clauses.

Gen 2:17 וּמֵעֵץ הַדַּעַת טוֹב וָרָע לֹא תֹאכַל מִמֶּנּוּ כִּי בְּיוֹם אֲכָלְךָ מִמֶּנּוּ מוֹת תָּמוּת׃

And from the tree of the knowledge of good and evil you shall not eat, because in the day of **your eating (when you eat)** from it you shall surely die.

Gen 2:4; 5:1; 30:41; Exod 12:4; 32:18; Lev 12:2; 25:50

2. With a preposition (§79a; 78c, g, h) *d*

These constructions substitute for an adverbial accusative construction.

a) Temporal clause

The prepositions ב and כ connected with an infinitive construct usually translate, "when" or "as." הָיָה often provides the context for the tense of the infinitive construct. The notion of "before" is usually לִפְנֵי (or אֲשֶׁר לִפְנֵי) with the infinitive construct; "after" is אַחֲרֵי or אַחַר (or אֲשֶׁר אַחֲרֵי) with the infinitive construct; "until" is עַד (or אֲשֶׁר עַד) with the infinitive construct. These prepositional phrases substitute for an accusative of time, answering the question "when."

Gen 29:13[a] וַיְהִי כִשְׁמֹעַ לָבָן אֶת־שֵׁמַע יַעֲקֹב בֶּן־אֲחֹתוֹ וַיָּרָץ לִקְרָאתוֹ

And it happened, **when** Laban **heard** the report of Jacob, the son of his sister, that he ran to meet him.

Gen 13:10 וַיִּשָּׂא־לוֹט אֶת־עֵינָיו וַיַּרְא אֶת־כָּל־כִּכַּר הַיַּרְדֵּן כִּי כֻלָּהּ מַשְׁקֶה לִפְנֵי שַׁחֵת יְהוָה אֶת־סְדֹם וְאֶת־עֲמֹרָה כְּגַן־יְהוָה כְּאֶרֶץ מִצְרַיִם בֹּאֲכָה צֹעַר׃

And Lot lifted up his eyes and he saw all the plain of the Jordan (for all of it was watered) **before** the Lord **destroyed** Sodom and Gomorrah, as the garden of the Lord, as the land of Egypt.

Gen 2:4; 4:8; 5:7, 10; 8:7; 9:14; 11:2; 12:14; 13:10; 19:17, 22; 24:30(2x); 36:31; Exod 3:12; 1 Sam 2:6; 9:15; 23:6

b) Reason/Cause/Motive clause (§52; 53f) *e*

Commonly, the prepositions לְ, לְמַעַן, בַּעֲבוּר, יַעַן, or עַל with the infinitive construct expresses the reason, cause, motive, or purpose of the verbal action, answering the questions "why," or "for what reason/cause/purpose."

וַיֵּ֣רֶד יְהוָ֔ה לִרְאֹ֥ת אֶת־הָעִ֖יר וְאֶת־הַמִּגְדָּ֑ל אֲשֶׁ֥ר בָּנ֖וּ בְּנֵ֥י הָאָדָֽם׃ Gen 11:5

The Lord came down **(for the reason, purpose, intent of) seeing** the city and tower.

Exod 16:3; 23:1; 1 Sam 20:24, 33; 23:8(2x); Ezra 7:10; BA Ezra 5:3; 6:12(2x)

f c) Specification/Explanation[5]

These constructions limit and explain the verbal action or nominal statement. The verb expresses a general concept, and the infinitive construct *with* the preposition (לְ) narrows, limits, specifies, and thereby explains the general concept. This is common with:

i. Verbs that (usually) require an infinitive to complete/explain their meaning, such as verbs of willing, wishing, beginning, continuing, increasing, adding, completing, ceasing, hastening, being able, seeking, allowing, permitting, and doing again (return):

פֶּן־יֹסִ֗יף לְהַכֹּת֤וֹ עַל־אֵ֙לֶּה֙ מַכָּ֣ה רַבָּ֔ה Deut 25:3[b]

Lest he should add **(in terms of, in the sense of) striking him** upon these (forty) with a great striking.

The verb "add" is the general concept that the infinitive construct "to strike" specifies or explains.

לֹ֥א אָשׁ֖וּב לְשַׁחֵ֣ת אֶפְרָ֑יִם Hos 11:9[a]

I will not return **to destroy** Ephraim. (I will not destroy Ephraim again.)

Gen 4:2; 10:8; 18:27, 31; Exod 2:3, 18, 21; Deut 1:41; 1 Sam 19:8; BA Ezra 4:22; Dan 3:13, 32; 5:16, 20

g ii. Some stative verbs in the Hiphil, such as to be great, low, high, distant, deep, good, many, early, etc.:

הִרְבָּ֗ה לַעֲשׂ֥וֹת הָרַ֛ע בְּעֵינֵ֥י יְהוָ֖ה לְהַכְעִֽיס׃ 2 Kgs 12:6[b]

He has done much **(in terms of, in the sense of) doing** evil in the eyes of the Lord.

In 2 Kgs 21:6, the infinitive construct explains and limits the verb, "done much."

Gen 12:11; Exod 8:24; 1 Sam 16:17; 2 Kgs 2:10; 10:30; Jer 1:12

h iii. Any verb or nominal statement that needs specification or explanation:[6]

5. Strictly speaking, specification has to be a primary noun, not an infinitive, but the infinitive is "in the place of a specification" or substitutes for a specification since it limits and explains the verb (§13jj).

6. Explanation may often be expressed by the gerund: by asking, by eating, by ceasing. For example, "The people are sinning against the Lord by eating with the blood" (1 Sam 14:33).

1 Sam 12:17[b] וּדְעוּ וּרְאוּ כִּי־רָעַתְכֶם רַבָּה אֲשֶׁר עֲשִׂיתֶם בְּעֵינֵי יְהוָה לִשְׁאוֹל לָכֶם מֶלֶךְ׃

And know and see that your evil is great which you have done in the eyes of the Lord **(in terms of, in the sense of) asking** for yourselves a king.

1 Sam 14:33[a] וַיַּגִּידוּ לְשָׁאוּל לֵאמֹר הִנֵּה הָעָם חֹטְאִים לַיהוָה לֶאֱכֹל עַל־הַדָּם

And they reported to Saul saying, behold the people are sinning against the Lord **(in the sense of, in terms of) eating** with the blood.

1 Sam 12:23 גַּם אָנֹכִי חָלִילָה לִּי מֵחֲטֹא לַיהוָה מֵחֲדֹל לְהִתְפַּלֵּל בַּעַדְכֶם וְהוֹרֵיתִי אֶתְכֶם בְּדֶרֶךְ הַטּוֹבָה וְהַיְשָׁרָה׃

Moreover, as for me, far be it from me that I should sin against the Lord by ceasing **to pray** for you; but I will instruct you in the good and right way.

Exod 3:6; 5:2; 7:18; 8:24; 10:16; 12:4, 33(2x); 13:15; 14:11; 16:1, 28; 19:12(2x); Num 6:2; 14:44; 22:30; Deut 18:20; Judg 12:6; 1 Sam 19:2, 5, 10, 11; 20:33; 23:7, 28; 1 Kgs 14:9

d) Situation (§13z) *i*

The infinitive construct with ל preposition occasionally substitutes for an ACCUSATIVE OF SITUATION after הָיָה.

Josh 2:5[a] וַיְהִי הַשַּׁעַר לִסְגּוֹר בַּחֹשֶׁךְ וְהָאֲנָשִׁים יָצָאוּ

And the gate existed **(in the condition) of shutting** (The gate was about to be shut), at dark, that the men went out.

Gen 15:12[a] וַיְהִי הַשֶּׁמֶשׁ לָבוֹא

And the sun existed **(in the condition) of setting**. (The sun was about to set.)

Num 8:11; Isa 5:5; 37:26; Ezek 30:16

C. Accusative *j*

These usages are the same as the genitive with the preposition except the infinitives are without a preposition, and therefore, in the accusative. The genitive constructions are more common than the accusative constructions.

1. Direct object

Gen 21:6 וַתֹּאמֶר שָׂרָה צְחֹק עָשָׂה לִי אֱלֹהִים כָּל־הַשֹּׁמֵעַ יִצְחַק־לִי׃

And Sarah said, **A laughing** God has done for me; everyone who hears will laugh with me.

1 Kgs 3:7 וְעַתָּה יְהוָה אֱלֹהָי אַתָּה הִמְלַכְתָּ אֶת־עַבְדְּךָ תַּחַת דָּוִד אָבִי וְאָנֹכִי נַעַר קָטֹן לֹא אֵדַע צֵאת וָבֹא׃

And now, O Lord my God, You have made your servant king in place of my father David, yet I am but a little child. I do not know **how to go out or come in**.

Num 10:31

k 2. Adverbial Accusative

a) Reason/Cause/Motive clause (§52; 53f)

As an accusative, this construction is rare. Exod 4:24; Ezek 7:14

l b) Specification/Explanation[7]

These constructions limit and explain the verbal action or nominal statement. The verb expresses a general concept, and the infinitive construct *without* the preposition ל narrows, limits, specifies, and thereby explains the verb. This is common with:

i. Verbs that (usually) require an infinitive to complete/explain their meaning, such as verbs of willing, wishing, beginning, continuing, increasing, adding, completing, ceasing, hastening, being able (having power), seeking, allowing, permitting, and doing again (return):

בְּיֶדְכֶם נָתַן אֱלֹהִים אֶת־שָׂרֵי מִדְיָן אֶת־עֹרֵב וְאֶת־זְאֵב וּמַה־יָּכֹלְתִּי עֲשׂוֹת כָּכֶם — Judg 8:3[a]

In your hand God has given the leaders of Midian, Oreb and Ze'eb, and how do I have power **(in terms of) doing** like you.

וַיֹּאמֶר מֹשֶׁה כֵּן דִּבַּרְתָּ לֹא־אֹסִף עוֹד רְאוֹת פָּנֶיךָ׃ — Exod 10:29

And Moses said, Thus you have spoken, I will not add again **(in terms of, in the sense of) seeing** your face.

כִּי עַם מְרִי הוּא בָּנִים כֶּחָשִׁים בָּנִים לֹא־אָבוּ שְׁמוֹעַ תּוֹרַת יְהוָה׃ — Isa 30:9

For this is a rebellious people, false sons. Sons who refuse **to listen** to the instruction of the Lord.

Gen 4:12; 8:10; Exod 10:28; Deut 2:25, 31; Josh 3:7; Isa 24:20

m ii. Some stative verbs in the Hiphil, such as to be great, low, high, distant, deep, good, many, early, etc.:

הֵיטִיבִי נַגֵּן — Isa 23:16[b]

Do good **(in terms of, in the sense of) stringing (the instrument)**.

Gen 4:7; 31:28; Ezek 33:32; Micah 6:8, 13; Ps 55:8

n iii. Any verb or nominal statement that needs specification or explanation:

הִנֵּה לֹא־יָדַעְתִּי דַּבֵּר — Jer 1:6[a]

Behold I do not know **how to speak**.

o iv. A finite verb (with or without a Vav) may substitute for the infinitive construct of specification/explanation.

וַיּוֹסֶף עוֹד יִפְתָּח וַיִּשְׁלַח מַלְאָכִים — Judg 11:14

And Jephthah added again **and he sent** (And Jephthah sent again) messengers.

7. See footnote 5.

The second verb (sent) substitutes or stands in the place of an infinitive construct of specification/explanation. Compare this construction with the following infinitive construction.

וַיֹּסֶף עוֹד בָּלָק שְׁלֹחַ Num 22:15

And Balak added again **to send** (And Balak sent again).

Compare the following two verses that are similar in meaning. Deut 1:43 has two verbs; Deut 18:20 has a verb with an infinitive construct.

וַתָּזִדוּ וַתַּעֲלוּ הָהָרָה׃ Deut 1:43[b]

And you acted presumptuously and you went up (You acted presumptuously by going up) to the mountain.

אַךְ הַנָּבִיא אֲשֶׁר יָזִיד לְדַבֵּר דָּבָר בִּשְׁמִי Deut 18:20[a]

Indeed, a prophet who **acts presumptuously to speak** a word in my name.

When consecutive verbs refer to the same action and the second verb specifies or explains the first verb (you acted presumptuously by going up), the second verb substitutes for the infinitive construct of specification/explanation.

Gen 30:31; Num 13:20; 1 Sam 3:2; 19:21; 1 Kgs 8:47; 2 Kgs 21:6.

D. Negation of Infinitive Constructs (§52d) *p*

The particles (לְ)בִלְתִּי or אֵין (Eccl 3:14) negate the infinitive construct.

וַיָּשֶׂם יְהוָה לְקַיִן אוֹת לְבִלְתִּי הַכּוֹת־אֹתוֹ כָּל־מֹצְאוֹ׃ Gen 4:15[b]

And the Lord placed to Cain a mark **not to kill** him everyone who finds him (so that everyone who finds him will not kill him).

Gen 3:11; 19:21; 38:9; Exod 8:18, 25; 9:17

Exercises

I. Questions and Discussions

1. List and define the verbal nouns.
2. Which verbal nouns are abstract or concrete? Provide a translation that distinguishes between abstract and concrete verbal nouns.
3. Which verbal noun is also known as the "noun of the agent"? Why is it called the "noun of the agent"?
4. Which verbal form does the participle resemble? Why?
5. How does the participle differ from a verb? How is it similar to a verb?
6. How does the participle differ from a noun? How is it similar to a noun?
7. Ultimately, should the participle be viewed as a noun or verb? Why?
8. When a form may be parsed as either a verb or a participle, how can it be determined if the form is a verb or participle?
9. Compare and contrast the participle with the imperfect.
10. Discuss the uses of participles in the nominative as the subject.
11. Which verbal form does the participle, as subject and predicate, usually resemble in aspect when it has the article and when it does not have the article?
12. Discuss the variety of clauses where the participle may occur as a predicate.
13. When may participles omit their subjects?
14. How is a participle negated? How is it emphasized?
15. When the participle is in the genitive and in proper annexation, which prepositions may be implied between the participle and its governing noun? Which preposition may not be implied?
16. Discuss the uses of the participle in the accusative. Which uses have the article? Which do not have the article?
17. As an attributive adjective (descriptive noun), the participle agrees with its noun on what grammatical levels?
18. In which case (nominative, genitive, or accusative) may the infinitive absolute be emphatic? In which cases is it not emphatic?
19. Define absolute object. List and define the three uses of the absolute object. Which absolute objects precede their verbs, and which absolute objects follow their verbs?
20. How may the absolute object construction be "abbreviated"?
21. What is the difference between an "intensifying a statement" and "intensifying the action of the verb" for the absolute object?
22. How do the infinitive construct and absolute differ in emphasis?
23. What determines whether an infinitive construct is in the genitive or in the accusative?
24. Discuss the uses of the infinitive construct in the genitive and in the accusative.
25. What kind of verbs are used when the infinitive construct expresses specification/explanation?
26. How are infinitive constructs negated?

II. Drills

1. **In the following verses, there are words that may be parsed as a participle or a perfect. Determine whether the form is a participle or a perfect and justify your answer. The verses follow the numbering of the Masoretic Text.**

1 Sam 3:15 (1) וַיִּשְׁכַּב שְׁמוּאֵל֙ עַד־הַבֹּ֔קֶר וַיִּפְתַּ֖ח אֶת־דַּלְת֣וֹת בֵּית־יְהוָ֑ה וּשְׁמוּאֵל֙ יָרֵ֔א
מֵהַגִּ֥יד אֶת־הַמַּרְאָ֖ה אֶל־עֵלִֽי׃

Prov 26:11 (2) כְּ֭כֶלֶב שָׁ֣ב עַל־קֵא֑וֹ כְּ֝סִ֗יל שׁוֹנֶ֥ה בְאִוַּלְתּֽוֹ׃

Gen 19:30 (3) וַיַּעַל֩ ל֨וֹט מִצּ֜וֹעַר וַיֵּ֣שֶׁב בָּהָ֗ר וּשְׁתֵּ֤י בְנֹתָיו֙ עִמּ֔וֹ כִּ֥י יָרֵ֖א לָשֶׁ֣בֶת בְּצ֑וֹעַר
וַיֵּ֙שֶׁב֙ בַּמְּעָרָ֔ה ה֖וּא וּשְׁתֵּ֥י בְנֹתָֽיו׃

Gen 18:33 (4) וַיֵּ֣לֶךְ יְהוָ֔ה כַּאֲשֶׁ֣ר כִּלָּ֔ה לְדַבֵּ֖ר אֶל־אַבְרָהָ֑ם וְאַבְרָהָ֖ם שָׁ֥ב לִמְקֹמֽוֹ׃

Judg 3:19 (5) וְה֣וּא שָׁ֗ב מִן־הַפְּסִילִים֙ אֲשֶׁ֣ר אֶת־הַגִּלְגָּ֔ל וַיֹּ֕אמֶר דְּבַר־סֵ֥תֶר לִ֛י אֵלֶ֖יךָ
הַמֶּ֑לֶךְ וַיֹּ֣אמֶר הָ֔ס וַיֵּצְאוּ֙ מֵֽעָלָ֔יו כָּל־הָעֹמְדִ֖ים עָלָֽיו׃

Gen 33:1 (6) וַיִּשָּׂ֨א יַעֲקֹ֜ב עֵינָ֗יו וַיַּרְא֙ וְהִנֵּ֣ה עֵשָׂ֣ו בָּ֔א וְעִמּ֕וֹ אַרְבַּ֥ע מֵא֖וֹת אִ֑ישׁ וַיַּ֣חַץ
אֶת־הַיְלָדִ֗ים עַל־לֵאָה֙ וְעַל־רָחֵ֔ל וְעַ֖ל שְׁתֵּ֥י הַשְּׁפָחֽוֹת׃

Gen 37:30 (7) וַיָּ֥שָׁב אֶל־אֶחָ֖יו וַיֹּאמַ֑ר הַיֶּ֣לֶד אֵינֶ֔נּוּ וַאֲנִ֖י אָ֥נָה אֲנִי־בָֽא׃

1 Sam 15:11 (8) נִחַ֗מְתִּי כִּֽי־הִמְלַ֤כְתִּי אֶת־שָׁאוּל֙ לְמֶ֔לֶךְ כִּֽי־שָׁב֙ מֵאַחֲרַ֔י וְאֶת־דְּבָרַ֖י לֹ֣א
הֵקִ֑ים וַיִּ֙חַר֙ לִשְׁמוּאֵ֔ל וַיִּזְעַ֥ק אֶל־יְהוָ֖ה כָּל־הַלָּֽיְלָה׃

Judg 9:37 (9) וַיֹּ֨סֶף ע֣וֹד גַּ֘עַל֮ לְדַבֵּר֒ וַיֹּ֗אמֶר הִנֵּה־עָם֙ יוֹרְדִ֔ים מֵעִ֖ם טַבּ֣וּר הָאָ֑רֶץ
וְרֹאשׁ־אֶחָ֣ד בָּ֔א מִדֶּ֖רֶךְ אֵל֥וֹן מְעוֹנְנִֽים׃

Gen 24:1 (10) וְאַבְרָהָ֣ם זָקֵ֔ן בָּ֖א בַּיָּמִ֑ים וַיהוָ֛ה בֵּרַ֥ךְ אֶת־אַבְרָהָ֖ם בַּכֹּֽל׃

2. **Label the clauses in which the participle as predicate (announcement) occurs.**

Exod 9:3 (1) הִנֵּ֨ה יַד־יְהוָ֜ה הוֹיָ֗ה בְּמִקְנְךָ֙ אֲשֶׁ֣ר בַּשָּׂדֶ֔ה בַּסּוּסִ֤ים בַּחֲמֹרִים֙ בַּגְּמַלִּ֔ים
בַּבָּקָ֖ר וּבַצֹּ֑אן דֶּ֖בֶר כָּבֵ֥ד מְאֹֽד׃

Gen 15:12 (2) וַיְהִ֤י הַשֶּׁ֙מֶשׁ֙ לָב֔וֹא וְתַרְדֵּמָ֖ה נָפְלָ֣ה עַל־אַבְרָ֑ם וְהִנֵּ֥ה אֵימָ֛ה חֲשֵׁכָ֥ה גְדֹלָ֖ה
נֹפֶ֥לֶת עָלָֽיו׃

Gen 29:31 (3) וַיַּ֤רְא יְהוָה֙ כִּֽי־שְׂנוּאָ֣ה לֵאָ֔ה וַיִּפְתַּ֖ח אֶת־רַחְמָ֑הּ וְרָחֵ֖ל עֲקָרָֽה׃

1 Sam 10:5 (4) אַחַר כֵּן תָּבוֹא גִּבְעַת הָאֱלֹהִים אֲשֶׁר־שָׁם נְצִבֵי פְלִשְׁתִּים וִיהִי כְבֹאֲךָ שָׁם הָעִיר וּפָגַעְתָּ חֶבֶל נְבִיאִים יֹרְדִים מֵהַבָּמָה וְלִפְנֵיהֶם נֵבֶל וְתֹף וְחָלִיל וְכִנּוֹר וְהֵמָּה מִתְנַבְּאִים׃

1 Sam 24:10 (5) וַיֹּאמֶר דָּוִד לְשָׁאוּל לָמָּה תִשְׁמַע אֶת־דִּבְרֵי אָדָם לֵאמֹר הִנֵּה דָוִד מְבַקֵּשׁ רָעָתֶךָ׃

Gen 41:25 (6) וַיֹּאמֶר יוֹסֵף אֶל־פַּרְעֹה חֲלוֹם פַּרְעֹה אֶחָד הוּא אֵת אֲשֶׁר הָאֱלֹהִים עֹשֶׂה הִגִּיד לְפַרְעֹה׃

Exod 5:16 (7) תֶּבֶן אֵין נִתָּן לַעֲבָדֶיךָ וּלְבֵנִים אֹמְרִים לָנוּ עֲשׂוּ וְהִנֵּה עֲבָדֶיךָ מֻכִּים וְחָטָאת עַמֶּךָ׃

Deut 4:3 (8) עֵינֵיכֶם הָרֹאֹת אֵת אֲשֶׁר־עָשָׂה יְהוָה בְּבַעַל פְּעוֹר כִּי כָל־הָאִישׁ אֲשֶׁר הָלַךְ אַחֲרֵי בַעַל־פְּעוֹר הִשְׁמִידוֹ יְהוָה אֱלֹהֶיךָ מִקִּרְבֶּךָ׃

1 Sam 6:13 (9) וּבֵית שֶׁמֶשׁ קֹצְרִים קְצִיר־חִטִּים בָּעֵמֶק וַיִּשְׂאוּ אֶת־עֵינֵיהֶם וַיִּרְאוּ אֶת־הָאָרוֹן וַיִּשְׂמְחוּ לִרְאוֹת׃

1 Sam 6:12 (10) וַיִּשַּׁרְנָה הַפָּרוֹת בַּדֶּרֶךְ עַל־דֶּרֶךְ בֵּית שֶׁמֶשׁ בִּמְסִלָּה אַחַת הָלְכוּ הָלֹךְ וְגָעוֹ וְלֹא־סָרוּ יָמִין וּשְׂמֹאול וְסַרְנֵי פְלִשְׁתִּים הֹלְכִים אַחֲרֵיהֶם עַד־גְּבוּל בֵּית שָׁמֶשׁ׃

3. **Label the case and usage of the following participles.**

Gen 21:9 (1) וַתֵּרֶא שָׂרָה אֶת־בֶּן־הָגָר הַמִּצְרִית אֲשֶׁר־יָלְדָה לְאַבְרָהָם מְצַחֵק׃

Judg 5:11 (2) מִקּוֹל מְחַצְצִים בֵּין מַשְׁאַבִּים שָׁם יְתַנּוּ צִדְקוֹת יְהוָה צִדְקֹת פִּרְזוֹנוֹ בְּיִשְׂרָאֵל אָז יָרְדוּ לַשְּׁעָרִים עַם־יְהוָה׃

Lev 14:8 (3) וְכִבֶּס הַמִּטַּהֵר אֶת־בְּגָדָיו וְגִלַּח אֶת־כָּל־שְׂעָרוֹ וְרָחַץ בַּמַּיִם וְטָהֵר וְאַחַר יָבוֹא אֶל־הַמַּחֲנֶה וְיָשַׁב מִחוּץ לְאָהֳלוֹ שִׁבְעַת יָמִים׃

Gen 24:30 (4) וַיְהִי כִּרְאֹת אֶת־הַנֶּזֶם וְאֶת־הַצְּמִדִים עַל־יְדֵי אֲחֹתוֹ וּכְשָׁמְעוֹ אֶת־דִּבְרֵי רִבְקָה אֲחֹתוֹ לֵאמֹר כֹּה־דִבֶּר אֵלַי הָאִישׁ וַיָּבֹא אֶל־הָאִישׁ וְהִנֵּה עֹמֵד עַל־הַגְּמַלִּים עַל־הָעָיִן׃

Exod 5:6 (5) וַיְצַו פַּרְעֹה בַּיּוֹם הַהוּא אֶת־הַנֹּגְשִׂים בָּעָם וְאֶת־שֹׁטְרָיו לֵאמֹר׃

Gen 4:12 (6) כִּי תַעֲבֹד אֶת־הָאֲדָמָה לֹא־תֹסֵף תֵּת־כֹּחָהּ לָךְ נָע וָנָד תִּהְיֶה בָאָֽרֶץ׃

Exod 30:35 (7) וְעָשִׂיתָ אֹתָהּ קְטֹרֶת רֹקַח מַעֲשֵׂה רוֹקֵחַ מְמֻלָּח טָהוֹר קֹֽדֶשׁ׃

Deut 28:25 (8) יִתֶּנְךָ יְהוָה נִגָּף לִפְנֵי אֹיְבֶיךָ בְּדֶרֶךְ אֶחָד תֵּצֵא אֵלָיו וּבְשִׁבְעָה דְרָכִים תָּנוּס לְפָנָיו וְהָיִיתָ לְזַעֲוָה לְכֹל מַמְלְכוֹת הָאָֽרֶץ׃

Gen 3:24 (9) וַיְגָרֶשׁ אֶת־הָאָדָם וַיַּשְׁכֵּן מִקֶּדֶם לְגַן־עֵדֶן אֶת־הַכְּרֻבִים וְאֵת לַהַט הַחֶרֶב הַמִּתְהַפֶּכֶת לִשְׁמֹר אֶת־דֶּרֶךְ עֵץ הַחַיִּֽים׃

Exod 5:20 (10) וַֽיִּפְגְּעוּ אֶת־מֹשֶׁה וְאֶת־אַהֲרֹן נִצָּבִים לִקְרָאתָם בְּצֵאתָם מֵאֵת פַּרְעֹֽה׃

4. **Label the usage of the absolute object.**

Exod 21:17 (1) וּמְקַלֵּל אָבִיו וְאִמּוֹ מוֹת יוּמָֽת׃

Gen 37:8 (2) וַיֹּאמְרוּ לוֹ אֶחָיו הֲמָלֹךְ תִּמְלֹךְ עָלֵינוּ אִם־מָשׁוֹל תִּמְשֹׁל בָּנוּ וַיּוֹסִפוּ עוֹד שְׂנֹא אֹתוֹ עַל־חֲלֹמֹתָיו וְעַל־דְּבָרָֽיו׃

Gen 12:9 (3) וַיִּסַּע אַבְרָם הָלוֹךְ וְנָסוֹעַ הַנֶּֽגְבָּה׃

Exod 15:1 (4) אָז יָשִׁיר־מֹשֶׁה וּבְנֵי יִשְׂרָאֵל אֶת־הַשִּׁירָה הַזֹּאת לַיהוָה וַיֹּאמְרוּ לֵאמֹר אָשִׁירָה לַיהוָה כִּי־גָאֹה גָּאָה סוּס וְרֹכְבוֹ רָמָה בַיָּֽם׃

Exod 18:18 (5) נָבֹל תִּבֹּל גַּם־אַתָּה גַּם־הָעָם הַזֶּה אֲשֶׁר עִמָּךְ כִּי־כָבֵד מִמְּךָ הַדָּבָר לֹא־תוּכַל עֲשֹׂהוּ לְבַדֶּֽךָ׃

1 Sam 6:12 (6) וַיִּשַּׁרְנָה הַפָּרוֹת בַּדֶּרֶךְ עַל־דֶּרֶךְ בֵּית שֶׁמֶשׁ בִּמְסִלָּה אַחַת הָלְכוּ הָלֹךְ וְגָעוֹ וְלֹא־סָרוּ יָמִין וּשְׂמֹאול וְסַרְנֵי פְלִשְׁתִּים הֹלְכִים אַחֲרֵיהֶם עַד־גְּבוּל בֵּית שָֽׁמֶשׁ׃

Judg 5:23 (7) אוֹרוּ מֵרוֹז אָמַר מַלְאַךְ יְהוָה אֹרוּ אָרוֹר יֹשְׁבֶיהָ כִּי לֹא־בָאוּ לְעֶזְרַת יְהוָה לְעֶזְרַת יְהוָה בַּגִּבּוֹרִֽים׃

1 Sam 1:10 (8) וְהִיא מָרַת נָפֶשׁ וַתִּתְפַּלֵּל עַל־יְהוָה וּבָכֹה תִבְכֶּֽה׃

5. **Label the case and type of clause of the infinitive construct.**

1 Sam 19:1 (1) וַיְדַבֵּר שָׁאוּל אֶל־יוֹנָתָן בְּנוֹ וְאֶל־כָּל־עֲבָדָיו לְהָמִית אֶת־דָּוִד וִיהוֹנָתָן בֶּן־שָׁאוּל חָפֵץ בְּדָוִד מְאֹֽד׃

Gen 10:8 (2) וְכ֖וּשׁ יָלַ֣ד אֶת־נִמְרֹ֑ד ה֣וּא הֵחֵ֔ל לִהְי֥וֹת גִּבֹּ֖ר בָּאָֽרֶץ׃

Gen 5:4 (3) וַיִּֽהְי֣וּ יְמֵי־אָדָ֗ם אַֽחֲרֵי֙ הוֹלִיד֣וֹ אֶת־שֵׁ֔ת שְׁמֹנֶ֥ה מֵאֹ֖ת שָׁנָ֑ה וַיּ֥וֹלֶד בָּנִ֖ים וּבָנֽוֹת׃

Exod 23:1 (4) לֹ֥א תִשָּׂ֖א שֵׁ֣מַע שָׁ֑וְא אַל־תָּ֤שֶׁת יָֽדְךָ֙ עִם־רָשָׁ֔ע לִהְיֹ֖ת עֵ֥ד חָמָֽס׃

Judg 3:4 (5) וַֽיִּהְי֔וּ לְנַסּ֥וֹת בָּ֖ם אֶת־יִשְׂרָאֵ֑ל לָדַ֗עַת הֲיִשְׁמְעוּ֙ אֶת־מִצְוֺ֣ת יְהוָ֔ה אֲשֶׁר־צִוָּ֥ה אֶת־אֲבוֹתָ֖ם בְּיַד־מֹשֶֽׁה׃

Exod 3:19 (6) וַאֲנִ֣י יָדַ֔עְתִּי כִּ֠י לֹֽא־יִתֵּ֥ן אֶתְכֶ֛ם מֶ֥לֶךְ מִצְרַ֖יִם לַהֲלֹ֑ךְ וְלֹ֖א בְּיָ֥ד חֲזָקָֽה׃

Deut 2:31 (7) וַיֹּ֣אמֶר יְהוָה֮ אֵלַי֒ רְאֵ֗ה הַחִלֹּ֙תִי֙ תֵּ֣ת לְפָנֶ֔יךָ אֶת־סִיחֹ֖ן וְאֶת־אַרְצ֑וֹ הָחֵ֣ל רָ֔שׁ לָרֶ֖שֶׁת אֶת־אַרְצֽוֹ׃

Gen 3:19 (8) בְּזֵעַ֤ת אַפֶּ֙יךָ֙ תֹּ֣אכַל לֶ֔חֶם עַ֤ד שֽׁוּבְךָ֙ אֶל־הָ֣אֲדָמָ֔ה כִּ֥י מִמֶּ֖נָּה לֻקָּ֑חְתָּ כִּֽי־עָפָ֣ר אַ֔תָּה וְאֶל־עָפָ֖ר תָּשֽׁוּב׃

Mic 6:13 (9) וְגַם־אֲנִ֖י הֶחֱלֵ֣יתִי הַכּוֹתֶ֑ךָ הַשְׁמֵ֖ם עַל־חַטֹּאתֶֽךָ׃

1 Sam 19:15 (10) וַיִּשְׁלַ֤ח שָׁאוּל֙ אֶת־הַמַּלְאָכִ֔ים לִרְא֥וֹת אֶת־דָּוִ֖ד לֵאמֹ֑ר הַעֲל֨וּ אֹת֥וֹ בַמִּטָּ֛ה אֵלַ֖י לַהֲמִתֽוֹ׃

Chapter 5
PERSONAL AND DEMONSTRATIVE PRONOUNS

§19. Personal Pronouns *a*

Personal pronouns substitute for SUBSTANTIVES in the first, second, or third person. Personal pronouns may be implicit as in the third masculine singular of the perfect or explicit as in the first common singular of the perfect. Personal pronouns may attach to verbs, nouns, or particles, or they may be independent words. Personal pronouns were uninflected, like a particle, even during the pre-Biblical Hebrew era, though they stood in the place of the nominative, genitive, and accusative in the pre-Biblical Hebrew and Biblical Hebrew eras. Sometimes, of course, a masculine pronoun may refer to a feminine substantive and a plural pronoun may refer to a singular substantive, especially a collective noun.

A. Attached Pronouns *b*

1. Attached pronouns must connect to the end of their verb,[1] noun, or particle. Although connected to the first word in a clause, the attached pronoun cannot be the first word of a clause because it attaches to the end of its word. The suffixed pronoun of nouns and verbs, therefore, cannot be the subject of a nominal clause since it never stands first in a clause.
2. Subject (agent) pronouns suffixed to the perfect, imperfect, or imperative are in the nominative case.
3. Pronouns suffixed to nouns, including prepositions, are in the genitive case. In PROPER ANNEXATION, the attached suffix on the genitive may be translated in a variety of ways: Isa 56:7 "in the house of the prayer of me" (בְּבֵ֣ית תְּפִלָּתִ֔י) may be rendered "in my prayer house," "in my house of prayer," or "the house of my prayer." In Ps 18:47, "the God of the salvation of me" (אֱלוֹהֵ֥י יִשְׁעִֽי׃) may be rendered similar to the previous example ("my saving God," "my God of salvation," or "the God of my salvation"), but since the noun "salvation" is related to a verb, it may also be rendered, "the God (who) saves me." The attached suffix often refers to the entire annexation. Pronouns with prepositions may have a reflexive nuance (Jer 7:19).
4. Object pronouns suffixed to the perfect, imperfect, imperative, and some particles, such as הִנֵּה, are in the accusative case. *c*
5. In direct speech and poetry, object pronouns tend to attach directly to their verbs instead of being attached to the אֵת particle. The suffix attached to the אֵת particle may express a reflexive nuance (Ezek 29:3).
6. If two verbs (or verbal nouns) have the same object, the attached pronoun of the second verb, expected in English, is often omitted.

---

1. Preformatives of the imperfect are not pronouns, but are particles indicating the imperfect. These preformatives substitute for pronouns. The pronouns of the imperfect are the suffixes of the 2fs and 2, 3fp forms. The Vav of plurality in the 2, 3mp also implies a pronoun (§4a).

וַיְשַׁלְּחוּ אֶת־כְּתֹנֶת הַפַּסִּים וַיָּבִיאוּ אֶל־אֲבִיהֶם Gen 37:32[a]

And they sent **the tunic of many colors** and they brought **(it)** to their father.

Exod 2:17; BA Ezra 7:10 (infinitives)

d 7. The attached pronoun of הִנֵּה before a participle may also be omitted if the identity of the subject is clear from the context.

וַיִּמְצָאֵהוּ אִישׁ וְהִנֵּה תֹעֶה בַּשָּׂדֶה Gen 37:15[a]

And a man found him, and behold (**he** was) a wanderer in the field.

Ezek 37:11; 39:8; Amos 4:13; 7:1; Mal 3:1

8. The first person singular pronoun has two forms: ִי and נִי. The second form has a PROTECTIVE NUN which protects other grammatical forms from confusion, especially with second feminine singular verbal forms. The protective Nun also occurs with the particle הִנֵּה (הִנְּנִי/הִנֵנִי) and the preposition מִן (מִמֶּנִּי).

e **B. Independent Pronouns**

1. Independent pronouns, contrary to attached pronouns, may begin the clause, and therefore, may be the initiator of a nominal clause, with or without a finite verb.

f 2. Independent pronouns emphasize, contrast, and/or clarify the subject. They may also express a reflexive nuance—I myself, you yourself, etc.

g a) With finite verbs: The independent pronouns with finite verbs are emphatic.

i. Perfect: The independent pronoun after the perfect is more emphatic than the pronoun before the perfect, since the pronoun after the perfect immediately repeats the implied pronoun of the perfect.

וּבָאתָ אַתָּה וְזִקְנֵי יִשְׂרָאֵל אֶל־מֶלֶךְ מִצְרַיִם Exod 3:18[b]

And **you will come, you** and the elders of Israel to the king of Egypt.

The independent pronoun after the perfect is more emphatic than the next example, Gen 16:5.

וַתֹּאמֶר שָׂרַי אֶל־אַבְרָם חֲמָסִי עָלֶיךָ אָנֹכִי נָתַתִּי שִׁפְחָתִי בְּחֵיקֶךָ Gen 16:5[a]

And Sarai said to Abram, My injury is upon you, **I – I gave** my handmaid in your bosom.

Pronoun before the perfect: Gen 3:12, 20; 4:20–22, 26; 10:8–9; 14:23; 16:5; BA Dan 4:6, 27; 5:16

Pronoun after the perfect: Gen 34:30; 44:3; Exod 4:16(2x); 12:4; 18:19; 19:24; BA Dan 2:31

h ii. Imperfect: The independent pronoun before the imperfect is relatively common, and somewhat expected, since most imperfect forms lack a suffixed pronoun. This independent pronoun is emphatic since it could be omitted or implied (Judg 6:16).

וַיֹּאמֶר אַבְרָהָם אָנֹכִי אִשָּׁבֵעַ׃ Gen 21:24

And Abraham said, **I – I swear**.

Pronoun before the imperfect: Gen 3:15(2x)-16; 4:7; 15:4, 15; 16:12; 21:24; BA Dan 2:44; 6:17; 7:24

Pronoun after the imperfect: Gen 17:9; 20:7; 45:11; 47:19; Exod 4:14; 18:22, 26; Lev 10:9

iii. Imperative: *i*

צֵא מִן־הַתֵּבָה אַתָּה וְאִשְׁתְּךָ וּבָנֶיךָ וּנְשֵׁי־בָנֶיךָ אִתָּךְ׃ Gen 8:16

Go out from the ark, **you** and your wife and your sons and the wives of your sons with you.

Gen 7:1; Exod 7:1; 18:19; 20:19; Deut 5:27; Judg 7:10

b) With attached suffixes: These independent pronouns repeat and emphasize an attached pronoun. *j*

i. Suffixes on verbs:

וַיֹּאמֶר לְאָבִיו בָּרֲכֵנִי גַם־אָנִי אָבִי׃ Gen 27:34[b]

And he said to his father, Bless **me**, even **me**, my father.

Gen 27:38; Zech 7:5

ii. Suffixes on nouns and particles:

וְכֹה אָמַר בְּלֶכְתּוֹ בְּנִי אַבְשָׁלוֹם בְּנִי בְנִי אַבְשָׁלוֹם מִי־יִתֵּן מוּתִי אֲנִי תַחְתֶּיךָ 2 Sam 19:1[b]

And thus he said as he went, My son, Absalom, my son my son, Absalom, O that **I – I had died** instead of you. (lit. Who will give my dying – mine instead of you)

1 Kgs 21:19; Jer 27:7; Ezek 6:3; 34:11; Prov 23:15

iii. Suffixes on prepositions:

וַתִּפֹּל עַל־רַגְלָיו וַתֹּאמֶר בִּי־אֲנִי אֲדֹנִי הֶעָוֹן 1 Sam 25:42[a]

And she fell upon his feet, and she said, **on me – me** – my lord be the guilt.

Exod 18:14; 1 Kgs 1:26; Hag 1:4; Ruth 4:6; 2 Chr 35:21

§20. Demonstrative Pronouns *a*

Demonstrative pronouns have inherent meaning (this, that, these, those, here) and a referent (someone or something to which it refers).

A. Forms

	Near (this, these)		Far (that, those)	
	Masculine	Feminine	Masculine	Feminine
Singular	זֶה	זֹאת (זֹה, זוֹ)	הַהוּא	הַהִיא
Plural	אֵלֶּה (אֵל)		הָהֵם, הָהֵמָּה	הָהֵנָּה

b **B. Observations**

1. The simple forms of the near demonstrative pronouns, זֶה, זֹאת, אֵלֶּה, may be augmented with an "alerting ה," that is, a ה that excites attention:[2] הַזֶּה, הַזֹּאת, הָאֵלֶּה. The far demonstrative pronouns almost always[3] have the alerting ה: הַהוּא, הַהִיא, הָהֵמָּה, etc. The near demonstrative pronouns may be further augmented with the demonstrative ל: הַלָּז, הַלָּזֶה, הַלֵּזוּ (§33; 36a).

c 2. Demonstrative pronouns without the alerting ה are often used as initiators in nominal clauses (Gen 5:1). With the alerting ה, demonstrative pronouns are often used appositionally as semi-descriptive nouns modifying nouns (§23i; Gen 38:1).

d 3. The near demonstrative pronoun זֶה without the alerting ה is often a demonstrative of place and time.

a) Place: זֶה may be used as a demonstrative of near place (here).

וְהִנֵּה־זֶה מַלְאָךְ נֹגֵעַ בּוֹ 1 Kgs 19:5[b]

And behold **here** an angel was touching him.

The demonstrative of far place (there) is usually שָׁם.

Exod 11:1; 13:3, 19; 17:3; Num 13:17; Lam 3:37

e b) Time: The demonstrative is often used with a temporal adverb (now, then) or number.

וַתֹּאמֶר הָאִשָּׁה אֶל־אֵלִיָּהוּ עַתָּה זֶה יָדַעְתִּי כִּי אִישׁ אֱלֹהִים אַתָּה 1 Kgs 17:24[a]

And the woman said to Elijah, **Now then** I know that you are a man of God.

The singular near demonstrative pronouns and far demonstrative pronouns, without alerting ה, may occur after an interrogative pronoun to express time.

וַיֹּאמֶר הָעָם אִישׁ אֶל־רֵעֵהוּ מַה־זֶּה הָיָה לְבֶן־קִישׁ 1 Sam 10:11[b]

And the people said to one another, What **now** has happened to the son of Kish?

מַה־זֹּאת עָשִׂיתָ לִּי Gen 12:18[a]

What **now** have you done to me?

Exod 2:20; 5:22; Num 14:41; 1 Sam 20:8; 26:18; Isa 66:1; Jer 49:19

§21. Retrospective Pronouns and Adverbs

a Retrospective pronouns, pronouns "looking back" to their antecedent, may occur in situation or relative clauses. In situation clauses, the retrospective pronoun "looks back" to another noun in its related clause (§48). In relative clauses, retrospective pronouns and adverbs "look back" to their antecedent nouns. Relative clauses require a pronoun or adverb to define the role (as a nominative, genitive, or accusative) of the antecedent within the relative clause. If, however, the relationship between the relative clause and its antecedent is clear, the retrospective pronoun and adverb could be omitted, though implied. Retrospective pronouns are common before an adjective, a participle, or in a negative sentence. For English translation, these retrospective pronouns and adverbs are omitted.

---

2. Compare the English word, "hey."
3. For example, Gen 19:33; 40:16, 22.

A. Retrospective Pronouns with Situation Clauses *b*

וַיִּזְרַח־לוֹ הַשֶּׁמֶשׁ כַּאֲשֶׁר עָבַר אֶת־פְּנוּאֵל וְהוּא צֹלֵעַ עַל־יְרֵכוֹ׃ Gen 32:32

And the sun rose upon him as he passed over Penuel, **as he was limping upon his thigh.**

The retrospective pronoun (וְהוּא) "looks back" to "he (Jacob)" in its related clause.

B. Retrospective Pronouns and Adverbs with Relative Clauses (§43–46) *c*

1. Pronouns
   i. Nominative (subject)
      כָּל־רֶמֶשׂ אֲשֶׁר הוּא־חַי – "Every creeping thing which it (is) alive."
      The retrospective pronoun (הוּא) occurs before the adjective חַי.
      The retrospective pronoun defines the role of the antecedent "every creeping (thing)" as the nominative of the relative clause.

   ii. Genitive (usually a pronominal suffix)
      הָאִישׁ אֲשֶׁר לֹא־תִשְׁמַע לְשֹׁנוֹ – "The man who you will not hear his tongue (language)."
      The retrospective pronoun (3ms suffix on לְשֹׁנוֹ) defines the role of "the man" as a genitive to the word "language" in the relative clause.

   iii. Accusative
      אֲנִי יוֹסֵף אֲשֶׁר מְכַרְתֶּם אֹתִי – "I am Joseph whom you sold me."
      The retrospective pronoun (אֹתִי) defines the antecedent "Joseph."

2. Adverbs *d*
   These retrospective adverbs define the location (there, to there, or from there) of the antecedent (the place) in a relative clause.
   i. שָׁם:
      הַמָּקוֹם אֲשֶׁר אַתָּה שָׁם – "The place which you (are) there." = "The place where you are." The retrospective adverb שָׁם combines with אֲשֶׁר to mean "where." The adverb שָׁם "looks back" on הַמָּקוֹם.
      "The place" is defined as located "where you are."

   ii. שָׁמָּה:
      הַמָּקוֹם אֲשֶׁר אַתָּה בָא שָׁמָּה – "The place which you are entering there" = The place where you are entering. "The place" is defined as located "where you are entering."
      אֲשֶׁר . . . שָׁמָּה = where, to which

   iii. מִשָּׁם:
      הַמָּקוֹם אֲשֶׁר אַתָּה יֹצֵא מִשָּׁם – "The place which you are going out from there" = "The place from which you are going out." "The place" is defined as located "where you are coming out."
      אֲשֶׁר . . . מִשָּׁם = from which

Exercises

I. Questions and Discussions

1. Define personal pronouns.
2. Where are personal pronouns implicit?
3. Are personal pronouns attached to the beginning or end of their words?
4. How are the preformatives of the imperfect considered: pronouns or something else?
5. In what case should the attached pronominal suffix (not the object suffix) of the perfect, imperfect, and imperative be considered?
6. In what case should the attached pronominal suffix of nouns and prepositions be considered?
7. In what case should the object pronominal suffix of the perfect, imperfect, and imperative be considered?
8. When may object pronouns be omitted?
9. What is a "protective Nun"? Where does it occur?
10. What are the common usages of the independent pronoun? How are they used with verbs and attached suffixes?
11. Define demonstrative pronouns.
12. Define the ה element with the demonstrative pronoun. When do demonstrative pronouns lack the ה element?
13. Define and discuss the demonstrative pronouns of place and time.
14. Define retrospective pronoun and adverb. How do they connect the antecedent with the relative clause?

Chapter 6
APPOSITION

§22. Introduction

Apposition in Semitic is a broader category than in Greek, Latin, or English, because Semitic has a broader view of the noun than Greek, Latin, or English.[1] In Semitic, for instance, adjectives are a subset of the noun (a descriptive noun) and, therefore, appositives to their nouns. The same is true of attributive participles, numerals, adverbs, and so forth.

Apposition limits or modifies words in Hebrew. The appositive usually agrees in gender, number, case, and definiteness with its antecedent. There are five types of apposition: QUALIFIER, CORROBORATIVE, CONJUNCTIVE, EXPLICATIVE, and SUBSTITUTION.[2]

§23. Qualifier *a*

Qualifiers are DESCRIPTIVE NOUNS or SEMI-DESCRIPTIVE nouns that modify another noun through apposition. Descriptive nouns include adjectives, attributive participles, and nouns with the intensive/extensive formation. Semi-descriptive nouns, by contrast, function like adjectives in certain contexts.

A. Descriptive Nouns

1. Adjectives

An adjective describes one of the qualities inherent or permanent in its noun. An adjective in apposition with a noun is attributive and usually agrees with its noun in gender, number, case, and definiteness: טוֹב, גָּדוֹל.

אֶל־אֶרֶץ טוֹבָה וּרְחָבָה Exod 3:8[a]

To a **good** and **broad** land

Gen 4:25 (אַחֵר); 7:11 (רַבָּה); 12:2 (גָּדוֹל); 18:7 (רַךְ וָטוֹב); 25:27 (תָּם); Exod 9:18 (כָּבֵד); 10:14 (כָּבֵד), 19 (חָזָק); 18:26 (הַקָּשֶׁה); 1 Sam 24:15 (אֶחָד); BA Dan 7:5 (אָחֳרִי)

a) Comparatives: *b*

i. Hebrew commonly expresses the comparative with an adjective (or stative verb) followed by the מִן of comparison.
מַה־מָּתוֹק מִדְּבַשׁ – "What is sweet (apart) from honey?" = "What is sweeter than honey?" Judg 14:18
(Gen 41:40; 48:19; Exod 1:9)

ii. Hebrew expresses the correlative comparatives—greater/lesser – by a definite adjective הַגָּדוֹל: the greater (Gen 1:16; 19:31; 27:1; 29:26), and sometimes by indefinite adjectives (Gen 25:23). *c*

b) Superlatives: Hebrew expresses superlatives with adjectives or with annexation. *d*

---

1. Semitic has three parts of speech: noun, verb, and particle.
2. Griess, 191–215; Howell §131–158; Wechter, 28–30; Wright II, §136–140.

i. With adjectives:

① Simple definite adjective: הַקָּטֹן "the small(est)" (Gen 9:24; 42:13; Lev 21:10)

② Definite attributive adjective: בְּנוֹ הַקָּטֹן "His son, the small one" = "his youngest son" (Gen 43:29; Judg 9:5)

e ii. With annexation of nouns (§12d):

① Adjective or noun (without an article) as the first member of a construct package:
קְטֹן בָּנָיו – "The small (one) of his sons" = "the myoungest of his sons" (Exod 15:4; Deut 7:7)

② Annexation with two nouns of the same word, with the last word of the package in the plural:
שִׁיר הַשִּׁירִים – "The song of songs" = "the most excellent song"
Gen 9:25; Exod 29:37; Deut 10:14, 17; Ezek 26:7; Eccl 1:2; BA Dan 2:47

③ Proper annexation with the preposition מִן implied between the words, expressing the part/whole (partitive genitive) relationship:

חַכְמוֹת שָׂרוֹתֶיהָ תַּעֲנֶינָּה Judg 5:29[a]

The wise(est) (women) of her princesses would answer.

f 2. Participles (§16n)

Participles used appositionally are similar to attributive adjectives and are usually definite, qualifying their nouns with the verbal aspect of a perfect or imperfect.

a) Perfect: In these examples, the participles have the verbal aspect of a perfect.

וְנָקוּמָה וְנַעֲלֶה בֵּית־אֵל וְאֶעֱשֶׂה־שָּׁם מִזְבֵּחַ לָאֵל הָעֹנֶה אֹתִי בְּיוֹם צָרָתִי Gen 35:3

And let us rise and go up to Bethel that I might make there an altar, to the God **who answered** me on the day of my distress.

וְגַם־לְלוֹט הַהֹלֵךְ אֶת־אַבְרָם הָיָה צֹאן־וּבָקָר וְאֹהָלִים׃ Gen 13:5

And even Lot, **who went** with Abram, also had flocks and herds and tents.

Gen 12:7 (הַנִּרְאֶה); 36:35 (הַמַּכֶּה); 46:8 (הַבָּאִים); Exod 1:1 (הַבָּאִים), 5 (יֹצְאֵי); 4:19 (הַמְבַקְשִׁים); Lev 11:45 (הַמַּעֲלֶה); 1 Sam 24:15 (מֵת); Isa 40:28 (בּוֹרֵא)

g b) Imperfect: In these examples, the participles have the verbal aspect of an imperfect.

וּמֵת כָּל־בְּכוֹר בְּאֶרֶץ מִצְרַיִם מִבְּכוֹר פַּרְעֹה הַיֹּשֵׁב עַל־כִּסְאוֹ עַד בְּכוֹר הַשִּׁפְחָה Exod 11:5[a]

And every firstborn in the land of Egypt will die from the firstborn of Pharaoh **who sits** upon his throne unto the firstborn of the handmaid.

1 Sam 14:1 וַיְהִ֣י הַיּ֗וֹם וַיֹּ֨אמֶר יוֹנָתָ֤ן בֶּן־שָׁאוּל֙ אֶל־הַנַּ֙עַר֙ נֹשֵׂ֣א כֵלָ֔יו לְכָ֗ה וְנַעְבְּרָה֙ אֶל־מַצַּ֣ב פְּלִשְׁתִּ֔ים אֲשֶׁ֥ר מֵעֵ֖בֶר הַלָּ֑ז וּלְאָבִ֖יו לֹ֥א הִגִּֽיד׃

Now the day came that Jonathan, the son of Saul, said to the young man **who was carrying** his armor, Come and let us cross over to the Philistines' garrison that is on yonder side. But he did not tell his father.

Gen 1:11–12 (מַזְרִ֣יעַ, מַזְרִ֤יעַ), 26 (הָרֹמֵ֥שׂ); 24:65 (הַהֹלֵ֤ךְ); Exod 6:7 (הַמּוֹצִ֣יא); 10:5 (הַנִּשְׁאֶ֣רֶת, הַצֹּמֵ֥חַ); 12:49 (הַגָּ֥ר); 14:8 (יֹצְאִ֖ים); 19:22 (הַנִּגָּשִׁ֥ים); Num 23:28 (הַנִּשְׁקָ֖ף); Deut 1:38 (הָעֹמֵ֣ד); 2:4 (הַיֹּשְׁבִ֖ים), 8 (הַיֹּֽשְׁבִים֙); 18:7 (הָעֹמְדִ֥ים); Josh 19:13 (הַמְּתֹאָ֖ר); Judg 5:9 (הַמִּֽתְנַדְּבִ֖ים); 1 Sam 14:11 (יֹֽצְאִ֔ים), 39 (הַמּוֹשִׁ֙יעַ֙); 24:4 (יֹשְׁבִ֖ים); Isa 43:16 (הַנּוֹתֵ֥ן); 45:3 (הַקּוֹרֵ֥א); Jer 23:1 (מְאַבְּדִ֧ים וּמְפִצִ֛ים)

3. Intensive/Extensive Noun Formations *h*

These are descriptive nouns associated with the INTENSIVE/EXTENSIVE verbal formations.[3] These forms exaggerate the meaning of the word by describing someone intensively/extensively doing an activity, or by someone possessing the quality intensively/extensively. Hence, these noun formations are ideal for profession or habit.

Exod 21:29[a] וְאִ֡ם שׁ֣וֹר נַגָּ֩ח ה֨וּא מִתְּמֹ֜ל שִׁלְשֹׁ֗ם

And if an ox, (in the habit of) **goring** he (was) formerly.

1 Kgs 1:21 וְהָיָ֕ה כִּשְׁכַ֥ב אֲדֹנִֽי־הַמֶּ֖לֶךְ עִם־אֲבֹתָ֑יו וְהָיִ֨יתִי אֲנִ֜י וּבְנִ֧י שְׁלֹמֹ֛ה חַטָּאִֽים׃

Otherwise it will come about, as soon as my lord the king sleeps with his fathers, that I and my son Solomon will be considered **traitors (great sinners)**.

Gen 40:3 (הַטַּבָּחִ֑ים); Exod 20:5 (קַנָּ֔א); Deut 28:65 (רַגָּ֔ז); 1 Sam 8:13 (לְרַקָּח֥וֹת וּלְטַבָּח֖וֹת); 24:16 (לְדַיָּ֔ן); 1 Kgs 5:29 (סַבָּ֔ל); Jer 16:16 (לְדַיָּגִ֥ים); 48:27 (בְּגַנָּבִ֖ים); Ps 86:5 (וְסַלָּ֑ח); Dan 1:20 (הָֽאַשָּׁפִ֔ים); BA Dan 2:14 (טַבָּחַיָּ֖א); Ezra 7:24 (זַמָּֽרַיָּא֙ תָּֽרָעַיָּ֔א)

B. Semi-Descriptive Nouns *i*

1. Demonstrative and relative pronouns (§20c)

Gen 7:1[b] כִּֽי־אֹתְךָ֥ רָאִ֛יתִי צַדִּ֥יק לְפָנַ֖י בַּדּ֥וֹר הַזֶּֽה׃

For you I have seen as righteous before me in **this** generation.

In Gen 7:1, a demonstrative pronoun is the semi-descriptive noun qualifying "generation" as "this generation."

Demonstrative pronouns: Gen 12:7; 17:21

Gen 2:8 וַיִּטַּ֞ע יְהוָ֧ה אֱלֹהִ֛ים גַּן־בְּעֵ֖דֶן מִקֶּ֑דֶם וַיָּ֣שֶׂם שָׁ֔ם אֶת־הָֽאָדָ֖ם אֲשֶׁ֥ר יָצָֽר׃

And the Lord God planted a garden toward the east in Eden; and there He placed the man **whom** He had formed.

3. See §7g. Like the intensive/extensive verbs, not all intensive/extensive noun formation exaggerate the meaning of noun. For example, the noun (adjective) צַדִּיק, derived from a stative verb, does not have a intensive/extensive meaning. Compare the factitive Piel, §7d.

In Gen 2:8, a relative pronoun is the semi-descriptive noun qualifying "man."
Relative Pronouns: Gen 1:7(2x), 29; 2:2, 22.

j 2. NISBAH[4] NOUNS (Hireq-Yod suffix, §31)
The Hireq-Yod (rarely Patah/Qames-Yod) ending converts nouns into adjectives, cardinal numbers into ordinal numbers, nations into nationalities, and tribes into tribal names. The Hireq-Yod ending means "pertaining to" or "in relation to." Nisbah nouns may have explicit or implicit appositives.

Gen 39:1 וְיוֹסֵף הוּרַד מִצְרָיְמָה וַיִּקְנֵהוּ פּוֹטִיפַר סְרִיס פַּרְעֹה שַׂר הַטַּבָּחִים אִישׁ מִצְרִי

And Joseph had been taken down to Egypt. And Potiphar, an officer of Pharaoh, the captain of the bodyguard, **an Egyptian** (a man, a pertaining to Egypt man), bought him.

In Gen 39:1, the word מִצְרִי with the Hireq-Yod suffix changes a nation (Egypt) into a nationality (Egyptian), also called a gentilic noun, which qualifies the explicit appositive, אִישׁ.

Deut 23:8 לֹא־תְתַעֵב אֲדֹמִי כִּי אָחִיךָ הוּא ס לֹא־תְתַעֵב מִצְרִי כִּי־גֵר הָיִיתָ בְאַרְצוֹ׃

You must not despise **an Edomite** because he is your brother. You must not despise **an Egyptian** because you were a stranger in his land.

In Deut 23:8, the gentilic nouns have implicit appositives, אִישׁ.

1 Kgs 18:1 וַיְהִי יָמִים רַבִּים וּדְבַר־יְהוָה הָיָה אֶל־אֵלִיָּהוּ בַּשָּׁנָה הַשְּׁלִישִׁית לֵאמֹר לֵךְ הֵרָאֵה אֶל־אַחְאָב וְאֶתְּנָה מָטָר עַל־פְּנֵי הָאֲדָמָה׃

And many days occurred, then the word of the Lord came to Elijah in **the third** year, saying, Go, show yourself to Ahab, and I will give rain on the face of the earth.

In 1 Kgs 18:1, the word with the Hireq-Yod suffix changes the cardinal number (three) into an ordinal number (third).
Gen 1:13 (שְׁלִישִׁי), 19 (רְבִיעִי), 23 (חֲמִישִׁי); 10:16–18 (הַיְבוּסִי, הָאֱמֹרִי, הַגִּרְגָּשִׁי, הַחִוִּי, הַעַרְקִי, הַסִּינִי, הָאַרְוָדִי, הַצְּמָרִי, הַחֲמָתִי, הַכְּנַעֲנִי); 15:2 (עֲרִירִי); 25:25 (אַדְמוֹנִי); 31:15 (נָכְרִיּוֹת); 39:14 (עִבְרִי); 46:10 (הַכְּנַעֲנִית); Exod 6:25 (הַלְוִיִּם); 12:37 (רַגְלִי); 21:2 (עִבְרִי, וּבַשְּׁבִעִת), 8 (נָכְרִי); Lev 14:16 (הַיְמָנִית, הַשְּׂמָאלִית); 1 Sam 21:8 (הָאֲדֹמִי); BA Dan 2:39 (אָחֳרִי); 3:26 (עִלָּאָה, The Aleph represents the Yod of the Nisbah ending since intervocalic Yod and Aleph often interchange. In Aramaic the Nisbah ending is usually Qames-Yod [Aleph]).

k 3. Numbers (§30a–b): Numbers, when occurring after their NUMERABLE and not in the genitive to their numerable, are semi-descriptive nouns (adjectives) appositionally qualifying their numerable.

4. Nisbah is an Arabic word meaning "pertaining to" or "in relation to."

Num 29:13 וְהִקְרַבְתֶּם עֹלָה אִשֵּׁה רֵיחַ נִיחֹחַ לַיהוָה פָּרִים בְּנֵי־בָקָר שְׁלֹשָׁה עָשָׂר אֵילִם שְׁנָיִם כְּבָשִׂים בְּנֵי־שָׁנָה אַרְבָּעָה עָשָׂר תְּמִימִם יִהְיוּ׃

And you will offer a burnt offering, a fire offering of a soothing aroma to the Lord: bulls, sons of cattle, **thirteen**; rams **two**; lambs, sons of a year, **fourteen**, in the situation of unblemished they exist.

Gen 32:15–16; Exod 21:32; 36:17; Num 31:44–46; Josh 15:41, 44; 1 Kgs 5:27; 18:19

4. כֹּל: This word is a semi-descriptive noun when it precedes an indefinite noun. *l*

Gen 7:14 הֵמָּה וְכָל־הַחַיָּה לְמִינָהּ וְכָל־הַבְּהֵמָה לְמִינָהּ וְכָל־הָרֶמֶשׂ הָרֹמֵשׂ עַל־הָאָרֶץ לְמִינֵהוּ וְכָל־הָעוֹף לְמִינֵהוּ כֹּל צִפּוֹר כָּל־כָּנָף׃

They and **every** beast to its kind, and **all** the cattle to its kind, and **every** creeping thing creeping upon the earth to its kind, and **every** fowl to its kind, **every** bird and **every** winged creature.

Gen 1:21(2x); 2:9; 6:13; 7:21; 9:3; 17:23; Exod 1:5; 10:15; 11:5; 12:15; BA Dan 3:29

C. Clauses *m*

These clauses, often relative clauses (§44), qualify a noun.

1. Verbal

Gen 2:2[b] וַיִּשְׁבֹּת בַּיּוֹם הַשְּׁבִיעִי מִכָּל־מְלַאכְתּוֹ אֲשֶׁר עָשָׂה׃

And he rested on the seventh day his work **which he made**.

The verbal clause with an explicit relative pronoun qualifies the antecedent "from all (מִכָּל) his work (מְלַאכְתּוֹ)."

Gen 49:27[a] בִּנְיָמִין זְאֵב יִטְרָף

Benjamin (is) a wolf (that) **tears**.

The verbal clause, an implied relative clause in Gen 49:27, qualifies זְאֵב. Implied relative clauses are more common in poetry and direct speech than in prose (§47).

Exod 15:17 (מָכוֹן לְשִׁבְתְּךָ פָּעַלְתָּ); Job 3:3 (וְהַלַּיְלָה אָמַר, יוֹם אִוָּלֶד בּוֹ); 20:19 (בַּיִת גָּזַל וְלֹא יִבְנֵהוּ); 21:18 (וּכְמֹץ גְּנָבַתּוּ סוּפָה); Ps 51:10 (תָּגֵלְנָה עֲצָמוֹת דִּכִּיתָ); 58:9 (כְּמוֹ שַׁבְּלוּל תֶּמֶס יַהֲלֹךְ); 59:13 (וּמֵאָלָה וּמִכַּחַשׁ יְסַפֵּרוּ); 68:17; 74:2

2. Nominal *n*

Job 3:15[a] אוֹ עִם־שָׂרִים זָהָב לָהֶם

Or with princes (who) **gold (is) to them** (to whom is gold).

The nominal clause, an implied relative clause, qualifies שָׂרִים.

Gen 3:3 וּמִפְּרִי הָעֵץ אֲשֶׁר בְּתוֹךְ־הַגָּן אָמַר אֱלֹהִים לֹא תֹאכְלוּ מִמֶּנּוּ וְלֹא תִגְּעוּ בּוֹ פֶּן־תְּמֻתוּן׃

But from the fruit of the tree **which is in the middle of the garden**, God has said, You shall not eat from it or touch it, lest you die.

In Gen 3:3, the nominal clause (a relative clause) qualifies וּמִפְּרִי הָעֵץ. Gen 1:29 (אֲשֶׁר עַל־פְּנֵי כָל־הָאָרֶץ); 6:4 (אֲשֶׁר מֵעוֹלָם אַנְשֵׁי הַשֵּׁם׃); 7:19 (אֲשֶׁר־תַּחַת כָּל־הַשָּׁמָיִם); 14:15 (אֲשֶׁר מִשְּׂמֹאל לְדַמָּשֶׂק); 18:24 (אֲשֶׁר בְּקִרְבָּהּ); 22:17 (אֲשֶׁר עַל־שְׂפַת הַיָּם); Ps 32:9 (אֵין הָבִין)

o **D. Prepositional Phrase**

Prepositional phrases, like clauses, may qualify a noun.

Gen 3:8 וַיִּשְׁמְעוּ אֶת־קוֹל יְהוָה אֱלֹהִים מִתְהַלֵּךְ בַּגָּן לְרוּחַ הַיּוֹם

And they heard the voice of the Lord God **in the status of walker in the garden** at the cool of the day.

The prepositional phrase modifies the participle functioning as a substantive. Gen 3:6 (גַּם־לְאִישָׁהּ עִמָּהּ); 1 Kgs 13:4 (עַל־הַמִּזְבֵּחַ בְּבֵית־אֵל); Isa 6:1 (יֹשֵׁב עַל־כִּסֵּא); Ezek 26:8 (בְּנוֹתַיִךְ בַּשָּׂדֶה); 1 Chr 11:3 (כִּדְבַר יְהוָה בְּיַד־שְׁמוּאֵל)

p **E. Syntactical Uses of Qualifiers**

1. Clarifying the Definite
   Qualifiers clarify their definite noun by giving an attribute that distinguishes that noun from another noun.
2. Specializing the Indefinite
   Qualifiers specialize their noun by limiting or modifying an indefinite noun.

§24. Corroborative

a The corroborative strengthens or emphasizes its noun by confirming or establishing its noun "because of the fear of forgetfulness, inattentiveness, or lack of concern."[5] The corroborative is divided into verbal or conceptual.

A. Verbal Corroborative

Verbal corroborative repeats the noun, pronoun, verb, particle, phrase, or clause.

1. Nouns:

Exod 8:10[a] וַיִּצְבְּרוּ אֹתָם חֳמָרִם חֳמָרִם

And they piled them up in **heaps, heaps** (heaps everywhere).

2 Kgs 25:15[a] וְאֶת־הַמַּחְתּוֹת וְאֶת־הַמִּזְרָקוֹת אֲשֶׁר זָהָב זָהָב וַאֲשֶׁר־כֶּסֶף כָּסֶף

And the firepots and the bowls, those of **gold, gold** (pure gold) and those of **silver, silver** (pure silver).

Gen 7:14 הֵמָּה וְכָל־הַחַיָּה לְמִינָהּ וְכָל־הַבְּהֵמָה לְמִינָהּ וְכָל־הָרֶמֶשׂ
הָרֹמֵשׂ עַל־הָאָרֶץ לְמִינֵהוּ וְכָל־הָעוֹף לְמִינֵהוּ כֹּל צִפּוֹר
כָּל־כָּנָף׃

They and **every** living animal to its kind, and **all** the cattle to its kind, and **every** creeping thing creeping upon the earth to its kind, and **every** fowl to its kind, **every** bird and **every** winged creature.

Gen 1:21 (כָּל־); 14:10 (בֶּאֱרֹת בֶּאֱרֹת); 22:11 (אַבְרָהָם׀ אַבְרָהָם); Exod 34:6 (יְהוָה׀ יְהוָה); Deut 16:20 (צֶדֶק צֶדֶק); 2 Sam 19:5 (בְּנִי בְנִי, אַבְשָׁלוֹם׀ אַבְשָׁלוֹם); 1 Kgs 13:2 (מִזְבֵּחַ מִזְבֵּחַ); 2 Kgs 3:16 (גֵּבִים׀ גֵּבִים); Isa 21:2 (וְהַשּׁוֹדֵד׀ שׁוֹדֵד, הַבּוֹגֵד׀ בּוֹגֵד); 26:3 (שָׁלוֹם׀ שָׁלוֹם); 29:1 (אֲרִיאֵל אֲרִיאֵל); 57:19 (שָׁלוֹם׀ שָׁלוֹם); Ezek 21:14 (חֶרֶב חֶרֶב), 32 (עַוָּה עַוָּה עַוָּה)

5. Griess, 197.

2. Pronouns: *b*
   a) Repeating independent pronouns:

אָנֹכִ֨י אָנֹכִ֥י ה֛וּא מֹחֶ֥ה פְשָׁעֶ֖יךָ לְמַעֲנִ֑י Isa 43:25[a]

I – I (am) He (who) blots out your transgressions for my sake.

Exod 10:8 (מִ֥י וָמִֽי); Deut 32:39 (אֲנִ֤י אֲנִי֙); Isa 43:11 (אָנֹכִ֥י אָנֹכִ֖י); 48:15 (אֲנִ֥י אֲנִ֛י); 51:12 (אָנֹכִ֧י אָנֹכִ֛י); 57:6 (הֵ֥ם הֵ֖ם); Hos 5:14 (אֲנִ֨י אֲנִ֤י)

   b) An independent pronoun repeating an attached pronoun or an independent pronoun being repeated by an attached pronoun: *c*

וַתֹּ֨אמֶר שָׂרַ֣י אֶל־אַבְרָם֮ חֲמָסִ֣י עָלֶ֒יךָ֒ אָנֹכִ֗י נָתַ֤תִּי שִׁפְחָתִי֙ בְּחֵיקֶ֔ךָ Gen 16:5[a]

And Sarai said to Abram, My wrong be on you, **I – I** gave my handmaid in your bosom.

וַאֲנִי֙ מְתֵ֣י מִסְפָּ֔ר וְנֶאֶסְפ֤וּ עָלַי֙ וְהִכּ֔וּנִי וְנִשְׁמַדְתִּ֖י אֲנִ֥י וּבֵיתִֽי׃ Gen 34:30[b]

And I (being) few in number, and they will be gathered against me and they will strike me, and **I – I** and my house – will be destroyed.

Gen 27:34 (בָּרֲכֵ֥נִי גַם־אָ֖נִי); Exod 22:26 (הִ֤וא כְסוּתֹה֙ לְבַדָּ֔הּ); 1 Sam 8:20 (וְהָיִ֥ינוּ גַם־אֲנַ֖חְנוּ); 12:3 (הִנְנִ֣י עֲנ֣וּ בִ֡י); 20:42 (נִשְׁבַּ֨עְנוּ שְׁנֵ֤ינוּ אֲנַ֙חְנוּ֙); 1 Kgs 21:19 (אֶת־דָּמְךָ֖ גַּם־אָֽתָּה); 2 Kgs 19:15 (אַתָּה־ה֤וּא הָֽאֱלֹהִים֙ לְבַדְּךָ֔); Jer 26:14 (וַאֲנִ֖י הִנְנִ֣י); Neh 9:6 (אַתָּה־ה֣וּא יְהוָה֮ לְבַדֶּךָ֒)

3. Verb (clause): *d*

נַחֲמ֥וּ נַחֲמ֖וּ עַמִּ֑י יֹאמַ֖ר אֱלֹהֵיכֶֽם׃ Isa 40:1

Comfort – comfort my people. Says your God.

Exod 15:16 (עַד־יַעֲבֹ֤ר ... עַֽד־יַעֲבֹ֖ר); Judg 5:12 (ע֤וּרִי עוּרִי֙); 2 Sam 16:7 (צֵ֥א צֵ֛א); 20:16 (שִׁמְע֣וּ שִׁמְע֑וּ); 2 Kgs 6:21 (הַאַכֶּ֥ה אַכֶּ֖ה אָבִֽי); Isa 21:9 (נָֽפְלָ֤ה נָֽפְלָה֙); 51:17 (הִתְעוֹרְרִ֣י הִֽתְעוֹרְרִ֗י); 52:11 (ס֤וּרוּ ס֙וּרוּ֙); 57:14 (סֹֽלּוּ־סֹ֖לּוּ); 62:10 (עִבְר֤וּ עִבְרוּ֙, סֹ֤לּוּ סֹ֙לּוּ֙); Ezek 33:11 (שׁ֣וּבוּ שׁ֜וּבוּ); Ps 137:7 (עָר֤וּ ׀ עָ֑רוּ); Prov 30:15 (הַ֣ב ׀ הַ֑ב)

4. Particle: *e*

רִאשׁ֥וֹן לְצִיּ֖וֹן הִנֵּ֣ה הִנָּ֑ם Isa 41:27[a]

Formerly, (I said) to Zion, **See – see** they are.

Gen 7:19 (מְאֹ֥ד מְאֹ֖ד); 17:2 (בִּמְאֹ֥ד מְאֹֽד); Exod 7:28–29 (בְּבֵיתֶ֔ךָ, וּבַחֲדַ֥ר, וּבְבֵ֣ית, וּבְעַמֶּ֔ךָ, וּבְתַנּוּרֶ֖יךָ, וּבְמִשְׁאֲרוֹתֶֽיךָ, וּבְכָ֥ה, וּֽבְעַמְּךָ֖); 8:17 (בְּךָ֙, וּבַעֲבָדֶ֧יךָ, וּֽבְעַמְּךָ֛, וּבְבָתֶּ֖יךָ), 27 (מִפַּרְעֹ֔ה, מֵעֲבָדָ֖יו, וּמֵעַמּ֑וֹ); Num 5:22 (אָמֵ֥ן ׀ אָמֵֽן); 2 Sam 20:20 (חָלִ֤ילָה חָלִ֙ילָה֙); Jer 7:16 (אַל־תִּתְפַּלֵּ֣ל, וְאַל־תִּשָּׂ֧א, וְאַל־תִּפְגַּע־בִּ֑י); Ezek 16:23 (א֥וֹי א֖וֹי); Amos 5:16 (הוֹ־הֽוֹ); Ps 35:21 (הֶ֤אָ֣ח ׀ הֶאָ֑ח)

5. Phrase: *f*

אֶעְבְּרָ֣ה בְאַרְצֶ֔ךָ בַּדֶּ֥רֶךְ בַּדֶּ֖רֶךְ אֵלֵ֑ךְ Deut 2:27[a]

I will pass through your land, **in the road in the road (only in the road)** I will go.

Of course, words may be repeated without being corroborative (emphatic), as for example, to express an idiom (פָּנִ֣ים אֶל־פָּנִ֔ים Gen 32:31) or to express a distributive notion (§9b; 31), as in the following example:

אִ֣ישׁ־אִ֥ישׁ מִמְּלַאכְתּ֖וֹ אֲשֶׁר־הֵ֥מָּה עֹשִֽׂים׃ Exod 36:4[b]
A man, a man (every man) from his work which they were doing.
Jer 7:4 (הֵיכַ֤ל יְהוָה֙ הֵיכַ֣ל יְהוָ֔ה הֵיכַ֥ל יְהוָ֖ה)

g 6. Nominal Clause

מִֽי־כָמֹ֤כָה בָּֽאֵלִם֙ יְהוָ֔ה מִ֖י כָּמֹ֣כָה נֶאְדָּ֣ר בַּקֹּ֑דֶשׁ Exod 15:11[a]
Who is like you among the gods, Lord; **who is like you** majestic in holiness?

h **B. Conceptual Corroborative**

Conceptual corroborative does not repeat words, but strengthens the *concept* of the totality or the self of the appositive by using two words: עֶ֫צֶם or כֹּל/כָּל־.

1. Strengthening self: עֶ֫צֶם (bone, self, substance)

בְּעֶ֨צֶם הַיּ֤וֹם הַזֶּה֙ בָּ֣א נֹ֔חַ וְשֵׁם־וְחָ֥ם וָיֶ֖פֶת בְּנֵי־נֹ֑חַ Gen 7:13[a]
In the substance of this day (**on** this **very** day), Noah entered, and Shem and Ham and Japheth, the sons of Noah.
Gen 17:26; Exod 12:17, 41; 24:10; Job 21:23

i 2. Strengthening the totality: כֹּל/כָּל־. For a conceptual corroborative, כֹּל/כָּל־ will have an attached pronoun in apposition with its antecedent noun.

וְהַ֤ר סִינַי֙ עָשַׁ֣ן כֻּלּ֔וֹ Exod 19:18
And the mount Sinai became smoke, **all of it**.
Gen 13:10; 25:25; 42:11; Exod 12:33; 25:36; Num 17:27; Deut 1:22; 4:4; Josh 8:24; Isa 14:29; BA Dan 2:38; Ezra 6:20

§25. Conjunctive

a Conjunctive apposition links two or more words of the same case, or of the same part of speech, by the particles: וְ/וַ, אוֹ, לֹא, or כִּי.

A. וְ/וַ

1. Conjunctive Vav

יְהוָ֤ה ׀ סַֽלְעִ֥י וּמְצוּדָתִ֗י וּמְפַ֫לְטִ֥י Ps 18:3
The Lord is my rock **and** my fortress **and** my deliverer.

The nouns "my fortress" and "my deliverer" are in apposition to "my rock." The conjunctive Vavs link the appositives to their antecedent noun, hence the term "conjunctive apposition."

Exod 2:3 (בַחֵמָ֖ר וּבַזָּ֑פֶת), 12 (כֹּה֙ וָכֹ֔ה), 14 (לְאִ֨ישׁ שַׂ֤ר וְשֹׁפֵט֙); 3:8 (טוֹבָה֙ וּרְחָבָ֔ה), 16 (אֶתְכֶ֔ם וְאֶת־הֶעָשׂ֥וּי לָכֶ֖ם); 7:28–29 (וּבְכָ֖ה וּבְעַמְּךָ֣ וּבְכָל־עֲבָדֶ֑יךָ ,בְּבֵיתֶ֔ךָ וּבַחֲדַ֥ר מִשְׁכָּבְךָ֖); 1 Sam 12:23 (הַטּוֹבָ֖ה וְהַיְשָׁרָֽה) Jer 7:20, 22, 24; BA Dan 3:13

2. Successive Vav

The Vav may be temporally or logically successive.

וַיֵּשְׁב֣וּ לְפָנָ֔יו הַבְּכֹר֙ כִּבְכֹ֣רָת֔וֹ וְהַצָּעִ֖יר כִּצְעִרָת֑וֹ Gen 43:33[a]
And they sat before him, the firstborn according to his firstborn right **and then** the youngest according to his youth.

B. אוֹ b

וַיֹּאמֶר לוֹ אַבְנֵר נְטֵה לְךָ עַל־יְמִינְךָ אוֹ עַל־שְׂמֹאלֶךָ 2 Sam 2:21

And Abner said to him, Turn aside for yourself upon your right **or** upon your left.

Exod 19:13 (כִּי־סָקוֹל יִסָּקֵל אוֹ־יָרֹה יִיָּרֶה); Exod 21:4, 6, 37; 22:9(2x)

C. לֹא c

לֹא־כֵן הָרְשָׁעִים כִּי אִם־כַּמֹּץ אֲשֶׁר־תִּדְּפֶנּוּ רוּחַ׃ Ps 1:4

Not so the wicked, but as the chaff which the wind completely blows away.

Num 20:17 (נַעְבְּרָה־נָּא בְאַרְצֶךָ לֹא נַעֲבֹר בְּשָׂדֶה וּבְכֶרֶם); Deut 2:27; Isa 10:7; Ps 39:10; Lam 2:21

D. כִּי d

כִּי הַר יִהְיֶה־לָּךְ כִּי־יַעַר הוּא Josh 17:18

But the hill country will exist to you, **for** it is forest.

§26. Explicative

The explicative apposition *explains* its noun by clarifying or identifying it. The explicative apposition is a PRIMARY NOUN, not a DESCRIPTIVE NOUN. Like an adjective, the explicative agrees with its antecedent noun in definiteness, case, number, and gender. The adjective refers to an attribute of its noun. The explicative apposition, by contrast, clarifies its noun by revealing or identifying its noun. The antecedent noun of an explicative apposition is a general term; its explicative apposition is a specific term—the blessed tree, the olive tree. Most often an explicative apposition is a proper name, especially personal proper names—the servant of the Lord, Moses. The specific word, "Moses," identifies the general word, "servant of the Lord." If, therefore, the specific term (the explicative apposition) were dropped, the identity of the antecedent noun would be in doubt, or the general term would need clarification or specification. The antecedent noun, being a general term, could apply to many people or things, but its explicative apposition identifies or specifies the individual(s) or thing(s). To paraphrase this construction, one could join the antecedent noun with its explicative apposition by an implied clause: "who is identified as," "who/what is more specifically called," or "better known as." For example, the phrase, "the men, the Midianites" could be paraphrased "the men who are identified as the Midianites." "The men" could refer to many men, but the explicative apposition, "Midianites," identifies or reveals the exact "men" intended. In 2 Sam 3:31, הַמֶּלֶךְ דָּוִד "the king, (better known as) David"—"the king" could refer to many individuals, but the explicative apposition identifies the king more specifically as David.

וַיִּשְׁלַח הַמֶּלֶךְ רְחַבְעָם 1 Kgs 12:18

And the king, **Rehoboam** sent....

Gen 44:2 (גְּבִיעַ הַכֶּסֶף); Exod 1:11 (אֶת־פִּתֹם וְאֶת־רַעַמְסֵס); 2:6 (אֶת־הַיֶּלֶד), 14 (שַׂר וְשֹׁפֵט); 3:6 (אֱלֹהֵי אַבְרָהָם אֱלֹהֵי יִצְחָק וֵאלֹהֵי יַעֲקֹב); 18:6 (יִתְרוֹ); 1 Sam 15:1 (עַל־יִשְׂרָאֵל), 18 (אֶת־עֲמָלֵק); 17:58 (יִשַׁי); 19:4 (בְּדָוִד); Jer 7:15 (אֶת כָּל־זֶרַע אֶפְרָיִם), 20 (יְהוָה), 21 (אֱלֹהֵי יִשְׂרָאֵל); BA Dan 2:28 (נְבוּכַדְנֶצַּר)

§27. Substitution

a Substitution is also used with primary nouns, similar to the explicative, but instead of clarifying or identifying its antecedent noun, it substitutes for its antecedent noun. In other words, the antecedent noun transforms into its substitution. The substitution, consequently, has an exclusive or unique relationship with its antecedent noun, often like a title, position, or relationship. The antecedent of the substitution can be dropped without loss of meaning to the sentence since it substitutes for its noun.[6] Whereas the qualifier, corroborative, and explicative focus their meaning on their antecedent noun, the substitution receives the focus of the meaning of its antecedent noun, which merely prepares the way for its substitution. The substitution, therefore, repeats (emphasizes) its noun, similar to a corroborative. When repeating its antecedent noun, the substitution often repeats the same preposition or particle of its antecedent.[7]

The substitution is often the general word; its antecedent noun, the specific word.[8] It is never a personal proper name.[9] Sometimes a word may simply be substituted for another word—"the righteous paths, the paths of God." Moreover, a noun may substitute for a third person pronoun (Exod 2:6; Ezek 10:3). If the explicative apposition mentioned above, "the servant of Lord, Moses," were inverted, a substitution would occur, "Moses, the servant of the Lord." Now the phrase, "the servant of the Lord," is viewed as a title that repeats or corroborates Moses. In 2 Sam 13:39, דָּוִד הַמֶּ֫לֶךְ "David the king," the word "the king" substitutes for "David." "David" is now transformed into "the king." In later verses in the context, the substitution can be used independently of its antecedent, 2 Sam 14:1, 5, 8, 10, 18, 21, etc. Also see, 1 Kgs 12:6, 22–23.

1 Kgs 12:22 וַיְהִי֙ דְּבַ֣ר הָאֱלֹהִ֔ים אֶל־שְׁמַֽעְיָ֖ה אִישׁ־הָאֱלֹהִ֥ים לֵאמֹֽר׃
1 Kgs 12:23[a] אֱמֹ֗ר אֶל־רְחַבְעָ֤ם בֶּן־שְׁלֹמֹה֙ מֶ֣לֶךְ יְהוּדָ֔ה

And word of God came to Shemayah, **the man of God**, saying, "Say to Rehoboam, **the son of Solomon, the king of Judah**."

Gen 14:22 (אֵ֣ל עֶלְי֔וֹן קֹנֵ֖ה שָׁמַ֥יִם וָאָֽרֶץ); Exod 2:21 (בִּתּ֖וֹ); 4:22–23 (בְּנִ֥י בְכֹרִ֖י ,בִּנְךָ֥ בְּכֹרֶֽךָ); 6:14 (בְּכֹ֣ר יִשְׂרָאֵ֗ל); 13:3 (מִבֵּ֣ית עֲבָדִ֔ים); 14:31 (עַבְדּֽוֹ); 15:20 (הַנְּבִיאָ֜ה אֲח֧וֹת אַהֲרֹ֛ן);

6. This is sometimes difficult to determine since the author's intent is not always easy to discern. In the statement, "I delivered his brother, Aaron," the antecedent, "his brother," is the key term identified as "Aaron." If "his brother" is dropped, the meaning or intent is missed. On the other hand, in the statement, "I delivered Aaron, his brother," the antecedent "Aaron" prepares the way for its substitute, "his brother," the key term. If the antecedent is dropped, the meaning is left intact by its substitution (whose identity is considered known). The substitute repeats or corroborates, not identifies, its antecedent.
7. This excludes the particles of conjunctive apposition mentioned above.
8. Proper nouns (but not personal proper names) may also be a substitution. Hence, the substitution may be more specific at times than its antecedent noun. Context must determine if a proper noun is identifying or substituting for the antecedent noun. Authorities often differ on this point. Substitution will often repeat the prepositions and particles of its antecedent noun.
9. This substitution or transformation is similar in meaning to other forms of ABSOLUTE IDENTIFICATION (§11v; 16h). Substitution apposition, because it is absolute, is also called "all-for-all" or "whole-for-the-whole" substitution. The noun and its substitution, therefore, must be of the same essence or nature.

18:1 (כֹהֵן מִדְיָן חֹתֵן מֹשֶׁה; compare verses 12 and 14 where Jethro is referred to only by his substitution); 1 Sam 19:4 (אָבִיו); 20:32 (אָבִיו; cf. 33); 21:2 (הַכֹּהֵן), 11 (מֶלֶךְ גַּת); Jer 1:2(2x); 7:21, 28, 32; 26:18; BA Dan 4:14; Ezra 6:13; 7:11–12

Biblical Hebrew exhibits two types of substitution:

A. All-for-All Substitution *b*

This is the normal or typical substitution as discussed above. The substitution completely stands in the place of its antecedent noun.

B. Comprehended Substitution *c*

This substitution refers only to one aspect of the antecedent noun. The comprehended substitution must have a pronoun to connect it with its antecedent noun.

שְׁכֶם בְּנִי חָשְׁקָה נַפְשׁוֹ בְּבִתְּכֶם Gen 34:8[b]

Shechem, my son, **his soul** clings to your daughter.

"My son" is an all-for-all substitution for Shechem; "his soul" is the comprehended apposition, comprehending only Shechem's soul, not his entire person.

The distinction between substitution and explicative is, at times, very fine. *d* Authorities, on occasion, differ on specific examples. Sometimes, it is a judgment call whether an author intended a substitution or an explicative. Practically speaking, explicative apposition will most often be a personal proper name or sometimes the general to the specific (tree, oak tree). Substitution, by contrast, will not be a personal proper name and is sometimes the specific to the general (Moses, the servant of Lord). Often substitution puts two nouns together like English apposition: "upon my people, upon Israel."

Exercises

I. Questions and Discussions

1. Define apposition. The appositive agrees with its antecedent on what grammatical levels?
2. List and define the five types of apposition.
3. Define descriptive nouns. List and define the three types of descriptive nouns.
4. List and define the four types of semi-descriptive nouns.
5. Describe the clauses and phrases that may qualify a noun.
6. Discuss the syntactical uses of qualifiers.
7. List and define the two types of corroboratives.
8. List the particles for conjunctive apposition.
9. Discuss and contrast, in detail, explicative and substitution apposition.
10. List and discuss the two types of substitution.

II. Drills

For the following nouns, analyze the type of apposition. The verses follow the numbering of the Masoretic Text.

Gen 14:10 (1) וְעֵמֶק הַשִּׂדִּים בֶּאֱרֹת בֶּאֱרֹת חֵמָר וַיָּנֻסוּ מֶלֶךְ־סְדֹם וַעֲמֹרָה וַיִּפְּלוּ־שָׁמָּה וְהַנִּשְׁאָרִים הֶרָה נָּסוּ׃

Gen 25:25 (2) וַיֵּצֵא הָרִאשׁוֹן אַדְמוֹנִי כֻּלּוֹ כְּאַדֶּרֶת שֵׂעָר וַיִּקְרְאוּ שְׁמוֹ עֵשָׂו׃

Exod 11:3 (3) וַיִּתֵּן יְהוָה אֶת־חֵן הָעָם בְּעֵינֵי מִצְרָיִם גַּם ׀ הָאִישׁ מֹשֶׁה גָּדוֹל מְאֹד בְּאֶרֶץ מִצְרַיִם בְּעֵינֵי עַבְדֵי־פַרְעֹה וּבְעֵינֵי הָעָם׃

Exod 3:15 (4) וַיֹּאמֶר עוֹד אֱלֹהִים אֶל־מֹשֶׁה כֹּה־תֹאמַר אֶל־בְּנֵי יִשְׂרָאֵל יְהוָה אֱלֹהֵי אֲבֹתֵיכֶם אֱלֹהֵי אַבְרָהָם אֱלֹהֵי יִצְחָק וֵאלֹהֵי יַעֲקֹב שְׁלָחַנִי אֲלֵיכֶם זֶה־שְּׁמִי לְעֹלָם וְזֶה זִכְרִי לְדֹר דֹּר׃

Gen 6:4 (5) הַנְּפִלִים הָיוּ בָאָרֶץ בַּיָּמִים הָהֵם וְגַם אַחֲרֵי־כֵן אֲשֶׁר יָבֹאוּ בְּנֵי הָאֱלֹהִים אֶל־בְּנוֹת הָאָדָם וְיָלְדוּ לָהֶם הֵמָּה הַגִּבֹּרִים אֲשֶׁר מֵעוֹלָם אַנְשֵׁי הַשֵּׁם׃

Gen 14:20 (6) וּבָרוּךְ אֵל עֶלְיוֹן אֲשֶׁר־מִגֵּן צָרֶיךָ בְּיָדֶךָ וַיִּתֶּן־לוֹ מַעֲשֵׂר מִכֹּל׃

1 Sam 18:6 (7) וַיְהִי בְּבוֹאָם בְּשׁוּב דָּוִד מֵהַכּוֹת אֶת־הַפְּלִשְׁתִּי וַתֵּצֶאנָה הַנָּשִׁים מִכָּל־עָרֵי יִשְׂרָאֵל לָשִׁיר וְהַמְּחֹלוֹת לִקְרַאת שָׁאוּל הַמֶּלֶךְ בְּתֻפִּים בְּשִׂמְחָה וּבְשָׁלִשִׁים׃

Gen 32:10 (8) וַיֹּאמֶר יַעֲקֹב אֱלֹהֵי אָבִי אַבְרָהָם וֵאלֹהֵי אָבִי יִצְחָק יְהוָה הָאֹמֵר אֵלַי שׁוּב לְאַרְצְךָ וּלְמוֹלַדְתְּךָ וְאֵיטִיבָה עִמָּךְ׃

Gen 42:11 (9) כֻּלָּנוּ בְּנֵי אִישׁ־אֶחָד נָחְנוּ כֵּנִים אֲנַחְנוּ לֹא־הָיוּ עֲבָדֶיךָ מְרַגְּלִים׃

Gen 2:9 (10) וַיַּצְמַח יְהוָה אֱלֹהִים מִן־הָאֲדָמָה כָּל־עֵץ נֶחְמָד לְמַרְאֶה וְטוֹב לְמַאֲכָל וְעֵץ הַחַיִּים בְּתוֹךְ הַגָּן וְעֵץ הַדַּעַת טוֹב וָרָע׃

1 Sam 17:58 (11) וַיֹּאמֶר אֵלָיו שָׁאוּל בֶּן־מִי אַתָּה הַנָּעַר וַיֹּאמֶר דָּוִד בֶּן־עַבְדְּךָ יִשַׁי בֵּית הַלַּחְמִי׃

Gen 24:43 (12) הִנֵּה אָנֹכִי נִצָּב עַל־עֵין הַמָּיִם וְהָיָה הָעַלְמָה הַיֹּצֵאת לִשְׁאֹב וְאָמַרְתִּי אֵלֶיהָ הַשְׁקִינִי־נָא מְעַט־מַיִם מִכַּדֵּךְ׃

1 Sam 8:2 (13) וַיְהִי שֶׁם־בְּנוֹ הַבְּכוֹר יוֹאֵל וְשֵׁם מִשְׁנֵהוּ אֲבִיָּה שֹׁפְטִים בִּבְאֵר שָׁבַע׃

(14) Exod 2:21 וַיּוֹאֶל מֹשֶׁה לָשֶׁבֶת אֶת־הָאִישׁ וַיִּתֵּן אֶת־צִפֹּרָה בִתּוֹ לְמֹשֶׁה׃

(15) Exod 21:32 אִם־עֶבֶד יִגַּח הַשּׁוֹר אוֹ אָמָה כֶּסֶף ׀ שְׁלֹשִׁים שְׁקָלִים יִתֵּן לַאדֹנָיו וְהַשּׁוֹר יִסָּקֵל׃

(16) Exod 18:20 וְהִזְהַרְתָּה אֶתְהֶם אֶת־הַחֻקִּים וְאֶת־הַתּוֹרֹת וְהוֹדַעְתָּ לָהֶם אֶת־הַדֶּרֶךְ יֵלְכוּ בָהּ וְאֶת־הַמַּעֲשֶׂה אֲשֶׁר יַעֲשׂוּן׃

(17) Exod 5:17 וַיֹּאמֶר נִרְפִּים אַתֶּם נִרְפִּים עַל־כֵּן אַתֶּם אֹמְרִים נֵלְכָה נִזְבְּחָה לַיהוָה׃

(18) Exod 12:51 וַיְהִי בְּעֶצֶם הַיּוֹם הַזֶּה הוֹצִיא יְהוָה אֶת־בְּנֵי יִשְׂרָאֵל מֵאֶרֶץ מִצְרַיִם עַל־צִבְאֹתָם׃

(19) Num 32:14 וְהִנֵּה קַמְתֶּם תַּחַת אֲבֹתֵיכֶם תַּרְבּוּת אֲנָשִׁים חַטָּאִים לִסְפּוֹת עוֹד עַל חֲרוֹן אַף־יְהוָה אֶל־יִשְׂרָאֵל׃

(20) Exod 3:10 וְעַתָּה לְכָה וְאֶשְׁלָחֲךָ אֶל־פַּרְעֹה וְהוֹצֵא אֶת־עַמִּי בְנֵי־יִשְׂרָאֵל מִמִּצְרָיִם׃

Chapter 7
NUMERALS

§28. Introduction

The syntax of numerals has two elements, the number and the NUMERABLE, the thing counted. Because the numerable and the number often differ in gender (especially with the numbers 3–10), two sets of constructions are given: one for the masculine numerable with a feminine number and one for the feminine numerable with a masculine number.

§29. Cardinal Numbers *a*

A. Masculine Numerable with Feminine Number

1) שְׁלֹשָׁה בָנִים: The numerable (בָנִים) is an accusative of specification (§13kk), "A triad in terms of sons." Gen 6:10; Exod 2:2; 21:37; 1 Sam 25:5; BA Dan 4:20; 7:6

2) שְׁלֹשֶׁת בָּנִים: The numerable is a GENITIVE OF SPECIFICATION, "A triad in terms of sons." Exod 3:18; 7:25; 10:22; 12:15; 15:22; 16:26; 23:15; BA Ezra 7:14

3) בָּנִים שְׁלֹשָׁה: The number is a SEMI-DESCRIPTIVE NOUN (adjective, §23k) in apposition to the numerable, "Sons, a triad (or three)." Gen 32:16; Num 7:17(4x); 29:29

B. Feminine Numerable with Masculine Number *b*

1) שָׁלֹשׁ שָׁנִים: The numerable (שָׁנִים) is an accusative of specification (§13kk), "A triad in terms of years." Exod 2:16; Lev 19:23; BA Dan 7:2–3

2) שְׁלֹשׁ שָׁנִים: The numerable is a genitive of specification, "A triad in terms of years." Exod 4:9; 21:37; Jer 1:2

3) שָׁנִים שָׁלֹשׁ: The number is a semi-descriptive noun (adjective, §23k) in apposition to the numerable, "Years, a triad (or three)." Gen 32:16; BA Ezra 6:3

C. Substantive or Adjective (semi-descriptive noun, §23i–l) *c*

In English, cardinal numbers (three, four, five, etc) are adjectives; in Hebrew, they are usually SUBSTANTIVES (a "triad" instead of "three").[1] Word order determines whether a number is a substantive or a semi-descriptive noun functioning as an adjective in Hebrew. If the number precedes the numerable, the number is a substantive (triad). If the number follows the numerable, the number is a semi-descriptive noun (triad) functioning as an adjective (three); hence, either translation (triad or three) is strictly correct. In examples one and two above, the number is a substantive; in example three, the number is a

1. In Hebrew, the cardinal number "one" is usually an adjective like English; the cardinal number "two" may often be an adjective as well, but sometimes it is a substantive.

semi-descriptive noun functioning as an adjective. Of course, the translations offered here are technical translations. The general English translations, "three sons" or "three years," are practical for the constructions.

d **D. Gender Difference between Number and Numerable**

Especially for the numbers three through ten (including the three through nine in the numbers, 13–19, and in decade numbers, 23–29, 33–39, etc.), the gender of the numerable and the gender of the number are opposites: a masculine numerable will take a feminine number (Gen 6:10; Exod 6:18), and a feminine numerable will take a masculine number (Lev 19:23; Num 29:13).

Exod 6:18 וּבְנֵי קְהָת עַמְרָם וְיִצְהָר וְחֶבְרוֹן וְעֻזִּיאֵל וּשְׁנֵי חַיֵּי קְהָת שָׁלֹשׁ וּשְׁלֹשִׁים וּמְאַת שָׁנָה׃

And the sons of Kohath: Amram and Izhar and Hebron and Uzziel; and the years of life of Kohath were one hundred and **thirty-three** years [three and thirty and a hundred years].

In Exod 6:18, the feminine numerable takes a masculine number.

Num 29:13 וְהִקְרַבְתֶּם עֹלָה אִשֵּׁה רֵיחַ נִיחֹחַ לַיהוָה פָּרִים בְּנֵי־בָקָר שְׁלֹשָׁה עָשָׂר אֵילִם שְׁנָיִם כְּבָשִׂים בְּנֵי־שָׁנָה אַרְבָּעָה עָשָׂר תְּמִימִם יִהְיוּ׃

And you shall present a burnt offering, an offering by fire as a soothing aroma to the Lord: **thirteen** bulls, sons of cattle, two rams, **fourteen** male lambs one year old, in the situation of unblemished they exist.

In Num 29:13, the masculine numerable takes a feminine number. See also 1 Sam 24:3.

The decade numbers from 20 to 90, plural in form, are common (masculine and feminine) in gender. The numbers one and two (and eleven, twelve; twenty-one, twenty-two, etc.) usually agree with their numerable in gender, but can occur in either gender. BA Dan 4:26

e **E. The Numerable as Singular or Plural**

The numbers two to ten almost always takes a plural numerable (Gen 18:2). The numbers eleven to nineteen, decade numbers (twenty, thirty, forty, etc), and words for hundred and thousand usually take a singular numerable (accusative of specification, §13kk) with common nouns, such as, יוֹם (Exod 12:18; 24:18), שָׁנָה (Exod 6:16, 18, 20; 12:40), אִישׁ, נֶפֶשׁ (Exod 1:5); otherwise, they usually take a plural numerable (Exod 15:27; 21:32). Decade numbers with one through nine (21–29, 31–39, etc,) often take a singular numerable after them (as an accusative of specification, Gen 5:20) or a plural numerable before them (as a semi-descriptive noun, §23k, Dan 9:26).

Gen 18:2 וַיִּשָּׂא עֵינָיו וַיַּרְא וְהִנֵּה שְׁלֹשָׁה אֲנָשִׁים נִצָּבִים עָלָיו וַיַּרְא וַיָּרָץ לִקְרָאתָם מִפֶּתַח הָאֹהֶל וַיִּשְׁתַּחוּ אָרְצָה׃

And he lifted up his eyes and looked, behold, **three men** were standing opposite him; and he saw *them*, and he ran to meet them from the tent door, and bowed himself to the ground.

The numbers two to ten often take a plural numerable.
Gen 6:10; 11:13; 18:6; 29:34

Deut 1:2 אַחַד עָשָׂר יוֹם מֵחֹרֵב דֶּרֶךְ הַר־שֵׂעִיר עַד קָדֵשׁ בַּרְנֵעַ׃

(It is) **eleven in terms of a day** from Horeb by the way of Mount Seir to Kadesh-barnea.

The numbers eleven to nineteen, decade numbers, and words for hundred and thousand take a singular numerable, an accusative of specification, especially with common nouns, such as יוֹם, שָׁנָה, אִישׁ, נֶפֶשׁ, שֵׁבֶט.
Exod 28:21; Num 1:44; 7:3; 1 Sam 24:3 (accusative of specification)

Exod 21:32 אִם־עֶבֶד יִגַּח הַשּׁוֹר אוֹ אָמָה כֶּסֶף ׀ שְׁלֹשִׁים שְׁקָלִים יִתֵּן
לַאדֹנָיו וְהַשּׁוֹר יִסָּקֵל׃

If a male servant the ox gores or a female servant, *the owner* shall give its owner silver, **thirty shekels**, and the ox shall be stoned.

The decade number takes a plural if its numerable is not a common noun, such as יוֹם, שָׁנָה, אִישׁ, נֶפֶשׁ, שֵׁבֶט.

Gen 5:20 וַיִּהְיוּ כָּל־יְמֵי־יֶרֶד שְׁתַּיִם וְשִׁשִּׁים שָׁנָה וּתְשַׁע מֵאוֹת שָׁנָה וַיָּמֹת׃

And all the days of Jared were nine hundred and **sixty-two** in terms of **year**, and he died.

The decade number (sixty) with its one to nine digit (two) before its numerable often takes a singular numerable with common nouns.

Dan 9:26 וְאַחֲרֵי הַשָּׁבֻעִים שִׁשִּׁים וּשְׁנַיִם יִכָּרֵת מָשִׁיחַ וְאֵין לוֹ וְהָעִיר
וְהַקֹּדֶשׁ יַשְׁחִית עַם נָגִיד הַבָּא וְקִצּוֹ בַשֶּׁטֶף וְעַד קֵץ
מִלְחָמָה נֶחֱרֶצֶת שֹׁמֵמוֹת׃

And after **the sixty-two weeks**, the Messiah will be cut off without anything to him, and the city and the sanctuary the people of the prince who is to come will destroy. And its end *will come* with a flood; even to the end of war; desolations are determined.

The decade number (sixty) with a one-to-nine digit (two) after its numerable often takes a plural numerable.
Gen 17:20; 37:9; Num 17:17; 29:17; Josh 19:30; 21:41; Ezra 8:35; 1 Chr 12:29

F. Compound Numbers f

Compound numbers are numbers combining a decade number (10, 20, 30, etc.) with a one through nine (11, 22, etc.). The word order for compound numbers is usually the decade number followed by one through nine (Gen 46:15). The opposite word order, the word order of Arabic, occasionally occurs (Gen 11:12). The Vav of apposition connects the parts of the compound numbers. Contrary to Arabic, compound numbers, especially with hundred or thousand, may repeat the numerable (Gen 5:23).

Gen 46:15 אֵלֶּה ׀ בְּנֵי לֵאָה אֲשֶׁר יָלְדָה לְיַעֲקֹב בְּפַדַּן אֲרָם וְאֵת דִּינָה
בִתּוֹ כָּל־נֶפֶשׁ בָּנָיו וּבְנוֹתָיו שְׁלֹשִׁים וְשָׁלֹשׁ׃

These are the sons of Leah, whom she bore to Jacob in Paddan-aram, and his daughter Dinah; every soul of his sons and daughters (were) **thirty and three**.

Gen 46:15 represents the usual word order and employs the Vav of apposition: decade number (thirty), then the one-to-nine digit (three).
Gen 18:28; Deut 2:14; Josh 7:5

Gen 11:12 וְאַרְפַּכְשַׁד חַי חָמֵשׁ וּשְׁלֹשִׁים שָׁנָה וַיּוֹלֶד אֶת־שָׁלַח׃

And Arpachshad lived **five and thirty** years, and he became the father of Shelah.

Gen 11:12 represents the alternative, less usual, word order, and employs the Vav of apposition: the one-to-nine digit (five), then the decade number (thirty). Gen 11:20; Exod 7:7; 12:18; Num 1:21; 31:40

Gen 5:23 וַיְהִי כָּל־יְמֵי חֲנוֹךְ חָמֵשׁ וְשִׁשִּׁים שָׁנָה וּשְׁלֹשׁ מֵאוֹת שָׁנָה׃

So all the days of Enoch were five and sixty **years** and three hundred **years**.

Gen 5:23 shows the repetition of the numerable. Exod 12:40

g **G. Numbers and Definiteness**

Having inherent or quasi-definiteness,[2] cardinal numbers usually do not take the article even when its numerable is definite (Gen 18:28; 1 Kgs 7:27). When the numerable is without definiteness, the number specifies the numerable (Num 7:17). If a number refers back to a numerable, but not directly modifying the numerable, it may have the article.

Gen 18:28 אוּלַי יַחְסְרוּן חֲמִשִּׁים הַצַּדִּיקִם חֲמִשָּׁה הֲתַשְׁחִית בַּחֲמִשָּׁה אֶת־
כָּל־הָעִיר וַיֹּאמֶר לֹא אַשְׁחִית אִם־אֶמְצָא שָׁם אַרְבָּעִים וַחֲמִשָּׁה׃

Perhaps **the fifty with respect to the righteous** lack five, will you destroy for the five the whole city? And He said, I will not destroy if I find there forty and five.

1 Kgs 7:27 וַיַּעַשׂ אֶת־הַמְּכֹנוֹת עֶשֶׂר נְחֹשֶׁת אַרְבַּע בָּאַמָּה אֹרֶךְ הַמְּכוֹנָה
הָאֶחָת וְאַרְבַּע בָּאַמָּה רָחְבָּהּ וְשָׁלֹשׁ בָּאַמָּה קוֹמָתָהּ׃

And he made **the ten stands** of bronze; the length of each stand was four cubits and its width four cubits and its height three cubits.

In Gen 18:28 and 1 Kgs 7:27, the numbers are indefinite with definite numerables.
Exod 26:19; Num 7:85; 28:4

Num 7:17 וּלְזֶבַח הַשְּׁלָמִים בָּקָר שְׁנַיִם אֵילִם חֲמִשָּׁה עַתֻּדִים חֲמִשָּׁה
כְּבָשִׂים בְּנֵי־שָׁנָה חֲמִשָּׁה זֶה קָרְבַּן נַחְשׁוֹן בֶּן־עַמִּינָדָב׃

And for the sacrifice of peace offerings, **two oxen, five rams, five male goats, five one-year-old male lambs.** This was the offering of Nahshon the son of Amminadab.

2. This inherent definiteness is indicated when a number without definiteness has the demonstrative pronoun (Gen 9:19).

Gen 9:19 שְׁלֹשָׁה אֵלֶּה בְּנֵי־נֹחַ וּמֵאֵלֶּה נָפְצָה כָל־הָאָרֶץ׃

These three were the sons of Noah; and from these the whole earth was populated.

In Num 7:17, the indefinite number specifies the indefinite numerable.
Gen 32:15(4x)–16(4x)

Gen 14:9 אֵת כְּדָרְלָעֹמֶר מֶלֶךְ עֵילָם וְתִדְעָל מֶלֶךְ גּוֹיִם וְאַמְרָפֶל מֶלֶךְ שִׁנְעָר וְאַרְיוֹךְ מֶלֶךְ אֶלָּסָר אַרְבָּעָה מְלָכִים אֶת־הַחֲמִשָּׁה׃

Against Chedorlaomer king of Elam and Tidal king of Goiim and Amraphel king of Shinar and Arioch king of Ellasar – four kings against **five**.

In Gen 14:9, the number five is definite, referring back to the kings.
Gen 18:29; Num 16:35

H. Numbers with the Omission of Measure, Weight, or Time *h*

Certain numerables may require specifications, such as a measure, weight, or time, which may be omitted if the context implies the specified measure, weight, or time.

Gen 20:16 וּלְשָׂרָה אָמַר הִנֵּה נָתַתִּי אֶלֶף כֶּסֶף לְאָחִיךְ הִנֵּה הוּא־לָךְ כְּסוּת עֵינַיִם לְכֹל אֲשֶׁר אִתָּךְ וְאֵת כֹּל וְנֹכָחַת׃

And to Sarah he said, Behold, I have given **a thousand** *shekels* of silver to your brother. Behold, it is a covering of eyes to all who are with you, and everything you are vindicated.

In Gen 20:16, the word "shekels" is implied.
Gen 24:22; 37:28 (shekels); Num 15:4 (ephahs); Lev 23:17 (loaves)

§30. Ordinal Numbers

Ordinal numbers—first, second, third—for two through ten are formed by adding a Hireq-Yod[3] to the root of the cardinal number, for example, שְׁלִישִׁי (the ת marks the feminine, שְׁלִישִׁית), "third," from the root שלשׁ. The ordinal "first" is רִאשׁוֹן.[4] The cardinal numbers substitute for the ordinals tenth and above (Gen 7:11). Moreover, like Arabic, the cardinal numbers may substitute for the ordinal numbers first through ninth, especially with days of the month or with years (2 Kgs 18:1).

Gen 7:11 בִּשְׁנַת שֵׁשׁ־מֵאוֹת שָׁנָה לְחַיֵּי־נֹחַ בַּחֹדֶשׁ הַשֵּׁנִי בְּשִׁבְעָה־עָשָׂר יוֹם לַחֹדֶשׁ בַּיּוֹם הַזֶּה נִבְקְעוּ כָּל־מַעְיְנֹת תְּהוֹם רַבָּה וַאֲרֻבֹּת הַשָּׁמַיִם נִפְתָּחוּ׃

In the **six hundredth** year to the life of Noah, in the second month, on the **seventeenth** day of the month, on this day all the fountains of the great deep split open, and the windows of the heavens were opened.

In Gen 7:11, the cardinal numbers (six hundred and seventeen) substitute for the ordinal numbers (six hundredth and seventeenth).

3. This is the Nisbah ending, "pertaining to" or "in relation to." (§23j)
4. The ending וֹן also appears similar to a Nisbah ending, compare קַדְמוֹן (pertaining to the east) from קֶדֶם.

2 Kgs 18:1 וַיְהִי בִּשְׁנַת שָׁלֹשׁ לְהוֹשֵׁעַ בֶּן־אֵלָה מֶלֶךְ יִשְׂרָאֵל מָלַךְ
חִזְקִיָּה בֶן־אָחָז מֶלֶךְ יְהוּדָה׃

And it happened in the **third** year of Hoshea, the son of Elah king of Israel, that Hezekiah the son of Ahaz king of Judah became king.

In 2 Kgs 18:1, the cardinal number (three) substitutes for the ordinal number (third).

Deut 26:12 כִּי תְכַלֶּה לַעְשֵׂר אֶת־כָּל־מַעְשַׂר תְּבוּאָתְךָ בַּשָּׁנָה הַשְּׁלִישִׁת
שְׁנַת הַמַּעֲשֵׂר וְנָתַתָּה לַלֵּוִי לַגֵּר לַיָּתוֹם וְלָאַלְמָנָה וְאָכְלוּ
בִשְׁעָרֶיךָ וְשָׂבֵעוּ׃

When you finish paying all the tithe of your increase **in the third year**, the year of tithing, then you shall give *it* to the Levite, to the stranger, to the orphan and to the widow, that they may eat in your towns, and be satisfied.

In Deut 26:12, the ordinal number modifies the numerable, agreeing in gender, number, and case. Ordinals are semi-descriptive nouns like cardinals. Ordinal numbers, however, are more like adjectives than the cardinals since they agree in gender and definiteness with their numerable, as Deut 26:12 and the following example illustrate.

Exod 2:13[a] וַיֵּצֵא בַּיּוֹם הַשֵּׁנִי

And he went out **on the second (next) day**

Exod 4:8; 12:15–16; 16:1; 20:5(2x); 23:11

§31. Distributives (§9b; 24f)

Like Arabic, Hebrew may repeat cardinal numbers to form distributives—two by two, three by three, etc. (Gen 7:9). The numerable may be repeated as well as the cardinal (Josh 3:12). The preposition ל attached to a cardinal may also communicate distribution (Amos 4:4).

Gen 7:9 שְׁנַיִם שְׁנַיִם בָּאוּ אֶל־נֹחַ אֶל־הַתֵּבָה זָכָר וּנְקֵבָה כַּאֲשֶׁר צִוָּה
אֱלֹהִים אֶת־נֹחַ׃

Two by two, male and female, they entered the ark to Noah, as God had commanded Noah.

Isa 27:12 וְהָיָה בַּיּוֹם הַהוּא יַחְבֹּט יְהוָה מִשִּׁבֹּלֶת הַנָּהָר עַד־נַחַל
מִצְרָיִם וְאַתֶּם תְּלֻקְּטוּ לְאַחַד אֶחָד בְּנֵי יִשְׂרָאֵל׃

And it will happen in that day, that the Lord will thresh from the flowing stream of the Euphrates to the brook of Egypt. And you – you will be gathered up **one by one**, O sons of Israel.

Gen 7:2; Exod 12:3; 13:10; 1 Sam 29:2; 1 Kgs 18:13; 1 Chr 26:17

§32. Multiplicatives

Again like Arabic, Hebrew multiplicatives—one time, two times, three times, etc.—may be expressed by cardinal numbers (seven times, Lev 26:21), probably with פַּעַם (Gen 27:36) or something similar implied (Gen 31:7; 43:34; Exod 23:14). Furthermore, multiplicatives may be expressed by the dual/adverbial ending ַ֫יִם, שִׁבְעָתַיִם (seven times Gen 4:15).

Lev 26:21 וְאִם־תֵּלְכוּ עִמִּי קֶרִי וְלֹא תֹאבוּ לִשְׁמֹעַ לִי וְיָסַפְתִּי עֲלֵיכֶם מַכָּה שֶׁבַע כְּחַטֹּאתֵיכֶם׃

If you walk with me rebelliously and are unwilling to obey Me, then I will increase on you the plague **seven times** according to your sins.

Cardinal number: Lev 26:18, 21; Deut 25:3; dual/adverbial ending: Isa 30:26; Ps 12:7

Exercises

I. Questions and Discussions

1. The numerable and the number often differ in what grammatical category?
2. How are cardinal numbers understood grammatically in English and Hebrew? How are the cardinal numbers one and two understood in Hebrew?
3. How does word order between the number and numerable affect the grammatical analysis of cardinal numbers? How should the genitive numerable of the number be understood?
4. What is the gender of decade numbers 20–90?
5. Which numbers usually take a plural numerable? Which ones with certain common nouns may take a singular numerable? Which numbers take numerables as an accusative of specification? Which take adjectives/apposition?
6. What is the usual word order for compound numbers? What is the occasional alternative word order?
7. Why may the number be without the article, though its numerable has the article?
8. What kind of numerables may be omitted?
9. How are ordinal numbers formed? What may substitute for ordinal numbers?
10. Define distributives. How does Hebrew express distributives?
11. Define multiplicatives. How does Hebrew express multiplicatives?

II. Drills

Analyze the numerable (for example, accusative of specification, genitive of specification, or apposition) in the following sentences. The verses follow the numbering of the Masoretic Text.

(1) Gen 2:10 וְנָהָר֙ יֹצֵ֣א מֵעֵ֔דֶן לְהַשְׁק֖וֹת אֶת־הַגָּ֑ן וּמִשָּׁם֙ יִפָּרֵ֔ד וְהָיָ֖ה לְאַרְבָּעָ֥ה רָאשִֽׁים׃

(2) Gen 46:15 אֵ֣לֶּה׀ בְּנֵ֣י לֵאָ֗ה אֲשֶׁ֨ר יָלְדָ֤ה לְיַעֲקֹב֙ בְּפַדַּ֣ן אֲרָ֔ם וְאֵ֖ת דִּינָ֣ה בִתּ֑וֹ כָּל־נֶ֛פֶשׁ
בָּנָ֥יו וּבְנוֹתָ֖יו שְׁלֹשִׁ֥ים וְשָׁלֹֽשׁ׃

(3) Gen 5:9 וַיְחִ֥י אֱנ֖וֹשׁ תִּשְׁעִ֣ים שָׁנָ֑ה וַיּ֖וֹלֶד אֶת־קֵינָֽן׃

(4) Gen 7:2 מִכֹּ֣ל׀ הַבְּהֵמָ֣ה הַטְּהוֹרָ֗ה תִּֽקַּח־לְךָ֛ שִׁבְעָ֥ה שִׁבְעָ֖ה אִ֣ישׁ וְאִשְׁתּ֑וֹ וּמִן־הַבְּהֵמָ֡ה
אֲ֠שֶׁר לֹ֣א טְהֹרָ֥ה הִ֛וא שְׁנַ֖יִם אִ֥ישׁ וְאִשְׁתּֽוֹ׃

(5) Gen 5:6 וַֽיְחִי־שֵׁ֕ת חָמֵ֥שׁ שָׁנִ֖ים וּמְאַ֣ת שָׁנָ֑ה וַיּ֖וֹלֶד אֶת־אֱנֽוֹשׁ׃

(6) Exod 26:11 וְעָשִׂ֛יתָ קַרְסֵ֥י נְחֹ֖שֶׁת חֲמִשִּׁ֑ים וְהֵבֵאתָ֤ אֶת־הַקְּרָסִים֙ בַּלֻּ֣לָאֹ֔ת וְחִבַּרְתָּ֥
אֶת־הָאֹ֖הֶל וְהָיָ֥ה אֶחָֽד׃

(7) Gen 4:19 וַיִּֽקַּֽח־ל֥וֹ לֶ֖מֶךְ שְׁתֵּ֣י נָשִׁ֑ים שֵׁ֤ם הָֽאַחַת֙ עָדָ֔ה וְשֵׁ֥ם הַשֵּׁנִ֖ית צִלָּֽה׃

(8) Gen 32:15 עִזִּ֣ים מָאתַ֔יִם וּתְיָשִׁ֖ים עֶשְׂרִ֑ים רְחֵלִ֥ים מָאתַ֖יִם וְאֵילִ֥ים עֶשְׂרִֽים׃

(9) Gen 8:10 וַיָּ֣חֶל ע֔וֹד שִׁבְעַ֥ת יָמִ֖ים אֲחֵרִ֑ים וַיֹּ֛סֶף שַׁלַּ֥ח אֶת־הַיּוֹנָ֖ה מִן־הַתֵּבָֽה׃

(10) Gen 10:25 וּלְעֵ֥בֶר יֻלַּ֖ד שְׁנֵ֣י בָנִ֑ים שֵׁ֣ם הָאֶחָ֞ד פֶּ֗לֶג כִּ֤י בְיָמָיו֙ נִפְלְגָ֣ה הָאָ֔רֶץ וְשֵׁ֥ם
אָחִ֖יו יָקְטָֽן׃

Chapter 8
THE ARTICLE

§33. Introduction

Hebrew nouns may be definite or indefinite. Ibn Barun defines an INDEFINITE NOUN as, "Every thing common to its (whole) genus, and not any of its individuals being meant rather than another."[1] A SPECIALIZED NOUN,[2] a type of INDEFINITE NOUN, is an *unknown*[3] person or thing that is part of the whole (genus), one or some individuals or things being meant rather than other individuals or things. A definite noun, by contrast, is a *known* person or thing that is part of the whole (genus), one or some individuals or things being meant rather than other individuals or things. The article is "a tool to make definite" the indefinite noun.[4] The article, therefore, limits or defines a known noun by selecting certain persons or things of a genus (group, class), not the whole of the genus (class), and by referring to an individual or individuals of a class rather than other individuals within the class. The article particularizes the known noun from its class. As such, the noun becomes definite or defined from the rest of its class. The indefinite "man" refers to any man or to mankind as a class; the specialized "a man" refers to a particular, unknown man; and the definite noun "the man" refers to a particular, known man.

The Hebrew article[5] has two definite uses and a non-definite use. The two definite uses are particular and generic. The particular use of the article singles out certain individual(s), thing(s), or concept(s) from their broader group. It particularizes its word. The generic use of the article limits a group or class (genus) from other groups or classes (genera). The generic article particularizes groups, not individuals.[6] Finally, the non-definite use of the article has two categories, when the words are naturally particularized (excessive article) and when the article and its noun have become a proper name (article of dominance).[7]

1. Wechter, 155.
2. Specialized nouns are limited by an adjective, genitive, clause, or context. Usually translate specialized nouns with an indefinite article in English—"a new king" (Exod 1:8), especially when אֶחָד specializes a noun. (1 Sam 1:1, a man; 24:15, a flea)
3. In the sentence, "He saw a man, but the man did not see him," the indefinite, "a man," is grammatically *unknown* since previously unmentioned; the definite, "the man," is grammatically *known* since mentioned earlier.
4. A word also becomes definite when constructed (annexed) onto a definite word, including words constructed onto pronominal suffixes. Some words are naturally definite, including proper names, independent pronouns, demonstrative pronouns, and relative pronouns. Cardinal numbers are semi-definite or inherently definite.
5. The Hebrew article, like the Greek article, may be related to the demonstrative pronoun or particle. The Dagesh Forte of the Hebrew article may reflect the demonstrative particle ל of the Arabic article, of demonstrative pronouns, and of some Aramaic demonstrative pronouns (אֵלֵּין and אֵלֵּךְ), found in the Hebrew forms אֵלֶּה and הַלָּזֶה (§20b; Gen 37:19).
6. Nouns without the article or specialization are not particularized in any manner.
7. Griess, 71–74; Howell §262; Wright I, §345.

§34. Particular

a The particular article singles out a noun from its broader group (genus). There are four categories for the particular use of the article. First, an author may mention or imply an indefinite noun (grammatically unknown). When he mentions the noun again (now grammatically known), the author attaches a particularizing article. Second, an author may preconceive a noun as known in his mind. The author, therefore, attaches the particularizing article at the first mention of the noun. Third, a noun that is present to the author/speaker, and hence known, also may receive an article at its first mention (presence). Finally, one-of-a-kind words (unique) possess the article, such as moon and sun, because they are naturally particular and known.

A. Repetition (of a previously mentioned indefinite noun)

Commonly, a noun first occurs without the article, often specialized, later to be repeated with an article. In 1 Sam 1:1, Elkanah is first introduced as *a* (one) man, then in verse three, he is referred to again as "that man (that I mentioned earlier)" with the article. This is similar to the usage of the article in English: "he saw a man, but the man did not see him." Here the article particularizes the man mentioned earlier.

Gen 6:14[a] עֲשֵׂה לְךָ תֵּבַת עֲצֵי־גֹפֶר קִנִּים תַּעֲשֶׂה אֶת־הַתֵּבָה

Make for yourself an ark of gopher wood. (In the status of) cells you will make **the ark**.

Gen 9:14 (הַקֶּשֶׁת); 31:46 (הַגָּל); 37:15 (הָאִישׁ); Exod 21:4 (הָאִשָּׁה), 28 (הַשּׁוֹר); 25:31 (הַמְּנוֹרָה); 31:15 (הַשַּׁבָּת); Lev 20:16 (הָאִשָּׁה); Num 19:14 (הָאֹהֶל); 35:16 (הָרֹצֵחַ); 1 Sam 17:49 (הָאֶבֶן); 24:4 (הַמְּעָרָה); BA Dan 7:8 (בְּקַרְנָא־דָא)

b **B. Preconception**

If a noun has the article at its first occurrence, an author may have preconceived or regarded the noun as known. Render preconceived definite nouns with an English indefinite article. In Genesis 8:7, Noah, having a particular raven and dove in mind, sends out *the* raven, and later *the* dove. Of course, in English, since the raven and the dove had not been mentioned earlier, and hence unknown, the indefinite article would be used—Noah sent out *a* raven and *a* dove. If an English speaker were to ask a Hebrew speaker what raven or dove he was referring to by the article, the answer would be, "The raven or dove about which I am talking."

Gen 14:13[a] וַיָּבֹא הַפָּלִיט וַיַּגֵּד לְאַבְרָם הָעִבְרִי

And **the (a) fugitive** came and reported to Abram the Hebrew.

Gen 15:1[a] אַחַר הַדְּבָרִים הָאֵלֶּה הָיָה דְבַר־יְהוָה אֶל־אַבְרָם בַּמַּחֲזֶה

After these things the word of the Lord came to Abram **in the (a) vision**.

Gen 9:23 (הַשִּׂמְלָה); Exod 4:20 (הַחֲמֹר); Num 13:23 (בַמּוֹט)

c **C. Presence**

When a noun is present to a speaker, and therefore known, the noun may have an article at its first mention.

1. With demonstrative pronouns: The definite article and its demonstrative pronoun points to something that is present, in mind or in actuality, to the speaker.

    וַיֹּאמֶר אַבְרָהָם כִּי אָמַרְתִּי רַק אֵין־יִרְאַת אֱלֹהִים בַּמָּקוֹם הַזֶּה Gen 20:11[a]

    And Abraham said, Because I said, surely there is no fear of God **in this place**.

    וַיֹּאמֶר לָבָן הַגַּל הַזֶּה עֵד בֵּינִי וּבֵינְךָ הַיּוֹם Gen 31:48[a]

    And Laban said, **This heap** is a witness between you and me this day.

    In these two examples, the definite nouns and the demonstrative pronouns (with an excessive article [§36a]) indicate the notion of presence to the speaker—"this here heap."

    Gen 7:1 (בַּדּוֹר הַזֶּה), 13 (הַיּוֹם הַזֶּה); 12:7 (הָאָרֶץ הַזֹּאת)
    Gen 15:7, 18; 17:21, 23; 19:13; Exod 17:4

2. With a vocative: This article often occurs with people who are present.

    וַיֹּאמֶר אַבְנֵר חֵי־נַפְשְׁךָ הַמֶּלֶךְ אִם־יָדָעְתִּי׃ 1 Sam 17:55[b]

    And Abner said, (by) the life of your soul, **O king**, I do not know.

    וַיֹּאמֶר אֵלָיו שָׁאוּל בֶּן־מִי אַתָּה הַנָּעַר 1 Sam 17:58[a]

    And Saul said to him, The son of whom are you, **O lad**.

    Deut 32:1 (הַשָּׁמַיִם); Judg 3:19 (הַמֶּלֶךְ); 1 Sam 23:20 (הַמֶּלֶךְ); 1 Kgs 18:26 (הַבַּעַל); 2 Kgs 1:11 (אִישׁ הָאֱלֹהִים); BA Dan 2:4 (מַלְכָּא)

3. With present time: This is common with certain nouns of time such as day (1 Sam 24:11), night (Gen 19:34), year (Jer 28:16), time (Gen 2:23). The word הַיּוֹם may occur with or without הַזֶּה, but with the same meaning of "this day" or "today."

    הוּא אֲבִי־מוֹאָב עַד־הַיּוֹם׃ Gen 19:37[b]

    He is the father of the Moabites unto **today (this day)**.

    Gen 19:5 (הַלָּיְלָה); 24:12 (הַיּוֹם)
    Gen 30:15; Exod 9:18; 13:4; 14:13, 21; Judg 13:23; 2 Kgs 19:29

D. Unique Terms *d*

Unique things and titles naturally have the article since there is only one, not a group or class: the moon, sun, earth, or high priest, and so forth.[8]

וַיַּחֲלֹם עוֹד חֲלוֹם אַחֵר וַיְסַפֵּר אֹתוֹ לְאֶחָיו וַיֹּאמֶר הִנֵּה חָלַמְתִּי חֲלוֹם עוֹד וְהִנֵּה הַשֶּׁמֶשׁ וְהַיָּרֵחַ וְאַחַד עָשָׂר כּוֹכָבִים מִשְׁתַּחֲוִים לִי׃ Gen 37:9

And he dreamed still another dream, and he related it to his brothers, and said, Behold, I have dreamed another dream. And behold, **the sun and the moon** and eleven stars were bowing down to me.

Gen 1:1 (אֵת הַשָּׁמַיִם וְאֵת הָאָרֶץ)

8. GKC §126d

§35. Generic

a While English occasionally uses the article generically—"the Russian," for example, to refer to Russians generically, not to a particular Russian—Hebrew commonly uses the article generically. The generic article refers to groups without referring to particular individuals or things, and to the general but not to the specific. The generic article has three usages:

A. Essence/Quality of the Group

This usage refers to the whole as the whole, not to any particular individuals making up the whole. This generic article focuses on the quality or essence of the group. In Gen 6:1, (וַיְהִי כִּי־הֵחֵל הָאָדָם "And it happened that man began to multiply") the word הָאָדָם refers to humanity as a whole becoming numerous, not every man or a particular man. The article brings out the essence or quality of אָדָם as a genus—mankind, humanity—not "the man." This is common with terms, such as cattle, silver, gold, and fire.[9]

Gen 13:2 וְאַבְרָם כָּבֵד מְאֹד בַּמִּקְנֶה בַּכֶּסֶף וּבַזָּהָב׃

And Abram was very rich **in [the] cattle, in [the] silver and in [the] gold**.

Gen 2:12 (הַשֹּׁהַם ,הַבְּדֹלַח); 6:14 (בַּכֹּפֶר); Exod 2:3 (בַחֵמָר וּבַזָּפֶת); 5:3 (בַּדֶּבֶר ,בֶחָרֶב); 7:19 (וּבָעֵצִים וּבָאֲבָנִים), 27 (בַּצְפַרְדְּעִים); 8:17 (הֶעָרֹב ,הֶעָרֹב); 15:10 (כַּעוֹפֶרֶת); 16:18 (בָעֹמֶר), 32 (הָעֹמֶר); 21:6 (בַּמַּרְצֵעַ), 20 (בַּשֵּׁבֶט); Num 12:10 (כַּשָּׁלֶג)

Exod 22:23, 24, 30; 23:28; Num 11:8; 21:31; Deut 5:24; 8:3; Jer 17:5; 26:23; Job 4:17; 2 Chr 6:18

b **B. Totality of individuals of the group**

This usage refers to all the individuals of the whole, without referring to any in particular. In Gen 6:5[a], וַיַּרְא יְהוָה כִּי רַבָּה רָעַת הָאָדָם ("And God saw that the wickedness of man was great") the word הָאָדָם refers to the totality of individuals (that is, every אָדָם) that make up the group. To determine whether the essence/quality or the totality of individuals of the group is meant, one may insert "every" (כָּל) before the word in question. If "every" (כָּל) can be inserted, the article represents the totality of individuals of the group. If (כָּל) cannot be inserted, the generic article represents the essence/quality of the group. Moreover, if the plural of the definite noun would virtually communicate the same meaning, the article is the totality of individuals of the group. The totality of individuals is common with gentilics (§23j; the Canaanite) and with classes, such as the righteous, the wicked, the enemy, the lion.[10]

Ps 9:7[a] הָאוֹיֵב תַּמּוּ חֳרָבוֹת לָנֶצַח

The enemy (every enemy, i.e., the enemies) – they have ceased in everlasting ruins.

Note the plural verb with "the enemy" in Ps 9:7.

1 Sam 13:17[a] וַיֵּצֵא הַמַּשְׁחִית מִמַּחֲנֵה פְלִשְׁתִּים שְׁלֹשָׁה רָאשִׁים

And **the raider (every raider, i.e., the raiders)** went out from the camp of the Philistines in three heads.

9. GKC §126n
10. GKC §126m

Gen 1:25 (הַבְּהֵמָה, cf. Gen 7:14); 6:20 (מֵהָעוֹף, הַבְּהֵמָה, cf. Gen 7:14); 14:21 (הַנֶּפֶשׁ); Exod 4:11 (לָאָדָם); 8:13 (בָּאָדָם וּבַבְּהֵמָה); 10:15 (בָּעֵץ וּבְעֵשֶׂב); 11:5 (הַשִּׁפְחָה); 12:49 (לָאֶזְרָח, וְלַגֵּר); 13:2 (בָּאָדָם וּבַבְּהֵמָה); 22:19 (לָאֱלֹהִים); 23:14 (בַּשָּׁנָה); Num 26:6 (הַכַּרְמִי)

C. Abstract *c*

The article used with the abstract nouns is probably related to the generic usage, since the abstract may be viewed as a class or group.[11]

Gen 19:11[a] וְאֶת־הָאֲנָשִׁים אֲשֶׁר־פֶּתַח הַבַּיִת הִכּוּ בַּסַּנְוֵרִים מִקָּטֹן וְעַד־גָּדוֹל

And the men who were at the door of the house they struck **with [the] blindness**, both small and great.

Gen 32:11 (הָאֱמֶת, הַחֲסָדִים); Exod 15:6 (בַּכֹּחַ); 18:9 (הַטּוֹבָה); 1 Sam 24:18 (הָרָעָה, הַטּוֹבָה); Jer 7:28 (הָאֱמוּנָה); BA Dan 2:20 (חָכְמְתָא, וּגְבוּרְתָא), 37 (וִיקָרָא, וְתָקְפָּא, חִסְנָא); Dan 9:7 (הַצְּדָקָה)

§36. Non-Definite Article *a*

Sometimes the article occurs on a word that is naturally definite.

A. Excessive Article (§20b)

The article attaches to a definite noun. Excessive articles are usually found with demonstrative pronouns, הַזֶּה, הַזֹּאת, הָאֵלֶּה,[12] and proper nouns, הַיַּרְדֵּן, הַגִּלְגָּל, etc.

Josh 1:2 מֹשֶׁה עַבְדִּי מֵת וְעַתָּה קוּם עֲבֹר אֶת־הַיַּרְדֵּן הַזֶּה

Moses my servant is dead. And now rise, cross this **Jordan**.

Josh 1:4[a] מֵהַמִּדְבָּר וְהַלְּבָנוֹן הַזֶּה וְעַד־הַנָּהָר הַגָּדוֹל נְהַר־פְּרָת כֹּל אֶרֶץ הַחִתִּים

From the wilderness **and this Lebanon**, even as far as the great river, the river Euphrates, all the land of the Hittites. . . .

Gen 31:23 (הַגִּלְעָד); Num 13:28 (הָעֲנָק); 14:45 (הַחָרְמָה); 21:1 (הָאֲתָרִים), 33 (הַבָּשָׁן); 1 Sam 25:2 (בַּכַּרְמֶל)

B. Article of Dominance *b*

The article turns its noun into a proper noun, hence, a dominant meaning for the word. In Job 1:6, the word הַשָּׂטָן, the adversary, has become a proper name (Satan); therefore, it has a dominant meaning with the article (Judg 6:25; GKC §126e).

Gen 4:1 וְהָאָדָם יָדַע אֶת־חַוָּה אִשְׁתּוֹ וַתַּהַר וַתֵּלֶד אֶת־קַיִן וַתֹּאמֶר קָנִיתִי אִישׁ אֶת־יְהוָה׃

And the man (Adam) knew Eve, his wife, and she conceived and gave birth to Cain, and she said, I have acquired a male child with the Lord.

Gen 20:1 (הַנֶּגֶב); Lev 20:5 (הַמֹּלֶךְ); Jer 7:14 (לַבַּיִת)

11. GKC §126n
12. These "excessive articles" on the demonstrative pronouns are also known as "alerting particles," (§20b).

Exercises

I. Questions and Discussions

1. Define indefinite noun, specialized noun, and definite noun.
2. List and define the two definite uses of the article.
3. When does the article not particularize its noun?
4. List and define the four particularizing usages of the article.
5. List and define the three usages of "presence" for the particularizing usage of the article.
6. List and define the three generic usages of the article. How can the "essence/quality of the group" and the "totality of individuals of the group" be distinguished?
7. List and define the two non-definite usages of the article.

II. Drills

Analyze the usage of the article in the following verses. The verses follow the numbering of the Masoretic Text.

Gen 11:3 (1)
וַיֹּאמְרוּ אִישׁ אֶל־רֵעֵהוּ הָבָה נִלְבְּנָה לְבֵנִים וְנִשְׂרְפָה לִשְׂרֵפָה וַתְּהִי
לָהֶם הַלְּבֵנָה לְאָבֶן וְהַחֵמָר הָיָה לָהֶם לַחֹמֶר׃

Gen 12:5 (2)
וַיִּקַּח אַבְרָם אֶת־שָׂרַי אִשְׁתּוֹ וְאֶת־לוֹט בֶּן־אָחִיו וְאֶת־כָּל־רְכוּשָׁם אֲשֶׁר
רָכָשׁוּ וְאֶת־הַנֶּפֶשׁ אֲשֶׁר־עָשׂוּ בְחָרָן וַיֵּצְאוּ לָלֶכֶת אַרְצָה כְּנַעַן וַיָּבֹאוּ
אַרְצָה כְּנָעַן׃

Gen 41:1 (3)
וַיְהִי מִקֵּץ שְׁנָתַיִם יָמִים וּפַרְעֹה חֹלֵם וְהִנֵּה עֹמֵד עַל־הַיְאֹר׃

Exod 17:3 (4)
וַיִּצְמָא שָׁם הָעָם לַמַּיִם וַיָּלֶן הָעָם עַל־מֹשֶׁה וַיֹּאמֶר לָמָּה זֶּה הֶעֱלִיתָנוּ
מִמִּצְרַיִם לְהָמִית אֹתִי וְאֶת־בָּנַי וְאֶת־מִקְנַי בַּצָּמָא׃

2 Kgs 9:5 (5)
וַיָּבֹא וְהִנֵּה שָׂרֵי הַחַיִל יֹשְׁבִים וַיֹּאמֶר דָּבָר לִי אֵלֶיךָ הַשָּׂר וַיֹּאמֶר יֵהוּא
אֶל־מִי מִכֻּלָּנוּ וַיֹּאמֶר אֵלֶיךָ הַשָּׂר׃

Exod 3:2 (6)
וַיֵּרָא מַלְאַךְ יְהוָה אֵלָיו בְּלַבַּת־אֵשׁ מִתּוֹךְ הַסְּנֶה וַיַּרְא וְהִנֵּה הַסְּנֶה
בֹּעֵר בָּאֵשׁ וְהַסְּנֶה אֵינֶנּוּ אֻכָּל׃

Exod 11:5 (7)
וּמֵת כָּל־בְּכוֹר בְּאֶרֶץ מִצְרַיִם מִבְּכוֹר פַּרְעֹה הַיֹּשֵׁב עַל־כִּסְאוֹ עַד
בְּכוֹר הַשִּׁפְחָה אֲשֶׁר אַחַר הָרֵחָיִם וְכֹל בְּכוֹר בְּהֵמָה׃

Exod 20:7 (8)
לֹא תִשָּׂא אֶת־שֵׁם־יְהוָה אֱלֹהֶיךָ לַשָּׁוְא כִּי לֹא יְנַקֶּה יְהוָה אֵת אֲשֶׁר־
יִשָּׂא אֶת־שְׁמוֹ לַשָּׁוְא׃

Exod 13:4 (9)
הַיּוֹם אַתֶּם יֹצְאִים בְּחֹדֶשׁ הָאָבִיב׃

Num 35:25 (10)
וְהִצִּילוּ הָעֵדָה אֶת־הָרֹצֵחַ מִיַּד גֹּאֵל הַדָּם וְהֵשִׁיבוּ אֹתוֹ הָעֵדָה אֶל־עִיר
מִקְלָטוֹ אֲשֶׁר־נָס שָׁמָּה וְיָשַׁב בָּהּ עַד־מוֹת הַכֹּהֵן הַגָּדֹל אֲשֶׁר־מָשַׁח אֹתוֹ
בְּשֶׁמֶן הַקֹּדֶשׁ׃

Num 21:20 (11)
וּמִבָּמוֹת הַגַּיְא אֲשֶׁר בִּשְׂדֵה מוֹאָב רֹאשׁ הַפִּסְגָּה וְנִשְׁקָפָה עַל־פְּנֵי הַיְשִׁימֹן׃

Gen 7:11 (12)
בִּשְׁנַת שֵׁשׁ־מֵאוֹת שָׁנָה לְחַיֵּי־נֹחַ בַּחֹדֶשׁ הַשֵּׁנִי בְּשִׁבְעָה־עָשָׂר יוֹם לַחֹדֶשׁ
בַּיּוֹם הַזֶּה נִבְקְעוּ כָּל־מַעְיְנֹת תְּהוֹם רַבָּה וַאֲרֻבֹּת הַשָּׁמַיִם נִפְתָּחוּ׃

Exod 12:10 (13)
וְלֹא־תוֹתִירוּ מִמֶּנּוּ עַד־בֹּקֶר וְהַנֹּתָר מִמֶּנּוּ עַד־בֹּקֶר בָּאֵשׁ תִּשְׂרֹפוּ׃

(14) Gen 22:13 וַיִּשָּׂא אַבְרָהָם אֶת־עֵינָיו וַיַּרְא וְהִנֵּה־אַיִל אַחַר נֶאֱחַז בַּסְּבַךְ בְּקַרְנָיו וַיֵּלֶךְ אַבְרָהָם וַיִּקַּח אֶת־הָאַיִל וַיַּעֲלֵהוּ לְעֹלָה תַּחַת בְּנוֹ׃

(15) Exod 15:11 מִי־כָמֹכָה בָּאֵלִם יְהוָה מִי כָּמֹכָה נֶאְדָּר בַּקֹּדֶשׁ נוֹרָא תְהִלֹּת עֹשֵׂה פֶלֶא׃

(16) Exod 16:16 זֶה הַדָּבָר אֲשֶׁר צִוָּה יְהוָה לִקְטוּ מִמֶּנּוּ אִישׁ לְפִי אָכְלוֹ עֹמֶר לַגֻּלְגֹּלֶת מִסְפַּר נַפְשֹׁתֵיכֶם אִישׁ לַאֲשֶׁר בְּאָהֳלוֹ תִּקָּחוּ׃

(17) Exod 4:20 וַיִּקַּח מֹשֶׁה אֶת־אִשְׁתּוֹ וְאֶת־בָּנָיו וַיַּרְכִּבֵם עַל־הַחֲמֹר וַיָּשָׁב אַרְצָה מִצְרָיִם וַיִּקַּח מֹשֶׁה אֶת־מַטֵּה הָאֱלֹהִים בְּיָדוֹ׃

(18) Gen 21:26 וַיֹּאמֶר אֲבִימֶלֶךְ לֹא יָדַעְתִּי מִי עָשָׂה אֶת־הַדָּבָר הַזֶּה וְגַם־אַתָּה לֹא־הִגַּדְתָּ לִּי וְגַם אָנֹכִי לֹא שָׁמַעְתִּי בִּלְתִּי הַיּוֹם׃

(19) Exod 16:13 וַיְהִי בָעֶרֶב וַתַּעַל הַשְּׂלָו וַתְּכַס אֶת־הַמַּחֲנֶה וּבַבֹּקֶר הָיְתָה שִׁכְבַת הַטַּל סָבִיב לַמַּחֲנֶה׃

(20) Exod 21:28 וְכִי־יִגַּח שׁוֹר אֶת־אִישׁ אוֹ אֶת־אִשָּׁה וָמֵת סָקוֹל יִסָּקֵל הַשּׁוֹר וְלֹא יֵאָכֵל אֶת־בְּשָׂרוֹ וּבַעַל הַשּׁוֹר נָקִי׃

Chapter 9
VERBAL AND NOMINAL CLAUSES

§37. Introduction: Particles and Clauses[1]

Particles derive their meaning from context, and therefore, must accompany a verb or noun.[2] They cannot convey action like a verb. They cannot function as a subject about which something is asserted, nor can they function as a predicate which asserts something about a subject, like a noun. When used with verbs, particles may assist in determining the aspect, tense, and mood of the verb. When used with nouns, particles often emphasize them.[3]

Particles also introduce various clauses—temporal, causal, conditional, etc. Clauses, of course, may also be introduced without particles, context determining the type of clause: temporal, causal, conditional, etc.

§38. Verbal and Nominal Clauses

All clauses, independent or dependent, may be divided into two general categories: verbal or nominal. This distinction is essential to the proper understanding of the Hebrew clause, sentence, and syntax. All other clause types—temporal, causal, conditional, etc.—must be understood within the broader categories of verbal and nominal clauses.[4] *a*

I. The Verbal/Nominal Clauses and the Sentence

A sentence contains a subject, concerning which something is stated, asked, exclaimed, or commanded, and a predicate that states, asks, exclaims, or commands something concerning a subject. A sentence occurs when a subject and predicate express a meaningful thought at which it is appropriate to pause. The clause is similar to the sentence, having a subject and a predicate. Independent clauses, moreover, express a meaningful thought at which it is appropriate to pause and are, therefore, essentially sentences. Dependent clauses, by contrast, are not sentences since they do not express a meaningful thought at which it is appropriate to pause. All sentences, therefore, are clauses, but not all clauses are sentences.

The same holds true for Hebrew. Most verbal and nominal clauses are sentences, but dependent clauses are not sentences. The terms verbal and nominal clauses, consequently, are more useful than the terms verbal and nominal sentences.

1. For the chapters on the clauses, only the substantival clause will be given a larger font. All other chapters will be with normal font, since the examples are straightforward with particles or common idioms.
2. Particles include prepositions, conjunctions, article, interrogatives, negatives, and any word that is not a verb or noun.
3. Particles used with verbs and nouns are discussed in chapters 1–8.
4. Howell, Introduction, iv; Wright II, §113; ZW, 23–24.

b **II. Definition of Verbal and Nominal Clauses**

The distinction between verbal and nominal clauses[5] is essential to understanding Hebrew syntax. Verbal clauses place the verb before the agent (subject); nominal clauses are either without a finite verb, or they place the initiator (subject) before the announcement (verb).[6] Verbal clauses focus on the verb, its development and progress; nominal clauses focus on the initiator, its identity, description, and characterization.

c **III. The Verbal Clause (§11a, jj)**

Verbal clauses carry the Hebrew narrative. By placing the verb before the agent, the verbal clause renders the action of the verb prominent, relative to the agent. In calm speech or narrative statements, the verbal clause represents the primary, dominant word order in Hebrew. Verbal clauses communicate the action or event. Thus, relatively speaking, what the agent *does* is more significant than who or what the agent *is*—the action is more significant than the actor.

d **IV. The Nominal Clause**

Nominal clauses, by contrast, render the noun (or more precisely, the initiator) prominent. Nominal clauses come with or without finite verbs. Those without finite verb are purely descriptive—the initiator is similar to the announcement in some manner. Those clauses with finite verbs are descriptive with verbal action in the announcement. Such clauses, therefore, have "two faces" because they have nominal and verbal aspects. Nominal clauses represent an alternative word order, interrupting the series of verbal clauses to focus on the initiator, a "new start" for the narrative. The initiator of a nominal clause always expresses a contrast, explicitly or implicitly, with other possible initiators in the context.[7] Nominal clauses describe, emphasize, contrast, and clarify the initiator. Thus, relatively speaking, who the initiator *is* rather than what he *does* is more important—the actor is more significant than the action.

5. A third type of clause, the adverbial, has an adverb or prepositional phrase in the place of announcement (predicate) and a definite initiator (subject). See §11a, footnote 1.
6. For the basic structures and terms (agent/verb and initiator/announcement) of verbal and nominal clauses, see §11.
7. Wright II, §119.

V. The Meaning of Verbal and Nominal Clauses e

Of course, verbal and nominal clauses differ in both form and meaning. Verbal clauses are about the verb, its action, event, occurrence; nominal clauses are about the initiator, its description, character, and identification. Nominal clauses with finite verbs are particularly noteworthy because they add emphasis, contrast, and/or clarity to the description of the subject (initiator). Not every nominal clause with a finite verb equally describes, emphasizes, contrasts, and clarifies its initiator. Sometimes the description is stronger than the emphasis. Other times, the emphasis is stronger than the description. Yet, every nominal clause with a finite verb has some element of description, emphasis, contrast, and clarification. *As a general rule: The descriptive nuance is stronger than emphasis in narrative, and the emphatic nuance is stronger than the descriptive in direct speech and poetry.*

The distinction between verbal and nominal clauses may be compared to a stage play.[8] If an actor pounds an anvil with a hammer on stage, and the author wishes to focus on the action rather than the actor, then the spotlight will be on the hammer and anvil, not the actor. The audience, of course, sees the actor on the stage, but their attention is on the hammer striking the anvil. Similarly, when an author of Scripture wants the reader to focus on the action (verb) of a clause rather than the actor (subject), he spotlights the action with a verbal clause. If, however, the author wishes to focus on the actor rather than the action, then the spotlight will be on the actor, not the hammer and anvil. Again, the audience sees the action on the stage, but the attention of the audience is on the actor, not his striking of the anvil. Likewise, when an author of Scripture wants the reader to focus on the actor (subject) rather than the action (verb), he spotlights the actor with a nominal clause having a finite verb. Moreover, a nominal clause without a finite verb purely describes the subject (initiator) without any verbal notion. Verbal clauses, therefore, focus on the action; nominal clauses on the subject. f

The interplay between a play-by-play commentator and a color commentator for a sporting event furnishes another analogy for verbal and nominal clauses.[9] The verbal clause supplies the play-by-play of narrative actions and events of the agent: (he) barks out signals . . . drops back . . . runs from sideline to sideline . . . avoids a tackle . . . throws the ball . . . and scores the touchdown. The nominal clause furnishes the "color" for the actions of the verbal clauses by describing the initiator: the quarterback is sick today, the quarterback—he could not see out of his left eye, the quarterback—he did not see his other receivers, the quarterback is hurt. Verbal clauses, of course, like a play-by-play narrative in football, need the color of nominal clauses to furnish the contextual details for understanding the narrative of the verbal clauses. Nominal or verbal clauses alone relate a flat or partial narrative. Nominal clauses alone supply interesting details and

8. We are thankful to Ihab Griess for suggesting the idea of the stage.
9. This is particularly true when applied to Hebrew narrative.

description, but without the movement and action of the verb.[10] Verbal clauses alone provide movement and action, but without the color of description. Verbal and nominal clauses woven together, however, narrate an interesting and complete account with action and description. For entertaining narration of a football game, play-by-play and color commentating must be present and understood; for pleasing Hebrew narration, verbal and nominal clauses must be present and understood.

10. Of course, it is possible to relate a narrative with nominal clauses. Biblical Aramaic frequently does this with participles. Moreover, Biblical Hebrew may do this for a few verses. (Gen 41:1–2)

Chapter 10
SUBSTANTIVAL CLAUSE

§39. The Usages of the Substantival Clauses *a*

A SUBSTANTIVAL CLAUSE functions in the place of a noun as a nominative, genitive, or accusative.

I. Nominative

The clause functions as an initiator (subject).

וַיֹּאמֶר לָבָן טוֹב תִּתִּי אֹתָהּ לָךְ מִתִּתִּי אֹתָהּ לְאִישׁ אַחֵר Gen 29:19[a]

And Laban said, **My giving her to you** is better than my giving her to another man.

The clause/phrase, "My giving her to you," in Gen 29:19 is in the place of the nominative as subject.

II. Genitive (§12l–q) *b*

A. After a Noun

וַיְהִי בְּיוֹם דִּבֶּר יְהוָה אֶל־מֹשֶׁה בְּאֶרֶץ מִצְרָיִם׃ Exod 6:28

And it happened on the day of (which) **the Lord spoke to Moses in the land of Egypt**.

The verbal clause, דִּבֶּר יהוה אֶל־מֹשֶׁה בְּאֶרֶץ מִצְרָיִם, in Exod 6:28 is in the place of the genitive to its governing noun, בְּיוֹם.

תְּחִלַּת דִּבֶּר־יְהוָה בְּהוֹשֵׁעַ Hos 1:2[a]

The beginning of (the time when) **the Lord spoke to Hosea**.

The verb in Hos 1:2, דִּבֶּר, is in the position of the genitive after the construct noun, תְּחִלַּת.

1 Sam 25:15; 2 Sam 22:1; Isa 29:1; Jer 48:36; Ps 71:18; 74:3; 90:15

B. After a Preposition *c*

הַכֹּהֲנִים לֹא אָמְרוּ אַיֵּה יְהוָה וְתֹפְשֵׂי הַתּוֹרָה לֹא יְדָעוּנִי וְהָרֹעִים
פָּשְׁעוּ בִי וְהַנְּבִאִים נִבְּאוּ בַבַּעַל וְאַחֲרֵי לֹא־יוֹעִלוּ הָלָכוּ׃ Jer 2:8

The priests did not say, Where is the Lord? and the handlers of the law did not know me. And the shepherds transgressed against me, and the prophets prophesied by Baal. And after **they (who) do not profit**, they walked.

The verbal clause after the preposition אַחֲרֵי is in the place of the genitive.

With a perfect—Lev 14:43; 25:48; Josh 2:22; 1 Sam 14:19

With an imperfect—Gen 38:11; Exod 10:28; 15:16; Num 23:24; Deut 33:11; Josh 10:13

III. Accusative (§13k, q) *d*

A clause in the place of an accusative may follow the verb with or without particles. The verbs are often verbs of the senses, such as saying, knowing, thinking, seeing, hearing, etc.

A. Clauses Following a Verb without Particles:

וְאָמְרוּ אִשְׁתּוֹ זֹאת Gen 12:12[a]

And they will say, **This is his wife.**

The substantival clause, "This is his wife," is the accusative of the direct object of the verb.

וַיֹּאמֶר מֹשֶׁה זֶה הַדָּבָר אֲשֶׁר־צִוָּה יְהוָה תַּעֲשׂוּ Lev 9:6[a]

And Moses said, **This is the word which the Lord commanded you to do.**

e **B. Clauses Following a Verb with Particles:**

1. כִּי

וַתֵּרֶא הָאִשָּׁה כִּי טוֹב הָעֵץ לְמַאֲכָל Gen 3:6[a]

And the woman saw **that the tree was good for food.**

וַיַּאֲמֵן הָעָם וַיִּשְׁמְעוּ כִּי־פָקַד יְהוָה אֶת־בְּנֵי יִשְׂרָאֵל Exod 4:31

And the people believed and they heard **that the Lord had visited the Israelites.**

Gen 1:10; 3:7; 6:5; 8:11; 12:11; Exod 8:6, 11; 9:14

f 2. אֲשֶׁר

כִּי שָׁמַעְנוּ אֵת אֲשֶׁר־הוֹבִישׁ יְהוָה אֶת־מֵי יַם־סוּף מִפְּנֵיכֶם Josh 2:10[a]

For we have heard **that the Lord dried up the waters of the Red Sea before you.**

וַיַּרְא שָׁאוּל אֲשֶׁר־הוּא מַשְׂכִּיל מְאֹד 1 Sam 18:15[a]

And Saul saw **that he was prospering greatly.**

Gen 30:29; Exod 11:7; 19:4; 1 Sam 10:24; 18:15; 24:19; 1 Kgs 20:22

g **C. Clauses Following a Participle:**

הַאֵינְךָ רֹאֶה מָה הֵמָּה עֹשִׂים בְּעָרֵי יְהוּדָה Jer 7:17a

Are you not seeing **what they are doing in the cities of Judah?**

Chapter 11
NEGATIVE CLAUSES

§40. Introduction

Negative clauses cover a variety of constructions, negating words and clauses, negating absolutely, and negating in special constructions such as prohibitions, absolute negation, and categoric negation. The negatives לֹא and אַל negate verbs and some nouns; the negative אֵין negates participles, nominal clauses, and most nouns. Although there are exceptional uses and occasional overlapping, the negative particles do follow consistent principles. First, negatives usually come before the words that they negate. Moreover, if a word occurs between a negative and a finite verb, special emphasis is given to the inserted word (Gen 32:29; Exod 16:8). Secondly, a single negative may govern two or more verbs (Deut 7:25–26; 19:10; 22:1).

§41. Negative Particles: General Features *a*

A. לֹא

This negative is the most common and most flexible of the negative particles. לֹא negates the fact and statement of the indicative, contradicting and denying. לֹא often parallels Greek οὐ and Latin *non*. לֹא negates a verb or noun. It may be used with an interrogative particle or absolutely.

1. Verb
   a) Perfect (§3s)

      לֹא usually negates the perfect.[1]

      כִּי לֹא הִמְטִיר יְהוָה אֱלֹהִים עַל־הָאָרֶץ Gen 2:5[b]

      For the Lord God had not caused rain upon the earth.

   b) Imperfect *b*
      i. Indicative (§4i; 53e): לֹא normally negates the imperfect indicative.

         לֹא־יָדוֹן רוּחִי בָאָדָם לְעֹלָם Gen 6:3[a]

         My Spirit will not strive with man forever.

         Exod 5:7–8, 19; 11:9

      ii. Subjunctive (§4j–m): לֹא usually negates purpose clauses. *c*

         אִם־מִחוּט וְעַד שְׂרוֹךְ־נַעַל וְאִם־אֶקַּח מִכָּל־אֲשֶׁר־לָךְ וְלֹא Gen 14:23
         תֹאמַר אֲנִי הֶעֱשַׁרְתִּי אֶת־אַבְרָם׃

         (May God do to me and more) if from thread even unto a throng of a sandal (I take) and if I take from all that is to you, so that you might not say, I made Abraham rich.

         Gen 35:5; 42:2; Exod 4:21; 8:27; Lev 10:9

      iii. Jussive (§4n–v): לֹא with the jussive is very rare, probably standing *d*
         in the place of (or overlapping with) לֹא with the indicative.

---

1. Particles such as טֶרֶם (בְּטֶרֶם) and בִּלְתִּי may also negate the perfect.

כִּי תַעֲבֹד֙ אֶת־הָ֣אֲדָמָ֔ה לֹֽא־תֹסֵ֥ף תֵּת־כֹּחָ֖הּ לָ֑ךְ Gen 4:12[a]

When you work the ground, it will not add to give her strength to you.

In Gen 4:12 the jussive may substitute for an indicative.

Gen 24:8; 1 Sam 14:36; 1 Kgs 2:6; Ezek 48:14; Hos 9:15

e iv. Energic particles (§4r–u):

① נָא: Only אַל negates imperfects with נָא.

② Cohortative: לֹא rarely negates the cohortative.

וַיֹּ֣אמֶר יוֹאָ֔ב לֹא־כֵ֖ן אֹחִ֣ילָה לְפָנֶ֑יךָ 2 Sam 18:14[a]

And Joab said, Not thus will I delay before you.

③ Energic Nuns: לֹא is the exclusive negative for energic particles.[2]

וַיֹּ֤אמֶר בָּלָק֙ אֶל־בִּלְעָ֔ם גַּם־קֹ֖ב לֹ֣א תִקֳּבֶ֑נּוּ גַּם־בָּרֵ֖ךְ לֹ֥א תְבָרֲכֶֽנּוּ׃ Num 23:25

Balak said to Balaam, Both a cursing you must not curse him and a blessing you must not bless him.

Gen 37:21; 42:37; 44:32; Exod 21:29, 33, 36; 22:20; 2 Kgs 4:29

f c) Imperative

The imperative is never negated.

g 2. Noun

a) With noun clauses

The לֹא emphasizes the noun or adjective.

וַיֹּ֙אמֶר֙ יְהוָ֣ה אֱלֹהִ֔ים לֹא־ט֛וֹב הֱי֥וֹת הָֽאָדָ֖ם לְבַדּ֑וֹ Gen 2:18[a]

And the Lord God said, Not good the existing of man alone.

Gen 7:2; 15:16; Exod 18:17; Num 24:17; Deut 30:11; Amos 7:14

h b) With individual nouns, the negative resembles the English prefixes non- or un-.

חֶבְלֵ֥י יֽוֹלֵדָ֖ה יָבֹ֣אוּ ל֑וֹ הוּא־בֵן֙ לֹ֣א חָכָ֔ם Hos 13:13

The pains of one giving birth come to him, he is a son not wise (unwise).

Deut 32:6; Jer 51:5; Ps 36:5; 43:1; Job 41:2

i c) With Infinitive constructs (rare).

בָּעֵ֣ת הַהִ֗יא יֵאָמֵ֤ר לָֽעָם־הַזֶּה֙ וְלִיר֣וּשָׁלִַ֔ם ר֣וּחַ צַ֤ח שְׁפָיִים֙ בַּמִּדְבָּ֔ר דֶּ֖רֶךְ בַּת־עַמִּ֑י ל֥וֹא לִזְר֖וֹת וְל֥וֹא לְהָבַֽר׃ Jer 4:11

At that time it will be said to this people and to Jerusalem, A scorching wind of barren tracks will be in the wilderness in the way of the daughter of my people, not to winnow and not to purify.

Exod 33:16; Deut 7:7; Judg 1:19; 1 Sam 20:15; Isa 30:5; Amos 6:10

j d) Participle

This construction is also rare.

2. This is expected since the energic forms are indicative in Arabic.

2 Sam 3:34[a] יָדֶךָ לֹא־אֲסֻרוֹת וְרַגְלֶיךָ לֹא־לִנְחֻשְׁתַּיִם הֻגָּשׁוּ
Your hands are not bound, and your feet not to fetters they have been brought near.

Num 35:23; Deut 4:42; 28:61; 30:11; Ezek 4:14; Ps 38:15; BA Dan 4:4, 6

3. With an Interrogative Particle *k*

The interrogative particle with לֹא expresses two meanings.

a) Expecting an affirmative answer to a question (§56b, e)[3]

Gen 13:9[a] הֲלֹא כָל־הָאָרֶץ לְפָנֶיךָ
Is not all the land before you?

Gen 19:20[b] אִמָּלְטָה נָּא שָׁמָּה הֲלֹא מִצְעָר הִוא וּתְחִי נַפְשִׁי׃
Let me flee please there (Is it not small?) that my soul may live?

Gen 20:5; 27:36; 29:25; 31:15; 34:23; 37:13; 40:8; 42:22; 44:5, 15; Exod 4:11; Num 22:30; Deut 31:17; BA Dan 6:13

b) Affirming a well-known event or object *l*

Deut 3:11[a] כִּי רַק־עוֹג מֶלֶךְ הַבָּשָׁן נִשְׁאַר מִיֶּתֶר הָרְפָאִים הִנֵּה עַרְשׂוֹ עֶרֶשׂ בַּרְזֶל הֲלֹה הִוא בְּרַבַּת בְּנֵי עַמּוֹן
For only Og, king of Bashan, was left from the rest of the Rephaim, behold his bedframe was a bedframe of iron. Is it not in Rabbah of the sons of Ammon?

Gen 19:20; Exod 4:14; Deut 11:30; Josh 10:13; 1 Sam 21:12; 1 Kgs 11:41

4. Absolutely (without verb or noun) *m*

a) In answer to a question or statement

Gen 23:11[a] לֹא־אֲדֹנִי שְׁמָעֵנִי
No, my lord, hear me.

1 Sam 1:15[a] וַתַּעַן חַנָּה וַתֹּאמֶר לֹא אֲדֹנִי אִשָּׁה קְשַׁת־רוּחַ אָנֹכִי
And Hannah answered and said, No, my lord, a woman harsh of spirit am I.

Gen 42:10; Exod 10:11; Judg 12:5; Isa 28:28; Zech 4:5, 13; Ruth 1:13

b) In compound and/or indirect questions ("whether . . . or not," §57–58) *n*

Gen 18:21 אֵרְדָה־נָּא וְאֶרְאֶה הַכְּצַעֲקָתָהּ הַבָּאָה אֵלַי עָשׂוּ כָּלָה וְאִם־לֹא אֵדָעָה׃
I will go down now that I might see whether according to her cry coming to me they have done completely, or not, I will know.

Gen 18:21 illustrates a compound question as the "or" indicates. See §58 for indirect questions.

Gen 24:21; 27:21; 37:32; Exod 16:4; 17:7; Num 11:23; 13:20; Deut 8:2; Judg 2:22

B. אַל *o*

This particle is less common and less flexible than לֹא. אַל negates the will and

3. This resembles questions in Greek with οὐ or in Latin with *nonne*. In Hebrew, context determines whether a negative answer is expected.

thought of the jussive, rejecting and deprecating. Generally, אַל parallels Greek μή and Latin *ne*. אַל negates a verb or noun. It is used with נָא and absolutely.

1. Verb
   a) Perfect
      אַל occurs once with the perfect, 1 Sam 27:10.

p b) Imperfect
      i. Indicative: אַל occurs with the indicative form in the place of אַל with the jussive form.

וַיְהִי֩ כְהוֹצִיאָ֨ם אֹתָ֜ם הַח֗וּצָה וַיֹּ֙אמֶר֙ הִמָּלֵ֣ט עַל־נַפְשֶׁ֔ךָ Gen 19:17[a]
אַל־תַּבִּ֣יט אַחֲרֶ֔יךָ וְאַל־תַּעֲמֹ֖ד בְּכָל־הַכִּכָּ֑ר

And it happened as they caused them to go out to the outside that he said, Flee for your soul, do not look behind you and do not stand in all the valley.

The Hiphil verb in Gen 19:17 is an indicative form, not the expected jussive form with אַל.

Gen 21:16; 2 Chr 32:15

q ii. Subjunctive: אַל negates a purpose clause (subjunctive) on occasion.

תִּכְבַּ֧ד הָעֲבֹדָ֛ה עַל־הָאֲנָשִׁ֖ים וְיַעֲשׂוּ־בָ֑הּ וְאַל־יִשְׁע֖וּ Exod 5:9
בְּדִבְרֵי־שָֽׁקֶר׃

Let the servitude be heavy upon the men that they may work in it, so that they may not regard false words.

וְאִם־כָּ֣כָה ׀ אַתְּ־עֹ֣שֶׂה לִּ֗י הָרְגֵ֤נִי נָא֙ הָרֹ֔ג אִם־מָצָ֥אתִי חֵ֖ן Num 11:15
בְּעֵינֶ֑יךָ וְאַל־אֶרְאֶ֖ה בְּרָעָתִֽי׃

And if as thus you are the one doing to me, kill me please a killing if I have found grace in your eyes, that I might not see my calamity.

1 Sam 12:19

r iii. Jussive: אַל normally negates the jussive.

לְכוּ֙ וְנִמְכְּרֶ֣נּוּ לַיִּשְׁמְעֵאלִ֔ים וְיָדֵ֙נוּ֙ אַל־תְּהִי־ב֔וֹ Gen 37:27[a]

Come and we will sell him to the Ishmaelites, but our hand – let it not fall upon him.

Gen 19:17; Exod 3:5; 5:9; 8:25; 14:13; 16:19; 23:21; 33:15; 34:3; Num 4:18; 32:5; Prov 3:7

s iv. Energic particles

① נָא: Only אַל negates imperfects with נָא.

אַל־נָ֨א תְהִ֤י מְרִיבָה֙ בֵּינִ֣י וּבֵינֶ֔ךָ Gen 13:8[a]

Let there please not exist strife between me and you.

Gen 18:3, 30, 32; 47:29; Num 10:31; 12:11–12; 22:16; Judg 6:18; 19:23; 1 Sam 3:17; 25:25

② Cohortative: אַל negates the cohortative.

לְכ֨וּ וְנַכֵּ֣הוּ בַלָּשׁ֔וֹן וְאַל־נַקְשִׁ֖יבָה אֶל־כָּל־דְּבָרָֽיו׃ Jer 18:18[b]

Come and let us smite him with the tongue and let us not take heed to any of his words.

2 Sam 24:14; Jer 17:18; 18:18; Ps 25:2; 31:2, 18; 69:15; 71:1

③ Energic Nuns: אַל does not negate with the energic Nun.

c) Imperative *t*

The imperative is never negated.

2. Noun *u*

a) אַל does not govern noun clauses.

b) With individual nouns, the negative resembles the English prefixes non- or un-. 2 Sam 1:21; Isa 62:6; Prov 8:10; 12:28; 17:12

c) אַל does not govern infinitive constructs or participles.

3. נָא *v*

For greater emphasis, the נָא particle often occurs between אַל and its verb.

וַיֹּאמֶר אַבְרָם אֶל־לוֹט אַל־נָא תְהִי מְרִיבָה בֵּינִי וּבֵינֶיךָ Gen 13:8[a]

And Abram said to Lot, Let there not please exist strife between me and you.

Gen 18:3; 30, 32; 47:29; Num 10:31; 12:11–12; 22:16; Judg 6:18

4. Absolutely (without verb or noun) *w*

a) with נָא

וַיֹּאמֶר לוֹט אֲלֵהֶם אַל־נָא אֲדֹנָי׃ Gen 19:18

And Lot said to them, No please, my lord.

Gen 19:7; 33:10

b) without נָא, usually with vocatives[4]

אַל בְּנֹתַי כִּי־מַר־לִי מְאֹד מִכֶּם Ruth 1:13[b]

No, my daughters, but it is more bitter for me than for you.

Gen 23:11; 42:10; Judg 19:23; 1 Sam 2:24; 2 Sam 13:25; 2 Kgs 4:16

C. אֵין (אַיִן) *x*

אַיִן is a noun meaning "non-existence."[5] Its construct form אֵין often becomes a semi-verb, similar to יֵשׁ in usage but opposite in meaning. As a semi-verb, אֵין ("there does not exist") negates nouns and nominal clauses, but not a finite verb. As a "sister" to הָיָה in meaning and usage, אֵין (and its opposite יֵשׁ) takes a subject, usually as the genitive of a construct package (with a separate word, Gen 20:11, אֵין־יִרְאַת אֱלֹהִים "the non-existence of the fear of God," that is, the fear of God does not exist; or with an attached pronominal suffix, Gen 5:24, וְאֵינֶנּוּ "and the non-existence of him," that is, and he does not exist). Occasionally, the subject precedes אֵין for emphasis (Exod 5:16).

---

4. These may imply a negative wish like the Greek μὴ γένοιτο (Rom 3:6).
5. This non-existence may be complete non-existence (2 Sam 7:22) or the non-presence of someone or something (Gen 5:24; 39:11; Exod 17:1).

Also like הָיָה, אֵין (יֵשׁ) may take an accusative of situation, usually a participle or adjective, as predicate (§13z): 1 Sam 3:1, אֵין חָזוֹן נִפְרָץ "non-existence of a vision in the status of spread abroad," that is, a vision did not exist as widespread. (אֵין with subject as attached pronoun with accusative of situation: Gen 7:8; 20:7; 30:33; 39:9; 43:5; Exod 3:2; 5:10. אֵין with subject as noun with accusative of situation: Gen 39:23; Exod 5:16; 33:15; Lev 13:31; 14:21. יֵשׁ with subject as attached pronoun with accusative of situation: Gen 24:42, 49; 43:4; Deut 13:4; Judg 6:36. יֵשׁ with subject as noun with accusative of situation: Ps 58:12; Prov 18:24; Ruth 3:12; Eccl 7:15[2x])

אֵין negates the following nouns which function as a subject for the semi-verb אֵין:

1. Nouns
   a) Substantive

      Gen 41:49[b] עַד כִּי־חָדַל לִסְפֹּר כִּי־אֵין מִסְפָּר׃

      Until he ceased to count for there was no number.

      Gen 31:50; 45:6; Exod 12:30

y b) Pronoun

      Gen 5:24[b] וְאֵינֶנּוּ כִּי־לָקַח אֹתוֹ אֱלֹהִים׃

      And he was not, because God took him.

      Gen 7:8; 20:7; 30:33; 31:2; 42:13; Exod 12:30

z c) Participle (§16i)

      This is common.

      1 Sam 26:12 וַיִּקַּח דָּוִד אֶת־הַחֲנִית וְאֶת־צַפַּחַת הַמַּיִם מֵרַאֲשֹׁתֵי שָׁאוּל וַיֵּלְכוּ לָהֶם וְאֵין רֹאֶה וְאֵין יוֹדֵעַ וְאֵין מֵקִיץ

      And David took the spear and the flask of water from the places about the head of Saul, and they came to them, while there was no one who saw, and while there was no one who knew, and while there was no one who awoke.

      Gen 41:8, 24, 39; Exod 5:11; 22:9; Lev 26:17; Isa 5:29; Ps 7:3

aa d) Infinitive construct (§18p)

      Eccl 3:14[a] יָדַעְתִּי כִּי כָּל־אֲשֶׁר יַעֲשֶׂה הָאֱלֹהִים הוּא יִהְיֶה לְעוֹלָם עָלָיו אֵין לְהוֹסִיף וּמִמֶּנּוּ אֵין לִגְרֹעַ

      I know that all which God does, it happens forever; upon it there is nothing to add, and from it there is nothing to diminish.

      Num 20:5; 1 Sam 9:7; Hag 1:6; Ps 32:9; 40:6; Esth 8:8; Ezra 9:15

bb 2. Noun Clauses

   אֵין often expresses CATEGORIC NEGATION (§42g), negating the category or group.

   Gen 31:50[a] אִם־תְּעַנֶּה אֶת־בְּנֹתַי וְאִם־תִּקַּח נָשִׁים עַל־בְּנֹתַי אֵין אִישׁ עִמָּנוּ

   If you mistreat my daughters and if you take wives in addition to my daughters, there is no man with us.

   Gen 39:11; 47:4; Exod 14:11; 21:11; Num 11:6

D. Other negative particles *cc*

Other negative particles include: בַּל and בְּלִי which parallel לֹא in poetry; טֶרֶם (בְּטֶרֶם), *not yet*, which negates the perfect and imperfect; בִּלְתִּי (לְבִלְתִּי) which negates perfects, imperfects, nouns, and especially, infinitive constructs (Exod 8:18, 25); and פֶּן which negates subjunctive imperfects (Exod 5:3; 13:17).

§42. Negative Particles: In Special Constructions *a*

A. Prohibitions (§4i)

In prohibitions, לֹא takes the indicative and is the stronger, harsher negative, demanding obedience; אַל takes the jussive and is the weaker, softer negative, desiring obedience. In the words of the Talmudic Rabbis, לֹא requires lashes; אַל usually does not.[6] לֹא has authority; אַל has emotion. Of course, this is relative to the speaker. When a superior, such as God or the king, uses אַל in prohibitions, the command expresses desire less harshly than לֹא, but the prohibition demands obedience because of the position of the person making the command. Similarly, when an inferior, such as a petitioner to God, uses לֹא in prohibitions, the prohibition expresses a strong request, not an authoritative demand for obedience (Ps 40:12). אַל is often found in emotionally intense narratives (Gen 22:12); לֹא is found in legal texts, such as the Ten Commandments, and in texts where orders and charges are commanded (Gen 24:3).

1. אַל with the jussive *b*

Gen 22:12[a] וַיֹּאמֶר אַל־תִּשְׁלַח יָדְךָ אֶל־הַנַּעַר וְאַל־תַּעַשׂ לוֹ מְאוּמָה

And He said, Do not stretch out your hand to the lad and do not do to him anything.

Exod 8:25[b] רַק אַל־יֹסֵף פַּרְעֹה הָתֵל לְבִלְתִּי שַׁלַּח אֶת־הָעָם לִזְבֹּחַ לַיהוָה׃

Only may Pharaoh not add to trifle so as not to send away the people to sacrifice to the Lord.

Gen 22:12; 31:35; 37:22, 27; 44:18; 45:5, 20; Exod 8:25; 12:9; 16:19; 23:1; 32:22; 34:3; Lev 10:9; 1 Sam 20:3; 1 Kgs 8:57

2. לֹא with the indicative *c*

Gen 2:17[a] וּמֵעֵץ הַדַּעַת טוֹב וָרָע לֹא תֹאכַל מִמֶּנּוּ

And from the tree of good and evil you must not eat.

Exod 5:7 לֹא תֹאסִפוּן לָתֵת תֶּבֶן לָעָם לִלְבֹּן הַלְּבֵנִים כִּתְמוֹל שִׁלְשֹׁם הֵם יֵלְכוּ וְקֹשְׁשׁוּ לָהֶם תֶּבֶן׃

Exod 5:8[a] וְאֶת־מַתְכֹּנֶת הַלְּבֵנִים אֲשֶׁר הֵם עֹשִׂים תְּמוֹל שִׁלְשֹׁם תָּשִׂימוּ עֲלֵיהֶם לֹא תִגְרְעוּ מִמֶּנּוּ

You must not gather to give straw to the people to make bricks as formerly. They will go and gather for themselves straw. The quota of bricks which they were making formerly you will place upon them. You must not diminish from it.

Gen 3:1; 17:15; 24:3, 8; 30:31; 31:52; Exod 5:19; 8:24; 12:10, 22, 46; 20:4, 22:21; 1 Sam 14:34; 20:2(2x)

---

6. Talmud Yerushalmi, Pesachim 6:2. J. Neusner, *The Talmud of the Land of Israel*, Vol V (Atlanta: Scholars Press, 1998), 186.

d **B. Absolute Negation**

Absolute negation emphasizes the universality of the negative—a negative without exception. כֹּל with a (usually) indeterminate noun preceded or followed by לֹא expresses absolute negation.[7] אִישׁ may substitute for כֹּל; אַיִן may substitute for לֹא in nominal clauses.

1. לֹא . . . כֹּל

לֹֽא־תַעֲשֶׂה כָל־מְלָאכָה Exod 20:10[b]

You will not do any work at all.

Gen 3:1; Exod 9:4; 12:16, 20, 48; 13:7; Lev 14:36; 18:26; 26:14; Num 15:22; Deut 4:15; 8:9; 14:3, 21; 20:16; 28:14; 1 Sam 14:24; Jer 13:7; 18:18 (with אַל) reverse order כֹּל . . . לֹא, Exod 12:16, 20, 43; 15:26; 22:21; Lev 2:11; 3:17; 12:4; 16:17, 29; 17:14; BA Dan 2:10, 35; 4:6, 15; 6:5(2x)–6, 6, 16, 24.

e 2. אִישׁ . . . לֹא

אִישׁ מִמֶּנּוּ אֶת־קִבְרוֹ לֹא־יִכְלֶה מִמְּךָ מִקְּבֹר מֵתֶךָ׃ Gen 23:6[b]

A man from us will not withhold his burial plot from you to bury your dead.

f 3. אַיִן . . . כֹּל

וְלָרָשׁ אֵין־כֹּל כִּי אִם־כִּבְשָׂה אַחַת קְטַנָּה אֲשֶׁר קָנָה 2 Sam 12:3[a]

And to the poor man there was not anything but one small lamb which he acquired.

יְלָדִים אֲשֶׁר אֵין־בָּהֶם כָּל־מאוּם Dan 1:4[a]

Lads in whom there was no blemish.

Judg 19:19; 1 Sam 14:39; 2 Kgs 5:15; Jer 12:12; Ps 10:4; Eccl 1:9; 4:8

g **C. Categoric Negation**

Categoric negation absolutely negates the category or group. In categoric negation, an indefinite noun of the category or group is negated by אַיִן or לֹא. This negation resembles absolute negation by emphasizing the negation of the category, but without כֹּל. This construction asserts the negation of existence.[8]

1. אַיִן

אֵין עֹשֵׂה־טוֹב׃ ... אֵין עֹשֵׂה־טוֹב אֵין גַּם־אֶחָד׃ Ps 14:1, 3

There is no doer of good . . . there is no doer of good, there is not even one.

The entire category of those doing good is negated and rejected.

Gen 45:6; 47:4; Exod 12:30(2x); 14:11; 21:11; Num 11:6; 20:19; 21:5; 1 Sam 24:12; Ps 19:7; 72:12; BA Dan 4:10

h 2. לֹא

כִּי לֹא־נַחַשׁ בְּיַעֲקֹב וְלֹא־קֶסֶם בְּיִשְׂרָאֵל Num 23:23[a]

For no omen is against Jacob, and no divination is against Israel.

Gen 27:12; Num 23:19; Deut 32:20, 47; 2 Sam 20:1; 1 Kgs 12:16; Isa 29:9; 31:8; 53:9; Jer 10:14; BA Dan 2:27(4x)

---

7. Compare Rom 3:20, "οὐ δικαιωθήσεται πᾶσα σάρξ."
8. Compare §11f.

CHAPTER 12
RELATIVE CLAUSES

§43. Introduction *a*

Similar to an adjective, a relative clause modifies a noun: clarifying the definite and specializing the indefinite. The relative clause, a subordinate clause, almost always follows its antecedent.[1] Particles, usually אֲשֶׁר,[2] introduce a relative clause. Context, however, occasionally implies a relative clause without particles.

There are differences between Arabic and Hebrew relative clauses. In classical Arabic, a definite antecedent precedes a relative pronoun. Arabic omits the relative pronoun before an indefinite antecedent. Biblical Hebrew, by contrast, allows an indefinite antecedent before a relative particle.[3] Hebrew, however, resembles Arabic by having a definite antecedent before the relative pronoun and omitting the relative pronoun before indefinite antecedents.

Differences aside, Hebrew and Arabic relative clauses are essentially the same. *b*
Relative clauses in both languages consist of verbal, nominal, or ADVERBIAL CLAUSES. For instance, the relative clause in Gen 6:7, אֶמְחֶה אֶת־הָאָדָם אֲשֶׁר־בָּרָאתִי "I will blot out man which I created," illustrates the relative clause as a verbal clause. The relative clause in Gen 7:2, וּמִן־הַבְּהֵמָה אֲשֶׁר לֹא טְהֹרָה "And from the beast which it is unclean," illustrates the relative clause as a nominal clause. Finally, the relative clause in Gen 3:3, וּמִפְּרִי הָעֵץ אֲשֶׁר בְּתוֹךְ־הַגָּן "And from the fruit of the tree which (it is) in the midst of the garden," shows the relative clause as an ADVERBIAL CLAUSE, a clause with an implied RETROSPECTIVE PRONOUN as an initiator and an adverbial word(s) or a prepositional phrase as the announcement.

Relative clauses express an indicative statement (not imperative, jussive, interrogative, prohibitive, etc.), clarify the definite antecedent or specialize the indefinite antecedent, and have a RETROSPECTIVE PRONOUN (§21c) linking the relative clause to its antecedent. This retrospective pronoun may be implicit or explicit, as for example in Gen 5:29, מִן־הָאֲדָמָה אֲשֶׁר אֵרְרָהּ יהוה, "From the ground which the Lord cursed it." The verbal relative clause in this verse is an indicative statement, clarifying the definite with the explicit retrospective pronoun (it) looking back to the definite antecedent. The retrospective

---

1. Rarely, the relative clause precedes its antecedent, Judg 21:19; Isa 29:22. Moreover, a relative clause may modify a phrase or clause, not just a word, Jer 7:31.
2. Although אֲשֶׁר usually introduces a relative clause, it may introduce a variety of clauses including causal, purpose, or substantival clauses. Moreover, אֲשֶׁר may also function as a demonstrative pronoun: he who, they who, those of you who, and that which (Exod 14:13). The accusative marker אֵת frequently precedes אֲשֶׁר as a demonstrative pronoun (Gen 44:1; Num 22:6). The particle אֲשֶׁר may become an indefinite relative pronoun (whoever, whatever, wherever, *quicumque*, *quisquis*), when it occurs between the same verb, Exod 33:19[b], וְרִחַמְתִּי אֶת־אֲשֶׁר אֲרַחֵם "And I will show compassion on whomever I will show compassion."
3. GKC §155d states that an indeterminate noun with אֲשֶׁר lays "special stress on the indeterminate substantive (noun)." The words גּוֹי אֲשֶׁר may be precisely translated, "a nation of such a kind that." The Septuagint may suggest this in Lev 5:2; Num 14:8; Deut 2:36 by translating the relative particle as ἥτις instead of ἥ.

pronoun can also be implied, as for example in Gen 2:2[b], מִכָּל־מְלַאכְתּוֹ אֲשֶׁר עָשָׂה "From all His work which he made (it)." If the retrospective pronoun is a pronominal suffix (a genitive) on a noun in the relative clause, it must be explicit, Deut 28:49[b] גּוֹי אֲשֶׁר לֹא־תִשְׁמַע לְשֹׁנוֹ "A nation whose tongue you do not understand." The adverbial particle שָׁם may substitute, implicitly or explicitly, for the retrospective pronoun when the antecedent is a noun of place, Gen 3:23[b], לַעֲבֹד אֶת־הָאֲדָמָה אֲשֶׁר לֻקַּח מִשָּׁם "To work the ground which he was taken from there," that is, "the ground from which he was taken."

The particle אֲשֶׁר or other particles (זֶה, זוֹ, זוּ, and a demonstrative particle ה pointed like the article) usually introduce a relative clause. Context may also indicate a relative clause without particles by a retrospective pronoun (explicit or implicit) referring back to the antecedent. Relative clauses may be a verbal, nominal, or adverbial clause, expressing an indicative statement.

§44. Relative Clauses Introduced by the Particle אֲשֶׁר

a A. Verbal Clause

Gen 2:8[b] וַיָּשֶׂם שָׁם אֶת־הָאָדָם אֲשֶׁר יָצָר׃

And he placed there the man whom he had formed *him*.

In Gen 2:8, the relative clause has a definite antecedent and an implied retrospective pronoun.[4]

Gen 2:3, 22; 3:1; 5:5; 8:6

Gen 45:4[b] אֲנִי יוֹסֵף אֲחִיכֶם אֲשֶׁר־מְכַרְתֶּם אֹתִי מִצְרָיְמָה׃

I am Joseph your brother whom you sold [me] to Egypt.

Gen 45:4 has a definite antecedent, but contrary to Gen 2:8, it has an explicit retrospective pronoun.

Gen 5:29; 48:15; Exod 6:4, 26; 17:5; Dan 4:27

Gen 20:9 וַיִּקְרָא אֲבִימֶלֶךְ לְאַבְרָהָם וַיֹּאמֶר לוֹ מֶה־עָשִׂיתָ לָּנוּ וּמֶה־חָטָאתִי לָךְ כִּי־הֵבֵאתָ עָלַי וְעַל־מַמְלַכְתִּי חֲטָאָה גְדֹלָה מַעֲשִׂים אֲשֶׁר לֹא־יֵעָשׂוּ עָשִׂיתָ עִמָּדִי׃

And Abimelek called to Abraham and said to him, What have you done to us and how have I sinned against you? For you have brought upon me and upon my kingdom a great sin, deeds of such a kind that *they* should not be done you have done to me.

The antecedent in Gen 20:9 is indefinite with an implied retrospective pronoun in the verb.

Gen 15:17; 27:27; 29:27; 31:13; 44:8; Exod 4:28; 10:15

Exod 21:13[b] וְשַׂמְתִּי לְךָ מָקוֹם אֲשֶׁר יָנוּס שָׁמָּה׃

Then I will appoint for you a place where you will flee.

Exod 21:13 has an indefinite antecedent with a retrospective pronoun.

Exod 25:2; 30:36

b B. Nominal Clause

Deut 8:9[b] אֶרֶץ אֲשֶׁר אֲבָנֶיהָ בַרְזֶל

A land whose stones are iron

4. Italicized words, like *him* in Gen 2:8[b], indicate an implied retrospective pronoun.

In Deut 8:9, the antecedent is indefinite with a retrospective pronoun (her).

Gen 9:12[a] וַיֹּאמֶר אֱלֹהִים זֹאת אוֹת־הַבְּרִית אֲשֶׁר־אֲנִי נֹתֵן בֵּינִי וּבֵינֵיכֶם

And God said, This is the sign of the covenant which I am giving *it* between me and you.

In Gen 9:12, the relative clause has a definite antecedent with an implied retrospective pronoun.
Gen 39:6; 47:14; Exod 5:8

Num 14:8 אִם־חָפֵץ בָּנוּ יְהוָה וְהֵבִיא אֹתָנוּ אֶל־הָאָרֶץ הַזֹּאת וּנְתָנָהּ לָנוּ אֶרֶץ אֲשֶׁר־הִוא זָבַת חָלָב וּדְבָשׁ׃

If the Lord is pleased with us, then he will bring us into this land and will give it to us as a land which [it] is flowing with milk and honey.

The antecedent in Num 14:8 is indefinite with a retrospective pronoun.
Gen 1:12; 41:38; Num 27:18; Deut 8:9; 11:12; 29:17

Num 9:13[a] וְהָאִישׁ אֲשֶׁר־הוּא טָהוֹר

And the man who [he] is clean.

Num 9:13 has a definite antecedent with a retrospective pronoun.
Gen 13:14; 28:13; Exod 3:5; 8:17; 12:13; 18:5; BA Dan 4:5

C. Adverbial Clause *c*

Gen 3:3[a] וּמִפְּרִי הָעֵץ אֲשֶׁר בְּתוֹךְ־הַגָּן

And from the fruit of the tree which *it* is in the midst of the garden.

Gen 8:1[a] וַיִּזְכֹּר אֱלֹהִים אֶת־נֹחַ וְאֵת כָּל־הַחַיָּה וְאֶת־כָּל־הַבְּהֵמָה אֲשֶׁר אִתּוֹ בַּתֵּבָה

And God remembered Noah and every living thing and every animal which *they* were with him in the ark.

Gen 3:3 and 8:1 have definite antecedents and implied retrospective pronouns.
Gen 1:7(2x); 7:23; 14:5, 17; 22:17; 23:11, 17; 24:32; Exod 4:18; 7:17; Jer 1:1

§45. Relative Clauses Introduced by the Particles זֶה, זוֹ, זוּ, and a Demonstrative Particle ה Pointed Like the Article

These are rare, usually found in poetry.

Verbal Clause

Ps 104:26[b] לִוְיָתָן זֶה־יָצַרְתָּ לְשַׂחֶק־בּוֹ׃

Leviathan, this one (which) you formed *him* to play in it.

Ps 104:26 has a definite antecedent and an implied retrospective pronoun.

Isa 42:24 מִי־נָתַן לִמְשִׁסָּה יַעֲקֹב וְיִשְׂרָאֵל לְבֹזְזִים הֲלוֹא יְהוָה זוּ חָטָאנוּ לוֹ

Who gave Jacob for spoil and Israel to the spoilers, is it not the Lord, against whom we have sinned (which we have sinned against Him).

Ps 132:12[a] אִם־יִשְׁמְרוּ בָנֶיךָ בְּרִיתִי וְעֵדֹתִי זוֹ אֲלַמְּדֵם

If your sons will keep my covenant and my testimonies which I taught [them].

Isa 42:24 and Ps 132:12 have a definite antecedent and a retrospective pronoun.

Exod 15:13[a] נָחִ֥יתָ בְחַסְדְּךָ֖ עַם־ז֣וּ גָּאָ֑לְתָּ

You led in your grace a people whom you redeemed *them*.

Exod 15:13 has an indefinite antecedent and an implied retrospective pronoun.
Isa 43:21; Ps 9:16; 10:2; 31:5; 32:8; 142:4; 143:8

Josh 10:24[a] וַיִּקְרָ֨א יְהוֹשֻׁ֜עַ אֶל־כָּל־אִ֣ישׁ יִשְׂרָאֵ֗ל וַ֠יֹּאמֶר אֶל־קְצִינֵ֞י אַנְשֵׁ֤י הַמִּלְחָמָה֙ הֶהָלְכ֣וּא אִתּ֔וֹ

And Joshua called to every man of Israel, and he said to the officials of the men of war who *they* went with him.

Josh 10:24 has a definite antecedent and an implied retrospective pronoun. Other examples of the demonstrative particle ה include Gen 18:21; 46:27; 1 Kgs 11:9; Isa 51:10; 1 Chr 26:28.

§46. Relative Clauses by Context without Particles

a When a relative clause is without the relative particle, a retrospective pronoun (explicit or implicit) referring back to the antecedent is necessary.

A. Verbal Clause

Ps 34:9 טַעֲמ֣וּ וּ֭רְאוּ כִּֽי־ט֣וֹב יְהוָ֑ה אַֽשְׁרֵ֥י הַ֝גֶּ֗בֶר יֶחֱסֶה־בּֽוֹ׃

Taste and see that the Lord is good; blessed be the man (who) *he* takes refuge in Him.

Ps 34:9 has a definite antecedent and an implied retrospective pronoun.

Gen 49:27[a] בִּנְיָמִין֙ זְאֵ֣ב יִטְרָ֔ף

Benjamin is a wolf (that) *he* tears.

The relative clause in Gen 49:27 has an indefinite antecedent and an implied retrospective pronoun.

Ps 18:3[a] יְהוָ֤ה ׀ סַֽלְעִ֣י וּמְצוּדָתִי֮ וּמְפַלְטִ֪י אֵלִ֣י צ֭וּרִי אֶֽחֱסֶה־בּ֑וֹ

The Lord is my rock and my fortress and my deliverer, my God and my rock (whom) I take refuge [in Him] (in whom I take refuge).

Ps 18:3 has an definite antecedent and the retrospective pronoun.

b **B. Nominal Clause**

2 Sam 20:12[a] כִּ֡י אִ֞ישׁ מֵהַ֣ר אֶפְרַ֗יִם שֶׁ֣בַע בֶּן־בִּכְרִ֣י שְׁמ֔וֹ

But a man from the mountainous country of Ephraim, (which) Sheba, son of Bichri, is his name. (whose name is Sheba, son of Bichri)

The indefinite antecedent (אִ֗ישׁ) in 2 Sam 20:21 is specialized, the relative clause having a retrospective pronoun.

c **C. Adverbial Clause**

Gen 15:13[a] וַיֹּ֣אמֶר לְאַבְרָ֗ם יָדֹ֨עַ תֵּדַ֜ע כִּי־גֵ֣ר ׀ יִהְיֶ֣ה זַרְעֲךָ֗ בְּאֶ֙רֶץ֙ לֹ֣א לָהֶ֔ם

And he said to Abram, You indeed know that your seed will exist as an alien in a land (which) *it* is not to them.

Gen 15:13 has an indefinite antecedent and an implied retrospective pronoun.
Hab 1:6; Prov 26:17

Chapter 13
COMPARATIVE CLAUSES

§47. The Usages of Comparative Clauses a

Comparative clauses contrast or compare statements, introduced by particles or juxtaposed clauses.

I. Particles

A. כַּאֲשֶׁר . . . (כֵּן)

Usually, both particles are used, but כַּאֲשֶׁר may be used alone.

וְכַאֲשֶׁר֙ יְעַנּ֣וּ אֹת֔וֹ כֵּ֥ן יִרְבֶּ֖ה וְכֵ֣ן יִפְרֹ֑ץ Exod 1:12[a]

And as they were oppressing them, so they were becoming numerous and so they were increasing.

כַּאֲשֶׁ֨ר צִוָּ֧ה יְהוָ֛ה אֹתָ֖ם כֵּ֥ן עָשֽׂוּ׃ Exod 7:6[b]

As the Lord commanded them, so they did.

Gen 41:13; Exod 12:28, 50; 27:8; Lev 4:20; 24:19–20; Josh 11:15

B. ו (Vav of Comparison) b

Occurring in poetry, the Vav of comparison compares moral facts with physical facts.[1]

כִּֽי־אָ֭דָם לְעָמָ֣ל יוּלָּ֑ד וּבְנֵי־רֶ֝֗שֶׁף יַגְבִּ֥יהוּ עֽוּף׃ Job 5:7

For a man to trouble is born as the flames fly upward.

מַצְרֵ֣ף לַ֭כֶּסֶף וְכ֣וּר לַזָּהָ֑ב וּבֹחֵ֖ן לִבּ֣וֹת יְהוָֽה׃ Prov 17:3

A smelting pot for silver and a furnace for gold, so the Lord is a tester of the hearts.

II. Juxtaposing Clauses c

Context indicates these rare constructions.

קֹרֵ֤א דָגַר֙ וְלֹ֣א יָלָ֔ד עֹ֥שֶׂה עֹ֖שֶׁר וְלֹ֣א בְמִשְׁפָּ֑ט Jer 17:11[a]

As a partridge that hatches eggs that it has not laid, so he who makes wealth but not justly.

1. GKC §161a

Chapter 14
SITUATION CLAUSES

§48. Introduction

Situation clauses (§16e) resemble the accusative of situation (§13z; 16l). In the sentence וַיֵּרֶד יַעֲקֹב אָבֵל, "And Jacob went down as a mourner," the word אָבֵל is an accusative of situation. This accusative of situation, of course, can be expanded to a clause, וַיֵּרֶד יַעֲקֹב וְהוּא אָבֵל, "and Jacob went down (and) as he was a mourner." Both constructions function adverbially to another word or clause and are naturally descriptive, explaining how the verbal action was done or furnishing the situation, condition, status, or attending circumstances for another word or clause. Situation clauses, therefore, function similarly to English and Greek adverbial participial clauses and to Greek and Latin absolute clauses.

Being adverbial, the situation clause is closely related with another clause or word. A Vav (Vav of situation) and/or a retrospective pronoun often connects the situation clause to the related word or clause that it modifies. The retrospective pronoun may be implicit with a finite verb. Situation clauses usually follow their related clause.

The description or action of situation clauses may precede or occur contemporaneously with their related clause. Situation clauses with nouns and participles are contemporaneous with the verb of their related clause. The situation clauses with the perfect usually precede the action of the verb of their related clause. The situation clauses with the imperfect are contemporaneous with the verb (usually an imperfect or imperative) of their related clause.

§49. Situation Clauses with Nouns *a*

These clauses usually have nouns or pronouns as initiators and participles or prepositional phrases as announcements. These situation clauses with nouns (and participles) are contemporaneous with the verb of their related clauses.

A. Particles

1. Vav of situation with retrospective pronoun (§21a)

   The Vav of situation with its attached retrospective pronoun connects the situation clause to its related clause. These constructions are common, especially with participles, which are ideal for accusatives of situation and situation clauses. Translate the Vav of situation "as" or "while."

   Gen 18:1 וַיֵּרָא אֵלָיו יְהוָה בְּאֵלֹנֵי מַמְרֵא וְהוּא יֹשֵׁב פֶּתַח־הָאֹהֶל כְּחֹם הַיּוֹם׃

   And the Lord appeared to him (Abram) at the oaks of Mamre, as (or while) he was a sitter at the opening of the tent about the heat of the day.

   In Gen 18:1, the Vav of situation with its retrospective pronoun, וְהוּא, connects the situation clause to its related clause. This pronoun resumes the pronoun in the prepositional phrase of its related clause, אֵלָיו. This clause describes the situation, condition, or status of Abram, as a sitter at the opening of the tent, contemporaneous with the Lord's appearing to him.

Gen 14:12–13; 24:62; 32:32; Num 22:22; 25:6; 33:40; Judg 3:20; 4:2, 21; 10:1; 13:9; 19:16; 1 Sam 10:5; 22:9; 23:1; 24:12; 28:14; 2 Sam 4:5, 7; 11:4; 13:8; 15:30; 21:16; 1 Kgs 20:12; BA Dan 5:6(2x); Ezra 5:8(4x)

b 2. Vav of situation with noun

The noun may be repeated from a preceding clause and may have a retrospective pronoun attached to it.

וַיֵּלֶךְ וַיִּמְצָאֵהוּ אַרְיֵה בַּדֶּרֶךְ וַיְמִיתֵהוּ וַתְּהִי נִבְלָתוֹ מֻשְׁלֶכֶת בַּדֶּרֶךְ וְהַחֲמוֹר עֹמֵד אֶצְלָהּ וְהָאַרְיֵה עֹמֵד אֵצֶל הַנְּבֵלָה׃ 1 Kgs 13:24

And he went, and a lion found him in the road and killed him. And his corpse was thrown down in the road, as the donkey was standing beside it (the road), as the lion was standing beside the corpse.

The noun, וְהָאַרְיֵה, with its Vav of situation is repeated from its related clause. The noun, וְהַחֲמוֹר, with its Vav of situation is repeated from 1 Kgs 13:23.

Gen 40:17; Exod 9:24; Deut 4:11; Josh 3:14; Judg 16:12; 18:17; 1 Sam 17:41; 2 Sam 15:12; Esth 5:1; Neh 2:6; 2 Chr 13:14

וַיֹּאמְרוּ הָבָה ׀ נִבְנֶה־לָּנוּ עִיר וּמִגְדָּל וְרֹאשׁוֹ בַשָּׁמַיִם Gen 11:4[a]

And they said, Come, let us build for ourselves a city, and a tower whose top is in the heavens.

The situation clause in Gen 11:4 has a Vav of situation and a retrospective pronoun attached to the noun. The announcement of this situation clause is a prepositional phrase.

Gen 24:15; Exod 6:12; 14:7, 27; 1 Sam 17:40; 19:9; 22:6; 23:15; 24:4; 2 Sam 2:16; 13:24; 2 Kgs 11:8; Jer 1:13; BA Dan 2:49; 4:7–8; 6:11; 7:5

c 3. Vav of situation with הִנֵּה and retrospective pronoun

וַיָּבֹא אֵלָיו וְהִנּוֹ נִצָּב עַל־עֹלָתוֹ וְשָׂרֵי מוֹאָב אִתּוֹ Num 23:17[a]

And he came to him, while behold he was stationed beside his burnt offering with the officials of Moab beside him.

Gen 40:6; Exod 2:13; 4:6; 1 Kgs 11:22

d 4. Vav of situation with אֵין and a retrospective pronoun or noun

This is the common negative for situation clauses with nouns.

וַיְהִי כְּהַיּוֹם הַזֶּה וַיָּבֹא הַבַּיְתָה לַעֲשׂוֹת מְלַאכְתּוֹ וְאֵין אִישׁ מֵאַנְשֵׁי הַבַּיִת שָׁם בַּבָּיִת׃ Gen 39:11

And it happened on this day that he entered the house to do his work while there was no man of the men of the house there in the house.

וַתָּבֹא אֵלָיו אִיזֶבֶל אִשְׁתּוֹ וַתְּדַבֵּר אֵלָיו מַה־זֶּה רוּחֲךָ סָרָה וְאֵינְךָ אֹכֵל לָחֶם׃ 1 Kgs 12:5

And Jezebel his wife came to him, and she spoke to him, What now, your spirit is saddened, as you are not eating food?

Gen 41:8, 24; Exod 17:1; Lev 26:6, 17; Deut 22:27; 28:31–32; 32:12, 28, 39; Judg 19:15; 1 Sam 14:26; 22:8; 26:12; 2 Sam 14:6; Jer 32:33

5. עוֹד with retrospective pronoun *e*
This particle may or may not have a Vav of situation attached to it. If without a Vav of situation, a retrospective pronoun on the particle connects the situation clause to its related clause.

2 Sam 18:14 וַיֹּאמֶר יוֹאָב לֹא־כֵן אֹחִילָה לְפָנֶיךָ וַיִּקַּח שְׁלֹשָׁה שְׁבָטִים
בְּכַפּוֹ וַיִּתְקָעֵם בְּלֵב אַבְשָׁלוֹם עוֹדֶנּוּ חַי בְּלֵב הָאֵלָה׃

And Joab said, I will not now delay before you, and he took three spears in his hand, and he thrust them in the heart of Absalom, while he was alive in the middle of the oak tree.

The particle עוֹד functions virtually as a Vav of situation, perhaps stating more precisely than the Vav of situation that Absalom was still alive when the spears were thrown into his heart.

Job 2:3 וַיֹּאמֶר יְהוָה אֶל־הַשָּׂטָן הֲשַׂמְתָּ לִבְּךָ אֶל־עַבְדִּי אִיּוֹב כִּי אֵין
כָּמֹהוּ בָּאָרֶץ אִישׁ תָּם וְיָשָׁר יְרֵא אֱלֹהִים וְסָר מֵרָע וְעֹדֶנּוּ
מַחֲזִיק בְּתֻמָּתוֹ וַתְּסִיתֵנִי בוֹ לְבַלְּעוֹ חִנָּם׃

And the Lord said to Satan, Have you considered my servant Job, for there is not like him on earth, a blameless and righteous man; a fearer of God and who turns away from evil, while still he is holding on to his integrity although you entice me against him to devour him without cause.

The particle עוֹד has the Vav of situation attached in Job 2:3.
Gen 18:22; 25:6; 44:14; 1 Kgs 12:2; Jer 33:1

B. Without Particles *f*

These constructions are usually nouns with prepositional phrases.

Gen 12:8 וַיַּעְתֵּק מִשָּׁם הָהָרָה מִקֶּדֶם לְבֵית־אֵל וַיֵּט אָהֳלֹה בֵּית־אֵל
מִיָּם וְהָעַי מִקֶּדֶם וַיִּבֶן־שָׁם מִזְבֵּחַ לַיהוָה וַיִּקְרָא בְּשֵׁם יְהוָה׃

And he proceeded from there to the mountain range on the east of Bethel, and he pitched his tent, Bethel (being) on the west and Ai (being) on the east, and he built there an altar to the Lord, and he called on the name of the Lord.

Gen 32:12[b] כִּי־יָרֵא אָנֹכִי אֹתוֹ פֶּן־יָבוֹא וְהִכַּנִי אֵם עַל־בָּנִים׃

For I am fearing him, lest he come and smite me, mother upon children.

Gen 32:12 may be understood as an ACCUSATIVES OF SITUATION with a preposition instead of a situation clause: "lest he should come and smite me (in the status of) a mother with her children" (§13z; 16l–ii).
Exod 12:11(3x), 34; Num 22:24[b]; and perhaps Exod 33:11 though it should probably be understood as Gen 32:12 above as an accusative of situation with a prepositional phrase.

§50. Situation Clauses with Finite Verbs *a*

Finite verbs do not have a Vav of situation attached to them, though another word in the clause might have it, such as a pronoun or a repeated noun, retrospective to its related clause.

A. Perfect

The completed action of the perfect in a situation clause usually precedes the verbal action of its related clause. These may often be translated into English as past participles. They may also be translated as absolute clauses of Greek and Latin. These situation clauses often answer the questions: "how", "in what situation," or "in what condition," etc., to its related clause.

Exod 34:28[a] וַיְהִי־שָׁם עִם־יְהוָה אַרְבָּעִים יוֹם וְאַרְבָּעִים לַיְלָה לֶחֶם לֹא
אָכַל וּמַיִם לֹא שָׁתָה

And he was there with the Lord for forty days and forty nights, having not eaten bread nor having drunk water.

Moses was with the Lord for forty days and nights, in the situation of one who had not eaten or drunk.

Gen 48:14 וַיִּשְׁלַח יִשְׂרָאֵל אֶת־יְמִינוֹ וַיָּשֶׁת עַל־רֹאשׁ אֶפְרַיִם וְהוּא
הַצָּעִיר וְאֶת־שְׂמֹאלוֹ עַל־רֹאשׁ מְנַשֶּׁה שִׂכֵּל אֶת־יָדָיו כִּי
מְנַשֶּׁה הַבְּכוֹר׃

And Israel stretched out his right hand, and he placed (it) upon the head of Ephraim, he being the younger, and his left hand upon the head of Manasseh, having crisscrossed his hands, because Manasseh was the firstborn.

In Gen 48:14, Israel stretched out his hands in the manner of having crisscrossed them.

Gen 44:12[a] וַיְחַפֵּשׂ בַּגָּדוֹל הֵחֵל וּבַקָּטֹן כִּלָּה

And he searched, having begun with the oldest and having finished with the youngest.

The situation clause in Gen 44:12 relates how the search was conducted.

1 Kgs 13:28 וַיֵּלֶךְ וַיִּמְצָא אֶת־נִבְלָתוֹ מֻשְׁלֶכֶת בַּדֶּרֶךְ וַחֲמוֹר וְהָאַרְיֵה
עֹמְדִים אֵצֶל הַנְּבֵלָה לֹא־אָכַל הָאַרְיֵה אֶת־הַנְּבֵלָה וְלֹא
שָׁבַר אֶת־הַחֲמוֹר׃

And he went and found his corpse thrown down in the road while the donkey and the lion were standing beside the corpse, the lion having not eaten the corpse nor having torn the donkey.

In this last example, 1 Kgs 13:28, instead of using a retrospective pronoun, the noun (lion) is repeated from a nearby clause. The participle (עֹמְדִים) expresses contemporaneous actions with the verb (וַיִּמְצָא). The perfects express preceding action prior to the main verb.

Isa 3:9; Jer 7:26; BA Dan 4:19; 6:19(2x)

b **B. Imperfect**

The incomplete action of the imperfect in a situation clause is contemporaneous with the action of its related clause. These may often be translated into English as present participles. Indeed the imperfect is similar to the participle examples earlier, but the imperfect stresses the verbal action relative to the description of the participle. Like the perfect, they may also be translated as absolute clauses of Greek and Latin, answering the questions: "how", "in what situation," or "in what condition," etc., to its related clause.

Ps 35:8[a] תְּבוֹאֵ֣הוּ שׁוֹאָ֮ה לֹֽא־יֵ֫דָ֥ע

Let destruction come to him not knowing.

The situation clause in Ps 35:8 relates how or in what situation the destruction should come—"unawares." The destruction and the not knowing occur simultaneously.

Deut 2:27 אֶעְבְּרָ֣ה בְאַרְצֶ֔ךָ בַּדֶּ֥רֶךְ בַּדֶּ֖רֶךְ אֵלֵ֑ךְ לֹ֥א אָס֖וּר יָמִ֥ין וּשְׂמֹֽאול׃

Let me pass through your land, going only through the road, not turning aside to the right or left.

The situation clauses in Deut 2:27 express how or in what manner Israel is to pass through the land—going only through the road, not turning aside to the right or left. The act of going and not turning aside occurs contemporaneous with the passing through.

Exod 7:15; 10:26; 1 Kgs 1:42

Chapter 15
PURPOSE AND RESULT CLAUSES

§51. Introduction

Purpose clauses express the intent or reason for another action or situation—"For I have chosen him *to the intent that* (or *for the reason that*) he might command his house" (Gen 18:19). The result clause, by contrast, expresses the outcome, eventuality, or effect of another action or situation—"Those who fashion an idol, all of them are nothing, and their precious things do not profit, and their witnesses, they do not see, and they do not know *of the ultimate outcome that* (or *of the final effect/result that*) they are put to shame" (Isa 44:9).

For some contexts, distinguishing between purpose and result clauses is difficult. Two principles, however, distinguish between purpose and result clauses. First, an English infinitive frequently translates a purpose/intent clause, not a result clause. Secondly, a result clause usually expresses something unexpected, by surprise or disappointment. The ultimate outcome or result, therefore, is contrary to the intent or purpose. For example, Hos 8:4, states, "Their gold and silver they made for themselves into idols *so that* (*with the unexpected outcome that*) they may be cut off." Israel, of course, did not make idols with the hopeful or intended expectation of being cut off. On the contrary, their making idols brought the unexpected and disappointing outcome of their being cut off.

Various particles express purpose and result. Furthermore, these particles put the imperfect in the subjunctive and the infinitive construct and perfect in the position of the subjunctive.[1] All examples are purpose clauses, except those labeled result.

§52. Independent Particles (§4j–m; 18e) *a*

A. לְמַ֫עַן

This particle is used for purpose or result.

Gen 12:13 אִמְרִי־נָא אֲחֹתִי אָתְּ לְמַעַן יִיטַב־לִי בַעֲבוּרֵךְ וְחָיְתָה נַפְשִׁי
בִּגְלָלֵךְ׃

Say now, You are my sister, for the purpose (reason/intent) that it might be good for me on account of you and my soul might live because of you.

Jer 7:18 הַבָּנִים מְלַקְּטִים עֵצִים וְהָאָבוֹת מְבַעֲרִים אֶת־הָאֵשׁ וְהַנָּשִׁים
לָשׁוֹת בָּצֵק לַעֲשׂוֹת כַּוָּנִים לִמְלֶכֶת הַשָּׁמַיִם וְהַסֵּךְ נְסָכִים
לֵאלֹהִים אֲחֵרִים לְמַעַן הַכְעִסֵנִי׃

The sons are collecting wood, and the fathers are burning fire, and the women are kneading dough, to make cakes for the queen of heaven and to pour out libations to other gods with the (disappointed or unexpected) outcome/result of provoking me. (result)

Gen 18:19; 27:25; Exod 1:1; 8:6, 18; (with לְמַ֫עַן אֲשֶׁר) 9:16; 11:9; 13:9; Lev 17:5; Num 17:5; Deut 27:3; Josh 3:4; Jer 7:19 (result), 23

1. Arabic also uses various particles to place the verb in the subjunctive. For example, the Lamed (Lam) and other particles connected to the imperfect (subjunctive) expresses purpose.

b **B. בַּעֲבוּר**

This particle is used only for purpose.

Gen 21:30 וַיֹּ֗אמֶר כִּ֚י אֶת־שֶׁ֣בַע כְּבָשֹׂ֔ת תִּקַּ֖ח מִיָּדִ֑י בַּעֲבוּר֙ תִּֽהְיֶה־לִּ֣י
לְעֵדָ֔ה כִּ֥י חָפַ֖רְתִּי אֶת־הַבְּאֵ֥ר הַזֹּֽאת׃

And he said, Indeed, seven ewe lambs you will take from my hand, in order that (for the intent that, for the reason that) it may exist for me as a witness that I dug this well.

Gen 27:4, 19, 31; 46:34; (with אֲשֶׁר) 27:10; Exod 9:14, 16(2x), 19; 20:20(2x); 1 Sam 1:6

c **C. אֲשֶׁר**

This particle may be used for purpose or result.

Deut 4:10 הַקְהֶל־לִי֙ אֶת־הָעָ֔ם וְאַשְׁמִעֵ֖ם אֶת־דְּבָרָ֑י אֲשֶׁ֨ר יִלְמְד֜וּן
לְיִרְאָ֣ה אֹתִ֗י

Assemble to me the people that I might cause them to hear my words to the intent that they may learn to fear me.

Deut 4:10 could also be rendered well by an English infinitive . . . "to learn to fear me."

Gen 13:16 וְשַׂמְתִּ֥י אֶֽת־זַרְעֲךָ֖ כַּעֲפַ֣ר הָאָ֑רֶץ אֲשֶׁ֣ר ׀ אִם־יוּכַ֣ל אִ֗ישׁ לִמְנוֹת֙
אֶת־עֲפַ֣ר הָאָ֔רֶץ גַּֽם־זַרְעֲךָ֖ יִמָּנֶֽה׃

And I will make your seed as the dirt of the land, so that if a man is (unexpectedly) able to count the dirt of the land, even your seed can be counted. (result, perhaps)

Deut 6:3[a] וְשָׁמַעְתָּ֤ יִשְׂרָאֵל֙ וְשָׁמַרְתָּ֣ לַעֲשׂ֔וֹת אֲשֶׁר֙ יִיטַ֣ב לְךָ֔

Hear, Israel, and keep it carefully so that it may be well for you.

Compare Deut 6:3 with the following example:

Deut 5:29 מִֽי־יִתֵּ֡ן וְהָיָה֩ לְבָבָ֨ם זֶ֜ה לָהֶ֗ם לְיִרְאָ֥ה אֹתִ֛י וְלִשְׁמֹ֥ר
אֶת־כָּל־מִצְוֺתַ֖י כָּל־הַיָּמִ֑ים לְמַ֨עַן יִיטַ֥ב לָהֶ֛ם וְלִבְנֵיהֶ֖ם לְעֹלָֽם׃

Would that this their heart might exist to them to fear me and keep all my commandments always so that it might be good for them and for their sons forever.

The purpose nuance in Deut 6:3 with אֲשֶׁר parallels the meaning of לְמַ֫עַן in Deut 5:29.

Gen 11:7; Exod 5:2 (possibly result); Deut 4:40; 28:27, 51; Josh 3:7; 1 Kgs 3:13; 2 Kgs 9:37; Ps 58:6; 89:22; Neh 8:14

d **D. לְבִלְתִּי (§18b)**

This particle negates a perfect, imperfect, or infinitive construct in a purpose or result clause by putting the imperfect in the subjunctive and the infinitive construct or perfect in the position of the subjunctive.

Exod 20:20 וַיֹּ֨אמֶר מֹשֶׁ֣ה אֶל־הָעָם֮ אַל־תִּירָאוּ֒ כִּ֗י לְבַֽעֲבוּר֙ נַסּ֣וֹת אֶתְכֶ֔ם
בָּ֖א הָאֱלֹהִ֑ים וּבַעֲב֗וּר תִּהְיֶ֧ה יִרְאָת֛וֹ עַל־פְּנֵיכֶ֖ם לְבִלְתִּ֥י
תֶחֱטָֽאוּ׃

And Moses said to the people, Do not fear, for in order to test you God has come, and in order that his fear might exist before you to the intent that you might not sin.

Gen 4:15; 38:9; Exod 8:18, 25; 9:17; Lev 18:30; 20:4; 2 Sam 14:14; Jer 7:8 (result); 16:12; 23:14

E. פֶּן *e*

This particle also negates a purpose clause.

וַיֹּאמְרוּ הָבָה נִבְנֶה־לָּנוּ עִיר וּמִגְדָּל וְרֹאשׁוֹ בַשָּׁמַיִם וְנַעֲשֶׂה־לָּנוּ
שֵׁם פֶּן־נָפוּץ עַל־פְּנֵי כָל־הָאָרֶץ׃ Gen 11:4

And they said, Come, let us build for ourselves a city along with a tower whose top is in the heavens that we make for ourselves a name, lest (with the intent that) we should be scattered upon the face of all the earth.

Gen 3:3, 22; 19:17; 24:6; 26:7; Num 20:18

F. כִּי *f*

This particle expresses result, not purpose.

וַיִּקְרָא אֲבִימֶלֶךְ לְאַבְרָהָם וַיֹּאמֶר לוֹ מֶה־עָשִׂיתָ לָּנוּ
וּמֶה־חָטָאתִי לָךְ כִּי־הֵבֵאתָ עָלַי וְעַל־מַמְלַכְתִּי חֲטָאָה גְדֹלָה Gen 20:9[a]

Abimelek called to Abraham and said to him, What have you done to us and how have I sinned against you so that (with the unexpected outcome that) you have brought upon me and upon my kingdom great sin.

מָה־אֱנוֹשׁ כִּי־תִזְכְּרֶנּוּ וּבֶן־אָדָם כִּי תִפְקְדֶנּוּ׃ Ps 8:5

What is man, so that (with the unexpected outcome that) you should think about him?

Gen 40:15; Exod 3:11(2x); Deut 14:24; 1 Sam 18:18; 22:8; 2 Sam 13:15; Isa 22:1, 16; 36:5; 52:5; Mic 4:9; Hab 2:18

§53. Particles Connected to Words *a*

A. ו with Perfect (§6d, g, h)

This rare construction expresses purpose.

וַיֹּאמֶר לוֹ הַמֶּלֶךְ עֲשֵׂה כַּאֲשֶׁר דִּבֶּר וּפְגַע־בּוֹ וּקְבַרְתּוֹ
וַהֲסִירֹתָ דְּמֵי חִנָּם 1 Kgs 2:31

And the king said to him, Do as he spoke, and kill him and bury him, for the intent that you might remove innocent blood.

Alternatively, render the last clause of 1 Kgs 2:31 by an English infinitive, "to remove innocent blood."

Gen 35:5; 1 Sam 25:21; 1 Kgs 13:3

B. ו (Conjunctive Vav) with Jussive (§6u) *b*

This common construction substitutes for the subjunctive, expressing purpose or result.

כֹּה־אָמַר יְהוָה אֱלֹהֵי הָעִבְרִים שַׁלַּח אֶת־עַמִּי וְיַעַבְדֻנִי׃ Exod 9:1[b]

Thus says the Lord, the God of the Hebrews, Send away my people for the reason that (so that) they may serve me.

Num 23:19[a] לֹא אִישׁ אֵל וִיכַזֵּב וּבֶן־אָדָם וְיִתְנֶחָם

Not a man is God so that (so as to have the unexpected outcome that) he should lie, nor a son of man so that (so as to have the unexpected outcome that) he should change his mind. (result)

Gen 19:20; 20:7; 23:9; 24:49; 27:7, 9; 42:16; Exod 2:7; Hos 14:10

c **C. ו with Imperative (§6w)**

This construction may express purpose.

Gen 20:7[a] וְעַתָּה הָשֵׁב אֵשֶׁת־הָאִישׁ כִּי־נָבִיא הוּא וְיִתְפַּלֵּל בַּעַדְךָ וֶחְיֵה

And now, return the wife of the man for he is a prophet that he might pray for you to the intent that (so that) you might live.

Gen 18:4–5; 19:8, 34; Exod 3:10; 18:22; Judg 8:24; 19:24; 1 Sam 28:22

d **D. ו with Noun and Following Imperfect**

This rare construction occurs in poetry and direct speech. Here the noun separates the Vav from the imperfect for emphasis of the noun and/or the stylistic effect of the sentence.

Prov 8:29[a] בְּשׂוּמוֹ לַיָּם ׀ חֻקּוֹ וּמַיִם לֹא יַעַבְרוּ־פִיו

When he set for the sea its boundary, (he did so) with the intent that (so that) the waters might not transgress his commandment.

Job 10:18; 41:8; Prov 30:16

e **E. וְלֹא or וְאַל with the Imperfect (§4i; 41a-e)**

Because of the negative, the Vav detaches from the imperfect. This construction may negate a purpose or result clause.

Gen 14:23 אִם־מִחוּט וְעַד שְׂרוֹךְ־נַעַל וְאִם־אֶקַּח מִכָּל־אֲשֶׁר־לָךְ וְלֹא תֹאמַר אֲנִי הֶעֱשַׁרְתִּי אֶת־אַבְרָם׃

Not from thread even unto strap of the sandal (I am not taking) and I am not taking from all that belongs to you, for the intent that (so that) you do not say, I made Abram rich.

Gen 41:36; 42:2, 20; Exod 4:21; 7:21; 9:28; Lev 2:13; 8:35; 10:6, 9; 26:21; Num 15:39; BA Dan 6:3

f **F. מִן with Infinitive Construct**

This construction may also express a purpose clause.

Gen 31:29 יֶשׁ־לְאֵל יָדִי לַעֲשׂוֹת עִמָּכֶם רָע וֵאלֹהֵי אֲבִיכֶם אֶמֶשׁ ׀ אָמַר אֵלַי לֵאמֹר הִשָּׁמֶר לְךָ מִדַּבֵּר עִם־יַעֲקֹב מִטּוֹב עַד־רָע׃

There was in my power to do with you evil, but the God of your father last night said to me, keep yourself from speaking with Jacob (from the intent to speak) from good even unto evil.

Gen 18:25; 20:6; 23:6

G. ל with Infinitive Construct (§18e) *g*

This is a very common construction for expressing purpose or result.

וַיֵּ֣רֶד יְהוָ֔ה לִרְאֹ֥ת אֶת־הָעִ֖יר וְאֶת־הַמִּגְדָּ֑ל Gen 11:5[a]

And the Lord went down (with the intent) to see the city and the tower.

וְגַם֙ נֵ֣צַח יִשְׂרָאֵ֔ל לֹ֥א יְשַׁקֵּ֖ר וְלֹ֣א יִנָּחֵ֑ם כִּ֣י לֹ֥א אָדָ֛ם ה֖וּא לְהִנָּחֵֽם׃ 1 Sam 15:29

And even the glory of Israel, he does not lie and he does not change his mind, for he is not a man so that (so as to have the unexpected outcome that) he should change his mind. (result)

Gen 1:14–15, 18; 2:5, 10, 15, 19; Exod 5:21(2x); Deut 4:25; 2 Sam 12:10

H. ו of the Vav-Consecutive with Imperfect (§6n) *h*

This construction may negate a purpose or result clause.

וְֽאֶת־הָאֲנָשִׁ֞ים אֲשֶׁר־פֶּ֣תַח הַבַּ֗יִת הִכּוּ֙ בַּסַּנְוֵרִ֔ים מִקָּטֹ֖ן וְעַד־גָּד֑וֹל וַיִּלְא֖וּ לִמְצֹ֥א הַפָּֽתַח׃ Gen 19:11

And the men who were at the door of the house they (the angels) smote with blindness from the young to the old so that they groped to find the door.

Exod 10:15; 19:16; 1 Kgs 1:45

Chapter 16
INTERROGATIVE CLAUSES

§54. Introduction

Context or particles may introduce an interrogative clause. Interrogative clauses express questions for which the expected answer is uncertain, positive, or negative. Interrogative clauses may also express an exclamatory statement, terminating with an exclamation point instead of a question mark. Finally, interrogative clauses may be expressed indirectly after verbs of the senses (think, say, etc.).

§55. Interrogative Clauses with and without Vav *a*

Context determines whether a clause without an interrogative particle is an interrogative clause. In the spoken language, the speaker probably raised the voice at the beginning or end of these interrogative statements. These interrogative clauses may be with or without an initial Vav.

A. Interrogative Clauses without Initial Vav

Gen 18:12 וַתִּצְחַ֥ק שָׂרָ֖ה בְּקִרְבָּ֣הּ לֵאמֹ֑ר אַחֲרֵ֤י בְלֹתִי֙ הָֽיְתָה־לִּ֣י עֶדְנָ֔ה
וַֽאדֹנִ֖י זָקֵֽן׃

And Sarah laughed within herself saying, After I have become unable to bear children will delight happen to me, while my husband is old?

Gen 27:24[a] וַיֹּ֕אמֶר אַתָּ֥ה זֶ֖ה בְּנִ֣י עֵשָׂ֑ו

And he (Isaac) said, Are you [here] my son Esau?

B. Interrogative Clauses with an Initial Vav *b*

Exod 8:22 וַיֹּ֣אמֶר מֹשֶׁ֗ה לֹ֤א נָכוֹן֙ לַעֲשׂ֣וֹת כֵּ֔ן כִּ֚י תּוֹעֲבַ֣ת מִצְרַ֔יִם נִזְבַּ֖ח
לַֽיהוָ֣ה אֱלֹהֵ֑ינוּ הֵ֣ן נִזְבַּ֞ח אֶת־תּוֹעֲבַ֥ת מִצְרַ֛יִם לְעֵינֵיהֶ֖ם וְלֹ֥א
יִסְקְלֻֽנוּ׃

And Moses said, It is not right to do this, for an abomination of the Egyptians (it is) should we sacrifice to the Lord, our God. Behold, should we sacrifice an abomination of the Egyptians before them, [and] will they not stone us?

Jon 4:10 וַיֹּ֣אמֶר יְהוָ֔ה אַתָּ֥ה חַ֙סְתָּ֙ עַל־הַקִּ֣יקָי֔וֹן אֲשֶׁ֛ר לֹא־עָמַ֥לְתָּ בּ֖וֹ
וְלֹ֣א גִדַּלְתּ֑וֹ שֶׁבִּן־לַ֥יְלָה הָיָ֖ה וּבִן־לַ֥יְלָה אָבָֽד׃

Jon 4:11[a] וַאֲנִי֙ לֹ֣א אָח֔וּס עַל־נִֽינְוֵ֖ה הָעִ֣יר הַגְּדוֹלָ֑ה

[10]And the Lord said, You had compassion on the vine on which you did not labor and you did not cause to grow, it happened in a night, and perish in a night. [11]And should I not have compassion upon Nineveh the great city?

§56. Interrogative Clauses with Particles *a*

A. ה

The interrogative ה is a common interrogative particle that may attach to other particles, such as הֲכִי.

1. As an interrogative
   a) Expecting an uncertain answer

      Most interrogative clauses are uncertain as to the answer. The answer may be "yes" by repeating the important word in the clause, or "no" by a negative. Of course, the answer is not always given, nor is the answer always "yes" or "no."

Gen 24:58 וַיִּקְרְא֤וּ לְרִבְקָה֙ וַיֹּאמְר֣וּ אֵלֶ֔יהָ הֲתֵלְכִ֖י עִם־הָאִ֣ישׁ הַזֶּ֑ה וַתֹּ֖אמֶר אֵלֵֽךְ׃

And they summoned Rebekah and said to her, Will you go with this man? And she said, I will go (yes).

In Gen 24:58, the positive answer (yes) is indicated by repeating the verb.

Gen 29:6 וַיֹּ֥אמֶר לָהֶ֖ם הֲשָׁל֣וֹם ל֑וֹ וַיֹּאמְר֣וּ שָׁל֔וֹם

And he said to them, Is it well with him? And they said, Well (yes).

Judg 4:20 וַיֹּ֣אמֶר אֵלֶ֔יהָ עֲמֹ֖ד פֶּ֣תַח הָאֹ֑הֶל וְהָיָה֩ אִם־אִ֨ישׁ יָב֜וֹא וּשְׁאֵלֵ֗ךְ וְאָמַ֛ר הֲיֵשׁ־פֹּ֥ה אִ֖ישׁ וְאָמַ֥רְתְּ אָֽיִן׃

And he said to her, Stand at the opening of the tent, and it will happen if a man should enter and he should ask you, and should say, Is a man here, then you should say, No.

Gen 43:7[a] וַיֹּאמְר֡וּ שָׁא֣וֹל שָֽׁאַל־הָ֠אִישׁ לָ֣נוּ וּלְמֽוֹלַדְתֵּ֜נוּ לֵאמֹ֗ר הַעוֹד֩ אֲבִיכֶ֨ם חַי֙ הֲיֵ֣שׁ לָכֶ֣ם אָ֔ח

And they said, The man intently asked concerning us and concerning our kin saying, Is yet your father alive? Is there a brother to you? (A response is not given.)

1 Sam 23:11; Job 1:8

b
   b) Expecting a positive answer (§41k)

      Context determines if the question expects a positive answer.

1 Sam 2:27[b] הֲנִגְלֹ֤ה נִגְלֵ֙יתִי֙ אֶל־בֵּ֣ית אָבִ֔יךָ בִּֽהְיוֹתָ֥ם בְּמִצְרַ֖יִם לְבֵ֥ית פַּרְעֹֽה׃

Did I not in fact reveal myself to the house of your father when they were in Egypt to the house of Pharaoh? (Yes!)

In 1 Sam 2:27, the interrogative may also express an exclamation.

Gen 16:13; Num 12:2 (second question), 14; 1 Sam 10:24; 1 Kgs 21:19; 2 Kgs 6:32; Jer 31:20

c
   c) Expecting a negative answer

      Context determines if the question expects a negative answer.

Deut 4:33 הֲשָׁ֣מַֽע עָם֩ ק֨וֹל אֱלֹהִ֜ים מְדַבֵּ֧ר מִתּוֹךְ־הָאֵ֛שׁ כַּאֲשֶׁר־שָׁמַ֥עְתָּ אַתָּ֖ה וַיֶּֽחִי׃

Has a people heard the voice of God speaking from the midst of fire as you have heard and lived? (No)

2 Sam 7:5 לֵ֤ךְ וְאָֽמַרְתָּ֙ אֶל־עַבְדִּ֣י אֶל־דָּוִ֔ד כֹּ֖ה אָמַ֣ר יְהוָ֑ה הַאַתָּ֛ה תִּבְנֶה־לִּ֥י בַ֖יִת לְשִׁבְתִּֽי׃

Go and say to my servant David, thus says the Lord, Will you build for me a house for my dwelling? (No)

Compare 1 Chr 17:4, which is a negative question.
Gen 18:17; 30:2; 50:19; Num 11:23; 12:2 (first question); Deut 20:19; Isa 28:24; 57:6; Jer 15:12; 16:20

2. As an interrogative expressing exclamation *d*

הֲכִי֩ קָרָ֨א שְׁמ֜וֹ יַעֲקֹ֗ב וַֽיַּעְקְבֵ֙נִי֙ זֶ֣ה פַעֲמַ֔יִם Gen 27:36[a]

Indeed, does he call his name Jacob, namely, that he has cheated me now twice!

וַיֹּ֤אמֶר מֶֽלֶךְ־יִשְׂרָאֵל֙ אֶל־עֲבָדָ֔יו הַיְדַעְתֶּ֕ם כִּֽי־לָ֖נוּ רָמֹ֣ת גִּלְעָ֑ד 1 Kgs 22:3[a]

And the king of Israel said to his servants, Do you not (indeed) know that to us is Ramoth-Gilead? (Indeed, you should!)

B. הֲלֹא (§41k) *e*

This compound particle often expects a positive answer and expresses exclamation.

הֲלֹא־הֵ֜מָּה בְּעֵ֣בֶר הַיַּרְדֵּ֗ן אַחֲרֵי֙ דֶּ֚רֶךְ מְב֣וֹא הַשֶּׁ֔מֶשׁ בְּאֶ֙רֶץ֙ הַֽכְּנַעֲנִ֔י הַיֹּשֵׁ֖ב בָּעֲרָבָ֑ה מ֚וּל הַגִּלְגָּ֔ל אֵ֖צֶל אֵלוֹנֵ֥י מֹרֶֽה׃ Deut 11:30

Are they not beyond the Jordan to the west in the land of the Canaanites who dwell in the Arabah before Gilgal beside oaks of Moreh? (Indeed, they are!)

הֲל֤וֹא צִוִּיתִ֙יךָ֙ חֲזַ֣ק וֶאֱמָ֔ץ Josh 1:9[a]

Have I not (indeed) commanded you, Be strong and courageous?

The Septuagint and Vulgate express the nuance of exclamation, "Behold (ἰδού, *ecce*) I have commanded you." Here and in many other places, הֲלֹא equals הִנֵּה (§62d).

וְיֶ֙תֶר֙ דִּבְרֵ֣י שְׁלֹמֹ֔ה וְכָל־אֲשֶׁ֥ר עָשָׂ֖ה וְחָכְמָת֑וֹ הֲלוֹא־הֵ֣ם כְּתֻבִ֔ים עַל־סֵ֖פֶר דִּבְרֵ֥י שְׁלֹמֹֽה׃ 1 Kgs 11:41

And the rest of the deeds of Solomon and all that he did and his wisdom are they not (in fact) written upon the book of the deeds of Solomon?

1 Kgs 11:41 has הֲלֹא; 1 Kgs 14:19 furnishes the parallel construction הִנָּם, "Behold they are written upon the book of the deeds of the days to the kings of Israel."

The following verses imply a positive answer and most express exclamation (= הִנֵּה): Gen 13:9; 19:20; 20:5; 27:36; 29:25; Exod 4:11; Deut 3:11; 11:30; Judg 6:14; 1 Sam 21:12; 23:19; 26:1; 2 Sam 15:35; Ruth 2:9

C. מִי *f*

This interrogative pronoun for persons may occur in any case: nominative (Gen 3:11), genitive (1 Sam 6:20), or accusative (1 Sam 12:3). The pronoun זֶה or הוּא may be added to strengthen or to give "vividness" to the interrogative statement.[1]

1. Wright II, 170b

1. As an interrogative

וַתֹּ֣אמֶר אֶל־הָעֶ֗בֶד מִֽי־הָאִ֤ישׁ הַלָּזֶה֙ הַהֹלֵ֤ךְ בַּשָּׂדֶה֙ לִקְרָאתֵ֔נוּ Gen 24:65[a]

And she said to the servant, Who is this man who is walking in the field to meet us?

מִ֤י ה֣וּא זֶה֮ מֶ֤לֶךְ הַכָּב֥וֹד Ps 24:10[a]

Who is he [now], the king of glory!

Note the strengthening pronouns in Ps 24:10.

g 2. As an interrogative expecting a negative answer with exclamation

א֣וֹי לָ֔נוּ מִ֣י יַצִּילֵ֔נוּ מִיַּ֛ד הָאֱלֹהִ֥ים הָאַדִּירִ֖ים הָאֵ֑לֶּה 1 Sam 4:8[a]

Woe to us. Who can (indeed) save us from the hand of these mighty gods! (Nobody!)

Deut 9:2; 30:12; 1 Sam 6:20; 22:14; 26:9, 15

h 3. As an interrogative expressing contempt or humility

וַיֹּ֣אמֶר פַּרְעֹ֔ה מִ֤י יְהוָה֙ אֲשֶׁ֣ר אֶשְׁמַ֣ע בְּקֹל֔וֹ לְשַׁלַּ֖ח אֶת־יִשְׂרָאֵ֑ל Exod 5:2[a]

And Pharaoh said, Who is the Lord that I should listen to him to send away Israel?

The interrogative in Exod 5:2 expresses contempt.

a) Contempt: Judg 9:28; 1 Sam 17:26, 25:10; Isa 28:9
b) Humility: Exod 3:11; 1 Sam 18:18

i 4. As an interrogative expressing an exclamatory desire (§62c)

וּמִ֤י יִתֵּן֙ כָּל־עַ֤ם יְהוָה֙ נְבִיאִ֔ים Num 11:29[b]

And who will give all the people of the Lord as prophets (Would that all the people of the Lord were prophets).

וַיֹּ֙אמֶר֙ אַבְשָׁל֔וֹם מִֽי־יְשִׂמֵ֥נִי שֹׁפֵ֖ט בָּאָ֑רֶץ 2 Sam 15:4[a]

And Absalom said, Who will place me as judge in the land (Would that I were judge in the land).

Num 11:4, 18; Deut 28:67; 2 Sam 15:4; Mal 1:10; Ps 4:7; 60:11; 94:16

j **D. מַה**

This interrogative pronoun for things (instead of people) may be compounded with other particles, such as כַּמָּה. The pronoun זֶה (this or now) or הוא may be added to strengthen or to give "vividness" to the interrogative statement.

1. As an interrogative

וַיִּקְרָ֨א אֲבִימֶ֜לֶךְ לְאַבְרָהָ֗ם וַיֹּ֨אמֶר ל֜וֹ מֶה־עָשִׂ֤יתָ לָּ֙נוּ֙ וּמֶֽה־חָטָ֣אתִי לָ֔ךְ Gen 20:9[a]

And Abimelek summoned Abraham and said to him, What have you done to us? And How have I sinned against you?

וַיֹּאמֶר יְהוָה אֱלֹהִים לָאִשָּׁה מַה־זֹּאת עָשִׂית Gen 3:13[a]
And the Lord God said to the woman, What now have you done?

Note the strengthening pronoun in Gen 3:13.

k

2. As an interrogative expressing exclamation (§62a)

וּבֹקֶר וּרְאִיתֶם אֶת־כְּבוֹד יְהוָה בְּשָׁמְעוֹ אֶת־תְּלֻנֹּתֵיכֶם עַל־יְהוָה וְנַחְנוּ מָה כִּי תַלִּינוּ עָלֵינוּ׃ Exod 16:7
And in the morning then you will see the glory of the Lord when he hears your murmurings against the Lord. And what (indeed) are we that you should murmur against us? (Nothing!)

Gen 23:15; 27:37; 37:26; Num 16:11; Judg 8:3; 11:12; 1 Kgs 12:16
Also לָמָּה expresses the notion of exclamation.

לָמָּה זֶּה עֲזַבְתֶּן אֶת־הָאִישׁ Exod 2:20[b]
Why now have you left the man?

l

E. Adverbial Interrogative Particles

There are a variety of adverbial interrogative particles, for example אֵי, אַיֵּה, אָן, אָנָה, אֵיפֹה – where; אֵיךְ, אֵיכָה – how. These may be used with strengthening pronouns זֶה or הוּא.

וַיֹּאמְרוּ אֵלָיו אַיֵּה שָׂרָה אִשְׁתֶּךָ Gen 18:9[a]
And they said to him, Where is Sarah, your wife?

וַיֹּאמֶר הַגִּידָה־נָּא לִי אֵי־זֶה בֵּית הָרֹאֶה׃ 1 Sam 9:18[b]
And he said, Report please to me, where now is the house of the seer?

Exod 6:30

§57. Compound Interrogative Questions (§41n)

Compound interrogative questions, (whether . . . or . . ?) (. . . or . . ?), are usually expressed by (וְ)אִם . . . הֲ or אוֹ . . . הֲ.

הֶהָיְתָה זֹּאת בִּימֵיכֶם וְאִם בִּימֵי אֲבֹתֵיכֶם׃ Joel 1:2[b]
Did this exist in your days or in the days of your fathers?

וַיֹּאמֶר אַל־יוֹשִׁעֵךְ יְהוָה מֵאַיִן אוֹשִׁיעֵךְ הֲמִן־הַגֹּרֶן אוֹ מִן־הַיָּקֶב׃ 2 Kgs 6:27
And he said, (If) the Lord does not save you, whence shall I save you, whether from the threshing floor or from the vinepress?

וַיֹּאמֶר לוֹ הֲלָנוּ אַתָּה אִם־לְצָרֵינוּ׃ Josh 5:13[b]
And he (Joshua) said to him, Are you for us or for our enemies?

Gen 27:21; 37:32; Num 11:12

§58. Indirect Questions

Indirect questions, interrogative statements after verbs of the senses, may take (וְ)אִם or הֲ in a simple question.

Gen 8:8 וַיְשַׁלַּח אֶת־הַיּוֹנָה מֵאִתּוֹ לִרְאוֹת הֲקַלּוּ הַמַּיִם מֵעַל פְּנֵי הָאֲדָמָה׃

And he sent away a dove from him to see whether the waters had diminished from upon the face of the ground (or not).

Gen 18:21; 43:6; Exod 4:18

In compound indirect questions, both particles are used, (וְ)אִם . . . הֲ or אוֹ . . . הֲ.

Gen 24:21 וְהָאִישׁ מִשְׁתָּאֵה לָהּ מַחֲרִישׁ לָדַעַת הַהִצְלִיחַ יְהוָה דַּרְכּוֹ אִם־לֹא׃

And the man was looking at her, being silent to know whether the Lord would prosper his way or not.

Exod 16:4; Num 11:23; Deut 8:2

Chapter 17
EXCLAMATION

§59. Introduction

An exclamation clause expresses a sudden, vehement outcry, a strong outburst of emotion. Nouns, verbs, interrogative particles, and interjection particles may express exclamation.

§60. Nouns of Interjection

Context determines whether a noun is exclamatory. Repeating nouns often indicate exclamation.

הַפְּכְּכֶם אִם־כְּחֹמֶר הַיֹּצֵר יֵחָשֵׁב Isa 29:16[a]

Your turning! If he should be regarded as the clay of the potter.

In Isa 29:16, the context indicates that the first word is exclamatory.

וַיֹּאמֶר אֶל־אָבִיו רֹאשִׁי ׀ רֹאשִׁי 2 Kgs 4:19[a]

And he said to his father, My head, my head!

וְכֹה ׀ אָמַר בְּלֶכְתּוֹ בְּנִי אַבְשָׁלוֹם בְּנִי בְנִי אַבְשָׁלוֹם 2 Sam 19:1[b]

And thus he said while he walked, My son Absalom; my son, my son Absalom!

In 2 Kgs 4:19 and 2 Sam 19:1, the repeating noun indicates exclamation.

אַשְׁרֵי־הָאִישׁ אֲשֶׁר ׀ לֹא הָלַךְ בַּעֲצַת רְשָׁעִים Ps 1:1[a]

How blessed is the man who walks not in the counsel of the ungodly.

The noun **אַשְׁרֵי** is always exclamatory (GKC §93l).

Gen 22:11; 46:2; Exod 34:6; 1 Sam 3:10; 2 Sam 19:5; 1 Kgs 13:2; 2 Kgs 2:12; Isa 29:1; 57:19; Jer 4:19; 6:14; 22:29; Ezek 21:32(3x); Joel 4:14; Zech 4:7; Ps 22:2; Lam 1:16; 1 Chr 12:19

§61. Verbs of Interjection *a*

If context suggests, some verbs, especially imperatives, may communicate interjection/exclamation.

A. הַלְלוּ־יָהּ

הַלְלוּ־יָהּ כִּי־טוֹב יְהוָה Ps 135:3[a]

Praise the Lord! For the Lord is good.

Ps 102:19; 104:35; 105:45; 106:1, 48

B. רְאֵה *b*

אִם־תְּעַנֶּה אֶת־בְּנֹתַי וְאִם־תִּקַּח נָשִׁים עַל־בְּנֹתַי אֵין אִישׁ עִמָּנוּ רְאֵה אֱלֹהִים עֵד בֵּינִי וּבֵינֶךָ׃ Gen 31:50

If you humiliate my daughters or if you take wives besides my daughters with no one (being) with us, see – God is a witness between me and you!

Gen 27:27; 41:41; Exod 7:1; 31:2; 1 Sam 24:12

C. הַב *c*

This imperative functions as an interjection often before cohortatives.

וַיֹּאמְרוּ אִישׁ אֶל־רֵעֵהוּ הָבָה נִלְבְּנָה לְבֵנִים וְנִשְׂרְפָה לִשְׂרֵפָה Gen 11:3[a]
And they said to each other, Come now! Let us build with bricks and let us burn (them) with a burning.

Gen 11:7; 38:16; Exod 1:10

d **D.** לְכָה, לֵךְ, קוּמָה, קוּם

These imperatives, used before a cohortative, imperative, or jussive, may function as an interjection.

וְעַתָּה לְכָה נִכְרְתָה בְרִית אֲנִי וָאָתָּה Gen 31:44[a]
And now, come! Let us make a covenant, I and you.

הִתְנַעֲרִי מֵעָפָר קוּמִי שְּׁבִי יְרוּשָׁלִָם Isa 52:2[a]
Shake off for yourself the dust; rise, dwell Jerusalem!

Gen 13:17; 19:14–15; 21:18; 27:19, 43; 28:2; 37:13; Exod 4:19; 12:31; BA Dan 7:5

§62. Interrogative Particles

a Some interrogative particles may express exclamation. These are rhetorical questions conveying a variety of nuances, such as, astonishment, wonder, contempt, etc., that may be punctuated with an exclamation point instead of a question mark.

A. מָה **(§56k)**

This word "casts a shadow of greatness on the following word."[1] When מָה is rhetorical, it expresses exclamation. The pronoun זֶה or הוּא may be added to strengthen or to give "vividness" to the interrogative statement.[2]

וַיֹּאמֶר מֶה עָשִׂיתָ Gen 4:10[a]
And he (the Lord) said, What have you done!

וַיֹּאמֶר יְהוָה אֱלֹהִים לָאִשָּׁה מַה־זֹּאת עָשִׂית Gen 3:13[a]
And the Lord God said to the woman, What now have you done!

Note the strengthening pronoun זֹאת, "now" in Gen 3:13.

יְהוָה מָה־רַבּוּ צָרָי רַבִּים קָמִים עָלָי׃ Ps 3:2
Lord, how my adversaries have become many! (How) many are rising up against me!

Gen 20:9; 27:37; 28:17; 37:26; Num 16:11; 24:5; Judg 8:3; 11:12; 14:18; 2 Sam 6:20; 1 Kgs 12:16; Ps 8:2; 21:2; 31:20; 36:8; 66:3; 78:40; 84:2; 92:6; 104:24; 119:97; Job 6:25; 26:14; BA Dan 3:33

b **B.** אֵיךְ, אֵיכָה

אֵיךְ נָפְלוּ גִבֹּרִים בְּתוֹךְ הַמִּלְחָמָה 2 Sam 1:25[a]
How the mighty warriors have fallen in the midst of battle!

וְאֵיךְ אֶעֱשֶׂה הָרָעָה הַגְּדֹלָה הַזֹּאת וְחָטָאתִי לֵאלֹהִים׃ Gen 39:9[b]
And how shall I do this great evil and sin against God!

Gen 26:9; 44:8; Exod 6:12, 30; 2 Sam 1:27; 12:18; Isa 1:21; 4:4; Jer 48:17; Ps 73:19; Prov 5:12; Eccl 2:16; Lam 1:1

c **C.** מִי **(§56i)**

This interrogative particle may convey exclamation. With imperfect verbs, especially with נתן and שׂים, it may express an exclamatory wish or desire.

---

1. Griess, 189
2. Wright II, 170b

Mic 7:18[a] מִי־אֵל כָּמוֹךָ
Who is God like you!

Exod 3:11[a] וַיֹּאמֶר מֹשֶׁה אֶל־הָאֱלֹהִים מִי אָנֹכִי כִּי אֵלֵךְ אֶל־פַּרְעֹה
And Moses said to God, Who am I that I should go to Pharaoh!

Ps 24:10[a] מִי הוּא זֶה מֶלֶךְ הַכָּבוֹד
Who is he [now], the king of glory!

Note the strengthening pronouns in Ps 24:10.

2 Sam 15:4[a] וַיֹּאמֶר אַבְשָׁלוֹם מִי־יְשִׂמֵנִי שֹׁפֵט בָּאָרֶץ
And Absalom said, Who will appoint me as a judge in the land!

Num 11:29[b] וּמִי יִתֵּן כָּל־עַם יְהוָה נְבִיאִים
And who will give all the people of the Lord to be prophets!

2 Sam 15:4 and Num 11:29 express an exclamatory wish or desire.

Num 11:4, 18; Deut 28:67; 33:29; Mal 1:10; Ps 4:7; 60:11; 94:16

D. Interrogative ה or הֲכִי *d*

The interrogative ה or the composite particle הֲכִי may communicate exclamation.

1 Kgs 11:41 וְיֶתֶר דִּבְרֵי שְׁלֹמֹה וְכָל־אֲשֶׁר עָשָׂה וְחָכְמָתוֹ הֲלוֹא־הֵם כְּתֻבִים עַל־סֵפֶר דִּבְרֵי שְׁלֹמֹה׃
And the rest of the deeds of Solomon and all that he did and his wisdom are they not (in fact) written upon the book of the deeds of Solomon!

1 Kgs 11:41 has הֲלֹא; 1 Kgs 14:19 furnishes the parallel construction הִנָּם, "Behold they are written upon the book of the deeds of the days to the kings of Israel" (§56e).

1 Kgs 14:19[b] הִנָּם כְּתוּבִים עַל־סֵפֶר דִּבְרֵי הַיָּמִים לְמַלְכֵי יִשְׂרָאֵל׃
Behold are they not written upon the book of the deeds of the days to the kings of Israel!

Gen 29:15[a] וַיֹּאמֶר לָבָן לְיַעֲקֹב הֲכִי־אָחִי אַתָּה
And Laban said to Jacob, Surely, you are my brother!

Gen 27:36[a] וַיֹּאמֶר הֲכִי קָרָא שְׁמוֹ יַעֲקֹב
And he said, Surely, his name is called Jacob!

§63. Particles of Interjection *a*

Interjections are emphatic exclamatory particles expressing surprise, wonder, disappointment, lament, etc. The most common particles of interjection are:

A. הוֹי, אוֹי

Isa 1:4[a] הוֹי גּוֹי חֹטֵא עַם כֶּבֶד עָוֹן זֶרַע מְרֵעִים בָּנִים מַשְׁחִיתִים
Woe, sinning nation, a people laden with iniquity, seed of evil ones, sons who corrupt themselves!

Jer 23:1; Isa 5:8, 11, 18, 20–22

B. אֲהָהּ, הֶאָח *b*

Jer 1:6 וָאֹמַר אֲהָהּ אֲדֹנָי יְהוִה הִנֵּה לֹא־יָדַעְתִּי דַּבֵּר כִּי־נַעַר אָנֹכִי׃
And I said, Alas Lord God, behold I do not know how to speak for I am a youth!

Josh 7:7; Judg 6:22; 11:35; 2 Kgs 3:10; 6:5; Ezek 26:2; Ps 35:21

c C. הִנֵּה, הֵן

וְעַתָּ֕ה הִנֵּ֥ה אִשְׁתְּךָ֖ קַ֥ח וָלֵֽךְ׃ And now, behold your wife, take (her) and go!	Gen 12:19[b]
וּֽלְיִשְׁמָעֵאל֮ שְׁמַעְתִּיךָ֒ הִנֵּ֣ה׀ בֵּרַ֣כְתִּי אֹת֗וֹ וְהִפְרֵיתִ֥י אֹת֛וֹ וְהִרְבֵּיתִ֥י אֹת֖וֹ בִּמְאֹ֣ד מְאֹ֑ד And as for Ishmael, I have heard you, behold I will bless him and I will multiply him and I will make him very, very numerous!	Gen 17:20[a]
וַיַּ֤רְא אֱלֹהִים֙ אֶת־כָּל־אֲשֶׁ֣ר עָשָׂ֔ה וְהִנֵּה־ט֖וֹב מְאֹ֑ד And God saw all that he made and behold – very good!	Gen 1:31[a]

Gen 1:29; 6:12–13, 17; 8:11, 13; 9:9; 12:11; Exod 5:5; 7:16

d D. חָלִ֫ילָה

וַיֹּאמְר֣וּ אֵלָ֔יו לָ֚מָּה יְדַבֵּ֣ר אֲדֹנִ֔י כַּדְּבָרִ֖ים הָאֵ֑לֶּה חָלִ֙ילָה֙ לַעֲבָדֶ֔יךָ מֵעֲשׂ֖וֹת כַּדָּבָ֥ר הַזֶּֽה׃ And they said to him, Why does my lord speak according to these words? Far be it to your servants from doing this thing!	Gen 44:7

Gen 18:25; 44:17; Josh 22:29; 24:16; 1 Sam 2:30

e E. בִּי

בִּ֣י אֲדֹנָ֗י לֹא֩ אִ֨ישׁ דְּבָרִ֜ים אָנֹ֗כִי Please, Lord, I am not a man of words.	Exod 4:10[a]

Gen 44:18; Exod 4:13; Num 12:11; Judg 6:13; 1 Sam 1:26

Chapter 18
ASSEVERATIVE CLAUSES

§64. The Usages of Asseverative Clauses *a*

Clauses of exclamation (§59–§63) and oath (§65–§66) convey an asseverative statement, a strong assertion or statement. Various particles may also express an asseverative statement by strengthening individual nouns or entire clauses. Often a second asserverative particle further strengthens the statement. These particles may transform a normal statement into an earnest or severe assertion. Common asseverative particles include:

A. אֲבָל

Gen 42:21[a] וַיֹּאמְרוּ אִישׁ אֶל־אָחִיו אֲבָל אֲשֵׁמִים׀ אֲנַחְנוּ עַל־אָחִינוּ

And they said to one another, Indeed, we are guilty concerning our brother.

Gen 17:19; 2 Sam 14:5

B. אָמְנָה, אֻמְנָם (with interrogatives), אָמְנָם *b*

Gen 20:12[a] וְגַם־אָמְנָה אֲחֹתִי בַת־אָבִי הִוא

And surely **in fact**, my sister, daughter of my father she is.

The particle גַּם strengthens אָמְנָה.

2 Kgs 19:17 אָמְנָם יְהוָה הֶחֱרִיבוּ מַלְכֵי אַשּׁוּר אֶת־הַגּוֹיִם וְאֶת־אַרְצָם׃

Indeed, Lord, the kings of Ashur have made desolate the nations and their land.

Ruth 3:12 וְעַתָּה כִּי אָמְנָם כִּי אִם גֹאֵל אָנֹכִי וְגַם יֵשׁ גֹּאֵל קָרוֹב מִמֶּנִּי׃

And now, **in fact surely**, I am a redeemer, but truly there exists a redeemer closer than I.

The particle כִּי strengthens אָמְנָם.

Gen 18:13; 2 Kgs 8:27; Josh 7:20; Isa 37:18

C. אַךְ, אָכֵן *c*

Gen 26:9[a] וַיִּקְרָא אֲבִימֶלֶךְ לְיִצְחָק וַיֹּאמֶר אַךְ הִנֵּה אִשְׁתְּךָ הִוא

And Abimelek summoned Isaac and said, **Indeed**, behold your wife, she is (here).

The particle אַךְ strengthens הִנֵּה.

Gen 44:28[a] וַיֵּצֵא הָאֶחָד מֵאִתִּי וָאֹמַר אַךְ טָרֹף טֹרָף

And the one went out from me and I said, **Indeed**, he has been completely torn apart.

Gen 28:16[a] וַיִּיקַץ יַעֲקֹב מִשְּׁנָתוֹ וַיֹּאמֶר אָכֵן יֵשׁ יְהוָה בַּמָּקוֹם הַזֶּה

And Jacob awoke from his sleep and he said, **Surely**, the Lord exists in this place.

Exod 2:14 וַיֹּאמֶר מִי שָׂמְךָ לְאִישׁ שַׂר וְשֹׁפֵט עָלֵינוּ הַלְהָרְגֵנִי אַתָּה אֹמֵר כַּאֲשֶׁר הָרַגְתָּ אֶת־הַמִּצְרִי וַיִּירָא מֹשֶׁה וַיֹּאמַר אָכֵן נוֹדַע הַדָּבָר׃

But he said, Who made you a prince or a judge over us? Are you intending to kill me, as you killed the Egyptian? Then Moses became afraid, and said, **Surely** the matter has become known.

1 Sam 15:32 וַיֹּאמֶר שְׁמוּאֵל הַגִּישׁוּ אֵלַי אֶת־אֲגַג מֶלֶךְ עֲמָלֵק וַיֵּלֶךְ אֵלָיו אֲגַג מַעֲדַנֹּת וַיֹּאמֶר אֲגָג אָכֵן סָר מַר־הַמָּוֶת׃

Then Samuel said, Bring me Agag, the king of the Amalekites. And Agag came to him cheerfully. And Agag said, **Surely** the bitterness of death is past.

Gen 9:5; 29:14; Exod 31:13; Jer 10:19; Lam 2:16

d D. רַק

Gen 20:11[a] וַיֹּאמֶר אַבְרָהָם כִּי אָמַרְתִּי רַק אֵין־יִרְאַת אֱלֹהִים בַּמָּקוֹם הַזֶּה

And Abraham said, for I said, **Surely** there exists no fear of God in this place.

1 Kgs 21:25[a] רַק לֹא־הָיָה כְאַחְאָב אֲשֶׁר הִתְמַכֵּר לַעֲשׂוֹת הָרַע בְּעֵינֵי יְהוָה

Surely, there has not existed *one* like Ahab who has sold himself to do evil in the eyes of the Lord.

Gen 19:8; Deut 4:6; Josh 6:18; 2 Chr 28:10

e E. גַּם

Gen 20:12[a] וְגַם־אָמְנָה אֲחֹתִי בַת־אָבִי הִוא

And **surely** in fact, my sister, daughter of my father she is.

The particle גַּם strengthens אָמְנָה.

Ruth 3:12 וְעַתָּה כִּי אָמְנָם כִּי אִם גֹּאֵל אָנֹכִי וְגַם יֵשׁ גֹּאֵל קָרוֹב מִמֶּנִּי׃

And now, in fact surely I am a redeemer, but **truly** there exists a redeemer closer than I.

Gen 17:16; 27:33; 29:30

f F. אַף

Gen 18:13 וַיֹּאמֶר יְהוָה אֶל־אַבְרָהָם לָמָּה זֶּה צָחֲקָה שָׂרָה לֵאמֹר הַאַף אֻמְנָם אֵלֵד וַאֲנִי זָקַנְתִּי׃

And the Lord said to Abraham, Why now has Sarah laughed, Will **surely** indeed I bear a child though I am old?

The particle אַף strengthens אֻמְנָם.

Isa 46:11[b] אַף־דִּבַּרְתִּי אַף־אֲבִיאֶנָּה יָצַרְתִּי אַף־אֶעֱשֶׂנָּה׃

Indeed, I have spoken. **Indeed**, I will in fact cause it to happen. I have purposed; **indeed**, I will in fact do it.

אַף repeats three times for greater emphasis.

Gen 3:1; 18:23–24; 40:16; Num 16:14; Deut 33:3

g G. הִנֵּה

This is a particle of exclamation.

Gen 11:6[a] וַיֹּאמֶר יְהוָה הֵן עַם אֶחָד וְשָׂפָה אַחַת לְכֻלָּם

And the Lord said, **Behold**, one people and one language is to all of them.

Gen 12:11[b] וַיֹּאמֶר אֶל־שָׂרַי אִשְׁתּוֹ הִנֵּה־נָא יָדַעְתִּי כִּי אִשָּׁה יְפַת־מַרְאֶה אָתְּ׃

And he said to Sarai, his wife, **Behold** please, I know that a woman fair of form you are.

The particle הִנֵּה strengthens נָא.

Exod 1:9 וַיֹּאמֶר אֶל־עַמּוֹ הִנֵּה עַם בְּנֵי יִשְׂרָאֵל רַב וְעָצוּם מִמֶּנּוּ׃

And he said to his people, **Behold**, the people of the sons of Israel are more numerous and stronger than we.

Gen 1:29; 16:11; 19:8, 21; 42:28

H. כִּי *h*

1 Sam 17:25[a] וַיֹּ֣אמֶר ׀ אִ֣ישׁ יִשְׂרָאֵ֗ל הַרְּאִיתֶם֙ הָאִ֤ישׁ הָעֹלֶה֙ הַזֶּ֔ה כִּ֛י לְחָרֵ֥ף אֶת־יִשְׂרָאֵ֖ל עֹלֶ֑ה

And the men of Israel said, Have you seen this man who comes up? **Indeed** to reproach Israel he comes up.

Ruth 3:12 וְעַתָּה֙ כִּ֣י אָמְנָ֔ם כִּ֥י אם גֹאֵ֖ל אָנֹ֑כִי וְגַ֛ם יֵ֥שׁ גֹּאֵ֖ל קָר֥וֹב מִמֶּֽנִּי׃

And now, **in fact** surely I am a redeemer, but truly there exists a redeemer closer than I.

The particle כִּי strengthens **אָמְנָם**.

Gen 27:36; 29:32; Exod 3:12; Josh 2:24; 1 Sam 2:21; 1 Kgs 1:13; Isa 5:10; 63:16; Job 22:2

Chapter 19
OATH CLAUSES

§65. Introduction *a*

Oath clauses are the strongest assertions in Hebrew, or in any language, because they usually invoke a curse of God upon oneself or upon another person. Oath clauses with their curse formula, whether implicit or explicit, therefore, assure in the most solemn manner the truthfulness of a statement or the accomplishment (or non-accomplishment) of an action.

The oath clause may have three parts: the introductory formula, the curse formula, and the sworn statement. First, the introductory formula, which may be implied, consists of a verb of swearing or a clause such as, "As the Lord lives, by the life of my Lord, as I live, far be it from me," etc. Moreover, the introductory formula may be (or include) the physical gesture of raising the hand that accompanies the oath. The verb of swearing and the physical gesture of lifting the hands to take an oath may be combined (Dan 12:7). Second, the curse formula, "May God do to me (or someone) and may he add," is often implied because of the dreadfulness of the statement. Third, the sworn statement, the main part of the oath that cannot be omitted, is a truthful statement about what one has done, or more commonly, about what one will do. Usually, the sworn statement is preceded by the particles, אִם and/or כִּי. (See 1 Kgs 2:23–24; §67)

Because the oath clause is often abbreviated, the clause may challenge interpreters. *b* Sometimes by adding the implied curse formula, the sworn statement introduced with אִם is better understood. For example, in 2 Sam 11:11[b]:

2 Sam 11:11[b] חַיֶּךָ וְחֵי נַפְשֶׁךָ אִם־אֶעֱשֶׂה אֶת־הַדָּבָר הַזֶּה׃

by your life and the life of your soul, (may God do to me and may he add), if I do this thing.

Of course, the same applies when the negative follows the particle אִם, as in Josh 14:9[a]:

Josh 14:9[a] וַיִּשָּׁבַע מֹשֶׁה בַּיּוֹם הַהוּא לֵאמֹר אִם־לֹא הָאָרֶץ אֲשֶׁר דָּרְכָה רַגְלְךָ בָּהּ לְךָ תִהְיֶה לְנַחֲלָה וּלְבָנֶיךָ עַד־עוֹלָם

And Moses swore on that day saying, (May God do to me and may he add) if the land on which your foot treads will not exist for an inheritance to you and to your sons forever.

The particle כִּי is difficult to interpret when it introduces an oath because of its range of meaning within an oath clause: "if," "that," "indeed," etc. In any case, both particles אִם and כִּי are emphatic because they introduce a sworn statement[1] and should, therefore, be translated either together or separately as "if indeed," as context allows.

§66. Introductory Formula *a*

Although it may be implied, the introductory formula is common in oath clauses.

1. See, for example, Gen 42:15–16 (and 22:17), where the Septuagint translates the particle כִּי of verse 16 as ἦ μὴν, as it also translates the particle אִם by the same Greek particles ἦ μὴν in Exod 22:10.

A. שׁבע (sometimes with the ב preposition)

1 Sam 3:14 וְלָכֵ֥ן נִשְׁבַּ֖עְתִּי לְבֵ֣ית עֵלִ֑י אִם־יִתְכַּפֵּ֞ר עֲוֺ֧ן בֵּית־עֵלִ֛י בְּזֶ֥בַח
וּבְמִנְחָ֖ה עַד־עוֹלָֽם׃

And therefore I swore to the house of Eli, (May God do to me and may he add) if indeed the iniquity of the house of Eli be atoned for with sacrifice or offering forever.

1 Kgs 1:30[a] כִּ֠י כַּאֲשֶׁ֨ר נִשְׁבַּ֤עְתִּי לָךְ֙ בַּיהוָ֜ה אֱלֹהֵ֤י יִשְׂרָאֵל֙ לֵאמֹ֔ר כִּֽי־
שְׁלֹמֹ֤ה בְנֵךְ֙ יִמְלֹ֣ךְ אַחֲרַ֔י וְה֛וּא יֵשֵׁ֥ב עַל־כִּסְאִ֖י תַּחְתָּ֑י

For as I swore to you by the Lord, the God of Israel saying, Indeed Solomon your son will rule after me, and he will sit upon my throne in my place.

Cant 2:7 הִשְׁבַּ֨עְתִּי אֶתְכֶ֜ם בְּנ֤וֹת יְרוּשָׁלִַ֙ם֙ בִּצְבָא֔וֹת א֖וֹ בְּאַיְל֣וֹת
הַשָּׂדֶ֑ה אִם־תָּעִ֧ירוּ ׀ וְֽאִם־תְּעֽוֹרְר֛וּ אֶת־הָאַהֲבָ֖ה עַ֥ד שֶׁתֶּחְפָּֽץ׃

I adjure you daughters of Jerusalem by the gazelles or the does of the field, (May God do to you and may he add) if indeed you awaken or arouse love until she desires.

1 Sam 24:22; 2 Sam 19:8; Isa 45:23; Jer 49:13; Ps 89:4; 95:11; 110:4

b **B. חַי (חֵי)**

This word is pointed with Patah or with Sere in oaths. The Septuagint and Vulgate usually translate חֵי as "by the health of (someone)" and חַי as "the Lord (God) lives." Similarly, the Targums usually translate חֵי as "the life (health) of (someone)" and חַי as "He is the existing one, the Lord." In the following examples, the curse formula is probably implied by the phrases, "As the Lord lives, by the life of my Lord, as I live, far be it from me," etc.

1 Sam 14:45 וַיֹּ֨אמֶר הָעָ֜ם אֶל־שָׁא֗וּל הֲֽיוֹנָתָ֤ן ׀ יָמוּת֙ אֲשֶׁ֨ר עָשָׂ֜ה הַיְשׁוּעָ֨ה
הַגְּדוֹלָ֣ה הַזֹּאת֮ בְּיִשְׂרָאֵל֒ חָלִ֗ילָה חַי־יְהוָ֡ה אִם־יִפֹּל֩ מִשַּׂעֲרַ֨ת
רֹאשׁ֜וֹ אַ֗רְצָה כִּֽי־עִם־אֱלֹהִ֛ים עָשָׂ֖ה הַיּ֣וֹם הַזֶּ֑ה

And the people said to Saul, Will Jonathan be put to death who wrought this great salvation in Israel, far be it, by the life of the Lord, (May God do to me and may he add) if indeed (a hair) falls from the hair of his head to the ground, for with God he wrought (salvation) this day.

Judg 8:19 וַיֹּאמַ֕ר אַחַ֥י בְּנֵֽי־אִמִּ֖י הֵ֑ם חַי־יְהוָ֕ה ל֚וּ הַחֲיִתֶ֣ם אוֹתָ֔ם לֹ֥א
הָרַ֖גְתִּי אֶתְכֶֽם׃

And he said, They are my brothers, the sons of my mother, by the life of the Lord, (May God do to me and may he add) if indeed you had preserved them alive, I would not kill you.

Ruth 3:13[a] לִ֣ינִי ׀ הַלַּ֗יְלָה וְהָיָ֤ה בַבֹּ֙קֶר֙ אִם־יִגְאָלֵ֥ךְ טוֹב֙ יִגְאָ֔ל וְאִם־לֹ֨א
יַחְפֹּ֧ץ לְגָֽאֳלֵ֛ךְ וּגְאַלְתִּ֥יךְ אָנֹ֖כִי חַי־יְהוָ֑ה

Stay the night and it will happen in the morning if he redeems you, good, let him redeem, but if he is not pleased to redeem you, then I will redeem you, I, by the life of the Lord.

In Ruth 3:13, the introductory formula follows the sworn statement. The statement, "by the life of the Lord," probably implies the curse formula.

1 Sam 20:3
וַיִּשָּׁבַע עוֹד דָּוִד וַיֹּאמֶר יָדֹעַ יָדַע אָבִיךָ כִּי־מָצָאתִי חֵן בְּעֵינֶיךָ
וַיֹּאמֶר אַל־יֵדַע־זֹאת יְהוֹנָתָן פֶּן־יֵעָצֵב וְאוּלָם חַי־יְהוָה וְחֵי
נַפְשֶׁךָ כִּי כְפֶשַׂע בֵּינִי וּבֵין הַמָּוֶת׃

And David swore again and he said, Your father indeed knows that I have found grace in your eyes, and he said, do not let Jonathan know this lest he should be grieved. But nevertheless by the life of the Lord and by your life, indeed (there is) about a step between me and death.

In 1 Sam 20:3, the statement, "by the life of the Lord," probably implies the curse formula.

1 Sam 1:26; 14:39; 17:55; 19:6; 20:21; 25:26; 2 Sam 15:21; 1 Kgs 1:29; 2 Kgs 2:2

C. נשׂא יד or רום יד *c*

The lifting of the hand(s) relates the physical gesture for the taking of an oath.

Gen 14:22
וַיֹּאמֶר אַבְרָם אֶל־מֶלֶךְ סְדֹם הֲרִימֹתִי יָדִי אֶל־יְהוָה אֵל
עֶלְיוֹן קֹנֵה שָׁמַיִם וָאָרֶץ׃

Gen 14:23[a]
אִם־מִחוּט וְעַד שְׂרוֹךְ־נַעַל וְאִם־אֶקַּח מִכָּל־אֲשֶׁר־לָךְ

[22]And Abram said to the king of Sodom, I raise my hand to the Lord, the most high God, possessor of heaven and earth, [23](May God do to me and may he add) if indeed from thread even unto the sandal lace (I should take), and if I should take from anything which belongs to you.

Dan 12:7
וָאֶשְׁמַע אֶת־הָאִישׁ לְבוּשׁ הַבַּדִּים אֲשֶׁר מִמַּעַל לְמֵימֵי הַיְאֹר
וַיָּרֶם יְמִינוֹ וּשְׂמֹאלוֹ אֶל־הַשָּׁמַיִם וַיִּשָּׁבַע בְּחֵי הָעוֹלָם כִּי
לְמוֹעֵד מוֹעֲדִים וָחֵצִי וּכְכַלּוֹת נַפֵּץ יַד־עַם־קֹדֶשׁ תִּכְלֶינָה
כָל־אֵלֶּה׃

And I heard the man clothed in linen who was above the waters of the river, and he raised his right hand and his left hand to the heavens and he swore by the life of the Eternal One. For a time, times, and a half and as the completion of the shattering of the power of the holy people, all these will be finished.

The preceding example, Dan 12:7, combines two introductory formulae: the verb of swearing with the lifting of hands.

Deut 32:40
כִּי־אֶשָּׂא אֶל־שָׁמַיִם יָדִי וְאָמַרְתִּי חַי אָנֹכִי לְעֹלָם׃

For I lift to heaven my hand and I said, I live forever.

Ezek 36:7
לָכֵן כֹּה אָמַר אֲדֹנָי יְהוִה אֲנִי נָשָׂאתִי אֶת־יָדִי אִם־לֹא
הַגּוֹיִם אֲשֶׁר לָכֶם מִסָּבִיב הֵמָּה כְּלִמָּתָם יִשָּׂאוּ׃

Therefore, thus the Lord God said, I – I lifted my hand, (May God do to me and may he add) if indeed not the nations which are around about to you will bear their own reproach.[2]

Exod 6:8; Ezek 20:5–6, 15; Ps 106:26

2. Joüon and Muraoka doubt the presence of the curse formula since God would be cursing himself (JM §165h). Yet, God invokes a curse upon himself in making the covenant with Abram in Gen 15:17. "Since he could swear by no one greater, he swore by himself" (Heb 6:13).

d **D.** חָלִ֫ילָה

1 Sam 24:7[a] וַיֹּ֨אמֶר לַאֲנָשָׁ֜יו חָלִ֧ילָה לִּ֣י מֵיהוָ֗ה אִם־אֶעֱשֶׂ֨ה אֶת־הַדָּבָ֤ר
הַזֶּה֙ לַֽאדֹנִי֙ לִמְשִׁ֣יחַ יְהוָ֔ה לִשְׁלֹ֥חַ יָדִ֖י בּ֑וֹ

And he said to his men, Far be it to me from the Lord, (May God do to me and may he add) if I do this matter to my Lord to the anointed of the Lord to stretch out my hand against him.

e **E. Verb of Speaking**

Verbs of speaking, saying, etc., may introduce an oath.

Num 14:35 אֲנִ֣י יְהוָה֮ דִּבַּ֒רְתִּי֒ אִם־לֹ֣א ׀ זֹ֣את אֶֽעֱשֶׂ֗ה לְכָל־הָעֵדָ֤ה הָֽרָעָה֙
הַזֹּ֔את הַנּוֹעָדִ֖ים עָלָ֑י בַּמִּדְבָּ֥ר הַזֶּ֛ה יִתַּ֖מּוּ וְשָׁ֥ם יָמֻֽתוּ׃

I, the Lord, have spoken, (May God do to me and may he add) if indeed I do not do this to all this evil congregation, the men who have gathered against me. In this wilderness they will come to an end and there they will die.

§67. Curse Formula

The curse formula is: "May God do to me (or someone) and may he add."

1 Sam 25:22 כֹּה־יַעֲשֶׂ֧ה אֱלֹהִ֛ים לְאֹיְבֵ֥י דָוִ֖ד וְכֹ֣ה יֹסִ֑יף אִם־אַשְׁאִ֧יר מִכָּל־
אֲשֶׁר־ל֛וֹ עַד־הַבֹּ֖קֶר מַשְׁתִּ֥ין בְּקִֽיר׃

Thus may God do to the enemies of David and thus may he add if indeed I leave from all which is to him unto morning a man who urinates against the wall.

2 Sam 3:9 כֹּֽה־יַעֲשֶׂ֤ה אֱלֹהִים֙ לְאַבְנֵ֔ר וְכֹ֖ה יֹסִ֣יף ל֑וֹ כִּ֗י כַּאֲשֶׁ֨ר נִשְׁבַּ֤ע
יְהוָה֙ לְדָוִ֔ד כִּֽי־כֵ֖ן אֶֽעֱשֶׂה־לּֽוֹ׃

Thus may God do to Abner and thus may he add to him, if indeed as the Lord swore to David, certainly thus I will do for him.

2 Sam 19:14 וְלַעֲמָשָׂא֙ תֹּֽמְר֔וּ הֲל֛וֹא עַצְמִ֥י וּבְשָׂרִ֖י אָ֑תָּה כֹּ֣ה יַעֲשֶׂה־לִּ֤י
אֱלֹהִים֙ וְכֹ֣ה יוֹסִ֔יף אִם־לֹ֞א שַׂר־צָבָ֞א תִּהְיֶ֧ה לְפָנַ֛י כָּל־הַיָּמִ֖ים
תַּ֥חַת יוֹאָֽב׃

And to Amasa you say, Are you not my bone and flesh. Thus may God do to me and thus may he add, if indeed you do not exist as the commander of the army before me continually in the place of Joab.

1 Kgs 2:23 וַיִּשָּׁבַע֙ הַמֶּ֣לֶךְ שְׁלֹמֹ֔ה בַּֽיהוָ֖ה לֵאמֹ֑ר כֹּ֣ה יַעֲשֶׂה־לִּ֤י אֱלֹהִים֙
וְכֹ֣ה יוֹסִ֔יף כִּ֣י בְנַפְשׁ֔וֹ דִּבֶּר֙ אֲדֹ֣נִיָּ֔הוּ אֶת־הַדָּבָ֖ר הַזֶּֽה׃

1 Kgs 2:24 וְעַתָּ֗ה חַי־יְהוָה֙ אֲשֶׁ֣ר הֱכִינַ֗נִי וַיּֽוֹשִׁיבַ֙נִי֙ עַל־כִּסֵּא֙ דָּוִ֣ד אָבִ֔י
וַאֲשֶׁ֧ר עָֽשָׂה־לִ֛י בַּ֖יִת כַּאֲשֶׁ֣ר דִּבֵּ֑ר כִּ֣י הַיּ֔וֹם יוּמַ֖ת אֲדֹנִיָּֽהוּ׃

[23] And the king Solomon swore by the Lord saying, Thus may God do to me and thus may he add if indeed against his own life Adonijah has spoken this word. [24] And now by the life of the Lord who established me and caused me to sit upon the throne of David, my father, and who made for me a house as he spoke, surely today Adonijah will be put to death.

1 Kgs 2:23–24 furnishes a complete oath statement except for the physical gesture of the raising of hands. The passage begins with the introductory formula

given in the indirect speech of the narrator by the verb of swearing, "the king Solomon swore" (Direct speech would be, "and I swear . . ."). This is followed by another introductory formula, "by the Lord," again indirect speech for "by the life of the Lord" (Direct speech would be, "And I swear by the life of the Lord." This latter phrase is given directly in verse 24.) Then the curse formula is given (May God do to me and thus more), followed by the sworn statement of fact (indeed, against his own life Adonijah has spoken this word).

In verse 24, another statement of oath is given. In contrast with verse 23, the introductory formula is given as direct speech, "and now by the life of the Lord." The curse formula (May God do to me and thus more) is implied from the preceding verse and from the preceding introductory formula, "by the life of the Lord." Finally, the sworn statement is given, "Indeed, today Adonijah will die."

1 Sam 20:13; 2 Sam 3:25; Ruth 1:17

§68. Sworn Statement *a*

The particles אִם and כִּי are emphatic because they introduce the sworn statement.

A. אִם

1 Sam 3:17 וַיֹּאמֶר מָה הַדָּבָר אֲשֶׁר דִּבֶּר אֵלֶיךָ אַל־נָא תְכַחֵד מִמֶּנִּי כֹּה
יַעֲשֶׂה־לְּךָ אֱלֹהִים וְכֹה יוֹסִיף אִם־תְּכַחֵד מִמֶּנִּי דָּבָר מִכָּל־
הַדָּבָר אֲשֶׁר־דִּבֶּר אֵלֶיךָ׃

And he said, What is the word which he spoke to you? Do not hide now from me, may God do to you and may he add, if indeed you hide from me a word from every word which he spoke to you.

2 Sam 11:11 וַיֹּאמֶר אוּרִיָּה אֶל־דָּוִד הָאָרוֹן וְיִשְׂרָאֵל וִיהוּדָה יֹשְׁבִים
בַּסֻּכּוֹת וַאדֹנִי יוֹאָב וְעַבְדֵי אֲדֹנִי עַל־פְּנֵי הַשָּׂדֶה חֹנִים וַאֲנִי
אָבוֹא אֶל־בֵּיתִי לֶאֱכֹל וְלִשְׁתּוֹת וְלִשְׁכַּב עִם־אִשְׁתִּי חַיֶּךָ וְחֵי
נַפְשֶׁךָ אִם־אֶעֱשֶׂה אֶת־הַדָּבָר הַזֶּה׃

And Uriah said to David, The ark and Israel and Judah are dwelling in booths, and my lord Joab and the servants of my lord are camping upon the face of the ground. And I – I will enter into my house to eat and to drink and to lie with my wife? By your life and by the life of your soul, (May God do to me and he add) if indeed I do this thing.

B. כִּי *b*

Ruth 1:17[b] כֹּה יַעֲשֶׂה יְהוָה לִי וְכֹה יֹסִיף כִּי הַמָּוֶת יַפְרִיד בֵּינִי וּבֵינֶךָ׃

Thus may God do to me and may he add, indeed if (anything but) death should separate between me and you.

1 Sam 14:44 וַיֹּאמֶר שָׁאוּל כֹּה־יַעֲשֶׂה אֱלֹהִים וְכֹה יוֹסִף כִּי־מוֹת תָּמוּת
יוֹנָתָן׃

And Saul said, Thus may God do to me and thus add, indeed you will certainly be put to death, Jonathan.

c **C. כִּי and אִם**

וַיָּבֹ֣א כָל־הָעָ֗ם לְהַבְר֧וֹת אֶת־דָּוִ֛ד לֶ֖חֶם בְּע֣וֹד הַיּ֑וֹם וַיִּשָּׁבַ֨ע 2 Sam 3:35
דָּוִ֜ד לֵאמֹ֗ר כֹּ֣ה יַעֲשֶׂה־לִּ֤י אֱלֹהִים֙ וְכֹ֣ה יֹסִ֔יף כִּ֣י אִם־לִפְנֵ֧י
בֽוֹא־הַשֶּׁ֛מֶשׁ אֶטְעַם־לֶ֖חֶם א֥וֹ כָל־מְאֽוּמָה׃

And all the people came to cause David to eat bread while (it was) day, and David swore saying, Thus may God do to me and may he add, if indeed before the sun sets I taste bread or any other thing.

וַיֹּ֣אמֶר גֵּיחֲזִ֗י נַ֚עַר אֱלִישָׁ֣ע אִישׁ־הָאֱלֹהִים֒ הִנֵּ֣ה ׀ חָשַׂ֣ךְ אֲדֹנִ֗י 2 Kgs 5:20
אֶת־נַעֲמָ֤ן הָֽאֲרַמִּי֙ הַזֶּ֔ה מִקַּ֥חַת מִיָּד֖וֹ אֵ֣ת אֲשֶׁר־הֵבִ֑יא חַי־יְהוָה֙
כִּֽי־אִם־רַ֣צְתִּי אַחֲרָ֔יו וְלָקַחְתִּ֥י מֵאִתּ֖וֹ מְאֽוּמָה׃

And Gehazi, the servant of Elisha the man of God, said, Behold my lord has restrained Naaman, this Aramean, from taking from his hand that which he brought. By the life of the Lord, indeed I will run after him and take something from him.

Chapter 20
CAUSAL CLAUSES

§69. Introduction

Various particles and the prepositional particle עַל with the infinitive construct express causal clauses, that supply the reason, occasion, or basis of another action. Rarely, juxtaposing clauses suggest a causal clause.

§70. Particles *a*

Most of these particles may combine with other particles, especially אֲשֶׁר, to convey a causal clause. The following particles may express causality.

A. כִּי

Gen 2:3
וַיְבָ֤רֶךְ אֱלֹהִים֙ אֶת־י֣וֹם הַשְּׁבִיעִ֔י וַיְקַדֵּ֖שׁ אֹת֑וֹ כִּ֣י ב֤וֹ שָׁבַת֙
מִכָּל־מְלַאכְתּ֔וֹ
And God blessed the seventh day and he sanctified it because on it he rested from all his labor.

Gen 3:14[a]
וַיֹּאמֶר֩ יְהוָ֨ה אֱלֹהִ֥ים ׀ אֶֽל־הַנָּחָשׁ֮ כִּ֣י עָשִׂ֣יתָ זֹּאת֒ אָר֤וּר אַתָּה֙
And the Lord God said to the serpent, Because you did this, cursed are you.

Gen 22:16
וַיֹּ֕אמֶר בִּ֥י נִשְׁבַּ֖עְתִּי נְאֻם־יְהוָ֑ה כִּ֗י יַ֚עַן אֲשֶׁ֤ר עָשִׂ֙יתָ֙ אֶת־
הַדָּבָ֣ר הַזֶּ֔ה וְלֹ֥א חָשַׂ֖כְתָּ אֶת־בִּנְךָ֥ אֶת־יְחִידֶֽךָ׃
And he said, By myself I have sworn declares the Lord, because you did this thing and have not withheld your only begotten son.

In Gen 22:16, the particle כִּי combines with יַ֚עַן אֲשֶׁר.

Gen 2:23; 3:17, 20; 8:21; 11:9; 18:20; 19:13; 1 Sam 23:7; Jer 1:7

B. יַ֫עַן *b*

1 Sam 15:23
כִּ֤י חַטַּאת־קֶ֙סֶם֙ מֶ֔רִי וְאָ֥וֶן וּתְרָפִ֖ים הַפְצַ֑ר יַ֗עַן מָאַ֙סְתָּ֙ אֶת־דְּבַ֣ר
יְהוָ֔ה וַיִּמְאָסְךָ֖ מִמֶּֽלֶךְ׃
Because the sin of divination is rebellion, and presumption is iniquity and idolatry. Because you have rejected the word of the Lord, he has rejected you from (being) king.

1 Kgs 14:13
וְסָפְדוּ־ל֣וֹ כָל־יִשְׂרָאֵ֗ל וְקָבְר֣וּ אֹת֔וֹ כִּי־זֶה֙ לְבַדּ֔וֹ יָבֹ֥א
לְיָרָבְעָ֖ם אֶל־קָ֑בֶר יַ֣עַן נִמְצָא־ב֞וֹ דָּבָ֣ר ט֗וֹב אֶל־יְהוָ֛ה אֱלֹהֵ֥י
יִשְׂרָאֵ֖ל בְּבֵ֥ית יָרָבְעָֽם׃
And all Israel will mourn for him and will bury him because this one, he alone, will come to a grave belonging to Jeroboam because a good thing was found in him to the Lord God of Israel in the house of Jeroboam.

Deut 1:36
זוּלָתִ֞י כָּלֵ֤ב בֶּן־יְפֻנֶּה֙ ה֣וּא יִרְאֶ֔נָּה וְלֽוֹ־אֶתֵּ֧ן אֶת־הָאָ֛רֶץ אֲשֶׁ֥ר
דָּֽרַךְ־בָּ֖הּ וּלְבָנָ֑יו יַ֕עַן אֲשֶׁ֥ר מִלֵּ֖א אַחֲרֵ֥י יְהוָֽה׃
Except Celeb, son of Jephunneh – he will certainly see it, and to him I am giving the land on which he walked and to his sons because he was fully devoted to the Lord.

1 Kgs 3:11[a] וַיֹּאמֶר אֱלֹהִים אֵלָיו יַעַן אֲשֶׁר שָׁאַלְתָּ אֶת־הַדָּבָר הַזֶּה ...
וְלֹא שָׁאַלְתָּ נֶפֶשׁ אֹיְבֶיךָ

And God said to him, Because you have asked this thing, . . . and (because) you have not asked the life of your enemies.

In Deut 1:36 and 1 Kgs 3:11, the particle יַעַן combines with אֲשֶׁר.

Lev 26:43; Num 11:20; 20:12; Josh 14:14; Judg 2:20; 1 Sam 30:22; 1 Kgs 11:33

c **C.** אֲשֶׁר

Gen 30:18[a] וַתֹּאמֶר לֵאָה נָתַן אֱלֹהִים שְׂכָרִי אֲשֶׁר־נָתַתִּי שִׁפְחָתִי לְאִישִׁי

And Leah said, God has given my wage because I gave my handmaid to my husband.

Gen 34:13 וַיַּעֲנוּ בְנֵי־יַעֲקֹב אֶת־שְׁכֶם וְאֶת־חֲמוֹר אָבִיו בְּמִרְמָה וַיְדַבֵּרוּ
אֲשֶׁר טִמֵּא אֵת דִּינָה אֲחֹתָם׃

And the sons of Jacob answered Shechem and Hamor, his father, with deceit and they spoke, because he defiled Dinah, their sister.

Gen 39:9[a] אֵינֶנּוּ גָדוֹל בַּבַּיִת הַזֶּה מִמֶּנִּי וְלֹא־חָשַׂךְ מִמֶּנִּי מְאוּמָה כִּי
אִם־אוֹתָךְ בַּאֲשֶׁר אַתְּ־אִשְׁתּוֹ

There is no one greater in this house than I, and he has not withheld from me anything except you because you are his wife.

In Gen 39:9, the ב preposition combines with אֲשֶׁר to form a causal conjunction.

Gen 31:49; 34:27; Exod 5:21; Deut 3:24; Josh 4:7, 23; 22:31; Judg 9:17; Jer 1:16

d **D.** עֵקֶב

Num 14:24 וְעַבְדִּי כָלֵב עֵקֶב הָיְתָה רוּחַ אַחֶרֶת עִמּוֹ וַיְמַלֵּא אַחֲרָי
וַהֲבִיאֹתִיו אֶל־הָאָרֶץ

And my servant Celeb, because a different spirit existed in him, and (because) he was fully devoted to me that I will cause him to enter the land.

Deut 8:20 כַּגּוֹיִם אֲשֶׁר יְהוָה מַאֲבִיד מִפְּנֵיכֶם כֵּן תֹּאבֵדוּן עֵקֶב לֹא
תִשְׁמְעוּן בְּקוֹל יְהוָה אֱלֹהֵיכֶם׃

As the nations which the Lord is causing to perish from before you, thus you will perish, because you would not obey the Lord, your God.

Combinations:

a) with אֲשֶׁר

Gen 22:18 וְהִתְבָּרְכוּ בְזַרְעֲךָ כֹּל גּוֹיֵי הָאָרֶץ עֵקֶב אֲשֶׁר שָׁמַעְתָּ בְּקֹלִי׃

And all the nations of the earth will be blessed in your seed because you obeyed me.

b) with כִּי

2 Sam 12:10 וְעַתָּה לֹא־תָסוּר חֶרֶב מִבֵּיתְךָ עַד־עוֹלָם עֵקֶב כִּי בְזִתָנִי

And now, a sword will not depart from your house forever because you despised me.

Gen 26:5; Deut 7:12; 2 Sam 12:6, 10; Amos 4:12

e **E.** עַל (without infinitive construct)

Ps 119:136 פַּלְגֵי־מַיִם יָרְדוּ עֵינָי עַל לֹא־שָׁמְרוּ תוֹרָתֶךָ׃

As channels of water my eyes have gone down because they have not kept your law.

וַיִּגֹּ֥ף יְהוָ֖ה אֶת־הָעָ֑ם עַ֚ל אֲשֶׁ֣ר עָשׂ֣וּ אֶת־הָעֵ֔גֶל Exod 32:35

And the Lord smote the people because they made the calf.

יֵאָסֵ֤ף אַהֲרֹן֙ אֶל־עַמָּ֔יו כִּ֣י לֹ֤א יָבֹא֙ אֶל־הָאָ֔רֶץ אֲשֶׁ֥ר נָתַ֖תִּי Num 20:24
לִבְנֵ֣י יִשְׂרָאֵ֑ל עַ֧ל אֲשֶׁר־מְרִיתֶ֛ם אֶת־פִּ֖י לְמֵ֥י מְרִיבָֽה׃

And Aaron was gathered to his people because he could not enter the land which I gave to the sons of Israel because you rebelled against me at the waters of Meribah.

In Exod 32:35 and Num 20:24, the particle עַל combines with אֲשֶׁר.

Gen 31:20; Deut 29:24

F. Vav *f*

וַיֹּ֗אמֶר אַל־תִּשְׁלַ֤ח יָֽדְךָ֙ אֶל־הַנַּ֔עַר וְאַל־תַּ֥עַשׂ ל֖וֹ מְא֑וּמָּה כִּ֣י Gen 22:12
עַתָּ֣ה יָדַ֗עְתִּי כִּֽי־יְרֵ֤א אֱלֹהִים֙ אַ֔תָּה וְלֹ֥א חָשַׂ֛כְתָּ אֶת־בִּנְךָ֥ אֶת־
יְחִידְךָ֖ מִמֶּֽנִּי׃

And he said, Do not stretch out your hand to the lad, and do not do anything to him. For now I know that you are a fearer of God because (and) you did not withhold your only son from me.

In Gen 22:12, the Vav assumes the causal meaning of כִּי from the preceding clause.

וְגֵ֖ר לֹ֣א תִלְחָ֑ץ וְאַתֶּ֗ם יְדַעְתֶּם֙ אֶת־נֶ֣פֶשׁ הַגֵּ֔ר כִּֽי־גֵרִ֥ים הֱיִיתֶ֖ם Exod 23:9
בְּאֶ֥רֶץ מִצְרָֽיִם׃

And an alien, you must not oppress, because (and) you know the life of the alien for you were aliens in the land of Egypt.

§71. Particle עַל with Infinitive Construct

The particle עַל with the infinitive construct may express causality.

וַיִּקְרָא֙ שֵׁ֣ם הַמָּק֔וֹם מַסָּ֖ה וּמְרִיבָ֑ה עַל־רִ֣יב ׀ בְּנֵ֣י יִשְׂרָאֵ֗ל וְעַ֨ל Exod 17:7
נַסֹּתָ֤ם אֶת־יְהוָה֙

And he called the name of the place Massah and Meribah because of the contention of the sons of Israel and because of their putting the Lord to the test.

כֹּ֚ה אָמַ֣ר יְהוָ֔ה עַל־שְׁלֹשָׁה֙ פִּשְׁעֵי־צֹ֔ר וְעַל־אַרְבָּעָ֖ה לֹ֣א Amos 1:9
אֲשִׁיבֶ֑נּוּ עַל־הַסְגִּירָ֞ם גָּל֤וּת שְׁלֵמָה֙ לֶאֱד֔וֹם

Thus said the Lord, for three transgressions of Tyre and for four I will not in fact turn back because he (Tyre) took a whole captivity (of people) to Edom.

Jer 9:13; 16:18; Job 32:2; 1 Chr 29:9

§72. Context of Juxtaposing Clauses

Context determines the causality of juxtaposing clauses.

וְעָרֵ֣ל ׀ זָכָ֗ר אֲשֶׁ֤ר לֹֽא־יִמּוֹל֙ אֶת־בְּשַׂ֣ר עָרְלָת֔וֹ וְנִכְרְתָ֛ה הַנֶּ֥פֶשׁ Gen 17:14
הַהִ֖וא מֵעַמֶּ֑יהָ אֶת־בְּרִיתִ֖י הֵפַֽר׃

And an uncircumcised male, who is not circumcised with respect to his foreskin – even that soul will be cut off from his people (because) the covenant he has broken.

Chapter 21
CONCESSIVE CLAUSES

§73. Introduction

Concessive clauses grant a concession or allowance to another clause. Particles usually introduce concessive clauses. Moreover, some situation clauses may suggest a concessive notion. Some conditional, adversative, and causal clauses may be interpreted as concessive clauses, as some concessive clauses may be understood as conditional, adversative, or causal clauses.

§74. Particles a

A. כִּי and גַּם כִּי

Jer 49:16[b] כִּֽי־תַגְבִּיהַ כַּנֶּשֶׁר קִנֶּךָ מִשָּׁם אוֹרִידְךָ נְאֻם־יְהוָה׃

Although you make your nest high as an eagle, from there I will cause you to go down, declares the Lord.

Isa 1:15[a] וּבְפָרִשְׂכֶם כַּפֵּיכֶם אַעְלִים עֵינַי מִכֶּם גַּם כִּי־תַרְבּוּ תְפִלָּה אֵינֶנִּי שֹׁמֵעַ

And when you spread out your hands, I will hide my eyes from you. Although you make much your prayer, I will not be hearing.

Ps 23:4[a] גַּם כִּי־אֵלֵךְ בְּגֵיא צַלְמָוֶת לֹא־אִירָא רָע

Although I walk in the valley of deep darkness, I will fear no evil.

Gen 31:37; Deut 29:19; Isa 12:1; Jer 2:22; 4:30; 1 Chr 26:10

B. אִם b

Num 22:18 וַיַּעַן בִּלְעָם וַיֹּאמֶר אֶל־עַבְדֵי בָלָק אִם־יִתֶּן־לִי בָלָק מְלֹא בֵיתוֹ כֶּסֶף וְזָהָב לֹא אוּכַל לַעֲבֹר אֶת־פִּי יְהוָה אֱלֹהָי

And Balaam answered and said to the servants of Balak, Although Balak should give to me the fullness of his house, silver and gold, I would not be able to transgress the commandment of the Lord, my God.

Isa 1:18 לְכוּ־נָא וְנִוָּכְחָה יֹאמַר יְהוָה אִם־יִהְיוּ חֲטָאֵיכֶם כַּשָּׁנִים כַּשֶּׁלֶג יַלְבִּינוּ אִם־יַאְדִּימוּ כַתּוֹלָע כַּצֶּמֶר יִהְיוּ׃

Come now and let us reason together, says the Lord. Although your sins exist as scarlet, they will be white as snow. Although they are red like crimson, they will exist as wool.

Judg 13:16; 1 Sam 15:17; Jer 5:2; 14:7; Job 9:15; Neh 1:9

C. עַל c

The generally accepted examples are with negated nouns.

Isa 53:9 וַיִּתֵּן אֶת־רְשָׁעִים קִבְרוֹ וְאֶת־עָשִׁיר בְּמֹתָיו עַל לֹא־חָמָס עָשָׂה וְלֹא מִרְמָה בְּפִיו׃

And he gave his grave with the wicked, and with the wealthy in his death, although (upon the fact that) no violence he did and no deceit was in his mouth.

עַל לֹא־חָמָס בְּכַפָּי וּתְפִלָּתִי זַכָּה׃ Job 16:17

Although no violence was in my hands and my prayer was pure.

d **D. ו (Vav)**

וַיֹּאמֶר יְהוָה אֶל־הַשָּׂטָן הֲשַׂמְתָּ לִבְּךָ אֶל־עַבְדִּי אִיּוֹב כִּי אֵין
כָּמֹהוּ בָּאָרֶץ אִישׁ תָּם וְיָשָׁר יְרֵא אֱלֹהִים וְסָר מֵרָע וְעֹדֶנּוּ
מַחֲזִיק בְּתֻמָּתוֹ וַתְּסִיתֵנִי בוֹ לְבַלְּעוֹ חִנָּם׃ Job 2:3

And the Lord said to Satan, Have you considered my servant Job, for there is not like him on earth, a blameless and righteous man; a fearer of God and who turns away from evil, while still he is holding on to his integrity although you entice me against him to devour him without cause.

Gen 42:8; Josh 22:17; Jer 31:32

§75. Situation Clauses

Some situation clauses may be interpreted concessively.

וַיַּעַן אַבְרָהָם וַיֹּאמַר הִנֵּה־נָא הוֹאַלְתִּי לְדַבֵּר אֶל־אֲדֹנָי
וְאָנֹכִי עָפָר וָאֵפֶר׃ Gen 18:27

And Abraham answered and said, Behold now, I have undertaken to speak to my lord, although I am dirt and ashes.

וַיִּשְׁלַח יִשְׂרָאֵל אֶת־יְמִינוֹ וַיָּשֶׁת עַל־רֹאשׁ אֶפְרַיִם וְהוּא
הַצָּעִיר Gen 48:14[a]

And Israel stretched out his right hand and he placed it upon the head of Ephraim, although he was the younger.

Num 5:13; Josh 17:14; 1 Kgs 3:7; 18:12; Hos 5:2

Chapter 22
CONDITIONAL CLAUSES

§76. Introduction

Conditional clauses resemble temporal clauses (§77–79). Both use the כִּי particle and may be expressed by context with juxtaposing clauses without particles. Both occur in the present and future. Because they are so similar, distinguishing whether a clause is temporal or conditional may be difficult, especially with juxtaposing clauses without particles.

Conditional clauses are contingent on an independent clause. Fully expressed conditional clauses (sentences) consist of two clauses: the "if" (or condition) clause, known as the protasis, and the "then" (or conclusion) clause, known as the apodosis. The finite verbs are "tenseless" in conditional clauses. Context determines the tense, usually future. The conditional modality of the clauses often makes the meaning of the clause virtually the same, whether the perfect or imperfect is used in the protasis or apodosis. The perfect in the protasis represents the conditional as fulfilled.

Hebrew has two types of conditional statements. First, the particles אִם, כִּי, or context introduce simple conditions or suppositions (which may or may not occur, similar to the simple or general conditional clauses of Greek and Latin).[1] Secondly, the particles לוּ or לוּלֵא introduce contrary-to-fact conditions that did not happen or will not happen (similar to the unreal or contrary-to-fact conditional clause of Greek and Latin).[2]

Conditional clauses are expressed by independent particles or by juxtaposing clauses (with or without Vav).

§77. Independent Particles *a*

These particles introduce the protasis, which usually has a perfect, imperfect, or participle. The apodosis may be a variety of constructions.

A. אִם

This particle commonly introduces a simple or general conditional clause.

1. With a perfect verb in the protasis:

Gen 43:9[b] אִם־לֹא הֲבִיאֹתִיו אֵלֶיךָ וְהִצַּגְתִּיו לְפָנֶיךָ וְחָטָאתִי לְךָ כָּל־הַיָּמִים׃

If I do not bring him to you and set him before you, then I will sin against you forever.

Gen 18:3; 47:6, 16; Exod 22:2; Lev 13:56

2. With an imperfect verb in the protasis: *b*

Gen 18:26 וַיֹּאמֶר יְהוָה אִם־אֶמְצָא בִסְדֹם חֲמִשִּׁים צַדִּיקִם בְּתוֹךְ הָעִיר וְנָשָׂאתִי לְכָל־הַמָּקוֹם בַּעֲבוּרָם׃

And the Lord said, If I find in Sodom fifty righteous in the midst of the city, then I will forgive to all that place on account of them.

Gen 4:7; 13:16; 14:23; Exod 4:8–9; 12:4; BA Dan 2:5

---

1. Smyth 516–518, 523–528; Allen and Greenough 324–328.
2. Smyth 518–522; Allen and Greenough 328–330.

c 3. With a participle in the protasis:

וְעַתָּה אִם־יֶשְׁכֶם עֹשִׂים חֶסֶד וֶאֱמֶת אֶת־אֲדֹנִי הַגִּידוּ לִי Gen 24:49[a]

And now if you are showing (doing) grace and truth with my lord, tell me.

Gen 20:7; 27:46; 43:4–5; Exod 7:27; 8:17

d **B. כִּי**

This particle introduces a general conditional clause.

1. With a perfect verb in the protasis:

וְאַתְּ כִּי שָׂטִית תַּחַת אִישֵׁךְ וְכִי נִטְמֵאת וַיִּתֵּן אִישׁ בָּךְ אֶת־שְׁכָבְתּוֹ מִבַּלְעֲדֵי אִישֵׁךְ׃ Num 5:20

וְהִשְׁבִּיעַ הַכֹּהֵן אֶת־הָאִשָּׁה בִּשְׁבֻעַת הָאָלָה Num 5:21[a]

[20]And you, if you go astray under (the authority of) your husband and if you defile yourself and (another) man has relations with you apart from your husband, [21]then the priest will cause the woman to swear by the swearing an oath.

Lev 13:51; 1 Sam 14:30; Jer 12:5; Ezek 3:19, 21; Ruth 1:12

e 2. With an imperfect verb in the protasis:

כִּי תִקְנֶה עֶבֶד עִבְרִי שֵׁשׁ שָׁנִים יַעֲבֹד וּבַשְּׁבִעִת יֵצֵא לַחָפְשִׁי חִנָּם׃ Exod 21:2

If you purchase a Hebrew slave, six years he will serve. And in the seventh he will go out free without cost.

Gen 37:26; Exod 12:48; Lev 5:1, 21, 23; Num 10:32; Deut 6:25; 7:17; 28:2, 13; 1 Sam 24:20

f 3. With a participle in the protasis:

כִּי בַיהוָה נִשְׁבַּעְתִּי כִּי־אֵינְךָ יוֹצֵא אִם־יָלִין אִישׁ אִתְּךָ הַלַּיְלָה 2 Sam 19:8[b]

For by the Lord I have sworn, if you are not going out, surely a man will not spend with you the night.

Exod 12:15, 19

g **C. לוּ (or its negative לוּלֵא)**

This particle may introduce a contrary-to-fact condition.

1. With a perfect verb in the protasis:

לוּ חָכְמוּ יַשְׂכִּילוּ זֹאת Deut 32:29[a]

If they had been wise, they would understand this.

Judg 8:19; 1 Sam 14:30; Negative Gen 43:10; Judg 14:18; 2 Sam 2:27

h 2. With a participle in the protasis:

וַיֹּאמֶר הָאִישׁ אֶל־יוֹאָב וְלוּא אָנֹכִי שֹׁקֵל עַל־כַּפַּי אֶלֶף כֶּסֶף לֹא־אֶשְׁלַח יָדִי אֶל־בֶּן־הַמֶּלֶךְ 2 Sam 18:12[a]

And the man said to Joab, And had I been one who weighs upon my hands a thousand (shekels) of silver, I would not stretch out my hand against the son of the king.

Mic 2:11

§78. Clauses Juxtaposed without Conditional Particles *a*

Context determines whether juxtaposed clauses are conditional, temporal, etc.

A. With Vav Introducing the Apodosis:

Gen 33:13[b] וּדְפָקוּם יוֹם אֶחָד וָמֵתוּ כָּל־הַצֹּאן׃

And (if) they drive them for one day, then all the flock will die.

Gen 44:29 וּלְקַחְתֶּם גַּם־אֶת־זֶה מֵעִם פָּנַי וְקָרָהוּ אָסוֹן וְהוֹרַדְתֶּם
אֶת־שֵׂיבָתִי בְּרָעָה שְׁאֹלָה׃

And (if) you should take even this one from me and harm should happen to him, then you will bring my gray hair down in calamity to Sheol.

Josh 22:18 וְאַתֶּם תָּשֻׁבוּ הַיּוֹם מֵאַחֲרֵי יְהוָה וְהָיָה אַתֶּם תִּמְרְדוּ הַיּוֹם
בַּיהוָה וּמָחָר אֶל־כָּל־עֲדַת יִשְׂרָאֵל יִקְצֹף׃

And should you return today from after the Lord. And it will happen (if) you rebel today against the Lord, then tomorrow against the entire congregation of Israel he will be angry.

B. Without Vav Introducing the Apodosis: *b*

Num 12:14[a] וְאָבִיהָ יָרֹק יָרַק בְּפָנֶיהָ הֲלֹא תִכָּלֵם שִׁבְעַת יָמִים

And (if) her father indeed spit into her face, will she not be ashamed for seven days.

Neh 1:8[b] אַתֶּם תִּמְעָלוּ אֲנִי אָפִיץ אֶתְכֶם בָּעַמִּים׃

(If) you act unfaithfully, I will scatter you among the nations.

Prov 18:22[a] מָצָא אִשָּׁה מָצָא טוֹב

(If) he found a wife, he found a good thing.

1 Sam 2:16 וַיֹּאמֶר אֵלָיו הָאִישׁ קַטֵּר יַקְטִירוּן כַּיּוֹם הַחֵלֶב וְקַח־לְךָ
כַּאֲשֶׁר תְּאַוֶּה נַפְשֶׁךָ וְאָמַרו לֹא כִּי עַתָּה תִתֵּן וְאִם־לֹא
לָקַחְתִּי בְחָזְקָה׃

And (if) the man said to him, They must surely burn the fat first, and then take for yourself as much as you desire, then he would say, No, but you give now; and if not, I take it by force.

In 1 Sam 2:16, the perfect in the apodosis is a perfect of certitude, furthering the intimidation.

Chapter 23
TEMPORAL CLAUSES

§79. Introduction

Temporal clauses are adverbial, modifying another clause. Particles and context indicate a temporal clause. The particles may be independent particles, the inseparable prepositions בּ and כּ, or the Vav of the Vav-consecutive. The Vav-conjunctive may also join nominal clauses in a temporal relationship.

These independent temporal particles are in the position of an accusative (of time).[1] Although all particles are indeclinable, many Arabic particles and a few Hebrew particles, including particles of time, still have the accusative vowel (עַתָּה).

In temporal clauses, the perfect represents completed action in the past or future (English future perfect); the imperfect represents contingent, incomplete action in the future.

§80. Independent Particles *a*

A. אִם: when (if)

This particle, usually a conditional particle, may also be used temporally with the perfect or imperfect and in the past, present, or future.

וַיֵּ֣דַע אוֹנָ֔ן כִּ֛י לֹּ֥א ל֖וֹ יִהְיֶ֣ה הַזָּ֑רַע וְהָיָ֞ה אִם־בָּ֨א אֶל־אֵ֤שֶׁת אָחִיו֙ וְשִׁחֵ֣ת אַ֔רְצָה לְבִלְתִּ֥י נְתָן־זֶ֖רַע לְאָחִֽיו׃ Gen 38:9

And Onan knew that the seed would not become his, and it would be, when he entered into the wife of his brother that he would destroy (it) to the ground so as not to give seed to his brother.

Num 21:9; Judg 6:3; Isa 4:4; 24:13; Amos 7:2; Ps 78:34

B. אָז (also מֵאָז): then *b*

This temporal particle may be used for past, present, or future time. When used in past time with the perfect or imperfect, this particle is stronger than the Vav of the Vav-consecutive with the imperfect (without a verb Gen 12:6; 13:7; with perfect Gen 4:26; Exod 4:26; with imperfect Exod 15:1; Num 21:17). When used in future time and in poetry, this particle is usually emphatic.

אָ֣ז יַקְהֵ֣ל שְׁלֹמֹ֣ה אֶת־זִקְנֵ֣י יִשְׂרָאֵ֡ל אֶת־כָּל־רָאשֵׁ֣י הַמַּטּוֹת֩ נְשִׂיאֵ֨י הָאָב֜וֹת לִבְנֵ֧י יִשְׂרָאֵ֛ל אֶל־הַמֶּ֥לֶךְ שְׁלֹמֹ֖ה יְרוּשָׁלָ֑͏ִם 1 Kgs 8:1[a]

Then Solomon assembled the elders of Israel, all the heads of the tribes, the leaders of the fathers of the sons of Israel to king Solomon at Jerusalem.

אָ֚ז יִזְעֲק֣וּ אֶל־יְהוָ֔ה וְלֹ֥א יַעֲנֶ֖ה אוֹתָ֑ם Mic 3:4[a]

Then they will cry out to the Lord, but he will not answer them.

1. Of course, the entire temporal clause may be viewed as in the position of the accusative to its main clause.

With a perfect: Gen 39:5; 49:4; Exod 5:23; 2 Sam 5:24; Isa 33:23
With an imperfect: Isa 35:5–6
With an infinitive construct: Exod 4:10

c **C. אַחַר and אַחֲרֵי: after(wards)**

These particles may be used as temporal prepositions before nouns (especially before infinitives) and temporal conjunctions before verbs. They may take a variety of prepositions before them (מֵאַחֲרֵי, for example), and they may take אֲשֶׁר after them to form a conjunction.[2]

Gen 18:5[a] וְאֶקְחָה פַת־לֶחֶם וְסַעֲדוּ לִבְּכֶם אַחַר תַּעֲבֹרוּ

And let me take a piece of bread and sustain your heart, afterwards you may pass over.

Josh 7:8 בִּי אֲדֹנָי מָה אֹמַר אַחֲרֵי אֲשֶׁר הָפַךְ יִשְׂרָאֵל עֹרֶף לִפְנֵי אֹיְבָיו׃

Alas, my Lord, what can I say after Israel has turned the back of the neck before his enemies.

Gen 5:4, 7, 10; 13:14; 14:17; 18:12; 41:39; Exod 3:20; 5:1; 7:25

d **D. אֲשֶׁר and כַּאֲשֶׁר: when**

The particle אֲשֶׁר may introduce a temporal clause. Prepositions may become temporal conjunctions when attached to אֲשֶׁר.

Josh 4:21[b] אֲשֶׁר יִשְׁאָלוּן בְּנֵיכֶם מָחָר אֶת־אֲבוֹתָם לֵאמֹר מָה הָאֲבָנִים הָאֵלֶּה׃

When your sons ask tomorrow their fathers, What (are) these stones?

Gen 18:33[a] וַיֵּלֶךְ יְהוָה כַּאֲשֶׁר כִּלָּה לְדַבֵּר אֶל־אַבְרָהָם

The Lord departed when he finished speaking to Abraham.

Gen 40:13; Lev 4:22; Num 5:29–30; 15:23; Deut 2:22; 11:4; 18:22; 1 Sam 24:2, 5; Isa 31:4

e **E. טֶרֶם and more commonly בְּטֶרֶם: not yet, before (that)**

These particles are commonly used with the preterit imperfect.

Gen 2:5 וְכֹל שִׂיחַ הַשָּׂדֶה טֶרֶם יִהְיֶה בָאָרֶץ וְכָל־עֵשֶׂב הַשָּׂדֶה טֶרֶם יִצְמָח כִּי לֹא הִמְטִיר יְהוָה אֱלֹהִים עַל־הָאָרֶץ וְאָדָם אַיִן לַעֲבֹד אֶת־הָאֲדָמָה׃

And every shrub of the field, before it existed in the earth, and all vegetation of the field before it sprouted, for the Lord God had not yet caused it to rain upon the ground, nor was there a man to work the ground.

Gen 19:4; 24:15 (perfect); 27:4, 33; 37:18; 41:50; 1 Sam 3:7; Jer 1:5(2x)

f **F. כִּי: when**

This flexible particle, when used temporally, may be used for past time, with the perfect, and for present and future time, usually with the imperfect. A form of הָיָה often precedes this temporal particle.

---

2. These particles may function as conjunctions without אֲשֶׁר as well.

וַיְהִ֗י כִּ֣י אָֽרְכוּ־ל֥וֹ שָׁם֙ הַיָּמִ֔ים וַיַּשְׁקֵ֗ף אֲבִימֶ֙לֶךְ֙ מֶ֣לֶךְ פְּלִשְׁתִּ֔ים בְּעַ֖ד הַֽחַלּ֑וֹן And it happened, when the days were long to him there that Abimelek, the king of Philistines, looked down through the window.	Gen 26:8[a]
כִּֽי־הֶ֭חֱרַשְׁתִּי בָּל֣וּ עֲצָמָ֑י בְּ֝שַׁאֲגָתִ֗י כָּל־הַיּֽוֹם׃ When I was silent, my bones wasted away in my roaring all the day.	Ps 32:3

Gen 27:1; Exod 3:21; 7:9; 12:25–26; 13:5; 1 Sam 24:20; 2 Sam 6:13; 7:1; 19:26

G. לִפְנֵי: before *g*

This preposition may be used with nouns, especially the infinitive construct, to form temporal phrases and clauses.

וַיִּשָּׂא־ל֣וֹט אֶת־עֵינָ֗יו וַיַּרְא֙ אֶת־כָּל־כִּכַּ֣ר הַיַּרְדֵּ֔ן כִּ֥י כֻלָּ֖הּ מַשְׁקֶ֑ה לִפְנֵ֣י ׀ שַׁחֵ֣ת יְהוָ֗ה אֶת־סְדֹם֙ וְאֶת־עֲמֹרָ֔ה כְּגַן־יְהוָה֙ כְּאֶ֣רֶץ מִצְרַ֔יִם בֹּאֲכָ֖ה צֹֽעַר׃ And Lot lifted his eyes and he saw all the plain of Jordan (for all of it was well watered) before the Lord destroyed Sodom and Gomorrah, as the garden of the Lord, as the land of Egypt going into Zoar.	Gen 13:10

Gen 36:31; 1 Sam 9:15; 2 Sam 3:13, 35; Ezek 33:22; Joel 3:4

H. עַד: until (the time that), while *h*

This particle may be used as a preposition to an infinitive construct or as a conjunction to a verb to form temporal clauses. This particle, as a conjunction, may be preceded by אֲשֶׁר or rarely by כִּי.

וְהַיָּמִ֞ים אֲשֶׁר־הָלַ֣כְנוּ ׀ מִקָּדֵ֣שׁ בַּרְנֵ֗עַ עַ֤ד אֲשֶׁר־עָבַ֙רְנוּ֙ אֶת־נַ֣חַל זֶ֔רֶד שְׁלֹשִׁ֥ים וּשְׁמֹנֶ֖ה שָׁנָ֑ה And the days when we marched from Kadesh-Barnea until (the time that) we passed over the wadi Zered were thirty-eight years.	Deut 2:14[a]
וַיֵּלְכוּ֙ וַיָּבֹ֣אוּ הָהָ֔רָה וַיֵּ֤שְׁבוּ שָׁם֙ שְׁלֹ֣שֶׁת יָמִ֔ים עַד־שָׁ֖בוּ הָרֹדְפִ֑ים And they marched and came to the mountain region, and they dwelt there three days until (the time that) the pursuers returned.	Josh 2:22[a]

Gen 3:19; 8:7; 19:22; 27:45; Jer 1:3(2x); BA Ezra 5:5; Dan 2:9

§81. Attached Particles *a*

A. ב or כ Particle Attached to an Infinitive Construct

This construction commonly expresses a temporal clause, often preceded by a form of היה.

וַיָּבֹ֥א אִישׁ־אֱלֹהִ֖ים אֶל־עֵלִ֑י וַיֹּ֣אמֶר אֵלָ֗יו כֹּ֚ה אָמַ֣ר יְהוָ֔ה הֲנִגְלֹ֤ה נִגְלֵ֙יתִי֙ אֶל־בֵּ֣ית אָבִ֔יךָ בִּהְיוֹתָ֥ם בְּמִצְרַ֖יִם לְבֵ֥ית פַּרְעֹֽה׃ And the man of God came to Eli, and he said to him, Thus said the Lord, I truly revealed myself to the house of your fa-	1 Sam 2:27

ther when (lit. in the existing of them) they existed in Egypt to the house of Pharaoh.

Gen 24:30 וַיְהִי כִּרְאֹת אֶת־הַנֶּזֶם וְאֶת־הַצְּמִדִים עַל־יְדֵי אֲחֹתוֹ וּכְשָׁמְעוֹ
אֶת־דִּבְרֵי רִבְקָה אֲחֹתוֹ לֵאמֹר כֹּה־דִבֶּר אֵלַי הָאִישׁ וַיָּבֹא
אֶל־הָאִישׁ וְהִנֵּה עֹמֵד עַל־הַגְּמַלִּים עַל־הָעָיִן׃

And it happened, when (he) saw (lit. as the seeing of [him]) the ring and the bracelets upon the arms of his sister and when he heard (as the hearing of him) the words of Re-becca, his sister, thus the man spoke to me, then he came to the man and behold he was standing beside the camels beside the well.

Gen 9:14; 12:4; 19:17; Exod 3:12; 5:20; 7:5, 7; 9:29; 11:1; 12:27; 13:17; 1 Sam 23:6; 24:12; Jer 26:8

b **B. ב Particle Attached to a Noun in Construct**

The noun is usually a temporal word, such as יוֹם.

Jer 7:22[a] בְּיוֹם הוֹצִיאִי אוֹתָם מֵאֶרֶץ מִצְרָיִם

On the day (when) I brought them out from the land of Egypt

c **C. וְ: and**

The Vav often connects temporally related clauses.

1. Vav-consecutive with verbal clauses

   The Vav-consecutive constructions often express successive action.

   Exod 2:2[b] וַתֵּרֶא אֹתוֹ כִּי־טוֹב הוּא וַתִּצְפְּנֵהוּ שְׁלֹשָׁה יְרָחִים׃

   When (and) she saw him that he was handsome, then she hid him for three months.

   Ruth 3:3[a] וְרָחַצְתְּ וָסַכְתְּ וְשַׂמְתְּ שִׂמְלֹתַךְ עָלַיִךְ וְיָרַדְתְּ הַגֹּרֶן

   When you wash, anoint, and put your garments on yourself, then you will go down to the threshing floor.

d 2. Vav-conjunctive with nominal clauses (§16g)

   When connecting temporally related nominal clauses, the particle Vav usually expresses closely successive or (nearly) simultaneous actions.

   a) Perfect: These often convey a nearly simultaneous action.

      Gen 19:23 הַשֶּׁמֶשׁ יָצָא עַל־הָאָרֶץ וְלוֹט בָּא צֹעֲרָה׃

      The sun had (just) gone out upon the earth, when (and) Lot entered Zoar

      Gen 44:3; Judg 3:24; 1 Sam 9:5

   b) Participle: These express a (nearly) simultaneous action.

      1 Sam 9:14 וַיַּעֲלוּ הָעִיר הֵמָּה בָּאִים בְּתוֹךְ הָעִיר וְהִנֵּה שְׁמוּאֵל יֹצֵא
      לִקְרָאתָם לַעֲלוֹת הַבָּמָה׃

      They went up to the city. They were entering in the midst of the city, when (and) behold Samuel was going out to meet them to go up to the high place.

      2 Kgs 4:5

c) Participle and perfect:

1 Sam 9:11[a] הֵ֣מָּה עֹלִים֙ בְּמַעֲלֵ֣ה הָעִ֔יר וְהֵ֙מָּה֙ מָצְא֣וּ נְעָר֔וֹת יֹצְא֖וֹת לִשְׁאֹ֣ב מָ֑יִם

They were going up the ascent of the city, when (and) they found young maidens going out to draw water.

2 Kgs 13:21; Job 1:16

3. Nominal clause without a perfect or participle and another nominal clause with a perfect *e*

Gen 7:6 וְנֹ֕חַ בֶּן־שֵׁ֥שׁ מֵא֖וֹת שָׁנָ֑ה וְהַמַּבּ֣וּל הָיָ֔ה מַ֖יִם עַל־הָאָֽרֶץ׃

And Noah was six hundred years old, when (and) the flood happened

4. Verbal clause connected by Vav-conjunctive to a nominal clause *f*

1 Sam 7:10[a] וַיְהִ֤י שְׁמוּאֵל֙ מַעֲלֶ֣ה הָעוֹלָ֔ה וּפְלִשְׁתִּ֥ים נִגְּשׁ֖וּ

And Samuel existed in the status of one offering a whole burnt offering, when the Philistines approached.

Chapter 24
ADVERSATIVE AND EXCEPTIVE CLAUSES

§82. Introduction

Adversative clauses contrast actions, objects, or ideas, usually from the preceding clause. Exceptive clauses furnish exceptions to the preceding statement. Various particles introduce adversative and exceptive clauses.

§83. Adversative *a*

A. אוּלָם

The Septuagint sometimes translates אוּלָם with ἀλλά, indicating a strong adversative particle.

Gen 48:19 — וַיְמָאֵ֣ן אָבִ֗יו וַיֹּאמֶר֮ יָדַ֣עְתִּֽי בְנִי֒ יָדַ֔עְתִּי גַּם־ה֥וּא יִֽהְיֶה־לְּעָ֖ם וְגַם־ה֣וּא יִגְדָּ֑ל וְאוּלָ֗ם אָחִ֤יו הַקָּטֹן֙ יִגְדַּ֣ל מִמֶּ֔נּוּ וְזַרְע֖וֹ יִהְיֶ֥ה מְלֹֽא־הַגּוֹיִֽם׃

And his father refused and said, I know, my son, I know. Even he will exist as a people and even he will become great, **but nevertheless**, his younger brother will become greater than he and his seed will exist as a multitude of the nations.

Job 1:11[a] — וְאוּלָם֙ שְֽׁלַֽח־נָ֣א יָֽדְךָ֔ וְגַ֖ע בְּכָל־אֲשֶׁר־ל֑וֹ

But nevertheless, stretch forth now your hand and touch all which is to him.

Gen 28:19; Exod 9:16; Num 14:21; Judg 18:29; 1 Sam 20:3, 25:34

B. כִּי or כִּי אִם *b*

These adversative particles often occur after negative statements.

Gen 17:15 — לֹא־תִקְרָ֥א אֶת־שְׁמָ֖הּ שָׂרָ֑י כִּ֥י שָׂרָ֖ה שְׁמָֽהּ׃

You will not call her name Sarai, **but** Sarah is her name.

Gen 24:3 — וְאַשְׁבִּ֣יעֲךָ֔ בַּֽיהוָה֙ אֱלֹהֵ֣י הַשָּׁמַ֔יִם וֵֽאלֹהֵ֖י הָאָ֑רֶץ אֲשֶׁ֨ר לֹא־תִקַּ֤ח אִשָּׁה֙ לִבְנִ֔י מִבְּנוֹת֙ הַֽכְּנַעֲנִ֔י אֲשֶׁ֥ר אָנֹכִ֖י יוֹשֵׁ֥ב בְּקִרְבּֽוֹ׃

Gen 24:4[a] — כִּ֧י אֶל־אַרְצִ֛י וְאֶל־מוֹלַדְתִּ֖י תֵּלֵ֑ךְ

[3]And I cause you to swear by the Lord, God of heaven and earth, that you will not take a wife for my son from the daughters of the Canaanites in whose midst I am dwelling, [4]**but** to my land and to my kindred you will go.

Gen 15:4 — וְהִנֵּ֨ה דְבַר־יְהוָ֤ה אֵלָיו֙ לֵאמֹ֔ר לֹ֥א יִֽירָשְׁךָ֖ זֶ֑ה כִּי־אִם֙ אֲשֶׁ֣ר יֵצֵ֣א מִמֵּעֶ֔יךָ ה֖וּא יִֽירָשֶֽׁךָ׃

And behold the word of the Lord *came* to him, This one will not inherit, **but** that one who comes forth from your loins – he will inherit.

Gen 32:29; Lev 21:14; Num 10:30, 26:33

c C. ו (Vav)

Gen 2:20 וַיִּקְרָא הָאָדָם שֵׁמוֹת לְכָל־הַבְּהֵמָה וּלְעוֹף הַשָּׁמַיִם וּלְכֹל
חַיַּת הַשָּׂדֶה וּלְאָדָם לֹא־מָצָא עֵזֶר כְּנֶגְדּוֹ׃

And the man called names to every beast and to the fowl of the skies and to every living thing of the field, **but** to the man a helper was not found corresponding to him.

1 Sam 1:15 וַתַּעַן חַנָּה וַתֹּאמֶר לֹא אֲדֹנִי אִשָּׁה קְשַׁת־רוּחַ אָנֹכִי וְיַיִן
וְשֵׁכָר לֹא שָׁתִיתִי וָאֶשְׁפֹּךְ אֶת־נַפְשִׁי לִפְנֵי יְהוָה׃

And Hannah answered and said, No my lord, I am woman, harsh of spirit, and wine and drink I have not drunk, **but** I poured out my soul before the Lord.

Gen 39:8; Exod 4:23; Lev 11:5, 22:23; Num 22:35
וְלֹא Gen 8:9, 31:7, 33–35; 1 Sam 24:19; Jer 1:19

§84. Exceptive

a A. אֶפֶס כִּי

This exceptive clause follows a positive statement.

Num 13:27[b] וְגַם זָבַת חָלָב וּדְבַשׁ הִוא וְזֶה־פִּרְיָהּ׃
Num 13:28[a] אֶפֶס כִּי־עַז הָעָם הַיֹּשֵׁב בָּאָרֶץ

[27] And even it flows with milk and honey, and this is its fruit;
[28] **except that** the people who dwell in the land are strong.

Deut 15:4; Judg 4:9; 2 Sam 12:14

b B. בִּלְתִּי אִם or בִּלְתִּי

Gen 47:18[b] לֹא נִשְׁאַר לִפְנֵי אֲדֹנִי בִּלְתִּי אִם־גְּוִיָּתֵנוּ וְאַדְמָתֵנוּ׃

And there is not left before my lord **except** our body and our land.

Gen 43:3; Num 11:6, 32:12; Josh 11:19; Amos 3:3

c C. כִּי אִם

This exceptive clause follows a negative statement.

Gen 32:27[b] וַיֹּאמֶר לֹא אֲשַׁלֵּחֲךָ כִּי אִם־בֵּרַכְתָּנִי׃

And he said, I will not let you go away, **except** you will have blessed me.

Gen 39:9[a] אֵינֶנּוּ גָדוֹל בַּבַּיִת הַזֶּה מִמֶּנִּי וְלֹא־חָשַׂךְ מִמֶּנִּי מְאוּמָה כִּי
אִם־אוֹתָךְ בַּאֲשֶׁר אַתְּ־אִשְׁתּוֹ

There is no one in this house greater than I, and he has not withheld from me anything **except** you because you are his wife.

Gen 28:17, 32:29, 39:6; 47:18; Num 14:30, 35:33

d D. וְלֹא

Exod 3:19 וַאֲנִי יָדַעְתִּי כִּי לֹא־יִתֵּן אֶתְכֶם מֶלֶךְ מִצְרַיִם לַהֲלֹךְ וְלֹא
בְּיָד חֲזָקָה׃

I know that the king of Egypt will not allow you to go, **except** (if not) by a strong hand.

Exercises: Various Clauses

I. Questions and Discussions

1. Define adversative and exceptive clauses. How are these clauses expressed?
2. Define asseverative clause. How is this clause expressed? What clauses are naturally asseverative?
3. Define causal clause. How is this clause expressed?
4. Define comparative clause. How is this clause expressed?
5. Define concessive clause. How is this clause expressed?
6. Define conditional clause. How is this clause expressed?
7. Define protasis and apodosis.
8. What are the two types of conditional statements?
9. Define exclamation clause. How is this clause expressed?
10. Define interrogative clause. How is this clause expressed?
11. Discuss the general characteristics of the negative particle לֹא. What mood does it usually negate? What negatives does it parallel in Greek and Latin? Discuss its usages with verbs and nouns. How is it used in prohibitions?
12. Discuss the general characteristics of the negative particle אַל. What mood does it usually negate? What negatives does it parallel in Greek and Latin? Discuss its usages with verbs, nouns, and the particle נָא. How is it used in prohibitions?
13. Discuss the general characteristics of the negative particle אַיִן. Discuss its usage as a semi-verb and its relationship with הָיָה. Discuss its usages with various parts of speech.
14. Define and discuss absolute negation and categoric negation. Which negative particles are used in these constructions?
15. Define oath clause. How are they used?
16. What are the three parts of an oath clause? Which parts may be implied? Which parts must be explicitly furnished?
17. Define purpose and result clause. What are the two general principles that may distinguish between purpose and result clauses? How are purpose and result clauses expressed?
18. Define relative clause. How is this clause expressed?
19. Compare and contrast Hebrew and Arabic relative clauses. What must be true for every relative clause in Hebrew?
20. Define situation clause. How is this clause expressed? Discuss the similarity between the accusative of situation and the situation clause. Discuss the adverbial nature of the situation clause.
21. Define substantival clause.
22. Define temporal clause. How is this clause expressed?
23. How do the finite verbal forms express tense in conditional clauses?

II. Drills

1. In the following verses, analyze the following clauses.

Gen 32:29 (1) וַיֹּ֗אמֶר לֹ֤א יַעֲקֹב֙ יֵאָמֵ֥ר עוֹד֙ שִׁמְךָ֔ כִּ֖י אִם־יִשְׂרָאֵ֑ל כִּֽי־שָׂרִ֧יתָ עִם־אֱלֹהִ֛ים
וְעִם־אֲנָשִׁ֖ים וַתּוּכָֽל׃

Exod 9:16 (2) וְאוּלָ֗ם בַּעֲב֤וּר זֹאת֙ הֶֽעֱמַדְתִּ֔יךָ בַּעֲב֖וּר הַרְאֹתְךָ֣ אֶת־כֹּחִ֑י וּלְמַ֛עַן סַפֵּ֥ר
שְׁמִ֖י בְּכָל־הָאָֽרֶץ׃

Num 11:6[b] (3) וְעַתָּ֛ה נַפְשֵׁ֥נוּ יְבֵשָׁ֖ה אֵ֣ין כֹּ֑ל בִּלְתִּ֖י אֶל־הַמָּ֥ן עֵינֵֽינוּ׃

2 Kgs 19:17 (4) אָמְנָ֖ם יְהוָ֑ה הֶחֱרִ֜יבוּ מַלְכֵ֥י אַשּׁ֛וּר אֶת־הַגּוֹיִ֖ם וְאֶת־אַרְצָֽם׃

Gen 20:6 (5) וַיֹּאמֶר֩ אֵלָ֨יו הָֽאֱלֹהִ֜ים בַּחֲלֹ֗ם גַּ֣ם אָנֹכִ֤י יָדַ֙עְתִּי֙ כִּ֣י בְתָם־לְבָבְךָ֙ עָשִׂ֣יתָ
זֹּ֔את וָאֶחְשֹׂ֧ךְ גַּם־אָנֹכִ֛י אוֹתְךָ֖ מֵחֲטוֹ־לִ֑י עַל־כֵּ֥ן לֹא־נְתַתִּ֖יךָ לִנְגֹּ֥עַ אֵלֶֽיהָ׃

Gen 6:17 (6) וַאֲנִ֗י הִנְנִי֩ מֵבִ֨יא אֶת־הַמַּבּ֥וּל מַ֙יִם֙ עַל־הָאָ֔רֶץ לְשַׁחֵ֣ת כָּל־בָּשָׂ֗ר אֲשֶׁר־בּוֹ֙
ר֣וּחַ חַיִּ֔ים מִתַּ֖חַת הַשָּׁמָ֑יִם כֹּ֥ל אֲשֶׁר־בָּאָ֖רֶץ יִגְוָֽע׃

Num 20:13 (7) הֵ֚מָּה מֵ֣י מְרִיבָ֔ה אֲשֶׁר־רָב֥וּ בְנֵֽי־יִשְׂרָאֵ֖ל אֶת־יְהוָ֑ה וַיִּקָּדֵ֖שׁ בָּֽם׃

1 Sam 24:6[b] (8) עַ֚ל אֲשֶׁ֣ר כָּרַ֔ת אֶת־כָּנָ֖ף אֲשֶׁ֥ר לְשָׁאֽוּל׃

Gen 3:10[b] (9) וָאִירָ֛א כִּֽי־עֵירֹ֥ם אָנֹ֖כִי וָאֵחָבֵֽא׃

Exod 12:28[b] (10) כַּאֲשֶׁ֨ר צִוָּ֧ה יְהוָ֛ה אֶת־מֹשֶׁ֥ה וְאַהֲרֹ֖ן כֵּ֥ן עָשֽׂוּ׃

Exod 13:17 (11) וַיְהִ֗י בְּשַׁלַּ֣ח פַּרְעֹה֮ אֶת־הָעָם֒ וְלֹא־נָחָ֣ם אֱלֹהִ֗ים דֶּ֚רֶךְ אֶ֣רֶץ פְּלִשְׁתִּ֔ים כִּ֥י
קָר֖וֹב ה֑וּא כִּ֣י ׀ אָמַ֣ר אֱלֹהִ֗ים פֶּֽן־יִנָּחֵ֥ם הָעָ֛ם בִּרְאֹתָ֥ם מִלְחָמָ֖ה וְשָׁ֥בוּ מִצְרָֽיְמָה׃

1 Sam 14:39 (12) כִּ֣י חַי־יְהוָ֗ה הַמּוֹשִׁ֙יעַ֙ אֶת־יִשְׂרָאֵ֔ל כִּ֥י אִם־יֶשְׁנ֛וֹ בְּיוֹנָתָ֥ן בְּנִ֖י כִּ֣י מ֣וֹת יָמ֑וּת
וְאֵ֥ין עֹנֵ֖הוּ מִכָּל־הָעָֽם׃

Gen 43:9b (13) אִם־לֹ֨א הֲבִיאֹתִ֤יו אֵלֶ֙יךָ֙ וְהִצַּגְתִּ֣יו לְפָנֶ֔יךָ וְחָטָ֥אתִֽי לְךָ֖ כָּל־הַיָּמִֽים׃

Exod 15:26 (14) וַיֹּאמֶר֩ אִם־שָׁמ֨וֹעַ תִּשְׁמַ֜ע לְק֣וֹל ׀ יְהוָ֣ה אֱלֹהֶ֗יךָ וְהַיָּשָׁ֤ר בְּעֵינָיו֙ תַּעֲשֶׂ֔ה
וְהַֽאֲזַנְתָּ֙ לְמִצְוֺתָ֔יו וְשָׁמַרְתָּ֖ כָּל־חֻקָּ֑יו כָּל־הַמַּחֲלָ֞ה אֲשֶׁר־שַׂ֤מְתִּי בְמִצְרַ֙יִם֙
לֹא־אָשִׂ֣ים עָלֶ֔יךָ כִּ֛י אֲנִ֥י יְהוָ֖ה רֹפְאֶֽךָ׃

(15) Judg 13:23 וַתֹּאמֶר לוֹ אִשְׁתּוֹ לוּ חָפֵץ יְהוָה לַהֲמִיתֵנוּ לֹא־לָקַח מִיָּדֵנוּ עֹלָה וּמִנְחָה
וְלֹא הֶרְאָנוּ אֶת־כָּל־אֵלֶּה וְכָעֵת לֹא הִשְׁמִיעָנוּ כָּזֹאת׃

(16) Gen 42:38 וַיֹּאמֶר לֹא־יֵרֵד בְּנִי עִמָּכֶם כִּי־אָחִיו מֵת וְהוּא לְבַדּוֹ נִשְׁאָר וּקְרָאָהוּ
אָסוֹן בַּדֶּרֶךְ אֲשֶׁר תֵּלְכוּ־בָהּ וְהוֹרַדְתֶּם אֶת־שֵׂיבָתִי בְּיָגוֹן שְׁאוֹלָה׃

(17) Exod 3:4b וַיִּקְרָא אֵלָיו אֱלֹהִים מִתּוֹךְ הַסְּנֶה וַיֹּאמֶר מֹשֶׁה מֹשֶׁה וַיֹּאמֶר הִנֵּנִי׃

(18) Gen 23:15 אֲדֹנִי שְׁמָעֵנִי אֶרֶץ אַרְבַּע מֵאֹת שֶׁקֶל־כֶּסֶף בֵּינִי וּבֵינְךָ מַה־הִוא
וְאֶת־מֵתְךָ קְבֹר׃

(19) 1 Kgs 22:3 וַיֹּאמֶר מֶלֶךְ־יִשְׂרָאֵל אֶל־עֲבָדָיו הַיְדַעְתֶּם כִּי־לָנוּ רָמֹת גִּלְעָד וַאֲנַחְנוּ
מַחְשִׁים מִקַּחַת אֹתָהּ מִיַּד מֶלֶךְ אֲרָם׃

(20) Exod 2:7 וַתֹּאמֶר אֲחֹתוֹ אֶל־בַּת־פַּרְעֹה הַאֵלֵךְ וְקָרָאתִי לָךְ אִשָּׁה מֵינֶקֶת מִן
הָעִבְרִיֹּת וְתֵינִק לָךְ אֶת־הַיָּלֶד׃

(21) Gen 27:36 וַיֹּאמֶר הֲכִי קָרָא שְׁמוֹ יַעֲקֹב וַיַּעְקְבֵנִי זֶה פַעֲמַיִם אֶת־בְּכֹרָתִי לָקָח
וְהִנֵּה עַתָּה לָקַח בִּרְכָתִי וַיֹּאמַר הֲלֹא־אָצַלְתָּ לִּי בְּרָכָה׃

(22) Gen 4:9 וַיֹּאמֶר יְהוָה אֶל־קַיִן אֵי הֶבֶל אָחִיךָ וַיֹּאמֶר לֹא יָדַעְתִּי הֲשֹׁמֵר אָחִי
אָנֹכִי׃

(23) Gen 37:22 וַיֹּאמֶר אֲלֵהֶם רְאוּבֵן אַל־תִּשְׁפְּכוּ־דָם הַשְׁלִיכוּ אֹתוֹ אֶל־הַבּוֹר הַזֶּה
אֲשֶׁר בַּמִּדְבָּר וְיָד אַל־תִּשְׁלְחוּ־בוֹ לְמַעַן הַצִּיל אֹתוֹ מִיָּדָם לַהֲשִׁיבוֹ
אֶל־אָבִיו׃

(24) Gen 3:3 וּמִפְּרִי הָעֵץ אֲשֶׁר בְּתוֹךְ־הַגָּן אָמַר אֱלֹהִים לֹא תֹאכְלוּ מִמֶּנּוּ וְלֹא תִגְּעוּ
בּוֹ פֶּן־תְּמֻתוּן׃

(25) Gen 9:11 וַהֲקִמֹתִי אֶת־בְּרִיתִי אִתְּכֶם וְלֹא־יִכָּרֵת כָּל־בָּשָׂר עוֹד מִמֵּי הַמַּבּוּל
וְלֹא־יִהְיֶה עוֹד מַבּוּל לְשַׁחֵת הָאָרֶץ׃

(26) Exod 10:15b וְלֹא־נוֹתַר כָּל־יֶרֶק בָּעֵץ וּבְעֵשֶׂב הַשָּׂדֶה בְּכָל־אֶרֶץ מִצְרָיִם׃

(27) Exod 14:11 וַיֹּאמְרוּ אֶל־מֹשֶׁה הֲמִבְּלִי אֵין־קְבָרִים בְּמִצְרַיִם לְקַחְתָּנוּ לָמוּת בַּמִּדְבָּר
מַה־זֹּאת עָשִׂיתָ לָּנוּ לְהוֹצִיאָנוּ מִמִּצְרָיִם׃

(28) 1 Sam 15:29[b] כִּ֣י לֹ֥א אָדָ֛ם ה֖וּא לְהִנָּחֵֽם׃

(29) 1 Sam 3:17[b] כֹּ֣ה יַעֲשֶׂה־לְּךָ֤ אֱלֹהִים֙ וְכֹ֣ה יוֹסִ֔יף אִם־תְּכַחֵ֤ד מִמֶּ֙נִּי֙ דָּבָ֔ר מִכָּל־הַדָּבָ֖ר
אֲשֶׁר־דִּבֶּ֥ר אֵלֶֽיךָ׃

(30) 1 Sam 1:26 וַתֹּ֙אמֶר֙ בִּ֣י אֲדֹנִ֔י חֵ֥י נַפְשְׁךָ֖ אֲדֹנִ֑י אֲנִ֣י הָֽאִשָּׁ֗ה הַנִּצֶּ֤בֶת עִמְּכָה֙ בָּזֶ֔ה
לְהִתְפַּלֵּ֖ל אֶל־יְהוָֽה׃

(31) Ezek 38:29[b] אִם־לֹ֣א׀ בַּיּ֣וֹם הַה֗וּא יִֽהְיֶה֙ רַ֣עַשׁ גָּד֔וֹל עַ֖ל אַדְמַ֥ת יִשְׂרָאֵֽל׃

(32) Exod 4:5 לְמַ֣עַן יַאֲמִ֔ינוּ כִּֽי־נִרְאָ֥ה אֵלֶ֛יךָ יְהוָ֖ה אֱלֹהֵ֣י אֲבֹתָ֑ם אֱלֹהֵ֧י אַבְרָהָ֛ם אֱלֹהֵ֥י
יִצְחָ֖ק וֵאלֹהֵ֥י יַעֲקֹֽב׃

(33) Jer 7:18 הַבָּנִ֞ים מְלַקְּטִ֣ים עֵצִ֗ים וְהָֽאָבוֹת֙ מְבַעֲרִ֣ים אֶת־הָאֵ֔שׁ וְהַנָּשִׁ֖ים לָשׁ֣וֹת בָּצֵ֑ק
לַעֲשׂ֨וֹת כַּוָּנִ֜ים לִמְלֶ֣כֶת הַשָּׁמַ֗יִם וְהַסֵּ֤ךְ נְסָכִים֙ לֵאלֹהִ֣ים אֲחֵרִ֔ים לְמַ֖עַן
הַכְעִסֵֽנִי׃

(34) Deut 4:40 וְשָׁמַרְתָּ֞ אֶת־חֻקָּ֣יו וְאֶת־מִצְוֺתָ֗יו אֲשֶׁ֨ר אָנֹכִ֤י מְצַוְּךָ֙ הַיּ֔וֹם אֲשֶׁר֙ יִיטַ֣ב לְךָ֔
וּלְבָנֶ֖יךָ אַחֲרֶ֑יךָ וּלְמַ֜עַן תַּאֲרִ֤יךְ יָמִים֙ עַל־הָ֣אֲדָמָ֔ה אֲשֶׁ֨ר יְהוָ֧ה אֱלֹהֶ֛יךָ
נֹתֵ֥ן לְךָ֖ כָּל־הַיָּמִֽים׃

(35) Gen 1:17[b] לְהָאִ֖יר עַל־הָאָֽרֶץ׃

(36) Gen 4:11[b] מִן־הָֽאֲדָמָה֙ אֲשֶׁ֤ר פָּצְתָ֣ה אֶת־פִּ֔יהָ לָקַ֛חַת אֶת־דְּמֵ֥י אָחִ֖יךָ מִיָּדֶֽךָ׃

(37) Gen 9:3[a] כָּל־רֶ֙מֶשׂ֙ אֲשֶׁ֣ר הוּא־חַ֔י לָכֶ֥ם יִהְיֶ֖ה לְאָכְלָ֑ה

(38) Exod 15:16 תִּפֹּ֨ל עֲלֵיהֶ֤ם אֵימָ֙תָה֙ וָפַ֔חַד בִּגְדֹ֥ל זְרוֹעֲךָ֖ יִדְּמ֣וּ כָּאָ֑בֶן עַד־יַעֲבֹ֤ר עַמְּךָ֙
יְהוָ֔ה עַד־יַעֲבֹ֖ר עַם־ז֥וּ קָנִֽיתָ׃

(39) Jer 5:19 וְהָיָה֙ כִּ֣י תֹֽאמְר֔וּ תַּ֣חַת מֶ֗ה עָשָׂ֨ה יְהוָ֧ה אֱלֹהֵ֛ינוּ לָ֖נוּ אֶת־כָּל־אֵ֑לֶּה
וְאָמַרְתָּ֨ אֲלֵיהֶ֜ם כַּאֲשֶׁ֨ר עֲזַבְתֶּ֥ם אוֹתִ֛י וַתַּעַבְד֞וּ אֱלֹהֵ֤י נֵכָר֙ בְּאַרְצְכֶ֔ם כֵּ֚ן
תַּעַבְד֣וּ זָרִ֔ים בְּאֶ֖רֶץ לֹ֥א לָכֶֽם׃

(40) Gen 18:8[b] וְהֽוּא־עֹמֵ֧ד עֲלֵיהֶ֛ם תַּ֥חַת הָעֵ֖ץ וַיֹּאכֵֽלוּ׃

Num 22:5 (41) וַיִּשְׁלַח מַלְאָכִים אֶל־בִּלְעָם בֶּן־בְּעוֹר פְּתוֹרָה אֲשֶׁר עַל־הַנָּהָר אֶרֶץ בְּנֵי־עַמּוֹ לִקְרֹא־לוֹ לֵאמֹר הִנֵּה עַם יָצָא מִמִּצְרַיִם הִנֵּה כִסָּה אֶת־עֵין הָאָרֶץ וְהוּא יֹשֵׁב מִמֻּלִי׃

Deut 4:42 (42) לָנֻס שָׁמָּה רוֹצֵחַ אֲשֶׁר יִרְצַח אֶת־רֵעֵהוּ בִּבְלִי־דַעַת וְהוּא לֹא־שֹׂנֵא לוֹ מִתְּמֹול שִׁלְשֹׁום וְנָס אֶל־אַחַת מִן־הֶעָרִים הָאֵל וָחָי׃

Exod 3:2b (43) וַיַּרְא וְהִנֵּה הַסְּנֶה בֹּעֵר בָּאֵשׁ וְהַסְּנֶה אֵינֶנּוּ אֻכָּל׃

Exod 2:6 (44) וַתִּפְתַּח וַתִּרְאֵהוּ אֶת־הַיֶּלֶד וְהִנֵּה־נַעַר בֹּכֶה וַתַּחְמֹל עָלָיו וַתֹּאמֶר מִיַּלְדֵי הָעִבְרִים זֶה׃

Lev 14:46 (45) וְהַבָּא אֶל־הַבַּיִת כָּל־יְמֵי הִסְגִּיר אֹתוֹ יִטְמָא עַד־הָעָרֶב׃

1 Sam 5:9 (46) וַיְהִי אַחֲרָיו הֵסַבּוּ אֹתוֹ וַתְּהִי יַד־יְהוָה בָּעִיר מְהוּמָה גְּדוֹלָה מְאֹד וַיַּךְ אֶת־אַנְשֵׁי הָעִיר מִקָּטֹן וְעַד־גָּדוֹל וַיִּשָּׂתְרוּ לָהֶם טְחֹרִים׃

Gen 12:18 (47) וַיִּקְרָא פַרְעֹה לְאַבְרָם וַיֹּאמֶר מַה־זֹּאת עָשִׂיתָ לִּי לָמָּה לֹא־הִגַּדְתָּ לִּי כִּי אִשְׁתְּךָ הִוא׃

Gen 9:24 (48) וַיִּיקֶץ נֹחַ מִיֵּינוֹ וַיֵּדַע אֵת אֲשֶׁר־עָשָׂה־לוֹ בְּנוֹ הַקָּטָן׃

Gen 24:41 (49) אָז תִּנָּקֶה מֵאָלָתִי כִּי תָבוֹא אֶל־מִשְׁפַּחְתִּי וְאִם־לֹא יִתְּנוּ לָךְ וְהָיִיתָ נָקִי מֵאָלָתִי׃

Gen 6:1 (50) וַיְהִי כִּי־הֵחֵל הָאָדָם לָרֹב עַל־פְּנֵי הָאֲדָמָה וּבָנוֹת יֻלְּדוּ לָהֶם׃

Gen 4:8 (51) וַיֹּאמֶר קַיִן אֶל־הֶבֶל אָחִיו וַיְהִי בִּהְיוֹתָם בַּשָּׂדֶה וַיָּקָם קַיִן אֶל־הֶבֶל אָחִיו וַיַּהַרְגֵהוּ׃

Gen 6:4 (52) הַנְּפִלִים הָיוּ בָאָרֶץ בַּיָּמִים הָהֵם וְגַם אַחֲרֵי־כֵן אֲשֶׁר יָבֹאוּ בְּנֵי הָאֱלֹהִים אֶל־בְּנוֹת הָאָדָם וְיָלְדוּ לָהֶם הֵמָּה הַגִּבֹּרִים אֲשֶׁר מֵעוֹלָם אַנְשֵׁי הַשֵּׁם׃

Gen 11:2a (53) וַיְהִי בְּנָסְעָם מִקֶּדֶם וַיִּמְצְאוּ בִקְעָה בְּאֶרֶץ שִׁנְעָר וַיֵּשְׁבוּ שָׁם׃

2. **For the following verses, discuss the semi-verb אֵ֣ין, with its subject and predicate.**

Deut 1:32 (54) וּבַדָּבָ֖ר הַזֶּ֑ה אֵֽינְכֶם֙ מַאֲמִינִ֔ם בַּיהוָ֖ה אֱלֹהֵיכֶֽם׃

Judg 19:15 (55) וַיָּסֻ֣רוּ שָׁ֔ם לָב֖וֹא לָל֣וּן בַּגִּבְעָ֑ה וַיָּבֹ֗א וַיֵּ֙שֶׁב֙ בִּרְח֣וֹב הָעִ֔יר וְאֵ֥ין אִ֛ישׁ
מְאַסֵּֽף־אוֹתָ֥ם הַבַּ֖יְתָה לָלֽוּן׃

Composition

INTRODUCTION TO THE COMPOSITIONS

The compositions have four parts in addition to a glossary. First, the initial page is the composition without notes, used for the recitation of the composition in Hebrew. Second, the following pages are the same English text as the initial page but with notes to assist the student in composing the Hebrew. The notes also reinforce the syntax, so their mastery is essential. Moreover, the notes of the later compositions assume the notes of the earlier compositions. Third, the keys are provided for correcting mistakes. Fourth, the unpointed text (key) supplies practice for reading and reviewing the composition. An English to Hebrew glossary in the appendixes further aids the student in composing the Hebrew.

Suggested Method for Working the Compositions:

1. Compose the English text into Biblical Hebrew using the syntax, notes, and glossary. Carefully study the notes and review the sections of the syntax referenced in the composition. Cross references with numbers, such as 2.11, refer to composition two, footnote eleven. The symbol "§" followed by a reference refers to the section in the syntax.

2. Correct the composition using the key. There are acceptable variations to the key. For example, the prepositions, ל or אל, may be equally correct in many contexts; the accusative marker את may be present or absent in many context, and so forth.

3. Read the unpointed Hebrew (key) repeatedly until the composition is read accurately and fluently. When reading the Hebrew, identify constructions and review the syntax given in the notes.

4. Looking only at the English text without notes (the first page of each composition), recite the composition in Hebrew repeatedly and fluently until it is mastered.

5. After completing a composition, begin the next composition while the prior composition is still ingrained in the mind to accelerate the learning of the next composition.

For further study, read the Old Testament in Hebrew constantly, learn vocabulary by root, and memorize passages of the Old Testament in Hebrew.

For an alternative benefit of the compositions, use them as texts with syntactical commentary, especially the last three compositions, which are Biblical passages. This will aid the student in analyzing the text syntactically.

COMPOSITION ONE

(1) Now there was a young man from the land of Ur whose name (was) Abram, son of Terah. (2) And he went to the temple of Ur to sacrifice a sacrifice to the gods of his fathers and to their idols. (3) Now it would be when Abram would go up to the temple of Ur every year that he would sacrifice there upon the altar of his gods, and the priest would bless him, and then he would return to his house. (4) And it happened while Abram prayed to his gods in the temple of Ur that the Lord appeared to him at that time and said, "I (am) the Lord, the God of heaven and earth, walk about before me and be complete. (5) Forsake your gods and the idols of your fathers and then go, you and your wife, from your land and from the house of your father, and I will make you famous, and all the nations of the earth will be blessed in your seed." (6) Then Abram rose up early in the morning and he smashed the idols of his fathers and he went and recounted these words to his father and to the priest of Ur, but they did not believe him, and then the priest of Ur rebuked Abram and said, "Can a man see (the) gods or can a man hear (the) gods?" (7) And Abram answered and said, "I have forsaken my gods and the idols of my fathers I have smashed to pieces; and I trust in the Lord, and for his word I wait." (8) Then Terah said to Abram, "Leave my house and my land and go after your God; you must not return to me and you must not see my face again."

(9) Now Abram had taken a wife whose name (was) Sarai, and she heard the word which Abram spoke to his father, but she did not speak to Abram, her husband, a word, and she kept the matter in her heart.

(10) Then Abram rose up and went to Haran as the Lord had spoken to him, and Lot, the son of his brother, went with him, and they dwelt in Haran.

( ) – Not in Hebrew, but needed for English
[ ] – In the Hebrew, but not needed for English
* – Put the pronominal suffix directly on the verb
# – Put the pronominal suffix with energic Nun directly on the verb

(1) Now there was[1] a young man from the land of Ur whose name[2] (was) Abram, son of Terah. (2) And he went[3] to the temple of Ur[4] to sacrifice[5] a sacrifice[6] to the gods[7] of his fathers and to their idols.[8] (3) Now it would be[9] when Abram[10] would go up[11] to the temple of Ur every year[12] that he would sacrifice[13] there upon the altar of his gods, and the priest

1. Now there was – The Hebrew reads, "And a young man was." Use the Vav-consecutive with the imperfect (a jussive/preterit in form and preterit in meaning) of הָיָה (3.1). The word היה means "to exist, come to be, become, happen" (2.2). Hebrew lacks the English verb "to be," though Hebrew implies "to be" in clauses without verbs (1.2). The agent of verbal clauses is usually definite, but sometimes indefinite with הָיָה (§11nn). The Vav-consecutive (or sometimes the perfect, 1.29) is the tense of past narration. In narration, tense is usually stronger relative to aspect (1.9; §2c).
2. whose name (was) Abram – The Hebrew reads, "and his name (was) Abram." A Hebrew verbless clause implies a copula. For the first composition, the forms of "to be" will be placed in parentheses to indicate the implied copula. In future compositions, the parentheses will not be given.
3. And he went – Hebrew continues narrative in the past with the Vav-consecutive (with the preterit imperfect, §3p, 6n-o).
4. to the temple of Ur – Use the preposition אֶל־. Hebrew usually uses the preposition אֶל־ after verbs of motion, though the preposition לְ is sometimes found (Josh 1:15; 8:14). The preposition אֶל־ properly denotes "motion to" or "direction towards"; the preposition לְ, "direction towards," "with respect to," or "with reference to." The construct package or annexation is "proper," because the second word, "Ur," modifies the first word, "temple," and because a preposition (בְּ, לְ, מִן) can be inserted between the nouns for the meaning, "the temple *in* Ur." The preposition בְּ is the proper choice since "Ur" is a noun of place (§12b–c).
5. to sacrifice – This is a purpose clause, "for the intent that," "for the purpose (reason) that" (also called a final clause in JM §168). Hebrew expresses purpose clauses with a variety of particles and constructions (§51–53; JM §168). Use the infinitive construct with לְ (Gen 27:5; §18e, 53g; JM §168c, 124l).
6. a sacrifice – When a concrete (not abstract) direct object of the same root as the verb occurs, the expression is an idiomatic Hebrew (and Arabic) construction (that is, a Hebraic or Semitic way of saying something, §13b fn 35). If the concrete direct object were dropped, the meaning would not be affected. (Compare 1 Sam 1:4 with Gen 31:54.) This construction may also express greater clarity or provide "a more convenient way of connecting the verb with other members of the sentence" (GKC §117r).
7. to the gods – The preposition לְ is more common than אֶל־ for the verb "sacrifice" (1.4; BDB 257a I3).
8. and to their idols – Hebrew often repeats the preposition.
9. Now it would be – This English clause is a Hebrew verb, a Vav-consecutive with the perfect of הָיָה. This verb and the context (particularly, the following verbs) set the aspect and tense of the following narrative as past tense. The aspect of the verb is frequentative (that which *frequently* happens – Now it would happen from time to time). To communicate vivid narration in the past tense use the frequentative imperfect or a Vav-consecutive with a perfect (§4d). This verb, וְהָיָה, the Vav-consecutive with the perfect, is equivalent to an imperfect both in tense and aspect (§6e; JM §119a), the Vav adding the link to the preceding statement (Exod 17:11).
10. when Abram – Like purpose clauses, Hebrew variously expresses temporal clauses (§79–81; JM §166). Use the conjunction כַּאֲשֶׁר (1 Sam 1:24; Exod 17:11; §80d; JM §166n; BDB 455b 3).
11. Abram would go up – Abram would go up from time to time, that is, frequently. Use the (frequentative) imperfect indicative, as the context, especially the preceding verb, indicates (§4d).
12. every year – Repeating nouns may express the distributive idea of "every" or "each." The Hebrew reads, "year year" (§9b, 24f, 31; JM §135d; for numerals JM §142p).
13. that he would sacrifice – The Vav-consecutive with the perfect continues the prior frequentative imperfect. The word "that" translates the Vav of the Vav-consecutive (§6d–e).

would bless him, and then he would return to his house. (4) And it happened[14] while Abram prayed[15] to his gods in the temple of Ur that the Lord appeared[16] to him[17] at that time and said,[18] "I (am) the Lord, the God of heaven and earth,[19] walk about[20] before me and be com-

14. And it happened – The verb, the Vav-consecutive with the imperfect (preterit) of הָיָה, sets the tense and aspect of the following infinitive construct and verbs. The tense is past; the aspect is completed action (§6n). Sentence three represents a number of actions ongoing from time to time (frequentative) in the past; sentence four represents a finished action in the past. These terms for aspect (completed and incomplete) describe the "type of action" from the viewpoint or aspect of the speaker (writer). Furthermore, Hebrew verbal action may be viewed as ongoing (often occurring with Hebrew imperfects), as completed with continuing results (like a Greek perfect; this may occur with the Hebrew perfect), or as undefined (that is, like a Greek aorist, the simple action without ongoing action or completed action with continuing results; this occurs with Hebrew perfects and some imperfects). If an author views an action as incomplete in some manner (just having begun, ongoing, or just about to begin), he uses an imperfect (or its equivalent with Vav, Vᵊqatal). A Latin and Greek writer would use the present or imperfect. Similarly, a Hebrew author chooses an imperfect to convey an action as ongoing from time to time (action frequently done or repeatedly done, frequentative). Context or the meaning of the verb determines whether a specific imperfect is durative or frequentative (or just begun or about to begin). The meaning of certain verbs is naturally durative, as בִּקֵּשׁ (to seek), for example. The imperfect, especially when expressing ongoing action, vividly depicts events like a motion picture (§2a, 3b, 4c). The perfect, by contrast, presents events without motion, like a snapshot.
15. while Abram prayed – This time, use the infinitive construct with the כ preposition (the ב preposition is equally possible for this temporal clause; §18d, 81a; JM §166l–m).
16. that the Lord appeared – Render the word "that" by the Vav of the Vav-consecutive: "and the Lord appeared."
17. to him – The preposition with this verb is usually אֶל־ (occasionally לְ, BDB 908a 1a–b). Change the word order to: "that (he) appeared to him the Lord." Prepositional phrases that closely connect to the verb ("the Lord appeared to") and have pronominal suffixes as an object (not independent nouns) often occur between the verb and the subject (Gen 18:1; 26:2, 24; compare with Gen 35:9 where the word order changes when the object of the preposition is not a pronominal suffix). As always, there are exceptions: Exod 3:2.
18. and said – There are two possibilities for the thematic vowel when the Vav-consecutive of אָמַר occurs immediately before direct speech: Segol with a major disjunctive accent (Zaqeph or Rebia, Gen 21:7), or Patach with the word in pause (Zaqeph Qaton, Zaqeph Gadol, or Athnach, Gen 20:4).
19. the God of heaven and earth – Hebrew tends to repeat the first word (*nomen regens*, the ruling or governing noun; the end noun [*nomen rectum*] in a construct package is the genitive) in a compound construct package (Gen 24:3; Jer 8:1; JM §129b; GKC §128a; but there are numerous instances when the "governing noun" is not repeated: Gen 14:19; Num 20:5). This is proper annexation since the genitives (heaven and earth) modify the governing noun (God). For the meaning between the governing noun and the genitive, the preposition לְ should be understood: the God *with respect to* the heavens and the God *with respect to* the earth (§12e).
20. walk about – Use the Hithpael of הלך. The intensive verb communicates to walk or march about/around. The reflexive ת suggests "for his own benefit, at his own leisure" (§7c; JM §53; GKC §54f).

plete.[21] (5) Forsake your gods and the idols of your fathers and then go,[22] you and your wife,[23] from your land and from the house of your father, [24] and I will make you famous,[25] and all the nations of the earth will be blessed in your seed."[26] (6) Then Abram rose up early in the morning and he smashed the idols of his fathers and he went and recounted[27] these words to his father and to the priest of Ur,[28] but they did not believe him,[29] and then the priest of

---

21. and be complete – The Hebrew reads, "and exist complete." Use the verb of existence היה with the noun (adjective).
22. and then go – The nuance of "then" is communicated through the Vav of the Vav-consecutive with the perfect, which continues the imperative (forsake) with succession ("and then," §6h). If the meaning had been simply "forsake and go" then the second word would be an imperative with a connecting Vav (JM §119l).
23. you and your wife – These words, which could have been left out since the imperative implies them, are emphatic (§19i; JM §146c; GKC §135a; BDB 215b 1d). The meaning may be paraphrased: "you and your wife – not your father or your mother or some other person" (Exod 18:19; 24:1).
24. from your land and from the house of your father – Hebrew generally repeats the preposition when the same preposition governs more than one noun (JM §132g; the preposition is also frequently repeated in apposition, Gen 32:19 and JM §131i). This repetition of the preposition is similar to the repetition of the "governing noun" of the construct package (1.19). Many prepositions were originally "governing nouns" in a construct package. In Arabic (and Hebrew) the object of prepositions is in the genitive case, thus indicating the construct (annexation) relationship. Moreover, in Arabic (and Hebrew) the prepositions themselves are in the accusative case, usually as accusatives of time and place.
25. and I will make you famous – The Hebrew reads, "and I will make for you a great name."
26. and all the nations of the earth will be blessed in your seed – Change the word order to, "and (they) will be blessed in your seed, all the nations of the earth." This word order continues the Vav-consecutive chain and neatly delays the subject by placing it after the prepositional phrase.
27. Then Abram smashed the idols of his fathers and he went and recounted – The word "then" is the Vav of the Vav-consecutive. The Piel of שָׁבַר is intensive/extensive. The intensive/extensive Piel exaggerates the action by intensifying the force of the action (שָׁבַר, to break; שִׁבֵּר, to smash to pieces) and/or extending the action to many objects (to smash one object after another); therefore, its object is usually plural, or it has many objects. Intensive/extensive Piels are physical actions that are able to be intensified (burying and sacrificing, for example, cannot be done with more force) and have a similar meaning in the Qal and the Piel (Qal: breaking, Piel: smashing; these are similar in meaning). These physical actions are usually performed by the hands or feet, not by the senses, such as speaking, thinking, seeing, hearing, etc. Their objects are usually concrete, not abstract, and sometimes cease to exist after the action of the intensive/extensive Piel is completed. Usually, an intensive action is also extensive, but an extensive action may not be intensive, as זִבֵּחַ and קִבֵּר (§7c, g; Extensive action, a type of intensification, intensifies an action by extending the action to many objects, but not by increasing the force of action). Similarly, nouns built on the Piel stem exaggerate the meaning of the word by describing someone intensively/extensively doing an activity or someone possessing the quality intensively/extensively. These noun formations are ideal for indicating a profession (a job done time and time again, extensively, §23h; JM §88H a; GKC §84b a-b), so that a גַּנָּב is not a one-time thief, but a person who purloins professionally and continually (GKC §52f; Joüon 52d, French edition). For this context, the meaning of the Piel would be "Then Abram smashed the gods of his fathers into pieces one after another (until few or none were left)."
28. to his father and to the priest of Ur – Note the repetition of the preposition (1.24).
29. but they did not believe him – The adversative word "but" is the Hebrew particle Vav (connected to the negative). Context determines the meaning of particles. This Vav, especially with negatives, conveys antithesis or opposition, an adversative clause (Gen 8:9; 31:7; §83c; JM §172; GKC §163). The negative breaks the Vav-consecutive chain. Place the negative before the verb,

Ur rebuked Abram and said,[30] "Can a man see[31] (the) gods or can a man hear (the) gods?" (7) And Abram answered and said, "I have forsaken my gods[32] and the idols of my fathers I have smashed to pieces; and I trust in the Lord,[33] and for his word I wait."[34] (8) Then Terah said to Abram,[35] "Leave my house and my land and go[36] after your God; you must not return to me[37] and you must not see my face again."

---

which now must be a perfect for past, completed action. The next clause (and then the priest rebuked) begins a new Vav-consecutive chain. For the words "believe him," the Hebrew reads, "believe to (לְ) him." The preposition with its object receiving the action of the verb directly is an improper object (§13s).

30. and said – 1.18.
31. Can a man see – For questions in direct speech and in the present tense, use the imperfect (indicative, §4e). To emphasize the subject, place the subject before the verb (§11cc, 38e). In direct speech, the subject is often emphasized when placed before the verb – "Can (any) man (and therefore, especially you, Abram) see or hear God?"
32. I have forsaken my gods – Place "my gods" before the verb for emphasis (§11uu), but leave "the idols of my father" after the verb. The Hebrew perfect also communicates a variety of meanings, though not as much variety as the imperfect. This Hebrew perfect is like the Greek perfect: an action completed in the past, with the effects still continuing in the present. The verb may be paraphrased, "I have forsaken the idols in the past and I am forsaking them still in the present" (§3h; JM §112e; GKC §106g). Context determines whether a perfect is a simple past, as often found in narration (I forsook) or like a Greek perfect, as often found in direct speech and poetry (I have forsaken and I forsake still). The issue is whether the present is in view or not. If the perfect verb is completed up to and including the present (many Hebrew perfects, like Greek perfects, may be translated as present tense verbs), it is similar to a Greek perfect; if the verb does not apply to the present, it is usually a simple past tense.
33. and I trust in the Lord – The Hebrew reads "And in the Lord I trust." This verb often takes a ב preposition to complete its meaning (BDB 105a I3). The object is improper (1.29).
34. and for his word I wait – First person perfects expressing the exercise of the mind, will, or emotion, are often perfects of certitude. Often found in poetry and direct speech, the perfect of certitude conveys certainty and strong statements of the will. Three of the last four verbs (forsaken, trust, and wait) are perfects of certitude (§3i).
35. Then Terah said to Abram – The Hebrew reads, "And Terah said to Abram." Hebrew allows either אֶל־ or לְ as the preposition after אָמַר or דִּבֵּר: אֶל־ is more frequent, but לְ is also common (BDB 56a 1, 181b 3b-c).
36. and go – Use the connecting Vav with the imperative (1.22; §6v).
37. you must not return to me – The Hebrew reads, "to me you must not return." The word order emphasizes "to me." Normally, Hebrew expresses a prohibition by אַל with the jussive or לֹא with the imperfect indicative (second person). אַל with the jussive is the negative of the will and thought, rejecting or deprecating (Greek μή). לֹא with the imperfect indicative (second person) negates a statement or fact, contradicting or denying (Greek οὐ). In prohibitions, לֹא with the imperfect indicative (second person) is the stronger negative, demanding obedience, like a law or formal command/charge. Hence, the nuance "must" in the clause: you *must* not return, or thou *shalt* not return (§4i, 42a-c; JM §113m; GKC §107o). אַל with the jussive is the prohibition expressing emotion and volition, desiring obedience: do not return (GKC §109c). Either construction could have been used here. This construction, לֹא with the imperfect indicative, is a harsher, more uncompromising, more abrupt statement than אַל with the jussive.

(9) Now Abram had taken[38] a wife whose name (was) Sarai,[39] and she heard[40] the word which Abram spoke to his father, but[41] she did not speak to Abram, her husband, a word, and she kept[42] the matter in her heart.

(10) Then Abram rose up and went to Haran[43] as the Lord had spoken[44] to him, and Lot, the son of his brother, went with him,[45] and they dwelt in Haran.

---

38. Now Abram had taken – The distinction between the verbal and nominal clause is essential to a proper understanding of Hebrew syntax (§11b–c, x, §38). This important distinction between nominal and verbal clauses necessitated that grammarians distinguish their subjects and verbs. In a verbal clause, the subject is called the agent because it is the doer of the action; its verb is called the verb or action because it is the event. In nominal clauses, the subject is called the initiator because it starts a new beginning instead of another action of a verbal clause; its verb is called the announcement because it makes an announcement or some statement describing the initiator. Verbal clauses focus on the verb, its occurrence, development, and progress; nominal clauses focus on the initiator, its identity, description, and characterization.

    The nominal clause breaks the successive actions of the Vav-consecutives (verbal clauses) and describes its noun (the initiator, Abram) by supplying details important for the narrative. Since the initiator must precede its announcement and since a completed, past action is desired in this narrative, the announcement employs a perfect. Context determines the proper English tense for translating the perfect – in this case, an English past perfect. Although Semitic lacks a past perfect category, the Semitic perfect may include the notion of the past perfect (§3f). In this context, the Vav-consecutive would indicate that Abram married Sarai after Abram's conversation with Terah. The nominal clause depicts Abram as having taken a wife sometime in the past probably before his conversation with Terah. The next clause, another nominal clause, describes Abram's wife by supplying her name. The first nominal clause has a verbal clause as the predicate (announcement). This sentence, a nominal clause, parses as follows:

אִשָּׁה לָקַח	אַבְרָם
Verbal clause, predicate (announcement) of sentence. Implied "he" of third person verb is subject of verbal clause.	Subject of entire sentence

39. whose name – The Hebrew reads, "and her name (was)."
40. and she heard – The Vav-consecutive may continue the preceding perfect, but context here is against it. This Vav-consecutive is continuing the narrative after Abram's conversation with Terah. The preceding perfect added descriptive information about Abram and Sarai concerning what happened prior to the conversation. This Vav-consecutive continues or advances the narrative after Abram's conversation with his father.
41. but – A Vav introduces this adversative clause (1.29; §83c).
42. and she kept – This Vav-consecutive continues the adversative idea of the preceding verb.
43. to Haran – Use the accusative ending ָה (IBH 10.11).
44. Lord had spoken – The Hebrew perfect may, in certain contexts, be translated as a past perfect (§3f).
45. and Lot, the son of his brother, went with him – The word order is, "and (he) went with him, Lot, the son of his brother."

Key to Composition One

1 וַיְהִי־נַ֭עַר מֵאֶ֣רֶץ א֔וּר וּשְׁמ֖וֹ אַבְרָ֣ם בֶּן־תָּֽרַח׃

2 וַיֵּ֣לֶךְ אֶל־הֵיכַ֣ל א֔וּר לִזְבֹּ֥חַ זֶ֖בַח לֵֽאלֹהֵ֥י אֲבֹתָ֖יו וּלְגִלּוּלֵיהֶֽם׃

3 וְהָיָ֞ה כַּאֲשֶׁ֤ר יַֽעֲלֶה֙ אַבְרָ֔ם אֶל־הֵיכַ֣ל אוּר֙ שָׁנָ֣ה ׀ שָׁנָ֔ה וְזָבַ֥ח שָׁ֖ם עַל־מִזְבַּ֣ח אֱלֹהָ֑יו
וּבֵרַ֥ךְ אֹת֛וֹ הַכֹּהֵ֖ן וְשָׁ֥ב אֶל־בֵּיתֽוֹ׃

4 וַֽיְהִ֗י כְּהִתְפַּלֵּ֨ל אַבְרָ֜ם אֶל־אֱלֹהָיו֙ בְּהֵיכַ֣ל א֔וּר וַיֵּרָ֨א אֵלָ֤יו יְהוָה֙ בָּעֵ֣ת הַהִ֔יא וַיֹּ֖אמֶר
אֲנִ֣י יְהוָה֙ אֱלֹהֵ֤י הַשָּׁמַ֙יִם֙ וֵֽאלֹהֵ֣י הָאָ֔רֶץ הִתְהַלֵּ֥ךְ לְפָנַ֖י וֶהְיֵ֥ה תָמִֽים׃

5 עֲזֹ֨ב אֱלֹהֶ֜יךָ וְגִלּוּלֵ֣י אֲבוֹתֶ֗יךָ וְהָֽלַכְתָּ֤ אַתָּה֙ וְאִשְׁתְּךָ֙ מֵאַרְצְךָ֙ וּמִבֵּ֣ית אָבִ֔יךָ וְעָשִׂ֥יתִי
לְךָ֖ שֵׁ֣ם גָּד֑וֹל וְנִבְרְכ֣וּ בְזַרְעֲךָ֔ כָּל־גּוֹיֵ֖י הָאָֽרֶץ׃

6 וַיַּשְׁכֵּ֨ם אַבְרָ֜ם בַּבֹּ֗קֶר וַיְשַׁבֵּר֙ אֶת־גִּלּוּלֵ֣י אֲבֹתָ֔יו וַיֵּ֗לֶךְ וַיְסַפֵּר֙ אֶת־הַדְּבָרִ֣ים הָאֵ֔לֶּה
לְאָבִ֖יו וּלְכֹהֵן־א֑וּר וְלֹ֥א הֶאֱמִ֖ינוּ ל֑וֹ וַיּ֨וֹכַח כֹּהֵן־אוּר֙ אֶת־אַבְרָ֔ם וַיֹּ֖אמֶר הָאִ֣ישׁ
יִרְאֶ֣ה אֱלֹהִ֔ים א֖וֹ הָאִ֥ישׁ יִשְׁמַ֖ע אֱלֹהִֽים׃

7 וַיַּ֣עַן אַבְרָ֗ם וַיֹּ֙אמֶר֙ אֶת־אֱלֹהַ֣י עָזַ֔בְתִּי וְאֶת־גִּלּוּלֵ֥י אֲבוֹתַ֖י שִׁבַּ֑רְתִּי וּבַֽיהוָ֣ה בָּטַ֔חְתִּי
וְלִדְבָר֖וֹ קִוִּֽיתִי׃

8 וַיֹּ֣אמֶר תֶּ֗רַח אֶל־אַבְרָם֙ עֲזֹ֣ב בֵּיתִ֔י וְאַרְצִ֖י וְלֵ֣ךְ אַחֲרֵ֣י־אֱלֹהֶ֑יךָ אֵלַ֣י לֹ֣א תָשׁ֔וּב וְאֶת־
פָּנַ֖י לֹ֥א תִרְאֶ֖ה עֽוֹד׃

9 וְאַבְרָ֥ם לָקַ֛ח אִשָּׁ֖ה וּשְׁמָ֣הּ שָׂרָ֑י וַתִּשְׁמַ֣ע אֶת־הַדָּבָ֗ר אֲשֶׁ֨ר דִּבֶּ֤ר אַבְרָם֙ אֶל־אָבִ֔יו
וְלֹ֨א דִבְּרָ֜ה לְאַבְרָ֣ם אִישָׁהּ֙ דָּבָ֔ר וַתִּשְׁמֹ֥ר אֶת־הַדָּבָ֖ר בְּלִבָּֽהּ׃

10 וַיָּ֣קָם אַבְרָם֙ וַיֵּ֣לֶךְ חָרָ֔נָה כַּאֲשֶׁ֛ר דִּבֶּ֥ר אֵלָ֖יו יְהוָ֑ה וַיֵּ֤לֶךְ אִתּוֹ֙ ל֣וֹט בֶּן־אָחִ֔יו וַיֵּשְׁב֖וּ
בְּחָרָֽן׃

Unpointed Text of Composition One

1 ויהי־נער מארץ אור ושמו אברם בן־תרח׃

2 וילך אל־היכל אור לזבח זבח לאלהי אבתיו ולגלוליהם׃

3 והיה כאשר יעלה אברם אל־היכל אור שנה שנה וזבח שם על־מזבח אלהיו
וברך אתו הכהן ושב אל־ביתו׃

4 ויהי כהתפלל אברם אל־אלהיו בהיכל אור וירא אליו יהוה בעת ההיא ויאמר
אני יהוה אלהי השמים ואלהי הארץ התהלך לפני והיה תמים׃

5 עזב אלהיך וגלולי אבותיך והלכת אתה ואשתך מארצך ומבית אביך ועשיתי
לך שם גדול ונברכו בזרעך כל־גויי־הארץ׃

6 וישכם אברם בבקר וישבר את־גלולי אבתיו וילך ויספר את־הדברים האלה
לאביו ולכהן־אור ולא האמינו לו ויוכח כהן־אור את־אברם ויאמר האיש
יראה אלהים או האיש ישמע אלהים׃

7 ויען אברם ויאמר את־אלהי עזבתי ואת־גלולי אבותי שברתי וביהוה בטחתי
ולדברו קויתי׃

8 ויאמר תרח אל־אברם עזב ביתי וארצי ולך אחרי־אלהיך אלי לא תשוב ואת־
פני לא תראה עוד׃

9 ואברם לקח אשה ושמה שרי ותשמע את־הדבר אשר דבר אברם אל־אביו
ולא דברה לאברם אישה דבר ותשמר את־הדבר בלבה׃

10 ויקם אברם וילך חרנה כאשר דבר אליו יהוה וילך אתו לוט בן־אחיו וישבו
בחרן׃

COMPOSITION TWO

(1) After these things the word of the Lord came to Abram in Haran, saying, (2) "Go now from Haran and journey for yourself to the land which I shall in fact show you# that I might bless you* and make you famous. (3) Only command your sons and your house after you that they might keep the way of the Lord so that it might be well for you and for your house." (4) Then Abram answered and said to the Lord, "If I have found grace in your eyes, let me return please to my father and to my father's house that I might report to them concerning the covenant that you have made with me." (5) And the Lord said to Abram, "Return to the house of your father and say to your father, walk about in my ways so that you might live." (6) And Abram said, "Blessed be the Lord for his mercy is forever."

(7) Then Abram returned to his father's house and spoke to his father the word which the Lord commanded him.* (8) Then Terah rejoiced (with) a great rejoicing and said, "I will praise the Lord all the days and I will trust in his salvation forever. (9) Go now my son in peace, may the Lord my God bless you* and keep you* so that he might bring upon you all that he has promised you and that you might prosper your way.

(10) Then Abram and Sarai, his wife, rose up and went to Haran. (11) Then Abram said to Sarai, "Now we will journey to the land which the Lord has shown us* and we will keep the word of the Lord so that He might bless us and keep us in the way in which we will go. (12) Indeed, I know that the Lord will lead us* in all of his ways."

(13) Then Abram journeyed to the land of Canaan, and the Lord was with Abram and he prospered his way.

( ) – Not in Hebrew, but needed for English
[ ] – In the Hebrew, but not needed for English
* – Put the pronominal suffix directly on the verb
# – Put the pronominal suffix with energic Nun directly on the verb

(1) After these things[1] the word of the Lord came to[2] Abram in Haran, saying, (2) "Go now[3] from Haran and journey[4] for yourself[5] to the land[6] which I shall in fact show you[#] that I might bless[7]

---

1. After these things – A common temporal phrase (Gen. 15:1; 1.1; §80c; JM §166k; BDB 29b 2b). Frequently, וַיְהִי precedes this temporal phrase (Gen 22:1; 39:7).
2. the word of the Lord came to – The Hebrew word for "came" is היה. The appropriate preposition with this construction is אֶל־.
3. Go now – The nuance "now" is supplied by the energic (furnishing energy or emphasis) particle נָא. Arabic also preserves the energic particle נָא in special energic forms of the imperfect. The נָא particle adds an element of exhortation or urgency, especially when God uses the word (Gen 13:14; 15:5; 22:2). In other contexts, the נָא expresses politeness (please), an earnest request or appeal, or a softened command (§5e, 4r-u; JM §105c; GKC §105b and fn 1–2, p. 308; BDB 609a).
4. and journey – The conjunctive Vav unites two imperatives without the notion of succession or purpose (1.22, 36).
5. for yourself – This prepositional phrase is similar to the ethical dative of Greek and Latin, though Semitic lacks the dative case. Also called the dative of feeling, the ethical dative denotes the interest of the speaker, or it is used to secure the interest of the person spoken to, so that the verbal action is done *for* the subject. The preposition ל throws the action back to the subject so that the action is done to (or at) the pleasure or option of the subject; hence, the subject performs the action of the verb to his own satisfaction or interest. To communicate the ethical dative, Hebrew uses a first or second person verb with an agreeing pronoun connected to the preposition ל (third person for the dative of advantage or disadvantage). This construction, usually with verbs of motion and transitive verbs, is common with first person imperfects and imperatives. Semitic grammarians refer to this as a "ל of benefit" (Judg 1:1; JM §133d; GKC §119s; BDB 515b 5h).
6. to the land which I shall in fact show you – Use the accusative ending ה ָ for the noun and the energic suffix for the verb (§4r-u). The energic suffix lends more energy or emotion to the statement. The words "in fact" communicate the energic suffix. This is a covenantal statement, an assured promise, a guaranteed assertion. Moreover, this energic form probably indicates that the next two verbs are emphatic as well. In the following verb (bless), the pronominal suffix "hides" the energic cohortative form because the pronominal suffix conceals the final Qames-He of the cohortative. The last verb of the verse (make), an R3-weak verb, does not have cohortative forms. The cohortative of R3-weak verbs must be discerned by context. The verb with the energic suffix furnishes the context. Emphatic statements often come in clusters, not just in an isolated statements (Num 23:25–29; 24:10–11).
7. that I might bless – This is a purpose clause, but instead of using the ל with the infinitive construct, use the Vav-conjunctive connected to an imperfect (which is actually a hidden cohortative, see 2.6). Most imperfects with Vav-conjunctive (V^{ə}yiqtol) in narrative express purpose (§6u, 53c). This construction is another way that Hebrew expresses the subjunctive (§4j).

   Joüon calls this construction an indirect volitive (for the volitive, see IBH 18.4; JM §114). To Joüon, a (direct) volitive is a jussive, cohortative, or imperative (JM §114). An indirect volitive is a Vav-conjunctive connected to a jussive, cohortative, or imperative expressing purpose (or in Joüon's terminology, a consecutive clause, JM §116, 169). It would be misleading, however, to think that only jussives, cohortatives, and imperatives are "volitional." Most imperfects have a volitional element. The translation "will" of the imperfect often should be understood as indicating volition, not tense (1 Kgs 1:5; §4a). This volitional element may be strengthened by energic forms (cohortative and energic Nuns in suffixes), particles (especially, נָא), and independent pronouns preceding an imperfect.

   The Vav, like all particles, must derive its meaning from the context. When the Vav connects grammatical equals (for example, two nouns, boys and girls; two verbs, eat and drink), the Vav is juxtaposing words. When, however, the Vav does more than link grammatical equals, the Vav is said to be energic. That is, the meaning of the Vav has more energy of meaning than the juxtaposing "and." All Vayyiqtol forms are energic – and then, and so, etc. – as are most V^{ə}qatal and V^{ə}yiqtol forms. In direct speech and poetry, the V^{ə}yiqtol forms are sometimes

you* and make you famous.[8] (3) Only command[9] your sons and your house after you that they might keep[10] the way of the Lord so that it might be well[11] for you and for your house."[12] (4) Then Abram answered and said to the Lord, "If I have found grace in your eyes, let me return please[13] to my father and to my father's house that I might report to them concerning the covenant that you have made[14] with me." (5) And the Lord said to Abram, "Return to the house of your father and say to your father, walk about in my ways so that you might live."[15] (6) And Abram said, "Blessed be[16] the Lord for his mercy is forever."[17]

(7) Then Abram returned to his father's house[18] and spoke to his father the word which the Lord commanded him.* (8) Then Terah rejoiced (with) a great rejoicing[19] and

---

energic, sometimes juxtaposing, context deciding. There is, however, a general rule for narrative: the Vᵊyiqtol form is usually energic (§6u), expressing purpose when following imperfects (especially jussives and energic forms) and imperatives, or as Joüon says, "Indirect volitives usually follow direct volitives" (JM §116b, d, f; JM §115–116). For example, in this composition sentence, an indirect volitive follows (or connects to) the imperative (a direct imperative, "journey"), not the verb of the relative clause (show).

8. and make you famous – The Hebrew reads, "And I will make for you a great name." Again, attach a conjunctive Vav to the imperfect (which is actually a hidden cohortative, see 2.6).
9. command – In R3-Vav/Yod verbs, the ending for the imperative 2ms is usually ה ֵ (צַוֵּה); however, the imperative 2ms often apocopates (cuts off) the ending with a hovering Dagesh צַו (IBH 37.4.2.4 and 37.4.3; JM §79i-j).
10. that they might keep – This Vᵊyiqtol form conveys purpose and follows an imperative, "command" (2.7).
11. so that it might be well – Use Vᵊyiqtol again.
12. and for your house – Repeat the preposition (1.8).
13. let me return please – Use the cohortative with the energic particle נָא. The cohortative, an energic form, strongly expresses the emotion of an earnest request or urgent appeal (2.6; §4r-u). Common in prayers, the cohortative by itself or with נָא always expresses strong feelings or emotions.
14. you have made – The last letter of the verb כרת assimilates with the 2ms ending of the perfect.
15. so that you might live – This is also a purpose clause. This time, however, attach the Vav-conjunctive not to an imperfect, but to an imperative (Uqᵊtol). Purpose clauses with Vav-conjunctives attached to imperatives are rare. Imperatives with Vav-conjunctives are used for purpose clauses for second persons (you). In the first half of the sentence (return to the house of your father and say), two imperatives are connected by a conjunctive Vav (juxtaposition); in the latter half of the sentence, an imperative with energic Vav connects to the first imperative to express purpose. In form, these two constructions are identical, but in meaning, they are different. The first construction links two imperatives: "return and say." The second construction links a direct imperative with an indirect imperative: "walk about in my ways *to the intent that* you might live," not "walk about in my ways and live." Again, context decides whether a Vav is juxtaposing or energic. With imperatives, the Vav is usually juxtaposing, but occasionally energic (Gen 20:7 energic Vav; §6w; JM §116f).
16. Blessed be – This is the Qal passive participle of the root ברך.
17. for his mercy is forever – The Hebrew reads, "for forever (is) his mercy."
18. to his father's house – Use the accusative ending ה ָ. The Hebrew reads, "to the house of his father."
19. rejoiced [with] great rejoicing – This construction, though resembling the construction of 1.6, is different. The construction of 1.6 is idiomatic, without emphasis; this construction, the absolute object, is emphatic. The construction of 1.6 has a *concrete* object; the absolute object is an *abstract* object.

    Traditional Semitic grammarians (Medieval Arab and Jewish grammarians) considered the absolute object as "prior to all other objects" (Wechter, 52) and as "the truest object, since it expresses the very essence of the (abstract) action which the agent (subject) executes, causes, and brings into existence" (Ibid). Hence, the traditional grammarians call this construction "absolute,"

said,[20] "I will praise[21] the Lord all the days and I will trust[22] in his salvation forever. (9) Go now[23] my son in peace,[24] may the Lord my God bless you* and keep you*[25] so that he might bring upon you all that he has promised you so that you might prosper your way.[26]

(10) Then Abram and Sarai, his wife, rose up and went[27] to Haran.[28] (11) Then Abram said to Sarai, "Now[29] we will journey to the land which the Lord has shown us* and we will

---

because the object *is* the verbal action itself, without restriction or modification. This should be distinguished from the direct object, which receives the verbal action "directly," or the indirect (adverbial) accusative, which receives the verbal action "indirectly," usually translated adverbially.

Absolute objects have varied characteristics. Absolute objects may be infinitive absolutes or abstract nouns of action. Infinitive absolutes may be modified by another infinitive absolute (§13f) or a part of speech substituting for the infinitive absolute (§13g–i). The infinitive absolute cannot be pluralized. Abstract nouns of action are usually modified by an adjective or adverb and may be pluralized (§13e). Both types of absolute objects are indefinite, though they may be specialized. When the infinitive absolute lacks a modifier, it is more "absolute" than the infinitive absolute that is modified (restricted) or than the abstract noun (§13c). Finally, the subject executes, causes, and brings into existence the absolute object. If these characteristics are not present, the construction is probably idiomatic (1.6), not the absolute object.

In this context, the abstract noun (rejoicing) with its modifier (great) explains the verb by expressing the quality of the action (a rejoicing to remember) and the manner of the action (he rejoiced – with a great rejoicing).

The absolute object represents the verbal action in its purest, most ideal, *absolute* sense – or, put differently, the subject performs the verbal action in its purest, most ideal manner. Arab grammarians often translate such constructions, "Terah rejoiced – and what a rejoicing (it was)" (§13b–j, 17d–j; GKC §117p–r and fn 3, p. 367).

20. and said – 1.18.
21. I will praise – The imperfect indicative would adequately convey the volitional nuance of the verb (§4a). Use the cohortative to emphasize the determination of the speaker's will (§4r–u; JM §114b; GKC §108a): "I *will* praise." The word "will" expresses volition as much as or more than tense.
22. and I will trust – The Vav is a juxtaposing Vav (and) connecting two cohortatives.
23. Go now – Use the emphatic imperative, an energic form, to add urgency and emotion to the imperative (§4r).
24. in peace – Hebrew can express adverbial nuances through the prepositions ב and ל connected to a noun: "Go peaceably now." Driver describes this ב as, "the state or condition, whether material or mental, *in* which the action takes place" (BDB 88b I, 6). This construction substitutes for an accusative of situation (§13z, ii). The prepositions are encroaching on the fading case system of Biblical Hebrew.
25. and keep you – The Vav is juxtaposing, not energic.
26. that you might prosper your way – 2.15.
27. Then Abram and Sarai, his wife, rose up and went – This is an idiomatic expression meaning, "Abram and Sarai, his wife, *began to go* or *started out to go*." To express the incipient notion of "to begin, to start out," Hebrew employs the verb קום followed closely by another verb, usually a verb of motion, such as הלך, יצא, or עלה (Gen 13:17; 19:15; 27:43; 31:44; 1 Sam 3:9; BDB 878a 6c; GKC §120g). Similarly, the verb הלך may also be "weakened to (a) mere introductory word," such as "come (on)" (1 Sam 9:9; BDB 234a I5f).
28. to Haran – Use the accusative ending ָה.
29. Now – Use the Hebrew particle עַתָּה, not the emphatic particle נָא. עַתָּה usually occurs at the beginning of clauses; נָא after verbs or negative particles. The word, עַתָּה, originally a noun (related to עֵת) became a particle. Note the accusative ending, reflected in the Qames-He. This particle is always in the position of an accusative of time, expressing unspecified time (§13x).

keep[30] the word of the Lord so that he might bless us and keep us[31] in the way in which we will go.[32] (12) Indeed,[33] I know[34] that the Lord will lead us* in all of his ways."

(13) Then Abram journeyed to the land[35] of Canaan, and the Lord was[36] with Abram and he prospered his way.

---

30. and we will keep – Usually, the Vᵊqatal form denotes temporal succession: "and then we will keep." But a logical consecution (therefore, so, consequently) is also possible, "and, therefore (so, hence), we will keep" (§6g; JM §119d-e).
31. and keep us – 2.7.
32. in the way in which we will go – The Hebrew reads, "in the way which we will go in it." The retrospective pronoun (or particle) frequently defines or limits the relative pronoun אֲשֶׁר, which was probably a simple connective link. The retrospective pronoun (and preposition), "in it," clarifies the function and meaning of the antecedent בַּדֶּרֶךְ in the relative clause. (IBH 26.2.2. In relative clauses, retrospective pronouns frequently occur after adjectives, participles, and negative clauses. §43, 44a; GKC §155h-i)
33. Indeed – This is גַּם, the adverb that denotes addition (moreover, also) or emphasis on the following word, as here (BDB 169a 1).
34. I know – Render this perfect as a present tense. 1.32.
35. to the land of Canaan – Use the accusative ending ה ָ.
36. and the Lord was – Use the Vayyiqtol form for temporal consecution, "and then the Lord was" (§6o, 81c; JM §118h).

Key to Composition Two

1 אַחַ֣ר׀ הַדְּבָרִ֣ים הָאֵ֗לֶּה הָיָ֛ה דְּבַ֥ר יְהוָ֖ה אֶל־אַבְרָ֥ם בְּחָרָ֖ן לֵאמֹֽר׃

2 לֶךְ־נָא֙ מֵֽחָרָ֔ן וְסַ֣ע לְךָ֔ אַ֣רְצָה אֲשֶׁ֣ר אַרְאֶ֔ךָּ וַאֲבָֽרֶכְךָ֔ וְאֶֽעֱשֶׂה־לְּךָ֖ שֵׁ֥ם גָּדֽוֹל׃

3 רַ֗ק צַ֣ו בָּנֶ֙יךָ֙ וּבֵיתְךָ֣ אַחֲרֶ֔יךָ וְיִשְׁמְר֖וּ דֶּֽרֶךְ־יְהוָ֑ה וְיִיטַ֥ב לְךָ֖ וּלְבֵיתֶֽךָ׃

4 וַיַּ֣עַן אַבְרָ֗ם וַיֹּ֙אמֶר֙ אֶל־יְהוָ֔ה אִם־מָצָ֨אתִי חֵ֤ן בְּעֵינֶ֙יךָ֙ אָשֽׁוּבָה־נָּ֞א אֶל־אָבִ֣י וְאֶל־
בֵּית־אָבִ֗י וְאַגִּ֣יד לָהֶ֔ם עַל־הַבְּרִ֕ית אֲשֶׁ֥ר כָּרַ֖תָּ עִמִּֽי׃

5 וַיֹּ֨אמֶר יְהוָ֜ה אֶל־אַבְרָ֗ם שׁ֚וּב אֶל־בֵּ֣ית אָבִ֔יךָ וֶֽאֱמֹ֙ר אֶל־אָבִ֔יךָ הִתְהַלֵּ֥ךְ בִּדְרָכַ֖י
וֶֽחְיֵֽה׃

6 וַיֹּ֗אמֶר אַבְרָ֔ם בָּר֣וּךְ יְהוָ֔ה כִּ֥י לְעוֹלָ֖ם חַסְדּֽוֹ׃

7 וַיֵּ֤שֶׁב אַבְרָם֙ בֵּ֣יתָה אָבִ֔יו וַיְדַבֵּ֞ר אֶל־אָבִ֗יו אֶת־הַדָּבָ֔ר אֲשֶׁ֥ר צִוָּ֖הוּ יְהוָֽה׃

8 וַיִּשְׂמַ֤ח תֶּ֙רַח֙ שִׂמְחָ֣ה גְדוֹלָ֔ה וַיֹּ֕אמֶר אֲהַלְלָ֥ה אֶת־יְהוָ֖ה כָּל־הַיָּמִ֑ים וְאֶבְטְחָ֖ה
בִּֽישׁוּעָת֖וֹ לְעוֹלָֽם׃

9 לְכָ֤ה בְנִי֙ בְּשָׁל֔וֹם יְבָֽרֶכְךָ֖ יְהוָ֣ה אֱלֹהַ֑י וְיִשְׁמְרֶ֔ךָ וְיָבִ֤יא עָלֶ֙יךָ֙ כָּל־אֲשֶׁ֣ר דִּבֶּר־לָ֔ךְ
וְהִצְלִ֖יחַ אֶת־דַּרְכֶּֽךָ׃

10 וַיָּק֣וּמוּ וַיֵּֽלְכ֗וּ אַבְרָ֛ם וְשָׂרַ֥י אִשְׁתּ֖וֹ חָרָֽנָה׃

11 וַיֹּ֨אמֶר אַבְרָ֜ם אֶל־שָׂרַ֗י עַתָּ֞ה נִסַּ֤ע אֶל־הָאָ֙רֶץ֙ אֲשֶׁ֣ר הִרְאָ֣נוּ יְהוָ֔ה וְשָׁמַ֖רְנוּ אֶת־דְּבַ֣ר
יְהוָ֑ה וִיבָרֵ֣ךְ אֹתָ֔נוּ וְיִשְׁמֹ֖ר אֹתָ֙נוּ֙ בַּדֶּ֔רֶךְ אֲשֶׁ֥ר נֵֽלֶךְ־בָּֽהּ׃

12 גַּ֣ם יָדַ֔עְתִּי כִּ֥י יוֹלִיכֵ֖נוּ יְהוָ֑ה בְּכָל־דְּרָכָֽיו׃

13 וַיִּסַּ֥ע אַבְרָ֖ם אַ֣רְצָה כְּנָ֑עַן וַיְהִ֤י יְהוָה֙ עִם־אַבְרָ֔ם וַיַּצְלַ֖ח אֶת־דַּרְכּֽוֹ׃

Unpointed Text of Composition Two

1 אחר הדברים האלה היה דבר יהוה אל־אברם בחרן לאמר׃

2 לך־נא מחרן וסע לך ארצה אשר אראך ואברכך ואעשה־לך שם גדול׃

3 רק צו בניך וביתך אחריך וישמרו דרך־יהוה וייטב לך ולביתך׃

4 ויען אברם ויאמר אל־יהוה אם־מצאתי חן בעיניך אשובה־נא אל־אבי ואל־בית־אבי ואגיד להם על־הברית אשר כרת עמי׃

5 ויאמר יהוה אל־אברם שוב אל־בית אביך ואמר אל־אביך התהלך בדרכי וחיה׃

6 ויאמר אברם ברוך יהוה כי לעולם חסדו׃

7 וישב אברם ביתה אביו וידבר אל־אביו את־הדבר אשר צוהו יהוה׃

8 וישמח תרח שמחה גדולה ויאמר אהללה את־יהוה כל־הימים ואבטחה בישועתו לעולם׃

9 לכה בני בשלום יברכך יהוה אלהי וישמרך ויביא עליך כל־אשר דבר־לך והצלח את־דרכך׃

10 ויקומו וילכו אברם ושרי אשתו חרנה׃

11 ויאמר אברם אל־שרי עתה נסע אל־הארץ אשר הראנו יהוה ושמרנו את־דבר יהוה ויברך אתנו וישמר אתנו בדרך אשר נלך־בה׃

12 גם ידעתי כי יוליכנו יהוה בכל־דרכיו׃

13 ויסע אברם ארצה כנען ויהי יהוה עם־אברם ויצלח את־דרכו׃

COMPOSITION THREE

(1) And there came to be a famine in the land and Abram said to Sarai, his wife, and to Lot, son of his brother, "The famine is very severe; let us go down to Egypt that we may live and that we may not die." (2) Then they went down to Egypt and they dwelt there. (3) Now Abram had said to Sarai before they came to Egypt, "Do not say to the Egyptians, 'He is my husband,' so consequently they will kill me, but they will keep you alive." (4) Then the servants of Pharaoh saw Sarai, the wife of Abram, that she was very beautiful, and they praised her to Pharaoh, and then Pharaoh summoned Sarai and took her, and she became a wife for him.

(5) And it happened after Pharaoh took Sarai for a wife that Lot said to the servant of Pharaoh, "she is the wife of Abram." (6) And it happened when Pharaoh heard the words of Lot that he became angry and said, "Abram must die." (7) In that night, Pharaoh had a dream, and God said to Pharaoh, "Behold you, you are dead, but Abram, my servant, will live; you must not touch Sarai and you must not come near to her, because on the day that you touch her, you will surely die, you and your house. (8) Give to him sheep, [and] cattle, [and] silver, [and] gold, and Sarai his wife and then send him away lest you should die."

(9) And it happened in that night that Pharaoh summoned Abram and said to him, "Please I do not want to die, and now, behold Sarai, your wife, take and go to your land, do not hesitate. (10) Then Pharaoh gave to Abram sheep, cattle, silver, gold, and many servants. (11) In the morning, (just as) the sun came out, [and] Pharaoh sent away Abram and Sarai, his wife, from the land of Egypt and all which was to him, and the Lord removed his plagues from [upon] the house of Pharaoh. (12) Now God had plagued (with) great plagues the house of Pharaoh because of Sarai. (13) And it happened when Abram went up from Egypt that God removed his plagues from [upon] the house of Pharaoh. (14) So then Pharaoh lived and did not die.

(15) Now Abram went up from Egypt – he, [and] Sarai, his wife, and Lot, son of his brother. (16) And Abram rejoiced with Sarai, but he was angry with Lot because he had told Pharaoh that Sarai was the wife of Abram.

( ) – Not in Hebrew, but needed for English
[ ] – In the Hebrew, but not needed for English
* – Put the pronominal suffix directly on the verb
# – Put the pronominal suffix with energic Nun directly on the verb

(1) And there came to be[1] a famine in the land and Abram said to Sarai, his wife, and to Lot, son of his brother, "The famine is very severe;[2] let us go down[3] to Egypt[4] that we may live and that we may not die."[5] (2) Then they went down to Egypt[6] and they dwelt there. (3) Now Abram had said[7] to Sarai before they came to Egypt,[8] "Do not say[9] to the Egyptians,[10] 'He is my husband,' so consequently[11] they will kill me, but they will keep you alive."[12] (4) Then the

1. And there came to be – The Vayyiqtol form, the characteristic of Hebrew narrative, often begins a narrative or book (1 Sam 1:1; Ruth 1:1; contrast with 1 Kgs 1:1; §3p, 6n–s; JM §118c).
2. The famine is very severe – The Hebrew reads, "severe the famine very." The Hebrew word order emphasizes the word "severe."
3. let us go down – The cohortative plural often emphasizes the speaker's will for a proposed group action (§4s; JM §114b).
4. to Egypt – Use the accusative ending ָה .
5. and that we may not die – To negate a purpose clause, specifically a jussive with Vav-conjunctive, Hebrew usually uses לֹא, rarely אַל, with the imperfect indicative (§41c). For this construction, Hebrew must separate the Vav from the imperfect and connect the Vav to the negative. Another common way to negate a purpose clause is the negative בִּלְתִּי (לְבִלְתִּי) with the infinitive construct (§18p, 41cc).
6. to Egypt – Use the accusative ending ָה .
7. Now Abram had said – This is a descriptive statement concerning Abram. Form a nominal clause, therefore, by placing Abram (the initiator) with a conjunctive Vav before the announcement (verb). The initiator of a nominal clause always expresses, explicitly or implicitly, a contrast with other possible initiators in the context. In this context, it is implicit since no other initator is directly constrasted (3.24, 39; §38d). The Vav connected to Abram communicates the nuance of "now." Since the first verbal action of sentence three occurs before the verbal actions of sentence two, a perfect would be the appropriate form in Hebrew, and a past perfect would be an appropriate English rendering for the Hebrew perfect in this context. As often happens, the nominal clause breaks the chain of verbal clauses for descriptive information concerning the initiator (1.38; §11b–c, x, 38).
8. before they came to Egypt – For this temporal clause, use the particle בְּטֶ֫רֶם with the imperfect (Gen 27:33; 37:18; 41:50; §80e; JM §166k, 113j; GKC §107c, 164d–e). The imperfect with certain particles – אָז, טֶ֫רֶם, בְּטֶ֫רֶם, עַד – conveys a preterit meaning (past tense). These particles are in the position of accusatives of time (§80).
9. do not say – Compare this prohibition with לֹא and the imperfect (1.37; §42a–c). This prohibition is less abrupt, less forceful, a kinder, gentler negative.
10. to the Egyptians – The Hebrew reads, "to Egypt." The country stands for the inhabitants (BDB 595b 2b). Hebrew indicates gentilics (citizens of a nation) by a Hireq-Yod, meaning "pertaining to," or "in relation to" (Arabic, Nisbah; §23j): מִצְרִי (ms, a man related to Egypt), מִצְרִים (mp); the feminine ending is Hireq-Yod followed by a ת for the singular מִצְרִית; וֹת for the feminine plural מִצְרִיֹּת (BDB 596b; Notice the gemination of the Yod to prevent consecutive vowels).

    Hebrew, like Aramaic and Arabic, uses this Hireq-Yod ending (Nisbah) with ordinal numbers (first, second, third, etc.), שֵׁנִי (masc), שֵׁנִית (fem) – pertaining to, or related to two, that is, second; with nouns to form Nisbah adjectives, יְמָנִי "right" from יָמִין "right hand, side"; תַּחְתִּי "lower" from תַּ֫חַת "under" (GKC §86h-i; JM §88m,g).
11. so consequently – This Vᵊqatal indicates a logical consecution (not temporal succession), "and so consequently" (2.30; 1 Kgs 1:45; §6g; JM §119e).
12. but they will keep you alive – To express contrast, Hebrew must scrap the Vᵊqatal form to avoid its usual succession meaning. Hebrew frequently employs a nominal clause to convey contrast (JM §118f). But here use a verbal clause and place the object before the verb to contrast the actions.

    Hebrew forgoes the Vav-consecutive construction (in addition to conveying negative clauses or various adverbial words) to express: (1) description (3.7; §11a–c, 38; JM §118d), (2) contrast (§83c; JM §118e–f), (3) simultaneous or nearly simultaneous action (§81d; JM §118f), (4)

servants of Pharaoh saw[13] Sarai, the wife of Abram, that she was very beautiful,[14] and they praised[15] her to Pharaoh, and then Pharaoh summoned Sarai and took her, and she became a wife for him.[16]

(5) And it happened after Pharaoh took[17] Sarai for a wife that Lot said[18] to the servant of Pharaoh, "she is the wife of Abram." (6) And it happened when Pharaoh heard[19] the words of Lot that he became angry[20] and said, "Abram must die."[21] (7) In that night, Pharaoh had a dream,[22] and God said to Pharaoh, "Behold you,[23] you are dead, but Abram, my servant, will

emphasis of the subject (Exod 9:23; §11cc), or (5) beginning/shifting a narrative or introducing/changing to a new grammatical subject (Gen 4:1; §11b, 38d-e). Of course, these categories may overlap.

13. Then the servants of Pharaoh saw – The Vayyiqtol forms of sentence two and four focus on the action and advance the narrative. The nominal clause of sentence three focuses on and describes Abram (the initiator). Furthermore, the nominal clause has a verbal clause as its announcement; therefore, while describing Abram, the verbal clause also expresses action. Nominal clauses without a finite verb do not express action, but they only describe the subject. Nominal clauses with a finite verb as announcement describe the initiator (or give an announcement about the initiator) and express action (1.38; §38d).
14. that she was very beautiful – The Hebrew word order is "that beautiful she (was) very."
15. and they praised – In constructing this verb, watch the double SQeNeMLeVY (IBH, chapter 4, footnote 5).
16. and she became a wife for him – The Hebrew reads, "and she came to be to him for a wife." The verb היה takes its predicate in the accusative, not the nominative (§13aa fn 49). Hebrew lacks a "to be" verb like English, Greek (εἰμί), or Latin (*sum*), which take predicates in the nominative. Being closer to Greek γίνομαι, or Latin, *fio* in meaning, Hebrew היה – meaning "come to be," "happen," "came about," "exist," "become," "arise," etc. – take predicates in the accusative (usually, an accusative of situation, see 6.15 [1]; BDB 225b II 1a). The accusative following היה, usually an accusative of situation, describes the condition, state, status, or situation of the subject (§13z-hh). For example, Genesis 1:2 reads – Now the earth (subject) came to be (הָיְתָה) in a condition (or state) of form and void (accusatives). In this line, "and she became a wife for him," the ל of לְאִשָּׁה substitutes for the accusative of situation, thereby having the same meaning as the accusative of situation – Then she came to be to him *in the status of* a wife" (§13ii).
17. And it happened after Pharaoh took – For this temporal clause, use the preposition אַחַר and the infinitive construct of לָקַח (§80c).
18. that Lot said – This Vav introduces the apodosis for the preceding temporal clause. The protasis is the subordinate clause in a conditional or temporal sentence; the apodosis is the independent clause for conditional and temporal sentences. For example, in the sentence "If (When) I come, then I will see you," the first clause is the protasis, the second clause, the apodosis. Of course, this Vayyiqtol form continues the past actions of the narrative (§76).
19. when Pharaoh heard – Use the infinitive construct for this temporal clause (§18d, 81a).
20. that he became angry – This is another example of the Vav introducing the apodosis for a temporal clause (3.18). For the verb, the Hebrew reads, "his nose was hot."
21. Abram must die – Place the subject first for emphasis (§11cc). The notion of "must" expresses the volition of the imperfect (2.7; §4a).
22. Pharaoh had a dream – The Hebrew reads, "Pharaoh dreamed a dream" (1.6, contrast with 2.19).
23. Behold you – Attach the pronominal suffix to the particle הִנֵּה.

live;[24] you must not touch Sarai[25] and you must not come near to her, because on the day that you touch her,[26] you will surely die, you and your house.[27] (8) Give to him sheep, [and] cattle, [and] silver, [and] gold,[28] and Sarai his wife and then send him away lest you should die."

(9) And it happened in that night that Pharaoh summoned Abram and said to him, "Please, I do not want to die,[29] and now, behold Sarai, your wife, take[30] and go to your land,[31] do not hesitate.[32] (10) Then Pharaoh gave to Abram sheep, cattle, silver, gold, and many servants.[33] (11) In the morning, (just as) the sun came out,[34] [and] Pharaoh sent away Abram and Sarai, his wife, from the land of Egypt and all which was to him,[35] and the Lord removed his plagues from [upon]

---

24. You are dead, but Abram, my servant, will live – For emphasis, put the independent pronoun as the initiator before the participle (the announcement), "Behold you, *You* are dead, . . ." (§19f; JM §146a; GKC §135). For contrast, Hebrew may employ a nominal clause. Place "Abram, my servant," before the verb. Here the contrast is explicit between Abram and the earlier pronoun, "you" (3.7).
25. you must not touch Sarai – 1.37.
26. because on the day that you touch her – The Hebrew reads, "on the day of your touching her." The word בְּיוֹם, in construct with the infinitive construct and its object, introduces a temporal clause within a causal clause. בְּיוֹם can annex a verb, infinitive construct, or a clause to form a temporal clause (§12m, 81b; JM §129p; GKC §130d).
27. you will surely die, you and your house – A singular verb with multiple agents is common in Hebrew and Arabic. The repetition of the pronoun and the addition of the noun, "your house," after the verb are emphatic (1.23; §11ss; GKC §146f).
28. [and] cattle, [and] silver, [and] gold – Hebrew may place the Vav before all nouns in a series (Gen 12:16) or only before the last noun in a series (1 Kgs 9:20; §25a; JM §177o).
29. Please, I do not want to die – To give greater emphasis to נָא (please), place it between the negative and the verb (Gen 13:8; 18:3; §40). The cohortative, stressing the volition, supplies the nuance of "want" (§4r-s; JM §114b).
30. behold Sarai, your wife, take – Use the emphatic imperative to continue the energic language of the preceding cohortative (2.6).
31. go to your land – The Hebrew reads, "to your land, go!" Use the emphatic imperative again (2.6).
32. do not hesitate – Notice that Pharaoh, under duress, uses the kinder, gentler negative to Abram (1.37).
33. cattle, silver, gold, and many servants – 3.28.
34. (just as) the sun came out – Another way in which Hebrew expresses temporal clauses is with consecutive nominal clauses connected by conjunctive Vav. Usually, these nominal clauses have perfects or nouns, such as participles, as predicates (§81d).

    The Hebrew reads, "the sun went out." Form a nominal clause by placing the initiator before the announcement. When two or more of these nominal clauses with verbs occur consecutively, they may, if the context indicates it, refer to closely successive or nearly contemporaneous action, to be translated – as soon as, just as, the moment that, (or just) when: "As soon as (or, the moment that) the sun came out, Pharaoh sent away . . . and the Lord removed." Like most nominal clauses, they contrast the subjects and the actions. The subjects, therefore, cannot be the same for the verbs, nor can the verbs be the same for the subjects (§38e).
35. and he sent away Abram and Sarai, his wife, from the land of Egypt and all which was to him – Hebrew style occasionally breaks up a pair or a series of subjects, objects, or prepositional phrases with an intervening clause or phrase. Instead of writing, "and he sent away Abram and Sarai, his wife, and all which was to them from Egypt," a Hebrew writer with class and style inserts a phrase or clause (from the land of Egypt) before the last word in a series or pair (objects: Gen 1:16; 34:29; subjects: Gen 41:27; Judg 6:5; prepositions: Gen 28:14; Deut 7:14).

the house of Pharaoh.[36] (12) Now God had plagued (with) great plagues[37] the house of Pharaoh because of Sarai. (13) And it happened when Abram went up[38] from Egypt that God removed his plagues from [upon] the house of Pharaoh. (14) So then Pharaoh lived and did not die.

(15) Now Abram went up from Egypt – he, [and] Sarai, his wife, and Lot, son of his brother.[39] (16) And Abram rejoiced with Sarai, but he was angry with Lot[40] because he had told Pharaoh that Sarai was the wife of Abram.[41]

---

36. from [upon] the house of Pharaoh – Compound prepositions, common after verbs of motion, usually have מִן or אֶל as the first preposition in the compound preposition (JM §133j).
37. (with) great plagues – This absolute object with a pluralized abstract noun and modifier explains the verb (2.19).
38. And it happened when Abram went up – Use the conjunction כַּאֲשֶׁר with the perfect verb to express the temporal clause (1.10; §80d).
39. Now Abram went up from Egypt – he, [and] Sarai, his wife, and Lot, son of his brother – Place the initiator with a conjunctive Vav before the announcement. The initiator, in this context, indicates a new beginning within the story or a shifting of the story. This nominal clause describes Abram, who had already gone up from Egypt in sentence thirteen. The initiator implicitly contrasts with other possible initiators (3.7, 24). The pronoun after the verb and the following nouns are emphatic (1.23, 3.12 [5], cf. Gen 7:18–19; §38d-e).
40. but he was angry with Lot – To express the contrast between Sarai and Lot, place the object (Lot) before the verb (3.12). Placing the object first emphasizes Lot by contrast to Sarai and avoids the Vav-consecutive construction (3.12).
41. Sarai was the wife of Abram – The Hebrew reads, "the wife of Abram (was) Sarai."

Key to Composition Three

1 וַיְהִי רָעָב בָּאָרֶץ וַיֹּאמֶר אַבְרָם אֶל־שָׂרַי אִשְׁתּוֹ וְאֶל־לוֹט בֶּן־אָחִיו כָּבֵד הָרָעָב
מְאֹד נֵרְדָה מִצְרַיְמָה וְנִחְיֶה וְלֹא נָמוּת׃

2 וַיֵּרְדוּ מִצְרַיְמָה וַיֵּשְׁבוּ שָׁם׃

3 וְאַבְרָם אָמַר אֶל־שָׂרַי בְּטֶרֶם יָבֹאוּ אֶל־מִצְרַיִם אַל־תֹּאמְרִי אֶל־מִצְרַיִם אִישִׁי הוּא
וְהָרְגוּ אֹתִי וְאֹתָךְ יְחַיּוּ׃

4 וַיִּרְאוּ עַבְדֵי פַרְעֹה אֶת־שָׂרַי אֵשֶׁת־אַבְרָם כִּי־יָפָה הִיא מְאֹד וַיְהַלְלוּ אֹתָהּ אֶל־
פַּרְעֹה וַיִּקְרָא פַרְעֹה לְשָׂרַי וַיִּקַּח אֹתָהּ וַתְּהִי לוֹ לְאִשָּׁה׃

5 וַיְהִי אַחֲרֵי־קַחַת פַּרְעֹה אֶת שָׂרַי לְאִשָּׁה וַיֹּאמֶר לוֹט אֶל־עֶבֶד פַּרְעֹה אֵשֶׁת אַבְרָם הִיא׃

6 וַיְהִי כִּשְׁמֹעַ פַּרְעֹה אֶת־דִּבְרֵי לוֹט וַיִּחַר אַפּוֹ וַיֹּאמֶר אַבְרָם יָמוּת׃

7 בַּלַּיְלָה הַהוּא חָלַם פַּרְעֹה חֲלוֹם וַיֹּאמֶר אֱלֹהִים אֶל־פַּרְעֹה הִנְּךָ אַתָּה מֵת וְאַבְרָם עַבְדִּי
יִחְיֶה לֹא תִגַּע בְּשָׂרַי וְלֹא תִקְרַב אֵלֶיהָ כִּי בְּיוֹם נָגְעֲךָ בָּהּ מוֹת תָּמוּת אַתָּה וּבֵיתֶךָ׃

8 תֶּן־לוֹ צֹאן וּבָקָר וָכֶסֶף וְזָהָב וְשָׂרַי אִשְׁתּוֹ וְשִׁלַּחְתָּ אֹתוֹ פֶּן־תָּמוּת׃

9 וַיְהִי בַּלַּיְלָה הַהוּא וַיִּקְרָא פַרְעֹה לְאַבְרָם וַיֹּאמֶר אֵלָיו אַל־נָא אָמוּתָה וְעַתָּה הִנֵּה
שָׂרַי אִשְׁתְּךָ קְחָה וְאֶל־אַרְצְךָ לֵכָה אַל־תְּאַחֵר׃

10 וַיִּתֵּן פַּרְעֹה לְאַבְרָם צֹאן בָּקָר כֶּסֶף זָהָב וַעֲבָדִים רַבִּים׃

11 בַּבֹּקֶר הַשֶּׁמֶשׁ יָצָא וּפַרְעֹה שִׁלַּח אֶת־אַבְרָם וְאֶת־שָׂרַי אִשְׁתּוֹ מֵאֶרֶץ מִצְרַיִם וְאֶת־
כָּל־אֲשֶׁר־לוֹ וַיָּסַר יהוה אֶת־נְגָעָיו מֵעַל בֵּית פַּרְעֹה׃

12 וֵאלֹהִים נָגַף בֵּית־פַּרְעֹה מַגֵּפוֹת גְּדוֹלוֹת בַּעֲבוּר שָׂרָי׃

13 וַיְהִי כַּאֲשֶׁר עָלָה אַבְרָם מִמִּצְרָיִם וַיָּסַר אֱלֹהִים אֶת־נְגָעָיו מֵעַל בֵּית פַּרְעֹה׃

14 וַיְחִי פַּרְעֹה וְלֹא מֵת׃

15 וְאַבְרָם עָלָה מִמִּצְרָיִם הוּא וְשָׂרַי אִשְׁתּוֹ וְלוֹט בֶּן־אָחִיו׃

16 וַיִּשְׂמַח אַבְרָם אֶת־שָׂרַי וּבְלוֹט חָרָה אַפּוֹ כִּי הִגִּיד לְפַרְעֹה כִּי אֵשֶׁת־אַבְרָם שָׂרָי׃

Unpointed Text of Composition Three

1 ויהי רעב בארץ ויאמר אברם אל־שרי אשתו ואל־לוט בן־אחיו כבד הרעב
מאד נרדה מצרימה ונחיה ולא נמות׃

2 וירדו מצרימה וישבו שם׃

3 ואברם אמר אל־שרי בטרם יבאו אל־מצרים אל־תאמרי אל־מצרים אישי הוא
והרגו אתי ואתך יחיו׃

4 ויראו עבדי פרעה את־שרי אשת־אברם כי־יפה היא מאד ויהללו אתה אל־
פרעה ויקרא פרעה לשרי ויקח אתה ותהי לו לאשה׃

5 ויהי אחרי־קחת פרעה את שרי לאשה ויאמר לוט אל־עבד פרעה אשת אברם היא׃

6 ויהי כשמע פרעה את־דברי לוט ויחר אפו ויאמר אברם ימות׃

7 בלילה ההוא חלם פרעה חלום ויאמר אלהים אל־פרעה הנך אתה מת ואברם עבדי
יחיה לא תגע בשרי ולא תקרב אליה כי ביום נגעך בה מות תמות אתה וביתך׃

8 תן־לו צאן ובקר וכסף וזהב ושרי אשתו ושלחת אתו פן־תמות׃

9 ויהי בלילה ההוא ויקרא פרעה לאברם ויאמר אליו אל־נא אמותה ועתה הנה
שרי אשתך קחה ואל־ארצך לכה אל־תאחר׃

10 ויתן פרעה לאברם צאן בקר כסף זהב ועבדים רבים׃

11 בבקר השמש יצא ופרעה שלח את־אברם ואת־שרי אשתו מארץ מצרים ואת־
כל־אשר־לו ויסר יהוה את־נגעיו מעל בית פרעה׃

12 ואלהים נגף בית־פרעה מגפות גדולות בעבור שרי׃

13 ויהי כאשר עלה אברם ממצרים ויסר אלהים את־נגעיו מעל בית פרעה׃

14 ויחי פרעה ולא מת׃

15 ואברם עלה ממצרים הוא ושרי אשתו ולוט בן־אחיו׃

16 וישמח אברם את־שרי ובלוט חרה אפו כי הגיד לפרעה כי אשת־אברם שרי׃

COMPOSITION FOUR

(1) Now there came to be strife between Abram and Lot and they disputed with one another. (2) And Abram said, "Please, let there not come to be strife between me and you; choose for yourself the land in which you will dwell, and get yourself separated please from [upon] me." (3) And so Lot dwelt in the cities of the plain, but Abram dwelt in the land of Canaan.

(4) After these things, [and] the Lord appeared to Abram and said, "I am the Lord, God of heaven and earth; I am cutting a covenant of eternity with you. (5) To you I will certainly give this land, all the land of Canaan, for an eternal possession and to your seed after you so that all the nations might get themselves blessed in you. (6) And then He said, "Your name will not get called Abram again, but Abraham because a father of many nations I have appointed you."* (7) On that day, God cut a covenant with Abraham.

(8) And the men of Sodom were wicked and sinners to the Lord – greatly; now Abraham used to go down to Sodom to see Lot and he would dwell there for a few days. (9) And the Lord came to Abraham, as he was sitting in his tent, and the Lord said to Abraham, "I am destroying Sodom because the men of Sodom are wicked and they have sinned against me a very great sin, and so I will destroy them. (10) And now go down to Sodom and then say to Lot, 'The Lord is destroying this city.' (11) Rise, go out from this place; quickly flee to the mountain(s). You must not delay, you and your wife and both of your daughters."

(12) Then Abraham journeyed, journeying continually by stages to Sodom, and he came to Sodom while Lot was standing at the gate of the city. (13) Then Abraham told to Lot all the words which the Lord had spoken to him. Now to Lot (there were) two sons, and Lot told them, as they were eating and drinking, but they did not believe their father. (14) Now Abraham and Lot came to be jokers in the eyes of the sons of Lot, then the angel of the Lord came to them, saying, "Go out now; you must not tarry because I will completely destroy this place from upon the face of the earth."

(15) And it happened after they went out from the city that the Lord destroyed Sodom. (16) Then Abraham praised the Lord, but Lot wept bitterly.

( ) – Not in Hebrew, but needed for English
[ ] – In the Hebrew, but not needed for English
* – Put the pronominal suffix directly on the verb
# – Put the pronominal suffix with energic Nun directly on the verb

(1) Now there came to be strife between Abram and Lot[1] and they disputed with one another.[2] (2) And Abram said, "Please let there not come to be strife[3] between me and you; choose for yourself[4] the land in which you will dwell,[5] and get yourself separated please[6] from [upon] me."[7] (3) And so Lot dwelt in the cities of the plain, but Abram dwelt in the land of Canaan.

(4) After these things, [and] the Lord appeared to Abram[8] and said, "I am the Lord, God of heaven and earth; I am cutting[9] a covenant of eternity with

---

1. between Abram and Lot – The Hebrew reads, "between Abram and between Lot." Hebrew also allows the construction בֵּין ... לְ (Gen 1:6; 13:7; BDB 107b 1a–b).
2. with one another – The Hebrew reads, "a man with his brother." The reciprocal (mutual action or relationship concerning each of two or more persons) nuance of "one another" or "each other" or "the one ... the other" is expressed by אִישׁ...אָח or אִישׁ ...רֵעַ (BDB 36a; JM §147c) or זֶה...זֶה (BDB 260b 1b). Moreover, Niphals and Hithpaels may also denote the reciprocal idea (§7f, n; JM §51c, 53i).
3. Please, let there not come to be strife – To add emphasis to the נָא, place it between the negative and the verb (3.29). For the verb, use the jussive of הָיָה. Remember, the jussive takes אַל, not לֹא (1.37).
4. choose for yourself – The לְ of benefit. The construction may be paraphrased: choose for your own benefit and for your own satisfaction (2.5).
5. the land in which you will dwell – The Hebrew with the retrospective pronoun reads, "in the land which you will dwell in her" (2.32).
6. and get yourself separated please – The words, "get yourself separated," represent the reflexive Niphal. The passive assumes or implies a hidden agent: it was separated (by someone or something). The reflexive, by contrast, neither assumes nor implies an agent: it got separated. Context may indicate the agent, but the verbal form is "agentless." Reflexive action often expresses the result, state, or effect of verbal action on a direct object: He separated *it*; therefore, *it* got itself separated. In the previous sentence, the active verb explicitly indicates the agent (he) and relates the verbal action occurring to the direct object (*it*). The reflexive verb, however, disregards the agent and relates the result of the active verbal action on the object: it got (itself) separated. For the composition example, Lot is commanded (imperative) to get himself separated (reflexive). This would be the result of someone (or perhaps of Lot himself) separating him (active). The active verb in this case would be a Hiphil, since a Qal finite form does not exist for this verbal root (BDB 825a). Reflexive action often occurs with actions perceived by the senses (hit, break, separate, etc.), but they may also be used with actions that are not perceived by the senses (know, understand, etc.). Reflexives are often translated by English passives, as in the fifth sentence of the first composition ("be blessed," more literally, "get [themselves] blessed," not "bless themselves," §7a, e, k).

   Do not connect the נָא particle to the verb with the Maqqef. Instead, leave it as a separate word after the verb. This will usually retract the accent of the verb to avoid consecutive accented syllables. The accent of the verb usually retracts if the next to final syllable (penult) is open with a long vowel. Hebrew grammarians call this Nesiga (or retraction of stress; Gen 1:5, 11; 3:19; 1Kgs 8:26; JM §18j, 31c; GKC §29e). Also notice the retraction of stress on the preceding words, תֵּ֫שֶׁב בָּהּ.
7. from [upon] me – 3.36.
8. [and] the Lord appeared to Abram – The word order is, "and (he) appeared the Lord to Abram." Compare this word order with 1.17.
9. I am cutting – The participle is "the noun of the agent" or "the noun that does the action," hence, a verbal *noun* (§15, 16a). This clause, therefore, may be more precisely translated, "I am a cutter" or "I am he who cuts." The participle is often found in direct speech and poetry since the form is highly efficient: maximum description with implied verbal action. Hence, the participle is often used for repetitive actions, such as offices, professions, or occupations: אֹפִים (bakers), מַשְׁקִים (cupbearers). The finite verbal forms (perfect, imperfect, and imperative) convey verbal actions coming into existence and occurring; participles are descriptive nouns closely associated with verbal actions. They are doers or agents of verbal actions, but they do not convey a verbal

you.[10] (5) To you I will certainly give[11] this land, all the land of Canaan, for an eternal possession[12] and to your seed after you[13] so that all the nations might get themselves blessed in you.[14] (6) And then He said, "Your name will not get called Abram[15] again, but Abraham[16] because a father of many nations I have appointed you."*[17] (7) On that day, God cut a covenant with Abraham.[18]

(8) And the men of Sodom were wicked and sinners to the Lord – greatly;[19] now Abraham

---

occurrence. Wright (II §72) describes the difference between the participle and the imperfect, "The difference between them is, that the concrete verbal noun (participle) designates a person or thing, to which the verbal idea closely attaches itself and consequently remains immovable; whilst the imperfect, as a finite verb, expresses the verbal idea as movable and indeed in constant motion." Furthermore, Wright notes, "The Arab grammarians ascribe to the finite verb, in general, the idea of *the becoming new, the coming into existence or the act*; to the imperfect, in particular, that of *constant renewal* or *repetition*; to the verbal noun that of *fixedness, immobility*" (Wright, II page 198, footnote. Italics are his).

10. I am cutting a covenant of eternity with you – The word order is "I (am) a cutter with you a covenant of eternity." The preposition with the suffix (with you) usually occurs between the verb (or participle) and the noun (covenant). If the preposition has a noun as an object (instead of a pronominal suffix), the prepositional phrase occurs after the noun (covenant). For instance, the Hebrew word order is usually, "I (am) cutting a covenant with David." Of course, there are exceptions (1.17, 4.8; Gen 15:18).
11. I will certainly give – The nuance "certainly" reflects the infinitive absolute used as an absolute object, "giving I will give." Placing an infinitive absolute before (and sometimes after) a verb without modifiers strongly emphasizes the verb. This emphasis, to be sure, is varied. For example, the infinitive absolute vigorously asserts or affirms the verbal idea (as here), or it strengthens the modality of the verb, emphasizing doubt in a question (JM §123f), probability in a condition (JM §123g), or ability (or lack of ability) with a subjunctive verb (§4k; JM §123h). Moreover, it may intensify the action of the verb (2.19; JM §123j; GKC §113n-r; IBH 19.4). The imperfect expresses action in process, "I am (certainly) in the process of giving to you." Contrast the imperfect with the participle (4.9).
12. for an eternal possession – The Hebrew reads, "for a possession of eternity." This proper annexation implies the לְ preposition between the nouns (1.4).
13. to your seed after you – Notice the separation of the prepositional phrases "To you" and "to your seed after you" (1.32, 3.35).
14. so that all nations might get themselves blessed in you – Recast the Hebrew, "so that (they) might get themselves blessed in you all the nations" (1.26; 4.6, 10).
15. Your name will not get called Abram – Recast the Hebrew, "not Abram will (it) get said again your name." Placing a word between the negative and the verb accentuates the negative and the following word: "*Not Abram* will your name be called again" (3.29; §40; BDB 518b 1a[c], compare John 6:32). The imperfect is a future tense here as context, especially the particle עוֹד, indicates (4.9, 11). "Get called" represents the Niphal (4.6).
16. but Abraham – Use the adversative particles, כִּי אִם (or just כִּי), which are common after a negative clause, an oath, or a question (§83b; JM §172c; GKC §163a; BDB 474b 2a).
17. because a father of many nations I have appointed you – Notice the emphatic placement of the accusative of situation, "a father of many nations," before the verb (1.32; §11uu).
18. God cut a covenant with Abraham – The perfect functions as a past narrative tense (4.10; §3d).
19. And the men of Sodom were wicked and sinners to the Lord – greatly – This (verbless) nominal clause introduces and describes the men of Sodom and their character (1.38). The noun formation for the word "sinners" (חַטָּאִים), a descriptive noun (§23h) built on the intensive/extensive verbal formation exaggerates the meaning by describing someone possessing the quality intensively/extensively. The intensive/extensive formation is frequently used for occupations (Gen 39:1). These are professional sinners, engaged in their sin intensively and extensively.

used to go down to Sodom[20] to see Lot and he would dwell there for a few days.[21] (9) And the Lord came to Abraham, as he was sitting in his tent,[22] and the Lord said to Abraham, "I am destroying Sodom because the men of Sodom are wicked[23] and they have sinned against me a very great sin,[24] and so I will destroy them. (10) And now go down to Sodom[25] and then say to Lot, 'The Lord is destroying this city.' (11) Rise, go out[26] from this place; quickly[27] flee to the mountain(s).[28] You must not delay,[29] you and your wife and both of your daughters."

(12) Then Abraham journeyed, journeying continually by stages[30] to Sodom,[31] and he came to Sodom while Lot was standing at the gate of the city.[32] (13) Then Abraham told to Lot all the words which the Lord had spoken to him.[33] Now to Lot (there were) two sons,[34] and Lot told them, as they were eating and drinking, but they did not believe their father. (14) Now Abraham and Lot came to be jokers in the eyes of the sons of Lot,[35] then the

---

20. to Sodom – Use the accusative ending ָה.
21. for a few days – The Hebrew reads, "days few."
22. as he was sitting in his tent – The Hebrew reads, "and he (was) a sitter in his tent." This clause, closely associated with its main clause adverbially, functions as an accusative of situation (§13z) to the preceding clause, expressing the situation, status, or condition of Abraham when God appeared to him. Since the Vav on the pronoun introduces a situation clause, it is called a Vav of situation, often rendered "as." These clauses answer the adverbial questions of "in what situation, status, or condition" to its main clause. Modern grammars often call these circumstantial clauses, since the clause gives the circumstances under which the main clause occurs (§49a; JM §159; GKC §158).
23. the men of Sodom are wicked – The word order is "wicked (are) the men of Sodom," highlighting the adjective, "wicked."
24. and they have sinned against me a very great sin – The Hebrew reads, "and they (independent pronoun) sinned a sin great very to me." This is the absolute object with an abstract noun and modifiers, emphasizing and explaining the verb (2.19).
25. to Sodom – The accusative ending ָה.
26. Rise, go out – 2.27.
27. quickly – This is the Piel infinitive absolute of the root מהר. Placed before the verb, this infinitive absolute functions adverbially (2.19; §13e, 17j). In fact, BDB (555a) and KBL (2:553) analyze it as an adverb.
28. to the mountains – The accusative ending ָה. The Hebrew noun הַר can be a collective noun for a chain of mountains (BDB 250a 1b and 2; JM §135). This noun also has a plural form, often used intensively (§9b).
29. You must not delay – A temporally extensive Piel (1.27, 37; §7c).
30. journeying continually by stages – The Hebrew reads, "going and journeying by stages," two infinitive absolutes after the verb. The infinitive absolute of הלך after a verb of motion frequently expresses continuance. Moreover, a second infinitive absolute normally connects to the infinitive absolute of הלך to indicate what is continued: "journeying continually." Hence, the nuance becomes, "continuing journeying by stages." These two infinitive absolutes explain the verb adverbially with emphasis (2.19; §14f, 17j; GKC §113h–k; JM §123r–s).
31. to Sodom – The accusative ending ָה.
32. while Lot was standing at the gate of the city – A situation clause (4.22).
33. which the Lord had spoken to him – For the word order, see 1.17.
34. Now to Lot (there were) two sons – The Hebrew reads, "And to Lot two of sons." This construction asserts possession (§11f). As Hebrew (Arabic, Aramaic) does not have a "being" verb, it also does not have a verb that asserts possession.
35. Now Abraham and Lot came to be jokers in the eyes of the sons of Lot – This is an independent nominal clause, not a dependent situation clause since the clause does not function adverbially

angel of the Lord came to them, saying, "Go out now;[36] you must not tarry because I will completely destroy[37] this place from upon[38] the face of the earth."

(15) And it happened after they went out from the city that the Lord destroyed Sodom. (16) Then Abraham praised the Lord, but Lot wept bitterly.[39]

---

to a preceding clause. The participle מְצַחֲקִים, however, is an accusative of situation: they came to be (existed) *in the status of* jokers in the eyes of the sons of Lot (3.16).

36. Go out now – This infinitive absolute is an absolute object, its verb being assumed. The assumed verb is commonly an imperative, as here. (§17e–f; GKC §113aa–bb). Other assumed verbal forms, such as perfects and imperfects, etc., are also possible according to the context (§17g–h).
37. I will completely destroy – The Hebrew reads, "destroying I will destroy." The infinitive absolute, an absolute object, stresses the intensity and the completeness of the action (2.19; §13c, 17e; JM §123j; GKC §113n).
38. from upon – 3.36.
39. Lot wept bitterly – The Hebrew reads, "and Lot a weeping he wept." The English adverb "bitterly" effectively renders the intensifying infinitive absolute (an absolute object, 2.19, 4.36).

Key to Composition Four

1 וַיְהִי־רִיב בֵּין־אַבְרָם וּבֵין־לוֹט וַיָּרִיבוּ אִישׁ עִם־אָחִיו׃

2 וַיֹּאמֶר אַבְרָם אַל־נָא יְהִי רִיב בֵּינִי וּבֵינֶךָ בְּחַר לְךָ בָּאָרֶץ אֲשֶׁר תֵּשֶׁב בָּהּ וְהִפָּרֶד
נָא מֵעָלָי׃

3 וַיֵּשֶׁב לוֹט בְּעָרֵי הַכִּכָּר וְאַבְרָם יָשַׁב בְּאֶרֶץ כְּנָעַן׃

4 אַחַר׀ הַדְּבָרִים הָאֵלֶּה וַיֵּרָא יהוה אֶל־אַבְרָם וַיֹּאמֶר אָנֹכִי יהוה אֱלֹהֵי הַשָּׁמַיִם
וְהָאָרֶץ אֲנִי כֹּרֵת עִמְּךָ בְּרִית עוֹלָם׃

5 לְךָ נָתוֹן אֶתֵּן אֶת־הָאָרֶץ הַזֹּאת אֶת־כָּל־אֶרֶץ כְּנַעַן לַאֲחֻזַּת עוֹלָם וּלְזַרְעֲךָ אַחֲרֶיךָ
וְיִבָּרְכוּ בְךָ כָּל־הַגּוֹיִם׃

6 וַיֹּאמֶר לֹא אַבְרָם יֵאָמֵר עוֹד שְׁמֶךָ כִּי אִם־אַבְרָהָם כִּי אֲבִי־גוֹיִם רַבִּים נְתַתִּיךָ׃

7 בַּיּוֹם הַהוּא כָּרַת אֱלֹהִים בְּרִית אֶת־אַבְרָהָם׃

8 וְאַנְשֵׁי סְדֹם רָעִים וְחַטָּאִים לַיהוָה מְאֹד וְאַבְרָהָם יָרַד סְדֹמָה לִרְאוֹת אֶת־לוֹט
וְיָשַׁב שָׁם יָמִים אֲחָדִים׃

9 וַיָּבֹא יְהוָה אֶל־אַבְרָהָם וְהוּא יֹשֵׁב בְּאָהֳלוֹ וַיֹּאמֶר יהוה אֶל־אַבְרָהָם אֲנִי מַשְׁחִית
אֶת־סְדֹם כִּי רָעִים אַנְשֵׁי סְדֹם וְהֵמָּה חָטְאוּ חֲטָאָה גְדוֹלָה מְאֹד לִי וְהִשְׁמַדְתִּי אֹתָם׃

10 וְעַתָּה רֵד סְדֹמָה וְאָמַרְתָּ אֶל־לוֹט יְהוָה מַשְׁחִית אֶת־הָעִיר הַזֹּאת׃

11 קוּם צֵא מֵהַמָּקוֹם הַזֶּה מַהֵר הִמָּלֵט הָהָרָה לֹא תְאַחֵר אַתָּה וְאִשְׁתְּךָ וּשְׁנֵי בְנֹתֶיךָ׃

12 וַיִּסַּע אַבְרָהָם הָלוֹךְ וְנָסוֹעַ סְדֹמָה וַיָּבֹא אֶל־סְדֹם וְלוֹט עֹמֵד בְּשַׁעַר־הָעִיר׃

13 וַיַּגֵּד אַבְרָהָם לְלוֹט אֶת־כָּל־הַדְּבָרִים אֲשֶׁר־דִּבֶּר אֵלָיו יְהוָה וּלְלוֹט שְׁנֵי בָנִים וַיַּגֵּד
לוֹט לָהֶם וְהֵמָּה אֹכְלִים וְשֹׁתִים וְלֹא הֶאֱמִינוּ בַּאֲבִיהֶם׃

14 וְאַבְרָהָם וְלוֹט הָיוּ מְצַחֲקִים בְּעֵינֵי בְּנֵי לוֹט וַיָּבֹא אֲלֵיהֶם מַלְאַךְ יהוה לֵאמֹר
יָצוֹא לֹא תְאַחֲרוּ כִּי הַשְׁמֵד אַשְׁמִיד אֶת־הַמָּקוֹם הַזֶּה מֵעַל פְּנֵי־הָאֲדָמָה׃

15 וַיְהִי אַחֲרֵי צֵאתָם מִן־הָעִיר וַיַּשְׁחֵת יְהוָה אֶת־סְדֹם׃

16 וַיְהַלֵּל אַבְרָהָם אֶת־יְהוָה וְלוֹט בָּכֹה בָכָה׃

Unpointed Text of Composition Four

1 ויהי־ריב בין־אברם ובין־לוט ויריבו איש עם־אחיו׃

2 ויאמר אברם אל־נא יהי ריב ביני ובינך בחר לך בארץ אשר תשב בה והפרד נא מעלי׃

3 וישב לוט בערי הככר ואברם ישב בארץ כנען׃

4 אחר הדברים האלה וירא יהוה אל־אברם ויאמר אנכי יהוה אלהי השמים והארץ אני כרת עמך ברית עולם׃

5 לך נתון אתן את־הארץ הזאת את־כל־ארץ כנען לאחזת עולם ולזרעך אחריך ויברכו בך כל־הגויים׃

6 ויאמר לא אברם יאמר עוד שמך כי אם־אברהם כי אבי־גויים רבים נתתיך׃

7 ביום ההוא כרת אלהים ברית את־אברהם׃

8 ואנשי סדם רעים וחטאים ליהוה מאד ואברהם ירד סדמה לראות את־לוט וישב שם ימים אחדים׃

9 ויבא יהוה אל־אברהם והוא ישב באהלו ויאמר יהוה אל־אברהם אני משחית את־סדם כי רעים אנשי סדם והמה חטאו חטאה גדולה מאד לי והשמדתי אתם׃

10 ועתה רד סדמה ואמרת אל־לוט יהוה משחית את־העיר הזאת׃

11 קום צא מהמקום הזה מהר המלט ההרה לא תאחר אתה ואשתך ושני בנתיך׃

12 ויסע אברהם הלוך ונסוע סדמה ויבא אל־סדם ולוט עמד בשער־העיר׃

13 ויגד אברהם ללוט את־כל־הדברים אשר־דבר אליו יהוה וללוט שני בנים ויגד לוט להם והמה אכלים ושתים ולא האמינו באביהם׃

14 ואברהם ולוט היו מצחקים בעיני בני לוט ויבא אליהם מלאך יהוה לאמר יצוא לא תאחרו כי השמד אשמיד את־המקום הזה מעל פני־האדמה׃

15 ויהי אחרי צאתם מן־העיר וישחת יהוה את־סדם׃

16 ויהלל אברהם את־יהוה ולוט בכה בכה׃

COMPOSITION FIVE

(1) Now Abraham became old, and the Lord had blessed him all the days of his life. (2) And Abraham summoned Eliezer, his servant, and he said to him, "Behold, I am dying; go to my kin at Aram-Naharaim, and then take from there a wife for my son [for] Isaac. (3) You must not take a wife from the daughters of the Canaanites and you must not return my son to Aram because the land upon which we are dwellers is holy ground [it]."

(4) And Eliezer and many servants rose early in the morning, and they went to Aram. (5) And it happened when Eliezer came near to Aram that he prayed, "Oh Lord, God of Abraham my master and Isaac his son, bless please Abraham your servant and be gracious to me today that I might take from here a wife for Isaac." (6) Then he entered Aram-Naharaim to the city of Nahor, and the men of the city gate asked him,* "What are you seeking?" Eliezer answered and said, "A wife for Isaac, son of Abraham, my master, I am seeking."

(7) After this, Eliezer went to the broad place (of the city), as the daughters of the men of the city were going out to the well; then Eliezer lifted his eyes and looked, and behold, a young girl was walking with a pitcher on her head. (8) And the Lord said to Eliezer, "This is the girl whom I have chosen." (9) Then Eliezer greeted her and he told her that which the Lord spoke to him. (10) Then the girl went to her mother's house and told to Laban, her brother, as to these things.

(11) And it happened when Laban saw Eliezer and when he heard the words of Rebecca, his sister, that he said, "Did God really say these words to you?" (12) Then Eliezer said to Laban, "God has indeed said to me, 'The girl whom you are seeing [her], to Isaac I have given her* for a wife.'" (13) Then Laban asked Rebecca, his sister, "Are you willing to go after this man?" And she said, "I want to go."

(14) And then Eliezer praised the Lord and said, "The Lord, he is [the] God, there is none like you, and there is no God except you." (15) And Eliezer and Rebecca went out from Aram, rejoicing as he went out.

( ) – Not in Hebrew, but needed for English
[ ] – In the Hebrew, but not needed for English
* – Put the pronominal suffix directly on the verb
# – Put the pronominal suffix with energic Nun directly on the verb

(1) Now Abraham became old,[1] and the Lord had blessed him[2] all the days of his life. (2) And Abraham summoned Eliezer, his servant, and he said to him, "Behold, I am dying;[3] go to my kin at Aram-Naharaim,[4] and then take from there a wife for my son [for] Isaac.[5] (3) You must not take a wife[6] from the daughters of the Canaanites[7] and you must not return my son to Aram[8] because the land upon which we are dwellers is holy ground [it]."[9]

---

1. Now Abraham became old – The nominal clause supplies descriptive information for the following narrative (JM §159f). The verb for "became old" is the stative verb זָקֵן. This form may also be parsed as a participle: Abraham (was) old. With a verb, an event or action comes into existence and occurs; with a participle, the fixedness of a habitual or abiding state is conveyed. In this context, Abraham became or grew old (4.9; 5.3; §16a).
2. and the Lord had blessed him – This nominal clause describes the Lord as blessing Abraham.
3. Behold, I am dying – Connect the pronominal suffix (1cs) to the demonstrative particle, הִנֵּה. The form of this participle may also be parsed as a perfect 3ms (though the first person independent pronoun renders this parsing impossible). The participle communicates, "I (am) dying (or dead) one," equivalent to אֲשֶׁר אָמוּת. Abraham is in the state of dying. The perfect 3ms would indicate an action or event: I (Abraham) died (4.9; 5.1; §16a).
4. at Aram-Naharaim – The Hebrew reads, "to Aram-Naharaim."
5. for my son [for] Isaac – Hebrew often repeats the preposition (or the marker of the accusative) for its apposition. The apposition is explicative, explaining its antecedent by identifying or specifying. The explicative apposition is the specific term to its antecedent noun, the general term. Here the specific term, Issac, identifies its antecedent, my son, the general term. The construction may be paraphrased, "for my son, (identified or specified as) Isaac" (§26; JM §131i, 132g).
6. You must not take a wife – Because Abraham is talking to his servant, a superior to an inferior, לֹא with the imperfect indicative is common (1.37; JM §113m footnote 2).
7. of the Canaanites – The Hebrew reads, "of the Canaanite." Hebrew frequently uses the singular gentilic as a collective (§23j; BDB 489a 2b). In fact, Hebrew may use almost any noun in the singular collectively or generically to represent a plural (§9b; JM §135c). Moreover, the collective gentilic usually has the article, used generically to indicate the totality of the individuals within the group, every Canaanite. This is similar to English article when one refers to *the* Frenchman without a particular Frenchman in mind, but *the* typical or *the* generic Frenchman, that is, every Frenchman (§35b; JM §135c, 137i). For the gentilic, use the Hireq-Yod (Nisbah) ending (3.10).
8. to Aram – The accusative ending ָה.
9. because the land upon which we are dwellers is holy ground [it] – The Hebrew reads, "because the land which we (are) dwellers upon her, ground of holiness she (is)." These nominal clauses (sentences), similar to a separating pronoun, convey emphasis, clarity, smoothness of expression, or all of these. Such sentences may have nominal or verbal predicates. The word "land" is the subject (initiator) of the entire sentence (a nominal clause) with a modifying relative clause. Its predicate (announcement), "holy ground [she]," is also a nominal clause; הִיא, the "separating" pronoun, is the subject of the predicate, and אַדְמַת קֹדֶשׁ is the predicate of the predicate. The prepositional phrase ("upon her") has a retrospective pronoun (2.32). The following constructions are also regarded as casus pendens (preoccupation, 6.4 §14).

Subject of predicate　Predicate of predicate

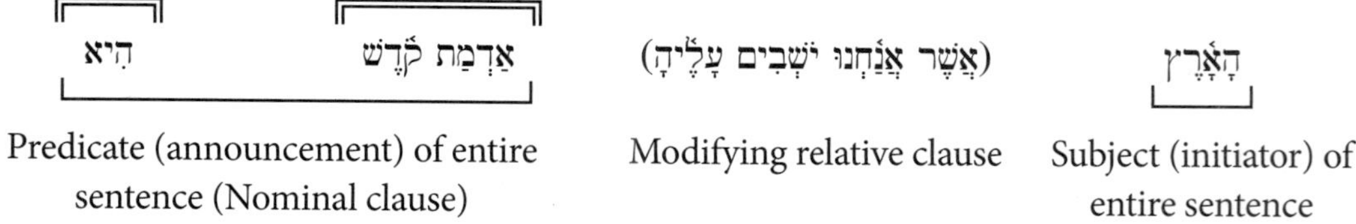

1. Nominal Clauses with a Nominal Clause Predicate

A. Subject (initiator) of the entire sentence (nominal clause) + nominal clause predicate (noun or adjective + subject, a pronoun usually): The subject of the entire sentence is often emphatic and the predicate of the predicate retains emphasis as well (Gen 31:16; 31:43; 34:21; 41:25; 47:6; 48:5; Exod 3:5; 16:36; Deut 1:17; §11w; JM §154i).

Subject of predicate — Predicate of predicate

הוא — לֵאלֹהִים — הַמִּשְׁפָּט

Predicate (announcement) of entire sentence (Nominal clause) — Subject (initiator) of entire sentence

"The judgment – to God [it] (is)" (Deut 1:17)

B. Subject (noun or pronoun) of the entire sentence (nominal clause) + nominal clause predicate (subject of predicate nominal clause, usually a pronoun, + predicate of predicate): This construction is the separating pronoun. The subject of the sentence and the subject of the predicate are very emphatic. This construction expresses absolute identification, the predicate is unique to the subject. Moreover, the construction is interchangeable: the predicate could become the subject, and the subject the predicate (Gen 42:6; Deut 3:22; 4:35; 7:9; 10:9; 2 Sam 7:28; Isa 37:16; 43:25; §11v; JM §154j).

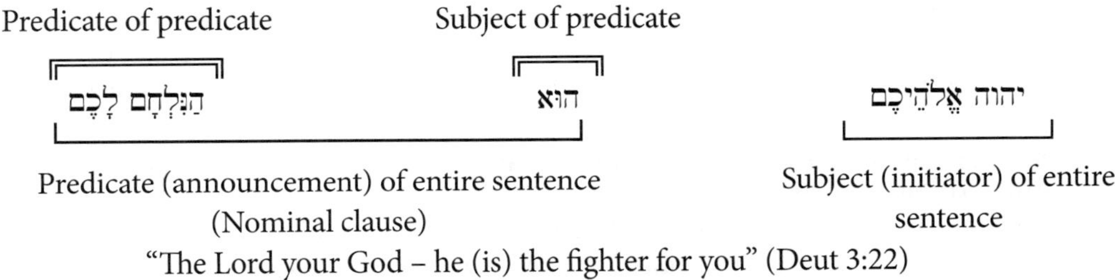

"The Lord your God – he (is) the fighter for you" (Deut 3:22)

2. Nominal Clauses with a Verbal Clause Predicate

A. Any clause where a subject precedes a finite verb is a nominal clause. The initial subject (initiator) is the subject (initiator) of the entire sentence. The finite verb is actually a verbal clause that is the predicate (announcement) of the nominal sentence. The subject of the verb is another (pro)noun or the pronoun implicit in the third masculine singular or third common verb. In prose, the subject of the entire sentence is usually described, having slight or no emphasis; in direct speech and poetry, the subject of the entire sentence is often emphatic, having some description as well (Gen 4:1; 20:4; 21:1; Ps 2:7; §11c).

Predicate (verb, subject implied)

Predicate (announcement; verbal clause) — Subject (initiator) of entire sentence

"And the man – he knew" (Gen 4:1)

B. Sometimes an additional pronoun for further emphasis is inserted between the subject of the sentence and the finite verb (Gen 3:12).

(4) And Eliezer and many servants[10] rose early in the morning, and they went to Aram.[11] (5) And it happened when Eliezer came near[12] to Aram that he prayed, "Oh Lord, God of Abraham my master and Isaac his son,[13] bless please Abraham your servant[14] and be gracious to me[15] today[16] that I might take from here a wife for Isaac." (6) Then he entered Aram-Naharaim[17] to the city of Nahor, and the men of the city gate asked him,* "What are you seeking?"[18] Eliezer answered and said, "A wife for Isaac, son of Abraham, my master, I am seeking."[19]

(7) After this, Eliezer went to the broad place (of the city), as the daughters of the men of the city were going out[20] to the well; then Eliezer lifted his eyes and looked, and behold, a young girl was walking with a pitcher on her head.[21] (8) And the Lord said to Eliezer, "This is the girl whom I have chosen." (9) Then Eliezer greeted her and he told her that which the Lord spoke to him. (10) Then the girl went to her mother's house[22] and told to Laban, her brother, as to these things.

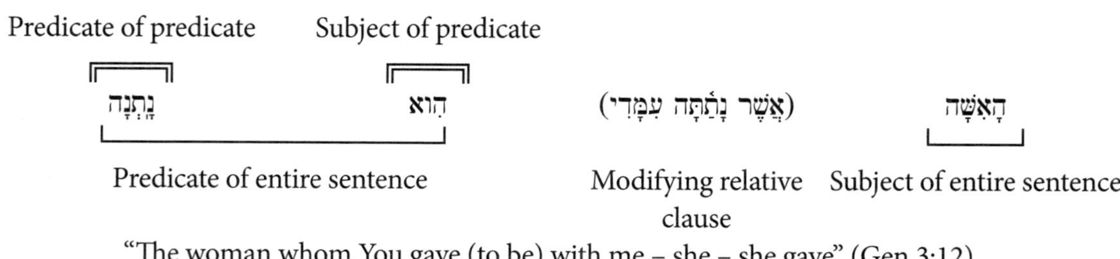

"The woman whom You gave (to be) with me – she – she gave" (Gen 3:12)

C. The subject of the sentence may be resumed in the predicate as a subject (implied subject of the verb, Gen 4:1), as a genitive (the pronominal suffix on the subject of the verb, Gen 34:8), or as an object (the pronominal suffix connected to the verb, Gen 28:13).

10. and many servants – 3.27; Gen 3:8; 7:7; 8:18; 24:50; 44:14; §11ss; GKC §146f.
11. to Aram – The accusative ending ה ָ.
12. when Eliezer came near – A temporal clause with ב and an infinitive construct (1.15; §18d, 81a).
13. and Isaac his son – The Hebrew reads, "and the God of Isaac, his son" (1.19).
14. Abraham your servant – Contrast this form of apposition with 5.5. This is substitution apposition, specifically, all-for-all substitution (§27a–b). Here, the appositive, "your servant," is the general term, and its antecedent, "Abraham" is the specific term. Substitution apposition substitutes for or transforms into its antecedent noun, much like a title – e.g. William the Conqueror. Since substitution actually corroborates (emphasizes) its noun, it is a form of absolute identification. The specific term, the antecedent noun, prepares the way for the substitution (§27; JM §131)j.
15. and be gracious to me – The Hebrew reads "and do with me lovingkindness." Note that the prepositional phrase with the pronominal suffix occurs before the object (1.17).
16. today – The Hebrew reads, "the day." When a particular noun is present to the speaker/writer, the article is often used at the first mention of the noun. This is common with nouns of time, such as day, night, time, year, etc. (§34c; JM §137f; GKC §126a-b).
17. Aram-Naharaim – The Hebrew reads, "to Aram-Naharaim."
18. What are you seeking? – The present, durative imperfect indicative is frequently found in questions (§4e; JM §113d).
19. I am seeking – Use the pronoun with the participle: "I (am) a seeker" (4.9).
20. as the daughters of the men of the city were going out – A situation clause (4.22). The Hebrew reads, "And the daughters of the men of the city were going out."
21. with a pitcher on her head – This is another situation clause. The Hebrew reads, "and a pitcher on her head" (§49b; IBH 26.3.2).
22. to her mother's house – The accusative ending ה ָ.

(11) And it happened when Laban saw[23] Eliezer and when he heard the words of Rebecca, his sister, that he said, "Did God really say[24] these words to you?" (12) Then Eliezer said to Laban, "God has indeed said[25] to me, 'The girl whom you are seeing [her], to Isaac I have given her* for a wife.'"[26] (13) Then Laban asked Rebecca, his sister, "Are you willing to go after this man?" And she said, "I want to go."[27]

(14) And then Eliezer praised the Lord and said, "The Lord, he is [the] God,[28] there is none like you, and there is no God except you." (15) And Eliezer and Rebecca[29] went out from Aram, rejoicing as he went out.[30]

---

23. when Laban saw – A temporal clause with כ and an infinitive construct (5.12).
24. Did God really say – The infinitive absolute (absolute object) before the verb underscores the doubt or hesitancy in a question, "Did God *really* (or *actually*) say?" (4.11; §17e; JM §123f).
25. God has indeed said – Here, the infinitive absolute (absolute object) strongly asserts or affirms the verb, "God has *certainly* said" (4.11; §17e; JM §123e).
26. the girl whom you are seeing [her], to Isaac I have given her for a wife – The word "[her]" is a retrospective pronoun (2.32). The word "girl" is the initiator of the entire sentence (a nominal clause). The announcement is a verbal clause. The object of the verb in the verbal clause refers back to the initiator of the entire sentence (5.9 2C). For the participle, see 4.9.
27. I want to go – The cohortative stresses the will or desire of the speaker, hence, the rendering "want" (2.21).
28. The Lord, he is [the] God – A very emphatic nominal clause expressing absolute identification (5.9 1B).
29. and Rebecca – 5.10.
30. rejoicing as he went out – the Hebrew reads, "going out and rejoicing." These infinitive absolutes, absolute objects, adverbially modify the verb, indicating how he went out: "he went out rejoicing." Consecutive infinitive absolutes after a verb often express the quality or manner of the action with emphasis (4.24, 27, 30; §13e, 17j; JM §123m).

Key to Composition Five

1 וְאַבְרָהָם זָקֵן וַיהוָה בֵּרַךְ אֹתוֹ כָּל־יְמֵי־חַיָּיו׃

2 וַיִּקְרָא אַבְרָהָם לֶאֱלִיעֶזֶר עַבְדּוֹ וַיֹּאמֶר אֵלָיו הִנְנִי מֵת לֵךְ אֶל־מוֹלַדְתִּי אֶל־אֲרַם
נַהֲרַיִם וְלָקַחְתָּ מִשָּׁם אִשָּׁה לִבְנִי לְיִצְחָק׃

3 לֹא תִקַּח אִשָּׁה מִבְּנוֹת הַכְּנַעֲנִי וְלֹא תָשִׁיב בְּנִי אֲדָמָה כִּי הָאָרֶץ אֲשֶׁר אֲנַחְנוּ
יֹשְׁבִים עָלֶיהָ אַדְמַת קֹדֶשׁ הִיא׃

4 וַיַּשְׁכֵּם אֱלִיעֶזֶר וַעֲבָדִים רַבִּים בַּבֹּקֶר וַיֵּלְכוּ אֲרָמָה׃

5 וַיְהִי בְּקָרֹב אֱלִיעֶזֶר אֶל־אֲרָם וַיִּתְפַּלֵּל יהוה אֱלֹהֵי אַבְרָהָם אֲדֹנִי וֵאלֹהֵי יִצְחָק
בְּנוֹ בָּרֶךְ־נָא אַבְרָהָם עַבְדֶּךָ וַעֲשֵׂה עִמִּי חֶסֶד הַיּוֹם וְאֶקַּח מִפֹּה אִשָּׁה לְיִצְחָק׃

6 וַיָּבֹא אֶל־אֲרַם נַהֲרַיִם אֶל־עִיר נָחוֹר וַיִּשְׁאָלֻהוּ אַנְשֵׁי הַשַּׁעַר מַה־תְּבַקֵּשׁ וַיַּעַן
אֱלִיעֶזֶר וַיֹּאמֶר אִשָּׁה לְיִצְחָק בֶּן־אַבְרָהָם אֲדֹנִי אֲנִי מְבַקֵּשׁ׃

7 אַחֲרֵי־כֵן הָלַךְ אֱלִיעֶזֶר אֶל־הָרְחוֹב וּבְנוֹת־אַנְשֵׁי הָעִיר יֹצְאוֹת אֶל־הַבְּאֵר וַיִּשָּׂא
אֱלִיעֶזֶר אֶת־עֵינָיו וַיַּרְא וְהִנֵּה נַעֲרָה הֹלֶכֶת וְכַד עַל־רֹאשָׁהּ׃

8 וַיֹּאמֶר יהוה אֶל־אֱלִיעֶזֶר זֹאת הַנַּעֲרָה אֲשֶׁר בָּחַרְתִּי׃

9 וַיְבָרֶךְ אֱלִיעֶזֶר אֹתָהּ וַיַּגֶּד־לָהּ אֶת־אֲשֶׁר דִּבֶּר אֵלָיו יהוה׃

10 וַתֵּלֶךְ הַנַּעֲרָה בֵּיתָה אִמָּהּ וַתַּגֵּד לְלָבָן אָחִיהָ כַּדְּבָרִים הָאֵלֶּה׃

11 וַיְהִי כִּרְאוֹת לָבָן אֶת־אֱלִיעֶזֶר וּכְשָׁמְעוֹ אֶת־דִּבְרֵי רִבְקָה אֲחֹתוֹ וַיֹּאמֶר הֶאָמוֹר
אָמַר אֱלֹהִים אֵלֶיךָ אֶת־הַדְּבָרִים הָאֵלֶּה׃

12 וַיֹּאמֶר אֱלִיעֶזֶר אֶל־לָבָן אָמוֹר אָמַר אֱלֹהִים אֵלַי הַנַּעֲרָה אֲשֶׁר אַתָּה רֹאֶה אֹתָהּ
לְיִצְחָק נְתַתִּיהָ לְאִשָּׁה׃

13 וַיִּשְׁאַל לָבָן אֶת־רִבְקָה אֲחֹתוֹ הֲתֹאבִי לָלֶכֶת אַחֲרֵי הָאִישׁ הַזֶּה וַתֹּאמֶר אֵלֵכָה׃

14 וַיְהַלֵּל אֱלִיעֶזֶר אֶת־יהוה וַיֹּאמֶר יהוה הוּא הָאֱלֹהִים אֵין־כָּמוֹךָ וְאֵין אֱלֹהִים זוּלָתֶךָ׃

15 וַיֵּצֵא אֱלִיעֶזֶר וְרִבְקָה מִן־אֲרָם יָצוֹא וְשָׂמוֹחַ׃

Unpointed Text of Composition Five

1 ואברהם זקן ויהוה ברך אתו כל־ימי־חייו׃

2 ויקרא אברהם לאליעזר עבדו ויאמר אליו הנני מת לך אל־מולדתי אל־ארם
נהרים ולקחת משם אשה לבני ליצחק׃

3 לא תקח אשה מבנות הכנעני ולא תשיב בני ארמה כי הארץ אשר אנחנו
ישבים עליה אדמת קדש היא׃

4 וישכם אליעזר ועבדים רבים בבקר וילכו ארמה׃

5 ויהי בקרב אליעזר אל־ארם ויתפלל יהוה אלהי אברהם אדני ואלהי יצחק
בנו ברך־נא אברהם עבדך ועשה עמי חסד היום ואקח מפה אשה ליצחק׃

6 ויבא אל־ארם נהרים אל־עיר נחור וישאלוהו אנשי השער מה־תבקש ויען
אליעזר ויאמר אשה ליצחק בן־אברהם אדני אני מבקש׃

7 אחרי־כן הלך אליעזר אל־הרחוב ובנות־אנשי העיר יצאות אל־הבאר וישא
אליעזר את־עיניו וירא והנה נערה הולכת וכד על־ראשה׃

8 ויאמר יהוה אל־אליעזר זאת הנערה אשר בחרתי׃

9 ויברך אליעזר אתה ויגד לה את־אשר דבר אליו יהוה׃

10 ותלך הנערה ביתה אמה ותגד ללבן אחיה כדברים האלה׃

11 ויהי כראות לבן את־אליעזר וכשמעו את־דברי רבקה אחתו ויאמר האמור
אמר אלהים אליך את־הדברים האלה׃

12 ויאמר אליעזר אל־לבן אמור אמר אלהים אלי הנערה אשר אתה ראה אתה
ליצחק נתתיה לאשה׃

13 וישאל לבן את־רבקה אחתו התאבי ללכת אחרי האיש הזה ותאמר אלכה׃

14 ויהלל אליעזר את־יהוה ויאמר יהוה הוא האלהים אין־כמוך ואין אלהים זולתך׃

15 ויצא אליעזר ורבקה מן־ארם יצוא ושמוח׃

COMPOSITION SIX

(1) Then Moses and Aaron came to Pharaoh and said, "The Lord, the God of the Hebrews, has appeared to us in the wilderness as (the) mighty God, and thus the Lord God said, 'I am the Lord, the God of all the earth, release my people that they may serve me.'"* (2) And Pharaoh said, "Who is the Lord that I should acknowledge him?" (3) And Moses said, "The Lord – his way is (the) way of truth and he will harden your heart that he might show you# his strength and that you might know his name always." (4) Then Pharaoh said, "The Lord I do not acknowledge, and moreover Israel I will not let go." (5) And Moses said, "(As for) the Lord, he is a jealous God, an avenger to his haters. (6) And he will completely harden your heart so that he might bring upon you and upon your house all his signs and wonders." (7) Then Pharaoh said, "You are worthy of death; go out from [with] me because I am not able to bear your words any longer."

(8) Then Pharaoh summoned his servants and the wise (men) of his house and said to them, "What shall we do?" (9) And his servants said, "We should smite him# mortally," but his wise men said, "No, but smite him* (on the) cheek and let us smite him* with a smiting that wounds, but do not kill him."* (10) And the words of his wise men pleased Pharaoh and then the wise men of Pharaoh and his servants went out to seize Moses and Aaron. (11) And they came near to Moses while he was standing beside the Nile with the staff of God in his hand. (12) Then Moses took water from the Nile and he poured (it) out (on) the dry ground, and the water became blood.

(13) And it happened when the servants of Pharaoh and the wise men saw this sign that they said to Pharaoh, "The Lord, he is fighting for them, what can we do since the Lord has done even this (sign)?" (14) But Pharaoh refused to listen to them, because God had hardened his heart and he said to them, "You are cowards, I will not release them."*

(15) Then the servants and wise men of Pharaoh said to each other, "Pharaoh is stiff-necked, why has he done this thing, namely, he refused to release them*; we shall all die as one man."

( ) – Not in Hebrew, but needed for English
[ ] – In the Hebrew, but not needed for English
* – Put the pronominal suffix directly on the verb
# – Put the pronominal suffix with energic Nun directly on the verb

(1) Then Moses and Aaron came to Pharaoh and said, "The Lord, the God of the Hebrews, has appeared[1] to us in the wilderness as (the) mighty God,[2] and thus the Lord God said, 'I am the Lord, the God of all the earth, release my people that they may serve me.'"* (2) And Pharaoh said, "Who is the Lord that I should acknowledge him?"[3] (3) And Moses said, "The Lord – his way is (the) way of truth[4] and he will harden your heart that he might show you[#] his strength and that you might know his name always."[5] (4) Then Pharaoh said, "The Lord I do not acknowledge,[6] and moreover Israel I will not let go."[7] (5) And Moses said, "(As for)

---

1. The Lord, the God of the Hebrews, has appeared – Put the subject before the verb for emphasis. For the gentilic (the Hebrews), see 3.10. The verb, "appeared," is a Niphal: "get (himself) seen" (4.6).
2. as (the) mighty God – The Hebrew reads, "in (the) mighty God." The ב is the ב *essentiae* (ב of the essence, being, or substance). The ב *essentiae* introduces the noun *in the being* or *in the person* which the noun reveals itself or *in the substance* of which the noun consists. Here, the Lord appeared to Israel in the wilderness *in the being of* (or *in the person* or *manifestation of*) mighty God or *revealed as* mighty God. The ב *essentiae*, especially when used as a predicate, may often be translated "as" (= כ). The classic example is Exodus 6:3, And I appeared to Abraham…*in the person of* (or *revealed as*) God Almighty (Num 26:53; Deut 1:13; 10:22; 26:14; BDB 88b I7; JM §133c; GKC §119i).
3. that I should acknowledge him – The word "that" is the particle אֲשֶׁר (Exod 5:2), expressing result. Result clauses usually express surprise, disapproval, or ridicule, often after questions that imply the same surprise, disapproval, or ridicule. It may be used for ridicule as here – "Who is the Lord (*with the final and ridiculously unexpected outcome*) that I should acknowledge him." The verb is a subjunctive imperfect (§4k). The particle כִּי would work as well to express result (Exod 3:11; BDB 83a 8a, 472b 1f).
4. The Lord – his way is (the) way of truth – The Hebrew reads, "The Lord – way of truth (is) his way." This construction is similar to the constructions in 5.9 (1A) except this construction lacks a separating pronoun.

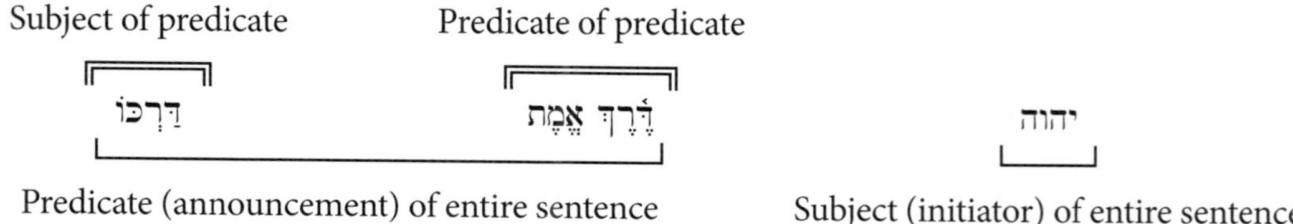

This construction, as the ones in 5.9, is a casus pendens. Native grammarians call these constructions, "preoccupation." The normal construction would read: the way of the Lord is (the) way of truth. By replacing the word, "Lord," with a pronominal suffix and by placing "Lord," the antecedent of the "Lord," at the beginning of the clause, the noun "way" (the subject of the predicate) is preoccupied with the pronominal suffix, emphasizing "Lord." The suspended noun—"Lord"—is resumed by the genitive, the pronominal suffix (§14d).

5. always – The Hebrew reads, "all the days."
6. I do not acknowledge – This imperfect describes, in the words of Arab grammarians, "what is going on and what is expected to go on in the future." Hence, this imperfect is present with the future also in view – "I do not acknowledge the Lord now, nor do I expect to acknowledge him in the future" (§4e).
7. and moreover Israel I will not let go – The particle גַּם functions as an accusative of situation modifying the noun "Israel" (§13ee). Place the direct object "Israel" at the beginning of the clause for emphasis (§11uu). Furthermore, Hebrew usually places the accusative marker אֵת before direct objects that precede the verb (2.33; §13n; JM §125e).

the Lord, he is a jealous God,[8] an avenger to his haters.[9] (6) And he will completely harden your heart so that he might bring upon you and upon your house all his signs and wonders."[10] (7) Then Pharaoh said, "You are worthy of death;[11] go out[12] from [with] me because I am not able[13] to bear[14] your words any longer."

(8) Then Pharaoh summoned his servants and the wise (men) of his house and said to them, "What shall we do?" (9) And his servants said, "We should smite him[#] mortally,"[15]

---

8. the Lord, he is a jealous God – The Hebrew reads, "the Lord, a God jealous he (is)." See 5.9 section 1A. For the intensive/extensive noun formation of the word "jealous," see 4.19.
9. his haters – This is a participle with a pronominal suffix. Moreover, the root נקם often takes the ל preposition (BDB 668a 1a).
10. all his signs and wonders – The Hebrew reads, "all his signs and all his wonders." מוֹפֵת reduces the Sere (actually, the original Hireq) in the open, pretonic position. This word is a participle in form and reduction pattern (IBH 19.2.3).
11. You are worthy of death – Recast the Hebrew, "son of death you (are)." The word order emphasizes "son of death." Genitive phrases with the words בֵּן, אִישׁ, בַּעַל, often express a possessor of a quality or characteristic, or a member of a class. These are "nouns of relations" because they express a relation of the person with a quality, characteristic, or class (metaphorically speaking), as a son is related to a father (§12i-k; JM §129j; GKC §128s-v; BDB 121b I7–8).
12. go out – Pharaohs might be expected to speak emphatically; therefore, use the infinitive absolute as the absolute object, with the imperative verb implied (4.36; §17f).
13. I am not able – The imperfect of the irregular verb יָכֹל (IBH 35.14) expresses a present tense with the future also in view: "I am not able (nor will I be able) to bear" (6.6).
14. to bear – The infinitive construct of this verb with the ל preposition is irregular (IBH 34.5.3).
15. We should smite him mortally – The Hebrew reads, "we should smite him soul." The last word "soul" is in the accusative in Hebrew. Hebrew formerly possessed case endings, as all Semitic languages did, and as formal Arabic still has. Semitic languages, including Hebrew, had three cases: nominative, genitive, and accusative. In Biblical Hebrew, these cases are preserved in certain common, archaic forms (JM §93; GKC §90). Biblical Hebrew occasionally preserved the *form* of the accusative case, as for instance, יוֹמָם (with final Mem and accusative vowel, Qames from an original Patah) and לַיְלָה (final Mem dropped, but accusative vowel retained). By the time of Biblical Hebrew, most final Mems were dropped and final short vowels (the case vowels) were dropped. Most case *functions*, however, continued during the Biblical Hebrew period, though the prepositions were encroaching on some case functions. The general rule in Biblical Hebrew is: if a noun, frequently indefinite, is not the subject, verb, direct object, object of the preposition, apposition, or the last word in a construct package (the genitive), the word is an (adverbial) accusative. Another way to detect the adverbial accusative is the need to smooth the translation of a particular noun, as in a sentence, such as, "we should smite him soul." The word "soul" cannot be translated smoothly, a possible indication of an adverbial accusative.

    Joüon and Muraoka label the adverbial accusative as the indirect accusative (JM §126; GKC §118 terms it, "the looser subordination of the accusative to the verb"), in contrast to the direct accusative (direct object; §13k–u), and to the absolute object (2.19; §13b–j). A more descriptive term, perhaps, is the "adverbial accusative" or "adverbial object" of Greek and Latin (§13v–qq).

    The major categories of adverbial accusatives include:

    1. Situation (Arabic Hal = situation, state, condition) – This accusative answers the questions: In what situation, state, or condition for nouns, and how or in what manner for verbs. It is frequently an indefinite, descriptive noun, that is, a participle (Num 16:27) or adjective (Lev 20:20), but it can be an indefinite (usually) primary noun if it has the sense of the כ preposition (as) implied before it (Gen 38:11). Finally, it may explain the manner of the verbal action (Gen 34:25). It describes more precisely the *situation* or *condition* in which an action takes place. Gen 15:2, וְאָנֹכִי הוֹלֵךְ עֲרִירִי "I am walking *as* (in the situation, state, or condition of) a barren one" (§13z–ii; JM §126a; GKC §118n–r).

but his wise men said,[16] "No, but[17] smite him* (on the) cheek[18] and let us smite him* with a smiting that wounds,[19] but do not kill him."*[20] (10) And the words of his wise men pleased Pharaoh[21] and then the wise men of Pharaoh and his servants[22] went out to seize Moses and

---

A. Adjectives: Gen 33:18; Judg 8:4; Ruth 1:21
B. Participle: Gen 21:9; Exod 2:11; Num 11:10; 16:27
C. Substantive: Gen 38:11; 1 Sam 13:17

There are also situation clauses that furnish the situation, state, or condition for another clause (§48).

2. Specification (Arabic Tamyiz = specification) – Specification is usually a primary noun, never a participle and rarely an adjective. It can never have a meaning of "as" of an implied כ preposition. Its sentence would be somewhat ambiguous without it, so it clarifies a statement by answering the questions, "in what terms of," "by what specifically," "with respect to what." Gen 41:40 is the classic example: רַק הַכִּסֵּא אֶגְדַּל מִמֶּךָּ "Only *with respect to* the throne, I will be greater than you" (Gen 3:15; 17:11; 37:21; Exod 6:3; Ps 3:8; JM §126g; GKC §118q though GKC combines situation and specification here). In the composition sentence, "We should smite him mortally," the accusative is specification: "We should smite him *specifically as to* soul" (§13jj–pp).
3. Time and Place (Arabic Zarf = vessel, since time and place are considered the vessels in which the verb occurs) – Accusatives indicating time and place are common.
   A. Time (§13x-y; JM §126i; GKC §118i–k)
      1) Answering the question: "when" (Gen 11:10; 14:4; Ps 5:4)
      2) Answering the question: "how long" (Gen 3:14; 7:4; 14:4; 15:13)
   B. Place (§13v-w; JM §126h; GKC §118d-g)
      1) Answering the question: "to what place" (after verbs of motion, Gen 10:11; 13:9; 24:27; 26:23; 27:3; 31:4; 1 Sam 20:11; GKC §118f). The accusative ending ָה works as well.
      2) Answering the question: "where" (after verbs of being, dwelling, and resting, Gen 18:1, 10; 24:23; 38:11; 1 Sam 17:15; GKC §118g. In these passages the accusative is the first word in the annexation). If a single word is used instead of annexation, the accusative of place is often avoided and the ב preposition with the single word occurs (2 Sam 7:6; 1 Kgs 3:17; 14:6; 2 Kgs 4:15), or the accusative ending ָה may be used (Gen 19:10; 43:16). With other verbs (other than, "being," "dwelling," and "resting") the accusative is often used with single words (Exod 4:9).

Adverbial (or indirect) accusatives (especially the accusatives of situation) resemble consecutive infinitive absolutes after verbs and situation clauses because they are all adverbial.

16. but his wise men said – The Hebrew reads, "and his wise men said." For this adversative clause, avoid the Vav-consecutive construction and use the nominal clause with its subject first (3.12; §83c).
17. No, but – Following a negative, כִּי often has the adversative nuance of "but" (§83b; JM §172c; GKC §163a; BDB 474a 3e).
18. smite him (on the) cheek – Adverbial accusative, specification (6.15 [2]). For the verb, use the plural imperative. Write the Vav of plurality defectively (IBH 1.8.2.2, footnote 6) since this commonly happens when another historic long vowel occurs in the next syllable (here with the pronominal suffix).
19. with a smiting that wounds – The Hebrew reads, "smiting and wounding." These infinitive absolutes explain and emphasize the manner or quality of the verbal action (5.30).
20. but do not kill him – The Hebrew reads, "and do not kill him." For the verb, see 6.18.
21. And the words of his wise men pleased Pharaoh – The Hebrew reads, "And (they) were good in the eyes of Pharaoh the words of his wise men."
22. the wise men of Pharaoh and his servants – Hebrew expresses compound genitival phrases in three ways: (1) The wise men of Pharaoh and his servants, חַכְמֵי פַּרְעֹה וַעֲבָדָיו, (2) The wise men

Aaron.[23] (11) And they came near to Moses while he was standing beside the Nile with the staff of God in his hand.[24] (12) Then Moses took water from the Nile and he poured (it)[25] out (on) the dry ground,[26] and the water became blood.[27]

(13) And it happened when the servants of Pharaoh and the wise men saw[28] this sign that they said to Pharaoh, "The Lord, he is fighting for them,[29] what can we do[30] since[31] the Lord has done even this (sign)?" [32] (14) But Pharaoh refused[33] to listen to them,[34] because[35] God had hardened[36] his heart and he said to them, "You are cowards,[37] I will not release them."*[38]

---

of Pharaoh and the servants, חַכְמֵי־פַרְעֹה וְהָעֲבָדִים, (3) the wise men and the servants which (are) to Pharaoh, הַחֲכָמִים וְהָעֲבָדִים אֲשֶׁר לְפַרְעֹה (6.28, 39; JM §129a).

23. to seize Moses and Aaron – To render the English "to seize," use the Hiphil of חזק with the ב preposition attached to the objects, "Moses and Aaron." Since these direct objects are attached to their verb by the ב preposition, they are called improper objects to distinguish them from proper objects, that is, direct objects (direct accusative) without prepositions. Often, prepositions with their objects are adverbial (indirect) to their verbs, but they may be in the position of the direct object as here (1.29; §13s).
24. with the staff of God in his hand – A situation clause, the Hebrew reads, "and the staff of God in his hand" (5.18–19; §49b).
25. and he poured (it) – If consecutive Hebrew verbs have the same object, Hebrew may drop the object with the second verb since context implies this object (Exod 2:5–6).
26. (on) the dry ground – This is an accusative of place (6.15 3B2). Moreover, the place is specified (§13w).
27. and the water became blood – The Hebrew reads, "and (they) became the water for blood." The preposition ל substitutes for the accusative of situation after the verb היה (3.16).
28. when the servants of Pharaoh and the wise men saw – For the temporal clause, use the infinitive construct with the כ preposition. For the compound genitival phrase, see 6.22.
29. The Lord, he is fighting for them – The Hebrew reads, "the Lord, he (is) the fighter for them." See 5.9 section 1B. The participle is a Niphal with an active meaning instead of the usual reflexive meaning. This is similar to a deponent verb of Greek or Latin.
30. what can we do – This is an imperfect indicative used in the present, as is common in questions (1.31).
31. since – Hebrew often connects *inseparable* prepositions to the relative particle אֲשֶׁר to form conjunctions. Moreover, *separable* prepositions are also placed before אֲשֶׁר to form conjunctions (BDB 83b 8f, 774b 2a–b). Here, the separable preposition before אֲשֶׁר is יַ֫עַן. Many prepositions, over time, became conjunctions even without אֲשֶׁר.
32. even this (sign) – Place the accusative marker before the demonstrative pronoun.
33. But Pharaoh refused – Occasionally, the Vav particle of the Vav-consecutive can express an adversative notion (1 Sam 1:15; §83c; JM §172a; GKC §163a).
34. to listen to them – The Hebrew reads, "to hear their words."
35. because – Use the conjunctive particle יַ֫עַן without אֲשֶׁר (6.31; BDB 774b 2c).
36. God had hardened – This Piel verb is factitive, meaning "to make," such as, "God made hard the heart." Factitive Piels are common with verbs that are stative in the Qal. For instance, the Qal stative כָּבֵד "to be heavy" becomes factitive in the Piel, putting its object into the state of the meaning of the Qal, "God put the heart of Pharaoh into a heavy (hard) state" (1.27; §7d; IBH 23.5.1.2; JM §52d).
37. You are cowards – The Hebrew reads, "men of fear you (are)" (6.11).
38. I will not release them – The pronominal suffix "hides" the final ה ָ of the cohortative form that emphasizes the will of the speaker.

(15) Then the servants and wise men of Pharaoh[39] said to each other,[40] "Pharaoh is stiffnecked,[41] why has he done this thing, namely, he refused[42] to release them*; we shall all die as one man."[43]

39. the servants and wise men of Pharaoh – The Hebrew reads, "the servants and the wise men which are to Pharaoh" (6.22).
40. to each other – The Hebrew reads, "a man to his brother" (4.2).
41. Pharaoh is stiffnecked – The Hebrew reads, "stiff of neck (is) Pharaoh." An adjective as the first word (*nomen regens*, governing noun) in annexation usually specifies the last word (the genitive) in the annexation, "stiff (*in terms of*) neck." This construction, when the first word of the annexation is a participle or adjective, is an "improper" or "impure" annexation between the words (§12f). The second word, always indefinite, does not define or identify the first word of the annexation. The indefinite second word, even if it were definite would not render the first word definite. The indefinite second word (the genitive) "specializes" the first word by specifying the affected area: "stiff with respect to the (or in the area of the) neck." Pharaoh's whole body is not stiff, but his neck is the affected area of his stiffness. This construction resembles the accusative of specification (6.15 [2]; §13nn; JM §129i).
42. namely, he refused – the Hebrew reads, "and he refused." The relationship between the clauses indicates an explanatory relationship. Translate the Vav of the Vav-consecutive as "namely" (§6r; JM §118j).
43. we shall all die as one man – The Hebrew reads, "we shall die, all of us, as one man." The phrase "all of us" is the noun כֹּל with a pronominal suffix. This appositional phrase emphasizes the subject, "We, the whole of us (everyone of us), are dead," to prevent forgetfulness, inattentiveness, or lack of concern. It is called conceptual emphasis because it strengthens the totality and pushes away other possibilities or options – "we shall die, everyone of us (and no others, so be attentive to the problem at hand), as one man" (§24i; BDB 481b 1d).

Key to Composition Six

1 וַיָּבֹאוּ מֹשֶׁה וְאַהֲרֹן אֶל־פַּרְעֹה וַיֹּאמְרוּ יְהוָה אֱלֹהֵי הָעִבְרִיִּים נִרְאָה אֵלֵינוּ
בַּמִּדְבָּר בֵּאלֹהִים גִּבּוֹר וְכֹה אָמַר יְהוָה אֱלֹהִים אָנֹכִי יְהוָה אֱלֹהֵי כָל־הָאָרֶץ
שַׁלַּח אֶת־עַמִּי וְיַעַבְדֻנִי׃

2 וַיֹּאמֶר פַּרְעֹה מִי יְהוָה אֲשֶׁר אֵדַע אֹתוֹ׃

3 וַיֹּאמֶר מֹשֶׁה יְהוָה דֶּרֶךְ אֱמֶת דַּרְכּוֹ וְכַבֵּד אֶת־לִבְּךָ וְיַרְאֲךָ אֶת־כֹּחוֹ וְתֵדַע אֶת־
שְׁמוֹ כָּל־הַיָּמִים׃

4 וַיֹּאמֶר פַּרְעֹה אֶת־יְהוָה לֹא אֵדָע וְגַם אֶת־יִשְׂרָאֵל לֹא אֲשַׁלֵּחַ׃

5 וַיֹּאמֶר מֹשֶׁה יְהוָה אֵל קַנָּא הוּא נֹקֵם לְשֹׂנְאָיו׃

6 וְכַבֵּד יְכַבֵּד אֶת־לִבֶּךָ וְיָבִיא עָלֶיךָ וְעַל־בֵּיתְךָ אֵת כָּל־אוֹתֹתָיו וְאֵת כָּל־מוֹפְתָיו׃

7 וַיֹּאמֶר פַּרְעֹה בֶּן־מָוֶת אַתָּה יָצוֹא מֵעִמִּי כִּי לֹא אוּכַל לָשֵׂאת אֶת־דְּבָרֶיךָ עוֹד׃

8 וַיִּקְרָא פַּרְעֹה לַעֲבָדָיו וּלְחַכְמֵי בֵיתוֹ וַיֹּאמֶר אֲלֵיהֶם מַה־נַּעֲשֶׂה׃

9 וַיֹּאמְרוּ עֲבָדָיו נַכֶּנּוּ נָפֶשׁ וַחֲכָמָיו אָמְרוּ לֹא כִּי־הַכֵּהוּ לְחִי וְנַכֵּהוּ הַכֵּה וּפָצֹעַ וְאַל
תַּהַרְגֻהוּ׃

10 וַיִּיטְבוּ בְּעֵינֵי פַּרְעֹה דִּבְרֵי חֲכָמָיו וַיֵּצְאוּ חַכְמֵי פַרְעֹה וַעֲבָדָיו לְהַחֲזִיק בְּמֹשֶׁה
וּבְאַהֲרֹן׃

11 וַיִּקְרְבוּ אֶל־מֹשֶׁה וְהוּא עֹמֵד עַל־יַד הַיְאֹר וּמַטֵּה אֱלֹהִים בְּיָדוֹ׃

12 וַיִּקַּח מֹשֶׁה מַיִם מִן־הַיְאֹר וַיִּשְׁפֹּךְ הַיַּבָּשָׁה וַיִּהְיוּ הַמַּיִם לְדָם׃

13 וַיְהִי כִּרְאוֹת עַבְדֵי פַרְעֹה וְהַחֲכָמִים אֶת־הָאוֹת הַזֶּה וַיֹּאמְרוּ אֶל־פַּרְעֹה יְהוָה הוּא
הַנִּלְחָם לָהֶם מַה־נַּעֲשֶׂה יַעַן־אֲשֶׁר עָשָׂה יְהוָה גַּם־אֶת־זֶה׃

14 וַיְמָאֵן פַּרְעֹה לִשְׁמֹעַ אֶת־דִּבְרֵיהֶם יַעַן כִּבֵּד אֱלֹהִים אֶת־לִבּוֹ וַיֹּאמֶר אֲלֵיהֶם אַנְשֵׁי
יִרְאָה אַתֶּם לֹא אֲשַׁלְּחֵם׃

15 וַיֹּאמְרוּ הָעֲבָדִים וְהַחֲכָמִים אֲשֶׁר לְפַרְעֹה אִישׁ אֶל־אָחִיו קְשֵׁה עֹרֶף פַּרְעֹה מַדּוּעַ
עָשָׂה אֶת־הַדָּבָר הַזֶּה וַיְמָאֵן לְשַׁלְּחָם נָמוּת כֻּלָּנוּ כְּאִישׁ אֶחָד׃

Unpointed Text of Composition Six

1 ויבאו משה ואהרן אל־פרעה ויאמרו יהוה אלהי העבריים נראה אלינו
במדבר באלהים גבור וכה אמר יהוה אלהים אנכי יהוה אלהי כל־הארץ
שלח את־עמי ויעבדני:

2 ויאמר פרעה מי יהוה אשר אדע אתו:

3 ויאמר משה יהוה דרך אמת דרכו וכבד את־לבך ויראך את־כחו ותדע את־
שמו כל־הימים:

4 ויאמר פרעה את־יהוה לא אדע וגם את־ישראל לא אשלח:

5 ויאמר משה יהוה אל קנא הוא נקם לשנאיו:

6 וכבד יכבד את־לבך ויביא עליך ועל־ביתך את כל־אותותיו ואת כל־מופתיו:

7 ויאמר פרעה בן־מות אתה יצוא מעמי כי לא אוכל לשאת את־דבריך עוד:

8 ויקרא פרעה לעבדיו ולחכמי ביתו ויאמר אליהם מה־נעשה:

9 ויאמרו עבדיו נכנו נפש וחכמיו אמרו לא כי־הכהו לחי ונכהו הכה ופצע ואל
תהרגהו:

10 וייטבו בעיני פרעה דברי חכמיו ויצאו חכמי פרעה ועבדיו להחזיק במשה
ובאהרן:

11 ויקרבו אל־משה והוא עמד על־יד היאר ומטה אלהים בידו:

12 ויקח משה מים מן־היאר וישפך היבשה ויהיו המים לדם:

13 ויהי כראות עבדי פרעה והחכמים את־האות הזה ויאמרו אל־פרעה יהוה הוא
הנלחם להם מה־נעשה יען־אשר עשה יהוה גם־את־זה:

14 וימאן פרעה לשמע את־דבריהם יען כבד אלהים את־לבו ויאמר אליהם אנשי
יראה אתם לא אשלחם:

15 ויאמרו העבדים והחכמים אשר לפרעה איש אל־אחיו קשה ערף פרעה מדוע
עשה את־הדבר הזה וימאן לשלחם נמות כלנו כאיש אחד:

COMPOSITION SEVEN

(1) Then the people saw that Moses did not come down from [upon] the mountain and the people got themselves gathered together at the door of (the) tent of meeting. (2) Then the people argued with Aaron saying, "Did you bring us up to this place to kill us?* (3) You have got yourself exalted over us – you and Moses – and now Moses is no more, and you cannot bring us# into this land. Enough of your being king over us because the entire congregation is holy to the Lord [it]. (4) We shall take now holy vessels and we will appoint rulers as our heads." But Aaron said, "No my brothers, do not strive with me please. Why are you tempting the Lord, who brought us out from Egypt?"

(5) Now Moses had gone up to the mountain to hear the word of the Lord as the mountain was burning with [the] fire. (6) And the Lord said to Moses, "Go down to the camp and then speak to the Israelites that they might turn from their evil ways lest I should smite them* greatly because from the least even to the greatest they have rebelled (against) me." (7) Then Moses went down from the mountain with the two [of] tablets of the Lord in his hand. And he entered the camp as the people were sinning greatly in the eyes of the Lord. (8) Then Moses became angry and smashed to pieces the two tablets of the Lord and said, "For forty days you have dwelled at Mount Sinai, and now you have rebelled (against) the Lord by worshipping the sun, [and] the moon, and the stars. (9) You are more wicked than the Amorites. Return to the Lord that he might deliver you from the plague." Then Moses said, "Who belongs to the Lord, come to me." (10) Then wild animals came into the camp and killed the ones sinning against the Lord and against Moses, as a lion would kill and eat. (11) Now the golden gods, which Aaron had made, Moses smashed them* and he caused the Israelites to drink (them).

(12) And it happened after these things that the people wept before the Lord as Moses was entering (the) tent of meeting. Then the Lord said to Moses, "Would that this people had a heart to obey me.* (13) Go out now to the people and say to them, 'Do not weep; go up to possess the land. Only obey me that you might lengthen your days upon the land.'"

(14) Then the people rose up and journeyed from Mount Sinai.

( ) – Not in Hebrew, but needed for English
[ ] – In the Hebrew, but not needed for English
* – Put the pronominal suffix directly on the verb
# – Put the pronominal suffix with energic Nun directly on the verb

(1) Then the people saw[1] that Moses did not come down from [upon] the mountain and the people got themselves gathered together at the door of (the) tent of meeting.[2] (2) Then the people argued with Aaron saying, "Did you bring us up to this place to kill us?*[3] (3) You have got yourself[4] exalted over us – you and Moses[5] – and now Moses is no more,[6] and you[7] cannot bring us#[8] into this land. Enough of your being king[9] over us because the entire congregation is holy to the Lord [it].[10] (4) We shall take now[11] holy vessels[12] and we will appoint rulers[13] as our heads."[14] But Aaron said, "No my brothers,

1. Then the people saw – 3.1.
2. got themselves gathered at the door of the tent of meeting – The verb is a Niphal (4.6). The preposition "at" represents an accusative of (specified) place (6:15 [3.B.2], 26; §13w).
3. to kill us – Use the Qal of הרג (BDB 247a), not the Hiphil of מות, which would be better for capital punishment or for war (BDB 560b).
4. You have got yourself exalted – The ת of the Hithpael conveys the reflexive nuance and the personal interest of the subject (4.6; §7b; JM §53i; GKC §54f). Moreover, since the Hithpael is often the reflexive of the Piel, as here, the Hithpael can be intensive/extensive (or any other meaning of the Piel): "You have got yourself intensely exalted." By using the Hithpael here, the speaker emphasizes that Aaron and Moses had got themselves appointed over the Israelites, suggesting that God had not appointed them.
5. you and Moses – 3.27, 5.10.
6. and now Moses is no more – The Hebrew reads, "And now Moses, he is not." The clause – "he is not" – is the particle of negation, the semi-verb אַיִן (in construct with a noun or with a suffix, the form appears as אֵין) with a 3ms energic suffix. This is another variation of the nominal clause with a clause for the predicate, "Moses – he is no more" (5.9 1.A).
7. and you – To contrast Aaron and Moses, use the independent pronoun, "Moses is no more, and *you* cannot bring us into this land" (3.12, 24, 34).
8. you cannot bring us – The Hebrew reads, "You are not (in the process of) bringing us" (§4e).
9. Enough of your being king – The Hebrew reads, "Much to you from being king." The last three English words of this idiomatic construction represent an infinitive construct with the מִן preposition (BDB 913a 1f).
10. the entire congregation is holy to the Lord [it] – The Hebrew reads, "The congregation, all of her (6.43), holy to the Lord she (is)" (5.9 [1A]). The word "all (of her)" is (conceptual) corroborative since it repeats its noun (congregation) and thus "strengthens or emphasizes its noun 'because of the fear of forgetfulness, inattentiveness, or lack of concern'" (§24i; for another type of corroborative, see 10.1).
11. We shall take now – Use the cohortative with the נָא particle to emphasize the rebellious will of the speakers. Use the cohortative with conjunctive Vav for the next verb (2.21).
12. holy vessels – The Hebrew reads, "vessels of holiness." Although it can modify nouns with adjectives, Hebrew usually modifies nouns with other nouns by annexation. This is proper annexation, the last noun (*nomen rectum*, end noun, the genitive) in the annexation modifies the first noun (*nomen regens*, governing noun). Assume a לְ preposition between the words in annexation for meaning: "vessels with respect to holiness" (1.4, 19; §12b, e; JM §129f 1; GKC §128p; IBH 11.9.2).
13. we will appoint rulers – The Hebrew reads, "we will appoint (give) men, rulers." The word "rulers" is an accusative of situation, "We will appoint men (to be) *in the situation, status, or condition of* rulers" (6.15 [1]; §13z; JM §131b). The accusative of situation is illustrating (§13aa) because it supplies new information (rulers) and is permanent (§13gg) because these rulers permanently replace Moses and Aaron.
14. as our heads – 6.2.

do not strive[15] with me please. Why are you tempting[16] the Lord, who brought us out[17] from Egypt?"

(5) Now Moses had gone up[18] to the mountain to hear the word of the Lord as the mountain was burning[19] with [the] fire.[20] (6) And the Lord said to Moses, "Go down to the camp[21] and then speak to the Israelites[22] that they might turn from their evil ways lest I should smite them* greatly[23] because from the least even to the greatest[24] they have rebelled (against) me."[25] (7) Then Moses went down from the mountain with the two [of] tablets of the Lord in his hand.[26] And he entered the camp as the people were sinning greatly[27] in the eyes of the Lord. (8) Then Moses became angry[28] and smashed to pieces the two tablets of the Lord and said, "For forty days[29] you have dwelled at Mount

---

15. do not strive – Use אַל with the jussive and the נָא particle since Aaron is pleading (not demanding) with the people (1.37, 3.9, 5.6).
16. Why are you tempting – 1.31, 5.18.
17. who brought us out – Use the participle with the article. The articular participle may have the aspect of a perfect or imperfect verb. Because the context indicates a past, completed action, the participle has the aspect of a perfect. For an example of a participle with the aspect of an imperfect, see 7.39. Indefinite participles usually have the aspect of an imperfect (4.9; §16n).
18. Now Moses had gone up – 1.38, 3.12.
19. as the mountain was burning – The Hebrew reads, "and the mountain was burning," a situation clause (4.22).
20. with [the] fire – Hebrew, more than English, uses the article generically (generally), where English uses the indefinite article or no article at all (5.7). This is especially true with materials and elements, such as, fire, silver, gold, oil, etc. (JM §137ia; GKC §126n). The article is the generic of the essence/quality of the group (§35a), focusing on the whole as a whole and not on every individual manifestation of fire (the totality of individuals within the group, §35b).
21. Go down to the camp – Use the accusative of (specified) place for the noun (7.2).
22. the Israelites – The Hebrew reads, "sons of Israel" (6.11).
23. lest I should smite them greatly – The Hebrew reads, "lest I should smite them a great smiting" (2.19).
24. from the least even to the greatest – The Hebrew reads, "from the small and unto the great." Hebrew can express the superlative (the least, the greatest) by the adjective with the article (§23d; JM §141j; GKC §133g; IBH 26.4.2.1.1).
25. they have rebelled (against) me – The Hebrew reads, "(against) me they have rebelled." Notice the emphatic placement of the direct object before the verb. The aspect of the verb is completed in the past up to the present, like a Greek perfect (1.14, 32; §3h).
26. with the two [of] tablets of the Lord in his hand – The Hebrew reads, "and the two [of] tablets of the Lord in his hand," a situation clause (5.18–19).
27. as the people were sinning greatly – The Hebrew reads, "and the people were sinning a great sin" (2.19, 4.22, 24; §13e, 17j). Use the imperfect for the verb and an absolute object with modifier that explains the quality or manner of the verbal action.
28. Then Moses became angry – The Hebrew reads, "And (it) became hot the nose of Moses."
29. For forty days – The Hebrew reads, "forty day." This is an adverbial accusative of (specified) time (6.15 [3A2]; §13y). The word "day," an accusative of specification, is singular in Hebrew: "forty *in terms of* day" (6:15 [2]; §13kk; JM §127b). With the numerals over eleven, certain commonly used nouns may be singular (§29e; JM §142e).

Sinai,[30] and now you have rebelled (against) the Lord[31] by worshipping[32] the sun, [and] the moon, and the stars.[33] (9) You are more wicked than[34] the Amorites.[35] Return to the Lord that he might deliver you[36] from the plague." Then Moses said, "Who belongs to the Lord,[37] come to me." (10) Then wild animals came[38] into the camp and killed the ones sinning against the Lord and against Moses,[39] as a lion[40] would kill and eat.[41] (11) Now the golden gods,[42] which Aaron had made, Moses smashed them* and he caused the Israelites[43] to drink (them).[44]

(12) And it happened after these things that the people wept before the Lord as Moses was entering[45] (the) tent of meeting. Then the Lord said to Moses, "Would

30. at Mount Sinai – The Hebrew reads, "Mountain of Sinai." The construct relationship is "proper" between the words, with the second word of the construct defining or identifying the first word of the construct. For this particular annexation, the relationship between the words is equivalent to a ב preposition inserted between them, "The mountain *in* Sinai" (1.4; JM §129f; GKC §128k, m).
31. you have rebelled (against) the Lord – The Hebrew reads, "you have rebelled (against) the mouth of the Lord."
32. by worshipping – Use the infinitive construct with the ל preposition. This infinitive construct explains or specifies how they rebelled against the Lord (§18h; JM §124o; GKC §114o). Note the English gerund, "by worshipping," for the explanatory or specification of infinitive constructs instead of the English infinitive, "to worship." This verb often takes an object with the preposition ל to complete the verbal meaning. The Hebrew reads, "to bow down to."
33. the sun, the moon, and the stars – The Hebrew reads, "the sun, *and* the moon, and the stars." The article is used for unique persons and objects (§34d; JM §137h; GKC §126d).
34. more wicked than – The adjective followed by the מִן preposition express the comparative (§23b; IBH 26.4.1.1).
35. the Amorites – Use the Hireq-Yod (Nisbah) ending on the singular noun (5.7). This generic use of the article could be the generic of the essence/quality of the group or the totality of individuals within the group. The former would mean the Amorites as a whole, as a group; the latter would mean all the individuals that make up the Amorite group. Here the essence/quality is better since a comparison is made between Israelites and Amorites as groups, not as every individual within the groups (§35a–b).
36. that he might deliver you – Use the jussive form with the conjunctive Vav (2.7; Hos 4:4).
37. who belongs to the Lord – The Hebrew reads, "Who (is) to the Lord."
38. Then wild animals came – The third feminine plural of בוא is תְּבוֹאנָה, תָּבֹאןָ, or תְּבֹאֶינָה. Use the last option.
39. the ones sinning against the Lord and against Moses – The participle conveys the durative aspect of their sinning (4.9, 7.17; §16a; JM §124c, f; GKC §116a). The participle often communicates the notion of office, occupation, or profession. They were professional sinners, as if sinning was their occupation or profession.
40. as a lion would kill – The Hebrew reads, "as the lion would kill." This article expresses the totality of individuals within the group (5.7). A particular lion is not in view, but the *typical* lion, every lion. Therefore, translate the word "lion" with an indefinite article (§35b; JM §137i). For the conjunctive "as," use כַּאֲשֶׁר, which is often followed by an imperfect for comparisons (BDB 445b 1.d).
41. would kill and eat – Connect the two imperfect indicatives (frequentatives) with a conjunctive Vav (1.11; §4d; JM §115a, 120). In this context, verbal aspect is stronger relative to tense (§ 2c; 3q).
42. Now the golden gods – The Hebrew reads, "And the gods of gold," proper annexation (7.12, 5.9 [2C]). Assume a מִן preposition between the annexation (§12d).
43. Israelites – The Hebrew reads, "the sons of Israel" (6.11).
44. (them) – Hebrew may omit the direct object from the second verb (6.25; §13r; JM §125x).
45. as Moses was entering – 4.22.

that this people had a heart to obey me.*[46] (13) Go out now[47] to the people and say to them,[48] 'Do not weep;[49] go up to possess the land.[50] Only obey me[51] that you might lengthen[52] your days upon the land.'"

(14) Then the people rose up and journeyed[53] from Mount Sinai.[54]

---

46. Would that this people had a heart to obey me – The Hebrew reads, "Who will give to this people a heart to obey (hear) me." The imperfect of the verb נָתַן may express a wish or desire, like a Greek optative (§56i, 62c; BDB 678b 1f).
47. Go out now – The infinitive absolute supplies the nuance of "now" (4.36). Use the infinitive absolute as the absolute object with the imperative implied.
48. and say to them – The Hebrew reads, "and say to *him*." "People" is a collective noun that may take a singular modifier or pronoun (4.28, 5.7; §9b; BDBa 1a).
49. Do not weep – Use אַל plus the jussive, though the form is indicative not jussive (7.15); therefore, use the long form of the verb, not the shortened form. אַל plus the jussive gives the command emotion and feeling.
50. go up to possess the land – The Hebrew reads, "go up, possess the land" (2.27; JM §177e; GKC §120g).
51. obey me – The Hebrew reads, "hear in my voice."
52. that you might lengthen – Use the conjunctive particle לְמַעַן with the imperfect subjunctive (2.15; Deut 16:3; 27:3; Josh 3:4; §4j; JM §116a).
53. Then the people rose up and journeyed – Because "people" is collective, it may take plural verbs or plural modifiers (2.27, 7.48; GKC §132g). Use the plural verb here.
54. from Mount Sinai – The Hebrew reads, "from (the) Mountain of Sinai" (7.30).

Key to Composition Seven

1 וַיַּרְא הָעָם כִּי לֹא־יָרַד מֹשֶׁה מֵעַל־הָהָר וַיִּקָּהֵל הָעָם פֶּתַח אֹהֶל מוֹעֵד׃

2 וַיָּרֶב הָעָם עִם־אַהֲרֹן לֵאמֹר הֶעֱלִיתָ אֹתָנוּ אֶל־הַמָּקוֹם הַזֶּה לְהָרְגֵנוּ׃

3 הִתְנַשֵּׂאתָ עָלֵינוּ אַתָּה וּמֹשֶׁה וְעַתָּה מֹשֶׁה אֵינֶנּוּ וְאַתָּה לֹא תְבִיאֵנוּ אֶל־הָאָרֶץ הַזֹּאת
רַב לְךָ מִמְּלֹךְ עָלֵינוּ כִּי הָעֵדָה כֻּלָּהּ קְדֹשָׁה לַיהוָה הִיא׃

4 נִקְחָה־נָּא כְּלֵי קֹדֶשׁ וְנִתְּנָה אֲנָשִׁים שָׂרִים בְּרָאשֵׁינוּ וַיֹּאמֶר אַהֲרֹן אַל־אַחַי אַל־
תָּרִיבוּ נָא עִמִּי לָמָּה תְנַסּוּ אֶת־יהוה הַמּוֹצִיא אֹתָנוּ מִמִּצְרָיִם׃

5 וּמֹשֶׁה עָלָה אֶל־הָהָר לִשְׁמֹעַ אֶת־דְּבַר יהוָה וְהָהָר בֹּעֵר בָּאֵשׁ׃

6 וַיֹּאמֶר יהוה אֶל־מֹשֶׁה רֵד הַמַּחֲנֶה וְדִבַּרְתָּ אֶל־בְּנֵי־יִשְׂרָאֵל וְיָשׁוּבוּ מִן־דַּרְכֵיהֶם
הָרָעִים פֶּן־אַכֶּם מַכָּה גְדוֹלָה כִּי מֵהַקָּטֹן וְעַד־הַגָּדוֹל אִתִּי מָרוּ׃

7 וַיֵּרֶד מֹשֶׁה מִן־הָהָר וּשְׁנֵי לֻחֹת יהוָה בְּיָדוֹ וַיָּבֹא הַמַּחֲנֶה וְהָעָם יֶחֱטָא חֲטָאָה
גְדוֹלָה בְּעֵינֵי יהוָה׃

8 וַיִּחַר־אַף מֹשֶׁה וַיְשַׁבֵּר אֶת־שְׁנֵי לֻחוֹת יהוָה וַיֹּאמֶר אַרְבָּעִים יוֹם יָשַׁבְתָּ הַר סִינַי
וְעַתָּה מָרִיתָ אֶת־פִּי יהוה לְהִשְׁתַּחֲוֹת לַשֶּׁמֶשׁ וְלַיָּרֵחַ וְלַכּוֹכָבִים׃

9 אַתָּה רָשָׁע מִן־הָאֱמֹרִי שׁוּב אֶל־יהוה וְיַצֵּל אֹתְךָ מִן־הַמַּגֵּפָה וַיֹּאמֶר מֹשֶׁה מִי
לַיהוָה לְכָה אֵלָי׃

10 וַתְּבֹאֶינָה אֶל־הַמַּחֲנֶה חַיּוֹת רָעוֹת וַתַּהֲרֹגְנָה אֶת־הַחֹטְאִים לַיהוה וּלְמֹשֶׁה כַּאֲשֶׁר
יַהֲרֹג הָאֲרִי וְיֹאכֵל׃

11 וֵאלֹהֵי זָהָב אֲשֶׁר עָשָׂה אַהֲרֹן שִׁבְּרָם מֹשֶׁה וַיַּשְׁקְ אֶת־בְּנֵי־יִשְׂרָאֵל׃

12 וַיְהִי אַחַר הַדְּבָרִים הָאֵלֶּה וַיֵּבְךְּ הָעָם לִפְנֵי־יהוה וּמֹשֶׁה בָּא אֹהֶל מוֹעֵד וַיֹּאמֶר
יהוה אֶל־מֹשֶׁה מִי יִתֵּן לָעָם הַזֶּה לֵב שָׁמְעֵנִי׃

13 יָצוֹא אֶל־הָעָם וְאָמַר אֵלָיו אַל־תִּבְכֶּה עֲלֵה רֵשׁ אֶת־הָאָרֶץ רַק שְׁמַע בְּקֹלִי לְמַעַן
תַּאֲרִיךְ יָמֶיךָ עַל־הָאֲדָמָה׃

14 וַיָּקוּמוּ הָעָם וַיִּסְעוּ מִן־הַר סִינָי׃

Unpointed Text of Composition Seven

1 וירא העם כי לא־ירד משה מעל־ההר ויקהל העם פתח אהל מועד:

2 וירב העם עם־אהרן לאמר ההעלית אתנו אל־המקום הזה להרגנו:

3 התנשאת עלינו אתה ומשה ועתה משה איננו ואתה לא תביאנו אל־הארץ הזאת
רב לך ממלך עלינו כי העדה כלה קדשה ליהוה היא:

4 נקחה־נא כלי קדש ונתנה אנשים שרים בראשינו ויאמר אהרן אל־אחי אל־
תריבו נא עמי למה תנסו את־יהוה המוציא אתנו ממצרים:

5 ומשה עלה אל־ההר לשמע את־דבר יהוה וההר בער באש:

6 ויאמר יהוה אל־משה רד המחנה ודברת אל־בני־ישראל וישובו מן־דרכיהם
הרעים פן־אכם מכה גדולה כי מהקטן ועד־הגדול אתי מרו:

7 וירד משה מן־ההר ושני לחות יהוה בידו ויבא המחנה והעם יחטא חטאה
גדולה בעיני יהוה:

8 ויחר־אף משה וישבר את־שני לחות יהוה ויאמר ארבעים יום ישבת הר סיני
ועתה מרית את־פי יהוה להשתחות לשמש ולירח ולכוכבים:

9 אתה רשע מן־האמרי שוב אל־יהוה ויצל אתך מן־המגפה ויאמר משה מי
ליהוה לכה אלי:

10 ותבאינה אל־המחנה חיות רעות ותהרגנה את־החטאים ליהוה ולמשה כאשר
יהרג הארי ויאכל:

11 ואלהי זהב אשר עשה אהרן שברם משה וישק את־בני־ישראל:

12 ויהי אחר הדברים האלה ויבך העם לפני־יהוה ומשה בא אהל מועד ויאמר
יהוה אל־משה מי יתן לעם הזה לב שמעני:

13 יצוא אל־העם ואמר אליו אל־תבכה עלה רש את־הארץ רק שמע בקלי למען
תאריך ימיך על־האדמה:

14 ויקומו העם ויסעו מן־הר סיני:

COMPOSITION EIGHT

(1) Now it happened before the death of David, the king of Israel, that he said, I have become old and grey, and behold, I am going in the way of all the earth. (2) The Lord, the God of Israel, has fulfilled his good word which he promised to me and to my house.

(3) Now Adonijah, the son of Haggith, was exalting himself saying, I reign. (4) And there existed for himself twelve chariots and thirty-six horsemen, with fifty men running before him. (5) And they went crying out as they went, king, live forever.

(6) And it was reported to David saying, Adonijah has become king, and he said, Solomon, son of Bathsheba, has become a traitor. (7) Then David summoned his servants and the people and Solomon, his son, and he said, today no food will be eaten at all until Solomon, my son, becomes king. (8) Far be it, (by) the life of the Lord who delivered me* from the hand of all my enemies, (thus may God do to you and thus may he add) if indeed (there) falls from a hair of the head of Solomon, my son, to the ground. (9) For he will indeed reign over all Israel this day. And they took Solomon, the son of David, and anointed him for a king over Israel.

(10) Then Adonijah and his men heard that David and the people made Solomon king over all Israel. (11) And the men belonging to Adonijah trembled and rose up and fled and got themselves hid in a cave. And there was a well of water and seven palm trees. (12) And Adonijah became afraid of Solomon and he arose and went and seized on the horns of the altar. (13) And it was reported to Solomon saying behold Adonijah is afraid of the king, Solomon, and he summoned Adonijah and commanded him* saying, you must not go out from this city. (14) For on the day of your going out of the city, you will most certainly die by the sword. And Adonijah said, Amen. (15) And it happened after six days, Adonijah went out of the city to meet the men who made him* king. (16) Then the king Solomon swore by the Lord saying, thus may God do to me and thus may he add if indeed against his own soul Adonijah has done this thing. (17) And now as the Lord lives, indeed today Adonijah will be put to death. Then Solomon sent his servant and he struck him down and so he died.

(18) Now the king Solomon was blessed, and the throne of David became established before the Lord on that day.

( ) – Not in Hebrew, but needed for English
[ ] – In the Hebrew, but not needed for English
* – Put the pronominal suffix directly on the verb
# – Put the pronominal suffix with energic Nun directly on the verb

(1) Now it happened before the death of David, the king of Israel,[1] that he said, I have become old and grey,[2] and behold, I[3] am going in the way of all the earth. (2) The Lord, the God of Israel,[4] has fulfilled[5] his good word which he promised to me and to my house.

(3) Now Adonijah, the son of Haggith, was exalting himself[6] saying, I reign.[7] (4) And there existed for himself twelve chariots[8] and thirty-six horsemen,[9] with fifty men running before him.[10] (5) And they went crying out as they went,[11] king,[12] live forever.

(6) And it was reported[13] to David saying, Adonijah has become king, and he

---

1. the king of Israel – substitution apposition (5.12)
2. I have become old and grey – The second perfect verb is attached to the first perfect verb by a connecting (conjunctive) Vav. If the Vav on the second perfect verb had been energic, the accent for the word would have been on the last syllable (Gen 28:21; Jer 29:14; 48:47; 50:19; Ezek 29:14; §6b; IBH 2.6).
3. and behold, I – Combine the first person pronoun with the particle.
4. The Lord, the God of Israel – Place this subject before the verb for emphasis (1.29, 3.12, 6.1). Note also the substitution apposition, the God of Israel (5.12, 8.1).
5. has fulfilled – The Hebrew reads, "has done."
6. was exalting himself – Use the participle of the Hithpael, therefore, the Hebrew reads, "he who got himself exalted" (4.6, 9).
7. I reign – Place the first person independent pronoun before the imperfect verb to stress the will of the speaker. This imperfect in direct speech often expresses action in process; the tense is present with the future also implied. The imperfect in direct speech and poetry often communicates what is going on and what you expect to go on in the future (4.11; §4e, h).
8. twelve chariots – The word "chariots" is a collective (§9b). The number "twelve" is a composite of two words. The first word, "two," is a masculine dual absolute: שְׁנַיִם (the construct is also possible, שְׁנֵי). The second word is the masculine singular absolute, עָשָׂר. Place the numeral "twelve" before the numerable "chariots." The numerable is an accusative of specification (§13kk). The numeral twelve agrees with its numerable in gender. The numbers three through nine and the decade numbers (twenty, thirty, forty, etc.) with the numbers three through nine (twenty-three, twenty-four, etc.) usually differ in gender between the numeral and the numerable, but for the numerals one and two (including decade numbers with one and two) the genders often agree (§29d, f).
9. horsemen – This noun formation is an intensive/extensive descriptive noun used for professions (4.19; §23h). Note the rejection of the Dagesh in the second root letter and the lengthening of the Patach to Qames under the first root letter because of the Resh.
10. with fifty men running in front of him – This is a situation clause (5.18–19). The numeral fifty or a decade number (twenty, thirty, forty, etc.) usually takes a singular numerable (§29e). Moreover, certain common nouns such as אִישׁ are also singular (§29e). Place the numeral in the absolute before its numerable, making the numerable an accusative of specification (§13kk). The Hebrew word for "running" is a participle, "runners."
11. crying out as they went – Usually, consecutive infinitive absolutes represent this construction, which would be proper here as well. For variation, however, substitute a Vav-perfect for the second infinitive absolute (Josh 6:13; 2 Sam 13:19; §13g; 17j).
12. king – This word is a word of address, a vocative. Use the article to convey that the noun is present to the speaker (§34c.)
13. And it was reported – To hide or omit the agent, use the passive (Hophal). This is done for a variety of reasons. First, the agent is well-known so there is no need to mention him, especially common when God is the agent. Secondly, the agent is unimportant so there is no need to mention him, especially common when a servant is the agent. Thirdly, the agent is hidden for security purposes, as here, to "protect the source." Another option for hiding an agent is to use impersonal third person verbs – "impersonal" because the identity of "they" or "he" is not revealed (§11vv–xx).

said,[14] Solomon, son of Bathsheba,[15] has become a traitor.[16] (7) Then David summoned his servants and the people and Solomon, his son, and he said, today[17] no food will be eaten at all[18] until Solomon, my son, becomes king.[19] (8) Far be it, (by) the life of the Lord[20] who delivered me* from the hand of all my enemies, (thus may God do to you and thus may he add)[21] if indeed[22] (there) falls from a hair[23] of the head of Solomon, my son, to the ground. (9) For he will indeed reign over all Israel this[24] day. And they took Solomon, the son of David, and anointed him for a king over Israel.

(10) Then Adonijah and his men[25] heard that David and the people[26] made[27] Solomon king over all Israel. (11) And men belonging to Adonijah[28] trembled and rose up and fled

---

14. and he said – Use the pausal form to introduce the direct discourse (1.18).
15. son of Bathsheba – substitution apposition (5.12, 8.1, 4)
16. traitor – This noun formation is also an intensive/extensive descriptive noun (4.19). This noun also functions an accusative of situation (illustrating and permanent) after הָיָה (7.13).
17. today – Place this word first in the clause for emphasis (§11uu). The Hebrew reads, "the day" (5.17).
18. no food will be eaten at all – The Hebrew reads, "it (she) will not be eaten all food." This is absolute negation, a universal negative without exception. Place the negative לֹא before the verb and the noun כֹּל before the (usually) indeterminate agent (Gen 9:11; Exod 10:15; 20:10; Josh 11:11; 2 Sam 15:11; §42d).
19. becomes king – The Hebrew reads, "becomes for a king." Use the imperfect for the verb. The noun, "king," has the לְ preposition which substitutes for the accusative of situation (3.16; §13ii).
20. Far be it, (by) the life of the Lord – These words are introductory formula for statements of oath. If the word, "life of," is annexed to "the Lord," as here, the pointing of the word is חַי. If it is annexed to a word other than "the Lord," the pointing of the word is חֵי (§65, 66b; BDB 311b 1a).
21. (thus may God do to you and thus may he add) – This is the implied curse formula. On occasion, the curse formula is explicitly written (1 Sam 3:17; 14:44; 20:13; 25:22; 2 Sam 3:9; 3:35; 19:14; 1 Kgs 2:23; 19:2; 20:10; 2 Kgs 6:31; Ruth 1:17), but usually the curse formula is omitted, perhaps because of the dreadfulness of the statement. Often the placement of the implied curse formula within the oath statement is easily discerned. In such cases, it may be simply assumed by the context (§67).
22. if indeed – This begins the sworn statement, which is introduced by אִם or כִּי or by both particles כִּי אִם. Here use the first option with אִם. Since these particles introduce a sworn statement, they are emphatic, hence the word "indeed." While the curse formula and even the introductory formula may be implied, the sworn statement must be explicit (§68).
23. a hair – The word is a singular feminine noun used for a singular example (שַׂעֲרָה, a single hair) of a class furnished by the masculine form (usually a collective, שֵׂעָר, hair). Grammarians call this feminine noun used for the singular example, nomen unitatis, "the noun of one (example)" (§9a; GKC §122t).
24. this – The demonstrative pronoun is inherently determined; therefore, the article is "excessive" (§36a). The demonstrative pronoun with the article indicates something that is present in mind or in actually to the speaker (§20a-b, 36c).
25. Then Adonijah and his men – To make a new "beginning" for the story, form a nominal clause by placing "Adonijah and his men" before the verb as initiators. The nominal clause focuses on Adonijah and his men by contrasting them with David, Solomon, and the people (1.38, 3.7, 12–13, 24).
26. and the people – 3.27; 5.10
27. made . . . king – The word "made" represents the causation of the Hiphil. The Hebrew reads, "David and the people caused Solomon (to be) king."
28. And the men belonging to Adonijah – The Hebrew reads, "And the men which (are) to Adonijah."

and got themselves hid[29] in a cave.[30] And there was a well of water[31] and seven palm trees.[32] (12) And Adonijah[33] became afraid[34] of[35] Solomon and he arose and went and seized on[36] the horns of the altar. (13) And it was reported[37] to Solomon saying behold Adonijah is afraid of[38] the king, Solomon,[39] and he summoned Adonijah and commanded him* saying,

---

29. got themselves hid – 4.6; §7k
30. in a cave – The Hebrew reads, "in the cave." The usage of the article is the particular preconception. It is particular because a particular, known cave is referred to. Contrast the particular use with the generic use which does not refer to a particular object or person within a group but to a group generically, not to any particular object or person within a group. It is preconception because the word "cave" is preconceived or regarded as known in the mind of the author. If the reader were to ask an author concerning the cave to which he referred, the author would say, "The one about which I am writing." The article of preconception is usually translated into English with the indefinite article because they are unknown. To illustrate the notion of "known" and "unknown," consider the following statement, "A man is at the door." "A man" is a particular but unknown man. If one were then to ask about "a man" at the door, "have you seen the man before"? Notice the use of the definite article in English because "the man" is now considered grammatically known since he was already mentioned as "a man." Of course, the terms "known" and "unknown" do not refer to acquaintances, but whether a person or thing has already been mentioned and therefore grammatically or contextually known. Hebrew does not have an indefinite article (though there are substitutes for the indefinite article in Hebrew); therefore, for particular, unknown persons and things Hebrew uses the article. English, by contrast, for particular, unknown persons and things may use the indefinite article (§34b; JM §137m–o; GKC §126q–t; BDB 207a 1d).
31. And there was a well of water – The Hebrew reads, "And there a well of water." Usually, the initiator is definite, but when an initiator is preceded by a prepositional phrase or an adverbial word or phrase indicating time or place, the initiator is usually indefinite (1 Sam 21:8–9). This construction asserts existence; hence, the translation, "there was." Moreover, the preposition phrase or adverbial expression, if expressing time or place, usually precede the initiator in the clause. If, however, the initiator is specialized as here, the word order may be reversed, the initiator preceding the announcement. Since with a specialized initiator the word order is usually the initiator after the announcement, place the initiator after the adverbial here (§11f, gg).
32. and seven palm trees – Place the numeral (seven) after the numerable (palm trees). This word order makes the numeral a semi-descriptive noun (functioning as an adjective) in apposition to its numerable (§23k, 29c). Contrast this word order with the word order of "twelve chariots" in 8.8. The numerals two through ten take a plural numerable; the numerals three through ten take the opposite gender of its numerable (§29d).
33. And Adonijah – Place the initiator before the verb, a nominal clause, to contrast Adonijah's actions with those of his co-conspirators who fled to a cave in the preceding verse (8.25).
34. became afraid – This form, יָרֵא, may be a perfect verb or a participle. Here, as the English indicates, a perfect verb is the correct parsing because an action or event came into existence and occurred. The participle would have described the subject like an adjective (apposition): Adonijah (was) a fearer of, or more idiomatically, Adonijah was afraid (§16a).
35. of – The Hebrew reads, "from the face of." This is a common idiom after the verbal root, ירא, to fear (Deut 5:5; Josh 11:6; 1 Sam 7:7; BDB 431a 2).
36. seized on – The verb takes an improper object with בְּ (1.29, 6.23)
37. And it was reported – 8.13
38. Adonijah is afraid of – Again the form for the announcement is יָרֵא, either a perfect verb or a participle. This time, in contrast with verse twelve (8.34), the form should be parsed as a participle, not a perfect verb because no event or action came into existence and occurred. The participle is much like an adjective to the initiator, as the English indicates, "Adonijah is afraid of," literally, "Adonijah (was) a fearer of" (§16a).
39. the king, Solomon – Explicative apposition (5.5)

you must not go out[40] from this[41] city. (14) For on the day of your going out[42] of[43] the city, you will most certainly die by the sword.[44] And Adonijah said, Amen. (15) And it happened after six days,[45] Adonijah went out of the city to meet[46] the men who made[47] him* king. (16) Then the king Solomon[48] swore[49] by the Lord saying, thus may God do to me and thus may he add[50] if indeed[51] against his own[52] soul Adonijah has done this thing.[53] (17) And now as the Lord lives,[54] indeed today[55] Adonijah will be put to death.[56] Then Solomon sent his servant and he struck him down[57] and so he died.

(18) Now the king Solomon[58] was blessed, and the throne of David[59] became established[60] before the Lord on that[61] day.

---

40. you must not go out – 1.37.
41. this – 8.24.
42. the day of your going out – Use the infinitive construct with the pronominal suffix. The infinitive construct is in the place of the genitive after the noun, "day" (§12m, 81b).
43. of – The Hebrew reads, "from."
44. by the sword – Since there is not a particular sword in view, the article is generic. More precisely, it is the generic of the essence/quality of the group, referring to the whole as the whole, not to any particular person or thing (sword) making up the whole. Death by sword, instead of by rope, by impaling, or by some other type of capital punishment is in view (§35a).
45. after six days – Put the numeral "six" in construct to the numerable "days." The numerable (days) is a genitive of specification (§29a). The numeral differs with its numerable in gender (§29d), and the numerable is plural with numerals two through ten (§29e).
46. to meet – The Hebrew verbal root, קרא (to meet, encounter), has an irregular infinitive construct in the Qal: לִקְרַאת (with לְ). GKC §19k.
47. made – 8.27.
48. The king Solomon – Explicative apposition (5.5).
49. swore – The Hebrew reads, "got himself put under oath" (4.6). This Niphal is a reflexive to the Hiphil stem of this verb (§7k). This is an introductory formula for oath clauses (8.20; §66).
50. thus may God do to me and thus may he add – On occasion, the curse formula is written explicitly (8.21; §66).
51. if indeed – Use the כִּי particle (8.22).
52. against his own soul – The Hebrew reads, "in his soul." The pronominal suffix may suggest a reflexive notion, "his own soul. " The notion of "in exchange for" is the ב of price, "in the exchange of the price of his own soul" (BDB 90a III 3a).
53. if indeed against his own soul Adonijah has done this thing – This is the sworn statement (8.22; §68).
54. And now as the Lord lives – Another introductory statement for an oath clause (8.20). The curse formula (thus may God do to you and thus may he add) is probably implied, but not easily inserted into the grammar.
55. today – Place this word before the verb and agent for emphasis (8.17).
56. indeed today Adonijah will be put to death – This is the sworn statement (8.22).
57. struck him down – The pronoun (him) has a ב preposition attached, probably as an improper object (8.36).
58. The king Solomon – Explicative apposition (5.5).
59. and the throne of David – The initiator of a nominal clause (8.25).
60. established – This is an accusative of situation (as always after הָיָה), illustrating and permanent (8.16).
61. that – 8.24.

Key to Composition Eight

1 וַיְהִי לִפְנֵי־מוֹת דָּוִד מֶלֶךְ יִשְׂרָאֵל וַיֹּאמֶר אֲנִי זָקַנְתִּי וָשַׂבְתִּי וְהִנְנִי הֹלֵךְ בְּדֶרֶךְ
כָּל־הָאָרֶץ׃

2 יהוה אֱלֹהֵי יִשְׂרָאֵל עָשָׂה דְבָרוֹ הַטּוֹב אֲשֶׁר דִּבֶּר לִי וּלְבֵיתִי׃

3 וַאֲדֹנִיָּהוּ בֶן־חַגִּית מִתְנַשֵּׂא לֵאמֹר אֲנִי אֶמְלֹךְ׃

4 וַיְהִי לוֹ שְׁנֵים עָשָׂר רֶכֶב וּשְׁלֹשִׁים וְשִׁשָּׁה פָּרָשִׁים וַחֲמִשִּׁים אִישׁ רָצִים לְפָנָיו׃

5 וַיֵּלְכוּ הָלוֹךְ וְזָעֹקוּ הַמֶּלֶךְ חַיֶּה לְעוֹלָם׃

6 וַיֻּגַּד לְדָוִד לֵאמֹר מָלַךְ אֲדֹנִיָּהוּ וַיֹּאמֶר שְׁלֹמֹה בֶן־בַּת־שֶׁבַע הָיָה חַטָּא׃

7 וַיִּקְרָא דָוִד לַעֲבָדָיו וּלְהָעָם וְלִשְׁלֹמֹה בְנוֹ וַיֹּאמַר הַיּוֹם לֹא תֵאָכֵל כָּל־אָכְלָה עַד־
אֲשֶׁר יִהְיֶה שְׁלֹמֹה בְנִי לְמֶלֶךְ׃

8 חָלִילָה חַי־יְהוָה אֲשֶׁר הִצִּילַנִי מִיַּד־כָּל־אֹיְבַי אִם־יִפֹּל מִשַּׂעֲרַת רֹאשׁ שְׁלֹמֹה בְנִי אָרְצָה׃

9 כִּי־מָלוֹךְ יִמְלֹךְ עַל־כָּל־יִשְׂרָאֵל הַיּוֹם הַזֶּה וַיִּקְחוּ אֶת־שְׁלֹמֹה בֶן־דָּוִד וַיִּמְשְׁחוּ אֹתוֹ
לְמֶלֶךְ עַל־יִשְׂרָאֵל׃

10 וַאֲדֹנִיָּהוּ וַאֲנָשָׁיו שָׁמְעוּ כִּי הִמְלִיךְ דָּוִד וְהָעָם אֶת־שְׁלֹמֹה עַל־כָּל־יִשְׂרָאֵל׃

11 וַיֶּחֶרְדוּ הָאֲנָשִׁים אֲשֶׁר לַאֲדֹנִיָּהוּ וַיָּקֻמוּ וַיָּנֻסוּ וַיֵּחָבְאוּ בַּמְּעָרָה וְשָׁם בְּאֵר מַיִם
וּתְמָרִים שִׁבְעָה׃

12 וַאֲדֹנִיָּהוּ יָרֵא מִפְּנֵי־שְׁלֹמֹה וַיָּקָם וַיֵּלֶךְ וַיַּחֲזֵק בְּקַרְנוֹת הַמִּזְבֵּחַ׃

13 וַיֻּגַּד לִשְׁלֹמֹה לֵאמֹר הִנֵּה אֲדֹנִיָּהוּ יָרֵא אֶת־הַמֶּלֶךְ שְׁלֹמֹה וַיִּקְרָא לַאֲדֹנִיָּהוּ וַיְצַוֵּהוּ
לֵאמֹר לֹא תֵצֵא מֵהָעִיר הַזֹּאת׃

14 כִּי בְּיוֹם צֵאתְךָ מֵהָעִיר מוֹת תָּמוּת בֶּחָרֶב וַיֹּאמֶר אֲדֹנִיָּהוּ אָמֵן׃

15 וַיְהִי אַחֲרֵי שֵׁשֶׁת יָמִים יָצָא אֲדֹנִיָּהוּ מֵהָעִיר לִקְרַאת הָאֲנָשִׁים אֲשֶׁר הִמְלִיכֻהוּ׃

16 וַיִּשָּׁבַע הַמֶּלֶךְ שְׁלֹמֹה בַּיהוָה לֵאמֹר כֹּה יַעֲשֶׂה־לִּי אֱלֹהִים וְכֹה יוֹסִיף כִּי בְנַפְשׁוֹ
עָשָׂה אֲדֹנִיָּהוּ אֶת־הַדָּבָר הַזֶּה׃

17 וְעַתָּה חַי־יְהוָה כִּי־הַיּוֹם יוּמַת אֲדֹנִיָּהוּ וַיִּשְׁלַח שְׁלֹמֹה אֶת־עַבְדּוֹ וַיִּפְגַּע־בּוֹ וַיָּמֹת׃

18 וְהַמֶּלֶךְ שְׁלֹמֹה בָּרוּךְ וְכִסֵּא דָוִד הָיָה נָכוֹן לִפְנֵי־יְהוָה בַּיּוֹם הַהוּא׃

Unpointed Text of Composition Eight

1 ויהי לפני־מות דוד מלך ישראל ויאמר אני זקנתי ושבתי והנני הלך בדרך כל־הארץ׃

2 יהוה אלהי ישראל עשה דברו הטוב אשר דבר לי ולביתי׃

3 ואדניהו בן־חגית מתנשא לאמר אני אמלך׃

4 ויהי לו שנים עשר רכב ושלשים וששה פרשים וחמשים איש רצים לפניו׃

5 וילכו הלוך וזעקו המלך חיה לעולם׃

6 ויגד לדוד לאמר מלך אדניהו ויאמר שלמה בן־בת־שבע היה חטא׃

7 ויקרא דוד לעבדיו ולהעם ולשלמה בנו ויאמר היום לא תאכל כל־אכלה עד־אשר יהיה שלמה בני למלך׃

8 חלילה חי־יהוה אשר הצילני מיד־כל־איבי אם־יפל משערת ראש שלמה בני ארצה׃

9 כי־מלוך ימלך על־כל־ישראל היום הזה ויקחו את־שלמה בן־דוד וימשחו אתו למלך על־ישראל׃

10 ואדניהו ואנשיו שמעו כי המליך דוד והעם את־שלמה על־כל־ישראל׃

11 ויחרדו האנשים אשר לאדניהו ויקמו וינסו ויחבאו במערה ושם באר מים ותמרים שבעה׃

12 ואדניהו ירא מפני־שלמה ויקם וילך ויחזק בקרנות המזבח׃

13 ויגד לשלמה לאמר הנה אדניהו ירא את־המלך שלמה ויקרא לאדניהו ויצוהו לאמר לא תצא מהעיר הזאת׃

14 כי ביום צאתך מהעיר מות תמות בחרב ויאמר אדניהו אמן׃

15 ויהי אחרי ששת ימים יצא אדניהו מהעיר לקראת האנשים אשר המליכהו׃

16 וישבע המלך שלמה ביהוה לאמר כה יעשה־לי אלהים וכה יוסיף כי בנפשו עשה אדניהו את־הדבר הזה׃

17 ועתה חי־יהוה כי־היום יומת אדניהו וישלח שלמה את־עבדו ויפגע־בו וימת׃

18 והמלך שלמה ברוך וכסא דוד היה נכון לפני־יהוה ביום ההוא׃

COMPOSITION NINE

(1) Now these are the words which Moses spoke to the Israelites when they camped [in] beyond the Jordan and Moses said, (2) "The Lord, God of Abraham, (and) Isaac, and Jacob, has delivered you* from Egypt, from bondage, with a strong hand and with an outstretched arm. And the Egyptians pressed upon you to send you away quickly. (3) Then you revolted against the Lord at the Red Sea saying: 'Surely, (it is) better for us to serve the Egyptians than to die in the wilderness.' Then the Lord delivered you again, by splitting the Red Sea and by leading you upon [the] dry ground and by destroying the army of Pharaoh. (4) After this, the Lord gave to you his laws and he said, 'All who obeys my commandments, that soul will live, and everyone who revolts against my words, that soul will surely die.' (5) Continually that generation revolted against the Lord and they cried out an exceedingly great and bitter cry; therefore, the Lord was pleased to kill that generation.

(6) And now, sanctify the seventh day; you must not do any work at all. Serve the Lord your God, he alone; you must not make for yourselves any idol or any representation at all. (7) And the Lord your God, who created the heavens and the earth and all that is in them, and who chose your fathers, Abraham, [and] Isaac, and Jacob, and who redeemed you from Egypt, and who led you in that great and fearful wilderness, he will send the angel of the covenant before you and he will cause you to inherit this land." (8) Then Moses sang this song before all Israel.

(9) **"Hear, heavens, and I will speak.**
And give ear, earth, to the words of my mouth.

(10) **I, to the Lord, I – I will sing.**
I will make music to the Lord, the God of Israel.

(11) **The name of the Lord I will call (upon).**
And give greatness to our God.

(12) **(As for) the rock, his work is perfect.**
For all his ways are justice.
A God of fidelity without unrighteousness,
righteous and just is he.

(13) **Woe, a sinning nation,**
a people heavy of iniquity,
they abandoned the God (who) made them.
Then they treated the rock of their salvation as a fool.

(14) **They – they made me jealous with a non-god.**
They provoked me with their idols.
And I – I will make them jealous with a non-people.
With a foolish nation I will provoke them.

(15) **Blessed are you, Israel,**
who is like you, a people saved by the Lord.
The Lord is your shield of help.
He reigns for forever and ever."

( ) – Not in Hebrew, but needed for English
[ ] – In the Hebrew, but not needed for English
* – Put the pronominal suffix directly on the verb
# – Put the pronominal suffix with energic Nun directly on the verb

(1) Now these are the words which Moses spoke to the Israelites when they camped[1] [in] beyond the Jordan and Moses said, (2) "The Lord, God of Abraham, (and) Isaac, and Jacob, has delivered you*[2] from Egypt, from bondage,[3] with a strong hand and with an outstretched[4] arm. And the Egyptians pressed upon you to send you away quickly.[5] (3) Then you revolted against the Lord at the Red Sea[6] saying:[7] "Surely, (it is) better for us to serve the Egyptians than to die in the wilderness."[8] Then the Lord delivered you again,[9] by splitting[10] the Red Sea and by leading[10] you upon [the] dry ground and by destroying[10] the army of Pharaoh. (4) After this, the Lord gave to you his laws and he said, "All who obeys my commandments,[11] that soul will live,[12] and everyone who revolts against my words, that soul will surely die.[13] (5) Continually[14] that generation revolted against the

1. when they camped – Use the infinitive construct (1.15; §18d, 81a; JM §166l) without the preceding וַיְהִי.
2. has delivered you – For this composition (except for the last verse) use the plural ("you") for the pronominal suffix.
3. from bondage – The Hebrew reads, "from the house of slaves" (Exod 20:2).
4. outstretched – The Qal passive participle of נטה (IBH 37.4.5.2).
5. to send you away quickly – The Hebrew reads, "to do quick to send away you." The first infinitive construct ("to do quick") is the general term, rendered in English by an adverb ("quickly"). The second infinitive construct ("to send away") is the more precise term, rendered by the English infinitive. The infinitive constructs specify/explain the main verb (pressed) (§18f, h).
6. at the Red Sea – The English preposition "at" represents the Hebrew accusative of (specified) place (6.15 [3B2], 7.2; §13w).
7. saying – The particle כִּי may add force to a statement – surely, indeed, in fact (BDB 472b 1e; JM §164b; GKC §159ee). This is common when other particles are combined with כִּי (BDB 472a 1d). The particle כִּי also may introduce direct discourse, similar to English quotation marks – Then you revolted against the Lord at the Red Sea saying: "(It is) better for us to serve the Egyptians than to die in this wilderness" (BDB 471b 1b; JM §157c footnote 2; GKC §157b).
8. (It is) better for us to serve the Egyptians than to die in the wilderness – The Hebrew reads, "good for us to serve the Egyptians than our dying (infinitive construct) in the wilderness."
9. Then the Lord delivered you again – The particle עוֹד may communicate the notion of "again" (Gen 9:11; BDB 729a 1b) or Hebrew may use the verb יסף in the Qal or more commonly in the Hiphil with a following infinitive construct (Gen 4:2; Lev 26:18; BDB 414b and 415b 2a). Moreover, Hebrew often adds the particle עוֹד to the verb יסף and the following infinitive construct (Gen 8:12, 21; BDB 414b and 415 2a). The Hebrew reads, "and the Lord added to deliver you again."
10. by splitting . . . by leading . . . and by destroying – These infinitive constructs with לְ specify, limit, and explain the verbal action (§18f-h; JM §124o; GKC §114o). Usually, the verb furnishes the general concept and the infinitive construct narrows the meaning of the verb by specifying and explaining the verb. These infinitives explains how God delivered the Israelites, by splitting . . . by leading . . . and by destroying. Translate these infinitive constructs by English gerunds.
11. All who obeys my commandments – The Hebrew reads, "Every man who listens to my commandments." This is the singular participle of שׁמע with the article followed by the preposition אֶל־ (BDB 1034a 1k). These words are in Casus Pendens to the following words, "that soul will live" (5.9 [2A]; §14).
12. that soul will live – The Hebrew reads, "then that soul will live." The conjunctive Vav on the perfect verb expresses the word "then."
13. that soul will surely die – 4.11.
14. Continually – Place this first in the sentence for emphasis (1.32, 3.21, 24; §11uu).

Lord and they cried out an exceedingly great and bitter cry;[15] therefore, the Lord was pleased to kill[16] that generation.

(6) And now, sanctify the seventh[17] day; you must not do any work at all.[18] Serve the Lord your God, he alone;[19] you must not make for yourselves[20] any idol or any representation at all.[21] (7) And the Lord your God, who created[22] the heavens and the earth and all that is in them, and who chose[19] your fathers, Abraham, [and] Isaac, and Jacob, and who redeemed[19] you from Egypt, and who led[19] you in that great and fearful wilderness,[23] he will send[24] the angel of the covenant before you and he will cause you to inherit this land. (8) Then Moses sang this song before all Israel.

(9) "Hear, heavens, and I will speak.
And give ear, earth, to the words of my mouth.

(10) I, to the Lord, I – I will sing.[25]
I will make music to the Lord, the God of Israel.

(11) The name of the Lord I will call (upon).
And give[26] greatness to our God.

---

15. and they cried out an exceedingly great and bitter cry – The Hebrew reads, "and they cried out a cry, great and bitter, exceedingly." Render the word "exceedingly" by מְאֹד (force, might) or עַד־מְאֹד (unto force or might) (BDB 547a–b), rendering the emphatic absolute object even more emphatic (2.19; §13e).
16. to kill – Use the Hiphil of the root מות (7.3).
17. seventh – For this ordinal number, use the Hireq-Yod (Nisbah) ending (3.10, 5.7).
18. you must not do any work at all – The words "any . . . at all" express absolute negation, an emphatic negative that allows no exceptions: the Hebrew reads, "All work you must not do" (8.18; §42d; GKC §152b; BDB 482a 1e; Exod 12:16, 19–20, 43, 48; 20:4, 10. Compare these with Mark 13:20; Luke 1:37; Gal 2:16). Joüon's and Muraoka's statement (JM §160k) concerning כֹּל and לֹא used together as "ambiguous" is misleading because their examples (Gen 3:1 and Lev 16:2) are clearly different constructions from the examples mentioned in Exodus above.
19. he alone – The particle for "alone" is לְבַד (with respect to separation, with respect to aloneness) with the pronominal suffix of singular nouns, לְבַדּוֹ (BDB 94b b).
20. you must not make for yourselves – 2.5.
21. any idol or any representation at all – 8.18, 9.18.
22. who created . . . and who redeemed . . . and who led – The relative pronoun "who" is אֲשֶׁר (§43a footnote 2; JM §145a; GKC §138a; BDB 82a 1).
23. in that great and fearful wilderness – The Hebrew reads, "in the wilderness great and fearful that."
24. he will send – Use the independent pronoun to emphasize "he" (§19f, h).
25. I will sing – Use the cohortative to emphasize the will of the speaker (2.21).
26. and give – For variety use the verb יהב.

(12) **(As for) the rock,[27] his work is perfect.[28]**
For all his ways are justice
A God of fidelity without unrighteousness,[29]
righteous and just is he.

(13) **Woe, a sinning nation,**
a people heavy of iniquity,
they abandoned the God[30] (who) made them.[31]
Then they treated the rock of their[32] salvation as a fool.[33]

(14) **They – they made me jealous with a non-god.[34]**
They provoked me with their idols.
And I – I will make them jealous with a non-people.
With a foolish nation I will provoke them.

(15) **Blessed[35] are you, Israel,**
who is like you, a people saved by the Lord.[36]
The Lord is your shield of help.[37]
He reigns for forever and ever."

---

27. (As for) the rock – 5.9 [2B].
28. his work is perfect – To emphasize the adjective, place the adjective before the noun: "perfect (is) his work (§11ff).
29. without unrighteousness – The Hebrew reads, "and non-existence of unrighteousness." The negative particle אַיִן means "non-existence, nothing." For its various usages and meanings, see BDB 34–35.
30. They abandoned the God – Use a word for God found often in poetry, אֱלוֹהַּ (BDB 43a).
31. (who) made them – Hebrew, like English, may omit the relative pronoun: The book (that) I wrote. This may occur in poetry and commonly with an indeterminate noun (as in Arabic; Gen 49:27, Benjamin is a wolf [who] robs. Job 18:21; Ps 34:9; §43a–b, 46; JM §158a–db. Joüon and Muraoka use the term "asyndetic" [not in the syntax] to describe the omitted relative and "syndetic" [in the syntax] to describe the relative clause with the relative pronoun JM §158e). The Hebrew reads, "(who) made him." The singular pronoun refers to a collective noun (9.32).
32. their – The Hebrew reads, "his." The word, "his," refers to the people. As a collective noun, עַם may take a singular pronoun (4.28, 7.48).
33. they treated . . . as a fool – This is the factitive Piel (6.36): "They put the rock of their salvation into a foolish state."
34. with a non-god – The Hebrew is בְּלֹא־אֵל. Commonly in poetry, the negative לֹא is used with a substantive "expressing pointedly its antithesis or negation" (BDB 519b 2d).
35. Blessed – This word occurs only in the plural construct form אַשְׁרֵי. Attach the pronoun (you) to this noun. The noun expresses interjection and exclamation: How blessed! The plural conveys intensity: blessed with all kinds of blessings and every kind of blessing (4.28, 10.48; §9b, 60; GKC §124e; 94l). The verse may be paraphrased, "How blessed with all kinds of blessings and every kind of blessing are you, Israel."
36. by the Lord – The ב preposition ("by") may be used with passive verbs (BDB 89b 2c; §41g–h).
37. your shield of help – In a construct package, only the last word (the genitive) may have a pronominal suffix, although the suffix may actually go with the entire construct package. For example, הַר־קָדְשִׁי, "hill of my holiness" (Ps 2:6), means "my hill of holiness" or "my holy hill." So here, the Hebrew reads, "the shield of your help" meaning "your shield of help" or "your helping shield" (§19b; GKC §128r).

Key to Composition Nine

1 וְאֵ֣לֶּה הַדְּבָרִ֗ים אֲשֶׁ֨ר דִּבֶּ֤ר מֹשֶׁה֙ אֶל־בְּנֵֽי־יִשְׂרָאֵ֔ל בַּחֲנוֹתָ֖ם בְּעֵ֣בֶר הַיַּרְדֵּ֑ן וַיֹּ֖אמֶר מֹשֶֽׁה׃

2 יְהוָ֞ה אֱלֹהֵ֣י אַבְרָהָ֗ם יִצְחָ֣ק וְיַעֲקֹב֒ הִצִּילְכֶ֣ם מִמִּצְרַ֔יִם מִבֵּ֣ית עֲבָדִ֔ים בְּיָ֤ד חֲזָקָה֙
וּבִזְר֣וֹעַ נְטוּיָ֔ה וַיְחַזֵּ֥ק מִצְרַ֛יִם עֲלֵיכֶ֖ם לְמַהֵ֣ר לְשַׁלַּ֣ח אֶתְכֶֽם׃

3 וַתִּפְשְׁע֞וּ בַּיהוָה֙ יַם־ס֔וּף לֵאמֹ֕ר כִּ֣י ט֥וֹב לָ֛נוּ עֲבֹ֖ד אֶת־מִצְרַ֑יִם מִמֻּתֵ֖נוּ בַּמִּדְבָּ֑ר
וַיּ֣וֹסֶף יְהוָ֞ה לְהַצִּ֤יל אֶתְכֶם֙ ע֔וֹד לְבַקַּ֥ע אֶת־יַם־ס֖וּף וּלְהוֹלִ֣יךְ אֶתְכֶם֙ עַל־הַיַּבָּשָׁ֔ה
וּלְהַאֲבִ֖יד אֶת־חֵ֥יל פַּרְעֹֽה׃

4 אַחֲרֵי־כֵ֞ן נָתַ֤ן יְהוָה֙ לָכֶ֔ם אֶת־תּוֹרֹתָ֖יו וַיֹּ֑אמֶר כָּל־הַשֹּׁמֵ֔עַ אֶל־מִצְוֺתַ֖י וְחָיְתָ֣ה הַנֶּ֣פֶשׁ
הַהִ֑יא וְכָל־הַפֹּשֵׁ֔עַ בִּדְבָרַ֖י מ֥וֹת תָּמ֖וּת הַנֶּ֥פֶשׁ הַהִֽיא׃

5 כָּל־הַיָּמִ֞ים פָּשַׁ֤ע הַדּ֣וֹר הַהוּא֙ בַּיהוָ֔ה וַיִּצְעֲק֣וּ צְעָקָ֔ה גְּדוֹלָ֖ה וּמָרָ֣ה עַד־מְאֹ֑ד עַל־כֵּ֔ן
חָפֵ֣ץ יְהוָ֔ה לְהָמִ֖ית אֶת־הַדּ֥וֹר הַהֽוּא׃

6 וְעַתָּ֗ה קַדְּשׁוּ֙ הַיּ֣וֹם הַשְּׁבִיעִ֔י כָּל־מְלָאכָ֖ה לֹ֣א תַעֲשׂ֑וּן עֲבֹ֞ד אֶת־יְהוָ֤ה אֱלֹהֵיכֶם֙ לְבַדּ֔וֹ
כָּל־פֶּ֙סֶל֙ וְכָל־תְּמוּנָ֔ה לֹ֥א תַעֲשׂ֖וּ לָכֶֽם׃

7 וַיהוָ֣ה אֱלֹהֵיכֶ֗ם אֲשֶׁ֨ר בָּרָ֜א אֶת־הַשָּׁמַ֣יִם וְאֶת־הָאָ֗רֶץ וְאֶת־כָּל־אֲשֶׁר־בָּם֒ וַאֲשֶׁ֣ר ׀
בָּחַ֣ר בַּאֲבֹתֵיכֶ֗ם אַבְרָהָ֛ם וְיִצְחָ֥ק וְיַעֲקֹ֖ב וַאֲשֶׁ֣ר פָּדָ֔ה אֶתְכֶם֙ מִמִּצְרַ֔יִם וַאֲשֶׁ֤ר הוֹלִיךְ֙
אֶתְכֶ֣ם בַּמִּדְבָּ֔ר הַגָּד֖וֹל וְהַנּוֹרָ֑א הַה֗וּא ה֚וּא יְשַׁלַּ֣ח אֶת־מַלְאַ֣ךְ הַבְּרִית֙ לִפְנֵיכֶ֔ם
וְהוֹרִ֥ישׁ אֶתְכֶ֖ם אֶת־הָאָ֥רֶץ הַזֹּֽאת׃

8 וַיָּ֤שַׁר מֹשֶׁה֙ אֶת־הַשִּׁ֣יר הַזֶּ֔ה לִפְנֵ֖י כָּל־יִשְׂרָאֵֽל׃

9 שִׁמְע֤וּ הַשָּׁמַ֙יִם֙ וַאֲדַבֵּ֔רָה וְהַאֲזִ֥ינִי הָאָ֖רֶץ לְאִמְרֵי־פִֽי׃

10 אָנֹכִ֗י לַֽיהוָה֙ אָנֹכִ֣י אָשִׁ֔ירָה אֲזַמֵּ֕ר לַֽיהוָ֖ה אֱלֹהֵ֥י יִשְׂרָאֵֽל׃

11 שֵׁ֥ם יְהוָ֖ה אֶקְרָ֑א וְהָב֥וּ גֹ֖דֶל לֵאלֹהֵֽינוּ׃

12 הַצּוּר֙ תָּמִ֣ים פָּעֳל֔וֹ כִּ֥י כָל־דְּרָכָ֖יו מִשְׁפָּ֑ט אֵ֤ל אֱמוּנָה֙ וְאֵ֣ין עָ֔וֶל צַדִּ֥יק וְיָשָׁ֖ר הֽוּא׃

13 אוֹי֙ גּ֣וֹי חֹטֵ֔א עַ֖ם כֶּ֣בֶד עָוֺ֑ן נָטְשׁוּ֙ אֱל֣וֹהַּ עָשָׂ֔הוּ וַיְנַבֵּ֖ל צ֥וּר יְשֻׁעָתֽוֹ׃

14 הֵ֚ם קִנְא֣וּנִי֙ בְלֹא־אֵ֔ל כִּעֲס֖וּנִי בְּהַבְלֵיהֶ֑ם וַאֲנִי֙ אַקְנִיאֵ֣ם בְּלֹא־עָ֔ם בְּג֥וֹי נָבָ֖ל
אַכְעִיסֵֽם׃

15 אַשְׁרֶ֨יךָ יִשְׂרָאֵ֜ל מִ֣י כָמ֗וֹךְ עַ֚ם נוֹשַׁ֣ע בַּיהוָ֔ה יְהוָה֙ מָגֵ֣ן עֶזְרֶ֔ךְ יִמְלֹ֖ךְ לְעֹלָ֥ם וָעֶֽד׃

Unpointed Text of Composition Nine

1 ואלה הדברים אשר דבר משה אל־בני־ישראל בחנותם בעבר הירדן ויאמר משה:

2 יהוה אלהי אברהם יצחק ויעקב הצילכם ממצרים מבית עבדים ביד חזקה ובזרוע נטויה ויחזק מצרים עליכם למהר לשלח אתכם:

3 ותפשעו ביהוה ים־סוף לאמר כי טוב לנו עבד את־מצרים ממתנו במדבר ויוסף יהוה להציל אתכם עוד לבקע את־ים־סוף ולהוליך אתכם על־היבשה ולהאביד את־חיל פרעה:

4 אחרי־כן נתן יהוה לכם את־תורתיו ויאמר כל־השמע אל־מצותי וחיתה הנפש ההיא וכל־הפשע בדברי מות תמות הנפש ההיא:

5 כל־הימים פשע הדר ההוא ביהוה ויצעקו צעקה גדולה ומרה עד־מאד על־כן חפץ יהוה להמית את־הדר ההוא:

6 ועתה קדשו היום השביעי כל־מלאכה לא תעשון עבד את־יהוה אלהיכם לבדו כל־פסל וכל־תמונה לא תעשו לכם:

7 ויהוה אלהיכם אשר ברא את־השמים ואת־הארץ ואת־כל־אשר־בם ואשר בחר באבתיכם אברהם ויצחק ויעקב ואשר פדה אתכם ממצרים ואשר הוליך אתכם במדבר הגדול והנורא ההוא הוא ישלח את־מלאך הברית לפניכם והוריש אתכם את־הארץ הזאת:

8 וישר משה את־השיר הזה לפני־כל־ישראל:

9 שמעו השמים ואדברה והאזיני הארץ לאמרי־פי:

10 אנכי ליהוה אנכי אשירה אזמר ליהוה אלהי ישראל:

11 שם יהוה אקרא והבו גדל לאלהינו:

12 הצור תמים פעלו כי כל־דרכיו משפט אל אמונה ואין עול צדיק וישר הוא:

13 אוי גוי חטא עם כבד עון נטשו אלוה עשהו וינבל צור ישעתו:

14 הם קנאוני בלא־אל כעסוני בהבליהם ואני אקניאם בלא־עם בגוי נבל אכעיסם:

15 אשריך ישראל מי כמוך עם נושע ביהוה יהוה מגן עזרך ימלך לעלם ועד:

COMPOSITION TEN

(1) Comfort, comfort my people,
says your God.

(2) Speak upon the heart of Jerusalem and call to her that her warfare is completed, that her iniquity has been satisfied,
that she has received from the hand of the Lord double in exchange for all her sins.

(3) A voice calling, in the wilderness clear the way for the Lord.
Make straight in the desert a highway for our God.

(4) Every valley will get itself lifted up and every mountain and hill will be low.
And the steep ground will become level; the impassible lands (will become) a broad valley.

(5) And the glory of the Lord will get itself revealed.
And all flesh will see (it) together because the mouth of the Lord has spoken.

(6) A voice of one saying, Call out. And he said, What will I call out?
All [the] flesh is grass, and all its beauty is as the flower of the field.

(7) (The) grass has dried up, (the) flower has faded because the breath of the Lord has blown on it.
Surely the people are grass.

(8) (The) grass has dried up, (the) flower has faded.
But the word of our God stands forever.

(9) Upon a high mountain, go up for yourself, bearer of good news (to) Zion; lift up with strength your voice, bearer of good news (to) Jerusalem.
Lift up, do not fear, speak to the cities of Judah, Behold your God.

(10) Behold, the Lord God with strength comes, and his arm is ruling for him.
Behold, his reward is with him, and his wage is before him.

(11) Like a shepherd, his flock he shepherds; with his arm he gathers lambs; in his bosom he lifts (them) up.
Nursing ewes he leads.

(12) All the nations are as nothing before him.
Of nothing and emptiness they are regarded to him.

(13) And to whom will you liken God?
And what likeness will you compare to him?

(14) (The) craftsman cast the idol and (the) smelter plates it# indeed with gold.
And chains of silver (the) smelter (attaches to it indeed).

(15) The poor man with respect to an offering, wood which does not rot he selects.
A skilled craftsman seeks for himself to prepare an idol (that) does not totter.

( ) – Not in Hebrew, but needed for English
[ ] – In the Hebrew, but not needed for English
* – Put the pronominal suffix directly on the verb
# – Put the pronominal suffix with energic Nun directly on the verb

(1) Comfort, comfort[1] my people,
says[2] your[3] God.

(2) Speak upon the heart of Jerusalem[4] and call to her that her warfare is completed, that her iniquity has been satisfied,
that she has received[5] from the hand of the Lord double[6] in exchange for[7] all her sins.

(3) A voice calling, in the wilderness clear the way for the Lord.[8]
Make straight[9] in the desert a highway for our God.

(4) Every valley[10] will get itself lifted up and every mountain and hill will be low.[11]
And the steep ground will become level; the impassible lands (will become) a broad valley.[12]

---

1. Comfort, comfort – Verbal corroborative, a category of corroborative apposition, repeats its word for emphasis "because of fear of forgetfulness, inattentiveness, or lack of concern" (Griess, 197; §24a, d). Compare this with conceptual corroborative (6.43)
2. says – This passage is both poetry and direct speech. Indeed, these largely overlapped in the Biblical period. In historical narrative, context usually makes the tense past. In poetry, however, context does not always indicate tense so clearly (for example, Ps 1, 15). In such cases, verbal aspect becomes more important for understanding a passage. In prophetic passages, the context ordinarily suggests a future time, but the prophet may present his message as happening in the present or in past time (prophetic perfect, §3m). This context is after the prophet's time, but Isaiah presents his message as occurring in the present, with some events occurring in the future. In this passage, pay particular attention to verbal aspect. Here the Lord is in the process of saying (§4c, h).
3. your – Use the plural.
4. Jerusalem – Like the name of most cities and countries, Jerusalem is a feminine noun: "mothers of the inhabitants" (§9a). For much of the passage, therefore, the verbs and pronouns will be feminine.
5. for her warfare is completed, for her iniquity has been satisfied, for she has received – The three perfect verbs convey a completed aspect. These actions are not in process like the aspect of the imperfect, but they are finished actions. Though the events are to happen in the future, Isaiah represents them as completed in the present (§3b, q). The three כִּי particles are a verbal corroborative (10.1). The כִּי particles and their perfects express a judicial finality, as if God is closing Israel's case with three verdicts of hope.
6. double – Use the dual with the noun כֶּפֶל (*i*).
7. in exchange for – This is the בְּ of price or exchange (8.52; Ps 15:5; BDB 90a III 3a).
8. A voice calling, in the wilderness clear the way for the Lord – Since the Zaqeph Qaton occurs before the Zaqeph Gadol, the Zaqeph Qaton is the stronger break. The translation according to the Masoretic Text, therefore, should be "A voice calling, in the wilderness clear the way for the Lord," not "A voice calling in the wilderness, clear the way for the Lord." The prepositional phrase "in the wilderness" connects with the following words, not with the preceding words, "A voice calling."
9. Make straight – A factitive Piel (6.36, 9.32)
10. Every valley – The word כָּל followed by an indefinite noun is a semi-descriptive noun (§23l).
11. will be low – Put this stative verb in pause. Place the initiators before their announcement (verb) for emphasis (1.31, 3.12, 21; §11cc). The same applies to the preceding announcement (verb), "lifted up."
12. level . . . broad valley – Place a לְ on these nouns. The לְ and their nouns substitute for accusatives of situation (3.16, 8.19).

(5) And the glory of the Lord will get itself revealed.
And all flesh[13] will see (it) together because the mouth of the Lord[14] has spoken.

(6) A voice of one saying,[15] Call out. And he said,[16] What will I call out?[17]
All [the] flesh is grass,[18] and all its beauty is as the flower of the field.

(7) (The) grass has dried up,[19] (the) flower has faded[20] because the breath of the Lord[21] has blown[22] on it.
Surely[23] the people are grass.[24]

(8) (The) grass has dried up, (the) flower has faded.
But the word of our God[25] stands[26] forever.[27]

---

13. all flesh – 10.10.
14. mouth of the Lord – Place this phrase before the announcement (verb) for emphasis (10.11).
15. A voice of one saying – The last word of this annexation is a participle.
16. And he said – Use the Vᵊqatal form. This Vav is not energic, but a conjunctive Vav connected to a perfect. Context must determine whether a Vav is energic or connecting (§6b–d).
17. What shall I call out – 1.31.
18. All [the] flesh is grass – Nominal clauses normally have definite initiators (§11e) and indefinite announcements when the announcement is a noun (§11u).
19. (The) grass has dried up – Context suggests that the perfect has the sense of a Greek perfect: The grass dried up and is dried up still (1.14, 32). Notice also that the agent of the verb is indefinite. In prose, indefinite agents are exceptional (§11ll), but in poetry and direct speech they are more common (§11mm).
20. has faded – The accent on this word (Munach) retracts to the first syllable to avoid consecutive accented syllables with the next word. This is known as "retraction of stress" (GKC §29e-g, The Metheg prevents the Sere from becoming a Segol in the closed unaccented syllable, GKC §29f; 16f).
21. the breath of the Lord – Place this annexation, the initiator, before its announcement (verb) (10.11).
22. has blown – The accent is retracted to the first syllable of the verb (10.20). The verb conveys the sense of a Greek perfect (10.19).
23. Surely – Use the asseverative particle אָכֵן (§64c).
24. the people are grass – For emphasis, place the announcement before its initiator (§11ff). The asseverative particle before the announcement further emphasizes the announcement.
25. But the word of our God – The Hebrew reads, "And the word of our God." Place this annexation, the initiator, before its announcement (verb) (10.11).
26. stands – The aspect of this imperfect is in process, conveying "what is going on what is expected to continue in the future" (6.6, 10.2; §4e). The following word, "forever," reinforces the aspect of the verb as in process (§2b).
27. forever – Hebrew frequently forms adverbs by a preposition, usually לְ or בְּ, attached to a noun (2.24). Without the preposition, the noun would be an accusative of (specified) time; therefore, the construction with the preposition substitutes for an accusative of (specified) time (§13y).

(9) Upon a high[28] mountain, go up[29] for yourself,[30] bearer of good news[31] (to) Zion;[32] lift up with strength[33] your voice, bearer of good news (to) Jerusalem.[34]
Lift up, do not fear,[35] speak to the cities of Judah, Behold your[36] God.

(10) Behold, the Lord God[37] with strength[38] comes,[39] and his arm is ruling[40] for him.
Behold, his reward is with him, and his wage is before him.

(11) Like a shepherd, his flock he shepherds;[41] with his arm[42] he gathers lambs; in his bosom[43] he lifts (them) up.
Nursing ewes he leads.

(12) All the nations are as nothing before him.
Of[44] nothing and emptiness they are regarded[45] to him.[46]

---

28. high – This is an adjective. To Semitic grammarians adjectives are nouns, more precisely a subset of descriptive nouns in apposition to their antecedents (§23a).
29. go up – Make all imperatives in this verse feminine because they are addressed to feminine nouns.
30. for yourself – 2.5.
31. bearer of good news – This is a Piel participle feminine singular (T-form, IBH 19.2) of בשׂר. This does not suggest that this "bearer of good news" is a female. Feminine participles may furnish titles or offices that refers to males (Eccl 1:1; GKC §122r; Also see the masculine participles of the Targum and LXX).
32. bearer of good news (to) Zion – If the participle is in the absolute state, then "Zion" is the direct object to the participle (§16a). If the participle is in the construct state, then the annexation is improper with "Zion" functioning as a genitive of specification (6.41; §12h).
33. with strength – 10.27. Put the article on the abstract noun (§35c).
34. bearer of good news (to) Jerusalem – 10.31, 32.
35. do not fear – Use אַל with the jussive (1.36). Put the verb in pause by lengthening the thematic vowel (IBH 6.5.3).
36. your – Use the plural.
37. Lord God – In these compositions, the divine name has lacked vowels, יהוה. Normally, the Masoretes provide the divine name with the vowels of אֲדֹנָי to avoid pronouncing the divine name in accordance with Jewish tradition. In this verse, however, אֲדֹנָי precedes the divine name. To avoid pronouncing the same word (אֲדֹנָי) twice, the Masoretes give the divine name the vowels of אֱלֹהִים. The words אֲדֹנָי יהוה should be read אֲדֹנָי אֱלֹהִים.
38. with strength – 10.27, 33.
39. Lord God with strength comes – Place the initiator and the prepositional phrase before the announcement (verb) (10.11). The imperfect is in process (10.2, 26).
40. is ruling – This is a participle, a ruler. Retract the accent to avoid consecutive accented syllables since the following word is monosyllabic (10.20).
41. his flock he shepherds – Place the direct object before the verb for emphasis (1.30, 3.30). For the imperfects of this verse, see 10.2, 26.
42. with his arm – Place the prepositional phrase before the verb for emphasis (§11uu).
43. in his bosom – 10.42.
44. Of – The מן preposition.
45. they are regarded – The Hebrew reads, "they got themselves regarded" (4.6). The verbal aspect resembles the Greek perfect: they were regarded in the past and they are still regarded now (10.19).
46. to him – To avoid consecutive accented syllables, attach this prepositional phrase to the

(13) And to whom will you liken[47] God?[48]
And what likeness will you compare to him?[49]

(14) (The) craftsman cast the idol[50] and (the) smelter[51] with [the] gold[52] plates[53] it[#] indeed.[54]
And chains of silver (the) smelter (attaches to it indeed).[55]

(15) The poor man[56] with respect to an offering,[57] wood (which)[58] does not rot he selects.
A skilled craftsman seeks for himself[59] to prepare an idol (that)[60] does not totter.[61]

---

preceding verb with a Maqqef (IBH 5.5). If the verb had a open syllable in the next-to-last syllable, retraction of the accent may have occurred (10.20).

47. will you liken – This verb is an imperfect 2mp of דמה, the original final Yod is preserved in this form. Add to this form a final Nun, an old indicative ending as seen in Aramaic and Arabic (IBH 18.2.3.2 footnote 5). Contrast these imperfects with the perfect of the preceding verse. These imperfects are "what is going on and what you expect to continue to go on"; therefore, "what are you comparing God to and what will you expect to compare him to in the future" (10.17).
48. God – Use the shortened form אֵל, strong, mighty one. The more common plural form, אֱלֹהִים, is a plural of intensity, "He is mighty with all kinds of might and with every kind of might, the perfection of might" (4.28, 9.34; §9b). Notice the first word in this verse and this word are אל with Sere and Segol.
49. will you compare to him – Retract the accent of the verb. The Patach under the Ayin in the verb is an "added" (anaptyxis) vowel which does not count as a syllable. The Patach under the Tav is in an open syllable (10.20).
50. (The) craftsman cast the idol – The Hebrew reads, "The idol (the) craftsman cast." Place the object first for emphasis (10.41). If the article refers to a particular idol, then the article is preconceived (§34b). If the article is generic referring to the totality of idols, then *every* idol is in view (§35b). Since "idol" is compared to God, perhaps Isaiah alludes to idols generically, every idol. The word "craftsman" is an intensive/extensive noun formation often used for professions (4.19; §23h).
51. and (the) smelter – The Qal active participle often expresses occupations (4.9).
52. with [the] gold – 7.20, 8.44.
53. cast . . . plates – The Hebrew poets often alternate between the perfect and imperfect: an action viewed as completed followed by an action viewed as incomplete, and vice versa. They weave these two tenses (aspects) with occasional Vav-consecutives and other forms for poetic feeling and emotion (11.10).
54. and (the) smelter with [the] gold plates it indeed – The Hebrew reads, "and smelter with the gold plates it indeed." The word "indeed" represents the energic ending of the imperfect.
55. (attaches to it indeed) – Assume but do not compose the imperfect with energic ending (compare the Targum).
56. The poor man – A Pual participle of the root סכן. Attach the article with the rule of SQeNeMLeVY on the participle (IBH 4.3.3 footnote 5).
57. with respect to an offering – An accusative of specification (6.15 [2]; §13nn, pp).
58. (which) – The relative pronoun drops out with an indefinite antecedent, as is the rule in Arabic, though optional in Hebrew (9.29; §43a, 46).
59. for himself – 2.5, 10.30.
60. (that) – 10.58.
61. does not totter – The Hebrew reads, "does not get itself tottered (overturned)" (4.6).

KEY TO COMPOSITION TEN

1 נַחֲמ֥וּ נַחֲמ֖וּ עַמִּ֑י יֹאמַ֖ר אֱלֹהֵיכֶֽם׃

2 דַּבְּר֞וּ עַל־לֵ֤ב יְרוּשָׁלַ֙͏ִם֙ וְקִרְא֣וּ אֵלֶ֔יהָ כִּ֤י מָלְאָה֙ צְבָאָ֔הּ כִּ֥י נִרְצָ֖ה עֲוֺנָ֑הּ כִּ֤י לָקְחָה֙
מִיַּ֣ד יְהוָ֔ה כִּפְלַ֖יִם בְּכָל־חַטֹּאתֶֽיהָ׃

3 ק֣וֹל קוֹרֵ֔א בַּמִּדְבָּ֕ר פַּנּ֖וּ דֶּ֣רֶךְ יְהוָ֑ה יַשְּׁרוּ֙ בָּעֲרָבָ֔ה מְסִלָּ֖ה לֵאלֹהֵֽינוּ׃

4 כָּל־גֶּיא֙ יִנָּשֵׂ֔א וְכָל־הַ֥ר וְגִבְעָ֖ה יִשְׁפָּ֑לוּ וְהָיָ֤ה הֶֽעָקֹב֙ לְמִישׁ֔וֹר וְהָרְכָסִ֖ים לְבִקְעָֽה׃

5 וְנִגְלָ֖ה כְּב֣וֹד יְהוָ֑ה וְרָא֤וּ כָל־בָּשָׂר֙ יַחְדָּ֔ו כִּ֛י פִּ֥י יְהוָ֖ה דִּבֵּֽר׃

6 ק֤וֹל אֹמֵר֙ קְרָ֔א וְאָמַ֖ר מָ֣ה אֶקְרָ֑א כָּל־הַבָּשָׂ֣ר חָצִ֔יר וְכָל־חַסְדּ֖וֹ כְּצִ֥יץ הַשָּׂדֶֽה׃

7 יָבֵ֤שׁ חָצִיר֙ נָ֣בֵל צִ֔יץ כִּ֛י ר֥וּחַ יְהוָ֖ה נָ֣שְׁבָה בּ֑וֹ אָכֵ֥ן חָצִ֖יר הָעָֽם׃

8 יָבֵ֥שׁ חָצִ֖יר נָ֣בֵֽל צִ֑יץ וּדְבַר־אֱלֹהֵ֖ינוּ יָק֥וּם לְעוֹלָֽם׃

9 עַ֣ל הַר־גָּבֹ֤הַ עֲלִי־לָךְ֙ מְבַשֶּׂ֣רֶת צִיּ֔וֹן הָרִ֤ימִי בַכֹּ֙חַ֙ קוֹלֵ֔ךְ מְבַשֶּׂ֖רֶת יְרוּשָׁלָ֑͏ִם הָרִ֙ימִי֙
אַל־תִּירָ֔אִי אִמְרִי֙ לְעָרֵ֣י יְהוּדָ֔ה הִנֵּ֖ה אֱלֹהֵיכֶֽם׃

10 הִנֵּ֨ה אֲדֹנָ֤י יְהוִה֙ בְּחָזָ֣ק יָב֔וֹא וּזְרֹע֖וֹ מֹ֣שְׁלָה ל֑וֹ הִנֵּ֤ה שְׂכָרוֹ֙ אִתּ֔וֹ וּפְעֻלָּת֖וֹ לְפָנָֽיו׃

11 כְּרֹעֶה֙ עֶדְר֣וֹ יִרְעֶ֔ה בִּזְרֹעוֹ֙ יְקַבֵּ֣ץ טְלָאִ֔ים וּבְחֵיק֖וֹ יִשָּׂ֑א עָל֖וֹת יְנַהֵֽל׃

12 כָּל־הַגּוֹיִ֖ם כְּאַ֣יִן נֶגְדּ֑וֹ מֵאֶ֥פֶס וָתֹ֖הוּ נֶחְשְׁבוּ־לֽוֹ׃

13 וְאֶל־מִ֖י תְּדַמְּי֣וּן אֵ֑ל וּמַה־דְּמ֖וּת תַּ֥עַרְכוּ לֽוֹ׃

14 הַפֶּ֙סֶל֙ נָסַ֣ךְ חָרָ֔שׁ וְצֹרֵ֖ף בַּזָּהָ֣ב יְרַקְּעֶ֑נּוּ וּרְתֻק֥וֹת כֶּ֖סֶף צוֹרֵֽף׃

15 הַמְסֻכָּ֣ן תְּרוּמָ֔ה עֵ֥ץ לֹֽא־יִרְקַ֖ב יִבְחָ֑ר חָרָ֤שׁ חָכָם֙ יְבַקֶּשׁ־ל֔וֹ לְהָכִ֥ין פֶּ֖סֶל לֹ֥א יִמּֽוֹט׃

Unpointed Text of Composition Ten

1 נחמו נחמו עמי יאמר אלהיכם׃

2 דברו על־לב ירושלים וקראו אליה כי מלאה צבאה כי נרצה עונה כי לקחה
מיד יהוה כפלים בכל־חטאתיה׃

3 קול קורא במדבר פנו דרך יהוה ישרו בערבה מסלה לאלהינו׃

4 כל־גיא ינשא וכל־הר וגבעה ישפלו והיה העקב למישור והרכסים לבקעה׃

5 ונגלה כבוד יהוה וראו כל־בשר יחדו כי פי יהוה דבר׃

6 קול אמר קרא ואמר מה אקרא כל־הבשר חציר וכל־חסדו כציץ השדה׃

7 יבש חציר נבל ציץ כי רוח יהוה נשבה בו אכן חציר העם׃

8 יבש חציר נבל ציץ ודבר־אלהינו יקום לעולם׃

9 על הר־גבה עלי־לך מבשרת ציון הרימי בכח קולך מבשרת ירושלים
הרימי אל־תיראי אמרי לערי יהודה הנה אלהיכם׃

10 הנה אדני יהוה בחזק יבוא וזרעו משלה לו הנה שכרו אתו ופעלתו לפניו׃

11 כרעה עדרו ירעה בזרעו יקבץ טלאים ובחיקו ישא עלות ינהל׃

12 כל־הגוים כאין נגדו מאפס ותהו נחשבו־לו׃

13 ואל־מי תדמיון אל ומה־דמות תערכו לו׃

14 הפסל נסך חרש וצרף בזהב ירקענו ורתקות כסף צורף׃

15 המסכן תרומה עץ לא־ירקב יבחר חרש חכם יבקש־לו להכין פסל לא ימוט׃

COMPOSITION ELEVEN

(1) Blessed is the man who has not walked in the counsel of (the) wicked.
And in the path of sinners he has not stood, and in the seat of scorners he has not sat.

(2) But in the law of the Lord is his delight.
And in his law he meditates day and night.

(3) And he will be as a tree planted upon channels of water:
whose fruit it gives in its time, and its leaf does not wither, and all that it does prospers.

(4) (But) not so the wicked,
but as the chaff that (the) wind drives [it][#] away.

(5) Therefore, (the) wicked will not stand in the judgment,
and sinners in (the) congregation of (the) righteous.

(6) For the Lord is knowing (the) path of (the) righteous
but (the) path of (the) wicked is about to perish.

(7) Why have (the) nations raged
and (the) peoples mutter emptiness?

(8) (The) kings of (the) earth got themselves stationed, and (the) rulers got themselves counsel together –
against the Lord and against his Messiah.

(9) We will tear their bonds to pieces one after another,
and we will throw down from us their ropes.

(10) (The) dweller in the heavens laughs
the Lord mocks [at] them.

(11) Then he speaks to them in his anger
and in his fury he terrifies them.

(12) But I – I have installed my king
upon Zion, my holy mountain.

(13) I will surely declare concerning (the) decree.
The Lord said to me, my son you are. I – today – I have begotten you.

(14) Ask of me, and I will indeed give nations as your inheritance.
And as your possession (the) ends of (the) world.

(15) You break them with a rod of iron.
As (the) vessel of (the) potter you smash them to pieces.

(16) And now, kings, show insight.
Receive discipline, judges of (the) earth.

(17) Serve the Lord with fear.
And rejoice with trembling.

(18) Kiss (the) son lest he become angry and you perish in (the) way. For his wrath will burn quickly. Blessed is all who take refuge in him.

( ) – Not in Hebrew, but needed for English
[ ] – In the Hebrew, but not needed for English
* – Put the pronominal suffix directly on the verb
# – Put the pronominal suffix with energic Nun directly on the verb

(1) Blessed[1] is the man who[2] has not walked[3] in the counsel of (the) wicked.
And in the path of sinners[4] he has not stood,[5] and in the seat of scorners[6] he has not sat.

(2) But in the law of the Lord[7] is his delight.[8]
And in his law[9] he meditates[10] day and night.[11]

(3) And he will be[12] as a tree planted upon channels of water:[13]

---

1. Blessed – 4.28, 9.34, 10.48.
2. who – The relative pronoun with a definite antecedent (the man) is the rule in Arabic and the general pattern in Hebrew (§43a). Contrast this construction with 10.58.
3. has not walked – Most modern translations render the perfect as a present tense. The past up to the present is in view, similar to a Greek perfect – "The man who has not walked and does not walk still" (1.14, 32, 10.19). The same applies to other perfects in the verse.
4. sinners – 4.19.
5. And in the path of sinners he has not stood – Notice the inverted word order of this and the next clause, forming a chiastic relationship with the first clause, a popular stylistic devise of Semitic writers.
6. scorners – The Qal participle depicts the scorners as professionals, as if their occupation (4.9, 7.39).
7. in the law of the Lord – The prepositional phrase receives force by its placement before the initiator (10.24; §11ff).
8. But in the law of the Lord is his delight – An adversative clause (§83b).
9. And in his law – Placed before the verb for emphasis (10.42).
10. he meditates – The Hebrew poets delight in alternating between the aspects of the perfect and imperfect. This alternation is rare in prose, occasional in direct speech, and frequent in poetry (10.53). In these poetic sections, aspect is usually more prominent than tense (10.2). He is mediating now and expects to continue mediating in the future (10.17, 47). The following words (day and night) fit well with the ongoing aspect of the imperfect.
11. day and night – These accusatives of specified time (§13y) preserve the old accusative endings. The word יוֹמָם maintains the Mem that ended Hebrew nouns (still seen in the masculine plural ending) in pre-Biblical Hebrew and the Qames that represents the original accusative vowel (Patach). The word לַ֫יְלָה has dropped the final Mem, but it retained the accusative vowel (The original Patach lengthened to a Qames). Being accusatives, these words may suggest the meaning, "*throughout* the day and *throughout* the night."
12. And he will be – In poetry and direct speech, the Vav of the Vᵊqatal form is commonly connecting or energic (in prose it is usually energic). Here it is energic since the verb has the meaning of the imperfect.
13. And he will be as a tree planted upon channels of water – As a general rule in poetry (also in prose as well), the first half of the verse (before the main disjunctive) expresses the main or general idea of the verse. The second half of the verse then supplements, qualifies, explains, and/or specifies the first half of the verse. Here the second half of the verse relates how the blessed man is like a tree planted beside the channels of waters. Notice how this general principle or tendency works throughout the Psalms and other poetical passages.

    The location of the main accent, Ole Veyored, suggests that the following words refer to the tree and not directly to the blessed man. (The whole verse, of course, by analogy refers to the blessed man.) All pronouns, therefore, are rendered "it." Had the Ole Veyored occurred after "wither," as in BHS, then the last words would directly refer to the blessed man with the pronouns rendered, "he" – "all that he does prospers."

whose fruit[14] it gives[15] in its time, and its leaf[16] does not wither, and all that it does[17] prospers.[18]

(4) (But) not so[19] the wicked,[20]
but[21] as the chaff[22] that (the) wind drives[23] [it]# completely away.[24]

(5) Therefore, (the) wicked will not stand in the judgment,[25]
and sinners[26] in (the) congregation of (the) righteous.

(6) For the Lord is knowing[27] (the) path of (the) righteous
but (the) path of (the) wicked[28] is about to perish.[29]

(7) Why have (the) nations raged
and (the) peoples[30] mutter[31] emptiness?

14. whose fruit – The Hebrew reads, "which (the) fruit of it (him)." The noun "fruit" by occurring before the verb receives weight in the clause (10.11).
15. gives – 11.10.
16. its leaf – Prominent by placement before its verb (announcement) (10.11).
17. and all that it does – 11.16.
18. prospers – 11.10.
19. (But) not so – As the negative לֹא emphasizes its noun, so here it emphasizes its particle (§41g). The context suggests that this verse is adversative to the preceding clause, a "but" is implied. Also note the parallelism of כִּי . . . לֹא־כֵן and כִּי . . . עַל־כֵּן that connects verse five and six closely together.
20. the wicked – The article is probably generic of the totality of the individuals of the group, "every wicked person" (5.7, 7.20, 10.50; §35b).
21. but – The Hebrew particles introduce an adversative clause (11.8).
22. as the chaff – The article is probably generic of the essence/quality of the group (5.7, 7.20, 10.50; §35a).
23. drives – 11.10.
24. completely away – This represents the energic ending on the imperfect.
25. in the judgment – The Targum interprets the article as particular, namely, *the* (final) judgment (§34a). Another interpretation of the article may suggest generic abstract – in judgment (§35c).
26. and sinners – 11.4.
27. For the Lord is knowing – The Hebrew reads, "For a knower is the Lord" (11.6).
28. but (the) path of (the) wicked – Note the chiastic word order of this verse (11.5).
29. is about to perish – This imperfect differs from the other imperfects in this Psalm (11.10). This is not what is going on now and what is expected to go on. But this is something that has not started yet. Its start, therefore, is imminent. His judgment, like a sword ready to fall, may begin at any moment (1.14; §4f, h).
30. and (the) peoples – The chiastic structure places the initiator before the announcement, giving prominence to the initiator (11.5).
31. raged . . . mutter – Notice the shift from the perfect to the imperfect (10.2, 53, 11.10).

(8) (The) kings of (the) earth got themselves stationed,[32] and (the) rulers[33] got themselves counsel together[34] –
against the Lord and against his Messiah.[35]

(9) We will tear their[36] bonds to pieces one after another.[37]
And we will throw down from us their ropes.

(10) (The) dweller[38] in the heavens laughs[39]
the Lord[40] mocks [at] them.[41]

(11) Then[42] he speaks to them[43] in his anger
and in his fury[44] he terrifies[45] them.[46]

32. got themselves stationed – This is the reflexive Hithpael (7.4). This verse echoes the verbal aspects of the preceding verse.
33. and (the) rulers – 11.5, 30.
34. got themselves counsel together – A reciprocal Niphal (§7n). David varies the aspect again with the perfect (11.31).
35. Messiah – *The* Anointed One.
36. their – Use the alternative ending, found in poetry, מוֹ.
37. We will tear their bonds to pieces one after another – The imperfect is an intensive/extensive Piel. Notice the plural concrete object, common with intensive/extensive Piels. The words "to pieces" represent the force of the intensive action; the words, "one after another," extends the action numerically to all the bonds (1.27). The LXX and Vulgate use intensive (or perfective) prepositions connected to the verb to express the intensive/extensive Piel. The cohortative emphasizes the determination of their rebellious volition (2.21, 3.3, 29, 5.25, 7.11, 9.25). The word "will" conveys volition more than tense. The verbal aspect is in process: "we are in the process of tearing and we expect to be tearing in the future."
38. (The) dweller – 11.6.
39. (The) dweller in the heavens laughs – Emphasize the initiator and the prepositional phrase by placing them before the announcement (11.16). For the aspect of the imperfect, see 11.10.
40. the Lord – 11.16.
41. [at] them – Use an alternative suffix found in poetry for the 3mp with ל preposition: לָמוֹ (11.36; GKC §91f).
42. Then – The particle אָז often precedes an imperfect preterit in prose (§4n). This particle, however, may precede a present/future imperfect, especially in poetry and in direct speech. This particle is stronger than the Vav of a Vav-consecutive form, expressing a "sudden turning of the action." The laughing and mocking of the preceding verse suddenly turns to God's speaking and terrifying. "In poetry," BDB states, "אז is sometimes used to throw emphasis on a particular feature of the description" (BDB 23a 1c). In the preceding verse, God laughs and mocks, *then* he acts by speaking in his anger and by his terrifying them in his fierce wrath.
43. to them – Use the poetical 3mp ending connected to the אל preposition (11.36, 41).
44. and in his fury – 11.5.
45. terrifies – This may be a factitive Piel (6.36, 9.32, 10.9). If the Qal root signifies, "to be excited or agitated," then the factitive means, "to put in an excited or agitated state."
46. them – 11.43.

(12) But I[47] – I have installed[48] my king
upon Zion, my holy mountain.[49]

(13) I will surely declare[50] concerning (the) decree.[51]
The Lord[52] said to me, my son you are. I[53] – today[54] – I have begotten[55] you.

(14) Ask of me, and I will indeed give[56] nations as your inheritance.[57]
And as your possession (the) ends of (the) world.[58]

(15) You break them[59] with[60] a rod of iron.[61]
As (the) vessel of (the) potter[62] you smash them to pieces.[63]

---

47. But I – Use the independent pronoun for emphasis (3.24, 9.24; §19f). The Vav is adversative (§83c).
48. I have installed – "I have installed, and he is installed still" (11.3). The perfect aspect contrasts with the imperfect aspect of the preceding verse (11.10, 31). The context suggests that the action of the perfect was completed before the rebellion of the preceding verses.
49. my holy mountain – Substitution apposition (5.12, 8.1, 15).
50. I will surely declare – Emphasize God's determination by using the cohortative. The cohortative communicates the meaning of "surely." The "will" of the translation expresses strong volition (11.37).
51. concerning (the) decree – The Masoretes place the main accent of the verse, Ole Veyored, on the word, "decree." "The Lord," therefore, is emphatically placed before the following verb, instead of an annexation with "decree" ("the decree of the Lord," so BHS). The "decree" by context refers to the "Lord's decree." The LXX and Vulgate interpret the "decree" as the "decree of the Lord," then repeat the word "Lord" for emphasis before the announcement. The Targum also interprets the decree as "the decree of the Lord" without repeating "the Lord" for emphasis with the following verb.
52. The Lord – Placed before its announcement for emphasis (11.16).
53. I – 11.46.
54. today – Emphasize this word by placing it before the announcement (verb) (11.9, 10.42). The Hebrew reads, "the day" (5.14).
55. I have begotten – 11.47, 11.3. Notice the Hireq thematic vowel, perhaps reflecting an old stative formation or the attenuation of Patach to Hireq in closed, unaccented syllables (GKC §27s). The Arabic verb of the same verbal root has a Hireq thematic vowel as well.
56. I will indeed give – The cohortative conveys "indeed" (11.37, 50).
57. nations as your inheritance – The verb takes two objects that may form a nominal clause: "Nations are your inheritance" (§13u). The first object is the direct object; the second object is an accusative of situation (illustrating and permanent, §13z, aa, gg).
58. And as your possession (the) ends of (the) world – These two objects may also form a nominal clause: "the ends of the earth are your possession." Note the chiastic arrangement of the four objects. The first object is an accusative of situation as in the preceding footnote; the second object is the direct object. Also notice the main accent of the verse, the Athnach, separates the four objects for parallelism.
59. You break them – The imperfect is in process: "You are breaking them, and you are expected to continue to break them" (11.10).
60. with – The בּ preposition often has the notion of instrument or means (BDB 89b III 2).
61. a rod of iron – A proper annexation with the meaning of a מִן preposition implied between the words: "a rod made of (from) iron" (7.42; §12d). The genitive (iron) is the material from which the governing noun (rod) is made.
62. As (the) vessel of (the) potter – This proper annexation expresses possession, implying the meaning of a לְ preposition between the words: "a vessel belonging to the potter" (1.19; §12e). Notice the chiastic construction in this verse.
63. you smash them to pieces – This verb only occurs in the Piel and in the Qal infinitive and participle. This often excludes the intensive meaning for the Piel, but the physical nature of this verb

(16) And now, kings, show insight.
Receive discipline, judges of (the) earth.[64]

(17) Serve the Lord with fear.
And rejoice with trembling.[65]

(18) Kiss[66] (the) son lest[67] he become angry and you perish in (the) way.[68] For his wrath will burn[69] quickly.[70] Blessed[71] is all who takes refuge in him.[72]

---

suggests the intensive/extensive (1.27; §7g). You smash them with great force (intensive) one after another until few or none are left (numerically extensive).

64. And now, kings, show insight. Receive discipline, judges of (the) earth – For the inverted word order, see 11.5. For the clause, "Receive discipline," the Hebrew reads, "Get yourselves disciplined" (4.6).
65. with fear . . . with trembling – 10.27.
66. Kiss – This extensive Piel is not extended to many objects (numerically extensive), but to the same object time and time again (frequentatively extensive, §7c): "Kiss the Son *time and time again*" (12.4).
67. lest – This particle introduces a subjunctive verb (§4j).
68. in (the) way – An accusative of specified place (6.15 [3b], 7.2, 9.6; §13w).
69. will burn – The context seems to indicate that the action of the imperfect has not begun. The imperfect expresses imminent action – what is about to happen (11.29).
70. quickly – The Hebrew reads, "as a little of his anger."
71. Blessed – 11.1.
72. all who takes refuge in him – The Hebrew reads, "all the refuge takers [of] in you." The participle, "the refuge takers" (who takes refuge), is in the construct to a prepositional phrase (in him). The prepositional phrase is in the place of the genitive (§12q).

Key to Composition Eleven

1 אַ֥שְֽׁרֵי הָאִ֗ישׁ אֲשֶׁ֤ר ׀ לֹ֥א הָלַךְ֮ בַּעֲצַ֪ת רְשָׁ֫עִ֥ים וּבְדֶ֣רֶךְ חַ֭טָּאִים לֹ֥א עָמָ֑ד וּבְמוֹשַׁ֥ב לֵ֝צִ֗ים לֹ֣א יָשָֽׁב׃

2 כִּ֤י אִ֥ם בְּתוֹרַ֥ת יְהוָ֗ה חֶ֫פְצ֥וֹ וּֽבְתוֹרָת֥וֹ יֶהְגֶּ֗ה יוֹמָ֥ם וָלָֽיְלָה׃

3 וְֽהָיָ֗ה כְּעֵץ֮ שָׁת֪וּל עַֽל־פַּלְגֵ֫י מָ֥יִם אֲשֶׁ֤ר פִּרְי֨וֹ ׀ יִתֵּ֬ן בְּעִתּ֗וֹ וְעָלֵ֥הוּ לֹֽא־יִבּ֑וֹל וְכֹ֖ל אֲשֶׁר־יַעֲשֶׂ֣ה יַצְלִֽיחַ׃

4 לֹא־כֵ֥ן הָרְשָׁעִ֑ים כִּ֥י אִם־כַּ֝מֹּ֗ץ אֲֽשֶׁר־תִּדְּפֶ֥נּוּ רֽוּחַ׃

5 עַל־כֵּ֤ן ׀ לֹא־יָקֻ֣מוּ רְ֭שָׁעִים בַּמִּשְׁפָּ֑ט וְ֝חַטָּאִ֗ים בַּעֲדַ֥ת צַדִּיקִֽים׃

6 כִּֽי־יוֹדֵ֣עַ יְ֭הוָה דֶּ֣רֶךְ צַדִּיקִ֑ים וְדֶ֖רֶךְ רְשָׁעִ֣ים תֹּאבֵֽד׃

7 לָ֭מָּה רָגְשׁ֣וּ גוֹיִ֑ם וּ֝לְאֻמִּ֗ים יֶהְגּוּ־רִֽיק׃

8 יִ֥תְיַצְּב֨וּ ׀ מַלְכֵי־אֶ֗רֶץ וְרוֹזְנִ֥ים נֽוֹסְדוּ־יָ֑חַד עַל־יְ֝הוָ֗ה וְעַל־מְשִׁיחֽוֹ׃

9 נְֽ֭נַתְּקָה אֶת־מ֣וֹסְרוֹתֵ֑ימוֹ וְנַשְׁלִ֖יכָה מִמֶּ֣נּוּ עֲבֹתֵֽימוֹ׃

10 יוֹשֵׁ֣ב בַּשָּׁמַ֣יִם יִשְׂחָ֑ק אֲ֝דֹנָ֗י יִלְעַג־לָֽמוֹ׃

11 אָ֤ז יְדַבֵּ֣ר אֵלֵ֣ימוֹ בְאַפּ֑וֹ וּֽבַחֲרוֹנ֥וֹ יְבַהֲלֵֽמוֹ׃

12 וַ֭אֲנִי נָסַ֣כְתִּי מַלְכִּ֑י עַל־צִ֝יּ֗וֹן הַר־קָדְשִֽׁי׃

13 אֲסַפְּרָ֗ה אֶֽ֫ל חֹ֥ק יְֽהוָ֗ה אָמַ֘ר אֵלַ֥י בְּנִ֥י אַ֑תָּה אֲ֝נִ֗י הַיּ֥וֹם יְלִדְתִּֽיךָ׃

14 שְׁאַ֤ל מִמֶּ֗נִּי וְאֶתְּנָ֣ה ג֭וֹיִם נַחֲלָתֶ֑ךָ וַ֝אֲחֻזָּתְךָ֗ אַפְסֵי־אָֽרֶץ׃

15 תְּ֭רֹעֵם בְּשֵׁ֣בֶט בַּרְזֶ֑ל כִּכְלִ֖י יוֹצֵ֣ר תְּנַפְּצֵֽם׃

16 וְ֭עַתָּה מְלָכִ֣ים הַשְׂכִּ֑ילוּ הִ֝וָּסְר֗וּ שֹׁ֣פְטֵי אָֽרֶץ׃

17 עִבְד֣וּ אֶת־יְהוָ֣ה בְּיִרְאָ֑ה וְ֝גִ֗ילוּ בִּרְעָדָֽה׃

18 נַשְּׁקוּ־בַ֡ר פֶּן־יֶאֱנַ֤ף ׀ וְתֹ֬אבְדוּ דֶ֗רֶךְ כִּֽי־יִבְעַ֣ר כִּמְעַ֣ט אַפּ֑וֹ אַ֝שְׁרֵ֗י כָּל־ח֥וֹסֵי בֽוֹ׃

Unpointed Text of Composition Eleven

1 אשרי־האיש אשר לא הלך בעצת רשעים ובדרך חטאים לא עמד ובמושב
לצים לא ישב׃

2 כי אם בתורת יהוה חפצו ובתורתו יהגה יומם ולילה׃

3 והיה כעץ שתול על־פלגי מים אשר פריו יתן בעתו ועלהו לא־יבול וכל
אשר־יעשה יצליח׃

4 לא־כן הרשעים כי אם־כמץ אשר־תדפנו רוח׃

5 על־כן לא־יקמו רשעים במשפט וחטאים בעדת צדיקים׃

6 כי־יודע יהוה דרך צדיקים ודרך רשעים תאבד׃

7 למה רגשו גוים ולאמים יהגו־ריק׃

8 יתיצבו מלכי־ארץ ורוזנים נוסדו־יחד על־יהוה ועל־משיחו׃

9 ננתקה את־מוסרותימו ונשליכה ממנו עבתימו׃

10 יושב בשמים ישחק אדני ילעג־למו׃

11 אז ידבר אלימו באפו ובחרונו יבהלמו׃

12 ואני נסכתי מלכי על־ציון הר־קדשי׃

13 אספרה אל חק יהוה אמר אלי בני אתה אני היום ילדתיך׃

14 שאל ממני ואתנה גוים נחלתך ואחזתך אפסי־ארץ׃

15 תרעם בשבט ברזל ככלי יוצר תנפצם׃

16 ועתה מלכים השכילו הוסרו שפטי ארץ׃

17 עבדו את־יהוה ביראה וגילו ברעדה׃

18 נשקו־בר פן־יאנף ותאבדו דרך כי־יבער כמעט אפו אשרי כל־חוסי בו׃

COMPOSITION TWELVE

(1) And he said, I love you,* Lord, my strength.

(2) The Lord is my rock and my fortress and my deliverer
my God, my rock, in (whom) I take refuge, my shield and the horn of my salvation, my secure height.

(3) I call (upon) the Lord, in the status of one to be praised.
From my enemies I am saved.

(4) The cords of death have surrounded me.*
And torrents of worthlessness terrify me.*

(5) (The) cords of Sheol have surrounded me.*
(The) snares of death have confronted me.*

(6) In my distress, I cry out (to) the Lord, and to my God I call out for help.
He hears from his temple my voice, and my cry for help comes before him into his ears.

(7) And the earth shook and quaked, and (the) foundations of (the) mountains trembled.
They got themselves shaken violently for he became angry

(8) Smoke went up in his nostrils, and fire from his mouth consumed.
Coals were kindled by it.

(9) Then he bent (the) heavens and came down,
with a dark cloud under his feet.

(10) And he rode upon a cherub and flew.
And he moved swiftly upon (the) wings of (the) wind.

(11) He placed darkness as his hiding place, around him was his covering,
watery darkness, dark masses of clouds.

(12) From the brightness before him,
his dark masses (of clouds) passed, hail and coals of fire.

(13) Then the Lord thundered in the heavens, and the Most High utters his voice,
hail and coals of fire.

(14) And he sent his arrows, and he scattered them.*
And (he sent) lightning strikes in abundance, and he confounded them.*

(15) Then channels of water appeared, and (the) foundations of (the) world were revealed,
By your rebuke, Lord, by the exhale of the breath of your nostrils.

( ) – Not in Hebrew, but needed for English
[ ] – In the Hebrew, but not needed for English
* – Put the pronominal suffix directly on the verb
# – Put the pronominal suffix with energic Nun directly on the verb

(1) And he said,[1] I love you,*[2] Lord, my strength.[3]

(2) The Lord is my rock and my fortress and my deliverer[4]
my God,[5] my rock,[6] in (whom) I take refuge,[7] my shield[8] and the horn of my salvation,[9] my secure height.[10]

(3) I call (upon) the Lord, in the status of one to be praised.[11]
From my enemies I am saved.[12]

---

1. And he said – Use the pausal form with this Vayyiqtol form (IBH 30.4.3.2). Athnach cannot stand on the first word; therefore, Pazer substitutes for the Athnach.
2. I love you – The imperfect is in process: "I am loving you now, and I expect to love you in the future" (6.6, 10.17, 47, 11.10).
3. my strength – Substitution apposition (5.12, 8.1, 15, 11.49)
4. and my deliverer – This word conveys a physical action (to break through, to tear off) with concrete objects, having a similar meaning in the Qal, the ideal characteristics of an intensive/extensive Piel. God delivers or tears away David with great force (intensive). Usually extensive action is numerical, that is, the action is extended to many objects, one after another. This time, however, the extensive action is temporal, that is, the action is extended many times: God tears away with great force (intensive) David, *time and time again* (frequentatively extensive) (1.27, 11.37, 66; §7c). The Vav on this participle and the Vav on the preceding noun are conjunctive, appositional Vavs, which link two or more words to their antecedent, appositive noun, "the Lord" (§25a).
5. my God – Use the singular form, common in poetry, אֵל.
6. my rock – Although this word may also mean, "rocky cliff or hill," as סַלְעִי in the preceding verse, it may also mean boulder or rock (BDB 849b 1).
7. in (whom) I take refuge – The Hebrew reads, "(whom) I take refuge in him." The rule in Arabic and the tendency in Hebrew is for the relative pronoun to appear after definite antecedents, as here. Poetry allows more freedom for grammatical rules than prose (10.58, 11.2; §46a). For the aspect of the imperfect, see 12.2.
8. my shield – This word has a Dagesh Forte in the last root letter, perhaps to preserve the preceding short vowel (GKC §93ee, kk, pp).
9. and the horn of my salvation – 9.36.
10. my secure height – 12.8.
11. I call (upon) the Lord, in the status of one to be praised – The Hebrew reads, "in the status of one to be praised, I call (upon) the Lord." The participle, placed before the verb for prominence, is an accusative of situation, hence, the translation, "in the status of" (§16l). The passive participle (or imperfect) may aptly be rendered, "worthy to be praised" (§7a).
12. I am saved – The Hebrew reads, "I got (myself) saved" (4.6). This Niphal verb is reflexive of the Hiphil root (8.49). For the aspect of both verbs in this verse, see 12.2.

(4) The cords of death surrounded me.*[13]
And torrents of worthlessness terrify me.*[14]

(5) (The) cords of Sheol have surrounded me.*
(The) snares of death have confronted me.*[15]

(6) In my distress,[16] I cry out[17] (to) the Lord, and to my God I call out for help.[18]
He hears[19] from his temple my voice, and my cry for help comes before him[20] into[21] his ears.

---

13. The cords of death surrounded me – Place the verb before the agent. After describing God as his deliverer and fortress in the first three verses, David relates a particular occasion when God supernaturally delivered him from Saul. To describe a past event in prose, a Hebrew writer uses a series of Vayyiqtol forms. In poetry, an author may do the same (Ps 18:8; 78); however, more commonly he uses perfects to relate a past, completed action. As expected David begins with a perfect since the action occurred in the past. Since this psalm is recounting or narrating a particular event, the verbs carry tense as much as aspect. For most psalms, tense is a secondary consideration to aspect (10.2).
14. And torrents of worthlessness terrify me – Place the initiator first to form a chiastic structure with the first half of the verse. David changes aspect again (10.53, 11.10, 31, 34). The imperfect describes the past action in process as if David is reliving the terror.
15. (The) cords of Sheol have surrounded me. (The) snares of death have confronted me – Make the first clause (sentence) a nominal clause by placing the initiator before the announcement. Then form a chiastic construction by making the second clause a verbal clause – place the verb before the agent.
16. In my distress – The Hebrew reads, "in the distress to me." Placed before the verb, this prepositional phrase has emphasis (10.42, 11.9).
17. I cry out – Notice the change of aspect of this imperfect from the preceding perfects (10.53, 11.10, 12.11).
18. I call out for help – 12.17.
19. He hears – In the parallel passage, 2 Sam 22:7, this imperfect is a Vayyiqtol form. This may suggest taking the imperfect here as a preterit. There are, however, differences between the passages. Perhaps David intended this version to vary from 2 Sam 22:7 and to understand this imperfect as in process (12.12).
20. and my cry for help comes before him – Place the initiator, "my cry for help," and the prepositional phrase before the announcement (10.11, 12.14).
21. into – The ב preposition.

(7) And the earth shook and quaked,[22] and (the) foundations of (the) mountains[23] were trembling.[24]
And they got themselves shaken violently[25] for he became angry.[26]

(8) Smoke went up in his nostrils, and fire from his mouth consumed.[27]
Coals[28] were kindled by it.

(9) Then he bent (the) heavens and came down,[29]
with a dark cloud under his feet.[30]

(10) And he rode upon a cherub and flew.[31]
And he moved swiftly upon (the) wings of (the) wind.

(11) He placed[32] darkness as his hiding place,[33] around him was his covering,
watery darkness,[34] dark masses of clouds.

(12) From the brightness before him,[35]
his dark masses (of clouds)[36] passed, hail and coals of fire.[37]

---

22. And the earth shook and quaked – David now details how God answered his prayer for help. David narrates with Vayyiqtol forms, the characteristic of prose narrative, with occasional perfects and imperfects for poetic feeling. Notice the similar, onomatopoeic roots of quaking, געשׁ, רעשׁ, and רגז (10.53, 11.10, 31, 34, 48).
23. and (the) foundations of (the) mountains – Place the initiator before the announcement for emphasis (10.11).
24. were trembling – The aspect shifts to ongoing action, the imperfect vivifying the account by describing the mountains as in process of trembling (12.22).
25. And they got themselves shaken violently – The verbal aspect shifts back to completed action (11.48, 12.22). This is an intensive/extensive Hithpael: "They got themselves shaken one after another (extensively) violently (intensively)" (11.37). For the reflexive notion of the Hithpael (and Niphal), see 7.4, (4.6).
26. he became angry – The Hebrew reads, "it became hot to him." Retract the accent on the verb (10.20).
27. and fire from his mouth consumed – Form a chiastic structure with the preceding clause by placing the initiator before the announcement (12.13).
28. Coals – Emphasize this initiator by placing it before the announcement (10.11).
29. and came down – Put this verb in pause with a Patach for the thematic vowel.
30. with a dark cloud under his feet – A situation clause, rare in poetry (§49b).
31. and flew – Put this Vayyiqtol form in pause with a Holem thematic vowel.
32. He placed – A preterit imperfect with the jussive/preterit form (IBH 36.4.2.2.2). Retract the accent on the verb (10.20).
33. darkness as his hiding place – The verb takes two objects that may form a nominal clause: His hiding place is darkness (11.57; §13u). The second object is an accusative of situation, illustrating and temporary (§13aa, hh).
34. watery darkness – The Hebrew reads, "darkness of water." The word for darkness is feminine.
35. From the brightness before him – Notice the strong disjunctive accent, Ole Veyored, marking the emphasis of the words before the announcement (verb).
36. his dark masses (of clouds) – Place the initiator before its announcement.
37. hail and coals of fire – Probably the preceding verb is implied again: Hail and coals of fire (also passed).

(13) Then the Lord thundered in the heavens,[38] and the Most High utters his voice,[39]
hail and coals of fire.[40]

(14) And he sent his arrows, and he scattered them.*
And (he sent) lightning strikes in abundance,[41] and he confounded them.*

(15) Then channels of water appeared,[42] and (the) foundations of (the) world were revealed,[43]
By[44] your rebuke, Lord, by[45] the exhale of the breath of your nostrils.

38. Then the Lord thundered in the heavens – The word order is "thundered in the heavens the Lord."
39. and the most high utters his voice – Place the initiator before the announcement, forming a partial chiastic construction. Note the change of aspect (12.22).
40. hail and coals of fire – 12.37. The repetition (verse 12) indicates the awesomeness of the hail and coals of fire.
41. And (he sent) lightning strikes in abundance – Assume the first verb of the verse for this direct object: "And (he sent) lightning strikes." The words, "in abundance," represent an accusative of situation of the adjective רַב (רָב).
42. Then channels of water appeared – A verbal clause with a reflexive Niphal: "channels of water got themselves seen" (4.6; §7k).
43. and (the) foundations of (the) world were revealed – Another verbal clause and another reflexive Niphal, "They got themselves uncovered."
44. By – מִן.
45. by – מִן.

Key to Composition Twelve

1 וַיֹּאמַר אֶרְחָמְךָ יְהוָה חִזְקִי׃

2 יְהוָה׀ סַלְעִי וּמְצוּדָתִי וּמְפַלְטִי אֵלִי צוּרִי אֶחֱסֶה־בּוֹ מָגִנִּי וְקֶרֶן־יִשְׁעִי מִשְׂגַּבִּי׃

3 מְהֻלָּל אֶקְרָא יְהוָה וּמִן־אֹיְבַי אִוָּשֵׁעַ׃

4 אֲפָפוּנִי חֶבְלֵי־מָוֶת וְנַחֲלֵי בְלִיַּעַל יְבַעֲתוּנִי׃

5 חֶבְלֵי שְׁאוֹל סְבָבוּנִי קִדְּמוּנִי מוֹקְשֵׁי מָוֶת׃

6 בַּצַּר־לִי׀ אֶקְרָא יְהוָה וְאֶל־אֱלֹהַי אֲשַׁוֵּעַ יִשְׁמַע מֵהֵיכָלוֹ קוֹלִי וְשַׁוְעָתִי לְפָנָיו׀
תָּבוֹא בְאָזְנָיו׃

7 וַתִּגְעַשׁ וַתִּרְעַשׁ׀ הָאָרֶץ וּמוֹסְדֵי הָרִים יִרְגָּזוּ וַיִּתְגָּעֲשׁוּ כִּי־חָרָה לוֹ׃

8 עָלָה עָשָׁן׀ בְּאַפּוֹ וְאֵשׁ־מִפִּיו תֹּאכֵל גֶּחָלִים בָּעֲרוּ מִמֶּנּוּ׃

9 וַיֵּט שָׁמַיִם וַיֵּרַד וַעֲרָפֶל תַּחַת רַגְלָיו׃

10 וַיִּרְכַּב עַל־כְּרוּב וַיָּעֹף וַיֵּדֶא עַל־כַּנְפֵי־רוּחַ׃

11 יָשֶׁת חֹשֶׁךְ׀ סִתְרוֹ סְבִיבוֹתָיו סֻכָּתוֹ חֶשְׁכַת־מַיִם עָבֵי שְׁחָקִים׃

12 מִנֹּגַהּ נֶגְדּוֹ עָבָיו עָבְרוּ בָּרָד וְגַחֲלֵי־אֵשׁ׃

13 וַיַּרְעֵם בַּשָּׁמַיִם׀ יְהוָה וְעֶלְיוֹן יִתֵּן קֹלוֹ בָּרָד וְגַחֲלֵי־אֵשׁ׃

14 וַיִּשְׁלַח חִצָּיו וַיְפִיצֵם וּבְרָקִים רָב וַיְהֻמֵּם׃

15 וַיֵּרָאוּ׀ אֲפִיקֵי מַיִם וַיִּגָּלוּ מוֹסְדוֹת תֵּבֵל מִגַּעֲרָתְךָ יְהוָה מִנִּשְׁמַת רוּחַ אַפֶּךָ׃

Unpointed Text of Composition Twelve

1 ויאמר ארחמך יהוה חזקי׃

2 יהוה סלעי ומצודתי ומפלטי אלי צורי אחסה־בו מגני וקרן־ישעי משגבי׃

3 מהלל אקרא יהוה ומן־איבי אושע׃

4 אפפוני חבלי־מות ונחלי בליעל יבעתוני׃

5 חבלי שאול סבבוני קדמוני מוקשי מות׃

6 בצר־לי אקרא יהוה ואל־אלהי אשוע ישמע מהיכלו קולי ושועתי לפניו
תבוא באזניו׃

7 ותגעש ותרעש הארץ ומוסדי הרים ירגזו ויתגעשו כי־חרה לו׃

8 עלה עשן באפו ואש־מפיו תאכל גחלים בערו ממנו׃

9 ויט שמים וירד וערפל תחת רגליו׃

10 וירכב על־כרוב ויעף וידא על־כנפי־רוח׃

11 ישת חשך סתרו סביבותיו סכתו חשכת־מים עבי שחקים׃

12 מנגה נגדו עביו עברו ברד וגחלי־אש׃

13 וירעם בשמים יהוה ועליון יתן קלו ברד וגחלי־אש׃

14 וישלח חציו ויפיצם וברקים רב ויהמם׃

15 ויראו אפיקי מים ויגלו מוסדות תבל מגערתך יהוה מנשמת רוח אפך׃

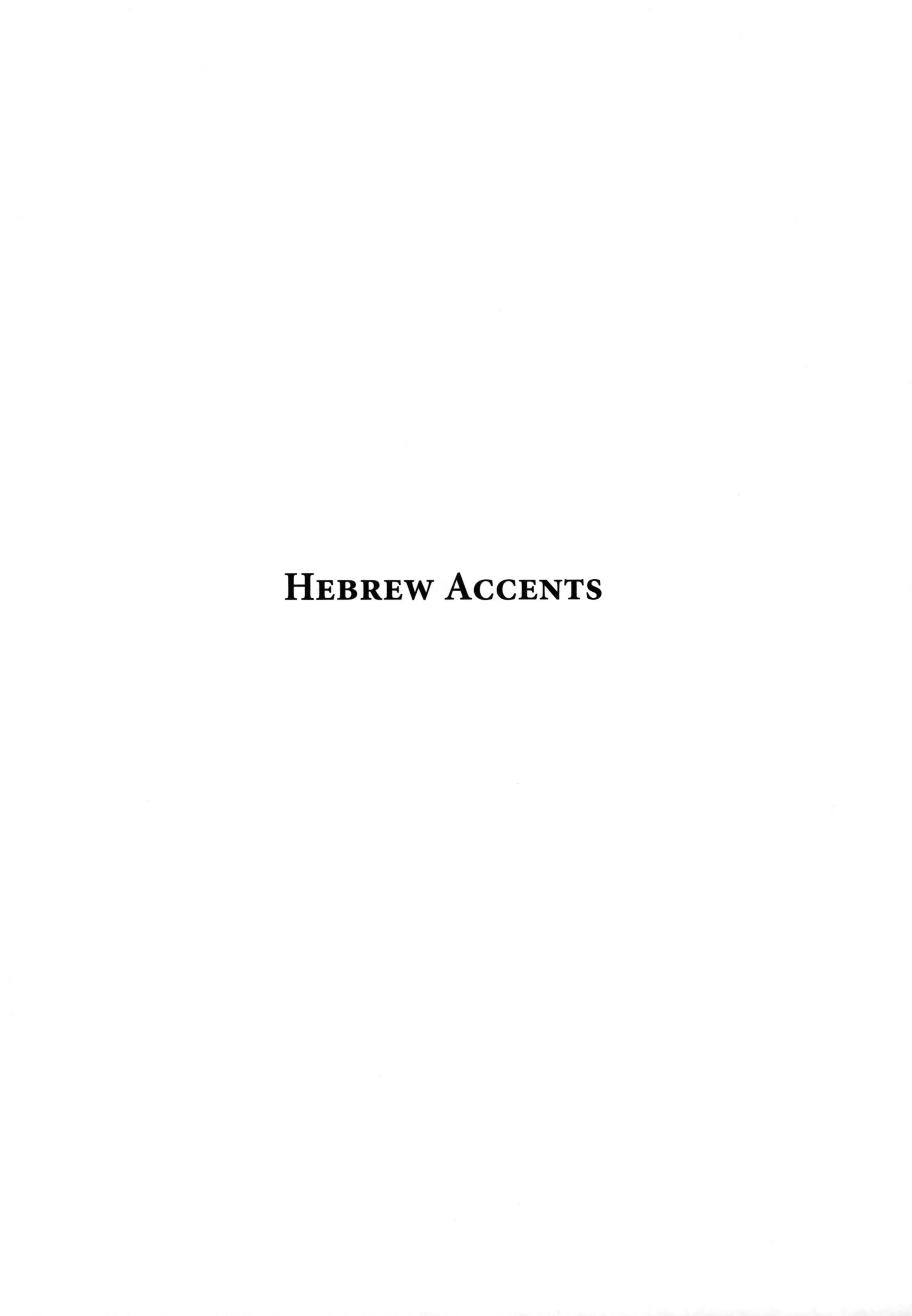

Hebrew Accents

HEBREW ACCENTS

Introduction

The Masoretes, the custodians and guardians of the Hebrew text of the Old Testament, inherited and handed down the traditional vocalizing and chanting of the text. This often indicates the traditional syntax and exegesis of the text. The vocalizing and chanting began centuries before Christ,[1] perhaps with the great scribe of Scripture, Ezra.[2] If so, then the

1. C. H. Roberts, *Two Biblical Papyri in the John Rylands Library* (Manchester, Manchester University Press, 1936), 28; E. J. Revell, *The Oldest Evidence for the Hebrew Accent System,* (Bulletin of John Rylands Library, LIV 1971), 214–222. In one sense, all unpointed texts are vocalized and their words grouped (which chanting indicates) any time they are read. What is meant here is that the traditional vocalization and chanting (or grouping of words), as reflected in the Masoretic tradition, most probably existed centuries before Christ.
2. The Babylonian Talmud (TB) states, "Has not Rabbi Iqa said in the name of Rabbi Hananel who had it from Rab: What is meant by the text, (Neh 8:8) *And they read in the book, in the law of God, with an interpretation, and they gave the sense, and caused them to understand the reading? And they read in the book, in the law*: this indicates the Bible; *with an interpretation*: this indicates the targum (interpretation); *and they gave the sense*: this indicates the verse stops; *and caused them to understand the reading*: this indicates the accentuation, or according to another version, the masoretic notes." TB Megillah 3a. Compare similarly, TB Nedarim 37b; TJ (Talmud Jerushalmi) Megillah 4:1 74d; Genesis Rabbah 36.8 (In the last two citations, the clause in Neh 8:8, "And they gave the sense in the reading," is connected to the accents). TB Nedarim 37b, discussing the same quotation in TB Megillah 3a, allows compensation for teaching the accents on the Sabbath because "the accents are also Biblical." Similarly, Rabbi Shefatiah states in the name of Rabbi Johanan: "If one reads the Scripture without a melody (as indicated by chanting the accents) or repeats the Mishnah without a tune, of him Scripture says, (Ezek 20:25) Wherefore I gave them also statues that were not good" (TB Megillah 32a). Rabbinic tradition sees the accentuation as given, or at least implied, by the biblical author – Raba made this exposition: "What was written in Scripture, (Eccl 12:9) And besides that Koheleth was wise, he also taught the people knowledge; yea, he pondered, and sought out, and set in order many proverbs? He also taught the people knowledge implies that he taught it with notes of accentuation and illustrated it by simile" (TB Erubin 21b). Commenting on TB Berakoth 62a, Rashi says that hand movements corresponded to the singing of the accents.

   Edwin Yamauchi, however, denies the Rabbinic interpretation of Neh 8:8, "But the Talmudic comment is clearly anachronistic as we have no evidence of targums from such an early date." Edwin Yamauchi, *Ezra and Nehemiah*, EBC 4 (Grand Rapids: Zondervan, 1988), 725. The earliest extant written targum is dated around 150–100 BC. Almost certainly, written targums predated 150 BC. Moreover, Rabbinic sources indicate other ancient targums no longer extant existed (TB Shabbath 115a; TJ Shabbath 15c). The current lack of evidence for a written targum during the time of Ezra does not make the rabbinic claim "anachronistic." Targums and their sources extend "several centuries" before the official targums of Onkelos and Jonathan, as Vermes and Millar write, "Though compiled in the third or fourth century A.D., there is no doubt that the Targums of Onkelos and Jonathan rely on older works and are the final outcome of a process covering several centuries. . . . In consequence, it is clear that the material used in the Targums of Onkelos and Jonathan is the product of the labour of previous generations, and that written Targums preceded the extant ones." Emil Schürer, *The History of the Jewish People in the Age of Jesus Christ, A New English Edition*, revised and edited by G. Vermes and F. Millar (Edinburgh: T & T Clark, 1973), I 102.

   Aaron ben Asher claimed that the Prophets, the Sopherim, with Ezra and the wise men [the Great Synagogue] originated the punctuation/accentual system. WW p. 5; Aaron ben Asher,

vocalizing and the chanting of the Scripture reflect the divinely inspired text.[3] If not, then the vocalizing and chanting of the Scripture represent an ancient rabbinic interpretation of Scripture, an invaluable resource for syntax and exegesis.

Many interpreters and grammarians have stressed the importance of the accents for syntax and exegesis. "Any interpretation which is not in accordance with the arrangement of the accents," Eben Ezra, the medieval rabbinic commentator, stated, "thou shalt not consent to it, nor listen to it."[4] Heinrich Ewald likewise recognized the importance of the accents for understanding Hebrew syntax:

> By further consideration and investigation in this way, there will always be found a beautiful harmony between the accentuation and the syntax, so that each may afford explanation and support to the other. Whether we start with the syntax, and come to understand it without knowing anything yet of the accentuation (as the author once actually did), or proceed from the latter to the former, accurate investigation will always lead to the same result, so that he who has a correct understanding of the syntax, has already nearly mastered the accentuation also, and he who understands the latter will always find himself more easily at home in the former. But this is, at the same time, the highest praise that can be given to the accentuation.[5]

Kautzsch also extolled the syntactical value of the accents for syntax.

Dikdukei Ha-Te'amim edited by Baer and Strack (Leipzig, 1879) xvi, 1. Ben Asher's claim resembles Pirke Aboth 1:1, "Moses received the law from Sinai, and he handed it down to Joshua, and Joshua (handed it down) to the elders, and the elders (handed it down) to the prophets, and the prophets handed it down to the men of the great synagogue." The verb "handed down" in Pirke Aboth 1:1 is the same root of the word Masorete (מסר).

3. When speaking of the divine inspiration of Scripture, theologians usually refer to the original manuscripts. This is certainly appropriate, but this definition should be extended to the canon of the Old Testament in the time of Ezra (which is the present Jewish and Protestant canon), the great scribe and final editor of Scripture. We refer to the Masoretic tradition being inspired as accurately preserving Ezra's inspired text, allowing for an isolated copyist mistake and/or a rare lapse in the tradition, for example, 1 Sam 13:1. The frequent emendations of the Masoretic Text by most modern translations are, therefore, unnecessary, speculative at best, and usually corrupting (See the text and footnotes of that mutant text known as BHS and the modern translations which follow its fantasies [dl, ins, om, tr-- scilicet] and corruptions [crrp]). Let the Masoretic tradition speak for itself, leaving opinion and conjecture to footnotes, commentaries, and the like. We, of course, accept Ben Asher's claim that his tradition reflects and preserves Ezra's inspired text (See footnote two above). The Formula of the Consensus Helvetica (1675) Canon II also reflects this claim, "But in particular, the Hebrew original of the Old Testament, which we have received and to this day do retain as handed down by the Jewish Church, unto whom formerly 'were committed the oracles of God' (Rom 3:2) is, not only in its consonants, but in its vowels – either the vowels points themselves, or at least the power of the points – not only in its matter, but in its words, inspired of God. . . ." A. A. Hodge, *Outlines of Theology* (Edinburgh: The Banner of Truth, 1879), 656. We would add, "not only in its consonants and the vowels, but the accents or the power of the accents," as well.
4. James D. Price, *The Syntax of Masoretic Accents in the Hebrew Bible* (Lewiston, NY: The Edwin Mellen Press, 1990), 9.
5. Ewald, §366.

> On the other hand, according to their original design they have also a twofold use which is still of the greatest importance for grammar (and syntax), viz. their value (a) as *marking the tone*, (b) as *marks of punctuation* to indicate the logical (syntactical) relation of single words to their immediate surroundings, and thus to the whole sentence.[6]

Joüon and Muraoka also confirm the value of the accents for syntax: "A knowledge of the accents is sometimes important for grammar and also for interpretation."[7] As these authorities intimate, students of Hebrew syntax should study the Masoretic accents and grasp their syntactical value. Indeed, the Hebrew word for these accents, טְעָמִים, means "understanding, sense," indicating that the understanding or sense of the syntax is communicated through the accents. Two cautions, however, must be mentioned. First, the accents follow their own rules of syntax based on musical considerations, which may on occasion formally contradict the grammatical syntax.[8] Secondly, the accents occasionally are difficult to interpret – allowing for different interpretations or being just simply difficult to understand. Happily, these cautions are rarely problematic. The chanting almost always conveys the syntax and meaning of the text clearly – the chanting, after all, must make sense.

The accents group words into units. As a rule, a clause of two words is grouped together with a conjunctive accent; a clause of three words, by contrast, introduces a disjunctive accent within the unit. The same is true of word or phrase units: a word or phrase unit of two words groups the words with a conjunctive accent; a word or phrase unit of three words introduces a disjunctive accent within the unit.

6. GKC, §15b.
7. JM, §15, especially 15k.
8. This is also true of modern hymns. Musical considerations may override the syntax. For example, in the hymn, *Sweeping This Way*, the beginning of the third verse reads, "Prophets have told it: In the last days . . . Hearts shall be filled with glorious praise." The words, "In the last days," are grouped with the words, "Prophets have told it," because of musical considerations, though syntactically they belong with the words, "Hearts shall be filled with glorious praise." The problem in Hebrew, as in English, rarely presents a problem for understanding the verse. In Gen 4:10, קֹ֖ול דְּמֵ֣י אָחִ֑יךָ "The voice of the blood of your brother," three words are in construct and, therefore, should syntactically be joined. Because of musical considerations, however, the first word often has a disjunctive accent.

Syntax of the Disjunctive and Conjunctive Accents for Prose

A. Disjunctive and Conjunctive Accents

Disjunctive Accents	
Soph Pasuq	דָבָֽר׃
Silluq	דָבָֽר
Athnach	דָבָ֑ר
Segolta	דָבָר֒
Shalsheleth	דָבָ֓ר ׀
Little Zaqeph	דָבָ֔ר
Great Zaqeph	דָבָ֕ר
Rebia	דָבָ֗ר
Tiphcha	דָבָ֖ר
Zarqa	דָבָר֮
Pashta	דָבָר֙
Yethib	דָ֚בָר
Tebir	דָבָ֛ר
Geresh	דָבָ֜ר
Gershaim	דָבָ֞ר
Pazer	דָבָ֡ר
Great Pazer	דָבָ֟ר
Great Telisha	דָ֠בָר
Legarmeh	דָבָ֣ר ׀

Conjunctive Accents	
Munach	דָבָ֣ר
Mehuppach	דָבָ֤ר
Merecha	דָבָ֥ר
Merecha Kepula	דָבָ֦ר
Darga	דָבָ֧ר
Azla	דָבָ֨ר
Little Telisha	דָבָר֩
Galgal	דָבָ֪ר
Mayela	דָ֖בָ֑ר

The Hebrew accents for prose are divided into disjunctive and conjunctive accents. Disjunctive accents disjoin a word or words from the next word, creating a pause between words; conjunctive accents join a word or words to the next word, without a pause between the words. Disjunctive accents possess rank, based on hierarchy. To illustrate their hierarchy and strength of disjunction, scholars divide the accents into the nobilities of emperor, kings, princes, dukes, and counts. Hence, the disjunctive accents are "lords" to the conjunctive accents. The conjunctive accents, "the servants," serve their disjunctive "lords."

B. Hierarchy of Disjunctive Accents

RANKS				
EMPEROR	Soph Pasuq (׃)			
KINGS	Silluq (ֽ)	Athnach (֑)		
PRINCES	Tiphcha (֖)	Zaqeph (֔)	Segolta (֒)	
DUKES	Tebir (֛)	Pashta (֙)	Zarqa (֘)	Rebia (֗)
COUNTS	Geresh (֜)	Great Telisha (֠)	Pazer (֡)	Legarmeh (׀ ֣)
SERVANTS	All conjunctive accents			

This hierarchy expresses the order of the disjunctive accents. Each lower rank is directly subordinate to its immediate superior: kings are directly subordinate to the emperor, as the princes are directly subordinate to kings, and so forth. Subordinates are divided into near subordinates and remote subordinates. The emperor Soph Pasuq, for instance, has a near subordinate, Silluq, and a remote subordinate, Athnach.

C. Disjunctive Accents: Ranks, Conjunctives, and Subordinates

COLUMN 1 **Ranks**	COLUMN 2 **Disjunctive Accent**	COLUMN 3 **Number of Conjunctive Accents (possible)**	COLUMN 4 **Near Subordinate**	COLUMN 5 **Remote Subordinate**
EMPEROR	Soph Pasuq (׃)	0	Silluq (ֽ)	Athnach (֑)
NEAR KING	Silluq (ֽ)	0–1 (֥)	Tiphcha (֖)	Zaqeph Qaton (֔)
REMOTE KING	Athnach (֑)	0–1 (֣)	Tiphcha (֖)	Zaqeph Qaton (֔), Segolta (֒)
NEAR PRINCE	Tiphcha (֖)	0–1 (֥)	Tebir (֛)	Rebia (֗)
REMOTE PRINCE	Zaqeph Qaton (֔)# Zaqeph Gadol [֕]	0–2 (֣)	Pashta (֙)	Rebia (֗)
REMOTE PRINCE	*Segolta (֒), Shalsheleth [֓]	0–1 (֣)	Zarqa (֘)	Rebia (֗)
NEAR DUKE	Tebir (֛)	0–2	Geresh (֜)	Pazer (֡), Great Telisha (֠)

Column 1 Ranks	Column 2 Disjunctive Accent	Column 3 Number of Conjunctive Accents (possible)	Column 4 Near Subordinate	Column 5 Remote Subordinate
Near Duke	*Pashta (֙) Yethib [֚]	0–2	Geresh (֜)	Pazer (֡), Great Telisha (֠)
Near Duke	*Zarqa (֮)	0–2	Geresh (֜)	Pazer (֡), Great Telisha (֠)
Remote Duke	Rebia (֗)#	0–3	Geresh (֜)	Pazer (֡), Great Telisha (֠)
Near Count	Geresh (֜), Garshaim [֞], Legarmeh (׀ ֣)	0–5 0–1 (֣) 0–2		
Remote Count	Pazer (֡)# [Great Telisha (֠), Great Pazer (֟)]	0–6 (֣) [for Great Pazer]		

1) Column one supplies the rank of subordination and its position as near or remote.

2) Column two gives the name of the disjunctive accent.
   i. The accents in the brackets [ ] indicate that the accent may substitute for the other accent. For example, a Zaqeph Gadol may substitute for a Zaqeph Qaton.

   ii. The asterisk (*) indicates prepositives and postpositives. Prepositives, always placed in the pre-position of a word (that is, at the beginning of the word), do not mark the accented syllable. Postpositives, always placed in the post-position of a word (that is, at the end of the word), do not mark the accented syllable of a word. Non-prepositive or non-postpositive accents mark the stress or tone of their words.

   iii. The sharp marks (#) indicate that a remote subordinate accent may be repeated. All remote subordinate accents may be repeated except for Athnach, Segolta, and Great Telisha. Near dukes, especially Pashta, appear to repeat. When Pashta or another duke appears to repeat, the first Pashta or duke (reading right to left) substitutes for a Rebia.

Jer 7:20 לָכֵ֞ן כֹּֽה־אָמַ֣ר ׀ אֲדֹנָ֣י יְהוִ֗ה הִנֵּ֨ה אַפִּ֤י וַחֲמָתִי֙ נִתֶּ֙כֶת֙ אֶל־הַמָּק֣וֹם הַזֶּ֔ה

Therefore, thus says the Lord God, Behold my anger and my wrath is being poured out unto this place.

The word with (double) Pasta (נִתְּכָ֙ה֙) is preceded by another word with a Pasta (וַחֲמָתִ֙י֙) which substitutes for a Rebia.

3) Column three gives the number of words with conjunctive accents that may intervene between the disjunctive accent in column two and its near subordinate in column four.[9] Zero means that no word (with a conjunctive accent) intervenes between the disjunctive accent in column two and its near subordinate in column four. One means that one word (with a conjunctive accent) may intervene between the disjunctive accent in column two and its near subordinate in column four.

4) Column four furnishes the near subordinate for the disjunctive accent in column two.

5) Column five furnishes the remote subordinate for the disjunctive accent in column two.

The conjunctive accents in column three are limited to Merecha and Munach for kings and princes. Dukes and counts, however, allow a greater number and variety of conjunctive accents to serve them, if necessary. The following chart illustrates the usage of conjunctive accents for dukes and counts.

D. Conjunctive Accents for Dukes and Counts in Prose[10]

	First Conjunctive		Second Conjunctive		Third Conjunctive
	Regular	Alternative	Regular	Alternative	
Rebia	◌֣		◌֧		◌֣
Tebir	◌֧	Merecha	Azla	Munach	
Pashta	◌֤	Merecha	Azla	Munach	
Zarqa	◌֣	**Merecha**	**Azla**	**Munach**	
Geresh	Azla		◌֩		◌֣
Garshaim	◌֣		◌֣		◌֣
Great Pazer	◌֪		◌֣		◌֣

9. The particular conjunctive accent is in the parenthesis. Disjunctives without parenthesis take more than one kind of conjunctive accent. For example, Pashta may take Mehuppach or Merecha for first conjunctive before it and an Azla or Munach for the second conjunctive before it.
10. This chart is adapted from Price, 35.

	First Conjunctive		Second Conjunctive		Third Conjunctive
	Regular	Alternative	Regular	Alternative	
Pazer	֣		֣		֣
Great Telisha	֣		֣		֣
Legarmeh	Merecha		Azla		

1) Dukes
   i. Rebia: The first conjunctive accent must be a Munach. If a second conjunctive occurs, it must be a Darga. The third must be a Munach.

      Num 4:14 וְנָתְנ֣וּ עָ֠לָיו אֶֽת־כָּל־כֵּלָ֞יו אֲשֶׁ֧ר יְשָׁרְת֣וּ עָלָ֛יו בָּהֶ֗ם
      And they will put on it all its equipment by which they serve concerning it.

      The word preceding the Rebia has a Munach, which is preceded by a word with Darga, which is preceded by a word with Munach.

   ii. Tebir, Pashta, and Zarqa: Each has its own particular accent for the first conjunctive; however, they may have an alternative for the first conjunctive, Merecha. For their second conjunctive, they all have Azla, which may be replaced with an alternative, Munach. If the Tebir, Pashta, or Zarqa appears to have Little Telisha as a third conjunctive accent, the first conjunctive accent (next to the Tebir, Pashta, or Zarqa) substitutes for a Geresh. Hence, that first conjunctive accent is considered a transformed Geresh. The transformed Geresh is chanted as a conjunctive accent, but understood syntactically as a disjunctive Geresh.

      Gen 2:14 וְשֵׁ֨ם הַנָּהָ֤ר הַשְּׁלִישִׁי֙ חִדֶּ֔קֶל
      And the name of the third river is Chideleth.

      In Gen 2:14, the Pashta has its normal conjunctives, preceded by a word with a Mehuppach, which is preceded by word with an Azla.

      Gen 14:16 וַיָּ֕שֶׁב אֵ֖ת כָּל־הָרְכֻ֑שׁ וְגַ֩ם אֶת־ל֨וֹט אָחִ֤יו וּרְכֻשׁוֹ֙ הֵשִׁ֔יב
      And he returned all the possessions, and even Lot, his brother, and his possessions he returned.

      In Gen 14:16, the Pashta appears to be served by three conjunctive accents: Mehuppach, Azla, and Little Telisha. The Mehuppach on the word preceding the Pashta, ho wever, substitutes for a transformed Geresh, with the Azla and Little Telisha serving as conjunctives to the transformed Geresh.

2) Counts

i. Geresh, Great Pazer, and Great Telisha: These may add two more Munachs beyond their third conjunctive accent.

ii. Pazer: It may add three more Munachs beyond the third conjunctive accent.

Diagrams of the Syntax of the Disjunctive Accents for Prose

A. Emperor

The emperor Soph Pasuq does not allow a conjunctive accent between it and the Silluq, its near subordinate. Hence, the Silluq must occur on the word directly before the Soph Pasuq. The Athnach, the remote subordinate of Soph Pasuq, may occur anywhere in a verse except for the last word. The Soph Pasuq governs the entire verse; the Silluq and the Athnach govern their own segments of the verse.

Genesis 1:1

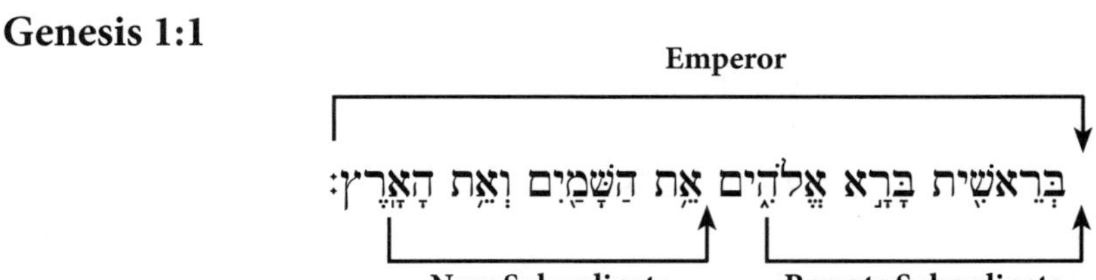

Emperor Soph Pasuq governs the entire verse. Its near subordinate Silluq governs to the Athnach; its remote subordinate Athnach governs to the beginning of the verse.

B. Kings

Like the Soph Pasuq, the kings, Silluq and the Athnach, govern their own near and remote subordinates, namely the princes. The Silluq and the Athnach may have one word with a conjunctive accent to intervene between them and the word with Tiphcha, their near subordinate. The conjunctive accent for Silluq is Merecha; for Athnach, it is Munach. Prince Zaqeph Qaton is the remote subordinate for Silluq and Athnach. While the placement of the word with Tiphcha is restricted (next to or one word away from the Silluq or Athnach), the placement of Zaqeph Qaton is unrestricted, based on the syntax and meaning of the verse. The Athnach segment (but not the Silluq segment) may substitute a Segolta for the Zaqeph Qaton.[11] For Athnach segments with more than one Zaqeph Qaton, the Segolta may substitute for the first Zaqeph Qaton. Unlike the kings and the other princes, the Zaqeph Qaton may repeat.[12]

11. In half-verses with repeating disjunctives, such as three Zaqeph Qatons, the first Zaqeph Qaton is a stronger disjunctive than the second Zaqeph Qaton, which is a stronger disjunctive than the third Zaqeph Qaton. When Segolta substitutes for the first Zaqeph Qaton, other Zaqeph Qatons in the same Athnach segment are weaker than the Segolta. Gen 1:7
12. Consider words with the dotted line under the governance of the near subordinate. Near subordinates require a dotted line for the word or words between them and their immediate superior. Their immediate superior governs the entire segment, not just the word or words between them and their near subordinate.

Genesis 4:9

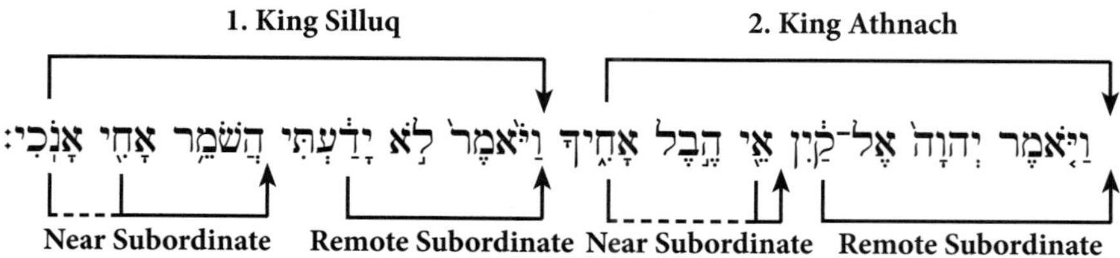

King Silluq (1) governs to the Athnach, and king Athnach (2) governs to the beginning of the verse. Their near subordinate, Tiphcha, governs to the Zaqeph Qaton, and their remote subordinate, Zaqeph Qaton, governs the rest of the segments. The words in the dotted lines are also under the government of their near subordinate Tiphcha.

C. Princes

The princes – Tiphcha, Zaqeph Qaton, and Segolta – also have near and remote subordinates. Tiphcha and Segolta may have one word (Segolta may rarely have two words) with a conjunctive accent between them and their near subordinates. The near subordinate for Tiphcha is Tebir, and for Segolta, the near subordinate is Zarqa. The word with Zaqeph Qaton allows up to two words (rarely two, usually it allows one word) with the conjunctive accent Munach between it and its near subordinate, Pashta. The remote subordinate for all princes is Rebia, whose placement, significant for interpretation, is determined by syntax and meaning of the verse. The princes govern their segments within the larger domain of the kings.

Genesis 7:13[b]

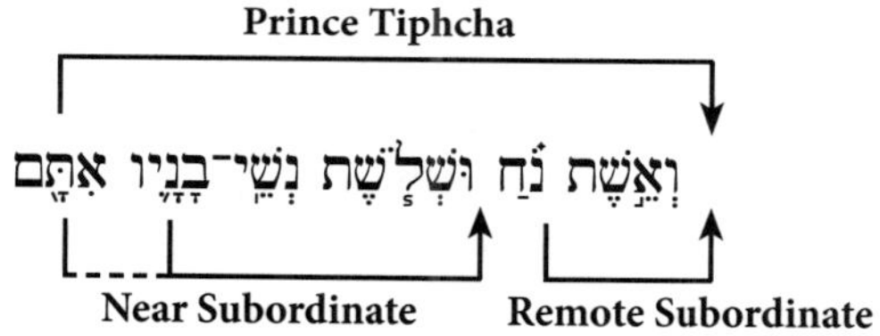

Prince Tiphcha governs the segment. Its near subordinate Tebir governs to the Rebia; the Rebia governs to the beginning of the segment.

Genesis 2:20[a]

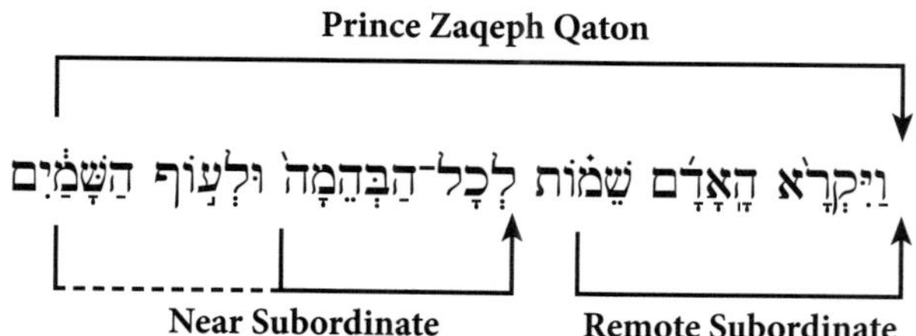

Prince Zaqeph Qaton governs the segment. Its near subordinate Pashta governs to the Rebia; Rebia governs to the beginning of the segment.

Genesis 24:7[a]

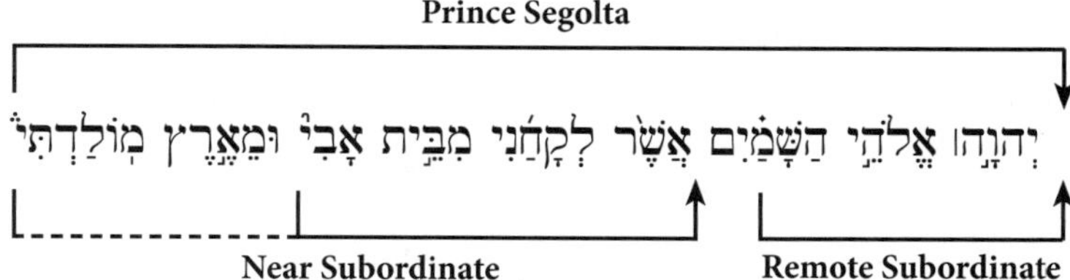

Prince Segolta governs the segment. Its near subordinate Zarqa governs to the Rebia; Rebia governs to the beginning of the segment.

D. Dukes

The dukes – Tebir, Pashta, Zarqa, and Rebia – have Geresh as their near subordinate and Great Telisha or Pazer as their remote subordinate. If both Pazer and Great Telisha occur in the same segment, Pazer is the stronger subordinate, with Great Telisha marking a minor break as a near subordinate. The Tebir, Pashta, and Zarqa may have two words with conjunctive accents serving them; the Rebia may have three words with conjunctive accents serving it.[13] A Rebia segment may be repeated. The dukes govern their segments within the larger domain of the princes.

Genesis 3:6

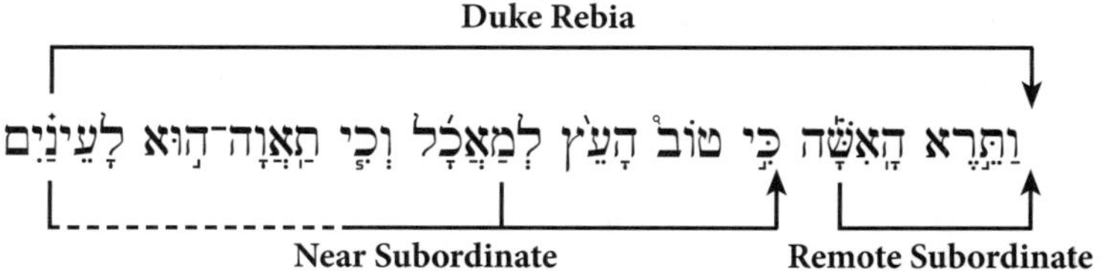

Duke Rebia governs the segment. Its near subordinate Geresh governs to the Pazer; Pazer governs to the beginning of the segment.

E. Counts

The counts – Geresh (Gershaim), Legarmeh, Great Telisha, and Pazer (Great Pazer) – do not have near or remote subordinates.[14] Occasionally, Paseq may be a subordinate to the Geresh, Pazer, or Great Telisha. The Paseq and Pazer may repeat. The counts govern their segments within the larger domain of the dukes.

---

13. The Rebia takes three conjunctives only ten times.
14. Paseq is a vertical line introducing a pause between words, often confused with the Legarmeh in the prose accents. Legarmeh occurs in Rebia's segment. Otherwise, vertical lines should be considered Paseqs.

Syntax of the Disjunctive and Conjunctive Accents for Poetry

A. Disjunctive and Conjunctive Accents

Disjunctive Accents		Conjunctive Accents	
Soph Pasuq	דָבָֽר׃	Munach	דָבָ֣ר
Silluq	דָבָֽר	Merecha	דָבָ֥ר
Ole Veyored	דָ֫בָ֥ר	Illuy	דָבָ֬ר
Athnach	דָבָ֑ר	Tarcha	דָבָ֖ר
Great Rebia	דָבָ֗ר	Galgal	דָבָ֪ר
Rebia Mugrash	דָ֝בָ֗ר	Mehuppach	דָבָ֤ר
Great Shalsheleth	דָבָ֓ר ׀	Azla	דָבָ֨ר
Sinnor	דָבָר֮	Little Shalsheleth	דָבָ֓ר
Little Rebia	דָבָ֗ר	Sinnorit-Merecha	דָ֘בָ֥ר
Dechi	דָבָ֭ר	Sinnorit-Mehuppach	דָ֘בָ֤ר
Pazer	דָבָ֡ר		
Mehuppach-Legarmeh	דָבָ֤ר ׀		
Azla-Legarmeh	דָבָ֨ר ׀		

As with the prose accents, the poetic accents (for Psalms, Proverbs, and most of Job) have disjunctive and conjunctive accents. The disjunctive accents, "the lords," have hierarchy of ranks and the conjunctive accents, "the servants," are equal in rank.

B. Hierarchy of Ranks

Ranks				
Emperor	Soph Pasuq (׃)			
Kings	Silluq (ֽ)	Ole Veyored (֫ ֥)	Athnach (֑) (if Ole Veyored does not occur in the verse)	
Princes	Rebia Mugrash (֝ ֗)	Dechi (֭)	Sinnor (֮)	Great Rebia (֗)
	Athnach (֑) (if Ole Veyored occurs in the verse)	Little Rebia (֗)		
Dukes	Legarmeh (׀)	Pazer (֡)		

Again, like the prose accents, each lower rank is directly subordinate to its immediate superior. There is, however, a major difference between disjunctives of prose and poetry: the remote disjunctives may sometimes occur without the near disjunctive, especially Rebia and Pazer. This usually happens for emphasis or for rhythm if long words (words with two or more syllables) occur between the remote and its governing accent.

C. Disjunctive Accents: Their Ranks, Conjunctives and Subordinates

Column 1	Column 2	Column 3	Column 4	Column 5
Rank	**Disjunctive**	**Conjunctive**	**Near**	**Remote**
Emperor	Soph Pasuq (:)	0	Silluq ( )	Ole Veyored ( ) Athnach ( ) (if Ole Veyored does not occur in the verse)
Near King	Silluq ( )	0–1 Munach ( ), Merecha ( ), Illuy ( )	Rebia Mugrash♣ ( ) (if Athnach occurs in the verse)	Athnach ( ) (if Ole Veyored occurs in the verse)
Remote Kings	Ole Veyored ( )	0–1 Galgal ( ), Mehuppach ( )	Sinnor ( ) or Little Rebia ( )	Great Rebia ( )
	Athnach ( ) (to Soph Pasuq)	0–1 Merecha ( ), Munach ( )	Dechi ( )	Great Rebia ( )
Near Princes	Rebia Mugrash ( )	0–3 Merecha ( ), Tarcha, Mehuppach	Empty	Empty
	*Sinnor ( )	0–1 Merecha ( ), Munach ( )	Legarmeh (	)	Pazer ( )
	*Dechi ( )	0–2 Munach ( )	Legarmeh (	)	Pazer ( )
	Little Rebia ( )	0–2 Merecha ( ), Mehuppach ( )	Legarmeh (	)	Empty
Remote Princes	Rebia ( )#	0–1 Illuy ( ), Mehuppach ( ), Sinnor-Mehuppach ( )	Legarmeh (	)♣	Pazer ( )
	Athnach ( ) (to Silluq)	Merecha ( ), Munach ( )	Dechi ( )	Great Rebia ( )
Near Duke	Legarmeh#	0–1 Illuy ( ), Mehuppach ( ), Sinnor-Mehuppach ( )	Legarmeh (	)	Empty
Remote Duke	Pazer ( )#	0–2 Galgal ( ), Mehuppach ( )	Legarmeh (	)	Empty

1) Column one supplies the rank of subordination and position of the subordinate as near or remote.

2) Column two gives the name of the disjunctive accent.
   i. The asterisk (*) marks prepositives and postpositives. Prepositives, always placed in the pre-position of a word (that is, at the beginning of the word), do not mark the accented syllable. Postpositives, always placed in the post-position of a word (that is, at the end of the word), do not mark the accented syllable of a word. Accents that are not prepositive or postpositive mark the accent or tone of the word.

   ii. The sharp mark (#) indicates that a remote subordinate accent may be repeated once. All remote subordinate accents may be repeated except for Ole Veyored and Athnach. Rarely, Legarmeh may repeat.

   iii. The spade mark (♠) indicates that a Legarmeh may occur between Silluq and Rebia Mugrash.

   iv. The clover mark (♣) indicates that the Legarmeh and Pazer may transpose positions. Pazer remains the stronger accent even after transposition. Ps 17:14

3) Column three gives the number of words with conjunctive accents that may intervene between the disjunctive accent in column two and its near subordinate in column four. Zero means that no word (with a conjunctive accent) intervenes between the disjunctive accent in column two and its near subordinate in column four. One means that one word (with a conjunctive accent) may intervene between the disjunctive accent in column two and its near subordinate in column four. Poetic accents limited to only one conjunctive accent may appear to take more conjunctives due to "transformed disjunctives." See section five below.

4) Column four furnishes the near subordinate for the disjunctive accent in column two.

5) Column five furnishes the remote subordinate for the disjunctive accent in column two.

Transformed Disjunctives

For musical reasons, disjunctive accents may transform into another disjunctive accent or a conjunctive accent. *Frequently, when a disjunctive accent has more than one conjunctive accent, the first conjunctive (or sometimes the second conjunctive) accent before the disjunctive accent functions syntactically as a disjunctive.*[15] This conjunctive accent, therefore, is called a transformed disjunctive accent. Transformed disjunctives are musically conjunctive, chanted as a conjunctive accent, but syntactically disjunctive.

A. Disjunctive Accents Transformed into Conjunctive Accents

1. Rebia Mugrash: When a Rebia Mugrash does not occur in a verse and less than

15. Rebia Mugrash, when not substituting for an Athnach, lacks subordinate disjunctive accents and may rarely take three conjunctives.

two syllables[16] occur between the syllable with Silluq and the first word before a Silluq, which has a conjunctive accent, the conjunctive accent is a transformed Rebia Mugrash. The transformed Rebia Mugrash is a conjunctive accent: Munach (usually), Merecha, or Illuy. The transformed Rebia Mugrash usually has a conjunctive, frequently Tarcha. If Silluq appears to have two or more conjunctive accents serving it, the first word from the Silluq is almost always a transformed Rebia Mugrash. The Rebia Mugrash, of course, can occur on the second or third word before the Silluq without transformation. In the following two examples, the first example has the Rebia Mugrash; in the second example, the first word from the Silluq has a transformed Rebia Mugrash.

a) Ps 18:4 וּמִן־אֹ֝יְבַ֗י אִוָּשֵֽׁעַ׃—Since there are two syllables between the syllable with the Silluq and the first word before the Silluq, a Rebia Mugrash appears.
b) Ps 18:5 בְלִיַּ֣עַל יְבַעֲת֥וּנִי׃—Since only one syllable occurs between the syllable with the Silluq and the first word before the Silluq, and the Rebia Mugrash does not appear anywhere in the second half of the verse, and the verse has an Athnach, the Munach is a transformed Rebia Mugrash.[17]

2. **Dechi**: The rules for Dechi resemble the rules for Rebia Mugrash. When less than two syllables occur between Athnach and Dechi, the Dechi transforms into a conjunctive accent: Munach (and sometimes Merecha) before Athnach. When an Athnach has more than one word with conjunctive accents, the first word before the Athnach has the transformed Dechi. The Dechi, of course, can occur on the second word before the Athnach without transformation.
   a) Ps 35:14 לִ֝י הִתְהַלָּ֑כְתִּי—Since two syllables occur between the syllable with the Athnach and the first word before the Athnach, a Dechi appears.
   b) Ps 35:4 יִסֹּ֣גוּ אָח֣וֹר וְיַחְפְּר֑וּ—Only one syllable occurs between the syllable with the Athnach and the first word before the Athnach. The Athnach also appears to govern two conjunctive accents (Munachs). The first Munach before the Athnach, however, represents a transformed Dechi.

3. **Legarmeh:**
   a) When Dechi appears to have more than one conjunctive accent, the first conjunctive accent before the Dechi (Munach) transforms into Legarmeh. Ps 4:3

16. When a long vowel followed by vocal shewa occurs between the syllable with Silluq and the first word before the Silluq, a Rebia Mugrash appears on the first word before the Silluq (Ps 27:5, 11). This is an exceptional case, probably due to the Metheg with the long vowel. (Inverting the accents of this exceptional case, with a vocal shewa followed by a long vowel, does not allow a Rebia Mugrash. Ps 15:5.) The shewa does not constitute a syllable, as Ps 2:9 and 5:4 indicate, since two vocal shewa do not constitute even one syllable. Moreover, added vowels (anaptyctic vowels) from consecutive vocal shewas or from segolate vowels also do not constitute a syllable (Ps 18:44). Words that have two syllables before the accented syllable, or a long vowel followed by vocal shewa before the accented syllable, are called "long words." Words that do not have two syllables before the accented syllable or a long vowel followed by vocal shewa before the accented syllables are called "short words."
17. This rule for long words applies only with the word having the Silluq, not with the final syllable of a preceding Milʿel word (Ps 2:3).

עַד־מֶ֥ה כְבוֹדִ֨י לִכְלִמָּ֗ה—The two conjunctive accents before Dechi, Munach and Illuy, indicate that the Munach is a transformed Legarmeh.

b) When a Dechi appears to have two conjunctive accents serving it, and the second word from the Dechi is a monosyllabic word, that second word is a transformed Legarmeh. This rule also applies with monosyllabic words when Little Rebia and Pazer appear to have two conjunctive accents serving them (Ps 1:2). Prov 15:17 טוֹב אֲרֻ֣חַת יָ֭רָק—The Dechi appears to have two conjunctive accents serving it. The second word from the Dechi, because it is monosyllabic, is a transformed Legarmeh.

c) Legarmeh also transforms into a conjunctive accent when it occurs on the first word before the Silluq and when Great Shalsheleth occurs on the third word from the Silluq (Ps 29:11).[18]

i. Ps 29:11 יְהוָ֤ה ׀ יְבָרֵ֖ךְ אֶת־עַמּ֣וֹ בַשָּׁלֽוֹם׃—The Silluq appears to have two conjunctive accents serving it. Since the Great Shalsheleth, a substitute for Rebia Mugrash, is on the third word from the Silluq, the first conjunctive before the Silluq is a transformed Legarmeh.

ii. Ps 10:14 יָ֝ת֗וֹם אַתָּ֤ה ׀ הָיִ֬יתָ עוֹזֵֽר׃—Contrast this example with the preceding. The Legarmeh occurs on the second word before the Silluq when Rebia Mugrash occurs on the third word from the Silluq.

B. Disjunctive Accents Transformed into Another Disjunctive Accent

1. **Athnach to Rebia Mugrash**: The Athnach may not stand on the first word before the Silluq. Instead it transforms into a Rebia Mugrash (often written defectively as Rebia) for musical reasons. Moreover, it may not stand on the second word before the Silluq if the first word before the Silluq and/or Silluq's word are short.[19] This Rebia Mugrash substitutes for the Athnach.

a) Ps 18:51 וּלְזַרְע֗וֹ עַד־עוֹלָֽם׃—When an Athnach would occur on the first word before the Silluq,[20] the first word before the Silluq transforms the Athnach into Rebia Mugrash (written defectively as Rebia).

b) Ps 119:2 עֵדֹתָ֑יו בְּכָל־לֵ֥ב יִדְרְשֽׁוּהוּ׃—The second word before the Silluq transforms the Athnach into Rebia Mugrash. The Athnach should appear on the second word before the Silluq, but word with Silluq and the first word before Silluq have less than two syllables between their accented syllable and the second word before the Silluq.[21] Only the syllable with Qames-Hatuph (בְּכָל) occurs between לֵב and עֵדֹתָיו.

18. The Great Shalsheleth substitutes for Rebia Mugrash. The first word with a conjunctive accent before the Silluq, therefore, is not a transformed Rebia Mugrash, since the Great Shalsheleth substitutes for the Rebia Mugrash.
19. See footnote 16 for the definition of "short word."
20. This is indicated by a verse lacking an Athnach and a Rebia Mugrash (or Rebia written defectively) occurring on the first word before the Silluq.
21. This is indicated again by a verse lacking an Athnach and a Rebia Mugrash (or Rebia written defectively) occurring on the second word before the Silluq. Moreover, this Rebia Mugrash (transformed from an Athnach) may take the subordinates of the Athnach, namely, Dechi and Rebia, Ps 119:48.

c) Ps 119:8 :אֶשְׁמֹ֑ר אַל־תַּעַזְבֵ֥נִי עַד־מְאֹֽד—Contrast this example with the preceding example. Two syllables occur between the accented syllable of the first word before the Silluq and the second word before the Silluq. (The Patachs under the Tav and Aleph are the syllables; the Patach under the Ayin is secondarily added [anaptyxis], like the added Segol of the Segolate noun.) Therefore, the Athnach occurs rather than the transformed Rebia Mugrash.

2. **Rebia Mugrash to Great Shalsheleth**: Rebia Mugrash transforms into Great Shalsheleth when Rebia Mugrash would stand on the third word from the Silluq, and a Legarmeh would stand on the first word before the Silluq. Athnach then appears on the fourth or fifth word before Silluq.
   a) Ps 29:11 :יְהוָ֓ה ׀ יְבָרֵ֖ךְ אֶת־עַמּ֣וֹ בַשָּׁלֽוֹם—Since the Rebia Mugrash would appear on the third word from the Silluq, and the first word before the Silluq has a transformed Legarmeh, the Rebia Mugrash transforms into a Great Shalsheleth.
   b) Ps 10:14 :יָ֝ת֗וֹם אַתָּ֤ה ׀ הָיִ֬יתָ עוֹזֵֽר—Contrast this example with the preceding example. The Legarmeh occurs on the second word from the Silluq; therefore, the Rebia Mugrash occurs on the third word from the Silluq.

3. **Great Rebia to Sinnor**: Two words must occur between Little Rebia and Great Rebia. If not, the Great Rebia transforms into a Sinnor (Ps 15:5; cf. Ps 20:7).
   a) Ps 15:5 בְּנֶ֗שֶׁךְ וְשֹׁ֥חַד עַל־נָקִ֗י לֹ֫א לָקָ֥ח—Only one word occurs between the Little Rebia and the word that should have the Great Rebia; therefore, the Great Rebia transforms into a Sinnor.
   b) Ps 20:7 יָדַ֗עְתִּי כִּ֤י הוֹשִׁ֥יעַ ׀ יְהוָ֗ה מְשִׁ֫יח֥וֹ—Contrast this example with the preceding example. Two words occur between the Little Rebia and the Great Rebia; therefore, the Great Rebia does not transform into a Sinnor.

Diagrams of the Syntax of the Disjunctive Accents for Poetry

A. Emperor

The emperor Soph Pasuq does not allow a conjunctive accent between it and the Silluq, its near subordinate. Hence, the Silluq occurs on the word before the Soph Pasuq. The Ole Veyored or the Athnach,[22] the remote subordinates of Soph Pasuq, may not occur on the last word or on the first word of a verse.[23] The Soph Pasuq governs the entire verse; the Silluq and the Ole Veyored or Athnach govern their own segments.

22. If the Athnach occurs in a verse with the Ole Veyored, the Ole Veyored is the remote disjunctive to the Soph Pasuq; the Athnach then is a remote subordinate to the Silluq. Athnach (or transformed into Rebia Mugrash) must occur in every verse. Moreover, it must be within five words of Silluq. Ole Veyored may occur on the fourth word from Silluq (rarely), on the fifth word from Silluq (commonly), and on the sixth word or further from the Silluq (always).
23. The Athnach may not appear on the second word from the Silluq if Silluq's word or the first word before the Silluq has less than two syllables before its accented syllable, Ps 1:2; 119:2. In such cases, Athnach transforms into Rebia Mugrash (often written defectively as Rebia).

Psalm 1:2

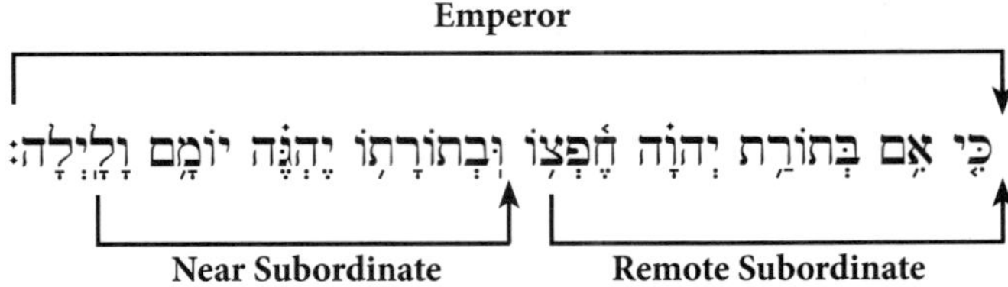

Emperor Soph Pasuq governs the entire verse. Its near subordinate Silluq governs to the Ole Veyored; the Ole Veyored governs to the beginning of the verse.

Psalm 1:4

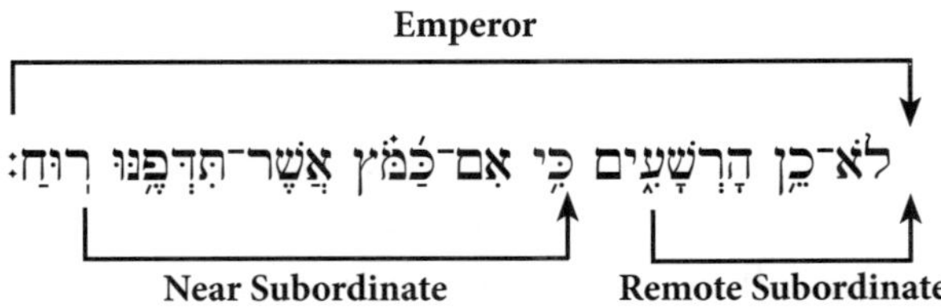

Emperor Soph Pasuq governs the entire verse. Its near subordinate Silluq governs to the Athnach; the Athnach governs to the beginning of the verse.

Psalm 1:1

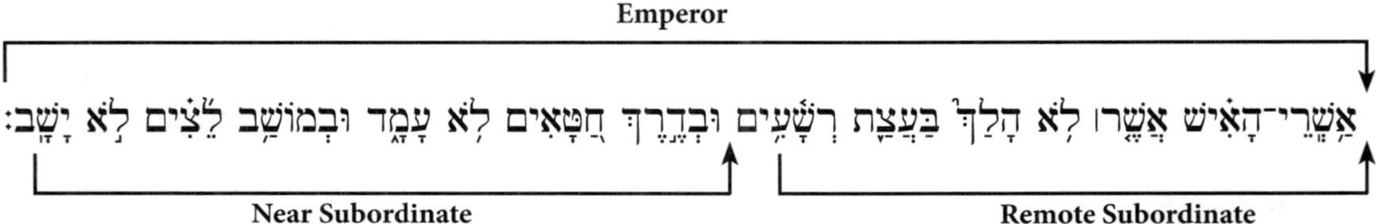

Emperor Soph Pasuq governs the entire verse. Its near subordinate Silluq governs to the Ole Veyored (the Athnach is the remote subordinate to Silluq, not the emperor Soph Pasuq); the Ole Veyored governs to the beginning of the verse.

B. Kings

Like the Soph Pasuq, the kings – Silluq, Ole Veyored, and Athnach – govern their own near and remote subordinate princes. The Silluq, Ole Veyored, and Athnach may have one word with a conjunctive accent to intervene between them and their near subordinate. Silluq governs a prince Rebia Mugrash[24] for the near subordinate and prince Athnach in verses with Ole Veyored.[25] Ole Veyored governs prince Sinnor for the near subordinate and prince Great

24. When more than one conjunctive accent occurs, the first conjunctive accent from the governing accent is usually a transformed disjunctive. Rebia Mugrash may exceptionally occur on the third word before its governing accent, Silluq.
25. When Athnach (or its substitutes) occurs in verses with Ole Veyored, the Athnach may be a near or remote subordinate prince to Silluq. In verses with Rebia Mugrash, Athnach, and

Rebia for a remote subordinate. Athnach governs prince Dechi for the near subordinate and prince Great Rebia for a remote subordinate, which may occur even without the near subordinate (Dechi). The placement of the near subordinates is restricted, occurring next to their superior or one word away from their superior. The placement of the remote subordinate, Great Rebia, is unrestricted, based on the syntax. The Great Rebia may repeat once in a segment.

Psalm 8:3

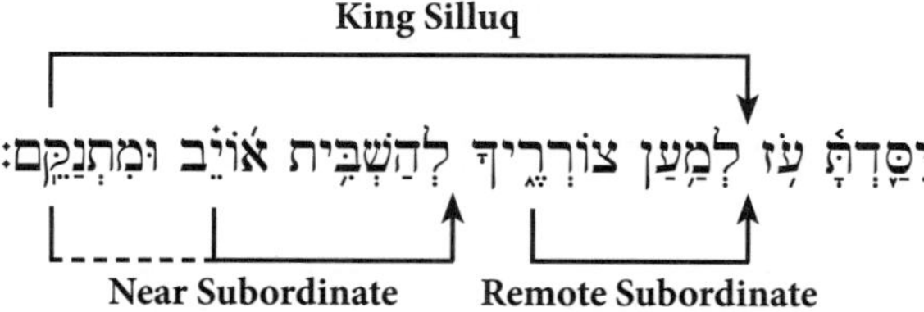

Silluq governs the entire segment. Its near subordinate Rebia Mugrash governs to the Athnach. Its remote subordinate Athnach governs to the Ole Veyored.

Psalm 39:2

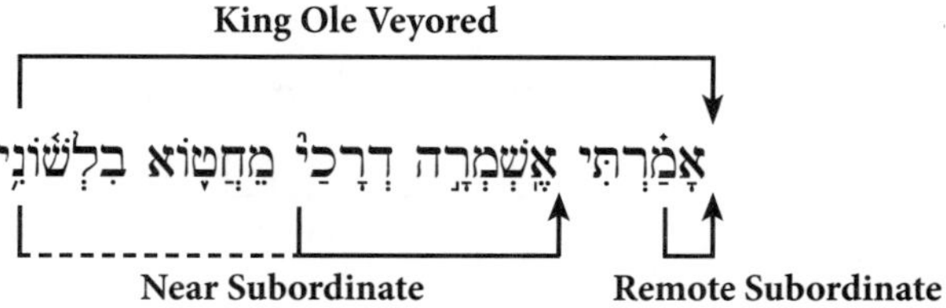

Ole Veyored governs the entire segment. Its near subordinate Sinnor governs to the Great Rebia. Its remote subordinate Great Rebia governs to the end of the segment.

Psalm 4:4

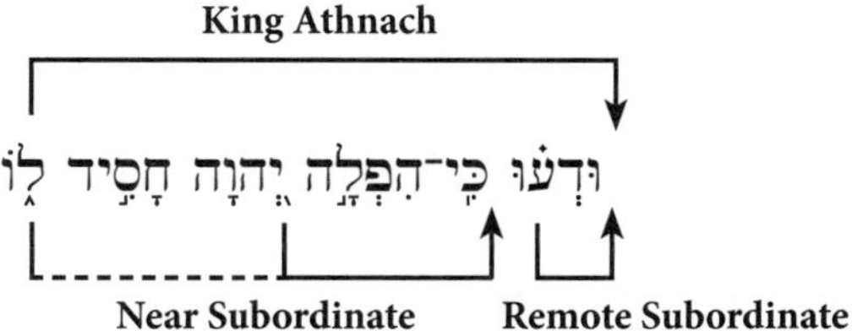

Athnach governs the entire segment. Its near subordinate Dechi governs to the Great Rebia. Its remote subordinate Great Rebia governs to the end of the segment.

C. Princes

The princes govern the dukes. Prince Rebia Mugrash does not govern a subordinate. The princes – Sinnor, Dechi, and Great Rebia – govern Legarmeh as a near subordinate and

Ole Veyored, the Athnach is the remote prince to the Silluq (Ps 1:1). In verses without Rebia Mugrash, but with Athnach and Ole Veyored, the Athnach is a near prince to Silluq (Ps 1:2). In verses without Ole Veyored, Athnach is a remote subordinate king to Soph Pasuq.

Pazer as a remote subordinate. If two conjunctives precede the Legarmeh, the Legarmeh becomes a Pazer (Ps 31:11). Moreover, Legarmeh and Pazer may transpose positions though Pazer is always the stronger accent. When Athnach is a prince (that is, when Ole Veyored occurs in the verse with Athnach), it takes Dechi and Great Rebia as subordinates. Prince Little Rebia takes only Legarmeh as a near subordinate.

Psalm 31:12

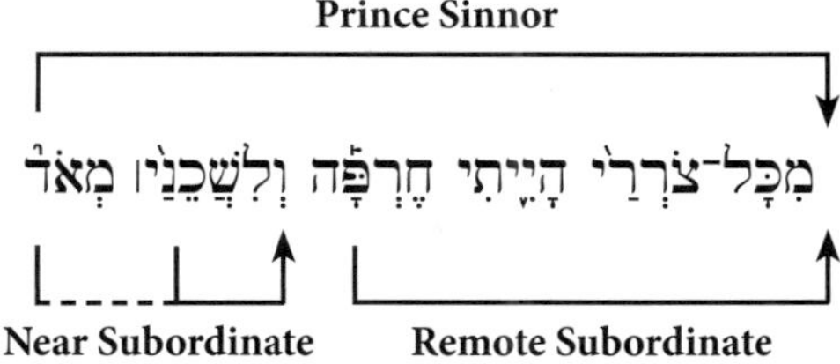

Sinnor governs the entire segment. Its near subordinate Legarmeh governs to the Pazer. Its remote subordinate Pazer governs to the end of the segment.

Psalm 98:1

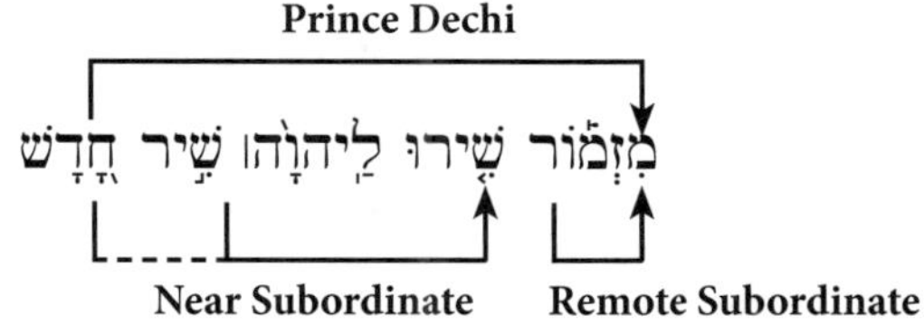

Dechi governs the entire segment. Its near subordinate Legarmeh governs to the Pazer. Its remote subordinate Pazer governs to the end of the segment.

D. Dukes

The duke Pazer may govern a near Legarmeh segment. The duke Legarmeh may rarely repeat.

Strength of the Disjunctive Accents in Prose and Poetry

As noted, the disjunctive accents have a hierarchy of order, reflecting their strength. The emperor is stronger than the kings, who in turn are stronger than the princes, and so forth. Their strength is particularly seen within a clause. For example, in Gen 22:15, a verbal clause, king Athnach, the strongest accent, indicates the main break of the sentence. The prince Tiphcha before the Athnach[26] is the second strongest accent/break, with duke Tebir on the verb, the third strongest accent/break – the disjunctive accents weakening as they move toward the verb. In Gen 18:18[a], a nominal clause, the strongest accent (prince Zaqeph) indicates the main break of the clause occurs with the nominal, Abraham. Within a clause, always note the rank and strength of the disjunctive accent.

26. In this context, the Tiphcha after the Athnach is very weak, a "musical foretone to the Silluq" according to Wickes, WW II, 61. The discussion in the next two paragraphs explains this.

Gen 22:15 וַיִּקְרָ֛א מַלְאַ֥ךְ יְהוָ֖ה אֶל־אַבְרָהָ֑ם שֵׁנִ֖ית מִן־הַשָּׁמָֽיִם׃
And the angel of the Lord called to Abraham a second time from heaven.

Gen 18:18[a] וְאַ֨בְרָהָ֔ם הָי֧וֹ יִהְיֶ֛ה לְג֥וֹי גָּד֖וֹל וְעָצ֑וּם
As for Abraham, he will indeed become a great and mighty nation.

Similarly, remote subordinate accents are stronger than their near subordinate counterparts, in part due to their flexibility in placement. When kings, princes, dukes, and counts function as subordinate accents to a superior, the subordinate may be either near or remote. The emperor, for instance, has a near subordinate king (Silluq) and a remote subordinate king (Athnach).[27] Similarly, the kings have a near subordinate prince (Tiphcha) and often a remote subordinate prince (Zaqeph or Segolta) if necessary. The placement of near subordinates is restricted, usually occurring one or two words from their governing accent.[28] If the main break of a governing accent occurs within two words of it, the near subordinate will be the strongest accent in the segment of the governing accent. Its remote subordinate counterpart, therefore, will be unnecessary. The main break, however, usually occurs two or more words away from the governing accent, making a remote subordinate necessary. The placement of the remote subordinate is virtually unlimited, determined by the syntax and meaning of the passage. If the remote subordinate occurs close to its near subordinate counterpart so that the near subordinate lacks subordinates, the near subordinate often becomes weaker, less valuable for marking the syntax and indicating the meaning.[29] But if the near subordinate governs its own subordinates, the near subordinate will strengthen, regaining value for syntax and meaning. In the end, though, however strong a near subordinate becomes, its corresponding remote subordinate, if it occurs, is always stronger.

For example, in Deut 6:22 (see below), the main break in Silluq's segment occurs one word away from the word with Silluq. Tichcha, the near subordinate of Silluq, therefore, marks this break and is the strongest accent in the segment (and, in this case, the verse). In Gen 22:17[b], on the other hand, the Zaqeph, a remote subordinate, must mark the main break in Silluq's segment because the break is beyond the reach of the near subordinate, Tiphcha, which can only extend one or two words before the Silluq. Moreover, the Zaqeph weakens the Tiphcha for syntax and meaning because of Zaqeph's proximity to the Tiphcha, which lacks subordinates. Now Tiphcha only prepares the chanter/reader for the coming Silluq as a foretone. In Gen 1:28[a], Segolta, a substitute for Zaqeph, breaks the Athnach segment. This time, however, the Segolta slightly weakens the Tiphcha since Zaqeph is distant from Tiphcha and since the Tiphcha governs its own near (Tebir) and remote (Rebia) subordinate accents.

27. Near subordinates usually occur; remote subordinates occur if the main break of a segment is over two words from their governing accent. A near subordinate may occur without a remote subordinate, but a remote subordinate rarely occurs without its near subordinate counterpart.
28. This is true with the kings, princes, and most dukes. The weaker counts allow more flexibility in their placement. The emperor decrees no variation in the placement of its near subordinate.
29. Of course, there are exceptions, especially in three word combinations, as in Gen 23:2[b], where the Tiphcha separates the final three words according to the sense and grammar. The presence of the Zaqeph still weakens the Tiphcha, the second strongest break in Silluq's segment.

Deut 6:22 וַיִּתֵּ֣ן יְהוָ֡ה אוֹתֹ֣ת וּ֠מֹפְתִים גְּדֹלִ֨ים וְרָעִ֧ים ׀ בְּמִצְרַ֛יִם בְּפַרְעֹ֥ה וּבְכָל־בֵּית֖וֹ לְעֵינֵֽינוּ׃

And the Lord gave great and terrible signs and wonders on Egypt, Pharaoh, and all his house before our eyes.

Gen 22:17[b] וְיִרַ֣שׁ זַרְעֲךָ֔ אֵ֖ת שַׁ֥עַר אֹיְבָֽיו׃

And your seed will possess the gates of his enemies.

Gen 1:28[a] וַיְבָ֣רֶךְ אֹתָם֮ אֱלֹהִים֒ וַיֹּ֨אמֶר לָהֶ֜ם אֱלֹהִ֗ים פְּר֥וּ וּרְב֛וּ וּמִלְא֥וּ אֶת־הָאָ֖רֶץ וְכִבְשֻׁ֑הָ

And God blessed them, and God said to them, Be fruitful and multiply and fill the earth and subdue it.

In short, for syntax and meaning, always notice remote subordinates. And notice near subordinates when they are the main breaks in a segment (that is, their remote counterpart is not present) or when they govern their own subordinates (and their remote counterpart is present).

Dividing Verses with the Accents

To interpret the accents correctly, first learn the general principles of dividing a verse with the accents, then advance to the specific principles of interpreting the verse with the accents.

The accents divide a verse into word groupings. The verse, of course, is a complete unit, a unified statement, understood and interpreted as a single entity. The accents break up the verse into word groupings, beginning with the Athnach, which divides the verse into halves. Then each half-verse is divided. Tiphcha divides the half-verse if the main break is one or two words away from the Athnach or Silluq. Zaqeph divides the half-verse if the main break is two words[30] or more words from the Athnach or Silluq. Now each of these half-verses are further divided, this process continuing until all words are paired or isolated as single words.[31] A group of three words usually receives a break, explicitly or implicitly. This continuous dividing furnishes the pieces, like a puzzle, for putting together the syntax, logic, and interpretation of the verse.

Keep in mind that the accents group and separate words on different levels. On a higher level, words are grouped; on a lower level, the same words are divided. On the Soph Pasuq level, for instance, all words are grouped together; on the Athnach level, the same words are divided into two groups. Similarly, the same words grouped together under Zaqeph's governance are divided under Rebia's governance, Zaqeph's remote subordinate. The following examples illustrate the principles.

30. Both Tiphcha and Zaqeph may occur on the second word before the Athnach or Silluq. Generally, if Athnach's or Silluq's word or the word before them is long – that is, there are two syllables before the accented syllable (a letter with shewa not counting as a syllable) or there is a long vowel followed by a vocal shewa before the accented syllable – then Zaqeph will usually occur on the second word. If the two words before the Athnach or Silluq are short, then a Tiphcha almost always occurs.
31. Wickes calls this, "continuous dichotomy." WW II, 29

A. Genesis 24:54

וַיֹּאכְלוּ וַיִּשְׁתּוּ הוּא וְהָאֲנָשִׁים אֲשֶׁר־עִמּוֹ וַיָּלִינוּ   וַיָּקוּמוּ בַבֹּקֶר וַיֹּאמֶר שַׁלְּחֻנִי לַאדֹנִי׃

And they ate and drank, he and the men who were with him, and they spent the night.
And they rose up in the morning, and he said, Send me away to my lord.

On the Soph Pasuq's level, the verse groups all words together. The Athnach divides the same words into two halves, separating the first six words (consider words joined by Maqqeph as one word) from the last five words.

1. **First Half of the Verse**
   a) Athnach Segment

   וַיֹּאכְלוּ וַיִּשְׁתּוּ הוּא וְהָאֲנָשִׁים אֲשֶׁר־עִמּוֹ   וַיָּלִינוּ

   Tiphcha, Athnach's near subordinate, breaks the segment, grouping the first five words from the last word. Since Tiphcha marks the main break of the half-verse, Zaqeph, Athnach's remote subordinate, cannot occur in the segment because Zaqeph would then mark the main break. Remote subordinates, if present, always furnish the main break of their governing accent. On Athnach's level, all words are grouped; on Tiphcha's level, the same words are divided.

   b) Tiphcha Segment

   וַיֹּאכְלוּ וַיִּשְׁתּוּ   הוּא וְהָאֲנָשִׁים אֲשֶׁר־עִמּוֹ

   Since Tiphcha's segment governs more than two words (five words[32]), subdivisions are required. Rebia, Tiphcha's remote subordinate, divides the segment. The Rebia governs, and therefore, connects with the preceding verb. The three words (the Tebir segment) after the Rebia to the Tiphcha are now also grouped. With a three-word grouping, another division is required. The first word, because it is the logical break for the three-word segment, receives a Tebir, the near subordinate of Tiphcha. This separates the pronoun (with the Tebir) from the noun with its relative clause. On the level of Tiphcha all words are grouped; on the level of Rebia, the same words are divided. On Tebir's level, Tiphcha's words are further divided since three words occur from the Tiphcha to the Rebia.

   c) Tebir Segment

   הוּא   וְהָאֲנָשִׁים אֲשֶׁר־עִמּוֹ

   The Tebir segment with its three words requires a minor break, isolating the pronoun from the noun and its relative clause.

2. **Second Half of the Verse**
   a) Silluq Segment

   וַיָּקוּמוּ בַבֹּקֶר   וַיֹּאמֶר שַׁלְּחֻנִי לַאדֹנִי׃

   Zaqeph, Silluq's remote subordinate, breaks the second half of the verse, grouping the first two words from the last three words. Zaqeph governs the preceding word, thereby forming a group with that word. Zaqeph's placement also groups the last three words. A three word group requires a break, here furnished by Tiphcha. On the Zaqeph level, the last three words are grouped; on the Tiphcha level, they are divided.

32. Technically, the Tiphcha also governs the word or words after it, so it actually governs six words.

b) Tiphcha Segment

וַיֹּ֖אמֶר שַׁלְּחֻ֥נִי לַאדֹנִֽי׃

The Tiphcha segment with its three words requires a break. Remember, if a remote subordinate is present (here Zaqeph), a near subordinate is virtually required (here Tiphcha).

B. Genesis 23:15

אֲדֹנִ֣י שְׁמָעֵ֔נִי אֶ֗רֶץ אַרְבַּ֨ע מֵאֹ֧ת שֶֽׁקֶל־כֶּ֛סֶף בֵּינִ֥י וּבֵינְךָ֖ מַה־הִ֑וא וְאֶת־מֵתְךָ֖ קְבֹֽר׃

My lord, hear me, a land of four hundred shekels of silver between me and you, what is it? Your dead bury.

On Soph Pasuq's level, all words are grouped. On Athnach's level, the same words are divided into two segments.

1. First Half of the Verse

a) Athnach Segment

אֲדֹנִ֣י שְׁמָעֵ֔נִי אֶ֗רֶץ אַרְבַּ֨ע מֵאֹ֧ת שֶֽׁקֶל־כֶּ֛סֶף בֵּינִ֥י וּבֵינְךָ֖ מַה־הִ֑וא

Two subordinates divide Athnach's segment. Zaqeph, Athnach's remote subordinate, divides Athnach's entire segment. The Zaqeph governs its preceding word, forming a word group. The Zaqeph also groups the seven words after it. Tiphcha, Athnach's near subordinate, divides the seven words after Zaqeph. Because it governs a near subordinate, Tiphcha's power is stronger here than the Tiphcha in the preceding example, Gen 24:54[b]. The Tiphcha in Gen 24:54[b] without any subordinates, is often "a mere foretone to the Silluq."[33]

b) Tiphcha Segment

אֶ֗רֶץ אַרְבַּ֨ע מֵאֹ֧ת שֶֽׁקֶל־כֶּ֛סֶף בֵּינִ֥י וּבֵינְךָ֖

Since there are six words from the Zaqeph to the Tiphcha, a division is required. Tebir, Tiphcha's near subordinate, divides the segment, grouping the first four words and the last two words.

c) Tebir Segment

אֶ֗רֶץ אַרְבַּ֨ע מֵאֹ֧ת שֶֽׁקֶל־כֶּ֛סֶף

Since the Tebir segment has four words, another division is required. The sense of the words demands the break on the word before the Tebir. Geresh usually cannot stand on the word before Tebir (nor before Pashta or Zarqa). In such cases, the Geresh transforms into a conjunctive accent. For the Tebir, the preceding conjunctive accent, usually Darga or Merecha, substitutes for the Geresh – hence, the term transformed Geresh. The Tebir with three conjunctive accents confirms the transformed Geresh since Tebir (as well as Pashta or Zarqa) may govern at most two conjunctive accents. If three or more conjunctive accents are present, then a transformed disjunctive occurs on the first word before the disjunctive. The transformed Geresh, a Darga, divides its word and the preceding two words from the word with the Tebir. Had the sense of the four words demanded a break on the second or third word before Tebir, a Geresh would have occurred without transformation. Geresh or transformed Geresh, minor disjunctive accents, may take more than two conjunctive accents. Their segments may have more than two words without division.

33. WW II, 61

2. **Second Half of the Verse**

וְאֶת־מֵתְךָ֖ קְבֹֽר׃

The foretone Tiphcha separates the last two words.

C. Genesis 1:9

וַיֹּ֣אמֶר אֱלֹהִ֗ים יִקָּו֨וּ הַמַּ֜יִם מִתַּ֤חַת הַשָּׁמַ֙יִם֙ אֶל־מָק֣וֹם אֶחָ֔ד וְתֵרָאֶ֖ה הַיַּבָּשָׁ֑ה וַֽיְהִי־כֵֽן׃

And God said, Let the waters from under the heavens be gathered into one place that the dry land might appear. And it happened thus.

The Soph Pasuq groups all words. The Athnach, the remote of Soph Pasuq, divides the same words, separating the first ten words from the last word.

1. **First Half of the Verse**
   a) Athnach Segment

   וַיֹּ֣אמֶר אֱלֹהִ֗ים יִקָּו֨וּ הַמַּ֜יִם מִתַּ֤חַת הַשָּׁמַ֙יִם֙ אֶל־מָק֣וֹם אֶחָ֔ד וְתֵרָאֶ֖ה הַיַּבָּשָׁ֑ה

   Two subordinates divide Athnach's segment. Zaqeph, Athnach's remote subordinate, breaks Athnach's entire segment. The Zaqeph governs its preceding words, forming a word group. The Zaqeph also groups the two words after it. Zaqeph can stand on the second word before Athnach since the word with Athnach or the word before it is long.[34] Tiphcha, Athnach's near subordinate, without subordinates functions as a foretone to the Athnach. On Athnach's level, all words are grouped; on Zaqeph's level, the same words are divided.

   b) Zaqeph Segment

   וַיֹּ֣אמֶר אֱלֹהִ֗ים יִקָּו֨וּ הַמַּ֜יִם מִתַּ֤חַת הַשָּׁמַ֙יִם֙ אֶל־מָק֣וֹם אֶחָ֔ד

   Two subordinates divide Zaqeph's segment. Rebia, Zaqeph's remote subordinate, breaks Zaqeph's entire segment. The Rebia governs its preceding word, forming a word group. The Rebia also groups the six words after it. Pashta, Zaqeph's near subordinate, furnishes the break for the six words after Rebia.

   יִקָּו֨וּ הַמַּ֜יִם מִתַּ֤חַת הַשָּׁמַ֙יִם֙ אֶל־מָק֣וֹם אֶחָ֔ד

   c) The Pashta Segment

   יִקָּו֨וּ הַמַּ֜יִם מִתַּ֤חַת הַשָּׁמַ֙יִם֙

   The Pashta segment has four words, requiring a break. The sense of the four words necessitates the break on the second word before the Pashta. Geresh, Pashta's near subordinate, furnishes the break. If the break had been on the first word before Pashta, a transformed Geresh would be required. See Gen 23:15[a] above.

2. **Second Half of the Verse**

   The Silluq governs the last clause/word.

D. Psalm 1:1

אַ֥שְֽׁרֵי־הָאִ֗ישׁ אֲשֶׁ֤ר ׀ לֹ֥א הָלַךְ֮ בַּעֲצַ֪ת רְשָׁ֫עִ֥ים וּבְדֶ֣רֶךְ חַ֭טָּאִים לֹ֥א עָמָ֑ד וּבְמוֹשַׁ֥ב לֵ֝צִ֗ים לֹ֣א יָשָֽׁב׃

Blessed is the man who has not walked in the counsel of the wicked. And in the path of the sinners he has not stood, and in the seat of the scornful he has not sat.

The poetical accents, the accent system of the books of Psalms, Job, and

34. See footnotes 16, 17, and 30.

Proverbs, differs from the other books. Ole Veyored, the remote subordinate of Soph Pasuq, divides the verse in half. In verses without Ole Veyored, Athnach is the remote subordinate of Soph Pasuq. On the Soph Pasuq level, all words are grouped together; on the Ole Veyored level, the same words are divided.

1. **First Half of the Verse**
   a) Ole Veyored Segment

   אַֽשְׁרֵי־הָאִ֗ישׁ אֲשֶׁ֤ר ׀ לֹ֥א הָלַךְ֮ בַּעֲצַ֪ת רְשָׁ֫עִ֥ים

   Two subordinates divide Ole Veyored's segment. Rebia, Ole Veyored's remote subordinate, breaks Ole Veyored's segment. Rebia's word is joined by Maqqeph, forming a single word group. The Rebia groups the five words after it. Sinnor, Ole Veyored's near subordinate, breaks the five words after Rebia.

   b) Sinnor Segment

   אֲשֶׁ֤ר ׀ לֹ֥א הָלַךְ֮

   In the poetical accents, the rule that three or more words grouped together requires a division is frequently observed. The Sinnor segment, therefore, requires a break – Legarmeh (with Mehuppach) – since it governs three words.

2. **Second Half of the Verse**
   a) Silluq Segment

   וּבְדֶ֣רֶךְ חַ֭טָּאִים לֹ֣א עָמָ֑ד וּבְמוֹשַׁ֥ב לֵ֝צִ֗ים לֹ֣א יָשָֽׁב׃

   Two subordinates divide Silluq's segment. Athnach, Silluq's remote subordinate, breaks Silluq's segment. The Athnach governs its preceding three words, forming a word group. The Athnach also groups the four words after it. Rebia Mugrash, Silluq's near subordinate, breaks the four words after Zaqeph.

   b) Athnach Segment

   וּבְדֶ֣רֶךְ חַ֭טָּאִים לֹ֣א עָמָ֑ד

   Since the Athnach segment consists of four words, Dechi, Athnach's near subordinate, breaks the segment.

   c) Rebia Mugrash Segment

   וּבְמוֹשַׁ֥ב לֵ֝צִ֗ים לֹ֣א יָשָֽׁב׃

   The Rebia Mugrash separates the words in its segment.

Interpreting the Accents

The accents were designed to convey the meaning of the text. The accents disclose the meaning on three levels: the syntactic, the clausal, and the semantic. The syntactic operates on a single independent clause, grouping and separating words, phrases, and dependent clauses. The clausal operates on multiple independent clauses, grouping and separating them. Operating on both single and multiple independent clauses, the semantic breaks the normal tendencies and patterns of the syntactic and clausal to bring out the meaning by marking the weightiest words, phrases, and clauses in the verse. The syntactic and clausal represent the usual, the expected, the routine; the semantic represents the fascinating, the interesting, the unexpected.

The unexpected, however, has caused many to dismiss the accents. Their placement is not just unexpected, but at times their placement seems bizarre and illogical. But sing most hymns, recite almost any liturgical formula, or read any careful writer, and you will find the same thing – the breaking of the normal syntax and logic of a sentence to bring out the meaning and emphasis more fully. The author may further indicate this meaning and emphasis with italics, dashes, and exclamation marks. Biblical Hebrew may also further indicate meaning and emphasis, not with italics, dashes, and exclamation marks, *but with the accents.*

A. Interpreting an Independent Clause Syntactically: Verbal and Nominal Clauses

Verbal and nominal clauses have distinctive accentual patterns. In verbal clauses, the verb and agent are usually joined, with the object receiving a minor disjunctive. The stronger disjunctive accents usually occur later in the verbal clause, between the prepositional phrases and adverbials after the object. The prepositional phrases and adverbials normally supplement details, situations, locations, times, and so forth, for the verb, agent, and object. In nominal clauses, the stronger accents usually separate the initiator and announcement. Generally, verbal clauses have stronger accents at the end of the clause; nominal clauses, by contrast, have stronger accents at the beginning of the clause. These accentual patterns signal the distinctive meanings of the verbal and nominal clause.

1. **Verbal Clauses**

   a) Verbal Clauses Covering the Verse

   Num 33:49 וַֽיַּחֲנ֤וּ עַל־הַיַּרְדֵּן֙ מִבֵּ֣ית הַיְשִׁמֹ֔ת עַ֖ד אָבֵ֣ל הַשִּׁטִּ֑ים בְּעַֽרְבֹ֖ת מוֹאָֽב׃

   And they camped beside the Jordan, from Beth-jesimoth as far as Abel-shittim in the plains of Moab.

   With verbal clauses, the accents usually become stronger towards the end of the clause, or viewed conversely, the accents become weaker as they approach the verb. The stronger accents usually divide prepositional phrases or adverbials (accusative of situation, etc.). In Numbers 33:49, for example, each prepositional phrase receives a stronger accent (Athnah, Athnach, and Silluq/Soph Pasuq) as the accents move farther from the verb. Gen 16:7; 20:18; 22:15; 23:19–20; 33:19; Judg 4:23; 1 Kgs 8:65

   b) Verbal Clauses Covering Part of the Verse

   Num 33:2 וַיִּכְתֹּ֨ב מֹשֶׁ֜ה אֶת־מוֹצָאֵיהֶ֛ם לְמַסְעֵיהֶ֖ם עַל־פִּ֣י יְהוָ֑ה

   And Moses wrote their starting out places for their journeyings by the command of the Lord.

   Again, the accents become stronger as they approach the end of the clause. Tiphcha, the main break, occurs between the prepositional phrases. The Tebir marks a smaller break between the object and the first prepositional phrase. The Geresh, the weakest break, slightly separates the agent from the object. The verb, agent, and object, often closely connected by the accents, provide the core statement, with the prepositional phrases and adverbials furnishing the details for the core statement.

   c) Parts of Speech Preceding the Verbal Clause

   If a direct object, prepositional phrase, adverbial, or particles precede the verb, their placement is emphatic. The accents usually reflect this by marking the part of speech with a strong disjunctive accent. Most pronouns, small prepositions, and some particles are exceptional, often receiving weaker disjunctive accents or even conjunctive accents before the verb. Moreover, in longer verbal clauses with prepositional phrases and adverbials (especially two or more) or long subordinate clauses, the words before the verb receive weaker disjunctive accents or even conjunctive accents.

Gen 13:15 וְגַם־לְל֔וֹט הַהֹלֵ֖ךְ אֶת־אַבְרָ֑ם הָיָ֥ה צֹאן־וּבָקָ֖ר וְאֹהָלִֽים׃

And even to Lot, the one going with Abram,
flock and cattle and tents existed.

In this verbal clause, the words preceding the verb are emphatic by placement. The Athnach, the strongest accent in the verse/clause, reflects this emphasis by its placement with the words before the verb.

Gen 27:16 וְאֵ֗ת עֹרֹת֙ גְּדָיֵ֣י הָֽעִזִּ֔ים הִלְבִּ֖ישָׁה עַל־יָדָ֑יו וְעַ֖ל חֶלְקַ֥ת צַוָּארָֽיו׃

And the skins of the kids of the goats wear upon his hands and
upon the smooth places of his neck.

This verbal clause is longer than the preceding example. Longer verbal clauses often command the main break after the verb, especially with two prepositional phrases. The verse/clause, therefore, breaks between the prepositional phrases. The direct object, emphatically placed before the verb, now receives the second strongest accent in the verse/clause.[35]

2. Nominal Clause

a) Nominal Clauses with Finite Verbs

Gen 6:8 וְנֹ֕חַ מָ֥צָא חֵ֖ן בְּעֵינֵ֥י יְהוָֽה׃

And Noah – he found grace in the eyes of the Lord.

In verbal clauses, the stronger accents occur at the end of the clause; in nominal clauses, the initiator – the nominal – receives the stronger accent at the beginning of the clause. In shorter nominal clauses, as in Gen 6:8, the initiator takes the strongest accent.

1 Sam 3:7[a] וּשְׁמוּאֵ֕ל טֶ֖רֶם יָדַ֣ע אֶת־יְהוָ֑ה

And Samuel – he had not yet known the Lord.

The Zaqeph-Gadol, the strongest accent in the clause, breaks the nominal clause at the initiator. If a nominal clause has a finite verb for an announcement, the rest of the clause after the verb will follow the accent pattern of a verbal clause. In such cases, the verbal clause is the predicate of the initiator.

Gen 7:19a וְהַמַּ֗יִם גָּ֥בְרוּ מְאֹ֛ד מְאֹ֖ד עַל־הָאָ֑רֶץ

And the waters – they prevailed very greatly upon the earth.

The Tiphcha breaks the clause since the nominal clause has a prepositional phrase and two adverbials. The initiator receives the second strongest accent in the clause, a Rebia. If the initiator is a pronoun (Gen 2:11; 5:1) or if the clause is lengthened with prepositional phrases or adverbials, the initiator takes a weaker disjunctive accent and sometimes a conjunctive accent (Gen 3:1; 13:13; 18:10: 24:35; Exod 15:18; longer clauses Deut 2:10; Josh 17:4; Isa 53:6). If the initiator is expanded by modifying words or clauses, it may receive strong accents in long clauses (Gen 3:12; 24:7).

35. The Rebia isolates the את particle from the following three words, tightly grouping the three words in construct. If the את had a conjunctive accent, the Zaqeph segment would awkwardly break at the word with Pashta.

b) Other Parts of Speech with the Initiator before the Announcement (Verb)
These often take strong accents because their placement is emphatic.

וִיהוֹשֻׁ֣עַ בִּן־נ֗וּן וְכָלֵב֙ בֶּן־יְפֻנֶּ֔ה מִן־הַתָּרִ֖ים אֶת־הָאָ֑רֶץ קָֽרְע֖וּ בִּגְדֵיהֶֽם׃ Num 14:6

And Joshua, son of Nun, and Caleb, son of Jephunneh,
from the spies of the land – they tore their clothes.

The Athnach, the leading disjunctive, divides the initiators from their announcement (the verbal clause) with a modifying prepositional phrase.

c) Nominal Clauses without Finite Verbs
   i. Clauses of two words:

יְהוָ֥ה רֹ֫עִ֗י Ps 23:1

The Lord is my shepherd.

Conjunctive accents usually connect clauses (nominal or verbal) of two words.

   ii. The initiator precedes the announcement: The initiator usually is separated from its announcement.

וְחֹ֖שֶׁךְ עַל־פְּנֵ֣י תְה֑וֹם Gen 1:2

And darkness was upon the face of the deep.

These brief clauses frequently resemble the initiator with finite verbs as announcements in their accentual pattern (the stronger accents with the initiator). Gen 13:13; 1 Sam 1:13

   iii. The announcement precedes the initiator: The announcement usually connects to its initiator, though sometimes a minor disjunctive may separate them. These accentual patterns resemble the verbal clause, the accents becoming stronger towards the end of the clause.

רִאשׁ֥וֹן הוּא֙ לָכֶ֔ם לְחָדְשֵׁ֖י הַשָּׁנָֽה Exod 12:2[b]

It is the first to you for the months of the year.

The announcement (the first word) connects to its initiator (the pronoun).

כִּֽי־קָר֥וֹב אֵלֶ֛יךָ הַדָּבָ֖ר מְאֹ֑ד Deut 30:14[a]

The word is very near to you.

On Tiphcha's level, the announcement connects to its initiator. On Tebir's level, a slight break occurs within the first three words. Gen 29:19; 1 Sam 3:13

B. Interpreting Multiple Independent Clauses Logically

Most verses have multiple clauses. For the verse, all clauses are grouped and should be read closely together. Within the verse, however, clauses are separated and grouped according to the meaning and sense of the verse. If a verse has two clauses, usually the Athnach or Ole Veyored divides them (Gen 3:4). If a verse has more than two clauses, then the Athnach or Ole Veyored separates and groups the clauses. The grouping of clauses impacts the meaning by indicating which clauses should be read more closely together.

1. Dividing Whole Verses

וְאֶֽעֶשְׂךָ֙ לְג֣וֹי גָּד֔וֹל וַאֲבָ֣רֶכְךָ֔ וַאֲגַדְּלָ֖ה שְׁמֶ֑ךָ וֶהְיֵ֖ה בְּרָכָֽה׃ Gen 12:2

And I will make you into a great nation, and I will bless you, and I
will make your name great. And (you will) become a blessing.

On the verse level, these four clauses are grouped together. Within the verse, the

Athnach divides the first three clauses from the last clause. Read the first three clauses closely together, with the last clause being more independent or disconnected from the other three clauses. The overall meaning suggests this division since the first three clauses are first person imperfect statements, followed by an imperatival clause. This division is expected and clausal.

Gen 40:10 וּבַגֶּ֖פֶן שְׁלֹשָׁ֣ה שָׂרִיגִ֑ם וְהִ֤וא כְפֹרַ֙חַת֙ עָלְתָ֣ה נִצָּ֔הּ הִבְשִׁ֥ילוּ אַשְׁכְּלֹתֶ֖יהָ עֲנָבִֽים׃

And on the vine there were three branches, and as it was sprouting, its bloom came up, its grapes ripened into grapes.

The Athnach clausally separates the first clause from the last three clauses. The first clause introduces the vine. The last three clauses describe the vine and relate its actions.

2. **Dividing Half-verses**

Tiphcha or Zaqeph divides half-verses. Tiphcha divides the half-verse one or two words before the Athnach or Silluq. Zaqeph divides the half-verse on the second word or further from the Athnach or Silluq.

Exod 7:19[a] וַיֹּ֨אמֶר יְהוָ֜ה אֶל־מֹשֶׁ֗ה אֱמֹ֣ר אֶֽל־אַהֲרֹ֡ן קַ֣ח מַטְּךָ֣ וּנְטֵֽה־יָדְךָ֩ עַל־מֵימֵ֨י מִצְרַ֜יִם עַֽל־נַהֲרֹתָ֣ם ׀ עַל־יְאֹרֵיהֶ֣ם וְעַל־אַגְמֵיהֶ֗ם וְעַ֛ל כָּל־מִקְוֵ֥ה מֵימֵיהֶ֖ם וְיִֽהְיוּ־דָ֑ם

And the Lord said to Moses, Say to Aaron, take your staff and stretch out your hand upon the waters of Egypt: upon their rivers, upon the tributaries of the Nile, and upon their ponds and upon all the places that gather their waters that they may become blood.

The Tiphcha divides the first three clauses from the final clause. The first Rebia separates the first clause from the next two clauses.

Exod 9:10[a] וַיִּקְח֞וּ אֶת־פִּ֣יחַ הַכִּבְשָׁ֗ן וַיַּֽעַמְדוּ֙ לִפְנֵ֣י פַרְעֹ֔ה וַיִּזְרֹ֥ק אֹת֛וֹ מֹשֶׁ֖ה הַשָּׁמָ֑יְמָה

And they took the soot of kiln, and they stood before Pharaoh, and Moses sprinkled it towards the heavens.

The Zaqeph divides the first two clauses from the final clause. Under Zaqeph's governance, the first two clauses are grouped together.

3. **Dividing Half-verses with Multiple Zaqephs**

In dividing half-verses with multiple Zaqephs, the first Zaqeph (or its substitute, Segolta) divides the half-verse. The first Zaqeph divides more strongly than the second Zaqeph, as the second divides more strongly than the third, and so forth. In a half-verse with five Zaqephs, for example, the first Zaqeph is the strongest Zaqeph, dividing the half-verse. This, in turn, groups the last four Zaqephs together. The second Zaqeph, the next strongest Zaqeph, is the second strongest break in the half-verse. The second Zaqeph groups the next three Zaqephs together. This process continues for the next three Zaqephs. On the level of the Athnach, all five Zaqephs are grouped. On the level of the first Zaqeph, the next four are grouped. On the level of the third Zaqeph, the next two are grouped.

Gen 12:7[a] וַיֵּרָ֤א יְהוָה֙ אֶל־אַבְרָ֔ם וַיֹּ֕אמֶר לְזַ֨רְעֲךָ֔ אֶתֵּ֖ן אֶת־הָאָ֣רֶץ הַזֹּ֑את

And the Lord appeared to Abram, and he said, To your seed I will give this land.

The first Zaqeph divides the first half of the verse, grouping the next two Zaqephs. On the level of the first Zaqeph, the second and third Zaqeph should be read together.

וַיֹּ֕אמֶר   לְזַ֨רְעֲךָ֔ אֶתֵּ֖ן אֶת־הָאָ֣רֶץ הַזֹּ֑את

The second Zaqeph, a Zaqeph-Gadol, divides its word from the last four words. On the level of the second Zaqeph, the last four words are grouped.

לְזַ֨רְעֲךָ֔   אֶתֵּ֖ן אֶת־הָאָ֣רֶץ הַזֹּ֑את

The third Zaqeph divides its word from the following three words. This Zaqeph affirms the emphatic placement of the prepositional phrase before its verb. This Zaqeph also groups the verb and object more closely together. The foretone Tiphcha furnishes a slight pause between the verb and its object/modifier.

Gen 3:17[a] וּלְאָדָ֣ם אָמַ֗ר כִּֽי־שָׁמַעְתָּ֮ לְק֣וֹל אִשְׁתֶּךָ֒   וַתֹּ֙אכַל֙ מִן־הָעֵ֔ץ אֲשֶׁ֤ר צִוִּיתִ֙יךָ֙
לֵאמֹ֔ר לֹ֥א תֹאכַ֖ל מִמֶּ֑נּוּ

And to Adam he said, Because you listened to the voice of your wife, and you ate from the tree which I commanded you saying, You must not eat from it.

The Segolta, the first Zaqeph's substitute, marks the break, grouping the following two Zaqephs together. On the level of the first Zaqeph, the next two Zaqephs should be read together.

וַתֹּ֙אכַל֙ מִן־הָעֵ֔ץ   אֲשֶׁ֤ר צִוִּיתִ֙יךָ֙ לֵאמֹ֔ר לֹ֥א תֹאכַ֖ל מִמֶּ֑נּוּ

The second Zaqeph, the next strongest break, separates the antecedent "tree" from its relative clause. On the level of the second Zaqeph, the next six words should be read together.

אֲשֶׁ֤ר צִוִּיתִ֙יךָ֙ לֵאמֹ֔ר   לֹ֥א תֹאכַ֖ל מִמֶּ֑נּוּ

The third Zaqeph divides those six words into two units of three words.
Gen 3:14, 17; 16:5; 28:15; 30:14; 47:28

But why have multiple Zaqephs? Although a number of possibilities exists, there are two main reasons. First, they allow Athnach's placement to be delayed in longer verses for strategic placement. Second, they allow greater flexibility to the accentual system. Near subordinates have fixed placements, most occurring a word or two from its superior. Multiple Zaqephs alleviates the problems of limited placement by allowing a major break before the near subordinates. Suppose, for example, a Zaqeph marks the main break of the verse half, but then the words after the Zaqeph to the Athnach (or to the Silluq) require a secondary major break to be on the third or further before the Athnach. Tebir or Rebia, the subordinates of Tiphcha, could not constitute the secondary major break since their presence would make the Tiphcha as the secondary major break. The only possible accent is another Zaqeph. Gen 26:4[a] illustrates this.

Gen 26:4[a] וְהִרְבֵּיתִ֤י אֶֽת־זַרְעֲךָ֙ כְּכוֹכְבֵ֣י הַשָּׁמַ֔יִם וְנָתַתִּ֣י לְזַרְעֲךָ֔ אֵ֖ת כָּל־הָאֲרָצֹ֣ת הָאֵ֑ל

I will be multiply your seed as the stars of heaven, I will give to your seed all these lands.

Again, the first Zaqeph divides the half verse, separating the two clauses. For the five words between the Zaqeph and Athnach, the major break should occur on the third word before the Athnach. The Tiphcha, therefore, could not mark it since it must occur one or two words before the Athnach. The Tebir cannot mark it since it is a subordinate to Tiphcha. With a Tebir, Tiphcha would mark the major break, awkwardly separating the last noun from its pronoun. Properly placing the major break on the third word requires a second Zaqeph. This second Zaqeph groups the first two words from the last three words. The second Zaqeph is clearly weaker than the first Zaqeph since the first Zaqeph divides clauses. The second Zaqeph, by contrast, divides within a clause. Moreover, if the second Zaqeph were considered stronger than the first Zaqeph, the main break of the half-verse would ineptly divide within a clause instead of between the clauses.[36]

4. Dividing Multiple Rebias in a Zaqeph Segment

Multiple Rebias work similarly to multiple Zaqephs. The first Rebia is stronger than the second Rebia, as the second is stronger than the third, and so forth. If a verse has three Rebias within the same segment, the first Rebia is the main break. This groups the next two Rebias together. Multiple Rebias usually make the placement of the first Zaqeph more flexible in a half-verse. Finally, the second (and third) Rebias furnish a major break between the first Rebia and its Zaqeph when that break is beyond the position of Pashta, usually the first or second word (rarely the third word) before the Zaqeph.

1 Sam 5:8[a] וַיִּשְׁלְחוּ וַיַּאַסְפוּ אֶת־כָּל־סַרְנֵי פְלִשְׁתִּים אֲלֵיהֶם וַיֹּאמְרוּ מַה־נַּעֲשֶׂה
לַאֲרוֹן אֱלֹהֵי יִשְׂרָאֵל

And they sent and gathered all the lords of the Philistines to them, and they said, What should we do to the ark of the God of Israel?

The first Zaqeph segment has three Rebias. (The second Rebia transformed into a Pashta since it is within three words of the first Rebia.) The first Rebia, the main break for the Rebias, separates the five words under its governance and five words after it. This groups the next two Rebias together.

וַיֹּאמְרוּ מַה־נַּעֲשֶׂה לַאֲרוֹן אֱלֹהֵי יִשְׂרָאֵל

The major break within these five words comes on the first word, this requires the second Rebia, transformed into a Pashta.

מַה־נַּעֲשֶׂה לַאֲרוֹן אֱלֹהֵי יִשְׂרָאֵל

For the remaining four words, the major break is on the first word again, so it gets the third Rebia. The three Rebias delay the placement of the first Zaqeph in the half-verse.

Gen 25:30[a] וַיֹּאמֶר עֵשָׂו אֶל־יַעֲקֹב הַלְעִיטֵנִי נָא מִן־הָאָדֹם הָאָדֹם הַזֶּה כִּי עָיֵף אָנֹכִי

And Esau said to Jacob, Allow me to eat please from this red food because I am faint.

The two Rebias (the second Rebia being the first Pashta) delay Zaqeph's placement.

וַיֹּאמֶר עֵשָׂו אֶל־יַעֲקֹב הַלְעִיטֵנִי נָא מִן־הָאָדֹם הָאָדֹם הַזֶּה

The first Rebia breaks the Zaqeph segment, separating the three words that its governs and the five words following it.

הַלְעִיטֵנִי נָא מִן־הָאָדֹם הָאָדֹם הַזֶּה

36. There are contexts in which a main break may properly occur within a clause instead of between clauses, such as Num 20:11[a], where Tiphcha is the main break separating the final adverb from the two preceding clause. In this context, the adverb modifies both clauses, so the Tiphcha is properly the main break in the half verse.

Since the major break in the last five words occurs on the third word from the Zaqeph, the second Rebia (transformed into Pashta because three words usually need to come between Rebias) is required. The Pashta cannot mark the break on the third word since it is usually limited to the first or second word before Zaqeph.
Gen 3:22; 19:9; 24:27; 25:30; 26:9,18; 34:21

5. **The Principle for Dividing Multiple Clauses Clausally**
The principle is that the break occurs at the most logical placement for the verse, the half-verse, and so forth. This aids interpretation by indicating the logic and grouping of the clauses. The following categories are selective and representative, not exhaustive.

a) Dividing a verse with two independent clauses

וַיַּרְא אֱלֹהִים אֶת־הָאוֹר כִּי־טוֹב וַיַּבְדֵּל אֱלֹהִים בֵּין הָאוֹר וּבֵין הַחֹשֶׁךְ׃ Gen 1:4

And God saw the light that it was good. And God distinguished between the light and the darkness.

The Athnach divides the two independent clauses.
Gen 3:2, 4, 8, 21; 5:4–23

b) Dividing a verse with more than two independent clauses

וַיִּקְרָא אֱלֹהִים׀ לָאוֹר יוֹם וְלַחֹשֶׁךְ קָרָא לָיְלָה וַיְהִי־עֶרֶב וַיְהִי־בֹקֶר יוֹם אֶחָד׃ Gen 1:5

And God called to the light day, but to the darkness he called night. The evening was and the morning was, first day.

The Athnach divides God's calling of the day and night from the statements of the first evening and morning. The first two clauses are divided from the last two clauses. Gen 1:7, 10; 3:7; 4:2

c) Dividing a verse with an independent clause and a dependent clause

וְאַבְרָם בֶּן־שְׁמֹנִים שָׁנָה וְשֵׁשׁ שָׁנִים בְּלֶדֶת־הָגָר אֶת־יִשְׁמָעֵאל לְאַבְרָם׃ Gen 16:16

Now Abram was eighty-six years old when Hagar gave birth to Ishmael to Abram.

The Athnach divides the independent clause from the dependent temporal clause. Gen 3:20, 23

d) Dividing between protasis and apodosis

וַיֹּאמֶר יְהוָה אִם־אֶמְצָא בִסְדֹם חֲמִשִּׁים צַדִּיקִם בְּתוֹךְ הָעִיר וְנָשָׂאתִי לְכָל־הַמָּקוֹם בַּעֲבוּרָם׃ Gen 18:26

And the Lord said, If I find in Sodom fifty righteous in the midst of the city, then I will forbear to all the place for them.

The Athnach divides the protasis and apodosis. The same holds true for half verses, with Zaqeph dividing them, Gen 18:3[b], or Tiphcha, Gen 24:49.

e) Dividing the introductory narrative from direct speech

וַיֹּאמֶר אֵלָיו אֲנִי יְהוָה אֲשֶׁר הוֹצֵאתִיךָ מֵאוּר כַּשְׂדִּים לָתֶת לְךָ אֶת־הָאָרֶץ הַזֹּאת לְרִשְׁתָּהּ׃ Gen 15:7

And he said to him, I am the Lord who brought you out from Ur of the Chaldeans to give to you this land to possess it.

The Athnach divides the introductory narrative (and he said, etc.) from the direct speech. Gen 3:4; 14:22; 15:8

f) Dividing the closing appendage from the rest of the verse.

Lev 19:18 לֹֽא־תִקֹּ֤ם וְלֹֽא־תִטֹּר֙ אֶת־בְּנֵ֣י עַמֶּ֔ךָ וְאָֽהַבְתָּ֥ לְרֵעֲךָ֖ כָּמ֑וֹךָ אֲנִ֖י יְהוָֽה׃

Do not maintain vengeance against the sons of your people, but you shall love you neighbor as yourself. I am the Lord.

The closing refrain attracts the Athnach before it. Lev 19:3–4; Isa 51:15; Jer 10:16

C. Interpreting a Single Independent Clause or Multiple Independent Clauses Semantically

In addition to separating and grouping multiple clauses and dividing up the syntax of single independent clauses, the accents often pinpoint the most meaningful words and statements. The Athnachs, Zaqephs, and other important disjunctive accents were not wasted on insignificant words or introductory clauses. Although they often follow the general patterns for single and multiple independent clauses, the accents just as often break the general patterns to locate the most meaningful clauses and words. The accents, therefore, do not always follow the most syntactical or most logical pattern. They often bypass the syntactical and logical to highlight meaning. This flexibility frees the accents from being merely syntax and clause markers. The accents now indicate – to their fullest extent and design – the meaning of the verse.

The following principles are general. Many factors – their placement within the verse, the syntax of the accents themselves, or the syntax of the grammar, among others – influence the placement of the accents. Sometimes the accents represent a more syntactical arrangement; at other times, a more logical arrangement of clauses; and still at other times, a more semantic arrangement, suited to the overall meaning of the verse. There are even times, of course, when the syntactical division and the semantic division are the same. One cannot always predict the arrangement, whether mostly syntactical, clausal, or semantical. These frequently overlap, but usually one is more prominent than the others.

1. **The Accents with a Single Clause, with Two Clauses, and with Multiple Clauses**

The following examples contrast syntactical and semantic divisions. Both divisions have significance for meaning. Syntactical division follows the logic of the grammar more closely; the semantic division locates the meaning more closely.

a) The Accents with a Single Clause

i. Syntactical Division

Gen 23:20 וַיָּקָם֩ הַשָּׂדֶ֨ה וְהַמְּעָרָ֥ה אֲשֶׁר־בּ֛וֹ לְאַבְרָהָ֖ם לַאֲחֻזַּת־קָ֑בֶר מֵאֵ֖ת בְּנֵי־חֵֽת׃

The field and the cave which was in it was confirmed to Abraham for a possession of burial from the sons of Heth.

Gen 23:20 follows the usual syntactical pattern for verbal clauses, illustrating syntactical division.

ii. Semantic Division

Gen 1:1 בְּרֵאשִׁ֖ית בָּרָ֣א אֱלֹהִ֑ים אֵ֥ת הַשָּׁמַ֖יִם וְאֵ֥ת הָאָֽרֶץ׃

In the beginning God created the heavens and the earth.

Words before the verb in verbal clauses often receive the main break, as in Isa 37:18. In Gen 1:1, however, the Athnach moves from its expected location on the prepositional phrase to the verb and agent for emphasis – *God created.*

b) The Accents with Two Clauses

i. Clausal Division

In verses with two clauses, the Athnach usually divides between the clauses.

Gen 21:21 וַיֵּ֖שֶׁב בְּמִדְבַּ֣ר פָּארָ֑ן וַתִּֽקַּֽח־ל֥וֹ אִמּ֛וֹ אִשָּׁ֖ה מֵאֶ֥רֶץ מִצְרָֽיִם׃

And he resided in the wilderness of Paran, and his mother took a wife from the land of Egypt.

ii. Semantic Division

Sometimes, however, the Athnach divides within one of the two clauses, usually within the second clause. This sometimes occurs when the first clause is introductory, and the second clause carries the meaning for the verse.

Gen 12:1 וַיֹּ֤אמֶר יְהוָה֙ אֶל־אַבְרָ֔ם לֶךְ־לְךָ֛ מֵאַרְצְךָ֥ וּמִמּֽוֹלַדְתְּךָ֖ וּמִבֵּ֣ית אָבִ֑יךָ
אֶל־הָאָ֖רֶץ אֲשֶׁ֥ר אַרְאֶֽךָּ׃

And the Lord said to Abram, Go for yourself from your land and from your kindred and from the house of your father to the land which I will indeed show you.

In Gen 12:1 the first independent clause takes a Zaqeph, not the Athnach, since it is an introductory clause. The second independent clause, containing the meaning, takes the Athnach. Athnach's placement highlights God's command to Abram. Placing the Athnach after the first independent clause, though logical, would squander the semantic weight of the Athnach.

Gen 22:10 וַיִּשְׁלַ֤ח אַבְרָהָם֙ אֶת־יָד֔וֹ וַיִּקַּ֖ח אֶת־הַֽמַּאֲכֶ֑לֶת לִשְׁחֹ֖ט אֶת־בְּנֽוֹ׃

And Abraham stretched out his hand and he took the knife to slay his son.

Again, the Athnach divides within the second clause, supplying a suspenseful pause emphasizing Abram's obedience.

c) The Accents with Three or More Clauses

i. Clausal Division

Gen 4:17 וַיֵּ֤דַע קַ֙יִן֙ אֶת־אִשְׁתּ֔וֹ וַתַּ֖הַר וַתֵּ֣לֶד אֶת־חֲנ֑וֹךְ וַֽיְהִי֙ בֹּ֣נֶה עִ֔יר וַיִּקְרָא֙
שֵׁ֣ם הָעִ֔יר כְּשֵׁ֖ם בְּנ֥וֹ חֲנֽוֹךְ׃

And Cain knew his wife, and she conceived and gave birth to Enoch, and he was a builder of a city, and he called the name of the city according to the name of his son, Enoch.

The Athnach separates the first three clauses from the last two clauses. Also, in the first half of the verse, the Zaqeph separates the first clause from the next two clauses.

ii. Semantic Division

Gen 3:5 כִּ֚י יֹדֵ֣עַ אֱלֹהִ֔ים כִּ֗י בְּיוֹם֙ אֲכָלְכֶ֣ם מִמֶּ֔נּוּ וְנִפְקְח֖וּ עֵֽינֵיכֶ֑ם וִהְיִיתֶם֙
כֵּֽאלֹהִ֔ים יֹדְעֵ֖י ט֥וֹב וָרָֽע׃

For God knows that on the day of your eating from it that your eyes will be opened. And you will exist as God, knowing good and evil.

As with the verses with two clauses, the Athnach may locate the most meaningful clause in the verse. In such cases, the Athnach bypasses the most logical grouping to pinpoint the most meaningful clause. Now, division may occur within clauses instead of between them; within the protasis or apodosis instead of between them; or within the direct speech instead of at the clause that introduces the direct speech. In Gen 3:5, for example, the Athnach does not occur between the protasis and the apodosis – the logical placement – but within the apodosis, highlighting it: *And your eyes will be opened* (Deut 23:25).

The logical placement is often bypassed (semantically) for the meaning. Independent clauses are passed over to divide at a dependent clause, Exod 24:4; Isa 42:24. Words introducing direct speech are passed over to divide within the direct speech, Gen 26:2; 28:16; 2 Sam 12:7. Instead of dividing logically before a כִּי clause, the break occurs within the כִּי clause, Gen 31:15. Instead of breaking logically between contrasts, the break comes within the contrast, Gen 22:5. Closing refrains and opening superscriptions are often ignored for the meaning within the verse, Lev 19:10; Isa 1:20; Jer 48:43; Gen 6:9 (superscription).

2. **Principles for Semantic Division**

These principles are tendencies, general rules for the main break and for secondary breaks in the verse.

a) The Athnach's placement is often delayed until the main statement, word, or action of the verse occurs. The segment after the Athnach often furnishes a conclusion, result, supplemental statement, closing comment, or details, among other things, to the *last* statement, clause, or word of the first half of the verse.[37] The second half of the verse is often, in the words of Ihab Griess, "the tail on the dog." Sometimes, the second half of the verse supplements the entire first half of the verse. More often, though, it supplements only the *last part* of the first half – that is, the clause, phrase, or word that ends with Athnach.

The Athnach often passes over many clauses – especially, introductory statements, such as, "and he rose up early in the morning"; clauses that introduce direct speech, commands, oaths; and even opening superscriptions, such as "these are the generations of" – to locate the meaning. For narrative, the direct speech usually carries the meaning. The Athnach, therefore, frequently lands within direct speech if the direct speech continues to the end of the verse (Gen 43:20; 44:16–17). If the direct speech ends within the verse, look for the Athnach at the end of the direct speech (Gen 44:4; 1 Sam 7:6). Furthermore, watch for the Athnach after dependent clauses ending within the verse, in particular, situation clauses, הִנֵּה clauses, and כִּי clauses (Gen 43:21; 44:14). Look also for concluding clauses that supplement the preceding clause or the first half of the verse (Gen 12:19). The Athnach often precedes concluding clauses.

37. WW II, 32

1 Sam 5:8 וַיִּשְׁלְחוּ וַיַּאַסְפוּ אֶת־כָּל־סַרְנֵי פְלִשְׁתִּים אֲלֵיהֶם וַיֹּאמְרוּ מַה־נַּעֲשֶׂה לַאֲרוֹן
אֱלֹהֵי יִשְׂרָאֵל וַיֹּאמְרוּ גַּת יִסֹּב אֲרוֹן אֱלֹהֵי יִשְׂרָאֵ֑ל וַיַּסֵּבּוּ
אֶת־אֲרוֹן אֱלֹהֵי יִשְׂרָאֵל׃

And they sent and gathered all the lords of the Philistines to them, and they said, What should we do to the ark of the God of Israel, and they said, Let the ark of the God of Israel go around to Gath. Then they brought the ark of the God of Israel around.

The Athnach, bypassing many introductory statements, lands on the most significant statement of the verse: the answer to their problem. Notice the three Zaqephs and three Rebias used to delay the Athnach's placement. The delaying of the Athnach does not always require multiple Zaqephs or Rebias, but it requires the passing over of clauses and phrases until the main point arrives.

The second half of the verse supplies the conclusion or result of the answer to their problem: they sent the ark around to different cities. The second half primarily concludes the last statement that ends with the Athnach, not the entire Athnach segment (or the entire first half of the verse).

Exod 10:3 וַיָּבֹא מֹשֶׁה וְאַהֲרֹן אֶל־פַּרְעֹה וַיֹּאמְרוּ אֵלָיו כֹּה־אָמַר יְהוָה אֱלֹהֵי
הָעִבְרִים עַד־מָתַי מֵאַנְתָּ לֵעָנֹת מִפָּנָ֑י שַׁלַּח עַמִּי וְיַעַבְדֻנִי׃

And Moses and Aaron came to Pharaoh, and they said to him, Thus said the Lord, the God of the Hebrews, How long will you refuse to humble yourself before me? Send away my people that they may serve me.

In Exod 10:3, the Athnach passes over a series of introductory statements to land on the direct speech, the meaning of the verse. If the division were more logical, it would be after the initial introductory statement or after the words introducing the direct discourse. Such a placement, though legitimate, would waste the semantic importance of the Athnach.

The second half of the verse supplements the preceding statement by telling Pharaoh how he should humble himself before the Lord. The second half primarily augments the final statement with the Athnach.

The accents consistently bypass words introducing direct speech to place the break within the direct speech, Gen 26:2; 28:16; 2 Sam 12:7.

Jer 24:3 וַיֹּאמֶר יְהוָה אֵלַי מָה־אַתָּה רֹאֶה יִרְמְיָהוּ וָאֹמַר תְּאֵנִ֑ים הַתְּאֵנִים
הַטֹּבוֹת טֹבוֹת מְאֹד וְהָרָעוֹת רָעוֹת מְאֹד אֲשֶׁר לֹא־תֵאָכַלְנָה מֵרֹעַ׃

And the Lord said to me, What are you seeing, Jeremiah? And I said, Figs! The good figs are very good and the bad figs are very bad which should not be eaten because of badness.

The Athnach marks the word of the verse – figs! The more syntactical break would be after the words introducing the direct discourse, after the question, or even after the word, within the direct discourse, that introduces the direct discourse. But again, these clauses just lead up to the direct speech. The Athnach marks the meaningful word in the direct speech.

The second half of the verse elaborates on "figs," detailing their condition. Note again how the second half of the verse focuses on the word "figs," not on the entire first half of the verse.

Gen 3:22 וַיֹּאמֶר ׀ יְהוָה אֱלֹהִים הֵן הָאָדָם הָיָה כְּאַחַד מִמֶּנּוּ לָדַעַת טוֹב וָרָע וְעַתָּה ׀
פֶּן־יִשְׁלַח יָדוֹ וְלָקַח גַּם מֵעֵץ הַחַיִּים וְאָכַל וָחַי לְעֹלָם׃

And the Lord God said, Behold, the man has become as one of us to know good and evil. And now lest he stretch out his hand and take even from the tree of life and should eat and live forever.

This principle also often works in the half-verse. In both halves of Gen 3:22, the Zaqeph marks the main idea of the half verse. The words after the Zaqeph supplement the main idea of the half verse by explaining "how man has become like one of us" in the first half, and by explaining the consequences of allowing man to take from the tree of life in the second half. For the whole verse, the Athnach illustrates the same principle again by marking the meaning of the verse. Then the words following the Athnach speak of the possible consequences of man's knowing of good and evil.

Jer 1:10 רְאֵה הִפְקַדְתִּיךָ ׀ הַיּוֹם הַזֶּה עַל־הַגּוֹיִם וְעַל־הַמַּמְלָכוֹת לִנְתוֹשׁ וְלִנְתוֹץ
וּלְהַאֲבִיד וְלַהֲרוֹס לִבְנוֹת וְלִנְטוֹעַ׃

See, I have appointed you this day over the nations and over kingdoms to tear down, and to tear apart, and to cause to perish, and to demolish; and to build and to plant.

The Athnach divides within the infinitives, the significant words that summarize the negative and positive aspects of Jeremiah's ministry.

Num 16:32 וַתִּפְתַּח הָאָרֶץ אֶת־פִּיהָ וַתִּבְלַע אֹתָם וְאֶת־בָּתֵּיהֶם וְאֵת כָּל־הָאָדָם אֲשֶׁר
לְקֹרַח וְאֵת כָּל־הָרְכוּשׁ׃

And the earth opened its mouth and swallowed them and their houses, and every man which was to Korah and every possession.

The most logical placement of the Athnach would divide the clauses. The remarkable feature of the verse, however, is the particulars: the people, houses, and possessions—hence, the location of the Athnach. Gen 3:14; 14:16; Neh 9:34

Gen 24:22 וַיְהִי כַּאֲשֶׁר כִּלּוּ הַגְּמַלִּים לִשְׁתּוֹת וַיִּקַּח הָאִישׁ נֶזֶם זָהָב בֶּקַע מִשְׁקָלוֹ וּשְׁנֵי
צְמִידִים עַל־יָדֶיהָ עֲשָׂרָה זָהָב מִשְׁקָלָם׃

And it happened as the camels finished drinking that the man took a ring of gold, a half shekel by weight, and two bracelets upon her wrists, ten shekels of gold by weight.

In addition to dividing particulars, the Athnach often separates pairs as well, especially if they are the outstanding components of the verse. Again, notice how independent clauses are passed over to divide the pair. Lev 21:22; Ezek 48:21; Amos 1:3

b) If, however, the meaning comes early in the verse, the Athnach often comes early as well. The principle is still the same: the Athnach locates the meaning. The segment after the Athnach still furnishes a conclusion, result, supplemental statement, closing comment, or details, among other things, for the first half of the clause. The tail is usually larger than the dog here. Moreover, early statements of direct speech frequently attract the Athnach, especially the first clause of direct speech, which often has the Athnach or Zaqeph. Also, when the first word is the important element of a verse, it receives the Athnach, with the remainder of the verse explaining, supplementing, or augmenting the first word of the verse.

2 Sam 12:7 וַיֹּ֧אמֶר נָתָ֛ן אֶל־דָּוִ֖ד אַתָּ֣ה הָאִ֑ישׁ כֹּֽה־אָמַ֞ר יְהוָ֣ה אֱלֹהֵ֣י יִשְׂרָאֵ֗ל אָנֹכִ֞י
מְשַׁחְתִּ֤יךָ לְמֶ֙לֶךְ֙ עַל־יִשְׂרָאֵ֔ל וְאָנֹכִ֥י הִצַּלְתִּ֖יךָ מִיַּ֥ד שָׁאֽוּל׃

And Nathan said to David, You are the man! Thus said the Lord, the God of Israel, I anointed you as a king over Israel, and I delivered you from the hand of Saul.

The Athnach marks the statement of the verse—"You are the man." The Athnach often marks the first clause of the direct speech. This allows the second half of the verse to supplement the first clause with the Athnach.

Gen 16:5[a] וַתֹּ֨אמֶר שָׂרַ֣י אֶל־אַבְרָם֮ חֲמָסִ֣י עָלֶ֒יךָ֒ אָנֹכִ֗י נָתַ֤תִּי שִׁפְחָתִי֙ בְּחֵיקֶ֔ךָ וַתֵּ֙רֶא֙ כִּ֣י
הָרָ֔תָה וָאֵקַ֖ל בְּעֵינֶ֑יהָ

And Sarai said to Abram, My harm is upon you. I gave my handmaid into your bosom, and she saw that she conceived, then I was small in her eyes.

The same is true for the half-verse. The Segolta, Zaqeph's substitute, marks the first clause of the direct speech. The clauses after the Segolta detail the wrong which was done to Sarah.

Ezek 34:19 וְצֹאנִ֕י מִרְמַ֥ס רַגְלֵיכֶם֙ תִּרְעֶ֔ינָה וּמִרְפַּ֥שׂ רַגְלֵיכֶ֖ם תִּשְׁתֶּֽינָה׃

And as for my sheep – the trampling of your feet they will graze, and the trampling of your feet they will drink.

When the key word occurs first in the verse, the Athnach marks it.[38] The rest of the verse explains or supplements that word. Ezra 10:26–29; BA Dan 5:26–28

c) Parenthesis

The accents can indicate parenthesis.[39] For short parenthetical statements (usually two words), a near subordinate disjunctive may set off a parenthesis, starting after the near subordinate and ending with its governing accent. For example, the words *after* a Tebir, a near subordinate disjunctive accent, up to and including the word with Tiphcha (Tebir's governing accent), may express parenthesis. For longer parenthetical statements (more than two words), a remote subordinate may set off a parenthesis ending with its governing accent. For instance, the words *after* a Rebia, a remote subordinate, up to and including the word with Zaqeph, Rebia's governing accent, may express parenthesis. Keep in mind that these accentual patterns, which indicate parenthesis, are also used frequently for non-parenthetical statements. Context must confirm the parenthesis.

---

38. In the poetical accents, the Athnach or Ole Veyored cannot occur on the first word of the verse. When they are due on the first word, they occur on another word (usually close to the first word), or Pazer will substitute for Athnach (Ps 25:1), and Azla-Legarmeh will substitute for Ole Veyored (Ps 26:1). Context must determine whether they truly belong to the other word (Ps 18:13) or the first word (Ps 102:8). The same is true for the next to last word in a verse: the Athnach must convert into Rebia Mugrash or Transformed Rebia Mugrash if it is due to occur on the word before Silluq. Context must determine whether it was due there (Ps 119:20). The Ole Veyored may occur on the fourth word or further from the Silluq.

39. Whole verses may also be parenthetical, Deut 2:10–12; 3:9, 11. Moreover, the beginning of verses may rarely be parenthetical, 1 Kgs 8:42[a]; 9:11[a].

i. Near subordinate disjunctive accent to its governing accent:
Words in apposition often take this form of parenthesis.

וַיִּשְׁלַח אֲבִימֶלֶךְ מֶלֶךְ גְּרָר וַיִּקַּח אֶת־שָׂרָה׃ Gen 20:2[b]

Abimelech, king of Gerar, sent and took Sarah

The accents indicate parenthesis for the appositional phrase, "king of Gerar," by the Pashta on "Abimelech" and the Zaqeph on "Gerar." The parenthesis starts *after* the near subordinate (Pashta) and ends with the governing accent (Zaqeph).

וּמַלְכִּי־צֶדֶק מֶלֶךְ שָׁלֵם הוֹצִיא Gen 14:18[a]

Melchizedek, king of Salem, brought out

Again, the accents indicate parenthesis for the appositional phrase, "king of Salem." The parenthesis starts *after* the near subordinate (Pashta) and ends with the governing accent (Zaqeph). Exod 18:2

ii. Remote subordinate disjunctive accent to its governing accent:
① Between independent clauses

In the following examples, the parenthesis occurs between independent clauses. Usually, for these constructions, render the parenthesis by inserting parentheses. Many dependent clauses are treated parenthetically between clauses: כַּאֲשֶׁר clause (Gen 12:4), for instance.

כִּי יֶחֶטְאוּ־לָךְ כִּי אֵין אָדָם אֲשֶׁר לֹא־יֶחֱטָא וְאָנַפְתָּ בָם 1 Kgs 8:46[a]

When they sin against you (for there is no man who does not sin), and you become angry against them. . . .

The accents indicate the parenthesis by the Rebia on "against you" and the Zaqeph on the verb "does not sin." The parenthesis begins after the remote subordinate, Rebia, and ends with its governing accent, Zaqeph. The overall meaning of the verse (context) confirms the parenthesis.

אִמָּלְטָה נָּא שָׁמָּה הֲלֹא מִצְעָר הִוא וּתְחִי נַפְשִׁי׃ Gen 19:20[b]

I will flee now there (is it not small?) that my soul may live.

This time the parenthesis begins after a Rebia and ends with Tiphcha, its governing accent. 2 Sam 14:26; 21:2

② Within a clause

In the following examples, the parenthesis occurs within a clause. For most of these constructions, render the parenthesis by inserting commas before and after the parenthesis or by inserting parenthesis marks.

וַיִּתֵּן אֶל־מֹשֶׁה כְּכַלֹּתוֹ לְדַבֵּר אִתּוֹ בְּהַר סִינַי שְׁנֵי לֻחֹת הָעֵדֻת Exod 31:18[a]

And he gave to Moses, when he finished speaking to him in Mount Sinai, both tablets of stone.

The parenthetical temporal clause, beginning after the Rebia and ending before the Zaqeph, interrupts the verb and object within the same clause. Commas indicate the parenthesis.

וְנֵר אֱלֹהִים טֶרֶם יִכְבֶּה וּשְׁמוּאֵל שֹׁכֵב בְּהֵיכַל יְהוָה 1 Sam 3:3
אֲשֶׁר־שָׁם אֲרוֹן אֱלֹהִים׃

And the lamp of God had not yet gone out (now Samuel was lying down) in the temple of the Lord where the ark of God was.

The parenthesis begins after the Zaqeph, the remote subordinate, and ends at the Athnach, its governing accent. Because the parenthesis is abrupt, insert parenthesis marks. Most modern translations improperly render – "And Samuel was lying down in the temple of the Lord, where the ark of God was." Samuel did not sleep in the holy place or the most holy place! Such a translation would require the Athnach to occur where the first Zaqeph occurs, and a different Bible.
Gen 11:11, 13; Amos 6:14[a]

Isa 38:8[a] הִנְנִ֣י מֵשִׁ֣יב אֶת־צֵ֣ל הַמַּעֲל֡וֹת אֲשֶׁ֣ר יָרְדָ֠ה בְּמַעֲל֨וֹת אָחָ֥ז בַּשֶּׁ֛מֶשׁ
אֲחֹרַנִּ֖ית עֶ֣שֶׂר מַעֲל֑וֹת

Behold, I am turning the shadow of the stairs, which went down on the stairs of Ahaz in the sun, backward ten steps.

The parenthesis begins after the Pazer, the remote subordinate, and ends at the Tebir, its governing accent. Relative clauses often are treated parenthetically within a clause. Gen 21:3, 9; 13:3[b]; 27:17; 44:8; Exod 34:18; Lev 2:8; verbal clause followed by כִּי clause, Deut 3:19

2 Chr 32:9 אַחַ֣ר זֶ֗ה שָׁלַ֞ח סַנְחֵרִ֧יב מֶֽלֶךְ־אַשּׁ֛וּר עֲבָדָ֖יו יְר֣וּשָׁלַ֑יְמָה וְהוּא֙
עַל־לָכִ֔ישׁ וְכָל־מֶמְשַׁלְתּ֖וֹ עִמּ֑וֹ עַל־יְחִזְקִיָּ֙הוּ֙ מֶ֣לֶךְ יְהוּדָ֔ה
וְעַל־כָּל־יְהוּדָ֛ה אֲשֶׁ֥ר בִּירוּשָׁלַ֖͏ִם לֵאמֹֽר׃

After this Sennacherib, king of Asshur, sent his servants to Jerusalem (while he was at Lachish and all his kingdom was with him), to Hezekiah, king of Judah and to all Judah which was in Jerusalem.

In addition to the relative clause, other clauses, such as the situation clauses here, may be parenthetically inserted in a clause. Notice here that the parenthesis starts after the *first* Zaqeph and ends at the Athnach. In verses with repeating Zaqeph indicating parenthesis, the parenthesis starts after the first Zaqeph and ends at its governing accent, Athnach. Deut 3:19; Jer 41:9[a]; 1 Chr 8:13

Gen 41:45[a] וַיִּתֶּן־ל֣וֹ אֶת־אָֽסְנַ֗ת בַּת־פּ֥וֹטִי פֶ֛רַע כֹּהֵ֥ן אֹ֖ן לְאִשָּׁ֑ה

And he gave to him Asenath, daughter of Potiphera priest of On, for a wife.

The parenthetical apposition begins after the Rebia and ends with the Tiphcha. This apposition is longer than two words; therefore, the remote subordinate is needed, instead of the near subordinate, to mark the parenthesis.

iii. Near subordinate disjunctive parenthesis followed by a remote subordinate disjunctive parenthesis.

Jer 20:1 וַיִּשְׁמַע֙ פַּשְׁח֣וּר בֶּן־אִמֵּ֔ר הַכֹּהֵ֔ן וְהוּא־פָקִ֥יד נָגִ֖יד בְּבֵ֣ית יְהוָ֑ה
אֶֽת־יִרְמְיָ֔הוּ נִבָּ֖א אֶת־הַדְּבָרִ֥ים הָאֵֽלֶּה׃

And Pashur, son of Immer the priest (now he was an overseer, a leader in the house of God), heard Jeremiah prophesying these words.

The first parenthesis with a near subordinate begins after the Pashta and ends at the Zaqeph: "son of Immer the priest." This parenthesis is followed by another parenthesis with a remote subordinate, beginning after the Zaqeph and ending with the Athnach.

iv. Parenthesis over Multiple Verses

Sometimes a parenthesis extends over a Soph Pasuq into other verses.

Isa 52:14–15 כַּאֲשֶׁר שָׁמְמוּ עָלֶיךָ רַבִּים כֵּן־מִשְׁחַת מֵאִישׁ מַרְאֵהוּ וְתֹאֲרוֹ מִבְּנֵי אָדָם׃ כֵּן יַזֶּה גּוֹיִם רַבִּים

As many were astonished at you – thus his form was marred more than a man, and his form more than the sons of man – so he will sprinkle (startle) many nations . . .

There is a double parenthesis: the first one starting after the Zaqeph and ending at the Athnach, the second one starting after the Athnach and ending with Soph Pasuq. The main statement extends over two verses.

1 Chr 5:1, 3[a] וּבְנֵי רְאוּבֵן בְּכוֹר־יִשְׂרָאֵל כִּי הוּא הַבְּכוֹר וּבְחַלְּלוֹ יְצוּעֵי אָבִיו נִתְּנָה בְּכֹרָתוֹ לִבְנֵי יוֹסֵף בֶּן־יִשְׂרָאֵל . . . בְּנֵי רְאוּבֵן בְּכוֹר יִשְׂרָאֵל...

[1] And the sons of Reuben, the firstborn of Israel, for he was the firstborn, and when he defiled the bed of his father, his firstborn rights were given to the sons of Joseph, son of Israel. . . . [3] The sons of Reuben, the firstborn of Israel, are. . . .

The parenthesis extends over three verses. The parenthesis begins with a near subordinate parenthesis, starting after the Zarqa and ending at the Segolta. Then the remote subordinate Segolta begins another parenthesis that continues through the first half of verse three.

1 Kgs 12:2–3 (after the second verbal clause); 18:3–4 (to the start of verse five); 2 Kgs 9:14–15[a]; Esth 2:12–13[a]; 2 Chr 5:11–13[a]

Interpreting Biblical Poetry: Syntactically, Clausally, and Semantically

For biblical poetry, the first half of the verse usually furnishes the main or general idea; the second half echoes, supplements, explains, details, and so forth, the first half of the verse. This principle, similar to the prose principle of delaying the Athnach until the main statement appears, is especially clear through parallelism, the distinguishing feature of Hebrew poetry, and often of direct discourse. The second half of the verse often parallels the syntax, vocabulary, and meaning of the first half.

Biblical poetry and its parallelism, of course, is as flexible as the soul of the poet. Sometimes, the parallel parts are precise and exact, each word and construction closely corresponding. More frequently, however, the parallel parts are less precise and exact, being more approximate and general. Indeed, at times just word or phrase may be in parallel. Often additional, non-parallel statements occur with parallel statements. They may be independent sentences that variously connect to the parallel statements, or they may be dependent clauses, phrases, and words connected to the parallel statements. Furthermore, the dividing of syntactical pairs or groups may create parallelism. Some verses of biblical poetry, in fact, lack any parallelism, the poetic lines appearing prosaic.

General Principle: The first half of the verse usually furnishes the main or general idea; the second half echoes, supplements, explains, details, and so forth, the first half of the verse.[40] The first half, therefore, usually has extra words to establish the main idea that are not paralleled in the second half.

40. WW I, 25

Ps 9:18 יָשׁ֣וּבוּ רְשָׁעִ֣ים לִשְׁא֑וֹלָה כָּל־גּ֝וֹיִ֗ם שְׁכֵחֵ֥י אֱלֹהִֽים׃
The wicked will turn to Sheol,
(and) all people who forget God.

The first line gives the general idea of the verse. The second half explains or supplements the first half by relating "the wicked" with "all peoples who forget God." The parallelism of the second half matches with one word of the first half, "the wicked."

Ps 1:3 וְֽהָיָ֗ה כְּעֵץ֮ שָׁת֢וּל עַֽל־פַּלְגֵ֫י מָ֥יִם אֲשֶׁ֤ר פִּרְי֨וֹ ׀ יִתֵּ֬ן בְּעִתּ֗וֹ וְעָלֵ֥הוּ לֹֽא־יִבּ֑וֹל
וְכֹ֖ל אֲשֶׁר־יַעֲשֶׂ֣ה יַצְלִֽיחַ׃
And he will exist as a tree planted upon channels of water;
whose fruit it gives in its time and whose leaf does not whither,
and all that it does prospers.

Again, the first half presents the main idea of the verse; the second half details the analogy of how the tree resembles the blessed man.

A. Syntactic placement of the division

The accents divide syntactically in verses or sentences with one independent clause. These sentences lack parallelism within them and in accentual pattern resemble verbal and nominal clauses of prose.

Ps 2:6 וַ֭אֲנִי נָסַ֣כְתִּי מַלְכִּ֑י עַל־צִ֝יּ֗וֹן הַר־קָדְשִֽׁי׃
I have set my king,
upon Zion, my holy hill.

This verse/clause, without parallelism, follows the accent pattern for nominal clauses in prose. Ps 25:22; 33:14; 48:3, 8; 70:4; 74:6; 89:12; 116:15; 121:4; 124:5

B. Clausal placement of the division

The accents divide verses clausally with two or more independent clauses. This commonly occurs in verses with parallel lines. The lines may parallel each other precisely and exactly, the members of each line matching with each other, or they may parallel each other approximately and generally, the members of each line more or less matching with each other. In either case, the lines *mostly* parallel each other. For verses with three parallel lines, the accents usually divide the first parallel line from the other two parallel lines. Furthermore, the accents clausally divide verses with non-parallel clauses, much like prose. With verses that combine parallel lines and non-parallel lines, the accents clausally separate the parallel lines from the non-parallel line(s).

1. Between Parallel Lines

The following examples will be more or less in parallel. The important issue is that *most* or *all* of the verse is parallel.

a) Two Parallel Lines

Ps 19:2 הַשָּׁמַיִם֮ מְֽסַפְּרִ֢ים כְּבֽוֹד־אֵ֑ל וּֽמַעֲשֵׂ֥ה יָ֝דָ֗יו מַגִּ֥יד הָרָקִֽיעַ׃
The heavens declare the glory of God;
And the works of his hands the sky relates.

The chiastic parallelism precisely and exactly aligns each part of the first half with the second half. The first half expresses the main idea; the second half explains the first half with matching statements. "The glory of God," for example, corresponds to "the works of his hands." In this verse, the second half defines God's glory as his marvelous works, not as the Shekinah glory of the temple. Ps 6:2; 8:5; 19:3, 8–10; Prov 13:7; 15:1; 25:21

Ps 1:2 כִּ֤י אִ֥ם בְּתוֹרַ֥ת יְהוָ֗ה חֶ֫פְצ֥וֹ וּֽבְתוֹרָת֥וֹ יֶהְגֶּ֗ה יוֹמָ֥ם וָלָֽיְלָה׃

But in the law of the Lord is his delight;
and in his law he meditates day and night.

The parallelism approximately and generally aligns "his delight" of the first line to "he meditates day and night." "In the law of the Lord" approximately parallels "and his law." The second half explains or supplements the first half by relating how he delights in God's law by mediating on it day and night. Ps 2:5, 9; 6:6; 8:7; 9:2

b) Three Parallel Lines

Ps 1:1 אַ֥שְֽׁרֵי־הָאִ֗ישׁ אֲשֶׁ֤ר ׀ לֹ֥א הָלַךְ֮ בַּעֲצַ֪ת רְשָׁ֫עִ֥ים וּבְדֶ֣רֶךְ חַ֭טָּאִים לֹ֥א עָמָ֑ד
וּבְמוֹשַׁ֥ב לֵ֝צִ֗ים לֹ֣א יָשָֽׁב׃

Blessed is the man who has not walked in the council of the wicked.
And in path of sinners he has not stood, and in the seat of the scorner he has not sat.

For verses with three parallel lines, the first line usually gets the break, with the next two lines echoing and supplementing the first line. Ps 7:15; 38:4; 53:7; 115:12; 139:12; Job 31:7

c) Four Lines with Two Parallel Pairs

Ps 11:4 יְהוָ֤ה ׀ בְּֽהֵיכַ֬ל קָדְשׁ֗וֹ יְהוָה֮ בַּשָּׁמַ֪יִם כִּ֫סְא֥וֹ עֵינָ֥יו יֶחֱז֑וּ עַפְעַפָּ֥יו יִ֝בְחֲנ֗וּ בְּנֵ֣י
אָדָֽם׃

The Lord is in his holy temple; the Lord – his throne is in the heavens.
His eyes – they see; his eyelids – they test the sons of man.

This verse has four lines. The break divides the first two parallel lines from the last two parallel lines. Ps 18:16; 30:6; 31:11; 51:6

2. Between Non-parallel Lines

These non-parallel lines, resembling prose statements, are divided clausally.

Ps 3:5 ק֭וֹלִי אֶל־יְהוָ֣ה אֶקְרָ֑א וַיַּעֲנֵ֨נִי מֵהַ֖ר קָדְשׁ֣וֹ סֶֽלָה׃

My voice to the Lord I raised;
he answered me from his holy mountain. Selah.

Ps 3:3 רַבִּים֮ אֹמְרִ֪ים לְנַ֫פְשִׁ֥י אֵ֤ין יְֽשׁוּעָ֓תָה לּ֬וֹ בֵֽאלֹהִ֬ים סֶֽלָה׃

Many are saying to my soul,
there is no salvation for him in God. Selah.

Ps 3:6, 7; 31:23

3. Between Two Parallel Lines and a Non-parallel Line

The parallel lines are grouped together, with the non-parallel line coming before or after the parallel lines.

Ps 24:7 שְׂא֤וּ שְׁעָרִ֨ים ׀ רָֽאשֵׁיכֶ֗ם וְֽ֭הִנָּשְׂאוּ פִּתְחֵ֣י עוֹלָ֑ם וְ֝יָב֗וֹא מֶ֣לֶךְ הַכָּבֽוֹד׃

Lift up, O gates, your heads, and lift up, O ancient doors;
That the king of glory may come in.

The break separates the parallel lines from the following non-parallel line. Ps 39:6; 40:10; 50:7; 54:5; 55:16; 71:6

Ps 24:8 מִי זֶה מֶלֶךְ הַכָּבוֹד יְהוָה עִזּוּז וְגִבּוֹר יְהוָה גִּבּוֹר מִלְחָמָה׃
Who is this king of glory?
The Lord strong and valiant; the Lord is valiant in battle.

The break separates the non-parallel line from the following parallel lines. Ps 16:11; 31:8; 35:10; 67:5; 78:21, 50

C. Semantic placement of the division

The clausal, however, often must yield to the semantic. This is common in verses with *partial* parallelism, with perhaps only a word or a few words in parallel between the lines. In such cases, the break will often bypass its syntactical or clausal placement to highlight the parallelism. Furthermore, the clausal may also yield to the semantic in verses of three lines, two parallel (usually fully parallel) and one non-parallel. Abandoning its clausal placement of dividing two parallel lines from a non-parallel line, the break now separates the parallel lines, linking a non-parallel line with one of the parallel lines. "In such instances," writes William Wickes, "attention seems to be drawn to the close connection between the idea contained in the parallelism, and the new idea introduced by the third (non-parallel) member."[41]

Also keep in mind that the first half of the verse usually furnishes the main or general idea, with the second half echoing, supplementing, explaining, or detailing the first half.

1. **Partial Parallelism**

a) One Independent Clause (Syntactic)

Ps 28:2 שְׁמַע קוֹל תַּחֲנוּנַי בְּשַׁוְּעִי אֵלֶיךָ בְּנָשְׂאִי יָדַי אֶל־דְּבִיר קָדְשֶׁךָ׃
Hear the voice of my cry for grace when I cry for help to you;
when I lift up my hands to your innermost holy place.

The syntactic break should come after the independent clause, but before the first temporal clause. The Athnach bypasses this break to form the parallelism between the infinitive clauses. Only the last clause of the first line is parallel with the second line, the first clause lacking parallelism in the second line.

Ps 31:20 מָה רַב־טוּבְךָ אֲשֶׁר־צָפַנְתָּ לִּירֵאֶיךָ פָּעַלְתָּ לַחֹסִים בָּךְ נֶגֶד בְּנֵי אָדָם׃
How great is your goodness which you have treasured up to those who fear you;
(which) you have done to those who seek refuge in you before the sons of men!

The syntactic break should occur after the independent clause or after the second dependent (relative) clause. The semantic break occurs after the first relative clause to form the parallelism. Again, the independent clause lacks parallelism in the second line. Ps 31:20; 115:14; 135:12; 140:13; Job 20:4

b) Two or More Independent Clauses (Clausal)

Ps 2:8 שְׁאַל מִמֶּנִּי וְאֶתְּנָה גוֹיִם נַחֲלָתֶךָ וַאֲחֻזָּתְךָ אַפְסֵי־אָרֶץ׃
Ask of me, and I will give the nations as your inheritance;
And as your possession the ends of the earth.

The most logical placement of the break is between the independent clauses. The actual break highlights the parallelism and allows for the main idea to

41. WW I, 27

come in the first half of the verse. This is a common pattern in partial parallelism (only the direct objects are parallel): the parallelism gets the break, and the first half of the verse is the more complete statement of the verse.

Ps 21:5 חַיִּים׀ שָׁאַל מִמְּךָ נָתַתָּה לּוֹ אֹרֶךְ יָמִים עוֹלָם וָעֶד׃

Life he asked of you, you have given to him
length of days forever and ever.

The break logically should separate the clauses. But again, the break stresses the parallelism (life and length of days, forever and ever), and it allows the main statement of the verse to occur in the first half. Ps 18:8; 22:9; Prov 1:33; 35:5

Ps 18:51 מַגְדִּיל יְשׁוּעוֹת מַלְכּוֹ וְעֹשֶׂה חֶסֶד׀ לִמְשִׁיחוֹ לְדָוִד וּלְזַרְעוֹ עַד־עוֹלָם׃

(It is) he who makes great salvations to his king;
(It is) he who does mercy to his anointed one, to David and to
his seed forever.

In this example, the non-parallel element is in the last line. In the preceding examples, it was in the first line. Logically, the break should come before the prepositional phrases—to David and to his seed forever – but again the break separates the parallel clauses semantically. The first line still gives the main idea; the second lines supplements the first line with a parallel clause and a non-parallel element. Usually, the non-parallel element is in the first line. Ps 21:12; 27:11; 37:40; 141:8

2. Progressive Parallelism

Progressive parallelism divides the same parts of speech within a clause or within the same grammatical construction. "When two parallel expressions," writes Wickes, "follow one another in the course of a continuous construction (*progressive parallelism* this has been termed), they are often separated by the caesura, so as to produce *parallelismus membrorum*."[42] For verses with a single independent clause, the same parts of speech – usually nouns, infinitives or prepositional phrases – are often divided, with additional words coming at the end of the clause (hence, "in the course of continuous construction"). Similarly, for verses with multiple independent clauses, the clauses are divided, with additional words coming at the end of the clause.

a) One independent clause

Ps 50:4 יִקְרָא אֶל־הַשָּׁמַיִם מֵעָל וְאֶל־הָאָרֶץ לָדִין עַמּוֹ׃

He calls to the heavens above
and to the earth, to judge his people.

The syntactical placement of the break would be before the infinitive. By dividing between the prepositional phrases, however, progressive parallelism is created. Notice that the division comes between the parallel members, with other words after the parallel members. Job 5:15; Ps 107:17

Prov 3:2 כִּי אֹרֶךְ יָמִים וּשְׁנוֹת חַיִּים וְשָׁלוֹם יוֹסִיפוּ לָךְ׃

For length of days and years of life;
And peace, they will add to you.

42. WW I, 25

Again, the syntactic placement of the break would be after the third parallel noun, but for progressive parallelism, the break occurs after the second parallel noun phrase. This time the nouns are divided at the beginning of the verse. The pause between parallel members focuses attention on the meaning of the parallel members. This separation between parallel members has a similar effect of separating the same parts of speech in narrative, for example, Deut 6:17, or to separating details in narrative, for instance, Exod 10:9. Is 19:7; Ps 145:5; Job 4:8, 10; 32:8; 37:13; Prov 7:6, 12, 15; 8:2–3 (these four examples have parallel prepositional phrases instead of nouns); 25:3

b) Two or more independent clauses

Isa 64:3 וּמֵעוֹלָ֥ם לֹא־שָׁמְע֖וּ לֹ֣א הֶאֱזִ֑ינוּ עַ֣יִן לֹֽא־רָאָ֗תָה אֱלֹהִים֙ זוּלָ֣תְךָ֔
יַעֲשֶׂ֖ה לִמְחַכֵּה־לֽוֹ׃

And from old, have they not heard, have not their ears heard, (their) eye has it not seen – a God, except you, who works for the one hoping for him.

Logically, the break should occur after the third verb. Yet, the break occurs after the second verb for progressive parallelism. The three verbs (independent clauses) occur in the middle of the verse, all having the same direct object. The break focuses the meaning on the parallel verbs. Ps 66:14; 90:2 (Notice how all three parallel statements, including the prepositional phrases which are not strictly parallel, all connect to the final statement, "You are God."); Ps 21:12; Job 11:10; Prov 21:30; 30:32

3. Two Parallel Clauses with a Non-Parallel Clause

Ps 93:1 יְהוָ֣ה מָלָךְ֮ גֵּא֪וּת לָ֫בֵ֥שׁ לָבֵ֣שׁ יְ֭הוָה עֹ֣ז הִתְאַזָּ֑ר אַף־תִּכּ֥וֹן תֵּ֝בֵ֗ל בַּל־תִּמּֽוֹט׃

The Lord reigns; he has put on majesty.
The Lord has put on; he has girded himself with strength. Moreover, the world is established; it will not move.

The break logically should occur at the Athnach instead of the Ole Veyored, keeping the parallel lines together, separated from the non-parallel line. The break in Ps 93:1, according to Wickes, associates the non-parallel line closely in meaning with the second parallel line. The context gives a conclusion to the Lord's girding himself with strength – the earth, therefore, is established. It cannot totter (lose its establishment). Ps 27:5; 37:5: 69:5; 116:16; 143:12; Isa 54:1

Ps 3:8 ק֘וּמָ֤ה יְהוָ֨ה ׀ הוֹשִׁ֘יעֵ֤נִי אֱלֹהַ֗י כִּֽי־הִכִּ֣יתָ אֶת־כָּל־אֹיְבַ֣י לֶ֑חִי שִׁנֵּ֖י
רְשָׁעִ֣ים שִׁבַּֽרְתָּ׃

Rise, Lord; Save me, my God, for you have smitten all my enemies on the cheek.
The teeth of the wicked you have smashed to pieces.

This example is similar to Ps 93:1 above, except the non-parallel line goes with the first parallel line instead of the second parallel line. Ps 4:3; 6:7; 7:6; 13:6; 23:4; 25:5; 27:6; 38:13; 105:10; 148:13; Job 9:21

COMMENTARY ON THE ACCENTS OF COMPOSITION 7 AND PSALM 1 (IN COMPOSITION 11)

Introduction

The two commentaries are given to reinforce the principles given in the preceding chapter. The commentaries review the principles for dividing the verse by the accents and the principle for interpreting the accents for exegesis. To understand the commentaries, give attention to the following general considerations:

1. The division of disjunctive accents will be classified as:
   A. syntactical, when dividing within a clause
   B. clausal, when dividing between clauses
   C. semantical, when the dividing highlights (or emphasizes) the meaning of the text. The semantic category often overlaps with the other categories. When the semantical and syntactical overlap, stronger disjunctive accents occur on the highlighted or emphasized words within a clause. In the usual word order of a verbal clause – verb, subject, object, prepositional phrase/adverbial – the stronger disjunctive accents occur at the end of the verse with the prepositional phrase/adverbial, with the disjunctives weakening as they approach the verb. When the object or prepositional phrase/adverbial occurs before the verb, the stronger accents usually precede the verb indicating the semantical or emphatic placement of the word order. The same is true for the nominal clause. The nominal before the verb often takes the strongest disjunctive of the clause or the second strongest.

      When the semantical and clausal overlap, the strongest disjunctive accents still divide clauses, but they do not occur at the most logical location. For example, instead of occurring on the clause introducing direct speech, the most logical placement, the strongest accents occur within the direct speech clauses where the meaning is most telling.

      The semantical is also detected when the strongest disjunctive accents, especially Athnach or the main break in half verses, occur within a clause instead of between clauses when multiple clauses are present.

2. The term "clause" refer to a grammatical clause; the term "segment" refers to a group of words under the governance of a disjunctive accent.

3. The length of words often influence the choice of accents.
   A. Zaqeph may occur on the second word before Silluq or Athnach if the word with Silluq/Athnach or the word before them is long, that is, a word having at least two syllables before its accented syllable (shewas not counting as syllables) or a word having a long vowel followed by a vocal shewa. If Silluq's or Athnach's word is short, then Tiphcha occurs on the second word before Silluq or Athnach, not Zaqeph.

B. If Zaqeph's segment has only two words, Zaqeph's word must be long for the preceding word to have Pashta (or Yetib, its substitute). If Zaqeph's word is short in a two-word segment, then the preceding word has a conjunctive accent (Munach).

4. For half verses, the main break will be divided into Zaqeph or Tiphcha segment and final segment.

5. Remember that when disjunctive accents divide words, they are often joining other words at the same time. For example, when an Athnach divides a verse in half, it is also joining together the words of each half. The disjunctive accents, therefore, will often be described as grouping or joining words before and after them.

Commentary on the Accents of Composition Seven

A. Verse One

וַיַּ֣רְא הָעָ֔ם כִּֽי־לֹ֥א יָרַ֛ד מֹשֶׁ֖ה מֵעַל־הָהָ֑ר וַיִּקָּהֵ֣ל הָעָ֔ם פֶּ֖תַח אֹ֥הֶל מוֹעֵֽד׃

The Athnach divides the verse clausally. The A-half of the verse has an independent clause followed by a dependent כִּי clause (substantival). The B-half is an independent clause.

וַיַּ֣רְא הָעָ֔ם כִּ֚י לֹֽא־יָרַ֛ד מֹשֶׁ֖ה מֵעַל־הָהָ֑ר

1. A-half: Zaqeph divides the A-half clausally, separating the independent clause from its dependent כִּי clause.
   a) Zaqeph segment: The word before the Zaqeph must have a Munach, since Zaqeph's word is short and the segment has only two words.
   b) Final segment: Tiphcha indicates the main break in the final segment. The break is syntactical since it breaks within a clause. Within verbal clauses, the main break usually occurs towards the end of the clause, before prepositional phrases or adverbial constructions. Since three words occur in Tiphcha's segment, another break is necessary. Tebir divides Tiphcha's segment, separating the כִּי particle from the verb and subject, thus joining the verb and subject closely together. Tebir's break is syntactical. If the כִּי had to be connected to the following words, a Maqqeph would be necessary.

וַיִּקָּהֵ֣ל הָעָ֔ם פֶּ֖תַח אֹ֥הֶל מוֹעֵֽד׃

2. B-half: The Zaqeph syntactically divides the verbal clause, separating the verb and its subject from the adverbial accusative (accusative of place).

   What if Tebir occurred instead of the Zaqeph? By rule this would be possible since the Tebir is a near subordinate to the Tiphcha. This, however, would make the Tiphcha the main break in the B-half, awkwardly breaking up the construct package and marring the meaning of the clause. The Zaqeph is necessary to keep the three words in construct together.

a) Zaqeph segment: A Munach is required before the Zaqeph since Zaqeph's word is short and the segment has only two words.
b) Final segment: By rule the Tiphcha must occur on the first or second word before the Silluq (or Athnach). In a three word construct package, the disjunctive (Tiphcha), if necessary, usually occurs on the first word of the package. This rule that Tiphcha occurs on the first or second word before Athnach overrides the syntax, since words in annexation should be connected. The Zaqeph, however, compensates for this rule of Tiphcha since Zaqeph's presence (as the main break) and location (before the three words) groups the three word construct package together. Tiphcha's role in such contexts is a "mere foretone" to the Silluq (Athnach) – a formal break without effecting the meaning of the annexation.

B. Verse Two

וַיָּ֥רֶב הָעָ֖ם עִם־אַהֲרֹ֣ן לֵאמֹ֑ר   הַֽהֶעֱלִ֤יתָ אֹתָ֙נוּ֙ אֶל־הַמָּק֣וֹם הַזֶּ֔ה לְהָרְגֵֽנוּ׃

In medium and short verses, (לֵאמֹר) often takes a major disjunctive. Here it receives the Athnach, dividing the verse clausally.

וַיָּ֥רֶב הָעָ֖ם   עִם־אַהֲרֹ֣ן לֵאמֹ֑ר

1. A-half: Segments with לֵאמֹר present special challenges. In segments with לֵאמֹר, one expects a major break before it to isolate it. (In Gen 1:22, the break of the A-half occurs before the לֵאמֹר. See also Gen 17:3[b]; 23:5). More frequently, however, לֵאמֹר does not get the break before it, perhaps to avoid monotony. Instead, it is often ignored, as if it were absent. This brings words together with לֵאמֹר unexpectedly (Gen 2:16; 8:15). Here in verse two, לֵאמֹר is combined with the preceding word with the Tiphcha.

הַֽהֶעֱלִ֤יתָ אֹתָ֙נוּ֙ אֶל־הַמָּק֣וֹם הַזֶּ֔ה   לְהָרְגֵֽנוּ׃

2. B-half: The Tiphcha furnishes the main break for the B-half; therefore, Zaqeph cannot occur in the B-half. Now, only subordinates of Tiphcha can occur. Zaqeph would occur if the break of the B-half occurred on at least the second word (under certain conditions) or further from the Silluq.

   Since Tiphcha's segment has four words, the Tebir divides the words syntactically, separating the verb and its object from the prepositional phrase.

C. Verse Three

רַב־לָךְ֒   הִתְנַשֵּׂ֣אתָ עָלֵ֙ינוּ֙ אַתָּ֣ה וּמֹשֶׁ֔ה וְעַתָּ֖ה מֹשֶׁ֣ה אֵינֶ֑נּוּ וְאַתָּ֗ה לֹ֤א תְבִיאֵ֙נוּ֙ אֶל־הָאָ֣רֶץ הַזֹּ֔את
מִמְלֹ֥ךְ עָלֵ֖ינוּ כִּ֥י הָעֵדָ֛ה כֻּלָּ֥הּ קְדֹשָׁ֖ה לַיהוָ֥ה הִֽיא׃

The Athnach breaks the verse clausally, separating the first three clauses from the last two clauses.

הִתְנַשֵּׂאתָ עָלֵינוּ אַתָּה וּמֹשֶׁה   וְעַתָּה מֹשֶׁה אֵינֶנּוּ וְאַתָּה לֹא תְבִיאֵנוּ אֶל־הָאָרֶץ הַזֹּאת

1. A-half: Segolta breaks the A-half, separating the first clause from the next two clauses.
   a) Segolta segment: Zarqa divides the segment syntactically and semantically, separating the pronoun "you" and "Moses" from the verb and its prepositional phrase. This separation emphasizes the pronoun since it repeats the pronoun inherent in the verb and "Moses" by placement after the prepositional phrase.
   b) Final segment: The Zaqeph Qaton clausally divides the final segment, with Pashta breaking before Zaqeph Qaton since its segment has three words. The Zaqeph Gadol is the main break after the Zaqeph Qaton syntactically and semantically, by separating and highlighting the emphatic pronoun from the rest of the clause. Since the clause is short, having a verb of motion and an emphatic pronoun, the prepositional phrase receives a minor disjunctive (Tiphcha) before it. Usually, small words, such as pronouns, do not receive the most important break of a clause. Prepositions and adverbials usually have the break of the clause before them, especially when the subject, verb, and object (if present) express a complete meaning with the prepositional phrase and/or adverbial being merely supplemental to the meaning. In this verse, the prepositional phrase is essential to the verb of motion, so the pronoun receives the main break.

רַב לְךָ מִמְּלָךְ עָלֵינוּ   כִּי הָעֵדָה כֻּלָּהּ קְדֹשָׁה לַיהוָה הִיא׃

2. B-half: The first Zaqeph divides the B-half clausally.
   a) The Zaqeph segment: Since the Zaqeph segment has four words, the Pashta syntactically separates the prepositional phrase from the beginning of the segment. If the break had been on the first word of the segment, Rebia would be necessary. A Pashta, as a minor break on the second or third word in the segment, would then be necessary since three words would be between the Rebia and the Zaqeph.
   b) The Final segment: The second Zaqeph divides syntactically and semantically within the final clause (and segment), separating and highlighting the Casus Pendens. The Pashta also divides semantically, furnishing an emphatic pause before the corroborative apposition, "all of her." The Tiphcha marks a minor pause before the pronoun.

D. Verse Four

נִקְחָה־נָּא כְּלִי קֹדֶשׁ וְנִתְּנָה אֲנָשִׁים שָׂרִים בְּרָאשֵׁינוּ   וַיֹּאמֶר אַהֲרֹן אַל־אַחַי אַל־תָּרִיבוּ נָא עִמִּי
לָמָּה תְנַסּוּ אֶת־יהוה הַמּוֹצִיא אֹתָנוּ מִמִּצְרָיִם׃

The Athnach separates the verse clausally, dividing the first two clauses from the rest of the clauses.

נִקְחָה־נָּא כְּלֵי קֹדֶשׁ   וְנִתְּנָה אֲנָשִׁים שָׂרִים בְּרָאשֵׁינוּ

1. A-half: Zaqeph divides the A-half clausally.
   a) Zaqeph segment: Since Zaqeph's segment has three words, a Pashta divides the segment syntactically, separating the verb from its object. This separation groups the direct object, a construct package, together.
   b) Final segment: Since the final segment has four words, a disjunctive accent is necessary. Moreover, since the break of these four words occurs on the word before the Athnach, Tiphcha furnishes the break. If the division had occurred on the second word before the Athnach, Tiphcha again would have provided the break, since the word with Athnach and the word before it are short. If the division had occurred on the third word before Athnach, Zaqeph would have furnished the break. Finally, since Tiphcha's segment has three words, a Tebir must separate the verb/subject from the object/apposition.

וַיֹּאמֶר אַהֲרֹן אַל־אַחַי אַל־תָּרִיבוּ נָא עִמִּי   לָמָּה תְנַסּוּ אֶת־יהוה הַמּוֹצִיא אֹתָנוּ מִמִּצְרָיִם׃

2. B-half: The first Zaqeph divides the B-half clausally and semantically. The most logical place to divide the clauses is after the first clause which introduces the direct discourse. The main division, as indicated by the first Zaqeph, however, moves down from the first clause to mark the most meaningful place of the B-half. The meaning overrules the logical. The accentuators did not waste important disjunctives on introductory words. Instead, they often reserved the main break (or other important breaks) for the meaning of the verse, half-verse, or segment. The clauses after the main break of the B-half may explain, supplement, and detail the clause(s) before the main break of the B-half.
   a) Zaqeph segment: The Rebia breaks the segment clausally. Since four words occur between the Zaqeph and the Rebia, another break occurs. Furthermore, since the break of these four words is on the third word before the Zaqeph, a Rebia is required because Pashta cannot occur on the third word before the Zaqeph. But a Rebia cannot be placed here because two Rebias cannot occur within three words of each other. The Rebia, therefore, transforms into a Pashta. The first Pashta, a transformed Rebia, breaks these four words syntactically.
   b) Final segment: The second Zaqeph divides the final segment clausally, separating the clauses (the last clause being participial). Yetib, a substitute for Pashta when the accent is on the first letter of the word, separates the particle from the verb and its object in the first half of Zaqeph's segment. Tiphcha marks a minor dichotomy before the prepositional phrase in the second half of the final segment.

E. Verse Five

וּמֹשֶׁה עָלָה אֶל־הָהָר לִשְׁמֹעַ אֶת־דְּבַר יהוה   וְהָהָר בֹּעֵר בָּאֵשׁ׃

The Athnach divides the verse clausally. The second half of the verse furnishes the situation in which the events of the first half occurred. The second half of the verse often supplements the first half.

וּמֹשֶׁה עָלָה אֶל־הָהָר   לִשְׁמֹעַ אֶת־דְּבַר יְהוָה

1. A-half: The Zaqeph divides the clauses (the second clause is infinitival).
   a) Zaqeph segment: Zaqeph's segment has three words, so Pashta divides the initiator from its announcement.
   b) Final segment: These words are grouped similar to verse one, B-half. The three words form a construct package, with the first word receiving the Tiphcha as a foretone.

וְהָהָר   בֹּעֵר בָּאֵשׁ׃

2. B-half: The B-half has three words; therefore, the Tiphcha supplies a break, separating the initiator from its announcement, as is common. Participles often connect to a following object or prepositional phrase.

F. Verse Six

וַיֹּאמֶר יְהוָה אֶל־מֹשֶׁה רֵד הַמַּחֲנֶה וְדִבַּרְתָּ אֶל־בְּנֵי־יִשְׂרָאֵל וְיָשׁוּבוּ מִן־דַּרְכֵיהֶם הָרָעִים פֶּן־אַכֶּם
מַכָּה גְדוֹלָה   כִּי מֵהַקָּטֹן וְעַד־הַגָּדוֹל אִתִּי מָרוּ׃

The Athnach separates the last clause from the rest of the clauses in the verse. The main break is often delayed until the main statement of the verse is given, with the words after the main break explaining, specifying, defining, etc. It supplies "the tail on the dog." Here it gives the reason why God is about to judge the people.

וַיֹּאמֶר יְהוָה אֶל־מֹשֶׁה רֵד הַמַּחֲנֶה וְדִבַּרְתָּ אֶל־בְּנֵי־יִשְׂרָאֵל   וְיָשׁוּבוּ מִן־דַּרְכֵיהֶם הָרָעִים פֶּן־אַכֶּם
מַכָּה גְדוֹלָה

1. A-half: The first Zaqeph divides the A-half, separating the direct speech of God to Moses from God's indirect speech to Israel through Moses.
   a) Zaqeph segment: Rebia breaks the segment clausally, with Geresh providing a minor break (syntactically) within the Rebia segment and with Pashta furnishing a minor break (clausally) after the Rebia segment. The Rebia segment introduces the direct discourse.
   b) Final segment: The second Zaqeph breaks the segment clausally, with (double) Pashta supplying a minor break before Zaqeph and with Tiphcha marking the minor break after the Zaqeph. These minor divisions syntactically group the nouns and their adjectives together.

כִּי מֵהַקָּטֹן וְעַד־הַגָּדוֹל   אִתִּי מָרוּ׃

2. B-half: The Tiphcha divides the B-half syntactically and semantically by reinforcing the emphatic placement of the prepositional phrases before the object and verb.
   a) Tiphcha segment: Since the segment has three words, Tebir divides the כִּי particle from the prepositional phrase. The Tiphcha also joins the direct object to its verb.
   b) Final segment: These two words are joined by a conjunctive accent, Merecha.

G. Verse Seven

וַיֵּ֣רֶד מֹשֶׁה֙ מִן־הָהָ֔ר וּשְׁנֵ֛י לֻחֹ֥ות יהו֖ה בְּיָד֑וֹ וַיָּבֹא֙ הַֽמַּחֲנֶ֔ה וְהָעָ֥ם יֶֽחֱטָ֛א חֲטָאָ֥ה גְדוֹלָ֖ה בְּעֵינֵ֥י
יהוֽה׃

The Athnach divides the verse clausally, separating the first two clauses from the last two clauses.

וַיֵּ֣רֶד מֹשֶׁה֙ מִן־הָהָ֔ר   וּשְׁנֵ֛י לֻחֹ֥ות יהו֖ה בְּיָד֑וֹ

1. A-half: The Zaqeph divides the A-half clausally, separating the main clause from its situation clause.
   a) Zaqeph segment: Pashta divides the segment syntactically, separating the verb/subject from the prepositional phrase. Conjunctive accents often connect verbs and their subjects in verbal clauses.
   b) Final segment: Tiphcha divides the four-word segment. The three-word construct package requires a disjunctive accent, since Tiphcha may have only one conjunctive accent. The first word in the package usually gets the disjunctive, hence, the placement of the Tebir.

וַיָּבֹא֙ הַֽמַּחֲנֶ֔ה   וְהָעָ֥ם יֶֽחֱטָ֛א חֲטָאָ֥ה גְדוֹלָ֖ה בְּעֵינֵ֥י יהוֽה׃

2. B-half: The Zaqeph divides the B-half clausally, separating the main clause from its situation clause.
   a) Zaqeph segment: The Zaqeph segment is two words. Since the word with Zaqeph is long, the preceding word has a Pashta. See verse one, B-half.
   b) Final segment: Tiphcha breaks the segment syntactically, separating the prepositional phrase from the rest of the clause. Since Tiphcha's segment has four words and the break comes on the second word, Tebir furnishes the minor break.

H. Verse Eight

וַיִּֽחַר־אַ֣ף מֹשֶׁ֔ה וַיְשַׁבֵּ֛ר אֶת־שְׁנֵ֥י לֻחֹ֖ות יהו֑ה וַיֹּ֗אמֶר אַרְבָּעִ֥ים יוֹם֙ יָשַׁ֣בְתָּ֙ הַ֣ר סִינַ֔י וְעַתָּ֗ה מָרִ֙יתָ֙
אֶת־פִּ֣י יהו֔ה לְהִֽשְׁתַּחֲוֺ֗ת לַשֶּׁ֛מֶשׁ וְלַיָּרֵ֖חַ וְלַכּוֹכָבִֽים׃

The Athnach divides the verse clausally.

וַיִּֽחַר־אַ֣ף מֹשֶׁ֔ה   וַיְשַׁבֵּ֛ר אֶת־שְׁנֵ֥י לֻחֹ֖ות יהו֑ה

1. A-half: The first Zaqeph divides the A-half clausally.
   a) Zaqeph segment: Because Zaqeph's word is short and in a two-word segment, the conjunctive Munach is required before it.
   b) Final segment: Since four words occur between the Athnach and the Zaqeph Qaton, a division is required. Since the break of these four words is on the third word before the Athnach, a Zaqeph (Gadol) is required. If the break

had been on the first or second word before the Athnach, Tiphcha would have marked the break instead of the Zaqeph. The Zaqeph Gadol divides syntactically. This separates the verb from the following words and groups the next three words together since they form a construct package.

וַיֹּ֫אמֶר אַרְבָּעִים יוֹם יָשַׁבְתָּ הַר סִינַי   וְעַתָּה מָרִיתָ אֶת־פִּי יהוה לְהִשְׁתַּחֲוֹת לַשֶּׁמֶשׁ וְלַיָּרֵחַ וְלַכּוֹכָבִים׃

2. B-half: The first Zaqeph divides the B-half semantically since its placement is delayed into the direct speech where the meaning is located. The division is also clausal, but it does not divide after the first verb (clause), the most logical place because it introduces the direct speech.
   a) Zaqeph segment: The Rebia divides the segment clausally. The first Pashta is actually a transformed Rebia (Pashta cannot repeat), separating syntactically the accusative of time from the rest of the clause, since its placement is emphatic. The double Pashta divides the verb from the following construct package.
   b) Final segment: The second Zaqeph divides the segment clausally (considering the second half as an infinitival clause). Pashta furnishes a minor break before the Zaqeph. The third Zaqeph divides the clause syntactically, grouping the prepositional phrases together, with the Tiphcha supplying a foretone to the Silluq.

I. Verse Nine

אַתָּה רָשָׁע מִן־הָאֱמֹרִי שׁוּב אֶל־יהוה וְיַצִּל אֹתְךָ מִן־הַמַּגֵּפָה   וַיֹּאמֶר מֹשֶׁה מִי לַיהוָה לְכָה אֵלָי׃

The Athnach divides the verse clausally.

אַתָּה רָשָׁע מִן־הָאֱמֹרִי   שׁוּב אֶל־יהוה וְיַצִּל אֹתְךָ מִן־הַמַּגֵּפָה

1. A-half: The first Zaqeph divides the A-half clausally and semantically. The Zaqeph segment relates the condition of the people; the last segment commands the people what they should do because of their condition.
   a) Zaqeph segment: Pashta divides the segment syntactically before the prepositional phrase.
   b) Last segment: The second Zaqeph breaks the last segment clausally. Since Zaqeph's word is long and its segment has only two words, the preceding word has Pashta. The Tiphcha divides the words after the Zaqeph syntactically.

וַיֹּאמֶר מֹשֶׁה   מִי לַיהוָה לְכָה אֵלָי׃

2. B-half: The Zaqeph divides the B-half clausally. Since the direct speech is brief, the introductory words mark the break.
   a) Zaqeph segment: Zaqeph's segment has a Munach since Zaqeph's word is short.
   b) Final segment: Tiphcha divides the final segment clausally.

J. Verse Ten

וַתְּבֹאֶינָה אֶל־הַמַּחֲנֶה חַיּוֹת רָעוֹת   וַתַּהֲרֹגְנָה אֶת־הַחֹטְאִים לַיהוה וּלְמֹשֶׁה כַּאֲשֶׁר יַהֲרֹג הָאֲרִי וְיֹאכֵל׃

The Athnach divides the verse clausally.

וַתְּבֹאֶינָה אֶל־הַמַּחֲנֶה   חַיּוֹת רָעוֹת

1. A-half: Because of the exceptional word order of the subject after the verb and prepositional phrase, the Tiphcha marks the break before the subject. This delays and highlights the subject. Tiphcha's break, therefore, is both syntactical and semantic. If the word order were normal, verb-subject-prepositional phrase, the Tiphcha before the prepositional phrase would be simply syntactical.

וַתַּהֲרֹגְנָה אֶת־הַחֹטְאִים לַיהוה וּלְמֹשֶׁה   כַּאֲשֶׁר יַהֲרֹג הָאֲרִי וְיֹאכֵל׃

2. B-half: The Zaqeph divides the B-half clausally.
   a) Zaqeph segment: In Zaqeph's segment, the Pashta furnishes the break, since the break is next to the word with Zaqeph. This allows the participle and the prepositional phrase to join together. It also gives some emphasis to "and to Moses" since words connected by Vav are often joined. The Geresh is a minor break under the governance of the Pashta. This also links the participle to the prepositional phrase.
   b) Last segment: The Tiphcha divides clausally. The Tebir is necessary since Tiphcha's segment has the three words.

K. Verse Eleven

וֵאלֹהֵי זָהָב אֲשֶׁר עָשָׂה אַהֲרֹן שִׁבְּרָם מֹשֶׁה   וַיַּשְׁקְ אֶת־בְּנֵי־יִשְׂרָאֵל׃

The Athnach breaks the verse clausally.

וֵאלֹהֵי זָהָב אֲשֶׁר עָשָׂה אַהֲרֹן   שִׁבְּרָם מֹשֶׁה

1. A-half: The Tiphcha breaks the A-half syntactically and semantically, setting off the Casus Pendens and its relative clause from the rest of the clause. The accents for the relative clause resemble the pattern of parenthesis for the accents, starting after the Rebia, the remote subordinate, and ending at its governing accent Tiphcha – "and the gods of gold (which Aaron made) Moses smashed them."
   a) Tiphcha segment: The Rebia is the main break within the segment. Tebir marks a minor break because of the three-word segment from the Tiphcha to the Rebia.
   b) Final segment: The Munach joins the words of the final segment.

וַיַּשְׁקְ   אֶת־בְּנֵי־יִשְׂרָאֵל׃

2. B-half: In this two-word segment, the Tiphcha is required.

L. Verse Twelve

וַיְהִ֞י אַחַ֣ר הַדְּבָרִ֣ים הָאֵ֗לֶּה וַיֵּ֥בְךְּ הָעָ֖ם לִפְנֵ֣י־יְהוָ֑ה וּמֹשֶׁ֨ה בָּ֜א אֹ֣הֶל מוֹעֵ֗ד וַיֹּ֧אמֶר יהו֙ה אֶל־מֹשֶׁ֔ה
מִ֥י יִתֵּ֛ן לָעָ֥ם הַזֶּ֖ה לֵ֥ב שָׁמְעֵֽנִי׃

The Athnach divides the verse clausally.

וַיְהִ֞י אַחַ֣ר הַדְּבָרִ֣ים הָאֵ֗לֶּה וַיֵּ֥בְךְּ הָעָ֖ם לִפְנֵ֣י־יְהוָ֑ה

1. A-half: The Zaqeph divides the segment clausally.
   a) Zaqeph segment: The Rebia breaks the segment syntactically, thereby grouping the next three words after the Rebia. The Pashta provides a minor break for the three-word grouping between Zaqeph and Rebia.
   b) Last segment: The Tiphcha breaks the segment syntactically before the prepositional phrase.

וּמֹשֶׁ֨ה בָּ֜א אֹ֣הֶל מוֹעֵ֗ד וַיֹּ֧אמֶר יהו֙ה אֶל־מֹשֶׁ֔ה מִ֥י יִתֵּ֛ן לָעָ֥ם הַזֶּ֖ה לֵ֥ב שָׁמְעֵֽנִי׃

2. B-half: The first Zaqeph divides the B-half.
   a) Zaqeph segment: Pashta divides the verb (announcement) from the accusative of place, a two-word construct package.
   b) Last segment: The second Zaqeph divides the segment, separating the introductory words from the direct speech. The Pashta divides the words before the Zaqeph, separating the prepositional phrase from the verb/subject. Tiphcha divides the words after the Zaqeph, separating the infinitive clause from the preceding words. Within Tiphcha's segment, Tebir is the main break, with Gershaim supplying a minor break under the governance of Tebir, since Tebir's segment has four words.

M. Verse Thirteen

יָצ֜וֹא אֶל־הָעָ֗ם וְאָמַ֣רְתָּ אֵלָ֔יו אַל־תִּבְכֶּ֑ה עֲלֵ֖ה רֵ֣שׁ אֶת־הָאָ֑רֶץ רַ֚ק שְׁמַ֣ע בְּקֹלִ֔י לְמַ֙עַן֙ תַּאֲרִ֣יךְ
יָמֶ֔יךָ עַל־הָאֲדָמָֽה׃

The Athnach divides the verse clausally.

יָצ֜וֹא אֶל־הָעָ֗ם וְאָמַ֣רְתָּ אֵלָ֔יו אַל־תִּבְכֶּ֑ה עֲלֵ֖ה רֵ֣שׁ אֶת־הָאָ֑רֶץ

1. A-half: Zaqeph divides the A-half semantically. The most logical location would be the preceding words with the Pashta which introduce the direct speech, but the break is delayed to mark the meaning in the direct speech.
   a) Zaqeph segment: Pashta breaks the segment (the most logical placement for the A-half). Within Pashta's four-word segment, Geresh separates the segment clausally.
   b) Last segment: Tiphcha separates the last segment clausally.

רַק שְׁמַע בְּקֹלִי   לְמַעַן תַּאֲרִיךְ יָמֶיךָ עַל־הָאֲדָמָה׃

2. B-half: Zaqeph breaks the B-half clausally.
   a) Zaqeph segment: Yetib, the substitute for Pashta when the word is accented on the first letter, divides the segment.
   b) Last segment: Tiphcha breaks the segment syntactically before the prepositional phrase, Tebir supplying the minor break within the Tiphcha segment.

N. Verse Fourteen

וַיָּקוּמוּ הָעָם   וַיִּסְעוּ מִן־הַר סִינָי׃

In this small verse, the Zaqeph divides clausally.

וַיָּקוּמוּ הָעָם

1. A-half: Because Zaqeph's word is short and its segment is only two words, Munach is required on the word before Zaqeph.

וַיִּסְעוּ   מִן־הַר סִינָי׃

2. B-half: Tiphcha breaks the B-half syntactically, separating the verb from the prepositional phrase.

Commentary on the Accents of Psalm 1

A. Verse One

אַשְׁרֵי־הָאִישׁ אֲשֶׁר ׀ לֹא הָלַךְ בַּעֲצַת רְשָׁעִים   וּבְדֶרֶךְ חַטָּאִים לֹא עָמָד וּבְמוֹשַׁב לֵצִים לֹא יָשָׁב׃

The Ole Veyored breaks the verse clausally, highlighting the parallelism. When the main break occurs further than the fifth word from the word with Silluq, Ole Veyored is required. Athnach, which in some form appears in every verse, must occur no further than the fifth word from the word with Silluq. This verse has three parallel lines. The first parallel line is set off by the Ole Veyored, grouping the next two parallel lines together. The first half gives the main or general idea; the second half complements, details, explains, or corresponds to the first half in some manner.

אַשְׁרֵי־הָאִישׁ   אֲשֶׁר ׀ לֹא הָלַךְ בַּעֲצַת רְשָׁעִים

1. A-half: The Great Rebia breaks the A-half, separating the first two words from the following five words, a relative clause.
   a) Rebia segment: This segment has two words, joined by a conjunctive accent.
   b) Final segment: The Sinnor breaks the five words of the final segment. Sinnor's segment now has more than two words (three); therefore, Legarmeh separates the relative particle from the verb and its negative.

וּבְדֶ֣רֶךְ חַ֭טָּאִים לֹ֣א עָמָ֑ד   וּבְמוֹשַׁ֥ב לֵ֝צִ֗ים לֹ֣א יָשָֽׁב׃

2. B-half: The Athnach divides the B-half. Since Ole Veyored occurs in the verse, Athnach is the remote subordinate to Silluq, functioning similar to Zaqeph in the prose accents.
   a) Athnach segment: Since Athnach's segment has four words and since the break occurs on the second word from the Athnach, Dechi divides the segment. If the break had occurred on the third word from the Athnach, then Great Rebia would have occurred. If the break had occurred on the first word from the Athnach, then the Dechi would have transformed into a conjunctive accent (Munach), since Athnach's word is short.
   b) Final Segment: Since the final segment has four words, Rebia-Mugrash separates syntactically the prepositional phrase from the verb and its negative.

B. Verse Two

כִּ֤י אִ֥ם בְּתוֹרַ֥ת יְהוָ֗ה חֶ֫פְצ֥וֹ   וּֽבְתוֹרָת֥וֹ יֶהְגֶּ֗ה יוֹמָ֥ם וָלָֽיְלָה׃

The Ole Veyored divides the verse clausally, highlighting the parallelism. The Ole Veyored rarely occurs on the fourth word from the word with Silluq, as here. The Ole Veyored cannot occur any closer to the word with Silluq.

כִּ֤י אִ֥ם בְּתוֹרַ֥ת יְהוָ֗ה   חֶ֫פְצ֥וֹ

1. A-half: The Little Rebia divides the A-half since the break is on the word before the word with Ole Veyored. If the break had occurred on the second word, Sinnor would have been used, as in Ps 3:3. If the break had occurred on the third word or further, Great Rebia would have been used, as in Ps 1:1.
   a) Little Rebia segment: Leningrad Codex and Aleppo Codex differ in their reading on the word אִם – Leningrad has Tarcha; Aleppo, Merecha. Either reading should be understood as a substitute for a Maqqeph. Mehuppach, functioning as a transformed Legarmeh, separates the כִּי particle from the rest of the segment. This groups the אִם particle with the following construct package.
   b) Final segment: The final segment is the word with the Ole Veyored.

וּֽבְתוֹרָת֥וֹ יֶהְגֶּ֗ה   יוֹמָ֥ם וָלָֽיְלָה׃

2. B-half: The transformed Athnach divides the clause syntactically.
   a) Transformed Athnach segment: Since every verse must have an Athnach and since an Athnach does not appear after the Ole Veyored, the Rebia-Mugrash, written defectively as Rebia, is a transformed Athnach.
   b) Final Segment: The last two words are joined by a conjunctive accent (Merecha).

C. Verse Three

וְהָיָה כְּעֵץ שָׁתוּל עַל־פַּלְגֵי מָיִם   אֲשֶׁר פִּרְיוֹ ׀ יִתֵּן בְּעִתּוֹ וְעָלֵהוּ לֹא־יִבּוֹל וְכֹל אֲשֶׁר־יַעֲשֶׂה
יַצְלִיחַ׃

The Ole Veyored divides the verse clausally and semantically. The Ole Veyored extends over two words, when the accent is on the first syllable of the second word (and a shewa does not begin the word. Also, the last syllable on the first word must be considered unaccented with an implied Maqqeph). This brings together the two words, similar to words joined by Maqqeph. The position of the Ole Veyored is important for interpretation (semantics), since it indicates whether the last two clauses of the verse refer to the blessed man of verse one or the planted tree of verse two. Ole Veyored's position indicates that the last two clauses refer to the planted tree ("and all that *it* does prospers"). If the Ole Veyored were located at the position of the Athnach, then the last words might refer to the blessed man ("and all that *he* does prospers").

וְהָיָה   כְּעֵץ שָׁתוּל עַל־פַּלְגֵי מָיִם

1. A-half: Since the break in this segment occurs on the third word from the Ole Veyored, Great Rebia is required.
   a) Great Rebia segment: The Great Rebia separates the segment clausally.
   b) Final segment: Since three words occur in the final segment and the second word receives the break, Sinnor separates the first word from the next two words (the Ole Veyored words are considered one word). The Sinnor also groups the participle and the following prepositional phrase together.

אֲשֶׁר פִּרְיוֹ ׀ יִתֵּן בְּעִתּוֹ וְעָלֵהוּ לֹא־יִבּוֹל   וְכֹל אֲשֶׁר־יַעֲשֶׂה יַצְלִיחַ׃

2. B-half: The Athnach divides the half verse clausally.
   a) Athnach segment: Great Rebia divides the segment clausally and semantically by highlighting the parallelism in Athnach's segment. Great Rebia, Athnach remote subordinate, occasionally occurs on the second word before the Athnach instead of Dechi, Athnach's near subordinate. This may happen when the word with Athnach or the word before it is long and when the Great Rebia would provide a stronger break than Dechi. In the prose accents, the remote subordinate accent cannot usurp the near subordinate. In the poetic books, however, the remote subordinate may supplant the near subordinate, furnishing a more definitive break syntactically, clausally, or semantically (WW I, p. 59). Since Rebia's segment has four words, Legarmeh furnishes the break.
   b) Final Segment: Since three words remain in the final segment, Rebia-Mugrash, should occur on the next-to-last word between the clauses. But since Silluq's word is short, the Rebia-Mugrash transforms into a conjunctive accent, Munach. The Munach, the transformed Rebia-Mugrash, is chanted conjunctively, but is analyzed disjunctively.

D. Verse Four

לֹא־כֵ֥ן הָרְשָׁעִ֑ים   כִּ֥י אִם־כַּ֝מֹּ֗ץ אֲשֶׁר־תִּדְּפֶ֥נּוּ רֽוּחַ׃

The Athnach divides the verse clausally. This verse supplies an antithesis to the preceding verse. The parallelism between the verses is faint.

לֹא־כֵ֥ן הָרְשָׁעִ֑ים

1. A-half: In this two-word segment, a Merecha joins the words. In the prose accents, when the Athnach segment has only two words, Tiphcha is required on the first word. Poetical accents are more flexible than the prose accents on this point by allowing a conjunctive accent.

כִּ֥י אִם־כַּ֝מֹּ֗ץ   אֲשֶׁר־תִּדְּפֶ֥נּוּ רֽוּחַ׃

2. B-half: Since the final segment has four words, Rebia-Mugrash supplies the break, separating the antecedent from its relative clause.

E. Verse Five

עַל־כֵּ֤ן ׀ לֹא־יָקֻ֣מוּ רְ֭שָׁעִים בַּמִּשְׁפָּ֑ט   וְ֝חַטָּאִ֗ים בַּעֲדַ֥ת צַדִּיקִֽים׃

The Athnach divides the verse clausally, highlighting the partial parallelism.

עַל־כֵּ֤ן ׀ לֹא־יָקֻ֣מוּ רְ֭שָׁעִים   בַּמִּשְׁפָּ֑ט

1. A-half: Dechi breaks the A-half at the prepositional phrase, as expected in a verbal clause. Dechi appears since Athnach's word is long. If Athnach's word were short, the Dechi would transform into Munach.
   a) Dechi segment: The Dechi segment has three words; therefore, Legarmeh divides the initial particle from the verb and its subject. Legarmeh's division groups the verb and its subject together.
   b) Final segment: The final segment is the word with Athnach.

וְ֝חַטָּאִ֗ים   בַּעֲדַ֥ת צַדִּיקִֽים׃

2. B-half: Since the B-half has three words, Rebia-Mugrash separates the first word from the final two words, thus joining the construct package tightly together.

F. Verse Six

כִּֽי־יוֹדֵ֣עַ יְ֭הוָה דֶּ֣רֶךְ צַדִּיקִ֑ים   וְדֶ֖רֶךְ רְשָׁעִ֣ים תֹּאבֵֽד׃

The Athnach divides the verse clausally, highlighting the partial parallelism.

כִּֽי־יוֹדֵ֣עַ יְ֭הוָה   דֶּ֣רֶךְ צַדִּיקִ֑ים

1. A-half: The Dechi supplies the break on the second word. Had the break been on the first word of the verse, Great Rebia would have been used, with Dechi marking a minor break since three word would be left between the Great Rebia and the Athnach.

וְדֶ֖רֶךְ רְשָׁעִ֣ים   תֹּאבֵֽד׃

2. B-half: Since the B-half has three words, a Rebia-Mugrash should appear. Rebia-Mugrash, however, cannot occur since Silluq's word is short and the break is needed on the next-to-last word. The Rebia-Mugrash, therefore, is transformed in a conjunctive accent (Munach). If the Rebia-Mugrash occurred on the second word before the word with Silluq, then Rebia-Mugrash would appear without transformation, such as in the preceding verse.

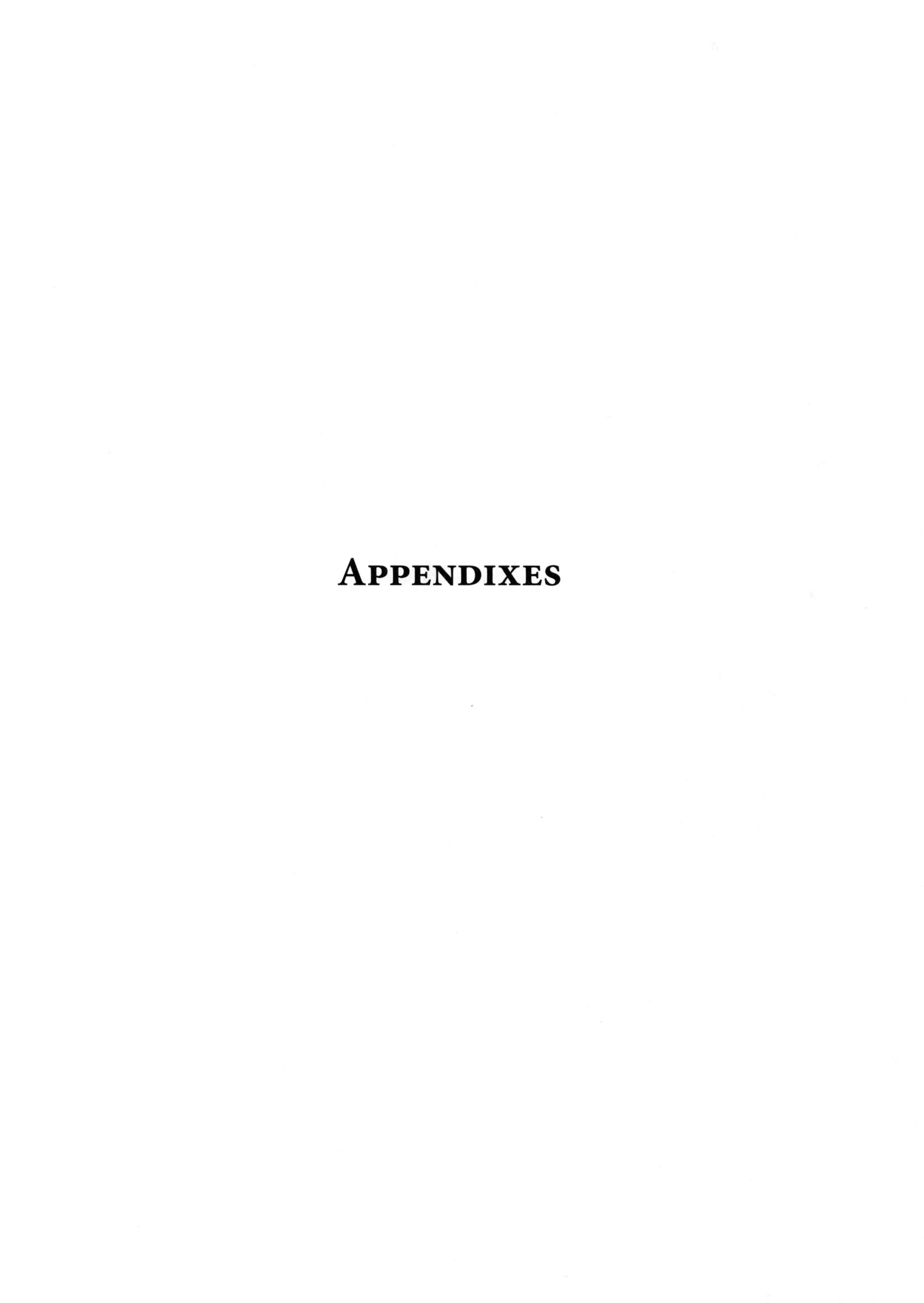

APPENDIXES

GLOSSARY TO SYNTAX

The words in small caps after an entry is a cross reference to a related entry.

ABSOLUTE IDENTIFICATION: Absolute identification implies that the subject is exclusively and completely identified as, identical to, or equated with the predicate or with its antecedent. The subject and its predicate, therefore, are interchangeable, as in Greek when both subject and predicate have the article – "The Spirit is the One making alive, or the One making alive is the Spirit." Absolute identification also applies to substitution apposition. SUBSTITUTION APPOSITION

ABSOLUTE NEGATION: Absolute negation emphasizes the universality of the negative – a negative without exceptions. Absolute negation is formed by כֹּל with a noun (usually indeterminate) preceded or followed by לֹא. אִישׁ may substitute for כֹּל. אֵין may substitute for לֹא in nominal clauses. CATEGORIC NEGATION

ABSOLUTE OBJECT: Absolute objects are infinitive absolutes or abstract nouns expressing verbal actions or states having the same root letters as their governing verb (שָׂמַח שִׂמְחָה גְדוֹלָה "he rejoiced a rejoicing," קָטוֹל קָטַל "Killing he killed"). This object is called absolute because the verb is not restricted by the person or thing (accusative of direct object) to whom the action is done, nor is it restricted in the time, place, manner, or specification (adverbial accusatives) in which or by which the action is done, but *the object is the verbal action itself*. DIRECT OBJECT, ADVERBIAL OBJECT

ACCUSATIVE: The accusative case is the case for objects of verbs and for adverbial expressions.

ACCUSATIVE OF SITUATION: The accusative of situation, a type of adverbial accusative and usually a descriptive noun, describes the situation, condition, or status of a noun. Accusatives of situation are divided into illustrating or strengthening and permanent or temporary. SITUATION CLAUSE, DESCRIPTIVE NOUN, PRIMARY NOUN

ACCUSATIVE OF SPECIFICATION: The accusative of specification, usually a primary noun, specifies the field of application for another noun when the specification clarifies the entire nature or essence of something. The accusative of specification also specifies the field of application by clarifying an attribute of a subject and its verb (or predicate) or by clarifying an attribute of a verb and its object. Finally, an accusative of specification specifies the field of application for impersonal passive verbs.

ADVERBIAL ACCUSATIVE: The adverbial object (accusative) limits its verb, subject, or object, adverbially. Since it does not receive the action of the verb directly, the adverbial accusative is also called the indirect accusative. There are five types of adverbial accusatives: time, place, situation, specification, purpose. ABSOLUTE OBJECT, DIRECT OBJECT

ADVERBIAL CLAUSE: A third category of clauses along with verbal and nominal clauses, the adverbial clause usually expresses time and place with the adverbial word(s) or a prepositional phrase occurring as the announcement. These clauses have definite initiators (subjects). See §11a, footnote 1. Some authorities view these as a variant of the nominal clause.

AGENT: The subject of a verbal clause. VERB, VERBAL CLAUSE

ANNEXATION: The construct package is called annexation because the governing noun is annexed or attached to another noun (in the genitive). Annexation occurs when a noun is attached to another noun, when a noun is attached to a pronominal suffix, or when a preposition is attached to a noun. IMPROPER ANNEXATION, PROPER ANNEXATION

ANNOUNCEMENT: The predicate of a nominal clause. NOMINAL CLAUSE, INITIATOR

ASPECT: Aspect is the manner of the verbal action, as conceived or portrayed by the author. For Hebrew the perfect represents the manner of action as completed (and, therefore, finished and done); the imperfect represents the manner of action as incomplete (and, therefore, in progress, about to begin, or just begun). TENSE

CATEGORIC NEGATION: Categoric negation absolutely negates the category or group. In categoric negation an indefinite noun, the category or group, is negated by אַיִן or לֹא. This negation, similar to absolute negation but without the כֹּל, emphasizes the universality of the negation, a negation without exception. ABSOLUTE NEGATION

CAUSATIVE: This is the characteristic usage of the Hiphil and Hophal verbal stems. Causatives usually add the nuance of causation to verbs in the Qal. For example, the Qal verb יצא "to go out" when conjugated in the Hiphil conveys "to cause (someone or something) to go out." Many intransitive verbs in the Qal take a single direct object in the Hiphil. Many transitive verbs in the Qal take two direct objects in the Hiphil.

COHORTATIVE: The cohortative, "exhorting together" (let us . . .), is an energic form expressing exhortation or fixed determination, often communicating the self interest of the speaker.

CONJUNCTIVE (APPOSITION): Conjunctive apposition links two or more words of the same case or of the same part of speech by the particles: וְ/וּ, אוֹ, לֹא, and כִּי.

CORROBORATIVE (APPOSITION): A type of apposition, the corroborative strengthens or emphasizes its noun by confirming or establishing its noun because of the fear of forgetfulness, inattentiveness, or lack of concern. The corroborative is divided into verbal or conceptual.

DECLARATIVE: Declarative intensives/extensives and causatives declare or consider someone or something to the verbal notion. For example, the declarative Piel of the verb ברך means "to declare or consider someone or something blessed."

DEFINITE NOUN: A definite noun is a *known* person or thing that is part of the whole (genus), one or some individuals or things being meant rather than other individuals or things. INDEFINITE NOUN, SPECIALIZED NOUN

DENOMINATIVE VERBS: Denominative verbs are derived from nouns. These usually occur in intensives/extensives and causatives verbs. For example, "to phone (someone)" is a denominative in English.

DESCRIPTIVE NOUN: The opposite of a primary noun, a descriptive noun is an adjective, participle, or some nouns with the intensive/extensive formation. PRIMARY NOUN, SEMI-DESCRIPTIVE NOUN

DIRECT OBJECT: The object is direct when the verbal action of the agent goes directly to the object. ADVERBIAL OBJECT, ABSOLUTE OBJECT

ENERGIC VAV: To be distinguished from a connecting Vav, which simply connects two parts of speech, the energic Vav adds more meaning (energy) to the Vav – "so that," "in order that," "then." Used with a perfect, the energic Vav often "converts" the perfect into the usages of the imperfect. With the imperfect, the energic Vav often "converts" the imperfect into a preterit verb or a purpose clause.

EXPLICATIVE APPOSITION: The explicative apposition *explains* its noun by clarifying or identifying it. The antecedent noun of an explicative apposition is a general term; its explicative apposition is a specific term – "the servant of the Lord, Moses." SUBSTITUTION APPOSITION.

EXTENSIVE PLURAL: The extensive plural extends something over an area/surface (for place) or time (for time). INTENSIVE PLURAL

FACTITIVE: From a Latin word meaning "to make," a factitive (Piel) puts someone or something into the state expressed by a Qal verb. This is common with stative verbs. For example, the Qal of the verb כָּבֵד (to be heavy) when used in the Piel is a factitive verb meaning "to make heavy" (honor) or "to put into a heavy state."

FREQUENTATIVE: Frequentative action describes the action as occurring *frequently*. It is also called repeated or iterative action.

FUTURE PERFECT: A future perfect is an action in the future that precedes another future action – "The boy will have gone to the store before the store closes."

GENITIVE: The genitive case is the case for the packaging of nouns to modify or to limit one noun by another noun. In a two-word construct package or annexation, the second word is in the genitive. A pronominal suffix is in the genitive when it is attached to a noun. Clauses also can be in the place of a genitive after words in the construct state.

GENITIVE OF SPECIFICATION: In improper annexations, the genitive specifies the field of application for its governing noun, which must be an adjective or an intransitive participle – "beautiful (specified in the field of application of the) face."

GENTILIC NOUN: A gentilic noun is a noun that refers to nationality – Egyptian, Israelite – usually formed by adding a Nisbah ending to a noun indicating a nation, e.g., יִשְׂרְאֵלִי. NISBAH ENDING, SEMI-DESCRIPTIVE NOUN

GREEK PERFECT: A Greek perfect expresses a completed action in the past with continuing results or effects in the present – "The boy has gone to the store (and he is still gone)." For Hebrew, the perfect may express a Greek perfect usually in poetry and direct speech.

IMPERATIVE: The imperative is a verbal mood expressing command, strong request, or exhortation.

IMPERFECT: The imperfect, "not thoroughly done," describes the verbal aspect, in the Yiqtol form. For tense, an author or speaker uses the imperfect when the verbal action occurs during or after the time of enunciation or narration. For aspect, an author or speaker uses the imperfect to depict verbal action as in process, ongoing in some manner, not yet started, or about to start.

IMPROPER ANNEXATION: Improper annexation occurs when the last word of the annexation (construct package) does not limit or identify its governing word (the annexation, therefore, does not form one unit of meaning), but the last word of the announcement is the object of the first word or the last word of the announcement specifies (genitive of specification) the first word – "a doer of righteousness (he who does righteousness)" or "beautiful (specifically in terms of) face."

IMPROPER OBJECT: An improper object occurs when a preposition with its genitive stands in the place of an accusative that receives the action of the verb directly (a direct object). Compare English, "I know of him," where "know of" has become the verb. Similarly, in Hebrew, to convey "to trust" is בטח with ב preposition taking the (direct or improper) object.

INDEFINITE NOUN: An indefinite noun is defined as every thing common to its (whole) genus, and not any of its individuals being meant rather than another. SPECIALIZED NOUN, DEFINITE NOUN

INDICATIVE MOOD: The indicative ("indicates") is one of the five verbal moods of Hebrew, expressing a statement as fact or reality – "the boy went to the store."

INFINITIVE: Meaning "without limits" (of person, number, and gender of the finite verb), infinitives are abstract verbal nouns – "dreaming," but not "dreamer"; "teaching," but not "teacher." PARTICIPLE

INITIATOR: The initiator is the subject of a nominal clause. ANNOUNCEMENT, NOMINAL CLAUSE

INNER CAUSATIVE: The inner causative is a usage of the Hiphil when the subject of the verb is also the object, so that the object is contained *within* the verb. The Qal of these inner causative verbs are usually stative and/or intransitive.

INTENSIVE/EXTENSIVE: This is the characteristic usage, but not necessarily the most common usage, of the Piel, Pual, and Hithpael verbal stems. Intensive action refers to an action done with great force or energy. Extensive action refers to an action extending (and, therefore, repeating the action) to many subjects or, more commonly, to many objects. Extensive action often occurs without intensification, but intensive action usually occurs with the extension of the action. Intensive/extensive action, therefore, is "busying oneself eagerly in an action" or "constant, firm action." Although not increasing the force of an action, extensive action is type or subset of intensive action.

INTENSIVE PLURAL: An intensive plural is a plural that amplifies and/or intensifies a noun or adjective. Intensive plural nouns are often abstract nouns and names of natural objects found in poetry and direct speech. For abstract noun, the intensive plural often has the idea of "having all kinds and every kind of something" – "the perfection of that something." For example, for the intensive plural "holy," it means "all and every kind of holiness" – "the perfection of holiness." EXTENSIVE PLURAL

JUSSIVE MOOD: The jussive, from the Latin word meaning "command," expresses a wish or desire – "Let the boy go to the store."

LOGICAL SUCCESSION: An action following or succeeding another action logically – "The store was closed, so the boy came home."

MOOD: Mood refers to an author's attitude or opinion toward the factuality or likelihood of an action or condition. Hebrew has four moods: indicative (expressing fact), subjunctive (expressing purpose, or intent), jussive (expressing wish or command), and imperative (expressing wish or command). The Preterit, a tense similar in form to the jussive, is an indicative.

NISBAH ENDING: Nisbah is an Arabic word meaning "pertaining to" or "in relation to." The Nisbah ending on a noun in Hebrew is a Hireq-Yod. This makes a noun a semi-descriptive noun. SEMI-DESCRIPTIVE NOUN, GENTILIC NOUN

NOMINAL CLAUSE: A nominal clause occurs when a clause does not have a finite verb (perfect, imperfect, or imperative) or when an initiator (subject) precedes a finite verb. VERBAL CLAUSE, INITIATOR, ANNOUNCEMENT

NOMINATIVE: The nominative case is the case for almost all subjects (agents and initiators) and for predicates in clauses without finite verbs.

NOUN: A noun is a word (person, place, or thing) with inherent meaning, but not with tense/aspect. VERB, PARTICLE

NOUNS OF RELATION: Nouns of relation are annexations with the governing nouns אִישׁ, בַּעַל, or בֵּן (or their plurals or their feminine forms) and their genitives that express a quality, characteristic, or class. ANNEXATION

Numerable: A numerable is the thing counted by a number – "three men," the word "men" is the numerable, the thing counted.

Participle: Participles, so-called because they participate in or partake of the verb and adjective, are *concrete* verbal nouns, more precisely, verbal adjectives, indicating the person or thing described by the verbal idea inherent in the participle – "one who dreams," "a dreamer"; "one who teaches," "a teacher." Infinitive

Particle: A word without inherent meaning and without tense/aspect, the particle's meaning is dependent upon context. Noun, Verb

Past Perfect: A verbal tense indicating a past action that precedes another action in the past or an action completed in the past with continuing results in the past – "the boy *had gone* to the store."

Perfect: The perfect, "thoroughly done," describing the verbal aspect, is the Qatal form. For tense, an author or speaker uses the perfect when the verbal action occurred before (and occasionally at) the time of enunciation or narration. For aspect, an author or speaker uses the perfect to present verbal action as done, finished, or completed.

Perfect of certitude: The perfect of certitude expresses an action in the present as completed, and therefore, with certainty or strong confidence – "I trust in the Lord." The perfect of certitude is usually found with verbs of the mind (know, hope, wait, trust, despise, choose, remember, love, hate, etc.), being in first person and in direct speech or poetry.

Preterit: A simple past tense verb with completed aspect.

Primary noun: Primary nouns are common nouns, such as king, son, tree, etc. Primary nouns exclude adjectives, participles, or a noun functioning as a superlative, all which are descriptive nouns. Descriptive noun

Proper annexation: Proper annexation occurs when the last word of the annexation (construct package) modifies the first word in some manner – "the man of God, that is, the godly man." In proper annexation, the meaning or relationship between the genitive and its governing noun may be understood by inserting one of three prepositions between them: ב, מִן, or לְ.

Prophetic perfect: Prophets often depict future events as an already completed by employing the perfect. This furnishes a certainty to a prophecy, similar to a perfect of certitude.

Protective Nun: A protective Nun protects a grammatical form from confusion. For example, the first common singular suffix form נִי has a protective Nun to avoid confusion with other grammatical forms.

Qualifier (apposition): A type of apposition, a qualifier is a descriptive or semi-descriptive noun that modifies another noun.

RECIPROCAL: The action is reciprocated by two or more individuals or groups.

REFLEXIVE: Reflexive action often expresses the result, state, or effect for the object of an active verb – נִחֲמוֹ וַיִּתְנַחֵם, He comforted him and so he got himself comforted (compare Gen 37:35). The action of the active verb (he comforted) affects the object (him). The result of this affect on the object is expressed by the reflexive verb. In reflexive action, the agent or agency is irrelevant, being neither implied or assumed. Reflexive action may express the personal interest of the subject.

RETROSPECTIVE PRONOUN AND ADVERB: Retrospective pronoun and adverbs occur in relative clauses to define the role (nominative, genitive, or accusative) of antecedent within the relative clause. If, however, the relationship between the relative clause and its antecedent is clear, the retrospective pronoun and adverb could be omitted, though implied. Retrospective pronouns also occur in situation clauses, often linking the situation clause to a word in its main clause.

SEMI-DESCRIPTIVE NOUN: Semi-descriptive nouns, in contrast to descriptive nouns, functions like an adjective in certain contexts. GENTILIC NOUN, DESCRIPTIVE NOUN

SEPARATING PRONOUN: A separating pronoun is an independent pronoun that separates between an initiator and its announcement. A similar construction has the pronoun after the initiator and its announcement.

SITUATION CLAUSE: Similar to the accusative of situation, the situation clause is an adverbial dependent clause that describes the situation, condition, or status of a noun in its independent clause. ACCUSATIVE OF SITUATION, VAV OF SITUATION

SPECIALIZATION, SPECIALIZE: Specialization limits a noun without making it definite. For example, an indefinite adjective may specialize an indefinite noun, and an indefinite genitive may specialize an indefinite governing noun.

SPECIALIZED NOUN: A specialized noun is a type of indefinite noun, an *unknown* person or thing that is part of the whole (genus), one or some individuals or things being meant rather than other individuals or things. In the sentence, "He saw a man, but the man did not see him," the indefinite, "a man," is regarded as grammatically *unknown* since previously unmentioned; the definite, "the man," is regarded now as grammatically *known* since mentioned earlier. INDEFINITE NOUN, DEFINITE NOUN

SPECIFICATION: Specification occurs when a noun (usually in the genitive or the accusative) conveys the field of application for another noun or verb. ACCUSATIVE OF SPECIFICATION, GENITIVE OF SPECIFICATION

STATIVE VERB: Originally, stative verbs are adjectives converted into verbs. They are often translated into English present tense verbs, though context determines the proper tense.

SUBJUNCTIVE MOOD: The subjunctive ("join under") mood is a contingent, hypothetical, or subordinate statement, joined under another statement. *He should (would, could, may, ought to) walk* is a subjunctive statement that is hypothetical statement of what should, but not necessarily will, happen. For Hebrew, the subjunctive mood is restricted to purpose/result clauses in the imperfect – "in order that the boy might go to the store."

SUBSTANTIVAL CLAUSE: A substantival clause is a clause functioning in the place of a noun as a nominative, genitive, or accusative.

SUBSTANTIVE: A substantive is a noun. Also any part of speech or clause functioning as a noun is a substantive. For example, a clause functioning as a direct object is a substantival use of the clause. English uses the plural adjective substantivally, "Only the *dead* have seen the end of war."

SUBSTITUTION APPOSITION: Substitution apposition substitutes for its antecedent noun, having an exclusive or unique relationship with its antecedent noun, often like a title, position, or relationship. The substitution, therefore, repeats (emphasizes) its noun, similar to a corroborative. The substitution apposition is often the general word; its antecedent noun, the specific word, but sometimes a word may simply be substituted for another word – "the righteous paths, the paths of God." EXPLICATIVE APPOSITION.

TEMPORAL SUCCESSION: An action following or succeeding another action in time – "The boy came to the house, and then he went to the store."

TENSE: Tense, a distinguishing characteristic of the verb, is simply time: past, present, and future. ASPECT

VAV-CONSECUTIVE: The Vav-consecutive is a perfect or imperfect with Vav, Vᵊqatal or Vayyiqtol, that expresses sequence or succession. The sequence or succession is usually temporal or logical.

VAV OF SITUATION: The Vav of situation is a conjunctive Vav connected to a noun, pronoun, or particle that introduces a situation clause. SITUATION CLAUSE

VERB: Having inherent meaning and tense/aspect, the verb (perfect, imperfect, or imperative) is the predicate of a verbal clause. NOUN, PARTICLE

VERBAL CLAUSE: A verbal clause consists of a finite verb (perfect, imperfect, or imperative) followed by a subject (agent). A verbal clause may also function as an announcement (predicate) to an initiator of a nominal clause.

VERBAL NOUN: Verbal nouns are nouns related to verbs. The verbal nouns are the infinitive absolute, the infinitive construct, and the participle.

KEY TO EXERCISES: DRILLS

Chapter 1. Hebrew Verbal System

1. Analyze the tense and usage (e.g. present, certitude) of the following perfects. The verses follow the numbering of the Masoretic Text. Context is the main factor for deciding the tense and usage. Other important factors include the meaning of the verb and the type of verb, for example, stative or a standard verb. For this chapter compare the renderings of the Septuagint (LXX), Vulgate, and Targums for their understandings of these examples.
    1) "Is dead," tense: present; usage: stative. Stative verbs often express the present tense. An English perfect tense (has died) is also possible since the action occurred in the past with *present* relevance.
    2) "Come," tense: future; usage: certitude/prophetic; "passed," future, certitude/prophetic. The context of the passage is future/prophetic; therefore, these perfects, with their completed action, express certain action in the future.
    3) "Says," tense: present; usage: completed action in the past with continuing results in the present, similar to a Greek perfect.
    4) "Dwelled," tense: past; usage: simple past. This is the simple, default tense and usage of the Perfect.
    5) "Had made," tense: past; usage: pluperfect. The verb is past (prior in time) relative to the preceding verb (repented). A pluperfect verb is past with results up to the time of the preceding verb (repented).
    6) "Declare," tense: present; usage: verbs of speaking. Verbs of speaking, especially in the first person, are often used in the present. The following noun (today) clinches the context of the present.
    7) "Will make," tense: future; usage: certitude. The context (see Exod 7:2) and the following verb (will exist) indicate the future. The completed action of the perfect in the future furnishes certainly to the statement. Another possibility is a present tense, translated with an English perfect, "I have appointed you." The statement is still certain in the present.
    8) "I am bereaved," tense: present; usage: stative verb. The stative expresses the present tense. The context confirms this.
    9) "Has found," tense: present; usage: perfect. The context indicates a past action with continuing relevance – he found grace in the past, and he *still* has found it.
    10) Exalts," tense: present; usage: certitude. The verb implies a past "exalting" that continues into the present – my heart exalted and still does. The perfect, with its completed action, expresses certainty. Usually, present statements of certitude occur with first person verbs. The noun, "my heart," substitutes for the first person.
    11) "Had taken," tense: past; usage: pluperfect. The context is past tense. Rachel's taking of the idols preceded Laban's entering her tent (the preceding verb); therefore, the usage is pluperfect. The action occurring in the past before another past action. The pluperfect verb also has relevance up to the other past action – Rachel had taken it (and still had it) when Laban entered her tent.

12) "Repent," tense: present; usage: perfect with completed action in the past with continuing results in the present. The Lord did not just repent sometime in the past, but he had repented in the past, and he still does.
13) "Waits," tense: present; usage: certitude. Similar to number ten above. "Our soul" substitutes for the first person verb.
14) "Has heard," tense: past; usage: perfect. Similar to number eleven above.
15) "Has given," tense: present/future; usage: present/future with certitude. The preceding verbs indicate a future time. The perfect expresses a certain action viewed as completed, though they did not possess it yet.

2. Analyze the mood, tense, and usage of the following imperfects.
 1) "That it might go well with me," subjunctive, future, simple action. This particle often signals the subjunctive (a purpose clause), which by definition implies the future.
 2) "The Lord will do this thing," indicative, future with simple action. The context, especially the word, "tomorrow," indicates the future. For the future the aspect is usually the simple action. If the action were in process, another word or the meaning of the verb would indicate this.
 3) "Let the labor be heavy on them," jussive/preterit, future, jussive. The context suggests the jussive for the mood and the usage. The jussive is naturally future.
 4) "He lifts the needy," indicative, present, action in process/durative action. This typical imperfect portrays action in process – God is in process now of lifting up the needy and causing them to inherit and he will be in the same process in the future.
 5) "Saul would send him, he would prosper," indicative, past, frequentative. The first verb in the verse sets the tense as past. The imperfect in the past is usually frequentative and indicative.
 6) "From the wicked comes forth wickedness, but my hand is not against you," indicative, present/future, general truths. Both the perfect and imperfect can communicate maxims, proverbs, or truisms. The imperfect stresses ongoing action, or something occurring time and time again. The present and future are implied with this indicative statement.
 7) "The Rephaim were regarded . . . they were called to them Emim," indicative, past, frequentative/durative. Similar to example five above, the context suggests the past tense. The verbs are frequentative or perhaps better durative (and indicative): The Rephaim were regarded as Anakim . . . and were called."
 8) "They dispossessed them," jussive/preterit, past, preterit. The surrounding verbs are the simple, past actions. Moreover, the past frequentative, though possible, is improbable. By process of elimination and the context, the form is a jussive/preterit, the tense past, and the usage preterit. Why not use a Vav-consecutive or a perfect? Apparently, the context was sufficient to allow a preterit imperfect. Although other constructions could have worked as well, Moses chose the preterit imperfect. For preterit imperfects, context must demand a past tense and simple action.
 9) "The king of Egypt will not grant you," indicative, present/future with action in process. Context suggests the present and future for the imperfect: "The king of Egypt is not granting to you now nor will he in the future grant you to leave."

10) "You shall impose, and you shall not diminish" indicative, future, volition/command. These imperfects as commands are future, though "from now on" (present/future) is contextually appropriate as well. Although the form is indicative, the usage insinuates the imperative mood.
11) "Moses would speak to God and God would answer him," indicative, past, frequentative. The first verb of the verse indicates the past tense. The imperfect conveys frequency the action: each time Moses would speak, each time God would answer. These imperfects are more descriptive, more dramatic than a perfect. It is as if the dialogue was still going back and forth.
12) "Keep distant from a false charge," indicative, future, volition/command. Similar to example ten above.
13) "What are you seeking," indicative, present, durative action. Interrogative statements often employ the imperfect indicative in present time with durative/ongoing action.
14) "Before they crossed," jussive/preterit, past, preterit. The particle and context indicates past tense and preterit usage.
15) "And Moses would take . . . everyone seeking the Lord would go out," indicative, past, frequentative. Similar to examples five and eleven above. The context indicates the past tense with frequent occurrences of the action: "As Moses would take from time to time . . . everyone seeking the Lord would go out from time to time."
16) "Lest you die," subjunctive, future, simple action. Like example fifteen, the particle indicates a subjunctive, therefore, a future and simple action: lest you *should* die.

3. Analyze the following Vav-perfect forms: connecting or energic Vav, then usage.
   1) "And it would melt," energic, past, frequentative. The energic Vav renders the verb similar to an imperfect in meaning. With connecting Vav, the perfect would retains its usual meaning. The first verb in the verse sets the time as past. The Vav-perfect functions similar to the imperfect frequentative in meaning. See section two above, examples five, eleven, and sixteen.
   2) "And fall down," energic, present, continuing imperfects. The first two imperfects express the usual imperfect meaning of what is happening now and what you expect will continue to happen. The Vav-perfect continues the preceding imperfects. The Targum and LXX may confirm this understanding.
   3) "Then you will say," energic, future, introducing the. The energic Vav-perfect resembles the imperfect in tense (future), perhaps with a hint of an imperatival meaning as well. The Vav-perfect also introduces the apodosis of the temporal clause.
   4) "And I am grey," connecting, simple connection. The Vav simply connects its perfect with the preceding perfect. Both perfects retain their normal meaning. If the Vav were energic, the Zaqeph accent would shift to the last syllable.
   5) "And you will gather," or "and gather," energic, future, continuing imperative. This Vav-perfect continues the preceding imperative in tense and in meaning.
   6) "And you will sow," energic, future, used independently after a nominal clause. Context indicates the future tense of the Vav-perfect and the energic use of the Vav. Usually, Vav-perfects continue preceding imperfects or imperatives, but they may be used in almost any context, as here after a nominal clause.

7) "And we will be fruitful," energic, future, used independently after a perfect. This is similar to the preceding example except the Vav-perfect follows a perfect. The preceding particle "now" gives the perfect a present orientation, smoothly continued by the present/future of the Vav-perfect.
8) "But I will confirm," energic, adversative. The future context suggests the energic Vav. Also, the Vav is adversative by context.
9) "And I will exist," energic, future, continuing imperfects. A typical Vav-perfect following an imperfect, expressing an energic Vav in the future.
10) "And they blew," connecting, simple connection. The Vav connects its perfect with its preceding perfect, both retaining their past tense and simple action.

4. Analyze the following Vav-imperfect and Vav-imperative forms.
   1) "And God will be," or "that God might be," connecting or energic Vav, future. The preceding verb and the context indicates the future tense. The Vav may be viewed as connecting with the meaning, "and": "and God will be with you," or as energic, "in order that God might be with you." The connecting Vav is preferred since it is the simplest option.
   2) "That they might keep the feast," energic, subjunctive, simple action. After an imperative, the Vav-imperfect is frequently subjunctive and simple action, requiring the energic Vav.
   3) "So I have come down," energic, past, logical succession. The context and the form suggest a past tense and an energic vav, with logical succession, "And so consequently . . ." instead of temporal succession, "And then (after the last action) . . ."
   4) "And subdues peoples under me," energic, present, continuing a participle. Particular in poetry, the Vav-imperfect continues the preceding form, here a participle. The Targum and Vulgate confirm this analysis. The Septuagint, however, seems to take it as a typical Vav-imperfect with a past meaning.
   5) "That you might refresh your heart," energic, subjunctive, simple action. Context indicates that the imperative functions as a purpose clause – "And I will take a piece of bread, that you may refresh your heart." A simple imperative with conjunctive Vav is also possible – "And I will take a piece of bread, and refresh your heart."
   6) "And trust in chariots," energic (connecting), present, continuing an imperfect. The Vav-imperfect continues the present tense of the preceding verb. The form of the Vav is energic, but the meaning of the Vav is connecting.
   7) "And it happened," energic, past, temporal succession. This is the typical Vav-imperfect: the Vav energic in the past tense expressing temporal succession.
   8) "That you might live," energic, subjunctive, simple action. The Vav-imperfect expresses a purpose (subjunctive) clause (Targum, and probably LXX and Vulgate).
   9) "And the Lord cuts off," energic, present, continuing prophetic perfects. The Vav-imperfect continues the preceding prophetic perfect. Notice the future tense of the Vulgate.
   10) "And she conceived and gave birth," energic, past, temporal succession. This is typical Vav-imperfect for temporal succession in narrative.

11) "But his wife looked," energic, past, adversative. This is similar to the preceding example in temporal succession except the Vav is adversative.
12) "That he might give to me," energic, subjunctive, simple action. As most conjunctive Vavs with imperfects, this Vav-imperfect indicates a purpose (Vulgate).

5. Analyze the usages of the Piel.
   1) "I will fulfill," Piel, factitive. When a stative verb occurs in the Piel, they are factitive: "I will make (something) full," or more literally, "I will put (something) in a full state."
   2) "He will send you away," Piel, intensive/extensive. The meanings of the verb in the Qal and Piel are similar, and the action is physical, suggesting an intensive action – "to send away completely." The plural object indicates an extensive meaning – "to send away completely each one of you."
   3) "The Lord hardened," Piel, factitive. Similar to the first example, the stative verb becomes factitive in the Piel: "The Lord made the heart of Pharaoh hard," or "The Lord put the heart of Pharaoh in a hardened state."
   4) "They drove them completely away," Piel, intensive/extensive. Similar to the second example, the verb expresses physical action with the same meaning in the Qal. The Piel intensifies the force of the action. Intensive action always carries extensive action as well, confirmed by the plural object.
   5) "To justify," Piel, declarative. Declaratives are less common than the factitive and intensive/extensive. Like the factitive, they are usually statives verbs in the Qal. They differ, however, by declaring or considering someone or something the meaning of the verb: "to declare you righteous," or "to consider you righteous."
   6) "It shattered," Piel, intensive/extensive. This classic intensive/extensive verb means to break in the Qal and to shatter to pieces in the intensive/extensive. This Piel frequently has a plural object. In this example, the idea conveyed is: "And every tree in the field it (the hail) shattered to pieces one after the other until none were left."
   7) "To act as a priest," Piel, denominative. The denominative is a verb derived from a noun, usually translated, "to act like the noun," or "to function like the noun." The idea is: "And they will function as a priest to me."

6. Analyze the usages of the Hiphil.
   1) "Cause light to shine," Hiphil, causative. This is the standard Hiphil causative.
   2) "Made red," Hiphil, inner causative. The subject and the object are the same in the inner causative – "They made themselves red. The inner causative verbs are usually stative or intransitive in the Qal."
   3) "Cause to come out," Hiphil, causative. Verbs of motion, intransitive in the Qal, become transitive in the Hiphil.
   4) "And he will let her be redeemed," Hiphil, allowance. Allowance, a type of causative, usually has its object passive or acted upon. For most causatives, the object acts upon the verb.
   5) "make righteous," Hiphil, declarative. Similar to the Piel, the Hiphil may also express the declarative notion: "I will not declare or consider the wicked righteous."
   6) "And you rose up early," Hiphil, denominative. This verb may come from the noun, "shoulder," meaning to get up early to load the shoulder of a beast for travel.

7. Analyze the usages of the Niphal conjugation.
    1) "Should get himself found," Niphal, reflexive. Someone found him, and so (the result is) he got himself found. This is the notion of the reflexive. The result of the action upon an object is communicated by the reflexive.
    2) "Get yourself humbled," Niphal, reflexive. The active may be from the Hiphil instead of the Qal.
    3) "Consulted together with," Niphal, reciprocal. These verbs are associated with plural nouns. The action goes back and forth between the subject and the associated noun. These Niphal reciprocals may have a reflexive nuance included as well, "he got himself counsel with colleagues."
    4) "Get yourselves on guard," Niphal, reflexive. This reflexive comes from the Qal verb: Someone guarded him, and so (the result is) he got himself in a guarded state.
    5) "I will get for myself honor," Niphal, reflexive. As with most reflexives, personal interest is implied. This Niphal may go back to the Hiphil of the root.
    6) "Then you would get yourselves destroyed," Niphal, reflexive. This reflexive corresponds to a Hiphil of same root: If someone would destroy you, then (the result is) you would have got yourself destroyed.

Chapter 3. The Cases

1. Analyze why the initiator or agent is indefinite.
    1) The initiator, "a mixed multitude," is indefinite because specialized by the adjective, "great."
    2) The verb היה may take an indefinite agent – in this case, the agent "hail."
    3) In negative clauses, the initiator may be indefinite.
    4) A prepositional phrase precedes the indefinite initiator. The construction asserts possession.
    5) Similar to example two, the verb היה may take an indefinite initiator. The indefinite initiator is emphatic.
    6) A prepositional phrase before the indefinite initiator asserts existence.
    7) The prepositional phrase specializes the indefinite agent.
    8) The indefinite agent is preceded by a negative clause, verb היה, and a jussive.

2. Analyze why the announcement is definite.
    1) The announcement has annexation and a pronoun for the initiator.
    2) The announcement has the article and a pronoun for the initiator.
    3) The announcement has the article and is preceded by a separating pronoun.
    4) The announcement is a proper name and has a pronoun for the initiator.
    5) The announcement is annexed to a pronominal suffix and has a pronoun for the initiator.
    6) The announcement has the article and expresses absolute identification.

3. Analyze the word order of the initiator and announcement.
    1) Since the announcement is an interrogative pronoun, the announcement must precede the initiator.
    2) Because emphatic, the initiator occurs before the announcement.

3) After certain particles – in this case אֵין, the initiator must precede announcement. The next particle הִנֵּה and its participle work similarly.
4) When the announcement is emphatic.
5) When both initiator and announcement are definite, the initiator must precede the announcement.
6) When the announcement is a prepositional phrase or adverb indicating place or time, the announcement may precede the initiator.
7) When both the initiator and announcement are indefinite, the initiator must precede announcement.

4. Analyze the following genitives as proper or improper. If proper, which preposition should be understood between the annexation. If improper, analyze its function.
   1) Since the first word in the annexation (the governing word) is an adjective, the annexation is improper. The second word is a genitive of specification.
   2) "Tumors of gold, mice of gold." The genitives are the materials out of which the governing noun is made – tumors and mice *made out of* gold. The מִן preposition, therefore, explains the relationship between the words. Since the genitive limits the governing noun, the annexation is proper.
   3) "Garden of Eden." The annexation is proper since the genitive limits the governing noun. The genitive is an adverb of place to its governing noun, therefore, the ב preposition explains the relationship between the words.
   4) "Shedder of blood." The annexation is improper with a participle as a governing noun. The genitive functions as a direct object.
   5) "Spirit of God," The annexation is proper since the genitive limits the governing noun. The ל is the preposition assumed between the words. This selection of the ל is often determined by eliminating the uses of the prepositions ב and מִן. The ל is the most common preposition for understanding the relationship between words in annexation.
   6) "In the land of Egypt." Similar to number three above.
   7) "A maker of wonders," The annexation is improper since the governing noun is a participle. The genitive functions as an accusative of direct object.
   8) "In the image of God." Similar to number five above.
   9) "Killer of Cain." Similar to number seven above.
   10) "Voice of the Lord God." Similar to number five above.
   11) "The land of Goshen." Similar to number three above.
   12) "The old one of his house." Similar to number one above.
   13) "Implements of silver and gold." Similar to number two above.

5. Analyze the following annexations.
   1) "Owner of words." The governing noun is a noun of relation. The genitive gives the quality, characteristic, or class for the governing noun. This idea is one who possesses words, therefore, an eloquent man.
   2) "Behold a son to Sarah." The preposition ל with noun substitutes for a genitive. This construction allows the governing noun to be indefinite with a definite genitive.
   3) "All the days he shut him in." The verbal clause is in the place of the genitive after the governing noun.

4) "Until the pursuers returned," Similar to the preceding example, but this time the clause in the place of the genitive after a preposition.
5) "From all to the sons of Israel," The prepositional phrase (to the sons of Israel) in the place of the genitive after the preceding noun in the construct.
6) "On the day the Lord spoke to Moses," Similar to number three above.
7) "Man of (the) field," Similar to number one above.

6. Find the accusatives in the following verses. Analyze the absolute objects, double direct objects, and adverbial accusatives (and their substitutes). Remember the general rule: if a word is not a subject, a verb, a genitive, a vocative, or a word in apposition to these, the word is an accusative.
   1) גֵּר "as a stranger," The verb היה often takes an accusative of situation. The accusative of situation, usually indefinite, is illustrating since it provides new information or an attribute to its subject. Moreover, accusative of situation is permanent in the "foreign land." Context determines whether the accusative of situation is permanent or temporary.
   2) בּוֹא "coming," The infinitive absolute is an absolute object, emphasizing the verb.
   3) רַק בַּיְאֹר "only in the Nile." This accusative of situation (only) does not provide new information or an attribute to its subject (as example one), but it strengthens the noun (Nile).
   4) מַכָּה רַבָּה מְאֹד "a very great smiting," The indefinite noun with its modifiers is an absolute object, explaining the quality or manner of the verbal action.
   5) שְׁמָהּ מָרָה "her name, Marah," The double objects are related, able to form a nominal clause, "Marah is her name."
   6) בָּנָיו שֹׁפְטִים "his sons in the status of judges." The verb takes related double objects (his sons are judges). The first object is a direct object. The second object is an accusative of situation, illustrating by providing new information or an attribute to its subject. The appointment is permanent.
   7) ךָ . . . נָבִיא "you in the status of a prophet." This is similar to the preceding example.
   8) אַרְבָּעִים יוֹם "forty in terms of a day." Specification of nature is common with numbers. "Forty" is the direct object; "day" is the specification of nature. As a specification of nature, a nominal clause is possible – the day(s) are forty.
   9) יוֹם הַשְׁכֵּם וְשָׁלֹחַ "daily, awaking early and sending." The infinitive absolutes are absolute objects, explaining the verb adverbially. The noun "day" (daily) is an accusative of situation (illustrating and permanent).
   10) הַבַּדִּים עֲצֵי שִׁטִּים "the poles, in the condition of acacia wood." Similar to examples six and seven.
   11) מִצְרָיִם "to Egypt," The noun is an accusative of (specified) place, common after verbs of motion.
   12) אֶת־מֹשֶׁה וְאֶת־אַהֲרֹן "specifically as to Moses and Aaron," These nouns are accusatives of specification after an impersonal passive verb. Usually, they are translated as subjects of the verb, but actually they are accusatives as the את particle confirms.
   13) וַיְהִי־לָהּ לְבֵן "as a son." The ל with its genitive substitutes for an accusative of situation. Without the ל, the noun would be in the accusative and the meaning

would be the same with or without the ל. Like most case languages, Hebrew substituted prepositional phrases for the cases, as the cases began to fade in the language. This substitute is also illustrating, permanent as an accusative of situation.

14) מָחָר "tomorrow," The noun is an accusative of (specified) time.
15) רָאֹה "seeing," Similar to example two, the absolute object emphasizes the verb.
16) הוּ... עֵץ ... "him, a tree," The verb takes unrelated double objects.
17) סְבִיבֹת הַיְאֹר "places around the Nile," The governing noun of the annexation is accusative of unspecified place. Its genitive specifies the places.
18) דַבֵּר "speaking," Similar to numbers fifteen and two, an absolute object emphasizes the verb.
19) רֵיקָם "empty-handed," Notice the accusative ending on the word with Memation (the final Mem is also found on the plural absolute nouns in Hebrew; in Aramaic and Arabic it would be a final Nun, or Nunation). This indefinite noun is an accusative of situation, illustrating and permanent.
20) תְּרוּעָה גְדוֹלָה "great shouting," Similar to number four, but without the additional emphatic word (מְאֹד), the absolute object explains the quality or manner of the verbal action.
21) נְתֻנִים "given over," The noun is an accusative of situation, permanent and strengthening the verb by virtually restating it with a different root.
22) לֶחִי "cheek," The noun is an accusative of specification of the attribute, clarifying and specifying the attribute smitten on the object (all my enemies): namely, their cheek.
23) שִׁבְעַת יָמִים "seven days," The governing noun, the number, is an accusative of time. The genitive specifies the time in term of days.
24) אִישׁ מִצְרִי מַכֶּה "an Egyptian man, one who smites," The verb takes two related double objects. The first is a direct object; the second, an accusative of situation, illustrating and temporary. This is similar to six and seven.
25) לְחָרָבָה "as dryness," Similar to the preceding example, the prepositional phrase substitutes for an accusative of situation, illustrating and temporary. If the LAMED were dropped, the noun would be a related double accusative to the verb.
26) עֹלֶה וּבוֹכֶה "ascending and weeping" Similar to number nine without the extra accusative, the absolute objects explains the manner of the verbal action – how David ascended the Mount of Olives.
27) שְׁקָלִים "specifically as to shekels." The noun "shekels" specifies the preceding number (30), similar to number eight. As a specification of nature, a nominal clause is possible – The shekels are thirty.
28) זָהָב "specifically as to gold," The noun of quality specifies of nature of the two Cheribim – they are golden Cheribim or two Cheribim specifically as to gold. As a specification of nature, a nominal clause is possible: The two Cheribim are gold.

7. Find the words in Casus Pendens. Then identify the case that resume the Casus Pendens.
   1) וִיהוֹשֻׁעַ בִּן־נוּן וְכָלֵב בֶּן־יְפֻנֶּה "And Joshua, son of Nun, and Celeb, son of Yefunneh": The implicit pronoun in the verb (they), a nominative, resumes the suspended nouns.
   2) יִתְרָה . . . וּפְקֻדָּתָם "Abundance and their stored up stuff": The pronominal suffix on the verb, an accusative, resumes the suspended nouns.

3) הַדָּבָר (אֲשֶׁר יָשִׂים אֱלֹהִים בְּפִי) "The word (which God placed in my mouth)": The pronoun with the accusative marker resumes the suspended noun.
4) וּפִילַגְשׁוֹ "And his concubine": The genitive pronoun (her name) resumes the suspended noun. Also the independent pronoun, a nominative, after the verb resumes the suspended noun.
5) וְהָאֲנָשִׁים (אֲשֶׁר־שָׁלַח מֹשֶׁה לָתוּר אֶת־הָאָרֶץ) "And the men (whom Moses sent to spy the land)": The implicit pronoun in the verb (they), a nominative, resumes the suspended noun.
6) כָּל־הַזָּהָב (הֶעָשׂוּי לַמְּלָאכָה בְּכֹל מְלֶאכֶת הַקֹּדֶשׁ) "All the gold (which is made for all the work of the sanctuary)": The phrase "The gold of the offering" resumes the suspended noun.
7) וְהַלֻּחֹת "And the tablets": The independent pronoun resumes the suspended noun. וְהַמִּכְתָּב "The writing": The independent pronoun resumes the suspended noun.
8) הָעַלְמָה (הַיֹּצֵאת לִשְׁאֹב) "The maiden (the one coming to draw water)": The pronoun (genitive) with the preposition resumes the suspended noun.
9) אֲשֶׁר־יְדַבֵּר יְהוָה "That which the Lord speaks": The pronoun with the accusative marker resumes the suspended clause.
10) שָׂרַי אִשְׁתְּךָ "Sarai, your wife": The pronoun (genitive) connected to the noun (name) resumes the suspended noun.
11) וְכָל־הַבְּאֵרֹת (אֲשֶׁר חָפְרוּ עַבְדֵי אָבִיו בִּימֵי אַבְרָהָם אָבִיו) "And all the wells (which the servants of his father dug in the days of Abraham, his father)": The pronominal suffixes (accusatives) of both verbs resumes the suspended noun.
12) יְהוָה "The Lord": the pronoun (genitive) connected to the participle (those who strive) resumes the suspended noun. Also the Lord is resumed as a nominative implicitly in the verbs (nominative).
13) הָעָם (הַהֹלְכִים בַּחֹשֶׁךְ) "The people (walking in darkness)": The implicit pronoun (nominative) in the verb resumes the suspended noun. יֹשְׁבֵי בְּאֶרֶץ צַלְמָוֶת "The dwellers in the land of the shadow of death": The pronoun (genitive) with the preposition resumes the suspended nouns.
14) כָּל־הַמֹּפְתִים (אֲשֶׁר־שַׂמְתִּי בְיָדֶךָ) "All the wonders (which I placed in your hand)": The pronominal suffix on the verb (accusative) resumes the suspended noun.
15) וּמֹשֶׁה "And Moses": The implicit pronoun (nominative) in the verb resumes the suspended noun.
16) רַק חַטֹּאֵי יָרָבְעָם בֶּן־נְבָט (אֲשֶׁר הֶחֱטִיא אֶת־יִשְׂרָאֵל) "Only the sins of Jeroboam, the son of Nebat, (which he caused Israel to sin)": The pronoun (genitive) with the preposition resumes the suspended noun.
17) מַעֲכָה אִמּוֹ "Maacah, his mother": The pronominal suffix on the verb, an accusative, resumes the suspended noun.
18) הַבְּרָכָה הַזֹּאת (אֲשֶׁר־הֵבִיא שִׁפְחָתְךָ לַאדֹנִי) "This blessing (which your handmaid brought to my lord)": The implicit pronoun (nominative) in the verb resumes the suspended noun.
19) הַמְדַבֵּר אֵלֶיךָ "The speaker to you": The pronominal suffix on the verb, an accusative, resumes the suspended nouns.
20) וְהָעֹמֶר "And the omer": The independent pronoun resumes the suspended noun.

21) וְיִשְׂרָאֵל "And Israel": The implicit pronoun (nominative) in the verb resumes the suspended noun.
22) נָהָר "A river": The pronoun (genitive) connected to the noun resumes the suspended noun. פְּלָגָיו "Its streams": The implicit pronoun (nominative) in the verb resumes the suspended noun.
23) דִּבְרֵי עֲוֺנֹת "Words of iniquities": The implicit pronoun (nominative) in the verb resumes the suspended noun. פְּשָׁעֵינוּ "Our sins": The pronominal suffix on the verb, an accusative, resumes the suspended noun.
24) אֲשֶׁר כָּל־שֹׁמְעוֹ "Which everyone hearing it": The pronoun (genitive) connected to the noun resumes the suspended noun.
25) אַתָּה "You": The explicit pronoun (nominative) in the verb resumes the suspended noun. קַיִץ וָחֹרֶף "Summer and winter": The pronominal suffix on the verb, an accusative, resumes the suspended nouns.

Chapter 4. Verbal Nouns

1. In the following verses, there are words that may be parsed as a participle or a perfect. Determine whether the form is a participle or a perfect and justify your answer.
   1) Participle. An event did not take place here: and Samuel became afraid. This would probably suggest an Vav-consecutive construction. Instead, the construction describes Samuel's habitual state of being: a man who is afraid, a fearful man.
   2) Participle. The participle, a descriptive noun, portrays habitual activity: a returning dog or a dog that returns. An event or occurrence did not happen: as a dog returned to his vomit. The participle in the second half of the verse confirms the analysis.
   3) Perfect. An event probably occurs here: Lot feared, or Lot became afraid. The causal clause is based on Lot's act of becoming afraid to dwell in Zoar, not his state of being afraid. The Targum and LXX suggest the same analysis.
   4) Perfect. Clearly an event happened: Abraham returned to his place. Abraham's action contrasts with the Lord's action of walking.
   5) Perfect. The perfect expresses a completed event: He returned. The participle, by contrast, would describe a habitual activity or state: he was a returning man (that is, a man who was returning).
   6) Participle. The participle depicts Esau as a man that was coming, a coming man. He had not already arrived (completed action), as the perfect would suggest.
   7) Participle. Similar to the preceding example, the perfect would suggest a completed occurrence – where have I come. Instead, the participle expresses an habitual activity – where will I be a man who comes.
   8) Perfect. Similar to number three above, the causal clause suggests God's regret because Saul had turned from after him – a completed action. The participle would suggest: For (he is) a man returning from behind me. Saul is not described as engaged in the activity, but he had completed the activity.
   9) Participle. Similar to number six.
   10) Perfect; perfect. Both forms are probably perfects, expressing completed actions. The half verse is still descriptive since both verbs are the predicates of nominal clauses. Participles would relate a continuing state of being (he who was being

old) and a continuing activity (a man who enters the days). The perfect views the actions as completed, done – he had become old and he had entered the days.

2. Label the clauses in which the participle as predicate (announcement) occurs.
   1) The participle as predicate is with הִנֵּה and is an independent clause. The participle as predicate is common in the first clause of a verse.
   2) The participle as predicate occurs in a situation clause with הִנֵּה. "And deep sleep fell upon Abram, as behold terror and great darkness was falling upon him."
   3) The participle as predicate occurs in a כִּי clause
   4) In the last clause of the verse, a situation clause, the participle functions as the predicate – You will meet a band of prophets . . . and they will be in the condition of ones prophesying (as you meet them).
   5) The participle as predicate is in an הִנֵּה and independent clause.
   6) The participle as predicate is in an relative clause.
   7) The first participle is in an independent clause, negated by אַיִן. The second participle is in an independent clause, but without the negative. The third is also in an independent clause with הִנֵּה.
   8) Since the participle as predicate has the article, it expresses absolute identification.
   9) The participle is in an independent clause. Context suggests a temporal clause.
   10) The participle as predicate is in a situation clause – The cows went straight . . . as the lords of the Philistines were in the status of those who walk behind them.

3. Label the case and usage of the following participles.
   1) Accusative, accusative of situation. If the indefinite participle is not an announcement, it is often an accusative of situation. The verb takes a double object. The objects are related: The son of Hagar is a man who laughs.
   2) Genitive, proper annexation. The participle in the genitive limits the governing noun.
   3) Nominative, agent. The participle, the noun of the agent, functions as the agent to the verb.
   4) Nominative, predicate or announcement. The participle is in a situation clause with הִנֵּה. The pronoun (הוּא) is often omitted before a participle after הִנֵּה.
   5) Accusative, direct object.
   6) Accusative, situation. היה commonly take participles as accusatives of situation.
   7) Genitive, improper annexation; accusative, situation. The first participle is in the genitive, a proper annexation since it limits its governing noun: "the work of a perfumer." The second participle is an accusative of situation, "in the condition of seasoned with salt."
   8) Accusative, situation. Similar to number one, the verb takes a double object, the second accusative an accusative of situation. "The Lord will give you over in a smitten condition."
   9) Accusative, apposition. The participle functions as an adjective (apposition) to the preceding annexation. The participle appears to modify the entire annexation; therefore, the participle follows the case of the governing noun, the accusative.
   10) Accusative, situation. If an indefinite participle is not an announcement, it is often an accusative of situation.

4. Label the usage of the absolute object. (The context and meaning of the verb determine the usage. The categories may overlap, especially, intensifying a statement or action.)
   1) Intensifying a statement. The infinitive absolute strengthens the assertion. The penalty will most certainly happen.
   2) Intensifying a statement. The infinitive absolute makes the interrogative statement more dubious – Will you *actually* rule over us. The infinitive absolute heightens Jacob's incredulity.
   3) Adverbial. The infinitive absolute when occurring after its verb is often adverbial – "Abram journeyed, journeying in stages as he went to the Negev."
   4) Intensifying the action of the verb. "He has gloriously triumphed."
   5) Intensifying the action of the verb and intensifying a statement. In this example, the categories overlap. The infinitive absolute intensifies the statement and the action.
   6) Adverbial. Similar to number three.
   7) Intensifying a statement. Similar to five.
   8) Intensifying the action of the verb.

5. Label the case and type of clause of the infinitive construct. The genitive is indicated by a preposition or a word in construct preceding the infinitive construct. Otherwise, the infinitive construct is usually in the accusative.
   1) Genitive, reason/cause/motive clause. This is the most common use of the infinitive construct. Context is the usual determining factor.
   2) Genitive, specification/explanation of a verb. The preceding verb (began) requires another word, usually an infinitive construct, to complete its meaning.
   3) Genitive, temporal clause. This preposition is common for temporal clauses.
   4) Genitive, reason/cause/motive clause. Similar to example one.
   5) Genitive, reason/cause/motive clause. Similar to example one and four, for both infinitive constructs in the verse.
   6) Genitive, specification/explanation of a verb. Similar to example two. The verb נתן sometimes requires an infinitive construct to complete its meaning.
   7) Accusative, specification/explanation of a verb. Similar to examples two and six.
   8) Genitive, temporal clause. This preposition usually indicates a temporal clauses.
   9) Accusative, specification/explanation of a stative verb. Statives verbs in the Hiphil often require an infinitive construct to complete their meaning – I have caused to be sick by the act of smiting you.
   10) Genitive, reason/cause/motive clause (for both infinitive constructs). Similar to example one.

Chapter 6. Apposition

For the following nouns, analyze the type of apposition. The verses follow the numbering of the Masoretic Text.

1) "In pits," corroborative, verbal. The corroborative, verbal apposition repeats the words.
2) "All of him," corroborative, conceptual, strengthening totality. The word כֹּל with the pronominal suffix often signals the corroborative, conceptual.

3) "Moses," explicative. The noun "Moses" reveals or identifies "the man."
4) "The God of your fathers," substitution. "The God of your fathers" functions as a title, substituting for the "Lord."
5) "Which is of old men of renown," qualifier, clause, nominal. The relative clause qualifies (limits) its antecedent, "mighty men."
6) "Most High," qualifier, descriptive noun, adjective. The adjective describes one of the qualities inherent or permanent in its noun.
7) "The king," substitution. Similar to number four.
8) "The one speaking," qualifier, descriptive noun, participle. Similar to number six, but the descriptive noun here is a participle.
9) "All of us," corroborative, conceptual, strengthening totality. See number two.
10) "In the midst of the garden," qualifier, prepositional phrase. Similar to five, but the prepositional phrase is qualifying the noun, "the tree of life."
11) "Jesse," explicative. The noun "Jesse" identifies "the son of your servant."
12) "The one going out," qualifier, descriptive noun, participle. See number eight.
13) "The firstborn," substitution. See number four.
14) "His daughter," substitution. Substitution is common after proper names when a family relationship is given.
15) "Thirty," qualifier, semi-descriptive noun, numbers. The number comes after its numerable in the absolute state.
16) "In which they go," qualifier, clause, verbal. The relative particle is assumed after its antecedent, "the way." The relative clause (also a verbal clause) qualifies the antecedent.
17) "Lazy," corroborative, verbal. See number one.
18) "In bone," corroborative, conceptual, strengthening self. This word, "bone," often signals the corroborative, conceptual when it modifies another word.
19) "Sinners," qualifiers, descriptive noun, intensive/extensive noun formation. Notice the Piel/Pael formation of the word.
20) "Sons of Israel," explicative. The noun "sons of Israel" identifies "my people."

Chapter 7. Numerals

Analyze the numerable (for example, accusative of specification, genitive of specification, or apposition) in the following sentences.

1) Accusative of specification. The number is not in construct to its numerable; therefore, the numerable is an accusative of specification.
2) Apposition. For apposition, the number comes after its numerable.
3) Accusative of specification. See example one.
4) Accusative of specification. Both numerables in the verse are accusative of specifications.
5) Accusative of specification; genitive of specification. The first numerable is a accusative of specification since its number is not in construct. The second numerable is a genitive of specification since its number is in construct.
6) Apposition. See number two above.
7) Genitive of specification. See the second example in chapter five.
8) Apposition. Four times in this verse the numerable is in apposition to its number.

9) Genitive of specification. See the second example in chapter five.
10) Genitive of specification. See the second example in chapter five.

Chapter 8. Article

Analyze the usage of the article in the following verses.

1) "The brick . . . and the mortar," generic, essence. The articles do not particularize a specific brick or lump of mortar, but it particularizing the categories of bricks and mortar. The article views the categories as a whole or as a single essence, not as every brick or lump of mortar that makes up the whole. It is, therefore, the generic of the essence, not of the totality of individuals or things. Also note that כֹּל cannot be inserted before the nouns, confirming the analysis.
2) "The soul," generic, totality of the group. Similar to the preceding except this example is generic, totality of the group instead of the essence. "The soul" do not refer to one individual, but to a category, much like the preceding word in the verse "property" is a category. The category of "the soul" refers to all the individuals that make up the whole, not the whole as one essence. The word כֹּל may be inserted for sense or the word may be pluralized: souls: "and every person that they purchased in Haran."
3) "The Nile," non-definite, dominance. The noun means "stream" or "canal." The article and its noun has become a proper noun, thereby, becoming a dominant use for the article, "The stream" (that we all know is the Nile), much like "The White House," whose dominant use refers to the residence of the President of the United States.
4) "For the water," generic, essence. See example one.
5) "The captain," particular, presence. Particular individuals are who are present to the speaker are in view.
6) "The bush," particular, preconception. The particular bush had not been mentioned before, hence, it is grammatically unknown. The Hebrew speaker, however, preconceived it as known since it is the bush he is talking about. Translate the first mention of these preconception indefinitely or with the English indefinite article.
7) "The slave girl," generic, totality of the group. See example two.
8) "To the vanity," generic, abstract. Abstract nouns are viewed as a class or group. Do not lift up the name of God in *the* (same) class as emptiness.
9) "The Abib," non-definite, excessive. The article is excessive since the noun is already definite. Excessive articles are common with proper names and demonstrative pronouns. With proper names, these may also be article of dominance as well a excessive.
10) "The high priest," particular, unique. The high priest, being a particular one-of-a-kind, receives the article.
11) "The Pisgah," non–definite, excessive. See example nine.
12) "This day," particular, presence. See example five, but this example refers to present time.
13) "In the fire," generic, essence. See example one.
14) "The ram," particular, repetition. A particular ram that was previously mentioned, hence, grammatically known, is mentioned again (repetition).
15) "In the holiness," generic, abstract. See example eight.
16) "To the head," generic, totality of the group. See example two.

17) “The donkey,” particular, preconception. See example six.
18) “The day,” particular, presence. See example twelve.
19) “The quail,” generic, essence. See example one.
20) “The ox,” particular, repetition. See example fourteen.

Chapter 24. Adversative and Exceptive Clauses
The analysis of the clauses depends on the particle and especially the context of the passage.

1) “But Israel,” adversative.
2) “But indeed for this reason I have caused you to stand,” adversative.
3) “Except our eyes are towards this manna,” exceptive.
4) “Indeed, Lord . . .” asseverative.
5) “Even I know,” asseverative.
6) “I, behold I am bringing a flood,” asseverative.
7) “These are the waters of Meribah because the Israelites contented with the Lord,” causal.
8) “Because he cut the edge of Saul’s robe,” causal.
9) “And I feared because I was naked,” causal.
10) “As the Lord commanded Moses and Aaron, so they did,” comparative.
11) “Though it was near,” concessive.
12) “Though it is in Jonathan, my son,” concessive.
13) “If I have not brought him to you and place him before you, I have sinned against you forever,” conditional, simple.
14) “And he said, if you will intently listen to the voice of the Lord, your God, and the right thing in his eyes you will do, and you will give hear to his commandments, and you will keep all his statutes, (then) every sickness which I placed on Egypt, I will not place on you. For I am the Lord who heals you.” conditional, simple.
15) “If the Lord were pleased to kill us, he would not have taken . . .” conditional, contrary-to-fact.
16) “And (if) harm shall meet him in the way,” conditional, simple.
17) “Moses, Moses,” exclamation, repeating noun.
18) “What is it?,” exclamation.
19) “Do you not know . . .” exclamation, interrogative.
20) “Shall I go . . . ?” interrogative, expecting a uncertain answer.
21) “Is indeed his name not called Jacob?” interrogative, expecting a positive answer.
22) “Am I my brother’s keeper?” interrogative, expecting a negative answer.
23) “Do not pour out blood,” prohibition with אַל and the jussive.
24) “You must not eat from it or touch it,” prohibition with לֹא and the indicative.
25) “No flesh will be cut off by waters of the flood again,” absolute negation.
26) “For all green vegetation will not be left,” absolute negation.
27) “Are there no graves in Egypt,” categoric negation.
28) “For not a man he is to repent,” categoric negation.
29) “Thus may God do to you and thus may he add, if indeed you hide a word from me from every word which he spoke to you,” oath clause.
30) “As your soul lives, my lord . . . ” oath clause.
31) “If indeed in that day a great shaking will happen upon the land of Israel,” oath clause.

32) "In order that they might believe," purpose clause.
33) "So as to provoke me," result. Notice the unexpected outcome.
34) "In order that it may go well," purpose.
35) "In order to shine light upon the earth," purpose.
36) "From the ground which opened its mouth to take the blood of your brother from your hand," relative clause, verbal clause with definite antecedent and explicit retrospective pronoun.
37) "Every creeping thing, which [it] is alive, exists to you for food," Relative clause, nominal clause with indefinite antecedent and explicit retrospective pronoun.
38) "The people which you have purchased," relative clause, verbal clause with indefinite antecedent and implicit retrospective pronoun.
39) "In a land which is not to you," relative clause, nominal clause (prepositional) with indefinite antecedent and implicit retrospective pronoun.
40) "As he was standing over them under the tree . . ." situation, Vav of situation with retrospective pronoun.
41) "And they [he] is dwelling before me," situation, Vav of situation with retrospective pronoun.
42) "And he was not a hater of him formerly," situation, Vav of situation with noun.
43) "As behold, the bush was burning with fire, but as the bush was not being consumed," two situation clauses.
44) "As behold the lad was weeping," situation.
45) "All the days (of) he shut him up," substantival clause, genitive (temporal).
46) "And it happened after they brought it around," substantival clause in the genitive (temporal).
47) "That she was your wife," substantival clause in the accusative.
48) "What his youngest son had done to him," substantival clause in the accusative.
49) "Then you will be innocent of my oath," temporal.
50) "When man began to multiply on the earth," temporal.
51) "When they were in the field," temporal.
52) "When the sons of God came into the daughters of man," temporal.
53) "And it happened in their journeying east," (when they journeyed east), temporal.
54) "But if you do not exist as one who sends away." The pronoun is the subject of אֵין, and the participle is an accusative of situation.
55) "A man does not exist as one who gathers them into a house to spend the night." The noun "man" is the subject of אֵין, and the participle is an accusative of situation.

GLOSSARY TO COMPOSITION

The verbs are usually unpointed. Most verbs are given thematic vowels (for example, A/O), but some verbs whose thematic vowels are indicated by the form (for example, third-guttural verbs) are not given.

A

Aaron	אַהֲרֹן
abandon	נטשׁ (A/O)
able (verb)	יכל (יָכֹל, יוּכַל)
Abraham	אַבְרָהָם
Abram	אַבְרָם
abundance	רֹב
acknowledge	ידע (ו)
add	יסף (Hiphil)
Adonijah	אֲדֹנִיָּהוּ
afraid (become)	ירא (E/A)
after (prep. & conj.)	אַחַר, אַחֲרֵי
after this	אַחֲרֵי־כֵן
again	עוֹד, יסף Hiphil or Qal +inf. cstr.
all	כָּל־, כֹּל
alone	לְבַד (+3ms לְבַדּוֹ)
altar	מִזְבֵּחַ
always	כָּל־הַיָּמִים
amen	אָמֵן
Amorite	אֱמֹרִי
angel	מַלְאָךְ
anger	אַף
angry (be/become)	אנף (A/A)
angry	חרה (+אַף) +ב of person, object (frequently)
animal	חַיָּה
anoint	משׁח
answer	ענה
any longer	עוֹד
appear	ראה (Niphal)
appoint	נתן (A/E)
Aram	אֲרָם
argue	ריב
argument	רִיב
arm	זְרוֹעַ
army	חַיִל, cstr. חֵיל
around	סָבִיב/סְבִיבָה
arrow	חֵץ
as (conjunction)	כַּאֲשֶׁר

ask	שׁאל
avenge	נקם (A/O) (with ל preposition)

B

Bathsheba	בַּת־שֶׁ֫בַע
be willing	אבה
bear	נשׂא (inf. cstr. with ל: לָשֵׂאת)
bearer of good news	בשׂר (Piel participle)
beast	חַיָּה
beautiful (adj.)	יָפָה
beauty	חֶ֫סֶד, יֳפִי, תִּפְאָרָה, צְבִי
because	בַּעֲבוּר, אֲשֶׁר, יַ֫עַן, כִּי
become	היה + ל, or just היה
before (conjunction)	טֶ֫רֶם, בְּטֶ֫רֶם (prep. & conj. לִפְנֵי)
beget	ילד (ו)
behold	הִנֵּה
believe	אמן (Hiphil) + ל or ב
bend	נטה
beside	עַל יָד
between	בֵּין
beyond	בְּעֵ֫בֶר
bitter (adj.)	מַר (root מרר)
bless	ברך (Piel, Niphal)
blessed (are)	אֶ֫שֶׁר (*a*) with plural suffix
blood	דָּם
blow	נשׁב (A/)
bond	מוֹסֵרָה/מוֹסֵר
bondage	בֵּית עֲבָדִים
bosom	חֵק/חֵיק
bow down	הִשְׁתַּחֲוָה
break	רעע
breath	רוּחַ
brightness	נֹ֫גַהּ
bring	בוא (Hiphil)
broad place (of a city)	רְחוֹב
broad valley	בִּקְעָה
brother	אָח
burn	בער (Qal)
but	כִּי אִם, ו

C

call out for help	שׁוע
came near	קרב (A/A)
came out	יצא (ו) (A/E)
came to (= enter)	בוא (A/Ô)
came to be	היה
came	בוא (היה with the "word of the Lord")
camp (noun)	מַחֲנֶה
camp (verb)	חנה
Canaan	כְּנַ֫עַן
Canaanite(s)	כְּנַ֫עַן, כְּנַעֲנִי
cast	נסך (A/)
cattle	בָּקָר
cave	מְעָרָה
chaff	מֹץ/מוֹץ
chain	רַתֻּקָה
channel	אָפִיק, פֶּ֫לֶג
chariots	רֶ֫כֶב
cheek	לְחִי
Cherub	כְּרוּב
choose	בחר (+ב usually)
city	עִיר (f), pl. עָרִים
city gate	שַׁ֫עַר (*a*)
clear	פנה
cloud	עָב
coal	גֶּ֫חֶל
come	בּוֹא
comfort	נחם
command	צוה (Piel)
commandment	מִצְוָה
compare	ערך (A/O)
complete (noun & adj.)	תָּם
complete (verb)	מלא (A/E)
concerning	עַל
confound	המם
confront	קדם (Piel)
congregation	עֵדָה
consume	אכל (IBH chapter 30)
continually	= all the days
cord	חֶ֫בֶל
counsel	עֵצָה
covenant	בְּרִית
covering	סֻכָּה
coward	אִישׁ־יְרֵאָה
craftsman	חָרָשׁ
create	ברא

cry (noun)	צְעָקָה
cry for help	שַׁוְעָה
cry out	צעק

D

dark cloud	עֲרָפֶל
dark masses	שַׁחַק
darkness	חֲשֵׁכָה (m), חֹשֶׁךְ (f)
daughter	בַּת
David	דָּוִד
day	יוֹם
death (put to)	מות (Hiphil, Hophal)
death	מָ֫וֶת, cstr. מוֹת
declare	ספר
decree	חֹק
delay	אחר (Piel)
delight	חֵ֫פֶץ
deliver	נצל (Hiphil)
deliverer	פלט (Piel participle)
desert	עֲרָבָה
destroy	שׁחת (Hiphil), שׁמד (Hiphil), אבד (Hiphil)
die	מות (A-e/Ū)
dispute	ריב
distress	צַר
do	עשׂה
door	פֶּ֫תַח
double	כֶּ֫פֶל
dream (noun)	חֲלוֹם
dream (verb)	חלם (A/O)
drink	שׁתה (Qal), שׁקה (cause to drink, Hiphil)
drive	נדף (A/O)
dry ground	יַבָּשָׁה
dry up	יבשׁ (י) (A-e/A)
dwell	ישׁב (ו) (A/E)

E

each other	אִישׁ ... אָחִיו
earth	אֶ֫רֶץ (*a*)
eat	אכל (IBH chapter 30)
Egypt (Egyptian)	מִצְרַ֫יִם
Eliezer	אֱלִיעֶ֫זֶר
emptiness	תֹּהוּ, רִיק
end	אֶ֫פֶס
enemy	אֹיֵב
enter (= came to)	בוא (A/Ô)
establish	כון (Niphal, Hiphil)

eternity	עוֹלָם
even	גַּם
ever	עַד (pause עֶד)
everyone	כָּל־, כֹּל
evil (verb)	רעה
evil	רֹעַ
exalt oneself	נשׂא (Hithpael)
exceedingly	עַד־מְאֹד
except	זוּלָה (+1cs זוּלָתִי)
exhale	נְשָׁמָה
eyes	עַ֫יִן, cstr. עֵין

F

face	פָּנִים
fade	נבל (A-e/O)
fall	נפל (A/O)
famine	רָעָב
far be it	חָלִ֫ילָה
father	אָב, pl. אָבוֹת
fear (noun)	יִרְאָה
fearful	ירא (E/A), Niphal participle
few (days)	(יָמִים) אֲחָדִים
fidelity	אֱמוּנָה
field	שָׂדֶה
fifty	חֲמִשִּׁים
fight	לחם (Niphal)
find	מצא
fire	אֵשׁ (f)
flee	מלט (Niphal), נוס
flesh	בָּשָׂר
flock	עֵ֫דֶר
flower	צִיץ
fly	עוף
food	אָכְלָה
foolish (adj.)	נָבָל
foot	רֶ֫גֶל
for	לְ
forever	לְעוֹלָם
forsake	עזב (A/O)
fortress	מְצוּדָה
forty	אַרְבָּעִים
foundation	מוֹסָד (m, f)
from	מִן
fruit	פְּרִי
fulfill	עשׂה
fury	חָרוֹן

G

gate — שַׂעַר (*a*)
gather together — קהל (Niphal)
gather — קבץ (Niphal, Piel)
generation — דֹּר
get up early — שׁכם (Hiphil)
girl — נַעֲרָה
give — נתן (A/E), יהב (/A)
glory — כָּבֹד/כָּבוֹד
go (went) — הלך (ו) (A/E)
go down — ירד (ו) (A/E)
go out — יצא (ו) (A/E)
go up — עלה
God — אֱלוֹהַּ, אֵל, אֱלֹהִים
gods — אֱלֹהִים
gold — זָהָב
good (adj.) — טוֹב
grace — חֵן (+1cs חִנִּי)
grass — חָצִיר
great (adj.) — גָּדוֹל
greatly — מְאֹד
greatness — גֹּדֶל (*o*)
greeted (= blessed) — ברך (Piel)
grey (verb) — שׂיב
ground — אֶרֶץ, אֲדָמָה (*a*)

H

Haggith — חַגִּית
hail — בָּרָד
hair — שַׂעֲרָה
hand — יָד (f)
happen — היה
Haran — חָרָן
harden — כבד (Piel)
hate — שׂנא (E/A)
head — רֹאשׁ
hear — שׁמע
heart — לֵב (+1cs לִבִּי), לֵבָב
heaven(s) — שָׁמַיִם
heavy (adj.) — כָּבֵד, cstr. כְּבֵד
Hebrew — עִבְרִי, (f) עִבְרִית, mp עִבְרִים or עִבְרִיִּים, see 3.10
help — עֵזֶר (*e*)
here — פֹּה
hesitate — אחר (Piel)
hide — חבא (Niphal)
hiding place — סֵתֶר

high גָּבֹהַּ
highway מְסִלָּה
hill גִּבְעָה
holiness קֹ֫דֶשׁ (*o*)
holy (adj.) קָדוֹשׁ
holy (noun) קֹ֫דֶשׁ (*o*)
horn קֶ֫רֶן (*a*) (f)
horseman פָּרָשׁ
house בַּ֫יִת
husband אִישׁ, בַּ֫עַל (*a*)

I
idol פֶּ֫סֶל, גִּלּוּל
if אִם
if indeed כִּי especially in oaths
impassible lands רֶ֫כֶס
in ב
in order that לְמַ֫עַן
indeed כִּי, גַּם
inheritance נַחֲלָה
iniquity עָוֹן
install נסך (A/)
into אֶל־, אֱל
Isaac יִצְחָק
Israel יִשְׂרָאֵל
Israelites בְּנֵי יִשְׂרָאֵל

J
Jacob יַעֲקֹב
jealous (be/become) קנא, make jealousy (Piel), provoke to jealousy (Hiphil)
jealous (noun) קַנָּא
Jerusalem יְרוּשָׁלַ֫יִם, יְרוּשָׁלַ֫ם
joker צחק (Piel participle)
journey נסע
Judah יְהוּדָה
judgment מִשְׁפָּט
just (adj.) יָשָׁר
justice מִשְׁפָּט

K
keep alive חיה (Piel)
keep שׁמר (A/O)
kill הרג (A/O), מות Hiphil 7.3
kin מוֹלֶ֫דֶת (*a*)
kindle בער
king (be/become) מלך (A/O) (Qal, Hiphil)

king	מֶ֫לֶךְ
kiss	נשׁק (A/A)
know	ידע (ו)

L

Laban	לָבָן
lamb	טָלֶה
land	אֶ֫רֶץ (*a*)
laugh at	שׂחק/צחק (Qal and Piel) +לְ
law	תּוֹרָה
lead	נהל (Piel), הלך (Hiphil)
leaf	עָלֶה
leave	עזב (A/O)
lengthen	ארך (Hiphil)
lest	פֶּן
let go	שׁלח (Piel)
level	מִישׁוֹר
life	חַיִּים (life of the Lord חַי־יהוה)
lift up	רום, נשׂא
lightning strike (noun)	בָּרָק
like (be/become)	דמה
like	כְּ (+1cs כָּמ֫וֹנִי)
likeness	דְּמוּת
lion	אֲרִי
listen	שׁמע
live	חיה, keep alive (Piel), as the Lord lives חַי־יהוה
looked (=saw, see)	ראה
Lord	יהוה
Lot	לוֹט
love	רחם
lovingkindness	חֶ֫סֶד (*a*)
low (be/become)	שׁפל (A-e/A)

M

make	עשׂה
make a covenant	כרת (A/O)
make music	זמר (Piel)
man	אִישׁ, young man נַ֫עַר (*a*), men אֲנָשִׁים
many (adj.)	רַב (pl. רַבִּים)
master	אֲדֹנִי
matter	דָּבָר
meditate	הגה
meet	קרא (inf. cstr. with לְ: לִקְרַאת)
men	אֲנָשִׁים
mercy	חֶ֫סֶד (*a*)
Messiah	מָשִׁיחַ

might (adj.)	חָזָק
mighty	גִּבּוֹר
mock	לעג
moon	יָרֵחַ
moreover	גַּם
morning	בֹּ֫קֶר
mortally	נֶ֫פֶשׁ (*a*) (in the accusative)
Moses	מֹשֶׁה
mother	אֵם (+1cs אִמִּי)
Mount Sinai (Mt. of Sinai)	הַר סִינַי
mountain(s)	הַר, pl. הָרִים
mouth	פֶּה, cstr. פִּי
move swiftly	דאה
much (adj.)	רַב
mutter	הגה

N

Naharaim	נַהֲרַ֫יִם
name	שֵׁם
nation	גּוֹי
night	לַ֫יְלָה
Nile	יְאוֹר
no more	אֵין
non-existence	אַ֫יִן, cstr. אֵין
nostril	אַף
not	לֹא, אַל
nothing	אַ֫יִן, אֶ֫פֶס
now	נָא (usually after volitives); עַתָּה (usually at beginning of a sentence or clause)
nursing (ewes)	עול

O

obey	שׁמע + קֹל or שׁמע + אל
offering	תְּרוּמָה
old (adj.)	זָקֵן
old (verb)	זקן (A-e/A)
on account of	בַּעֲבוּר
on	ב, עַל
one (adj.)	אֶחָד, cstr. אַחַת
only	רַק
or	אוֹ
outstretched	נטה Qal passive participle
over	עַל

P

palace	הֵיכָל

palm תָּמָר
path דֶּ֫רֶךְ (*a*)
peace שָׁלוֹם
people עַם, לְאוֹם/לְאֹם (+1cs suffix עַמִּי)
perfect (adj.) תָּמִים
perish אבד (IBH chapter 30)
Pharaoh פַּרְעֹה
pitcher כַּד
place (noun) מָקוֹם
place (verb) שׁית
plague (noun) מַגֵּפָה (+1cs מַגֵּפֹתַי), נֶ֫גַע (*i*)
plague (verb) נגף (A/O)
plain כִּכָּר
plant שׁתל (A/O)
plate רקע (Piel)
please (verb) (י)יטב (A/A), חפץ (A-e/A)
please (adv.) נָא
poor (be/become) סכן (Pual participle)
possess ירשׁ (י) (A/A)
possession אֲחֻזָּה
potter כְּלִי
pour (out) שׁפך (A/O)
praise הלל (Piel)
pray פלל (Hithpael)
prepare כון
press חזק (A/A)
priest כֹּהֵן
promise דבר (Piel +ל)
prosper צלח (Hiphil)
provoke כעס (Hiphil and Piel)

Q

quake רעשׁ
quickly מהר (Piel, inf. abs.), מְעַט/מְעָט

R

rage רגשׁ (A/)
Rebecca רִבְקָה
rebel (against) פֶּה + מרה
rebel (verb) מרה
rebuke (noun) גְּעָרָה
rebuke (verb) יכח (ו) (Hiphil)
receive discipline יסר (Niphal)
recount ספר (Piel)
Red Sea יַם־סוּף
redeem פדה

refuse	מאן (Piel)
regard	חשׁב (A/O)
reign	מלך (A/O)
rejoice	גִּיל
rejoice (verb)	שׂמח
rejoicing	שִׂמְחָה
release	שׁלח (Piel)
remove	סור (Hiphil)
report to	נגד (Hiphil or Hophal +ל usually)
representation	תְּמוּנָה
return	שׁוב
reveal	גלה
revolt (verb)	פשׁע (+ב against)
reward	שָׂכָר
righteous (adj.)	צַדִּיק
rise (up)	קום
rise early	שׁכם (Hiphil)
rock	צוּר
rocky cliff	סֶ֫לַע
rod	שֵׁ֫בֶט
rode	רכב (A/A)
rope	עֲבֹתָה/עֲבוֹת/עֲבֹת
rot	רקב (E/A)
rule (verb)	מלך (A/O), משׁל (A/O)
ruler	רֹזֵן, שַׂר, מֹשֵׁל
run	רוץ

S

sacrifice (noun)	זֶ֫בַח (*a*)
sacrifice (verb)	זבח
salvation	יְשׁוּעָה
sanctify	קדשׁ (Piel)
Sarai	שָׂרַי
sat (sit)	ישׁב (ו) (A/E)
satisfy	רצה
save	ישׁע (ו) (Niphal)
say	אמר (IBH chapter 30)
saying	לֵאמֹר
scatter	פוץ
scorner	לִיץ
secure height	מִשְׂגָּב
see	ראה
seed	זֶ֫רַע (*a*)
seek	בקשׁ (Piel)
seize	חזק (Hiphil +ב)
select	בחר

send	שׁלח send away (Piel)
separate	פרד (Niphal)
servant	עֶ֫בֶד (*a*)
serve (verb)	עבד (A/O)
seven	שִׁבְעָה (with masculine noun)
seventh	שְׁבִיעִי
severe (adj. & verb)	כָּבֵד
shake (shook)	געשׁ
sheep	צֹאן
Sheol	שְׁאוֹל
shepherd (noun)	רֹעֶה
shepherd (verb)	רעה
shield	מָגֵן
shook (see shake)	
show insight	שׂכל (Hiphil)
show	ראה (Hiphil)
sign	אוֹת
silver	כֶּ֫סֶף (*a*)
sin (noun)	חֲטָאָה
sin (verb)	חטא
sin against	חטא + ל
Sinai	סִינַי
sing	שׁיר
sinner	חַטָּא
sister	אָחוֹת
sit (sat)	ישׁב (ו) (A/E)
six	שִׁשָּׁה, cstr. שֵׁ֫שֶׁת
skilled (adj.)	חָכָם
small (adj.)	קָטֹן
smash (to pieces)	נפץ (Piel), שׁבר (Piel)
smelter	צֹרֵף
smite (verb)	נכה (Hiphil)
smiting (noun)	מַכֶּה
smoke	עָשָׁן
snare	מוֹקֵשׁ
so	כֹּה
Sodom	סְדֹם
Solomon	שְׁלֹמֹה
son	בֵּן
song	שִׁיר
soul	נֶ֫פֶשׁ (*a*) (f)
speak	דבר (Piel)
split	בקע
staff	מַטֶּה
stand	עמד, קום
star	כּוֹכָב

station — יצב (Hithpael)
steep ground — עָקֹב
stiffnecked — קְשֵׁה־עֹרֶף
straighten — ישׁר (י) (A/A)
strength — כֹּחַ, חֵ֫זֶק
strife — רִיב
strike down — פגע (ב+)
strive — ריב
strong (adj.) — חָזָק
summon — קרא (ל+)
sun — שֶׁ֫מֶשׁ
surely — כִּי
surround — אפף
swear — שׁבע (Niphal)
sword — חֶ֫רֶב (*a*) (f)

T

tablet — לוּחַ (f)
take — לקח
take counsel — יסד (ו) (Niphal)
takes refuge — חסה
tarry — אחר (Piel)
tear — נתק (Piel)
tell — נגד (Hiphil)
temple — הֵיכָל
tempt — נסה (Piel)
tent — אֹ֫הֶל (*o*)
tent of meeting — אֹהֶל מוֹעֵד
Terah — תֶּ֫רַח
terrify — בהל (Niphal, Piel), בעת (Piel)
test (verb) — נסה (Piel)
that (demonstrative pronoun) — הוּא (masc), הִיא (fem)
that (relative pronoun) — אֲשֶׁר
that which — אֲשֶׁר
there — שָׁם
there is none — אַיִן
therefore — עַל־כֵּן
thing — דָּבָר
this (after this) — כֵּן
this (thing) — זאת
throne — כִּסֵּא
throw down — שׁלך (Hiphil)
thunder — רעם (Hiphil)
thus — כֹּה, כֵּן
time — עֵת
to (direction) — אֶל, אֶל־, or the old accusative ending with certain nouns

today	הַיּוֹם
together	יַחְדָּו
torrent	נַ֫חַל
totter	מוט
touch	נגע (+ב frequently) (inf. cstr., root form *נְגֹעַ)
traitor	חַטָּא
treat as a fool	נבל (Piel)
tree	עֵץ
tremble	חרד (A/A), רגז (A/A)
trembling	רְעָדָה
trust	בטח
truth	אֱמֶת
turn	שׁוב
twelve	שְׁנֵי עָשָׂר (with masculine word)
two	שְׁנַ֫יִם, cstr. שְׁנֵי

U

unrighteousness	עָ֫וֶל (*a*), cstr. עֶ֫וֶל
until	עַד אֲשֶׁר or just עַד
upon	עַל
Ur	אוּר
utter	נתן (A/E)

V

valley	גַּיְא
vanity	הֶ֫בֶל (*a*)
very	מְאֹד
vessel	כְּלִי
voice	קוֹל

W

wage	פְּעֻלָּה
wait	קוה (Piel)
walk	הלך (ו) (A/E)
walk about	הלך (Hithpael)
want	אבה
warfare	צָבָא
was	היה
water	מַ֫יִם
way	דֶּ֫רֶךְ (*a*)
weep	בכה
well (noun)	בְּאֵר
well (verb)	יטב (י) (A/A)
went (go)	הלך (ו) (A/E)
what?	מַה־
which	אֲשֶׁר

while*	ב or כ with infinitive construct (usually), ו of situation in situation clauses
who, whom	אֲשֶׁר
who?	מִי
why	לָמָה, לָ֫מָּה, מַדּוּעַ
wicked (adj.)	רָשָׁע, רַע (pl. רָעִים)
wife	אִשָּׁה
wild (adj.)	רָעָה
wilderness	מִדְבָּר
willing (verb)	אבה
wind	רוּחַ
wing	כָּנָף
wise (man) (adj.)	חָכָם
with	אֵת (+1cs אִתִּי), עִם (+1cs עִמִּי); instrument or means, ב
wither	נבל (A-e/O)
woe	אוֹי
wonder	מוֹפֵת
wood	עֵץ
word	דָּבָר, אֹ֫מֶר (*i*) (poetry)
work	מְלָאכָה, פֹּ֫עַל (*o*)
world	תֵּ֫בֵל
worship	הִשְׁתַּחֲוָה (usually with a ל) (JM §79t)
worthlessness	בְּלִיַּ֫עַל
wound (verb)	פצע
wrath	אַף

<u>Y</u>

year	שָׁנָה
young man	נַ֫עַר (*a*)

<u>Z</u>

Zion	צִיּוֹן

SCRIPTURE INDEX

The initial letter "A" indicates "Hebrew Accent," and "C" "Compositions"; otherwise, those initializing in any number "Syntax." Examples: (1) 3b—Syntax, section(§) 3, b; (2) A9B5—Hebrew Accent, section(§) 9, B, 5; (3) C4.—Composition, 4, footnote 6. The books of the Old Testament are ordered according to the Leningrad Codex.

SUBJECT INDEX